## All the Derivation Rules of *SD* and Rules of Inference

*Modus Tollens* (*MT*)

$$\begin{array}{|l} \mathscr{P} \supset \mathscr{Q} \\ \sim \mathscr{Q} \\ \sim \mathscr{P} \end{array}$$

*Hypothetical Syllogism* (*HS*)

$$\begin{array}{|l} \mathscr{P} \supset \mathscr{Q} \\ \mathscr{Q} \supset \mathscr{R} \\ \mathscr{P} \supset \mathscr{R} \end{array}$$

*Disjunctive Syllogism* (*DS*)

$$\begin{array}{|l} \mathscr{P} \vee \mathscr{Q} \\ \sim \mathscr{P} \\ \mathscr{Q} \end{array} \quad \text{or} \quad \begin{array}{|l} \mathscr{P} \vee \mathscr{Q} \\ \sim \mathscr{Q} \\ \mathscr{P} \end{array}$$

## Rules of Replacement

*Commutation* (*Com*)

$$\mathscr{P} \,\&\, \mathscr{Q} :: \mathscr{Q} \,\&\, \mathscr{P}$$
$$\mathscr{P} \vee \mathscr{Q} :: \mathscr{Q} \vee \mathscr{P}$$

*Association* (*Assoc*)

$$\mathscr{P} \,\&\, (\mathscr{Q} \,\&\, \mathscr{R}) :: (\mathscr{P} \,\&\, \mathscr{Q}) \,\&\, \mathscr{R}$$
$$\mathscr{P} \vee (\mathscr{Q} \vee \mathscr{R}) :: (\mathscr{P} \vee \mathscr{Q}) \vee \mathscr{R}$$

*Implication* (*Impl*)

$$\mathscr{P} \supset \mathscr{Q} :: \sim \mathscr{P} \vee \mathscr{Q}$$

*Double Negation* (*DN*)

$$\mathscr{P} :: \sim\sim \mathscr{P}$$

*De Morgan* (*DeM*)

$$\sim(\mathscr{P} \,\&\, \mathscr{Q}) :: \sim \mathscr{P} \vee \sim \mathscr{Q}$$
$$\sim(\mathscr{P} \vee \mathscr{Q}) :: \sim \mathscr{P} \,\&\, \sim \mathscr{Q}$$

*Idempotence* (*Idem*)

$$\mathscr{P} :: \mathscr{P} \,\&\, \mathscr{P}$$
$$\mathscr{P} :: \mathscr{P} \vee \mathscr{P}$$

*Transposition* (*Trans*)

$$\mathscr{P} \supset \mathscr{Q} :: \sim \mathscr{Q} \supset \sim \mathscr{P}$$

*Exportation* (*Exp*)

$$\mathscr{P} \supset (\mathscr{Q} \supset \mathscr{R}) :: (\mathscr{P} \,\&\, \mathscr{Q}) \supset \mathscr{R}$$

*Distribution* (*Dist*)

$$\mathscr{P} \,\&\, (\mathscr{Q} \vee \mathscr{R}) :: (\mathscr{P} \,\&\, \mathscr{Q}) \vee (\mathscr{P} \,\&\, \mathscr{R})$$
$$\mathscr{P} \vee (\mathscr{Q} \,\&\, \mathscr{R}) :: (\mathscr{P} \vee \mathscr{Q}) \,\&\, (\mathscr{P} \vee \mathscr{R})$$

*Equivalence* (*Equiv*)

$$\mathscr{P} \equiv \mathscr{Q} :: (\mathscr{P} \supset \mathscr{Q}) \,\&\, (\mathscr{Q} \supset \mathscr{P})$$
$$\mathscr{P} \equiv \mathscr{Q} :: (\mathscr{P} \,\&\, \mathscr{Q}) \vee (\sim \mathscr{P} \,\&\, \sim \mathscr{Q})$$

(See reverse side)

IRV KATZ

# DERIVATION RULES OF *PD*

## All the Derivation Rules of *SD* and
## '∀' Rules

*Universal Introduction* (∀*I*)

$$\begin{array}{|l} \mathscr{P}(\boldsymbol{a}/\boldsymbol{x}) \\ (\forall \boldsymbol{x})\mathscr{P} \end{array}$$

Provided:
(i): $\boldsymbol{a}$ does not occur in an undischarged assumption.
(ii): $\boldsymbol{a}$ does not occur in $(\forall \boldsymbol{x})\ \mathscr{P}$.

*Universal Elimination* (∀*E*)

$$\begin{array}{|l} (\forall \boldsymbol{x})\mathscr{P} \\ \mathscr{P}(\boldsymbol{a}/\boldsymbol{x}) \end{array}$$

## '∃' Rules

*Existential Introduction* (∃*I*)

$$\begin{array}{|l} \mathscr{P}(\boldsymbol{a}/\boldsymbol{x}) \\ (\exists \boldsymbol{x})\mathscr{P} \end{array}$$

*Existential Elimination* (∃*E*)

$$\begin{array}{|l} (\exists \boldsymbol{x})\mathscr{P} \\ \quad \begin{array}{|l} \mathscr{P}(\boldsymbol{a}/\boldsymbol{x}) \\ \hline \\ \mathscr{Q} \end{array} \\ \mathscr{Q} \end{array}$$

Provided:
(i) $\boldsymbol{a}$ does not occur in an undischarged assumption.
(ii) $\boldsymbol{a}$ does not occur in $(\exists \boldsymbol{x})\mathscr{P}$.
(iii) $\boldsymbol{a}$ does not occur in $\mathscr{Q}$.

# DERIVATION RULES OF *PD* +

## All the Derivation Rules of *SD* + and of *PD* and

*Quantifier Negation* (*QN*)

$$\sim(\forall \boldsymbol{x})\mathscr{P} :: (\exists \boldsymbol{x}) \sim\mathscr{P}$$
$$\sim(\exists \boldsymbol{x})\mathscr{P} :: (\forall \boldsymbol{x}) \sim\mathscr{P}$$

# DERIVATION RULES OF *PDI*

## All the Derivation Rules of *PD* and
## '=' Rules

*Identity Introduction* (= *I*)

$$\begin{array}{|l} (\forall \boldsymbol{x})\boldsymbol{x} = \boldsymbol{x} \end{array}$$

*Identity Elimination* (= *E*)

$$\begin{array}{|l} \boldsymbol{a} = \boldsymbol{b} \\ \mathscr{P} \\ \mathscr{P}(\boldsymbol{a}//\boldsymbol{b}) \end{array} \quad \text{or} \quad \begin{array}{|l} \boldsymbol{a} = \boldsymbol{b} \\ \mathscr{P} \\ \mathscr{P}(\boldsymbol{b}//\boldsymbol{a}) \end{array}$$

# THE LOGIC BOOK

# THE LOGIC BOOK

*Second Edition*

*MERRIE BERGMANN* *Smith College*

*JAMES MOOR* *Dartmouth College*

*JACK NELSON* *Temple University*

McGRAW-HILL PUBLISHING COMPANY

New York St. Louis San Francisco Auckland Bogotá
Caracas Hamburg Lisbon London Madrid Mexico
Milan Montreal New Delhi Oklahoma City Paris
San Juan São Paulo Singapore Sydney Tokyo Toronto

**The Logic Book**



3 4 5 6 7 8 9 0 DOC DOC 9 5 4 3 2 1 0

P/N 004938-6
PART OF
ISBN 0-07-909524-0

This book was set in Baskerville by Science Typographers, Inc.
The editors were Steven Pensinger and Cynthia Ward;
The production supervisor was Louise Karam.
The cover was designed by Katherine Urban.
Project supervision was done by Science Typographers, Inc.
R. R. Donnelley & Sons Company was printer and binder.

Cover Photo: Jaco BAR-Portrait of *Luca Pacioli and an Unknown Man*, Capodimonte Museum, Naples. Photo SCALA/EPA, Inc.

**Library of Congress Cataloging-in-Publication Data**

Bergmann, Merrie.
The logic book/Merrie Bergmann, James Moor, Jack Nelson.—2nd ed.
p. cm.
Includes bibliographical references.
P/N 004938-6
1. Logic, Symbolic and mathematical. 2. Predicate (Logic)
I. Moor, James, (date). II. Nelson, Jack, (date). III. Title.
BC135.B435 1990
160—dc20 89-48698

# *ABOUT THE AUTHORS*

MERRIE BERGMANN received her Ph.D. in philosophy from the University of Toronto, and is currently an Assistant Professor in the Computer Science Department at Smith College. She has published articles in formal semantics and logic, philosophy of language, and computational linguistics.

JAMES MOOR received his Ph.D. from Indiana University in history and philosophy of science. He is a Professor of Philosophy at Dartmouth College. He has been involved in a variety of software projects for teaching logic such as *Bertie*, *Venn*, *The Gates of Logic*, and *Proof Designer*. His research interests include philosophy of science, logic, philosophy of mind, philosophy and artificial intelligence, and computer ethics.

JACK NELSON is currently Associate Vice Provost for Graduate Studies at Temple University. He received his Ph.D. in philosophy from the University of Chicago and has published in the areas of personal identity and epistemology, and is a coauthor of *Bertie*.

# CONTENTS

# *PREFACE*

In this second edition of *The Logic Book* we have maintained our original objective to write about symbolic logic in a way that is both pedagogically attractive and formally rigorous. This book does not presuppose that a student using the text has had any training in logic. It begins with a discussion of the relevance of logic to everyday life, develops sentential and predicate logic, and ends with a metatheoretic discussion of the semantic and syntactic techniques presented. Though every chapter has been improved, we have tried to preserve those features of the logical theory and the pedagogical presentation that have made *The Logic Book* sound, accessible, and enjoyable.

As in the first edition, there is sufficient material in the text for a one- or two-semester introductory course. There are many sequences of chapters that would form good syllabi for courses in symbolic logic. If an instructor has two quarters or two semesters (or one semester with advanced students), it is possible to work through the entire book. The instructor who does not want to emphasize metatheory can simply omit Chapters 6 and 11. The chapters on truth-trees and the chapters on derivations are independent so that it is possible to do truth-trees but not derivations, or vice versa. The chapters on truth-trees do depend on the chapters on semantics, that is, Chapter 4 depends on Chapter 3 and Chapter 9 depends on Chapter 8. And although most instructors will want to do semantics before doing the corresponding derivations, the opposite order is possible. The sections at the ends of Chapters 3, 5, 8, and 10 can also be omitted.

In this second edition the treatment of predicate logic has been expanded to include identity. New sections on identity appear in the predicate logic chapters on symbolization, semantics, truth-trees, derivations, and metatheory. Numerous specific refinements have been made throughout the book. For instance, the semantics for both sentential and predicate logic have been changed. Partial truth-value assignments have been eliminated in Chapter 3 and interpretations for predicate logic as well as satisfaction assignments have been defined along Tarskian lines. The presentations of interpretations and truth-functional expansions in Chapter 8 have been separated for clarity. The discussion of goal-analysis for derivations has been expanded in Chapter 5 and the rules of *SD* and *PD* have been renamed in Chapters 5 and 10 to better reflect their function. There is a new, improved rule in Chapter 9 for decomposing existentially quantified sentences. The metatheory in Chapters 6 and 11 has been rewritten to make it more perspicuous.

Many new exercises have been added throughout the book. Some instructors objected that there were not enough unanswered exercises—exercises not answered in the *Solutions Manual* for students—in the first edition. In this edition, half of the exercises are answered in the *Solutions Manual* for students and half are answered in the *Instructor's Manual*. We believe that because of the large number of exercises that we have added there will be plenty of answered problems for students to check their work and yet plenty of unanswered exercises for instructors to assign for homework if they wish.

We thank the students and teachers whose many insightful and valuable comments over the years have guided us in developing this second edition. We also appreciate the contributions made by reviewers and take this opportunity to acknowledge the help of Ellery Eels, University of Wisconsin; James Fahey, Rensselear Polytechnic Institute; Glen Helman, Pennsylvania State University; Andrew McCafferty, Louisiana State University; Ruth Anna Putman, Wellesley College; Glenn Ross, Franklin and Marshall College; Ruth Saunders, University of Washington; Niall Shanks, Southern Methodist University; Ralph Slaght, Lafayette College; and Sarah Stebbins, Columbia University. We wish to give special thanks to Austen Clark whose truth-tree program, *Twootie*, was used in producing many truth-trees for the book and whose software products are available for use with this edition of the book.

Merrie Bergmann
James Moor
Jack Nelson

*Chapter* **1**

# *BASIC NOTIONS OF LOGIC*

## 1.1 THE USES OF LOGIC

The study of logic as a formal discipline goes back at least to Aristotle. In more recent years, formal logic has been intimately connected with work in such disciplines as philosophy, physics, mathematics, computer science, and linguistics. But, logic is not a mere theoretical discipline. Logic has considerable importance for everyday life. All of us, logicians and nonlogicians, students and teachers, are, and must be, concerned with acquiring true beliefs about ourselves and the world around us. The emphasis here is on 'true' because, as agents constantly interacting with the world, we must care about whether our beliefs accurately picture the world. To be indifferent to the truth of one's beliefs or to think that the truth of a belief is a matter of how one feels about things, rather than how things are, is to court disaster. One who takes such a cavalier attitude toward truth will often end up thinking that such and such is the case when the world is really quite different. And the fact that the world is different will cause him or her at least consternation and very possibly serious harm.

The techniques of formal logic cannot generally tell us which claims or beliefs are true and which are false. Truth is usually a matter of how the world is, and logic does not tell us that. But the techniques we shall develop in this text can help us determine whether the beliefs or claims we are concerned with form a consistent group or set.

A group of beliefs or claims is *consistent* if and only if it is possible for all the members of the group to be true at the same time. A group of beliefs or claims is *inconsistent* if and only if it is not possible for all the members of the group to be true at the same time. When a group of claims is inconsistent, we say that one cannot *consistently assert* (claim, believe) all the members of that group.

Suppose someone believes all the following:

> Anyone who takes astrology seriously is a lunatic.
>
> Alice is my sister, and no sister of mine has a lunatic for a husband.
>
> Higgins is Alice's husband, and he reads the horoscope column every morning.
>
> Anyone who reads the horoscope column every morning takes astrology seriously.

A little reflection should show that these claims cannot all be true. At least one of them must be false. If the first, third, and fourth are true, the second cannot be. Alternatively, if the second, third, and fourth are true, the first cannot be. And so on. These sentences form an inconsistent set. Anyone who believes all of them has inconsistent beliefs and thus at least one false belief. So avoiding inconsistencies can help us avoid false beliefs.

Some inconsistencies, like that in our example, are fairly obvious. But not all inconsistent groups or sets of sentences are obviously inconsistent. The formal techniques we shall develop in this text will be of help in exposing nonobvious cases of inconsistency, as well as in explaining exactly why inconsistent sets are inconsistent. Of course, logic usually cannot tell us how to resolve an inconsistency. One or more of the members of the inconsistent set must be abandoned, on pain of irrationality. But which one or ones are to be abandoned depends upon the evidence available for the individual members of the group of sentences in question. Here we must appeal to our general familiarity with the way things are in the world, and to our own and others' expertise in specific disciplines.

As agents interacting with the world and with other agents we are constantly acquiring new beliefs from our observations, readings, and discussions with others, as well as by inferring new beliefs from old ones. The methods by which we reach new beliefs from old ones may be more or less rational, depending on the circumstances. When we attempt to justify or make plausible these new beliefs on the basis of old ones, to convince either ourselves or others of the acceptability of new claims, we are involved in giving *arguments*. Arguments in this sense are, of course, neither exercises in fisticuffs nor emotional outbursts. Rather, they are attempts to give supporting reasons for views we or others hold or are considering holding. A major part of this text will be devoted to the task of developing formal techniques for evaluating arguments.

It should be made clear from the start that what we shall be evaluating is not the psychological process by which an agent moves from some claims to others, but rather the arguments the agent or someone else presents as justifying his or her so moving. The motivating factor behind Mr. McAvarice's advocating the relaxing of air-pollution standards may be his ownership of stock in a company that produces coal with a high sulfur content. But McAvarice's view about pollution standards is not for that reason irrational or unsupported; he may have very good arguments for his view. In evaluating his position, we should address ourselves to these arguments or the lack of them, not to his ownership of stock or his bourgeois background or his unfortunate toilet training. Of course, if neither McAvarice nor anyone else can come up with good supporting reasons, good arguments, for the claim that pollution standards should be relaxed, McAvarice either ought to abandon that claim (if good arguments can be found to the effect that pollution standards should not be relaxed) or ought at least to be very tentative in his advocacy of that claim (if no good arguments can be found either for or against the claim). The force of 'ought' here is that of 'ought if one is interested in truth and wants to avoid falsity'. And all of us, as we have noted, must be so interested.

Good arguments are important in justifying our beliefs and expanding our knowledge. However, even arguments that lead to false claims can be useful if they force us to reexamine our beliefs and think critically about which claims we accept. Consider this simple line of reasoning. We know from elementary arithmetic that

$$2 \times 0 = 3 \times 0$$

and

$$0 = 0$$

By the principle that equals divided by equals are equal, we have

$$\frac{2 \times 0}{0} = \frac{3 \times 0}{0}$$

A factor which appears in both the numerator and denominator of a fraction can be canceled. Hence

$$2 = 3$$

Although this reasoning may seem plausible, clearly the result is not. 2 does not equal 3. Because this final claim is false and the logic of the argument is correct, at least one of the supporting claims on which the final claim is based must be false. In this case, the general principle that equals divided by equals are equal is false if it permits division by 0. Division by 0 is not defined. In order to retain the principle we must modify it. Equals divided by *nonzero* equals are equal.

The formal techniques we shall develop will make it easier to show that an argument is a good argument and why it is a good argument. These techniques will thus be of help in our attempt to avoid false beliefs and gain true ones. For, insofar as those techniques show that an argument is a good one and we have good reasons to believe the claims on which it rests, we also have good reasons to believe the claim the argument supports. On the other hand, if the supported claim is clearly false and our techniques show that the argument is a good one, we have good reason to reject at least one of the claims on which the argument is based.

Logic is not an unfailing antidote to sloppy thinking, but it can provide techniques that aid us in discovering inconsistencies and in evaluating arguments. And, if we do want to avoid falsity and gain truth, it is important to avoid having inconsistent beliefs and to accept only good arguments.

### 1.1E EXERCISES[1]

1. Explain why it is that, though logic can help expose inconsistencies in our beliefs, it cannot generally tell us how to resolve such inconsistencies.

*2. Explain why it is better to adopt the maxim 'Gain truth, and avoid error' than either just 'Gain truth' or just 'Avoid error'.

3. What is wrong with the view that truth is a matter of one's attitude toward a belief —that is, with the view that, if I believe something firmly enough or sincerely enough, then what I believe is true? Explain.

*4. Does showing that a belief was arrived at in some nonrational way amount to showing that that belief ought to be abandoned? Explain.

## 1.2 SENTENCES

In logic we are primarily interested in sentences that are either true or false (but not both). Often the truth or falsity of a sentence will depend upon the context in which it is asserted. For instance, the sentence

John is hungry

would normally be true if said about John immediately before he is to eat lunch but false if said about John immediately after he has eaten lunch. Sometimes, instead of talking of the truth or falsity of a sentence, we shall talk of its *truth-value*. If a sentence is true, we shall say that it has the *truth-value* **T**, and, if it is false, we shall say that it has the *truth-value* **F**.

Of course, not all sentences that are meaningful are either true or false (i.e., have a truth-value). In most contexts sentences like 'Are you feeling well?' and 'Run for your life!' are neither true nor false, yet they are perfectly meaningful. Generally speaking, the English sentences that are true or false are the declarative sentences. But it is a mistake to believe that picking out which sentences have a truth-value is a straightforward grammatical matter. We must be alert to how a particular sentence is used in a given context. For instance, the sentence 'You will finish your supper' would be true or false if given as a prediction about behavior. But, if the sentence is given in a context of a parent's talking to a child, with emphasis upon the word 'will', then the sentence is most likely being used as a command and as such is neither true nor false.

[1] Answers to the unstarred exercises are found in the companion volume *Solutions to Selected Exercises in The Logic Book*.

Many philosophical disputes arise about such basic concepts as sentences, meaning, context, and truth. For example, some philosophers argue that propositions are the kinds of entities that are really true or false, propositions being taken to be the meanings of sentences and to exist independently of any particular language. Other philosophers eschew propositions as unnecessary metaphysical baggage. Because we have to adopt some terminology and because all philosophers agree that sentences play some role in language, we shall talk of sentences as being true or false. But we consider such talk to be shorthand for talk of sentences that have certain meanings as used in particular contexts.

---

## 1.3 ARGUMENTS

An important use of language is to provide argumentation for beliefs. In an argument we give our reasons for a claim or assertion. For example, suppose we have a friend, Nancy, whom we regard as a hard worker and as someone who will be successful. If somebody challenges our belief that Nancy will be successful, we can, by appealing to our further belief that anyone who works hard will be successful, provide an argument for our prediction about Nancy's future:

> Anyone who works hard will be successful. So Nancy will be successful, for she works hard.

We are here using sentences (premises of the argument) to provide reasons for the truth of another sentence (the conclusion of the argument). We can display this argument more clearly by listing the premises first and the conclusion last.

> Anyone who works hard will be successful.
>
> Nancy works hard.
>
> ---
>
> Nancy will be successful.

> An *argument* is a set of sentences one of which (the *conclusion*) is taken to be supported by the remaining sentences (the *premises*).

In identifying arguments in ordinary conversation and writing, we must make reasonable judgments about how the sentences in question are being used. Consider the following passage:

> Our galaxy is made up of our sun and billions of other stars. The galaxy is a huge, flat spiral system that rotates like a wheel, and the myriads of stars move around its center somewhat as the planets revolve around our sun. In addition to our galaxy, there are millions of other galaxies.

This is a set of sentences, which are either true or false, but it is unlikely that they would be used in any context as an argument. Rather, this passage simply provides a description. Of course, it would be possible to use this set of sentences as an argument (though not a very good one). For one could consider one of the sentences as the conclusion and the others as premises offered in support of that conclusion. In short, whether or not we take a set of sentences to be an argument depends upon what we take the role of the sentences to be.

Once we have identified an argument in ordinary discourse, the next task is to decide which sentences are premises and which sentence is the conclusion. Grammar is not always a good guide here. For instance, even though

> Some animals that live in Kenya are endangered because lions are endangered animals and lions live in Kenya

is grammatically one sentence, we assume that it is being used to present an argument that might be expressed as follows:

> Lions are endangered animals.
>
> Lions live in Kenya.
>
> ---
>
> Some animals that live in Kenya are endangered.

We shall adopt this pattern as our standard form for paraphrases of arguments. First, we shall list the premises, then draw a line, and finally list the conclusion. In constructing paraphrases our aim is to capture as much of the content of the original argument as possible. Putting an argument into standard form will be the first step in analyzing it because until we can clearly state what the premises and the conclusion are, we cannot begin to evaluate the argument.

In paraphrasing an argument we need to pay attention to how key words indicate which sentences are being used as premises and which as the conclusion. In the last example, 'because' indicates that what follows is offered in support of the conclusion. Thus 'Lions are endangered animals' and 'Lions live in Kenya' are the premises of the argument. Incidentally, these two premises might have been taken together as one premise: 'Lions are endangered animals and lions live in Kenya'. What is left is the conclusion, 'Some animals that live in Kenya are endangered'.

There are many premise-indicator words in English. Some of them are

> since
> for
> because
> on account of
> inasmuch as
> for the reason that

Some conclusion-indicator words in English are

> therefore
> thus
> it follows that
> so
> hence
> consequently
> as a result

Premise-indicator words and conclusion-indicator words help us organize an argument even if the logic of the argument is less than perfect. Consider the following somewhat tortured reasoning inspired by Monty Python:

> If witches burn, they are made of wood. Wood floats, but stones do not. Thus, wooden ducks are witches, since ducks float.

Even bad arguments can be put into standard form. Notice that in this example the position of the word 'Thus' indicates that the conclusion occurs in the middle of the passage and the position of the word "since" indicates a premise comes after it. In standard form the argument is

> If witches burn, they are made of wood.
>
> Wood floats, but stones do not.
>
> Ducks float.
>
> ---
>
> Wooden ducks are witches.

Putting an argument into standard form is an important first step in the analysis of the argument.

### 1.3E EXERCISES

Paraphrase in standard form those of the following passages that contain arguments.

1. His power, we allow, is infinite; whatever he wills is executed; but neither man nor any other animal is happy; therefore, he does not will their happiness.

—David Hume

*2. It is right that men should value the soul rather than the body; for perfection of soul corrects the inferiority of the body, but physical strength without intelligence does nothing to improve the mind.

—Democritus

3. The table, which we see, seems to diminish, as we remove farther from it: but the real table, which exists independent of us, suffers no alteration: it was, therefore, nothing but its image, which was present to the mind.

—David Hume

*4. There cannot be any emptiness; for what is empty is nothing, and what is nothing cannot be.

—Melissus

5. We see that things which lack intelligence, such as natural bodies, act for an end, and this is evident from their acting always or nearly always, in the same way, so as to obtain the best result. . . . Now whatever lacks intelligence cannot move towards an end, unless it be directed by some being endowed with knowledge and intelligence; as the arrow is shot to its mark by the archer. Therefore, some intelligence exists by whom all natural things are directed to their end; and this being we call God.

—Thomas Aquinas

***6.** About the gods, I am not able to know whether they exist or do not exist, nor what they are like in form; for the factors preventing my knowledge are many: the obscurity of the subject, and the shortness of human life.

—Protagoras

**7.** It is by no means established that the brain of a woman is smaller than that of a man. If it is inferred merely because a woman's bodily frame generally is of less dimensions than a man's, this criterion would lead to strange consequences. A tall and large-boned man must on this showing be wonderfully superior in intelligence to a small man, and an elephant or a whale must prodigiously excel mankind.

—John Stuart Mill

***8.** In the beginning man was born from creatures of a different kind; because other creatures are soon self-supporting, but man alone needs prolonged nursing. For this reason he would not have survived if this had been his original form.

—Anaximenes

**9.** If the teacher happens to be a man of sense, it must be an unpleasant thing to him to be conscious, while he is lecturing his students, that he is either speaking or reading nonsense, or what is little better than nonsense. It must, too, be unpleasant to him to observe that the greater part of his students desert his lectures, or perhaps attend upon them with plain enough marks of neglect, contempt, and derision. If he is obliged, therefore, to give a certain number of lectures, these motives alone, without any other interest, might dispose him to take some pains to give tolerably good ones.

—Adam Smith

***10.** All the perceptions of the human mind resolve themselves into two distinct kinds, which I shall call *Impressions* and *Ideas*. The difference betwixt these consists in the degrees of force and liveliness with which they strike upon the mind, and make their way into our thought or consciousness. Those perceptions, which enter with most force and violence, we may name *impressions*; and under this name I comprehend all our sensations, passions and emotions, as they make their first appearance in the soul. By *ideas* I mean the faint images of these in thinking and reasoning.

—David Hume

**11.** This leads me to say a few words on what I have called Sexual Selection. This form of selection depends, not on a struggle for existence in relation to other organic beings or to external conditions, but on a struggle between the individuals of one sex, generally the males, for the possession of the other sex. The result is not death to the unsuccessful competitor, but few or no offspring. Sexual selection is, therefore, less rigorous than natural selection.

—Charles Darwin

***12.** The forces which we assume to exist by the tensions caused by the needs of the id are called instincts. They represent the somatic demands upon mental life. Though they are the ultimate cause of all activity, they are by nature conservative; the state, whatever it may be, which a living thing has reached, gives rise to a tendency to re-establish that state as soon as it has been abandoned.

—Sigmund Freud

**13.** Let us reflect in another way, and we shall see that there is great reason to hope that death is good; for one of two things—either death is a state of nothingness and utter unconsciousness, or as men say, there is a change and migration of the soul from this world to another. Now if you suppose that there is no consciousness, but a sleep like the sleep of him who is undisturbed even by dreams, death will be an unspeakable gain... for eternity is then only a single night. But if death is the journey to another place, and there, as men say, all the dead abide, what good, O my friends and judges, can be greater than this? ... Above all, I shall then be able to continue my search into true and false knowledge; as in this world, so also in the next; and I shall find out who is wise, and who pretends to be wise, and is not.

—Socrates

***14.** Geometry should not include lines that are strings, in that they are sometimes straight and sometimes curved, since the ratios between straight and curved lines are not known, and I believe cannot be discovered by human minds, and therefore no conclusion based upon such ratios can be accepted as rigorous and exact.

—René Descartes

**15.** [S]ome whales have been captured far north in the Pacific, in whose bodies have been found the barbs of harpoons darted in the Greenland seas. Nor is it to be gainsaid, that in some of these instances it has been declared that the interval of time between the two assaults could not have exceeded very many days. Hence, by inference, it has been believed by some whalemen, that the Nor'-West Passage, so long a problem to man, was never a problem to the whale.

—Herman Melville

## 1.4 EVALUATING ARGUMENTS

There are different ways of evaluating arguments and consequently different reasons for which we might accept an argument as a good one or reject it as a bad one. Consider the following argument:

All deaf persons are musically gifted.
Beethoven was deaf.
______________________________
Beethoven was musically gifted.

Is this argument a good one or a bad one? The answer to this question will depend on the *criteria* used to evaluate the argument. We might use the following criterion: The premises of an argument must all be true. If we then challenge the first premise—say, by citing examples of deaf persons who are not musically gifted—we would reject the argument as a bad one because not all the premises are true. A second criterion is this: If the premises are all true, the conclusion must be true as well. The argument about Beethoven satisfies this criterion, and on this basis of evaluation we would say that the argument is a good one. A third criterion is that if the premises are all true, the conclusion is probably true. The argument about Beethoven also satisfies this third criterion.

Once we make the criteria of evaluation explicit in this way, we see that an argument may meet one criterion but fail to meet another. A crucial step in evaluating arguments, therefore, is to determine what our criteria of evaluation are to be. In this section, certain logical criteria for evaluating arguments (and sentences) will be discussed.

One logical criterion mentioned was this: If all the premises of the argument are true, the conclusion must be true as well. An argument that satisfies this criterion is a *deductively valid argument*, or, more simply, a *valid argument*. An argument that fails to satisfy this criterion is a *deductively invalid argument* or, more simply, an *invalid argument*. When we use this criterion of evaluation we are not interested in which truth-values the premises and conclusion actually have. Rather, we ask whether it is *possible* for the premises to be true and the conclusion false. We may evaluate an argument by means of this criterion, and thus determine whether it is a deductively valid argument, independently of our evaluation on the basis of other criteria. The previous argument is a deductively valid argument; so is the following argument:

> All Indians are Buddhists.
>
> All Buddhists have two heads.
>
> Beethoven was an Indian.
>
> ---
>
> Beethoven had two heads.

Here it is impossible for the premises to be true and the conclusion false. (Of course, the premises are not all true. So, even though this is a deductively valid argument, the truth of the conclusion has not been established.) When we evaluate an argument by means of this criterion, we are using a deductive standard of evaluation.

The criterion may be restated in terms of consistency: An argument is a deductively valid argument if and only if it is not possible consistently both to assert the premises and to deny the conclusion.

| An argument is *deductively valid* if and only if it is not possible for the premises to be true and the conclusion false (i.e., it is not possible consistently both to assert the premises and to deny the conclusion). An argument is *deductively invalid* if and only if it is not deductively valid. |
|---|

Arguments need not be evaluated by deductive standards. For example, the following argument is a fairly good argument, although one can consistently both assert the premises and deny the conclusion:

> Public sentiment plays a large role in determining who will be U.S. presidential candidates.
>
> Most U.S. citizens believe that men make good presidents.
>
> Many U.S. citizens are reluctant to support a female candidate for the presidency.
>
> ---
>
> The next U.S. president will be a man.

This is a deductively invalid argument. But we may still say that it is a good argument if we evaluate it by means of our third criterion of evaluation: If the premises are true, the conclusion is *probably* true. An argument that is deductively invalid may fare quite well when evaluated by this criterion. Inductive logic is concerned with evaluating arguments by means of inductive standards. An argument is said to be *inductively strong* if the premises provide strong evidence for the truth of the conclusion. The more probable the truth of the conclusion, given the premises, the stronger the argument.

> An argument is *inductively strong* if and only if the conclusion is probably true given the premises. An argument is *inductively weak* if and only if it is not inductively strong.

The inductive strength of arguments is a matter of degree. For instance, the following is not a very strong inductive argument:

Three deaf persons in recorded history have been musically gifted.
Beethoven was deaf.

---

Beethoven was musically gifted.

Although we may be able to give good reasons for the conclusion, the premises of this argument are not among them. The following argument, with the opposite conclusion, is a much stronger inductive argument:

Ninety-nine percent of deaf persons have no musical talent.
Beethoven was deaf.

---

Beethoven had no musical talent.

The test for a strong inductive argument is not whether the conclusion is true. Rather, it concerns the evidence the premises provide in support of the conclusion.

In what follows we shall be concerned with deductive methods of evaluating arguments. We have seen that the first two arguments in this section are deductively valid and that the third is deductively invalid. The following argument is also deductively invalid:

Only plants undergo the process of photosynthesis.
Cacti are plants.

---

Cacti undergo the process of photosynthesis.

We can consistently both assert the premises and deny the conclusion of this argument. The first premise does not tell us that *all* plants undergo photosynthesis; it tells us that *only* plants undergo photosynthesis. This information alone leaves open the possibility that some plants do not undergo photosynthesis. And, if there were such plants and cacti were among them, the premises would be true and the conclusion false. So obviously it would be *possible* for the premises to be true and the conclusion false. Hence the argument is invalid. If we add 'All plants undergo the process of photosynthesis' as a premise, we shall have a valid argument:

Only plants undergo the process of photosynthesis.
All plants undergo the process of photosynthesis.
Cacti are plants.

---

Cacti undergo the process of photosynthesis.

It would be inconsistent both to assert the premises and to deny the conclusion of this argument.

Based on our examples of deductively valid arguments, we note that a deductively valid argument may have:

a. all true premises and a true conclusion
b. one or more false premises and a true conclusion
c. one or more false premises and a false conclusion

A deductively valid argument may *not* have all true premises and a false conclusion. There can be no such valid argument because, if an argument has all true premises and a false conclusion, then it is clearly *possible* for it to have true premises and a false conclusion. However, knowing that an argument satisfies condition a, b, or c is not sufficient for concluding that the argument is deductively valid. In evaluating arguments for deductive validity, we are not concerned with whether the sentences in the argument are actually true. Rather, we must ask whether it is *possible* for the premises to be true and the conclusion false, regardless of what the facts are. If it is not possible, the argument is valid; but, if it is possible, the argument is invalid.

At this point, you may be wondering why we should be concerned with determining whether or not an argument is deductively valid, since deductively valid arguments can have false conclusions. After all, one of the purposes of argumentation is to establish a point: that is, the conclusion of the argument! But deductive validity plays a role here. Although valid arguments may have false conclusions, we know that a deductively valid argument never leads from true premises to a false conclusion. So, if we determine that an argument is deductively valid and that the premises are all true, then we know that the conclusion is true.

An argument is *deductively sound* if and only if it is deductively valid and all its premises are true. An argument is *deductively unsound* if and only if it is not deductively sound.

The conclusion of a sound argument must be true. This follows from our definitions. For, if an argument has true premises and if it is not possible for the premises to be true and the conclusion false, then the conclusion must be true. The following is a sound argument:

Washington, D.C., is the capital of the United States.

The capital of the United States is in the eastern part of the United States.

---

Washington, D.C., is in the eastern part of the United States.

The argument is sound because it is deductively valid and has true premises. (It is deductively valid because one cannot consistently both assert the premises and deny the conclusion.)

The conclusion and the premises of a sound argument are all true. On the other hand, there are some arguments whose conclusion and premises are all true but that are not sound. Here is an example:

Washington, D.C., is the capital of the United States.

The capital of the United States is in the eastern part of the United States.

Colorado is not the capital of the United States.

---

Washington, D.C., is east of Colorado.

A sound argument must satisfy two criteria: It must have true premises, and it must be deductively valid. The present example is not a valid argument, and hence it is not sound. The argument is invalid because we can consistently both assert the premises and deny the conclusion. The premises do not give us enough information to rule out the possibility that Washington, D.C., is not east of Colorado.

There are some arguments that are valid but that cannot, for logical reasons, be sound. These arguments have premises that cannot all be true. For example,

Vitamin C prevents colds.

Vitamin C does not prevent colds.

---

Vitamin C is harmless.

This argument is valid because we cannot consistently both assert the premises and deny the conclusion. The reason here is that we cannot consistently assert both premises. If one is true, the other must be false. So, no matter what the facts about vitamin C are, we know that the argument is not, and cannot be, sound. Any argument whose premises cannot be consistently asserted is valid but unsound.

> A sentence is *logically false* if and only if it is not possible for the sentence to be true, that is, the sentence cannot be consistently asserted.

It is not possible for a logically false sentence to be true, no matter what the facts are. Examples of logically false sentences are

> There is a country that is not a country.
>
> Earth is a planet, and earth is not a planet.
>
> Some men are fathers, although no fathers are men.

Because a logically false sentence cannot be true, any set of sentences that contains a logically false sentence is inconsistent. Every argument that has at least one logically false premise is valid, no matter what the other sentences in the argument are. In such a case one cannot consistently both assert the premises and deny the conclusion because one cannot consistently assert the premises. Of course, every argument that has at least one logically false premise is unsound.

We can also identify *logically true* sentences.

| |
|---|
| A sentence is *logically true* if and only if it is not possible for the sentence to be false, that is, the sentence cannot be consistently denied. |

It is not possible for a logically true sentence to be false, no matter what the facts are. Here are some logically true sentences:

> A rose is a rose.
>
> Today is Tuesday unless today is not Tuesday.
>
> Either all ships are merchant vessels, or some ships are not merchant vessels.

Just as an argument with a logically false premise is valid, so an argument with a logically true conclusion is valid. For, if the conclusion cannot be consistently denied, it follows that we cannot consistently both assert the premises *and* deny the conclusion. Such an argument may or may not be sound, depending on whether the premises are true.

A *logically indeterminate* sentence, sometimes called a *contingent* sentence, can be consistently asserted and consistently denied.

| |
|---|
| A sentence is *logically indeterminate* if and only if it is neither logically true nor logically false. |

The majority of sentences that we encounter in everyday language are logically indeterminate. For example,

> Ivan is driving from Boston to New Orleans.
>
> Anyone who takes astrology seriously is a lunatic.
>
> McAvarice advocates the relaxation of air-pollution standards because he owns a lot of stock in a company producing coal with a high sulfur content.

We do not decide whether a sentence is logically true, logically false, or logically indeterminate simply by determining whether it is true or false. Rather, we must ask whether the sentence can possibly be true and whether it can possibly be false. Of course, if a sentence is actually true, it cannot be logically false; and, if it is actually false, it cannot be logically true.

Two sentences are *logically equivalent* if they always share the same truth-value.

> Two sentences are *logically equivalent* if and only if it is not possible for one of the sentences to be true while the other sentence is false, that is, it is not possible consistently both to assert one of the sentences and to deny the other sentence.

Here are pairs of sentences which are logically equivalent:

Beatrice beat Bob in bridge.

Bob was beaten by Beatrice in bridge.

The Blarney stone is at the top of Blarney Castle.

The Blarney stone is at the top of Blarney Castle.

Paris is in Japan and Moscow is in China.

Moscow is in China and Paris is in Japan.

Note that as special cases any two sentences which are logically true are logically equivalent and any two sentences which are logically false are logically equivalent.

The test for logical equivalence is not whether two sentences have the same truth-value, but, rather, whether the two sentences must have the same truth-value. Roughly speaking, one asks whether there is any imaginable situation in which one of the sentences would be true and the other would be false. If there is such a situation, then the sentences are not logically equivalent. For instance, here are two sentences which are not logically equivalent.

White wine is produced in California.

Red wine is produced in California.

Although both sentences happen to be true, it is nonetheless possible for one of the sentences to be true while the other is false.

### 1.4E EXERCISES

1. Which of the following are true, and which are false? Explain your answers, giving examples where appropriate.

a. All valid arguments have only true premises.

*b. A sound argument must be valid.

c. An argument with a false conclusion cannot be valid.

*d. An argument in which all the premises are true and the conclusion is true must be sound.
e. If a set of sentences has a logically false sentence as a member, then the set is inconsistent.
*f. A valid argument with all true premises must be sound.
g. A valid argument must be sound.
*h. An argument with true premises and a false conclusion may be valid.
i. An argument with true premises and a false conclusion may be sound.
*j. Two false sentences cannot be logically equivalent.
k. An argument in which all the premises are true and the conclusion is true must be valid.
*l. All arguments with true conclusions are valid.
m. An argument which has a conclusion which is logically equivalent to one of its premises is valid.

**2.** Answer each of the following:
a. Suppose that someone believes that New York is the capital of the United States. Does it follow that that person has inconsistent beliefs? Explain.
*b. Need one be engaged in a disagreement or dispute to have use for an argument, as we have been using the term 'argument'? Explain.
c. Explain why logic cannot normally tell us which valid arguments are sound. Under what conditions could we decide, on logical grounds alone, that an argument is sound?
*d. Suppose an argument is valid but has a false conclusion. What must be true of at least one of the premises? Why?
e. Suppose an argument has, as one of its premises, a logical falsehood. Explain why the argument must be deductively valid, no matter what the other premises are and no matter what the conclusion is.
*f. Suppose an argument has a premise which is logically equivalent to a logical falsehood. Must the argument be valid? Explain.
g. Suppose an argument has a logical truth for its conclusion. Explain why the argument must be valid, no matter what its premises are. Explain why such an argument may or may not be sound.
*h. Suppose the premises of an argument form an inconsistent set of sentences. Explain why the argument must be valid. Explain why it must be unsound.
i. Suppose a set of a million sentences is consistent. Now suppose a new set of sentences is constructed so that every sentence in the new set is logically equivalent to at least one of the sentences in the old set. Must the new set be consistent? Explain.

## GLOSSARY

CONSISTENCY: A set of sentences is *consistent* if and only if it is possible for all the members of the set to be true at the same time. A set of sentences is *inconsistent* if and only if it is not consistent.

ARGUMENT: An *argument* is a set of sentences one of which (the conclusion) is taken to be supported by the remaining sentences (the premises).

DEDUCTIVE VALIDITY: An argument is *deductively valid* if and only if it is not possible for the premises to be true and the conclusion false (i.e., it is not possible consistently both to assert the premises and to deny the conclusion). An argument is *deductively invalid* if and only if it is not deductively valid.

INDUCTIVE STRENGTH: An argument is *inductively strong* if and only if the conclusion is probably true given the premises. An argument is *inductively weak* if and only if it is not inductively strong.

DEDUCTIVE SOUNDNESS: An argument is *deductively sound* if and only if it is deductively valid and all its premises are true. An argument is *deductively unsound* if and only if it is not deductively sound.

LOGICAL TRUTH: A sentence is *logically true* if and only if it is not possible for the sentence to be false (i.e., the sentence cannot be consistently denied).

LOGICAL FALSITY: A sentence is *logically false* if and only if it is not possible for the sentence to be true (i.e., the sentence cannot be consistently asserted.)

LOGICAL INDETERMINACY: A sentence is *logically indeterminate* if and only if it is neither logically true nor logically false.

LOGICAL EQUIVALENCE: Two sentences are *logically equivalent* if and only if it is not possible for one of the sentences to be true while the other sentence is false (i.e., it is not possible consistently both to assert one of the sentences and to deny the other sentence).

# Chapter 2

# *SENTENTIAL LOGIC: SYMBOLIZATION AND SYNTAX*

## 2.1 SYMBOLIZATION AND TRUTH-FUNCTIONAL CONNECTIVES

Sentential logic, as the name suggests, is a branch of formal logic in which sentences are taken as the basic units. In this chapter we shall introduce *SL*, a symbolic language for sentential logic, which will facilitate our development of formal techniques for assessing the logical relationships among sentences and groups of sentences. The sentences of English that can be symbolized in *SL* are those sentences of English that are either true or false, that is, have truth-values.

In English there are various ways of generating sentences from other sentences. One way is to place a linking term such as 'and' between two sentences. The result, allowing for appropriate adjustments in capitalization and punctuation, will itself be a sentence of English. In this way we can generate

Socrates is wise and Aristotle is crafty

by writing 'and' between

Socrates is wise

and

Aristotle is crafty.

Some other linking terms of English are 'or', 'unless', 'before', and 'if and only if'. As used to generate sentences from other sentences these terms are called *sentential connectives* (they connect or join sentences to produce further sentences).

Some sentence-generating words and expressions do not join two sentences together but rather work on a single sentence. Examples are 'it is not the case that' and 'it is alleged that'. Prefacing a sentence with either of these expressions generates a further sentence. Since these expressions do not literally connect two sentences, the term 'sentential connective' is perhaps a little misleading. Nonetheless, such sentence-generating devices as these are commonly classified as sentential connectives, and we shall follow this usage.

Sentences generated from other sentences by means of sentential connectives are *compound sentences*. All other sentences are *simple sentences*. In developing sentential logic we shall be especially interested in the *truth-functional* use of sentential connectives. Intuitively, a compound sentence generated by a truth-functional connective is one in which the truth-value of the compound is a function of, or is fixed by, the truth-values of its components.

> A sentential connective is used *truth-functionally* if and only if it is used to generate a compound sentence from one or more sentences in such a way that the truth-value of the generated compound is wholly determined by the truth-values of those one or more sentences from which the compound is generated, no matter what those truth-values may be.

Few, if any, connectives of English are always used truth-functionally. However, many connectives of English are often so used. We shall call these connectives, as so used, 'truth-functional connectives'. A *truth-functionally compound* sentence is a compound sentence generated by a truth-functional connective.

In English 'and' is often used truth-functionally. Consider the compound sentence

Alice is in England and Bertram is in France.

Suppose that Alice is in Belgium, not England. Then 'Alice is in England' is false. The compound sentence is then clearly also false. Similarly, if 'Bertram is in France' is false, the compound 'Alice is in England and Bertram is in France' is also false. In fact, this compound will be true if and only if both of the sentences from which it is generated are true. Hence the truth-value of this compound is wholly determined by the truth-values of the component sentences from which it is generated. Given their truth-values, whatever they may be, we can always compute the truth-value of the compound in question. This is just what we mean when we say that 'and' is functioning as a truth-functional connective.

### *SENTENCES OF SENTENTIAL LOGIC*

In *SL* capital Roman letters are used to abbreviate individual sentences of English. Thus

Socrates is wise

can be abbreviated as

W

Of course, we could have chosen any capital letter for the abbreviation, but it is common practice to select a letter that reminds us of the sentence being abbreviated. In this case 'W' reminds us of the word 'wise'. But it is essential to remember that the capital letters of *SL* abbreviate entire sentences and *not* individual words within sentences.

To ensure that we have enough sentences in our symbolic language to represent any number of English sentences, we shall also count capital Roman letters with positive integer subscripts as sentences of *SL*. Thus all the following are sentences of *SL*:

$A, B, Z, T_{25}, Q_6$

In *SL* capital letters with or without subscripts are *atomic sentences*. Sentences of *SL* that are made up of one or more atomic sentences and one or more sentential connectives of *SL* are *molecular sentences*.

*CONJUNCTION*

We could abbreviate

Socrates is wise and Aristotle is crafty

in our symbolic language as 'A', but in doing so we would bury important information about this English sentence. This sentence is a compound made up of two simple sentences: 'Socrates is wise' and 'Aristotle is crafty'. Furthermore, in this case the word 'and', which connects the sentences, is serving as a truth-functional connective. This compound sentence is true if both of its component sentences are true and is false otherwise. We shall use '&' (ampersand) as the sentential connective of *SL* that captures the force of this truth-functional use of 'and' in English. Instead of symbolizing 'Socrates is wise and Aristotle is crafty' as 'A', we can now symbolize it as

W & C

where 'W' abbreviates 'Socrates is wise' and 'C' abbreviates 'Aristotle is crafty'. Remember that the letters abbreviate entire sentences, not merely the words 'wise' and 'crafty'. The compound sentence 'W & C' is an example of a molecular sentence of *SL*.

A sentence of the form

$\mathscr{P} \,\&\, \mathscr{Q}$

where $\mathscr{P}$ and $\mathscr{Q}$ are sentences of *SL*, is a *conjunction*.[1] $\mathscr{P}$ and $\mathscr{Q}$ are the *conjuncts* of the conjunction. Informally, we shall use the terms 'conjunction' and 'conjunct' in

[1] Our use of boldfaced script letters to talk generally about the sentences of *SL* is explained in Section 2.4.

talking of English sentences that can be symbolized as conjunctions of *SL*. The relation between the truth or falsity of a conjunction and the truth or falsity of its conjuncts can be simply put: A conjunction is true if and only if both of its conjuncts are true. This is summarized by the following table:

| $\mathscr{P}$ | $\mathscr{Q}$ | $\mathscr{P}$ & $\mathscr{Q}$ |
|---|---|---|
| T | T | T |
| T | F | F |
| F | T | F |
| F | F | F |

Such a table is called a *characteristic truth-table* because it defines the use of '&' in *SL*. The table is read horizontally, row by row. The first row contains three T's. The first two indicate that we are considering the case in which $\mathscr{P}$ has the truth-value **T** and $\mathscr{Q}$ has the truth-value **T**. The last item in the first row is a **T**, indicating that the conjunction has the truth-value **T** under these conditions. The second row indicates that when $\mathscr{P}$ has the truth-value **T** but $\mathscr{Q}$ has the truth-value **F**, the conjunction has the truth-value **F**. The third row shows that when $\mathscr{P}$ has the truth-value **F** and $\mathscr{Q}$ has the truth-value **T**, the conjunction has the truth-value **F**. The last row indicates that when both $\mathscr{P}$ and $\mathscr{Q}$ have the truth-value **F**, the conjunction has the truth-value **F** as well.

Sometimes an English sentence that is not itself a compound sentence can be paraphrased as a compound sentence. The sentence

Fred and Nancy passed their driving examinations

can be paraphrased as

<u>Both</u> Fred passed his driving examination <u>and</u> Nancy passed her driving examination.

We underscore the connectives in paraphrases to emphasize that we are using those connectives truth-functionally. We use '<u>both</u> . . . <u>and</u> . . . ', rather than just '<u>and</u>', to mark off the conjuncts unambiguously. Where the example being paraphrased is complex, we shall sometimes also use parentheses, '(' and ')', and brackets, '[' and ']', to indicate grouping. The foregoing paraphrase is an adequate paraphrase of the original sentence inasmuch as both the original sentence and the paraphrase are true if and only if 'Fred passed his driving examination' and 'Nancy passed her driving examination' are both true. The paraphrase is a conjunction and can be symbolized as

F & N

where 'F' abbreviates 'Fred passed his driving examination' and 'N' abbreviates 'Nancy passed her driving examination'.

Symbolizing English sentences in *SL* should be thought of as a two-step process. First, we construct in English a truth-functional paraphrase of the original

English sentence; next, we symbolize that paraphrase in *SL*. The paraphrase stage serves to remind us that the compounds symbolized as molecular sentences of *SL* are always truth-functional compounds.

The preceding example illustrates that the grammatical structure of an English sentence is not a completely reliable indication of its logical structure. Key words like 'and' are clues but not infallible guides to symbolization. The sentence

Two jiggers of gin and a few drops of dry vermouth make a great martini

cannot be fairly paraphrased as

Both two jiggers of gin make a great martini and a few drops of dry vermouth make a great martini.

Together these ingredients may make a great martini, but separately they make no martini at all. Such a paraphrase completely distorts the sense of the original sentence. Thus the original sentence must be regarded as a simple sentence and symbolized in *SL* as an atomic sentence, say

M

Many sentences generated by such other connectives of English as 'but', 'however', 'although', 'nevertheless', 'nonetheless', and 'moreover' can be closely paraphrased using 'and' in its truth-functional sense.

Susan loves country music, but she hates opera

can be paraphrased as

Both Susan loves country music and Susan hates opera.

The paraphrase can be symbolized as 'L & H', where 'L' abbreviates 'Susan loves country music' and 'H' abbreviates 'Susan hates opera'.

The members came today; however, the meeting is tomorrow

can be paraphrased as

Both the members came today and the meeting is tomorrow

which can be symbolized as 'C & M', where 'C' abbreviates 'The members came today' and 'M' abbreviates 'The meeting is tomorrow'.

Although George purchased a thousand raffle tickets, he lost

can be paraphrased as

Both George purchased a thousand raffle tickets and George lost

which can be symbolized as 'P & L', where 'P' abbreviates 'George purchased a thousand raffle tickets' and 'L' abbreviates 'George lost'.

In each of these cases the paraphrase perhaps misses part of the sense of the original English sentence. In the last example, for instance, there is the suggestion that it is surprising that George could have purchased a thousand raffle tickets and still have lost the raffle. Truth-functional paraphrases often fail to capture all the nuances present in the sentences of which they are paraphrases. This loss is usually not important for the purposes of logical analysis.

In symbolizing ordinary English sentences in *SL*, grammatical structure and key words provide important clues, but they are not infallible guides to correct symbolizations. Ultimately, we have to ask ourselves, as speakers of English, whether the sentence can be reasonably paraphrased as a truth-functional compound. If so, we can symbolize it as a molecular sentence of *SL*. If not, we have to symbolize it as an atomic sentence of *SL*.

## *DISJUNCTION*

Another sentential connective of English is 'or', used in such sentences as

Henry James was a psychologist or William James was a psychologist.

This English sentence contains two simple sentences as components: 'Henry James was a psychologist' and 'William James was a psychologist'. The truth-value of the compound wholly depends upon the truth-values of the component sentences. As long as at least one of the component sentences is true, the compound is true; but if both the components are false, then the compound is false. When used in this way 'or' is functioning as a truth-functional connective of English. In *SL* '$\vee$' (wedge) is the symbol that expresses this truth-functional relationship. Thus the sentence about Henry and William James can be symbolized as

$$H \vee W$$

where 'H' abbreviates 'Henry James was a psychologist' and 'W' abbreviates 'William James was a psychologist'. 'H $\vee$ W' is true if 'H' is true or 'W' is true, and it is false only when both 'H' and 'W' are false.

A sentence of the form

$$\mathscr{P} \vee \mathscr{Q}$$

where $\mathscr{P}$ and $\mathscr{Q}$ are sentences of *SL*, is a *disjunction*. $\mathscr{P}$ and $\mathscr{Q}$ are the *disjuncts* of the sentence. Informally, we shall use the terms 'disjunction' and 'disjunct' in talking of English sentences that can be symbolized as disjunctions of *SL*. A disjunction is true if and only if at least one of its disjuncts is true. This is summarized by the following characteristic truth-table:

| $\mathscr{P}$ | $\mathscr{Q}$ | $\mathscr{P} \vee \mathscr{Q}$ |
|---|---|---|
| **T** | **T** | **T** |
| **T** | **F** | **T** |
| **F** | **T** | **T** |
| **F** | **F** | **F** |

The only case in which a disjunction has the truth-value **F** is when both disjuncts have the truth-value **F**.

Sometimes sentences of English that do not contain the word 'or' can be paraphrased as disjunctions. For instance,

Tom will be late unless he gets an early start

might be paraphrased as

Either Tom will be late or Tom gets an early start

which can be symbolized as

T ∨ E

where 'T' abbreviates the sentence 'Tom will be late' and 'E' abbreviates 'Tom gets an early start'. Another example is

At least one of the two hikers, Jerry and Amy, will get to the top of the mountain.

This sentence can adequately be paraphrased as

Either Jerry will get to the top of the mountain or Amy will get to the top of the mountain.

This paraphrase can be symbolized as 'J ∨ A', where 'J' abbreviates 'Jerry will get to the top of the mountain' and 'A' abbreviates 'Amy will get to the top of the mountain'. Remember the letters abbreviate the entire sentences, not just the words 'Jerry' and 'Amy'. In paraphrasing English sentences as disjunctions of *SL* we use the 'either . . . or . . . ' construction to mark off the two disjuncts unambiguously.

In English sentences that can be paraphrased as disjunctions, 'or' does not always occur between full sentences. For example,

Nietzsche is either a philosopher or a mathematician

can be paraphrased as

Either Nietzsche is a philosopher or Nietzsche is a mathematician.

This truth-functional paraphrase can be symbolized as 'P ∨ M', where 'P' abbreviates 'Nietzsche is a philosopher' and 'M' abbreviates 'Nietzsche is a mathematician'.

We use the wedge to symbolize disjunctions in the *inclusive* sense. Suppose the following occurs on a menu:

With your meal you get apple pie or chocolate cake.

We might try to paraphrase this as:

Either with your meal you get apple pie or with your meal you get chocolate cake.

Since we use 'or' only in the inclusive sense in paraphrases, this paraphrase is true if either or both of the disjuncts are true. In ordinary English, on the other hand, 'or' is sometimes used in a more restrictive sense. In the present example, if someone orders both apple pie and cake, the waiter is likely to point out that either cake or pie, but *not* both, comes with the dinner. This is the exclusive sense of 'or' —either one or the other but not both. Although this sense of 'or' cannot be captured by '∨' alone, there is, as we shall soon see, a combination of connectives of *SL* that will allow us to express the exclusive sense of 'or'.

*NEGATION*

'It is not the case that' is a sentential connective of English. Consider the following compound generated by this connective:

It is not the case that Franklin Pierce was President.

This sentence is true if its component sentence 'Franklin Pierce was President' is false, and it is false if that component sentence is true. 'It is not the case that' is a truth-functional connective because the truth-value of the generated sentence is wholly determined by the truth-value of the component sentence. In *SL* '∼' (tilde) is the sentential connective that captures this truth-functional relationship. Thus the sentence in question can be symbolized as

∼ F

where 'F' abbreviates 'Franklin Pierce was President'. The tilde is a *unary connective*, because it "connects" only one sentence. On the other hand, '&' and '∨' are *binary connectives* since each connects two sentences. When '∼' is placed in front of a sentence, the truth-value of the generated sentence is just the opposite of the truth-value of the original sentence. So the characteristic truth-table for negation is

| $\mathscr{P}$ | $\sim \mathscr{P}$ |
|---|---|
| T | F |
| F | T |

Notice that, because '∼' is a unary connective, we need a truth-table of only two rows to represent all the possible "combinations" of truth-values that a single sentence to which '∼' is attached might have.

Putting a '∼' in front of a sentence forms the negation of that sentence. Hence '∼ A' is the negation of 'A' (though 'A' is *not* the negation of '∼ A'), '∼∼ A' is the negation of '∼ A' (though '∼ A' is not the negation of '∼∼ A'), and so forth. Informally, we shall use the term 'negation' in talking about sentences of English that can be symbolized as negations in *SL*. Thus

It is not the case that Franklin Pierce was President

is the negation of

Franklin Pierce was President.

Whether an English sentence should be symbolized as a negation depends on the context. As before, grammar and key words give us clues. Consider some examples:

Not all sailors are good swimmers

is readily paraphrased as

It is not the case that all sailors are good swimmers.

This paraphrase can be symbolized as ‘ $\sim$ G’, where ‘G’ abbreviates ‘All sailors are good swimmers’. But the following example is not as straightforward:

No doctors are rich.

One might be tempted to paraphrase this sentence as ‘It is not the case that all doctors are rich’, but to do so is to treat ‘No doctors are rich’ as the negation of ‘All doctors are rich’. This is a mistake because a sentence and its negation are always such that if one is true the other is false and vice versa. In fact, since there are some rich doctors and some doctors who are not rich, both ‘All doctors are rich’ and ‘No doctors are rich’ are false. Hence the latter cannot be the negation of the former. Rather, ‘No doctors are rich’ is the negation of ‘Some doctors are rich’. ‘No doctors are rich’ is true if and only if ‘Some doctors are rich’ is false, so the former sentence can be paraphrased as

It is not the case that some doctors are rich.

This can be symbolized as ‘ $\sim$ D’, where ‘D’ abbreviates ‘Some doctors are rich’.

Some further examples will be helpful here:

Chlorine is not a metal

can plausibly be understood as

It is not the case that chlorine is a metal.

This paraphrase can be symbolized as ‘ $\sim$ C’, where ‘C’ abbreviates ‘Chlorine is a metal’. Notice that ‘Chlorine is a metal’ and ‘Chlorine is not a metal’ are such that if either is true the other is false, which must be the case if the latter is to be the negation of the former. But now consider an apparently similar case:

Some humans are not male.

This sentence should not be paraphrased as ‘It is not the case that some humans are male’. The latter sentence is true if and only if *no* humans are male, which is not the claim made by the original sentence. The proper paraphrase is

It is not the case that all humans are male

which can be symbolized as ‘ $\sim$ H’, where ‘H’ abbreviates ‘All humans are male’.

Often sentences containing words with such prefixes as ‘un-’, ‘in-’, and ‘non-’ are best paraphrased as negations. But we must be careful here.

Kant was unmarried

can be understood as

It is not the case that Kant was married

and then symbolized as '∼ K', where 'K' abbreviates 'Kant was married'. 'Kant was unmarried' is the negation of 'Kant was married'. But

Some people are unmarried

should not be paraphrased as 'It is not the case that some people are married'. 'Some people are married' and 'Some people are unmarried' are both true. A proper paraphrase in this case is

It is not the case that all people are married

which can be symbolized as '∼ M', where 'M' abbreviates 'All people are married'.

### *COMBINATIONS OF SENTENTIAL CONNECTIVES*

So far we have discussed three types of truth-functional compounds—conjunctions, disjunctions, and negations—and the corresponding sentential connectives of *SL*—'&', '∨' and '∼'. These connectives can be used in combination to symbolize complex passages. Suppose we want to symbolize the following:

> Either Jane should finish her education or Jane should drop out of school, but Jane should not pay for her education without exerting an effort to learn.

The main connective is 'but', as indicated by the comma preceding it, and the sentence that it generates can be paraphrased as a conjunction. The left conjunct can be paraphrased as a disjunction and the right conjunct as a negation. Thus the truth-functional paraphrase is

> Both (either Jane should finish her education or Jane should drop out of school) and it is not the case that Jane should pay for her education without exerting an effort to learn.

This paraphrase can be symbolized as

$$(F \vee D) \;\&\; \sim P$$

where 'F' abbreviates 'Jane should finish her education', 'D' abbreviates 'Jane should drop out of school', and 'P' abbreviates 'Jane should pay for her education without exerting an effort to learn'. Here the parentheses in the paraphrase and the symbolic sentence are used to indicate how the components of these sentences are grouped. The placement of 'both' and 'either' in the paraphrase is also important. That 'both' precedes 'either' indicates that the paraphrase is a conjunction, rather than a disjunction.

The connectives '&', '∨', and '∼' can be used in combination to symbolize other sentential connectives in English, such as 'neither . . . nor . . .'. The sentence

Neither Sherlock Holmes nor Watson is fond of criminals

can be paraphrased as

Both it is not the case that Sherlock Holmes is fond of criminals and it is not the case that Watson is fond of criminals.

This can be symbolized as

~ H & ~ W

where 'H' abbreviates 'Sherlock Holmes is fond of criminals' and 'W' abbreviates 'Watson is fond of criminals'. Another equally good paraphrase of the original sentence is

It is not the case that either Sherlock Holmes is fond of criminals or Watson is fond of criminals.

This paraphrase can be symbolized using the abbreviations as

~ (H ∨ W)

Note that the original sentence, the paraphrases, and the symbolic sentences are all true if Sherlock Holmes is not fond of criminals and Watson is not fond of criminals, and they are all false otherwise. For just this reason it would be *incorrect* to paraphrase the original as

Either it is not the case that Sherlock Holmes is fond of criminals or it is not the case that Watson is fond of criminals

because this sentence is true if Sherlock Holmes is fond of criminals and Watson is not (since one of the disjuncts is true). But the original sentence 'Neither Sherlock Holmes nor Watson is fond of criminals' is false under these conditions.

A combination of the sentential connectives of *SL* can also be used to capture the exclusive sense of 'or' discussed earlier. Recall that the sentence

With your meal you get apple pie or chocolate cake

is true in the exclusive sense of 'or' if with your meal you get apple pie or chocolate cake but not both. We can paraphrase this as

Both (either with your meal you get apple pie or with your meal you get chocolate cake) and it is not the case that (both with your meal you get apple pie and with your meal you get chocolate cake).

This can be symbolized as

(A ∨ C) & ~ (A & C)

where 'A' abbreviates 'With your meal you get apple pie' and 'C' abbreviates 'With you meal you get chocolate cake'. Notice that the connective 'it is not the case that' in the example applies to an entire conjunction and not just to the first conjunct. We have indicated this by inserting parentheses in the paraphrase.

*MATERIAL CONDITIONAL*

One of the most common sentential connectives of English is 'if . . . then . . .'. A simple example is

If Jones got the job, then he applied for it.

This can be paraphrased as

Either it is not the case that Jones got the job or Jones applied for the job

which can be symbolized as

$\sim G \vee A$

where 'G' abbreviates 'Jones got the job' and 'A' abbreviates 'Jones applied for the job'. It will be convenient to have a symbol in *SL* that expresses the truth-functional sense of 'if . . . then . . .'; we introduce '$\supset$' (horseshoe) for this purpose. The sentence 'If Jones got the job, then Jones applied for the job' can then be symbolized as

$G \supset A$

A sentence of the form $\mathscr{P} \supset \mathscr{Q}$, where $\mathscr{P}$ and $\mathscr{Q}$ are sentences of *SL*, is a *material conditional*. $\mathscr{P}$, the sentence on the left of the '$\supset$', is the *antecedent*, and $\mathscr{Q}$, the sentence on the right of the '$\supset$', is the *consequent* of the conditional. It is important to remember that whenever we write a sentence of the form $\mathscr{P} \supset \mathscr{Q}$, we could express it as $\sim \mathscr{P} \vee \mathscr{Q}$. A sentence of the form $\sim \mathscr{P} \vee \mathscr{Q}$ is a disjunction, and a disjunction is false in only one case—when both disjuncts are false. Thus a sentence of the form $\sim \mathscr{P} \vee \mathscr{Q}$ is false when $\sim \mathscr{P}$ is false and $\mathscr{Q}$ is false, that is, when $\mathscr{P}$ is true and $\mathscr{Q}$ is false. This is also the only case in which a sentence of the form $\mathscr{P} \supset \mathscr{Q}$ is false, that is, when the antecedent is true and the consequent is false. The characteristic truth-table is

| $\mathscr{P}$ | $\mathscr{Q}$ | $\mathscr{P} \supset \mathscr{Q}$ |
|---|---|---|
| T | T | T |
| T | F | F |
| F | T | T |
| F | F | T |

Informally, we can regard the 'if' clause of an English conditional as the antecedent of that conditional and the 'then' clause as the consequent. Here is an example of an English conditional converted to a truth-functional paraphrase that is symbolized by the material conditional:

If Michelle is in Paris, then she is in France.

Expressed in a truth-functional paraphrase this becomes

If Michelle is in Paris then Michelle is in France.

The truth-functional paraphrase can be symbolized as a material conditional

$P \supset F$

Notice that both the original sentence and its truth-functional paraphrase are false if Michelle is in Paris but is not in France, that is, if the antecedent of the conditional is true and the consequent is false. But both the original sentence and its paraphrase are true under all other conditions. If Michelle is in Paris and in France, the sentences are true. If Michelle is not in Paris, but somewhere else in France, the sentences are true. If Michelle is not in Paris and not in France, the sentences are true.

However, the material conditional is not adequate as a complete treatment of conditional sentences in English. Material conditionals are truth-functional, but conditionals in English frequently convey information that exceeds a truth-functional analysis. For instance, 'if . . . then . . . ' constructions sometimes have a causal force that is lost in a truth-functional paraphrase. Consider

1. If this rod is made of metal then it will expand when heated.
2. If this rod is made of metal then it will contract when heated.

Each of these sentences can be used to make a causal claim, to assert a causal relationship between the substance of which the rod in question is composed and the reaction of the rod to heat. But sentence 1 is in accord with the laws of nature, and sentence 2 is not. So, as used to make causal claims, sentence 1 is true, and sentence 2 is false, even if it is false that the rod is made of metal. Now suppose we paraphrase these two sentences as material conditionals.

1a. If this rod is made of metal then this rod will expand when heated.
2a. If this rod is made of metal then this rod will contract when heated.

These paraphrases can be symbolized as

1b. $M \supset E$
2b. $M \supset C$

where 'M' abbreviates 'The rod is made of metal', 'E' abbreviates 'This rod will expand when heated', and 'C' abbreviates 'This rod will contract when heated'. Remember that a material conditional is true if the antecedent is false. If the rod in the example is not made of metal, then both sentences 1a and 2a, and consequently their symbolizations 1b and 2b, are true. Sentence 1 says more than either 1a or 1b, and sentence 2 says more than either 2a or 2b. The fact that sentence 2 is false, whereas 2a and 2b are both true, shows this. It follows that when they are used to assert a causal relation, sentences 1 and 2, like many other English conditionals, are not truth-functional compounds. When it is and when it is not appropriate to paraphrase such sentences as material conditionals will be discussed further in Section 2.3.

Here are further examples of English sentences that can be paraphrased by using 'if . . . then . . . ' in its truth-functional sense.

> Larry will become wealthy provided that he inherits the family fortune

can be paraphrased as

> If Larry inherits the family fortune then Larry will become wealthy

which can be symbolized as

> $F \supset W$

where 'F' abbreviates 'Larry inherits the family fortune' and 'W' abbreviates 'Larry will become wealthy'.

> The Democratic candidate will win the election if he wins in the big cities

can be paraphrased as

> If the Democratic candidate wins in the big cities then the Democratic candidate will win the election

which can be symbolized as '$C \supset E$', where 'C' abbreviates 'The Democratic candidate wins in the big cities' and 'E' abbreviates 'The Democratic candidate will win the election'.

> Betty is in London only if Betty is in England

can be paraphrased as

> If Betty is in London then Betty is in England

which can be symbolized as '$L \supset E$', where 'L' abbreviates 'Betty is in London' and 'E' abbreviates 'Betty is in England'. In this case be sure to notice the order in which the sentences are paraphrased. A common mistake in paraphrasing the sentential connective 'only if' is to ignore the word 'only' and reverse the order of the sentences. It is *incorrect* to paraphrase the original as 'If Betty is in England then Betty is in London'.

*MATERIAL BICONDITIONAL*

In English the connective 'if and only if' is used to express more than either the connective 'if' or the connective 'only if'.

> John will get an A in the course if and only if he does well on the final examination

can be paraphrased as

> Both (if John will get an A in the course then John does well on the final examination) and (if John does well on the final examination then John will get an A in the course).

We can symbolize the paraphrase as

$$(C \supset E) \ \& \ (E \supset C)$$

where 'C' abbreviates 'John will get an A in the course' and 'E' abbreviates 'John does well on the final examination'. The original sentence can also be paraphrased as

> Either (both John will get an A in the course and John does well on the final examination) or (both it is not the case that John will get an A in the course and it is not the case that John does well on the final examination).

Using the above abbreviations, this paraphrase is symbolized as

$$(C \ \& \ E) \vee (\sim C \ \& \sim E)$$

Both of these paraphrases and their corresponding symbolizations are truth-functional compounds. Each is true just in case either both atomic sentences are true or both atomic sentences are false. We introduce the connective '$\equiv$' (triple bar) to capture the truth-functional use of the connective 'if and only if'. The original English sentence can be symbolized as

$$C \equiv E$$

A sentence of the form

$$\mathcal{P} \equiv \mathcal{Q}$$

where $\mathcal{P}$ and $\mathcal{Q}$ are sentences of *SL*, is a *material biconditional*. Informally, we shall use the term 'material biconditional' when describing English sentences that can be symbolized as material biconditionals in *SL*. Here is the characteristic truth-table for '$\equiv$':

| $\mathcal{P}$ | $\mathcal{Q}$ | $\mathcal{P} \equiv \mathcal{Q}$ |
|---|---|---|
| T | T | T |
| T | F | F |
| F | T | F |
| F | F | T |

In this section we have been very careful to distinguish among the connectives 'if', 'only if', and 'if and only if'. This distinction is very important in logic, philosophy, and mathematics, and we shall be careful in our use of these connectives in this book. However, it is important to realize that not everyone makes these distinctions. For example, in everyday speech people sometimes use 'only if' for what we paraphrase as 'if and only if'.

## 2.1E EXERCISES

**1.** For each of the following sentences construct a truth-functional paraphrase and symbolize the paraphrase in *SL*. Use the following abbreviations:

A: Albert jogs regularly.
B: Bob jogs regularly.
C: Carol jogs regularly.

a. Bob and Carol jog regularly.
*b. Bob does not jog regularly, but Carol does.
c. Either Bob jogs regularly or Carol jogs regularly.
*d. Albert jogs regularly and so does Carol.
e. Neither Bob nor Carol jogs regularly.
*f. Bob does jog regularly; however, Albert doesn't.
g. Bob doesn't jog regularly unless Carol jogs regularly.
*h. Albert and Bob and also Carol do not jog regularly.
i. Either Bob jogs regularly or Albert jogs regularly, but they don't both jog regularly.
*j. Although Carol doesn't jog regularly, either Bob or Albert does.
k. It is not the case that Carol or Bob jogs regularly; moreover, Albert doesn't jog regularly either.
*l. It is not the case that Albert, Bob, or Carol jogs regularly.
m. Either Albert jogs regularly or he doesn't.
*n. Neither Albert nor Carol nor Bob jogs regularly.

**2.** Using the abbreviations given in exercise 1, construct idiomatic English sentences from the following sentences of *SL*:

a. $A \& B$
*b. $A \vee \sim A$
c. $A \vee C$
*d. $\sim (A \vee C)$
e. $\sim A \& \sim C$
*f. $\sim\sim B$
g. $B \& (A \vee C)$
*h. $(A \vee C) \& \sim (A \& C)$
i. $(A \& C) \& B$
*j. $\sim A \vee (\sim B \vee \sim C)$
k. $(B \vee C) \vee \sim (B \vee C)$

**3.** Assuming that 'Albert jogs regularly' is true, 'Bob jogs regularly' is false, and 'Carol jogs regularly' is true, which of the symbolic sentences in exercise 2 are true and which are false? Use your knowledge of the characteristic truth-tables in answering.

**4.** Paraphrase each of the following using the phrase 'It is not the case that'. Symbolize the results, indicating what your abbreviations are.

a. Some joggers are not marathon runners.
*b. Bob is not a marathon runner.

c. Each and every marathon runner is not lazy.
*d. Some joggers are unhealthy.
e. Nobody is perfect.

**5.** For each of the following sentences construct a truth-functional paraphrase and symbolize the paraphrase in *SL*. Use the following abbreviations:

A: Albert jogs regularly.
B: Bob jogs regularly.
C: Carol jogs regularly.
L: Bob is lazy.
M: Carol is a marathon runner.
H: Albert is healthy.

a. If Bob jogs regularly he is not lazy.
*b. If Bob is not lazy he jogs regularly.
c. Bob jogs regularly if and only if he is not lazy.
*d. Carol is a marathon runner only if she jogs regularly.
e. Carol is a marathon runner if and only if she jogs regularly.
*f. If Carol jogs regularly, then if Bob is not lazy he jogs regularly.
g. If both Carol and Bob jog regularly, then Albert does too.
*h. If either Carol or Bob jogs regularly, then Albert does too.
i. If either Carol or Bob does not jog regularly, then Albert doesn't either.
*j. If neither Carol nor Bob jogs regularly, then Albert doesn't either.
k. If Albert is healthy and Bob is not lazy then both jog regularly.
*l. If Albert is healthy, he jogs regularly if and only if Bob does.
m. Assuming Carol is not a marathon runner, she jogs regularly if and only if Albert and Bob both jog regularly.
*n. Although Albert is healthy he does not jog regularly, but Carol does jog regularly if Bob does.
o. If Carol is a marathon runner and Bob is not lazy and Albert is healthy, then they all jog regularly.
*p. If Albert jogs regularly, then Carol does provided Bob does.
q. If Albert jogs regularly if Carol does, then Albert is healthy and Carol is a marathon runner.
*r. If Albert is healthy if he jogs regularly, then if Bob is lazy he doesn't jog regularly.
s. If Albert jogs regularly if either Carol or Bob does, then Albert is healthy and Bob isn't lazy.

**6.** Using the abbreviations given in exercise 5, construct idiomatic English sentences from the following sentences of *SL*:

a. $L \vee \sim L$
*b. $M \supset C$
c. $A \equiv H$
*d. $C \;\&\; \sim B$
e. $\sim B \;\&\; \sim C$
*f. $[A \vee (B \vee C)] \supset [A \;\&\; (B \;\&\; C)]$
g. $(\sim A \vee \sim C) \supset B$
*h. $\sim (A \vee C) \supset B$

i. $C \supset (A \,\&\, \sim B)$
*j. $B \equiv (\sim L \,\&\, A)$
k. $C \,\&\, \sim C$
*l. $A \,\&\, (C \equiv B)$
m. $(L \supset L) \,\&\, B$
*n. $\sim\sim H \,\&\, \sim A$
o. $\sim A \supset (\sim B \supset \sim C)$
*p. $(C \supset A) \,\&\, (A \supset B)$
q. $\sim A \,\&\, (B \equiv \sim L)$
*r. $(H \supset A) \supset (\sim L \supset B)$

---

## 2.2 COMPLEX SYMBOLIZATIONS

Going through the paraphrase stage is useful when learning how to symbolize sentences. The paraphrases serve as reminders of exactly what is being symbolized in *SL*. Each sentence of a paraphrase will be either a simple sentence, a truth-functionally compound sentence, or a non-truth-functionally compound sentence. The simple sentences and non-truth-functionally compound sentences are to be symbolized as atomic sentences of *SL*. The truth-functionally compound sentences are to be symbolized as molecular sentences of *SL*. In constructing a paraphrase we must be alert to the grammar, wording, and context of the original passage. Sometimes there will be a loss of information in moving from the original passage to the paraphrase, but often the loss of information will not matter.

*GUIDELINES FOR PARAPHRASING*

Any sentence of the original passage that is going to be treated as a simple sentence, that will eventually be abbreviated as an atomic sentence in *SL*, can be copied as its own paraphrase.

Any sentence of the original passage that is going to be paraphrased as a truth-functionally compound sentence is to be paraphrased using one or more of the connectives ‘both . . . and . . .’, ‘either . . . or . . .’, ‘it is not the case that’, ‘if . . . then . . .’, and ‘if and only if’. We underscore these connectives in the paraphrases to emphasize their truth-functional usage.

Ambiguities should be eliminated in the paraphrase. For instance, sometimes it may be clearer to insert parentheses in the paraphrase to establish how sentences are to be grouped. If the connective ‘it is not the case that’ is applied to an entire material biconditional, rather than just to the first component, parentheses will show this; as in ‘It is not the case that (the Republican candidate will win if and only if he is supported by big business)’.

If the passage is an argument, put the paraphrased argument in standard form. That is, list the paraphrased premises first, draw a line, and then list the paraphrased conclusion.

Where an English passage contains two or more different wordings of the same claim, use just one wording in constructing a paraphrase of that passage.

The intent of the last of these guidelines can be made clear through the use of examples. Suppose someone offers the following rather trivial argument:

> If Sue and Bill got married yesterday, they are honeymooning today. They did get married yesterday. So they are honeymooning today.

The sentence 'They did get married yesterday' is not the antecedent of 'If Sue and Bill got married yesterday, they are honeymooning today'. Yet, in the context of this passage, 'they' refers to Sue and Bill. So the second premise of our paraphrase should be 'Sue and Bill got married yesterday', *not* 'They did get married yesterday'. The full paraphrase will be

> <u>If</u> Sue and Bill got married yesterday <u>then</u> Sue and Bill are honeymooning today.
>
> Sue and Bill got married yesterday.
>
> ---
>
> Sue and Bill are honeymooning today.

Note that we have replaced 'they' with 'Sue and Bill' throughout. Here is another example in which rewording is necessary in constructing a paraphrase.

> Either Jim will not pass the test or Jim spent last night studying logic. Jim's night was not spent poring over this logic text. Hence Jim will fail the test.

In constructing a paraphrase of this argument, it is important to word the premises and conclusion so that we can use a minimum number of sentential letters to symbolize the paraphrase. Suppose someone gives the following paraphrase:

> <u>Either</u> <u>it is not the case that</u> Jim will pass the test <u>or</u> Jim spent last night studying logic.
>
> <u>It is not the case that</u> Jim's night was spent poring over this logic text.
>
> ---
>
> Jim will fail the test.

To symbolize this argument, we need four sentence letters: 'J', 'S', 'O', and 'F'.

$$\sim J \vee S$$
$$\sim O$$

---

$$F$$

Here 'J' abbreviates 'Jim will pass the test', 'S' abbreviates 'Jim spent last night studying logic', 'O' abbreviates 'Jim's night was spent poring over his logic text', and 'F' abbreviates 'Jim will fail the test'. Symbolized in this way our argument is invalid. But the original English argument is valid. The following is a far better paraphrase:

> Either it is not the case that Jim will pass the test or Jim spent last night studying logic.
>
> It is not the case that Jim spent last night studying logic.
>
> ---
>
> It is not the case that Jim will pass the test.

'Jim will not pass the test' and 'Jim will fail the test' express the same claim in this context. So do 'He spent last night studying logic' and 'Jim's night was spent poring over his logic text'. Our second paraphrase reflects this, and allows us to give the following symbolization:

$\sim J \vee S$

$\sim S$

---

$\sim J$

This symbolic argument is valid, as our formal techniques will show.

We shall now present and symbolize more complex sentences and groups of sentences. In our first series of examples we shall consider sentences about an international yacht race in which there are just three major competitors, the Americans, the British, and the Canadians. In symbolizing these sentences we shall make use of the following abbreviations:

M: The Americans win the race.
R: The British win the race.
N: The Canadians win the race.
A: The Americans have good luck.
B: The British have good luck.
C: The Canadians have good luck.
E: Everyone is surprised.
T: A major tradition is broken.

Our first two examples illustrate the important difference between sentences compounded by 'if . . . then . . . ' and those compounded by 'only if':

1. The British will win if neither of the other two major competitors wins.
2. The British will win only if neither of the other two major competitors wins.

The first of these sentences tells us, in effect, that the British do not have to worry about the minor competitors. According to sentence 1, for the British to win all that is needed is that the Americans and Canadians not win. The second sentence makes a more modest claim—it expresses only the truism that for the British to win the other major competitors must not win. Here are our truth-functional paraphrases of these sentences:

1a. If both it is not the case that the Americans win the race and it is not the case that the Canadians win the race then the British win the race.

2a. If the British win the race then both it is not the case that the Americans win the race and it is not the case that the Canadians win the race.

The rule to remember here is that a sentence compounded by 'if' rather than by 'only if' should be paraphrased as a conditional whose *antecedent* is the sentence following 'if' in the original compound. A sentence compounded by 'only if' should be paraphrased as a conditional whose *consequent* is the sentence following 'only if' in the original compound. The symbolizations of these paraphrases will be:

1b. $(\sim M \,\&\, \sim N) \supset R$
2b. $R \supset (\sim M \,\&\, \sim N)$

In sentences 1 and 2 some of the verbs are in the present tense and some are in the future tense. But in these particular examples, the difference in tense does not reflect a difference in the temporal order of the events under discussion. ('The British will win if neither of the other two major competitors wins' does *not* mean that if neither of the other two major competitors wins *now*, then the British will win *later*.) Accordingly, in our paraphrases we have made all of the verbs present tense. We could, alternatively, have made them all future tense. In giving paraphrases it is often useful to make as many of the verbs as possible the same tense; but this should *only* be done when doing so does not distort the truth-functional connections between the sentences in the passage.

Often there is more than one correct paraphrase of a sentence. For example, in paraphrasing both sentence 1 and sentence 2 we could have used 'or' instead of 'and'. For sentence 1 we would then have

If it is not the case that either the Americans win the race or the Canadians win the race then the British win the race.

Here the symbolization is

$\sim (M \vee N) \supset R$

In general, a sentence of the form

neither $\mathscr{p}$ nor $\mathscr{q}$

where $\mathscr{p}$ and $\mathscr{q}$ are sentences of English, is equivalent both to the corresponding sentence of the form

not $\mathscr{p}$ and not $\mathscr{q}$

and to the corresponding sentence of the form

not either $\mathscr{p}$ or $\mathscr{q}$

That is, they are all true under just the same conditions. In *SL* a sentence of the form $\sim \mathcal{P} \;\&\; \sim \mathcal{Q}$ is equivalent to the corresponding sentence of the form $\sim (\mathcal{P} \vee \mathcal{Q})$. Similarly, in English

not $p$ or not $q$

and

not both $p$ and $q$

are equivalent forms, as are $\sim \mathcal{P} \vee \sim \mathcal{Q}$ and $\sim (\mathcal{P} \;\&\; \mathcal{Q})$ in *SL*.

Further examples will help make these relationships clear:

3. The Canadians will win if both the other major competitors do not have good luck.
4. The Canadians will win if either of the other major competitors does not have good luck.
5. The Canadians will win if not both of the other major competitors have good luck.

These are best paraphrased as

3a. If (both it is not the case that the Americans have good luck and it is not the case that the British have good luck) then the Canadians win the race.

4a. If (either it is not the case that the Americans have good luck or it is not the case that the British have good luck) then the Canadians win the race.

5a. If it is not the case that (both the Americans have good luck and the British have good luck) then the Canadians win the race.

In *SL* these become

3b. $(\sim A \;\&\; \sim B) \supset N$
4b. $(\sim A \vee \sim B) \supset N$
5b. $\sim (A \;\&\; B) \supset N$

Sentences 4a and 5a are equivalent, as are 4b and 5b. To say that either one or the other of the major competitors does not have good luck just is to say that they will *not both* have good luck. Where 'not' goes in relation to 'both' is important, as we shall see if we compare sentences 3 and 5. The phrase 'both . . . not . . . ' means that each of the two things in question does not have the property in question. But the phrase 'not both' means only that at least one of those two things does not have the property in question.

Here are two more examples:

6. The Americans will win unless they do not have good luck, in which case the British will win.
7. A major tradition will be broken if but only if no major competitor wins.

In sentence 6 the phrase 'in which case' is to be understood as 'in case the Americans do not have good luck'. The proper paraphrase is thus

6a. Both (either the Americans win the race or it is not the case that the Americans have good luck) and (if it is not the case that the Americans have good luck then the British win the race).

This is symbolized as

6b. $(M \vee \sim A) \& (\sim A \supset R)$

In paraphrasing sentence 7 we need only remember that there are exactly three major competitors: the Americans, the British, and the Canadians.

7a. A major tradition will be broken if and only if it is not the case that [either (either the Americans win the race or the British win the race) or the Canadians win the race].

In symbols this becomes

7b. $T \equiv \sim [(M \vee R) \vee N]$

(Here '$T \equiv \sim [M \vee (R \vee N)]$' is an equally good symbolization. The use of parentheses in grouping disjuncts will be discussed later.)

Sometimes sentences containing such quantity terms as 'at least', 'at most', and 'all' can be paraphrased as truth-functional compounds. This will be the case when the number of things or events or cases we are talking about is finite. All the following can be given truth-functional paraphrases.

8. At least one of the major competitors will have good luck.
9. Exactly one of the major competitors will have good luck.
10. At least two of the major competitors will have good luck.
11. Exactly two of the major competitors will have good luck.

Since there are three major competitors, to say that at least one of them will have good luck is equivalent to saying that either the first, the second, or the third will have good luck. So

8a. Either the Americans have good luck or (either the British have good luck or the Canadians have good luck).

And in symbols:

8b. $A \vee (B \vee C)$

The grouping here is arbitrary. We could just as well have written '$(A \vee B) \vee C$'. But grouping is necessary, since '$A \vee B \vee C$' is not a sentence of *SL*. (The connectives of *SL* are all, except for '$\sim$', *binary* connectives. That is, each connects *two* sentences. When the parentheses are removed from sentence 8b, there is no answer to the question 'which sentences does the first '$\vee$' connect?' So the expression is not well-formed; that is, it is not a sentence of *SL*.)

Since '$\vee$' is used to capture the inclusive sense of disjunction, we have to work some to say that one and only one of the three major competitors will have good luck. One way of doing it is this:

9a. Either [both the Americans have good luck and it is not the case that (either the British have good luck or the Canadians have good luck)] or (either [both the British have good luck and it is not the case that (either the Americans have good luck or the Canadians have good luck)] or [both the Canadians have good luck and it is not the case that (either the Americans have good luck or the British have good luck)]).

The symbolic version of sentence 9 is a good deal more perspicuous than is the paraphrase:

9b. $[A \;\&\sim (B \vee C)] \vee ([B \;\&\sim (A \vee C)] \vee [C \;\&\sim (A \vee B)])$

As sentence 9a illustrates, truth-functional paraphrases of complex English passages can themselves become very complex. Constructing truth-functional paraphrases is of most value when one is first learning to symbolize English sentences in *SL*. After some facility with the techniques of symbolization has been gained, the paraphrase stage can be skipped, except when there is something especially difficult or interesting about the passage being symbolized. Hence hereafter we shall sometimes omit the paraphrase stage. Sentence 10 is fairly readily symbolized as

10b. $(A \;\& B) \vee [(A \;\& C) \vee (B \;\& C)]$

Sentence 11 is a repeat of sentence 10 with the additional proviso that not all the teams have good luck. One appropriate symbolization is:

11b. $[(A \;\& B) \vee [(A \;\& C) \vee (B \;\& C)]] \;\& \sim [A \;\& (B \;\& C)]$

We shall now symbolize an argument, using the following abbreviations:

R: The Australians raise their spinnaker.
I: The wind increases.
A: The Australians win the race.
C: The Australians capsize.
L: The Australians look foolish.
J: The Australians strike their jib.
M: The Australians reef their main.

If the Australians raise their spinnaker then if the wind doesn't increase they will win the race, but if they raise their spinnaker and the wind does increase they will lose the race and look foolish. The wind will increase and the Australians will reef their main and strike their jib, and will not raise their spinnaker. So if they don't capsize the Australians will win the race.

In symbolizing this argument we shall identify losing the race with not winning the race. In the context this is surely permissible. Here is our symbolization of the argument:

$[R \supset (\sim I \supset A)] \;\& [(R \;\& I) \supset (\sim A \;\& L)]$

$[I \;\& (M \;\& J)] \;\& \sim R$

---

$\sim C \supset A$

Our formal techniques will reveal that this argument is truth-functionally invalid.

## 2.2E EXERCISES

**1.** Paraphrase the following sentences about the performance of the French, German, and Danish teams in the next Olympics and symbolize the paraphrases as sentences in *SL*:

F: The French team will win at least one gold medal.
G: The German team will win at least one gold medal.
D: The Danish team will win at least one gold medal.
P: The French team is plagued with injuries.
S: The star German runner is disqualified.
R: It rains during most of the competition.

a. At least one of the French, German, or Danish teams will win a gold medal.
*b. At most one of them will win a gold medal.
c. Exactly one of them will win a gold medal.
*d. They will not all win gold medals.
e. At least two of them will win gold medals.
*f. At most two of them will win gold medals.
g. Exactly two of them will win gold medals.
*h. They will all win gold medals.

**2.** Using the abbreviations given in exercise 1, construct idiomatic English sentences from the following sentences of *SL*:

a. $\sim F \,\&\, (\sim G \,\&\, \sim D)$
*b. $\sim (F \,\&\, (G \,\&\, D))$
c. $\sim (F \vee (G \vee D))$
*d. $\sim (F \vee G) \vee (\sim (G \vee D) \vee \sim (F \vee D))$
e. $(F \vee G) \vee ((G \vee D) \vee (F \vee D))$
*f. $(F \,\&\, G) \vee ((G \,\&\, D) \vee (F \,\&\, D))$
g. $F \,\&\, ((G \vee D) \,\&\, \sim (G \,\&\, D))$
*h. $(F \,\&\, G) \vee (F \,\&\, D)$

**3.** Paraphrase the following and using the abbreviations given in exercise 1 symbolize the resulting paraphrases as sentences in *SL*:

a. If any of them wins a gold medal so will the other two.
*b. The French will win a gold medal unless they are plagued with injuries, in which case they won't.
c. If the star German runner is disqualified, the Germans will win a gold medal only if neither of the other two teams does.
*d. Provided it doesn't rain during most of the competition and their star runner isn't disqualified, the Germans will win a gold medal if either of the other teams does.
e. The Danes will win a gold medal if and only if the French are plagued with injuries and the star German runner is disqualified.
*f. The Germans will win a gold medal only if it doesn't rain during most of the competition and their star runner is not disqualified.
g. If the French are plagued with injuries, they will win a gold medal only if neither of the other teams does and it rains during most of the competition.
*h. The Danes will win a gold medal unless it rains during most of the competition, in which case they won't but the other two teams will win gold medals.

4. Using the abbreviations given in exercise 1, construct idiomatic English sentences from the following sentences of *SL*:

a. (S ⊃ ~ G) & S
*b. ~ (F ∨ G) ⊃ D
c. ~ G ≡ (D & F)
*d. (P & S) ⊃ D
e. [(G ⊃ F) & (F ⊃ D)] ⊃ (G ⊃ D)
*f. R ⊃ [(~ F & ~ G) & ~ D]
g. [F ∨ (G ∨ D)] ∨ [P ∨ (S ∨ R)]
*h. D ∨ [(F & ~ P) ∨ (G & ~ S)]

5. Paraphrase and then symbolize the following passages, being careful to indicate the abbreviations you are using.

a. If the United States and Russia will negotiate seriously, the nuclear disarmament talks will succeed. The United States will negotiate seriously if there is a strong conventional military force in Europe, and the Soviet Union will negotiate seriously if and only if the Kremlin has something to gain. Of course, the Kremlin has something to gain and there's a strong conventional force in Europe. Thus the disarmament talks will succeed.

*b. Either George doesn't have a high cholesterol level or cholesterol is trapped in the walls of his arteries. If cholesterol is trapped in his arteries, then plaque will build up and block his arteries, and with such a build up and blockage he is a candidate for a heart attack. Hence George is a candidate for a heart attack.

c. Either the maid or the butler committed the murder unless the cook did it. The cook did it only if a knife was the murder weapon; moreover, if a knife was used, neither the butler nor the maid did it. The murder weapon was a knife. Therefore the cook did it.

*d. If neither Henry nor Fred will play the lawyer, then Morris will not be upset; and moreover, if Morris will not be upset the drama will be successful. Thus the drama will get good reviews. Afterall, both Henry and Fred will not play the part of the lawyer, and the drama will get good reviews if and only if the drama will be a success.

e. The candidate will win at least two of three key states—California, New York, and Texas, for if the candidate is perceived as conservative, she will not win New York but will win the other two. She is perceived as conservative if her advertising campaign is effective; and she has an effective advertising campaign.

*f. Assuming Betty is the judge, Peter won't get a suspended sentence. The trial will be long unless the district attorney is brief, but the district attorney is not brief. Fred is the defense lawyer. However, if Fred is the defense lawyer, Peter will be found guilty; and if Peter will be found guilty, he will be given a sentence. Consequently, after a long trial Peter will be given a sentence which won't be suspended by the judge.

## 2.3 NON-TRUTH-FUNCTIONAL CONNECTIVES

As stated in Section 2.1,

> A sentential connective is used *truth-functionally* if and only if it is used to generate a compound sentence from one or more sentences in such a way

that the truth-value of the generated compound is wholly determined by the truth-values of those one or more sentences from which the compound is generated, no matter what those truth-values may be.

The sentential connectives of *SL* have only truth-functional uses. Many sentential connectives of English have truth-functional uses, but many do not. And many of those that do are not always used truth-functionally.

Determining whether a particular connective is or is not being used in a truth-functional sense is a complex matter. But a good rule of thumb is this: If the connective is being used truth-functionally, one should be able to construct a truth-table that adequately characterizes that use. (This is just what we did for standard uses of the English connectives introduced in Section 2.1.) If a truth-table that adequately characterizes the use of a connective in a particular sentence cannot be constructed, then that connective is not being used truth-functionally in the sentence in question.

To see how this rule of thumb operates, consider the use of 'if . . . then . . . ' in the following sentence:

> If Germany's U-boats had been able to shut off the flow of supplies to Great Britain, then Germany would have won the war.

If 'if . . . then . . . ' is being used truth-functionally in this conditional, it is probably being used in the sense captured by the horseshoe of *SL*, in the sense characterized by the table

| $\mathscr{P}$ | $\mathscr{Q}$ | $\mathscr{P} \supset \mathscr{Q}$ |
|---|---|---|
| T | T | T |
| T | F | F |
| F | T | T |
| F | F | T |

The truth-functional paraphrase of the sentence would be

> If Germany's U-boats were able to shut off the flow of supplies to Great Britain then Germany won the war.

In fact, Germany's U-boats were not able to shut off the flow of supplies to Great Britain; that is, the antecedent of this material conditional is false. The material conditional is therefore true. But historians do not all think the original conditional is true. Some think it true, some false, depending upon their appraisal of the historical evidence.

One might still argue that in the example 'if . . . then . . . ' is being used in some truth-functional sense. If so, we should be able to construct a paraphrase and a truth-table that express that sense. But a little reflection will show that no rearrangement of the **T**'s and **F**'s in the final column of the table will produce such a table. This is because such conditionals are claims about what would happen in certain situations, regardless of whether or not those specified situations actually obtain. That is, knowledge of whether the situation described by the antecedent and consequent obtain is not sufficient to determine the truth-value of such conditionals. Some of these conditionals are true when the situations described do not hold ('If Germany had won World War II, Britain would have lost' is one), and some are false ('If Germany had invaded Spain, Germany would have won World War II').

Conditionals such as we have just been discussing are called *subjunctive conditionals* (because they are in the subjunctive, rather than the indicative, mood), and 'if ... then ...' as used in subjunctive conditionals is not truth-functional. In this case and in other cases in which connectives are not being used truth-functionally, the safest course is to abbreviate the compounds generated by the connectives as atomic sentences of *SL*.

But being safe has it costs. Many arguments do make use of subjunctive conditionals, and we do want to evaluate the validity of these arguments whenever it is possible to do so. Consider the case of a doctor testifying at an inquest. He claims that the deceased did not die of strychnine poisoning and, when asked by the coroner to support his claim, argues as follows:

> Had the deceased died of strychnine poisoning, there would have been traces of that poison in the body. The autopsy would have found those traces had they been there. The autopsy did not reveal any traces of strychnine. Hence the deceased did not die of strychnine poisoning.

Here the following truth-functional paraphrase seems appropriate:

> If the deceased died of strychnine poisoning then there were traces of strychnine in the body.
>
> If there were traces of strychnine in the body then the autopsy found traces of strychnine in the body.
>
> It is not the case that the autopsy found traces of strychnine in the body.
>
> ---
>
> It is not the case that the deceased died of strychnine poisoning.

Symbolizing this argument yields:

$$\begin{array}{l} S \supset T \\ T \supset R \\ \sim R \\ \hline \sim S \end{array}$$

This symbolic argument is valid. Hence so is the English paraphrase of our original argument. In constructing that paraphrase, we weakened the premises but not the conclusion. (A sentence $p$ is *weaker* than a sentence $q$ if and only if the truth of $q$ guarantees the truth of $p$ but not vice versa. If $p$ is weaker than $q$, $q$ is *stronger* than $p$.) Consequently, if the premises of the original argument are true, then so are those of the paraphrase. And, since the paraphrase is valid, its conclusion is true if its premises are. The conclusion of the paraphrase is just a rewording of the conclusion of the original argument. Hence, if the premises of the original argument are true, the conclusion of that argument is also true. That is, the original argument is also valid.

Here is another argument using subjective conditionals:

> If Hitler had kept his treaty with Stalin, he would have defeated England. Hitler did not keep his treaty with Stalin. Therefore if Hitler had kept his treaty with Stalin he would have freed all the Jews and disbanded the SS.

Suppose we construct the following truth-functional paraphrase:

> If Hitler kept his treaty with Stalin then Hitler defeated England.
> It is not the case that Hitler kept his treaty with Stalin.
>
> ---
>
> If Hitler kept his treaty with Stalin, then both Hitler freed all the Jews and Hitler disbanded the SS.

This paraphrase can be readily symbolized as

$$K \supset E$$
$$\sim K$$

---

$$K \supset (F \& D)$$

Here the conclusion is equivalent to '$\sim K \vee (F \& D)$' and hence accurately symbolizes only 'Either Hitler did not keep his treaty with Stalin or Hitler did free all the Jews and Hitler disbanded the SS'. This claim does validly follow from the second premise of the argument. So our paraphrase is valid (as, of course, is the symbolic version of it). But the original English argument is clearly invalid. What has happened is that, in paraphrasing that argument, we made the conclusion, which is a subjunctive conditional, a material conditional. And if we weaken a conclusion in constructing a truth-functional paraphrase, there can be no guarantee that the symbolic argument we obtain by symbolizing that paraphrase will be valid *only if* the original English argument is valid. It may well be impossible for certain premises to be true and a weak conclusion false, where it is *not* impossible for those same premises to be true and a stronger conclusion false. Parallel examples can be constructed using other non-truth-functional conditionals. In view of these examples, a further guideline for paraphrasing and symbolizing non-truth-functional compounds is in order:

> The safest policy in dealing with non-truth-functional compounds is to paraphrase them as single sentences. In constructing a paraphrase for an argument, if non-truth-functional compounds are paraphrased as truth-functional compounds, be sure that the paraphrased premises are not stronger than the original premises and that the paraphrased conclusion is not weaker than the original conclusion.

DIFFERENCE BETWEEN TRUTH FUNCTIONAL SENTENCES & NON-TRUTH FUNCTIONAL SENTENCES

There are many connectives of English that have no truth-functional senses. One such connective is 'before'. When placed between two English sentences 'before' does generate a further sentence (through sometimes an awkward one).

From the sentences 'Nixon was elected President' and 'Bush was elected President' we can in this way obtain

Nixon was elected President before Bush was elected President.

This compound is true. But writing 'before' between two true sentences does not always produce a true sentence. A case in point is

Nixon was elected President before Kennedy was elected President.

This compound is false, though the sentences from which it is generated are both true. Reflection should show that there is no truth-functional use of 'before', because there is no use of 'before' in which the truth-value of

$p$ before $q$

is determined, given only that $p$ and $q$ are both true. Similar considerations will show that 'after', 'when', and 'because' lack truth-functional senses in English.

There are also unary connectives of English that operate only non-truth-functionally. 'It is well known that' is one such connective. There is no use of this connective in which knowing only the truth-value of $p$ always allows one to calculate the truth-value of

It is well known that $p$.

For example, both 'Cleveland is a city in Ohio' and 'Arcadia is a town in Ohio' are true. And, though 'It is well known that Cleveland is a city in Ohio' is true, 'It is well known that Arcadia is a town in Ohio' is false. Such considerations show that this unary connective has no truth-functional use. Similar reasoning will show that such other unary connectives as 'necessarily', 'probably', 'possibly', 'it is alleged that', and 'many people fear that' have no truth-functional senses.

Such expressions as 'Tom believes that', 'Tom knows that', and 'Tom hopes that' can be attached to sentences to generate further sentences. But sentences generated in this way are not truth-functionally compound sentences. For example, 'Paris is in France' is true, but knowing this does not allow us to calculate the truth-value of

Tom believes that Paris is in France.

For all we know, Tom may believe that Paris is in Belgium, not France. Tom, like most of us, has some true beliefs and some false beliefs.

We have yet to consider the rather special case of a non-truth-functional connective generating a compound sentence from sentences that are themselves truth-functionally compound. For example,

<u>Either</u> Mary is late <u>or</u> the clock is wrong

is clearly a truth-functionally compound sentence. But

Tom believes that either Mary is late or the clock is wrong

is not. Nor should it be paraphrased as a truth-functional compound, for example,

> Either Tom believes that Mary is late or Tom believes that the clock is wrong.

Tom may well believe the disjunction about Mary and the clock without believing either disjunct, just as one might believe that one will either pass or fail a given course, without either believing that one will pass or believing that one will fail. (We can often reasonably predict that one or the other of two events will happen, without being able to predict *which* one will happen.)

Similarly,

> Probably the coin will come up heads or tails

cannot fairly be paraphrased as

> Either the coin will probably come up heads or the coin will probably come up tails.

In fact, if the coin is a fair coin the odds are very high that it will come up either heads or tails (that it will not stand on edge). But the odds that it will come up heads are slightly less than one in two, as are the odds that it will come up tails (it just might stand on edge). So the truth-functional paraphrase is false, even though the claim it allegedly paraphrases is true.

But now consider

> Probably Alice and Tom will both pass the course.

It certainly seems appropriate to paraphrase this sentence as

> Both probably Alice will pass the course and probably Tom will pass the course.

If a conjunction is probable, then each conjunct is probable. But a disjunction can be probable without either disjunct alone being probable. The same reasoning holds for such sentence-compounding expressions as 'necessarily' and 'certainly'. Roughly speaking, when either 'necessary' or 'probably' is attached to a sentence that can be paraphrased as a conjunction, the result can itself be paraphrased as a conjunction; but this is not the case when one of these terms is attached to a sentence that is a disjunction, or to other kinds of truth-functional compounds.

### 2.3E EXERCISES

**1.** Decide which of the following sentences are truth-functional compounds and explain why the remaining sentences are not. Symbolize all of the sentences in *SL*.

a. It's possible that every family on this continent owns a television set.

*b. Unless I am mistaken television is probably the most popular form of entertainment in the country.

c. Necessarily the coin will come up heads or tails.

*d. Tamara won't be visiting tonight because she is working late.
e. Although Tamara won't stop by, she has promised to phone early in the evening.
*f. If the defendant had originally pleaded guilty, the trial would have lasted twice as long.
g. John believes that our manuscript has been either lost or stolen.
*h. John believes that our manuscript has been stolen, and Howard believes that it has been lost.
i. The defendant relented only after much testimony was discredited.

**2.** Symbolize the following arguments in *SL*, being sure to state the abbreviations you are using.
a. The murder was committed by the maid unless she believed her life was in danger. Had the butler done it, it would have been done silently and the body would not have been mutilated. As a matter of fact it was done silently; however, the maid's life was not in danger. The butler did it if and only if the maid failed to do it. Hence the maid did it.
*b. If this piece of metal is gold, then it has atomic number 79. Nordvik believes this piece of metal is gold. Therefore Nordvik believes this piece of metal has atomic number 79.
c. If Charles Babbage had had the theory of the modern computer and had had modern electronic parts, then the modern computer would have been developed before the beginning of the twentieth century. In fact, although he lived in the early nineteenth century, Babbage had the theory of the modern computer. But he did not have access to modern electronic parts, and he was forced to construct his computers out of mechanical gears and levers. Therefore, if Charles Babbage had had modern electronic parts available to him, the modern computer would have been developed before the beginning of the twentieth century.

## 2.4 THE SYNTAX OF *SL*

Symbolic languages have a precision that everyday languages lack and that facilitates examination of the logical properties of sentences and arguments. We have already seen a large sample of sentences of *SL*. In this section a precise specification of the expressions of *SL* will be given. To ensure that our discussion of *SL* is as clear as possible, it will be helpful to draw some distinctions that are usually neither formulated nor observed in everyday language.

### *OBJECT LANGUAGE AND METALANGUAGE, USE AND MENTION*

We have been talking about the language *SL* in this chapter. When we talk about a language, we call that language the *object language*. In this text *SL* is an object language, and English is the metalanguage used to discuss it. A *metalanguage* is a language used to discuss or describe some object language. The distinction between object language and metalanguage is a relative one. If we talk about the German language in English, German is the object language and English the metalanguage. On the other hand, if we talk about the English language in German, then English is the object language and German the metalanguage.

Ordinarily, we employ words and expressions to talk about something other than those words themselves. But occasionally we do want to talk about expressions themselves, and we must use words to do so. For instance, in the sentence

Minnesota was the thirty-second state admitted to the Union

the word 'Minnesota' is being used to designate a political subdivision of the United States. On the other hand, in the sentence

'Minnesota' is an Indian word

the word 'Minnesota' itself is under discussion. When a word or expression is being talked about we say that that word or expression is being *mentioned*, rather than used. One way to mention an expression is to use a name of that expression, and the standard way to form the name of an expression is to enclose that expression in single quotation marks. Throughout this text we use this method of forming the names of expressions. Thus in

'Saratoga' contains four syllables

the word 'Saratoga' is mentioned, not used. Omitting the single quotation marks produces a false sentence:

Saratoga contains four syllables.

Saratoga is a city, not a word; it contains buildings and people, not syllables.

In discussing the object language *SL* we often need to refer to, that is, to mention, specific expressions. We do so by using names of those expressions. One way to form the name of an expression is to enclose that expression in single quotation marks. The sentence

'$\sim$ B' is a negation

is about the expression of *SL* enclosed within single quotation marks. We also mention expressions by displaying them. The expression

(A $\vee$ B)

is a sentence of *SL* and is mentioned here by being displayed.

Note that the names of expressions in a language we are talking about do not themselves have to be part of that language. In fact, the *names* of expressions of *SL* are not part of the language *SL*. So an expression like

'(A $\vee$ B)'

is not an expression of *SL*, although the expression named

(A $\vee$ B)

*is* an expression *SL*. This is because single quotation marks are not part of the vocabulary of the language *SL*. We use names of expressions of *SL* in order to talk about those expressions; hence in this text these names are part of the metalanguage that we are using.

*METAVARIABLES*

Besides naming specific expressions of *SL*, we sometimes want to talk about these expressions more generally. For this purpose, we use *metalinguistic variables, metavariables* for short. A metavariable is an expression in the metalanguage that is used to talk generally about expressions of the object language. In this text, we use the boldfaced script letters '$\mathscr{P}$', '$\mathscr{Q}$', '$\mathscr{R}$', and '$\mathscr{S}$' as metavariables that range over the expressions of our symbolic languages. (We used these metavariables in Section 2.1 in giving the characteristic truth-tables for the truth-functional connectives of *SL*.)

When we say

> If '$\sim$ (H $\vee$ I)' is an expression of *SL* consisting of a tilde followed by a sentence of *SL*, then '$\sim$ (H $\vee$ I)' is a negation

we are making a claim about a specific sentence of *SL*. But by using metavariables we can talk generally about expressions of *SL*. Thus we may write:

> If $\mathscr{P}$ is an expression of *SL* consisting of a tilde followed by a sentence of *SL*, then $\mathscr{P}$ is a negation.

Here '$\mathscr{P}$' is a metavariable that ranges over (is used to talk about) expressions of the object language. The displayed sentence means: Every expression of *SL* that consists of a tilde followed by a sentence is a *negation*. The displayed sentence is not about the metavariable '$\mathscr{P}$'; for '$\mathscr{P}$' is not an expression of *SL*. Rather, the sentence is about all the *values* of $\mathscr{P}$, that is, all those expressions that *are* expressions of *SL*. (When we want to talk about a metavariable, that is, to mention a metavariable, we place that metavariable in single quotation marks.)

*THE LANGUAGE* SL

We are now in a position to provide a rigorous definition of the sentences of the language *SL*. This is done in two steps: First the vocabulary of *SL* is specified and then the grammar. The specification of the vocabulary involves stating what the basic expressions of *SL* are. These are like the words and punctuation marks of English, in the sense that the items in the vocabulary of basic expressions of *SL* are the building blocks from which all sentences of *SL* are generated. The difference is that in *SL* we do not have words and punctuation marks; rather we have sentence letters, truth-functional connectives, and punctuation marks. The sentence letters are capitalized Roman letters (non-boldfaced) with or without positive integer subscripts:

$$A, B, C, \ldots, A_1, B_1, C_1, \ldots, A_2, B_2, C_2, \ldots$$

Note that a capitalized Roman letter with a numerical subscript counts as *one* sentence letter, so '$A_1$' is a *single* sentence letter. The connectives of *SL* are the five truth-functional connectives:

$\sim$ & $\vee$ $\supset$ $\equiv$

The connective '$\sim$' is a *unary* connective; the others are *binary* connectives. The punctuation marks consist of the left and right parentheses:

( )

Other expressions of *SL* are formed by writing one basic expression after another. But, just as the expression 'Some and vanity men will left' is not a sentence of the English language, although it is formed entirely of English words, so there are expressions that consist entirely of basic expressions of *SL* but are not themselves sentences of *SL*. We specify the grammar of *SL* by specifying what expressions of *SL* count as sentences of *SL*. The sentences of *SL* are defined as follows:

1. Every sentence letter is a sentence.
2. If $\mathscr{P}$ is a sentence, then $\sim \mathscr{P}$ is a sentence.[2]
3. If $\mathscr{P}$ and $\mathscr{Q}$ are sentences, then $(\mathscr{P} \,\&\, \mathscr{Q})$ is a sentence.
4. If $\mathscr{P}$ and $\mathscr{Q}$ are sentences, then $(\mathscr{P} \vee \mathscr{Q})$ is a sentence.
5. If $\mathscr{P}$ and $\mathscr{Q}$ are sentences, then $(\mathscr{P} \supset \mathscr{Q})$ is a sentence.
6. If $\mathscr{P}$ and $\mathscr{Q}$ are sentences, then $(\mathscr{P} \equiv \mathscr{Q})$ is a sentence.
7. Nothing is a sentence unless it can be formed by repeated application of clauses 1–6.

The sentences specified by the first clause—the sentence letters of *SL*—are the *atomic sentences* of *SL*. The second through the sixth clauses specify how sentences are built up from shorter sentences. The final clause specifies that only expressions that can be formed in accordance with clauses 1–6 are sentences. The

[2] The expression '$\sim \mathscr{P}$' is a hybrid insofar as the connective '$\sim$' belongs to the object language *SL*, whereas the metavariable '$\mathscr{P}$' does not. We use the expression

$\sim \mathscr{P}$

as an expression of our metalanguage to stand for any sentence of *SL* that consists of a tilde followed by a sentence of *SL*. Similarly,

$(\mathscr{P} \vee \mathscr{Q})$

is a metalinguistic expression that we use to stand for any sentence of *SL* that consists of the following sequence of expressions: a left parenthesis, a sentence of *SL*, a wedge, a sentence of *SL*, a right parenthesis.

In such contexts we do not place single quotes around these metalinguistic expressions because we want to talk about sentences of *SL*, rather than about the metalinguistic expressions. That is,

'$\sim \mathscr{P}$' is a sentence of *SL*

says *falsely* that the metavariable '$\mathscr{P}$' preceded by a tilde is a sentence of *SL*. When we do place single quotes around an expression containing a metavariable, it is because we want to talk about that expression, not about a sentence of *SL*.

We adopt the following conventions. Whenever we use expressions consisting of both metavariables and expressions of *SL*, we let the expressions of *SL* occurring therein function as their own names, while the metavariables continue to function as metavariables (*not* as their own names). Thus each symbol that occurs in such an expression is being used to designate some expression(s) of *SL*. Moreover, the order of the symbols in such an expression indicates the order of the symbols in the object language sentences that the expression stands for. (We shall observe the same conventions in the second half of this book when we discuss the language *PL*.)

definition provides the basis for an *effective* method of determining whether or not an expression is a sentence. This means that we can determine in a finite number of mechanical steps whether or not an expression is a sentence. We may show that an expression is a sentence by beginning with the sentence letters that occur in the expression and continually using the clauses of the definition until we have generated the sentence in question. To illustrate this, we shall use this definition to show that '(~ B & (~ B ∨ A))' is a sentence. By clause 1, 'A' and 'B' are sentences. By clause 2, ' ~ B' is a sentence. By clause 4, '(~ B ∨ A)' is a sentence. Finally, by clause 3, '(~ B & (~ B ∨ A))' is a sentence.

The following expressions are not sentences of *SL*:

(B ∨ C ∨ D)
~ & A
(BC ⊃ D)
(B ⊂ (C ∨ D))
(p ≡ q)
(((A & B) & (C ∨ D))

The reasons are

'(B ∨ C ∨ D)' needs another pair of parentheses because it contains two binary connectives.

'&A' is not a sentence, since '&' is a *binary* connective; so ' ~ & A' cannot be a sentence.

'(BC ⊃ D)' contains two consecutive sentence letters, but no rule allows us to form a sentence in which sentence letters appear consecutively.

'(B ⊂ (C ∨ D))' is not a sentence because ' ⊂ ' is not an expression of *SL*.

'(p ≡ q); contains symbols that are not expressions of *SL*—the two lower-case letters.

'(((A & B) & (C ∨ D))' contains more left parentheses than right, and the clauses that introduce parentheses introduce them in pairs.

We adopt the convention that the *outermost* parentheses of a sentence may be dropped whenever that sentence occurs by itself (when it is not part of another sentence). We followed this convention in earlier sections of this chapter. So we may write 'A ⊃ (B & C)' instead of '(A ⊃ (B & C))', but we may *not* write ' ~ B ∨ C' instead of ' ~ (B ∨ C)'. The second sentence is a negation; the first is not. Our convention also covers the *outermost* parentheses of metalinguistic expressions ranging over sentences of *SL*; for example, we write '𝒫 ∨ 𝒬' instead of '(𝒫 ∨ 𝒬)'. Finally, we adopt the convention, for both sentences of *SL* and metalinguistic expressions, that brackets may be used in place of parentheses. Thus '(A ∨ B) & C' may be written as '[A ∨ B] & C'.

In this section we have been discussing *SL* syntactically. The syntactical study of a language is the study of the expressions of the language and the relations among them, without regard to possible *interpretations* of these expressions. Thus, for example, we have defined sentences of *SL* only in terms of expressions of *SL*; nowhere in the definition are the possible interpretations of the expressions mentioned. Of course, we have certain interpretations of these expressions in mind. We intend the connective '&' to symbolize the English connective 'and' in its truth-functional sense, the sentence letters to abbreviate sentences of English, and so on. But we could have presented this syntactic discussion of *SL* without regard to the possible interpretations of the expressions. When we specify and investigate interpretations of the expressions of a language, we are looking at the *semantics* of the language. For instance, the specification of the characteristic truth-tables for the truth-functional connectives is part of the specification of a *semantics* for *SL*.

Before closing this section, we shall introduce four more syntactic concepts: the *main connective* of a sentence and the *immediate sentential components*, *sentential components*, and *atomic components* of a sentence. These are defined in terms of the specification of sentences as follows:

1. If $\mathscr{P}$ is an atomic sentence, $\mathscr{P}$ contains no connectives and hence does not have a main connective. $\mathscr{P}$ has no immediate sentential components.
2. If $\mathscr{P}$ is of the form $\sim \mathscr{Q}$, where $\mathscr{Q}$ is a sentence, then the main connective of $\mathscr{P}$ is the tilde that occurs before $\mathscr{Q}$, and $\mathscr{Q}$ is the immediate sentential component of $\mathscr{P}$.
3. If $\mathscr{P}$ is of the form $\mathscr{Q} \,\&\, \mathscr{R}$, $\mathscr{Q} \vee \mathscr{R}$, $\mathscr{Q} \supset \mathscr{R}$, or $\mathscr{Q} \equiv \mathscr{R}$, where $\mathscr{Q}$ and $\mathscr{R}$ are sentences, then the main connective of $\mathscr{P}$ is the connective that occurs between $\mathscr{Q}$ and $\mathscr{R}$, and $\mathscr{Q}$ and $\mathscr{R}$ are the immediate sentential components of $\mathscr{P}$.

The *sentential components* of a sentence include the sentence itself, its immediate sentential components, and the sentential components of its immediate sentential components. The *atomic components* of a sentence are all the sentential components that are atomic sentences.

### 2.4E EXERCISES

**1.** Which of the following are true and which are false?

a. Copper is copper.
*b. 'Copper' is the name of copper.
c. The chemical symbol 'Cu' names 'copper'.
*d. 'Copper' is copper.
e. Copper is the name of copper.
*f. Some coins are made of copper.
g. 'Copper' is a metal.

**2.** In each of the following sentences 'Deutschland' is either used or mentioned. Indicate where that word is being used or mentioned and explain how this is being done.

a. The only German word mentioned in the instructions to these exercises contains eleven letters.

*b. Some people think Deutschland and Germany are two different countries, but actually 'Deutschland' is the German name of Germany.
c. The German name of Germany is mentioned several times in these examples, but it only used once.
*d. 'Deutschland' is 'Deutschland'.
e. The word 'Deutschland' is not being used in this sentence.
*f. Deutschland is the German name of Germany.

**3.** Which of the following are sentences of *SL* and which are not? For those that are not explain why they are not.

a. B & Z
*b. & H
c. ~ O
*d. M ~ N
e. J ⊃ (K ⊃ (A ∨ N))
*f. $\mathscr{P} \vee \mathscr{Q}$
g. (I ∨ [T & E])
*h. (U & C & ~ L)
i. (F ≡ K) ⊃ [M ∨ K]
*j. [(G ∨ E) ⊃ (~ H & (K ∨ B)]

**4.** For each of the following sentences, specify the main connective and the immediate sentential components. Then list all the sentential components, indicating which ones are atomic.

a. ~ A & H
*b. ~ (A & H)
c. ~ (S & G) ∨ B
*d. K ⊃ (~ K ⊃ K)
e. (C ≡ K) ∨ (~ H ∨ (M & N))
*f. M ⊃ [~ N ⊃ ((B & C) ≡ ~ [(L ⊃ J) ∨ X])]

**5.** Which of the following sentences are of the form $\sim \mathscr{P} \supset \mathscr{Q}$? In each case justify your answer.

a. A ⊃ B
*b. ~ A ⊃ B
c. ~ A ⊃ ~ B
*d. ~~ A ⊃ B
e. ~ (A ⊃ B)
*f. ~~ A ⊃ ~ B
g. ~ (~ A ⊃ B)
*h. ~~ (A ⊃ B) ⊃ (C ⊃ D)
i. ~ (A ∨ ~ B) ⊃ ~ (C & ~ D)
*j. ~ (A ≡ B) & (~ C ⊃ D)

**6.** Which of the following characters can occur immediately to the left of '~' in a sentence of *SL*? When one can so occur, give a sentence of *SL* in which it does; when it cannot so occur, explain why. Which of these characters could occur immediately to the right of 'A' in a sentence of *SL*? When one can so occur, give a sentence of *SL* in which it does; when it cannot so occur, explain why.

a. H
*b. &
c. (
*d. )
e. [
*f. ~

## GLOSSARY

TRUTH-FUNCTIONAL USE OF A CONNECTIVE: A sentential connective is used truth-functionally if and only if it is used to generate a compound sentence from one or more sentences in such a way that the truth-value of the generated compound is wholly determined by the truth-values of those one or more sentences from which the compound is generated, no matter what those truth-values may be.

Chapter **3**

# SENTENTIAL LOGIC: SEMANTICS

| P | ~P |
|---|---|
| T | F |
| F | T |

| P | D |
|---|---|
| T | T |
| F | F |
| F | T |
| F | F |

| P & D |
|---|
| T |
| F |
| F |
| F |

| P | D |
|---|---|
| T | T |
| T | F |
| F | T |
| F | F |

| P v D |
|---|
| T |
| T |
| T |
| F |

| P | D |
|---|---|
| T | T |
| T | F |
| F | T |
| F | F |

| P ⊃ D |
|---|
| T |
| F |
| T |
| T |

## 3.1 TRUTH-VALUE ASSIGNMENTS AND TRUTH-TABLES FOR SENTENCES

In Chapter One we introduced logical concepts such as logical truth and deductive validity and used these to evaluate sentences and arguments stated in English. In this chapter we shall develop formal tests for truth-functional versions of the concepts introduced in Section 1.4, specifically truth-functional truth, falsity, and indeterminacy; truth-functional consistency; ~~truth-functional~~ entailment; and truth-functional validity. All these concepts fall within the realm of semantics: They concern the truth-values and truth-conditions of sentences. Before defining these truth-functional concepts for sentences and arguments of *SL*, our first task is to specify how truth-values and truth-conditions for sentences of *SL* are determined.

Every sentence of *SL* can be built up from its atomic components in accordance with the definition of sentences. Similarly, the truth-value of a sentence of *SL* is determined completely by the truth-values of its atomic components in accordance with the characteristic truth-tables for the connectives. We repeat the characteristic truth-tables here:

| $\mathscr{P}$ | $\sim \mathscr{P}$ |
|---|---|
| T | F |
| F | T |

| $\mathscr{P}$ | $\mathscr{Q}$ | $\mathscr{P}\ \&\ \mathscr{Q}$ |
|---|---|---|
| T | T | T |
| T | F | F |
| F | T | F |
| F | F | F |

| $\mathscr{P}$ | $\mathscr{Q}$ | $\mathscr{P} \vee \mathscr{Q}$ |
|---|---|---|
| T | T | T |
| T | F | T |
| F | T | T |
| F | F | F |

| $\mathscr{P}$ | $\mathscr{Q}$ | $\mathscr{P} \supset \mathscr{Q}$ |
|---|---|---|
| T | T | T |
| T | F | F |
| F | T | T |
| F | F | T |

| $\mathscr{P}$ | $\mathscr{Q}$ | $\mathscr{P} \equiv \mathscr{Q}$ |
|---|---|---|
| T | T | T |
| T | F | F |
| F | T | F |
| F | F | T |

These tables tell us how to determine the truth-value of a truth-functionally compound sentence given the truth-values of its immediate sentential components. And, if the immediate sentences of a truth-functionally compound sentence are themselves truth-functionally compound, we can use the information in the characteristic truth-tables to determine how the truth-value of each immediate component depends on the truth-values of *its* immediate components, and so on until we arrive at atomic components.

The truth-values of atomic sentences are fixed by truth-value assignments:

A truth-value assignment is an assignment of truth-values (**T**'s or **F**'s) to the atomic sentences of *SL*.

The concept of a truth-value assignment is the basic semantic concept of *SL*. Intuitively, each truth-value assignment gives us a description of a way the world *might* be, for in each we consider a combination of truth-values that atomic sentences might have. We assume that the atomic sentences of *SL* are truth-functionally independent, that is, that the truth-value assigned to one does not affect the truth-value assigned to any other. For generality, we stipulate that a truth-value assignment must assign a truth-value to every atomic sentence of *SL*. Thus a truth-value assignment gives a *complete* description of a way the world might be. It tells us of each atomic sentence of *SL* whether or not that sentence is true. The truth-values of truth-functionally compound sentences of *SL* are determined uniquely and completely by the truth-values of their atomic components; since every atomic sentence of *SL* is assigned a truth-value by a truth-value assignment, it follows that every truth-functionally compound sentence also has a truth-value on each truth-value assignment.

A truth-table for a sentence of *SL* is used to record its truth-value on each truth-value assignment. Because each truth-value assignment assigns truth-values to an infinite number of atomic sentences (*SL* has infinitely many atomic sentences), we cannot list an entire truth-value assignment in a truth-table. Instead we list all the possible combinations of truth-values that the sentence's atomic components may have on a truth-value assignment. As an example, here is the beginning of a truth-table for ‘ ~ B ⊃ C’:

| B | C | ~ B ⊃ C |
|---|---|---|
| T | T | |
| T | F | |
| F | T | |
| F | F | |

The atomic components of the sentence are ‘B’ and ‘C’ and there are four combinations of truth-values that these components might have, as indicated in the four rows of the table. (Rows in truth-tables go from left to right; columns go from top to bottom.) Each row represents an infinite number of truth-value assignments, namely, all of the truth-value assignments that assign to ‘B’ and ‘C’ the values indicated in that row. Since the truth-value of ‘ ~ B ⊃ C’ on a truth-value assignment depends only upon the truth-values that its atomic components have on that assignment (and not, say, on the truth-value of ‘D’), the four combinations that we have displayed will allow us to determine the truth-value of ‘ ~ B ⊃ C’ on any truth-value assignment. That is, no matter which of the infinitely many truth-value assignments we might select, that truth-value assignment will assign one of the four pairs of truth-values displayed in the table above to ‘B’ and ‘C’.

The first step in constructing a truth-table for a sentence $\mathscr{P}$ of *SL* is to determine the number of different combinations of truth-values that its atomic components might have. There is a simple way to do this. Consider first the case in which $\mathscr{P}$ has one atomic component. There are two different combinations of truth-values that the single atomic component may have: **T** and **F**. Now suppose that $\mathscr{P}$ is a sentence with two atomic components. In this case there are four combinations of truth-values that the atomic components of $\mathscr{P}$ might have, as we have seen in the case of ‘ ~ B ⊃ C’ above.

If $\mathscr{P}$ has three atomic components, there are eight combinations of truth-values that its atomic components might have. Suppose we were to add a third sentence letter to the truth-table for ‘ ~ B ⊃ C’:

| A | B | C | (~ B ⊃ C) & (A ≡ B) |
|---|---|---|---|
| | T | T | |
| | T | F | |
| | F | T | |
| | F | F | |

What truth-tables do we enter in the first row under ‘A’? The combination of truth-values that would be displayed by entering **T** there is different from the combination that would be displayed by entering **F**. And we see that the same holds for each row. So we need to list each of the four combinations of truth-values that 'B' and 'C' may have twice in order to represent all combinations of truth-values for the three atomic components.

| A | B | C | (~ B ⊃ C) & (A ≡ B) |
|---|---|---|---|
| T | T | T | |
| T | T | F | |
| T | F | T | |
| T | F | F | |
| F | T | T | |
| F | T | F | |
| F | F | T | |
| F | F | F | |

Extending this reasoning, we find that every time we add a new atomic sentence to the list the number of rows in the truth-table doubles. If $\mathscr{P}$ has $n$ atomic components, there are $2^n$ different combinations of truth-values for its atomic components.[1] (If the same sentence letters occurs more than once in $\mathscr{P}$, we do not count each occurrence as a different atomic component of $\mathscr{P}$. To determine the number of atomic components, we count the number of *different* sentence letters that occur in $\mathscr{P}$.)

In constructing a truth-table, we adopt a systematic method of listing the combinations of truth-values that the atomic components of a sentence $\mathscr{P}$ might have. We first list the atomic components of $\mathscr{P}$ to the left of the vertical line at the top of the truth-table, in alphabetical order.[2]

Under the first sentence letter listed, write a column of $2^n$ entries, the first half of which are **T**'s and the second half of which are **F**'s. In the second column, the number of **T**'s and **F**'s being alternated is half the number alternated in the first column. In the column under the third sentence letter listed, the number of **T**'s and **F**'s being alternated will again be half the number in the second column. We repeat this process until a column has been entered under each sentence letter to the left of the vertical line. The column under the last sentence letter in this list will then consist of single **T**'s alternating with single **F**'s. Thus, for a truth-table with $n$ sentence letters, the first column consists of $2^{n-1}$ **T**'s alternating with $2^{n-1}$ **F**'s, the second of $2^{n-2}$ **T**'s alternating with $2^{n-2}$ **F**'s, and in general the $i$th column consists of $2^{n-i}$ **T**'s alternating with $2^{n-i}$ **F**'s. (Note that $2^0 = 1$.)

Now we can complete the rest of the truth-table for '(~ B ⊃ C) & (A ≡ B)'. We first repeat under 'A', 'B', and 'C', wherever these occur, the columns

[1] $2^n$ is 2 if $n = 1$, $2 \times 2$ if $n = 2$, $2 \times 2 \times 2$ if $n = 3$, and so on.

[2] This is an extended sense of 'alphabetical order', since some sentence letters have subscripts. In this order, all the nonsubscripted letters appear first, then all letters subscripted with '1', then all letters subscripted with '2', and so on.

we have already entered to the left of the vertical line:

| A | B | C | (~ | B | ⊃ | C) | & | (A | ≡ | B) |
|---|---|---|---|---|---|---|---|---|---|---|
| T | T | T | | T | | T | | T | | T |
| T | T | F | | T | | F | | T | | T |
| T | F | T | | F | | T | | T | | F |
| T | F | F | | F | | F | | T | | F |
| F | T | T | | T | | T | | F | | T |
| F | T | F | | T | | F | | F | | T |
| F | F | T | | F | | T | | F | | F |
| F | F | F | | F | | F | | F | | F |

Next we may enter the column for the component '~ B' under its main connective, the tilde. In each row in which 'B' has the truth-value **T**, '~ B' has the truth-value **F**, and in each row in which 'B' has the truth-value **F**, '~ B' has the truth-value **T**:

| A | B | C | (~ | B | ⊃ | C) | & | (A | ≡ | B) |
|---|---|---|---|---|---|---|---|---|---|---|
| T | T | T | F | T | | T | | T | | T |
| T | T | F | F | T | | F | | T | | T |
| T | F | T | T | F | | T | | T | | F |
| T | F | F | T | F | | F | | T | | F |
| F | T | T | F | T | | T | | F | | T |
| F | T | F | F | T | | F | | F | | T |
| F | F | T | T | F | | T | | F | | F |
| F | F | F | T | F | | F | | F | | F |

The column for '~ B ⊃ C' is entered under the horseshoe:

| A | B | C | (~ | B | ⊃ | C) | & | (A | ≡ | B) |
|---|---|---|---|---|---|---|---|---|---|---|
| T | T | T | F | T | T | T | | T | | T |
| T | T | F | F | T | T | F | | T | | T |
| T | F | T | T | F | T | T | | T | | F |
| T | F | F | T | F | F | F | | T | | F |
| F | T | T | F | T | T | T | | F | | T |
| F | T | F | F | T | T | F | | F | | T |
| F | F | T | T | F | T | T | | F | | F |
| F | F | F | T | F | F | F | | F | | F |

The truth-values of the immediate components of 'A ≡ B' for each row have been recorded, so we can now complete the column for 'A ≡ B' in accordance with the characteristic truth-table for ‘ ≡ ’:

| A | B | C | (~ | B | ⊃ | C) | & | (A | ≡ | B) |
|---|---|---|---|---|---|---|---|---|---|---|
| T | T | T | F | T | T | T | | T | T | T |
| T | T | F | F | T | T | F | | T | T | T |
| T | F | T | T | F | T | T | | T | F | F |
| T | F | F | T | F | F | F | | T | F | F |
| F | T | T | F | T | T | T | | F | F | T |
| F | T | F | F | T | T | F | | F | F | T |
| F | F | T | T | F | T | T | | F | T | F |
| F | F | F | T | F | F | F | | F | T | F |

Remember that a material biconditional has the truth-value **T** on all truth-value assignments on which its immediate components have the same truth-value, and the truth-value **F** on all other truth-value assignments. Finally, we enter the column for ‘(~ B ⊃ C) & (A ≡ B)’ under its main connective, the ampersand:

| A | B | C | (~ | B | ⊃ | C) | ↓<br>& | (A | ≡ | B) |
|---|---|---|---|---|---|---|---|---|---|---|
| T | T | T | F | T | T | T | T | T | T | T |
| T | T | F | F | T | T | F | T | T | T | T |
| T | F | T | T | F | T | T | F | T | F | F |
| T | F | F | T | F | F | F | F | T | F | F |
| F | T | T | F | T | T | T | F | F | F | T |
| F | T | F | F | T | T | F | F | F | F | T |
| F | F | T | T | F | T | T | T | F | T | F |
| F | F | F | T | F | F | F | F | F | T | F |

We use arrows to indicate the main connective of the sentence for which a truth-table has been constructed. Each row of the truth-table displays, underneath the arrow, the truth-value that the sentence has on every truth-value assignment that assigns to the atomic components of that sentence the truth-values displayed to the left of the vertical line.

Here is the truth-table for the sentence ‘[A ≡ (B ≡ A)] ∨ ~ C’:

| A | B | C | [A | ≡ | (B | ≡ | A)] | ↓<br>∨ | ~ | C |
|---|---|---|---|---|---|---|---|---|---|---|
| T | T | T | T | T | T | T | T | T | F | T |
| T | T | F | T | T | T | T | T | T | T | F |
| T | F | T | T | F | F | F | T | F | F | T |
| T | F | F | T | F | F | F | T | T | T | F |
| F | T | T | F | T | T | F | F | T | F | T |
| F | T | F | F | T | T | F | F | T | T | F |
| F | F | T | F | F | F | T | F | F | F | T |
| F | F | F | F | F | F | T | F | T | T | F |

The column for ' ~ C' is constructed in accordance with the characteristic truth-table for the tilde. ' ~ C' has the truth-value **T** on all and only those truth-value assignments on which 'C' has the truth-value **F**, and ' ~ C' has the truth-value **F** on every assignment on which 'C' has the truth-value **T**. The column for ' ~ C' appears directly underneath the tilde. The immediate components of '(B ≡ A)' are 'B' and 'A'. The characteristic truth-table for ' ≡ ' tells us that a material biconditional has the truth-value **T** on all and only those truth-value assignments on which both of its immediate sentential components have the same truth-value (both have the truth-value **T** or both have the truth-value **F**). Thus '(B ≡ A)' has the truth-value **T** for the combinations of truth-values displayed in the first two and last two rows of the truth-table and the truth-value **F** for the other combinations.

Similarly, '[A ≡ (B ≡ A)]' has the truth-value **T** on exactly those truth-value assignments on which 'A' and '(B ≡ A)' have the same truth-value. The column for '[A ≡ (B ≡ A)]' appears directly underneath its main connective, which is the first occurrence of the triple bar. '[A ≡ (B ≡ A)] ∨ ~ C' has the truth-value **T** on exactly those truth-value assignments on which at least one disjunct has the truth-value **T**. The disjuncts are '[A ≡ (B ≡ A)]' and ' ~ C'. So '[A ≡ (B ≡ A)] ∨ ~ C' has the truth-value **T** on every truth-value assignment on which either '[A ≡ (B ≡ A)]' or ' ~ C' has the truth-value **T**. Where both disjuncts have the truth-value **F**, so does '[A ≡ (B ≡ A)] ∨ ~ C'. The truth-value of the entire sentence for each combination of truth-values assigned to its atomic components is written in the column directly underneath the wedge, the sentence's main connective.

Here is the truth-table for the sentence ' ~ [(U ∨ (W ⊃ ~ U)) ≡ W]':

| U | W | ↓ ~ | [(U | ∨ | (W | ⊃ | ~ | U)) | ≡ | W] |
|---|---|---|---|---|---|---|---|---|---|---|
| T | T | F | T | T | T | F | F | T | T | T |
| T | F | T | T | T | F | T | F | T | F | F |
| F | T | F | F | T | T | T | T | F | T | T |
| F | F | T | F | T | F | T | T | F | F | F |

The column under the first occurrence of the tilde represents the truth-value of the entire sentence ' ~ [(U ∨ (W ⊃ ~ U)) ≡ W]' for each combination of truth-values that its atomic components might have. The truth-table tells us that ' ~ [(U ∨ (W ⊃ ~ U)) ≡ W]' has the truth-value **T** on those truth-value assignments on which either 'U' is assigned the truth-value **T** and 'W' is assigned the truth-value **F**, or both 'U' and 'W' are assigned the truth-value **F**; the sentence is false on every other truth-value assignment.

Sometimes we are not interested in determining the truth-values of a sentence 𝒫 for every truth-value assignment but are interested only in the truth-value of $\mathscr{P}$ on a particular truth-value assignment. In that case, we may construct a shortened truth-table for $\mathscr{P}$, which records only the truth-values that its atomic components are assigned by that truth-value assignment. For example, suppose we want to know the truth-value of '(A & B) ⊃ B' on a truth-value assignment that assigns **F** to 'A' and **T** to 'B' and all the other atomic sentences of *SL*. We head the shortened truth-table as before, with the atomic components of the sentence to the left of the vertical line and '(A & B) ⊃ B' itself to the right. We list only one combination of truth-values for 'A' and 'B', namely, the truth-values they have on the assignment we are interested in:

| A | B | (A | & | B) | ↓ ⊃ | B |
|---|---|---|---|---|---|---|
| F | T | F | F | T | T | T |

The truth-values of '(A & B)' and '(A & B) ⊃ B' are determined in accordance with the characteristic truth-tables, as before. Thus '(A & B)' has the truth-value **F** on this truth-value assignment, for 'A' has the truth-value **F**. Since the antecedent of '(A & B) ⊃ B' has the truth-value **F** and the consequent the truth-value **T**, '(A & B) ⊃ B' has the truth-value **T**.

We emphasize that when we want to determine the truth-value of a sentence on a particular truth-value assignment, we do not display the full truth-value assignment in question. Truth-value assignments assign truth-values to *every* atomic sentence of *SL*. Rather, we display only the combinations of truth-values that the atomic components of the sentence in question have on that assignment. There is no loss here because the truth-value of a sentence on a truth-value assignment depends *only* upon the truth-values of its atomic components on that assignment. Conversely, each row of a truth-table for a sentence gives information about infinitely many truth-value assignments. It tells us the truth-value of the sentence on every truth-value assignment that assigns to the atomic components of the sentence the combination of truth-values displayed in that row (there are infinitely many such assignments).

To review: The truth-value of a sentence $\mathscr{P}$ on a truth-value assignment is determined by starting with the truth-values of the atomic components of $\mathscr{P}$ on that truth-value assignment and then using the characteristic truth-tables for the connectives of *SL* to compute the truth-values of larger and larger sentential components of $\mathscr{P}$ on that truth-value assignment. Ultimately, we determine the truth-value of the largest sentential component of $\mathscr{P}$, namely, $\mathscr{P}$ itself. This procedure is used in the construction of a truth-table for $\mathscr{P}$, where each row displays a different combination of truth-values for the atomic components of $\mathscr{P}$. The truth-value of $\mathscr{P}$ for each such combination is recorded directly underneath the main connective of $\mathscr{P}$ in the row representing that combination. (If $\mathscr{P}$ is atomic, the truth-value is recorded under $\mathscr{P}$.)

We also define the notions of being *true on a truth-value assignment* and *false on a truth-value assignment*:

> A sentence is *true on a truth-value assignment* if and only if it has the truth-value **T** on that truth-value assignment.
>
> A sentence is *false on a truth-value assignment* if and only if it has the truth-value **F** on that truth-value assignment.

## 3.1E EXERCISES

**1.** How many rows will be in the truth-table for each of the following sentences?

a. A ≡ (∼ A ≡ A) 2
*b. [∼ D & (B ∨ G)] ⊃ [∼ (H & A) ∨ ∼ D] ~~64~~ 32
c. (B & C) ⊃ [B ∨ (C & ∼ C)] 4

**2.** Construct truth-tables for the following sentences.

a. ∼ ∼ (E & ∼ E)
*b. (A & B) ≡ ∼ B
c. A ≡ [J ≡ (A ≡ J)]
*d. [A ⊃ (B ⊃ C)] & [(A ⊃ B) ⊃ C]
e. [∼ A ∨ (H ⊃ J)] ⊃ (A ∨ J)
*f. (∼ ∼ A & ∼ B) ⊃ (∼ A ≡ B)
g. ∼ (A ∨ B) ⊃ (∼ A ∨ ∼ B)
*h. ∼ D & [∼ H ∨ (D & E)]
i. ∼ (E & [H ⊃ (B & E)])
*j. ∼ (D ≡ (∼ A & B)) ∨ (∼ D ∨ ∼ B)
k. ∼ [D & (E ∨ F)] ≡ [∼ D & (E & F)]
*l. (J & [(E ∨ F) & (∼ E & ∼ F)]) ⊃ ∼ J
m. (A ∨ (∼ A & (H ⊃ J))) ⊃ (J ⊃ H)

**3.** Construct shortened truth-tables to determine the truth-value of each of the following sentences on the truth-value assignment that assigns **T** to 'B' and 'C', and **F** to 'A' and to every other atomic sentence of *SL*.

a. ∼ [∼ A ∨ (∼ C ∨ ∼ B)]
*b. ∼ [A ∨ (∼ C & ∼ B)]
c. (A ⊃ B) ∨ (B ⊃ C)
*d. (A ⊃ B) ⊃ (B ⊃ C)
e. (A ≡ B) ∨ (B ≡ C)
*f. ∼ A ⊃ (B ≡ C)
g. ∼ [B ⊃ (A ∨ C)] & ∼ ∼ B
*h. ∼ [∼ A ≡ ∼ (B ≡ ∼ [A ≡ (B & C)])]
i. ∼ [∼ (A ≡ ∼ B) ≡ ∼ A] ≡ (B ∨ C)
*j. ∼ (B ⊃ ∼ A) & [C ≡ (A & B)]

**4.** Construct a truth-table for each of the sentences in Exercise 1 of Section 2.2E.

**5.** Construct a truth-table for each of the sentences in Exercise 3 of Section 2.2E.

## 3.2 TRUTH-FUNCTIONAL TRUTH, FALSITY, AND INDETERMINACY

In Section 1.4 the semantic concepts of logical truth, logical falsity, and logical indeterminacy were defined in terms of consistency. A logically true sentence of English, it will be remembered, is one that cannot be consistently denied. And we took this to mean that the sentence cannot possibly be false. A sentence that is logically true may be true on purely truth-functional grounds. We shall accordingly introduce the notion of truth-functional truth, as well as truth-functional falsity and truth-functional indeterminacy, for the sentences of *SL*.

Truth-functional truth is defined in terms of truth-value assignments:

> A sentence $\mathscr{P}$ of *SL* is *truth-functionally true* if and only if $\mathscr{P}$ is true on every truth-value assignment.[3]

Since every sentence of *SL* has exactly one of the two truth-values on any truth-value assignment, it follows that a sentence $\mathscr{P}$ is truth-functionally true if and only if there is no truth-value assignment on which $\mathscr{P}$ is false.

Once the truth-table for a sentence has been constructed, it is a simple matter to determine whether the sentence is truth-functionally true. Just examine the column of truth-values under its main connective. The sentence is truth-functionally true if and only if that column consists solely of **T**'s. Since the rows of the truth-table represent *all* combinations of truth-values that may be assigned to the atomic components of the sentence by any truth-value assignment, the absence of **F**'s under the sentence's main connective shows that there is no truth-value assignment on which the sentence is false.

Here are the truth-tables for two truth-functionally true sentences:

| A | A | ↓ ∨ | ~ A |
|---|---|---|---|
| **T** | **T** | **T** | **F T** |
| **F** | **F** | **T** | **T F** |

| X | Z | Z | ↓ ⊃ | (X | ∨ | Z) |
|---|---|---|---|---|---|---|
| **T** | **T** | **T** | **T** | **T** | **T** | **T** |
| **T** | **F** | **F** | **T** | **T** | **T** | **F** |
| **F** | **T** | **T** | **T** | **F** | **T** | **T** |
| **F** | **F** | **F** | **T** | **F** | **F** | **F** |

[3] Truth-functionally true sentences are sometimes called *tautologies* or *truth-functionally valid* sentences. Truth-functionally false sentences (introduced below) are sometimes called *contradictions* or *self-contradictory* sentences. Truth-functionally indeterminate sentences (also to be introduced) are sometimes called *contingent* sentences.

The columns under the main connectives of 'A ∨ ~ A' and 'Z ⊃ (X ∨ Z)' contain only **T**'s. Note that the immediate sentential components of a truth-functionally true sentence need not themselves be truth-functionally true.

Truth-functional falsity is also defined in terms of truth-value assignments:

> A sentence 𝒫 of *SL* is *truth-functionally false* if and only if 𝒫 is false on every truth-value assignment.

It follows that if 𝒫 is truth-functionally false, there is no truth-value assignment on which 𝒫 is true. We can show that a sentence of *SL* is truth-functionally false by constructing a truth-table for the sentence; if the column of truth-values underneath the sentence's main connective contains only **F**'s, then the sentence is truth-functionally false. Here are truth-tables for two truth-functionally false sentences:

| A | A | ↓ & | ~ A |
|---|---|---|---|
| T | T | F | F T |
| F | F | F | T F |

| H | K | [(H | ∨ | K) | ⊃ | ~ | (H | ∨ | K)] | ↓ & | H |
|---|---|---|---|---|---|---|---|---|---|---|---|
| T | T | T | T | T | F | F | T | T | T | F | T |
| T | F | T | T | F | F | F | T | T | F | F | T |
| F | T | F | T | T | F | F | F | T | T | F | F |
| F | F | F | F | F | T | T | F | F | F | F | F |

Note that the immediate sentential components of a truth-functionally false sentence need not themselves be truth-functionally false. When we negate a truth-functionally true sentence, we end up with a truth-functionally false sentence:

| A | ↓ ~ | (A | ∨ | ~ A) |
|---|---|---|---|---|
| T | F | T | T | F T |
| F | F | F | T | T F |

If we add another tilde to obtain '~ ~ (A ∨ ~ A)', we will have a truth-functionally true sentence again.

Although the two sentences 'A ⊃ (B ⊃ A)' and '(A ⊃ B) ⊃ A' look very much alike, one is truth-functionally true and the other is not:

| A | B | A | ↓ ⊃ | (B | ⊃ | A) |
|---|---|---|---|---|---|---|
| T | T | T | T | T | T | T |
| T | F | T | T | F | T | T |
| F | T | F | T | T | F | F |
| F | F | F | T | F | T | F |

| A | B | (A | ⊃ | B) | ↓ ⊃ | A |
|---|---|---|---|---|---|---|
| T | T | T | T | T | T | T |
| T | F | T | F | F | T | T |
| F | T | F | T | T | F | F |
| F | F | F | T | F | F | F |

'A ⊃ (B ⊃ A)' is true on every truth-value assignment, whereas '(A ⊃ B) ⊃ A' is not. The latter sentence is truth-functionally indeterminate.

> A sentence $\mathscr{P}$ of *SL* is *truth-functionally indeterminate* if and only if $\mathscr{P}$ is neither truth-functionally true nor truth-functionally false.

A truth-functionally indeterminate sentence is true on at least one truth-value assignment and false on at least one truth-value assignment. We can use a truth-table to show that a truth-functionally compound sentence is truth-functionally indeterminate by showing that the column under its main connective contains at least one **T** and at least one **F**. Every atomic sentence of *SL* is truth-functionally indeterminate. For example, the truth-table for 'H' is

| H | ↓ H |
|---|---|
| T | T |
| F | F |

'H' is true on every truth-value assignment on which it is assigned the truth-value **T**, and false on every other truth-value assignment. Truth-tables for several truth-functionally indeterminate sentences appeared in Section 3.1. Every sentence of *SL* is either truth-functionally true, truth-functionally false, or truth-functionally indeterminate.

Sometimes we can show that a sentence is not truth-functionally true or is not truth-functionally false by displaying only one row of the sentence's truth-table—that is, by constructing a shortened truth-table. Consider the sentence '(A & ~ A) ∨ ~ A'. If this sentence is truth-functionally true, then there is no truth-value assignment on which it is false. So if we can show that the sentence is false for some combination of truth-values that its atomic components might have, then we can conclude that it is not truth-functionally true. The following shortened truth-table represents such a combination:

| A | (A | & | ~ A) | ↓<br>∨ | ~ A |
|---|---|---|---|---|---|
| T | T | F | F T | F | F T |

This shortened truth-table shows that the sentence '(A & ~ A) ∨ ~ A' is false on every truth-value assignment which assigns the truth-value **T** to 'A'. Note that the shortened table only shows that '(A & ~ A) ∨ ~ A' is not truth-functionally true. The table does not show whether the sentence is true on those truth-value assignments on which 'A' is assigned the truth-value **F**. If it is, then the sentence is truth-functionally indeterminate. If not, the sentence is truth-functionally false.

Similarly, we may construct a shortened truth-table to show that 'J & (~ K ∨ ~ J)' is not truth-functionally false:

| J | K | J | ↓<br>& | (~ K | ∨ | ~ J) |
|---|---|---|---|---|---|---|
| T | F | T | T | T F | T | F T |

This truth-table shows that the sentence is true on every truth-value assignment which assigns **T** to 'J' and **F** to 'K'. We thus know that the sentence is either truth-functionally indeterminate or truth-functionally true.

### 3.2E EXERCISES

**1.** Determine whether each of the following sentences is truth-functionally true, truth-functionally false, or truth-functionally indeterminate by constructing truth-tables.

a. ~ A ⊃ A
*b. J ⊃ (K ⊃ J)
c. (A ≡ ~ A) ⊃ ~ (A ≡ ~ A)
*d. (E ≡ H) ⊃ (~ E ⊃ ~ H)
e. (~ B & ~ D) ∨ ~ (B ∨ D)
*f. ([(C ⊃ D) & (D ⊃ E)] & C) & ~ E
g. [(A ∨ B) & (A ∨ C)] ⊃ ~ (B & C)
*h. ~ [[(A ∨ B) & (B ∨ C)] & (~ A & ~ B)]

i. $(J \vee \sim K) \equiv \sim\sim (K \supset J)$
*j. $\sim B \supset [(B \vee D) \supset D]$
k. $[(A \vee \sim D) \,\&\, \sim (A \,\&\, D)] \supset \sim D$
*l. $(M \equiv \sim N) \,\&\, (M \equiv N)$

**2.** For each of the following sentences either show that the sentence is truth-functionally true by constructing a full truth-table or show that the sentence is not truth-functionally true by constructing an appropriate shortened truth-table.
a. $(F \vee H) \vee (\sim F \equiv H)$
*b. $(F \vee H) \vee \sim (\sim F \supset H)$
c. $\sim A \supset [(B \,\&\, A) \supset C]$
*d. $A \equiv (B \equiv A)$
e. $[(C \vee \sim C) \supset C] \supset C$
*f. $[C \supset (C \vee \sim D)] \supset (C \vee D)$

**3.** For each of the following sentences either show that the sentence is truth-functionally false by constructing a full truth-table or show that the sentence is not truth-functionally false by constructing an appropriate shortened truth-table.
a. $(B \equiv D) \,\&\, (B \equiv \sim D)$
*b. $(B \supset H) \,\&\, (B \supset \sim H)$
c. $A \equiv (B \equiv A)$
*d. $[(F \,\&\, G) \supset (C \,\&\, \sim C)] \,\&\, F$
e. $[(C \vee D) \equiv C] \supset \sim C$
*f. $[\sim (A \,\&\, F) \supset (B \vee A)] \,\&\, \sim [\sim B \supset \sim (F \vee A)]$

**4.** Which of the following are true? Explain.
a. A conjunction with one truth-functionally true conjunct must itself be truth-functionally true.
*b. A disjunction with one truth-functionally true disjunct must itself be truth-functionally true.
c. A material conditional with a truth-functionally true consequent must itself be truth-functionally true.
*d. A conjunction with one truth-functionally false conjunct must itself be truth-functionally false.
e. A disjunction with one truth-functionally false disjunct must itself be truth-functionally false.
*f. A material conditional with a truth-functionally false consequent must itself be truth-functionally false.
g. A sentence is truth-functionally true if and only if its negation is truth-functionally false.
*h. A sentence is truth-functionally indeterminate if and only if its negation is truth-functionally indeterminate.
i. A material conditional with a truth-functionally true antecedent must itself be truth-functionally true.
*j. A material conditional with a truth-functionally false antecedent must itself be truth-functionally false.

**5.a.** Suppose that $\mathcal{P}$ is a truth-functionally true sentence and $\mathcal{Q}$ is a truth-functionally false sentence. On the basis of this information, can you determine whether $\mathcal{P} \equiv \mathcal{Q}$ is truth-functionally true, false, or indeterminate? If so, which is it?

*b. Suppose that 𝒫 and 𝒬 are truth-functionally indeterminate sentences. Does it follow that 𝒫 & 𝒬 is truth-functionally indeterminate?

c. Suppose that 𝒫 and 𝒬 are truth-functionally indeterminate. Does it follow that 𝒫 ∨ 𝒬 is truth-functionally indeterminate?

*d. Suppose that 𝒫 is a truth-functionally true sentence and that 𝒬 is truth-functionally indeterminate. On the basis of this information, can you determine whether 𝒫 ⊃ 𝒬 is truth-functionally true, false, or indeterminate? If so, which is it?

## 3.3 TRUTH-FUNCTIONAL EQUIVALENCE

We now introduce the concept of truth-functional equivalence.

> Sentences 𝒫 and 𝒬 of *SL* are *truth-functionally equivalent* if and only if there is no truth-value assignment on which 𝒫 and 𝒬 have different truth-values.

Hence, to show that 𝒫 and 𝒬 are truth-functionally equivalent, we construct a single truth-table for both 𝒫 and 𝒬 and show that in each row the two sentences have the same truth-value. The columns under the *main* connectives must be identical.

The sentences 'A & A' and 'A ∨ A' are truth-functionally equivalent, as shown by the following truth-table.

| A | A | ↓ & | A | A | ↓ ∨ | A |
|---|---|---|---|---|---|---|
| T | T | T | T | T | T | T |
| F | F | F | F | F | F | F |

On any truth-value assignment that assigns **T** to 'A', both 'A & A' and 'A ∨ A' are true. On any truth-value assignment which assigns **F** to 'A', both 'A & A' and 'A ∨ A' are false. The sentences '(W & Y) ⊃ H' and 'W ⊃ (Y ⊃ H)' are also truth-functionally equivalent:

| H | W | Y | (W | & | Y) | ↓ ⊃ | H | W | ↓ ⊃ | (Y | ⊃ | H) |
|---|---|---|---|---|---|---|---|---|---|---|---|---|
| T | T | T | T | T | T | T | T | T | T | T | T | T |
| T | T | F | T | F | F | T | T | T | T | F | T | T |
| T | F | T | F | F | T | T | T | F | T | T | T | T |
| T | F | F | F | F | F | T | T | F | T | F | T | T |
| F | T | T | T | T | T | F | F | T | F | T | F | F |
| F | T | F | T | F | F | T | F | T | T | F | T | F |
| F | F | T | F | F | T | T | F | F | T | T | F | F |
| F | F | F | F | F | F | T | F | F | T | F | T | F |

The columns under the main connectives of '(W & Y) ⊃ H' and 'W ⊃ (Y ⊃ H)' are identical, which shows that the two sentences have the same truth-value on every truth-value assignment.

It is important to remember that two sentences are truth-functionally equivalent only if they have the same truth-value on every truth-value assignment. That is, their truth-table columns (in the same truth-table) must be identical. Consider the following truth-table:

| E | H | J | E | ↓<br>∨ | H | (H | ∨ | J) | ↓<br>∨ | E |
|---|---|---|---|---|---|---|---|---|---|---|
| T | T | T | T | T | T | T | T | T | T | T |
| T | T | F | T | T | T | T | T | F | T | T |
| T | F | T | T | T | F | F | T | T | T | T |
| T | F | F | T | T | F | F | F | F | T | T |
| F | T | T | F | T | T | T | T | T | T | F |
| F | T | F | F | T | T | T | T | F | T | F |
| F | F | T | F | F | F | F | T | T | T | F |
| F | F | F | F | F | F | F | F | F | F | F |

The table shows that the sentences 'E ∨ H' and '(H ∨ J) ∨ E' are not truth-functionally equivalent, for they have different truth-values on any truth-value assignment that assigns **F** to 'E' and 'H' and **T** to 'J'. The fact that 'E ∨ H' and '(H ∨ J) ∨ E' have the same truth-value for all *other* truth-value assignments is irrelevant to the question of whether the two sentences are truth-functionally equivalent. When we show that two sentences are not truth-functionally equivalent, we will adopt the practice of circling at least one row of the truth-table in which the sentences do not have the same truth-value.

All truth-functionally true sentences are truth-functionally equivalent. This is because every truth-functionally true sentence has the truth-value **T** on every truth-value assignment. In a table for two truth-functionally true sentences the columns under the main connectives of those sentences will always be identical. For example, ' ~ (C & ~ C)' and 'A ⊃ (B ⊃ A)' are truth-functionally equivalent:

| A | B | C | ↓<br>~ | (C | & | ~ | C) | A | ↓<br>⊃ | (B | ⊃ | A) |
|---|---|---|---|---|---|---|---|---|---|---|---|---|
| T | T | T | T | T | F | F | T | T | T | T | T | T |
| T | T | F | T | F | F | T | F | T | T | T | T | T |
| T | F | T | T | T | F | F | T | T | T | F | T | T |
| T | F | F | T | F | F | T | F | T | T | F | T | T |
| F | T | T | T | T | F | F | T | F | T | T | F | F |
| F | T | F | T | F | F | T | F | F | T | T | F | F |
| F | F | T | T | T | F | F | T | F | T | F | T | F |
| F | F | F | T | F | F | T | F | F | T | F | T | F |

Likewise, all truth-functionally false sentences are truth-functionally equivalent.

But not all truth-functionally indeterminate sentences are truth-functionally equivalent. For example,

| B | D | B | ↓ & | D | ~ B | ↓ & | D |
|---|---|---|---|---|---|---|---|
| T | T | T | T | T | F T | F | T |
| T | F | T | F | F | F T | F | F |
| F | T | F | F | T | T F | T | T |
| F | F | F | F | F | T F | F | F |

On any truth-value assignment on which 'B' and 'D' are both true, or 'B' is false and 'D' is true, the sentences 'B & D' and '~ B & D' have different truth-values. Hence they are not truth-functionally equivalent. If $\mathscr{P}$ and $\mathscr{Q}$ are not truth-functionally equivalent we can construct a shortened truth-table to show this. The shortened truth-table will display a combination of truth-values for which one sentence is true and the other false. For example, the following shortened truth-table shows that 'A' and 'A ∨ B' are not truth-functionally equivalent:

| A | B | ↓ A | A | ↓ ∨ | B |
|---|---|---|---|---|---|
| F | T | F | F | T | T |

The shortened truth-table shows that on any truth-value assignment that assigns **F** to 'A' and **T** to 'B', 'A' is false and 'A ∨ B' is true. Hence the sentences are not truth-functionally equivalent. Note that if we construct a shortened truth-table that displays a row in which both sentences have the same truth-value, this is not sufficient to show that they are truth-functionally equivalent. This is because they are truth-functionally equivalent if and only if they have the same truth-value on *every* truth-value assignment. To show this, we must consider every combination of truth-values that their atomic components might have.

## 3.3E EXERCISES

**1.** Decide, by constructing truth-tables, in which of the following pairs the sentences are truth-functionally equivalent.

| | | |
|---|---|---|
| a. | ~ (A & B) | ~ (A ∨ B) |
| *b. | A ⊃ (B ⊃ A) | (C & ~ C) ∨ (A ⊃ A) |
| c. | K ≡ H | ~ K ≡ ~ H |
| *d. | C & (B ∨ A) | (C & B) ∨ A |
| e. | (G ⊃ F) ⊃ (F ⊃ G) | (G ≡ F) ∨ (~ F ∨ G) |
| *f. | ~ C ⊃ ~ B | B ⊃ C |
| g. | ~ (H & J) ≡ (J ≡ ~ K) | (H & J) ⊃ ~ K |
| *h. | ~ (D ∨ B) ⊃ (C ⊃ B) | C ⊃ (D & B) |

| | | |
|---|---|---|
| i. | $[A \vee \sim (D \& C)] \supset \sim D$ | $[D \vee \sim (A \& C)] \supset \sim A$ |
| *j. | $A \supset [B \supset (A \supset B)]$ | $B \supset [A \supset (B \supset A)]$ |
| k. | $F \vee \sim (G \vee \sim H)$ | $(H \equiv \sim F) \vee G$ |

**2.** For each of the following pairs of sentences, either show that the sentences are truth-functionally equivalent by constructing a full truth-table or show that they are not truth-functionally equivalent by constructing an appropriate shortened truth-table.

| | | |
|---|---|---|
| a. | $G \vee H$ | $\sim G \supset H$ |
| *b. | $\sim (B \& \sim A)$ | $A \vee B$ |
| c. | $(D \equiv A) \& D$ | $D \& A$ |
| *d. | $F \& (J \vee H)$ | $(F \& J) \vee H$ |
| e. | $A \equiv (\sim A \equiv A)$ | $\sim (A \supset \sim A)$ |
| *f. | $\sim (\sim B \vee (\sim C \vee \sim D))$ | $(D \vee C) \& \sim B$ |

**3.** Symbolize each of the following pairs of sentences, and determine whether the sentences are truth-functionally equivalent by constructing truth-tables.

a. Unless the sky clouds over, the night will be clear and the moon will shine brightly.
The moon will shine brightly if and only if the night is clear and the sky doesn't cloud over.

*b. Although the new play at the Roxy is a flop, critics won't ignore it unless it is canceled.
The new play at the Roxy is a flop, and if it is canceled, critics will ignore it.

c. If the *Daily Herald* reports on our antics, then the antics are effective.
If our antics aren't effective, then the *Daily Herald* won't report on them.

*d. The year 1972 wasn't a good vintage year, 1973 was, and neither 1974 nor 1975 was.
Neither 1974 nor 1972 was a good vintage year, and not both 1973 and 1975 were.

e. If Mary met Tom and she liked him, then Mary didn't ask George to the movies.
If Mary met Tom and she didn't like him, then Mary asked George to the movies.

*f. Either the blue team or the red team will win the tournament, and they won't both win.
The red team will win the tournament if and only if the blue team won't win the tournament.

**4.**a. Suppose that two sentences $\mathcal{P}$ and $\mathcal{Q}$ are truth-functionally equivalent. Are $\sim \mathcal{P}$ and $\sim \mathcal{Q}$ truth-functionally equivalent as well?

*b. Suppose that two sentences $\mathcal{P}$ and $\mathcal{Q}$ are truth-functionally equivalent. Show that it follows that $\mathcal{P}$ and $\mathcal{P} \& \mathcal{Q}$ are truth-functionally equivalent as well.

c. Suppose that two sentences $\mathcal{P}$ and $\mathcal{Q}$ are truth-functionally equivalent. Show that it follows that $\sim \mathcal{P} \vee \mathcal{Q}$ is truth-functionally true.

## 3.4 TRUTH-FUNCTIONAL CONSISTENCY

To define truth-functional consistency, we need the notion of a *set* of sentences that was informally introduced in Chapter One. A set of sentences of *SL* is a group, or collection, of sentences of *SL*. We have special notation for representing finite sets of sentences (sets consisting of a finite number of sentences): We write the names of the sentences, separated by commas, and enclose the whole list in braces. Thus {'A', 'B ⊃ H', 'C ∨ A'} is the set of sentences consisting of 'A', 'B ⊃ H', and 'C ∨ A'. We say that these three sentences are *members* of the set. For convenience, we will drop the single quotes from names of sentences when they are written between the braces; our convention is that this is just a way of abbreviating the set notation. So we may write

{A, B ⊃ H, C ∨ A}

instead of

{'A', 'B ⊃ H', 'C ∨ A'}

All sets of sentences which have at least one member are nonempty sets of sentences. '∅' is the name of the empty set; the empty set of sentences of *SL* is the set that contains no members at all. In what follows we shall use the variable 'Γ' (*gamma*), with or without a subscript, to range over sets of sentences of *SL*.

Truth-functional consistency may now be introduced.

> A set of sentences of *SL* is *truth-functionally consistent* if and only if there is at least one truth-value assignment on which all of the members of the set are true. A set of sentences of *SL* is *truth-functionally inconsistent* if and only if it is not truth-functionally consistent.

The set {A, B ⊃ H, B} is truth-functionally consistent, as is shown by the following truth-table:

| A | B | H | ↓ A | B | ↓ ⊃ | H | ↓ B |
|---|---|---|---|---|---|---|---|
| T | T | T | T | T | T | T | T |
| T | T | F | T | T | F | F | T |
| T | F | T | T | F | T | T | F |
| T | F | F | T | F | T | F | F |
| F | T | T | F | T | T | T | T |
| F | T | F | F | T | F | F | T |
| F | F | T | F | F | T | T | F |
| F | F | F | F | F | T | F | F |

The truth-table shows that on any truth-value assignment on which 'A', 'B', and 'H' are all true, all three set members are true. So the set is truth-functionally consistent. We have circled the row of the truth-table that shows this. (Sometimes when we construct a truth-table to test a set of sentences for truth-functional consistency, we will find that there is more than one row in which all of the members of the set are true. In such cases, we shall circle only one of those rows of the truth-table.)

The set of sentences {L, L ⊃ J, ~ J} is truth-functionally inconsistent:

| J | L | ↓<br>L | L | ↓<br>⊃ | J | ↓<br>~ J |
|---|---|---|---|---|---|---|
| T | T | T | T | T | T | F T |
| T | F | F | F | T | T | F T |
| F | T | T | T | F | F | T F |
| F | F | F | F | T | F | T F |

In each row, at least one of the three sentences has the truth-value **F** in the column under its main connective. Hence there is no single truth-value assignment on which all three set members are true. The following set of sentences is also truth-functionally inconsistent: {C ∨ ~ C, ~ C & D, ~ D}.

| C | D | C | ↓<br>∨ | ~ C | ~ C | ↓<br>& | D | ↓<br>~ D |
|---|---|---|---|---|---|---|---|---|
| T | T | T | T | F T | F T | F | T | F T |
| T | F | T | T | F T | F T | F | F | T F |
| F | T | F | T | T F | T F | T | T | F T |
| F | F | F | T | T F | T F | F | F | T F |

In this case, it does not matter that one of the sentences, 'C ∨ ~ C', is true on every truth-value assignment. All that matters for establishing truth-functional inconsistency is that there is no single truth-value assignment on which all three members are true.

We can show that a set of sentences is truth-functionally consistent by constructing a shortened truth-table that lists one row in which all of the set members are true. For instance, the following shortened truth-table shows that the set {(E ≡ H) ≡ E, H & ~ E} is truth-functionally consistent:

| E | H | (E | ≡ | H) | ↓<br>≡ | E | H | ↓<br>& | ~ E |
|---|---|---|---|---|---|---|---|---|---|
| F | T | F | F | T | T | F | T | T | T F |

The table shows that on any truth-value assignment on which 'E' is false and 'H' is true, the set members will all be true. Note that if we construct a shortened table which lists a row in which not all the members of the set are true, this is not sufficient to show that the set is truth-functionally inconsistent. This is because a set of sentences is truth-functionally inconsistent if and only if there is *no* truth-value assignment on which every member of the set is true. To show this, we would have to consider every combination of truth-values that the atomic components of the set members might have.

## 3.4E EXERCISES

**1.** Using truth-tables, determine which of the following sets are truth-functionally consistent.

a. $\{A \supset B, B \supset C, A \supset C\}$

*b. $\{B \equiv (J \& K), \sim J, \sim B \supset B\}$

c. $\{\sim [J \vee (H \supset L)], L \equiv (\sim J \vee \sim H), H \equiv (J \vee L)\}$

*d. $\{(A \& B) \& C, C \vee (B \vee A), A \equiv (B \supset C)\}$

e. $\{(J \supset J) \supset H, \sim J, \sim H\}$

*f. $\{U \vee (W \& H), W \equiv (U \vee H), H \vee \sim H\}$

g. $\{A, B, C\}$

*h. $\{\sim (A \& B), \sim (B \& C), \sim (A \& C), A \vee (B \& C)\}$

i. $\{(A \& B) \vee (C \supset B), \sim A, \sim B\}$

*j. $\{A \supset (B \supset (C \supset A)), B \supset \sim A\}$

**2.** For each of the following sets of sentences either show that the set is truth-functionally consistent by constructing an appropriate shortened truth-table or show that the set is truth-functionally inconsistent by constructing a full truth-table.

a. $\{B \supset (D \supset E), \sim D \& B\}$

*b. $\{H \equiv (\sim H \supset H)\}$

c. $\{F \supset (J \vee K), F \equiv \sim J\}$

*d. $\{\sim (\sim C \vee \sim B) \& A, A \equiv \sim C\}$

e. $\{(A \supset B) \equiv (\sim B \vee B), A\}$

*f. $\{H \supset J, J \supset K, K \supset \sim H\}$

**3.** Symbolize each of the following passages, and determine whether the set consisting of those sentences is truth-functionally consistent by constructing a truth-table.

a. If space is infinitely divisible, then Zeno's paradoxes are compelling. Zeno's paradoxes are neither convincing nor compelling. Space is infinitely divisible.

*b. Newtonian mechanics can't be right if Einsteinian mechanics is. But Einsteinian mechanics is right if and only if space is non-Euclidean. Space is non-Euclidean, or Newtonian mechanics is correct.

c. Eugene O'Neill was an alcoholic. His plays show it. But *The Iceman Cometh* must have been written by a teetotaler. O'Neill was an alcoholic unless he was a fake.

*d. Neither sugar nor saccharin is desirable if and only if both are lethal. Sugar is lethal if and only if saccharin is desirable. Sugar is undesirable if and only if saccharin isn't lethal.

e. If the Red Sox win next Sunday, then if Joan bet $5 she'll buy Ed a hamburger. The Red Sox won't win, and Joan won't buy Ed a hamburger.

*f. Either Johnson or Hartshorne pleaded guilty, or neither did. If Johnson pleaded guilty, then the newspaper story is incorrect. The newspaper story is correct, and Hartshorne pleaded guilty.

**4.**a. Prove that $\{\mathscr{P}\}$ is truth-functionally inconsistent if and only if $\sim \mathscr{P}$ is truth-functionally true.

*b. If $\{\mathscr{P}\}$ is truth-functionally consistent, must $\{\sim \mathscr{P}\}$ be truth-functionally consistent as well? Show that you are right.

c. If $\mathscr{P}$ and $\mathscr{Q}$ are truth-functionally indeterminate, does it follow that $\{\mathscr{P}, \mathscr{Q}\}$ is truth-functionally consistent? Explain your answer.

*d. Prove that if $\mathscr{P} \equiv \mathscr{Q}$ is truth-functionally true, then $\{\mathscr{P}, \sim \mathscr{Q}\}$ is truth-functionally inconsistent.

## 3.5 TRUTH-FUNCTIONAL ENTAILMENT AND TRUTH-FUNCTIONAL VALIDITY

Truth-functional entailment is a relation which may hold between a sentence of *SL* and a set of sentences of *SL*:

> A set Γ of sentences of *SL truth-functionally entails* a sentence $\mathscr{P}$ if and only if there is no truth-value assignment on which every member of Γ is true and $\mathscr{P}$ is false.

In other words, Γ truth-functionally entails $\mathscr{P}$ just in case $\mathscr{P}$ is true on every truth-value assignment on which every member of Γ is true. We have a special symbol for truth-functional entailment: the double turnstile '$\models$'. The expression

$$\Gamma \models \mathscr{P}$$

is read

Γ truth-functionally entails $\mathscr{P}$.

To indicate that Γ does not truth-functionally entail $\mathscr{P}$, we write

$$\Gamma \not\models \mathscr{P}$$

Thus

{A, B & C} $\models$ 'B'

and

{A, B ∨ C} $\not\models$ 'B'

mean, respectively:

{A, B & C} truth-functionally entails 'B'

and

{A, B ∨ C} does not truth-functionally entail 'B'

Henceforth we adopt the convention that, when using the turnstile notation, we drop the single quotation marks around the sentence following the turnstile. We also have a special abbreviation to indicate that a sentence is truth-functionally entailed by the empty set of sentences:

$$\models \mathscr{P}$$

The expression '$\models \mathscr{P}$' is an abbreviation for '$\varnothing \models \mathscr{P}$'. All and only truth-functionally true sentences are truth-functionally entailed by the empty set of sentences; the proof of this is left as an exercise in Section 3.6.

If Γ is a finite set, we can determine whether or not Γ truth-functionally entails $\mathcal{P}$ by constructing a truth-table for the members of Γ and for $\mathcal{P}$. If there is a row in the truth-table in which all the members of Γ have the truth-value **T** and $\mathcal{P}$ has the truth-value **F**, then Γ does not truth-functionally entail $\mathcal{P}$. If there is no such row, then Γ truth-functionally entails $\mathcal{P}$. We can see that {A, B & C} ⊨ B by checking the following truth-table:

| A | B | C | ↓ A | B | ↓ & | C | ↓ B |
|---|---|---|---|---|---|---|---|
| T | T | T | T | T | T | T | T |
| T | T | F | T | T | F | F | T |
| T | F | T | T | F | F | T | F |
| T | F | F | T | F | F | F | F |
| F | T | T | F | T | T | T | T |
| F | T | F | F | T | F | F | T |
| F | F | T | F | F | F | T | F |
| F | F | F | F | F | F | F | F |

There is only one row in which both members of {A, B & C} are true: namely, the row in which 'A', 'B', and 'C' all have the truth-value **T**. But since 'B' is true in this row, it follows that there is no combination of truth-values for the atomic components of all these sentences that will make both 'A' and 'B & C' true and 'B' false. Hence there is no truth-value assignment on which 'A' and 'B & C' are true and 'B' is false: {A, B & C} ⊨ B.

In the same way, we can show that {W ∨ J, (W ⊃ Z) ∨ (J ⊃ Z), ~ Z} ⊨ ~ (W & J):

| J | W | Z | W | ↓ ∨ | J | (W | ⊃ | Z) | ↓ ∨ | (J | ⊃ | Z) | ↓ ~ | Z | ↓ ~ | (W | & | J) |
|---|---|---|---|---|---|---|---|---|---|---|---|---|---|---|---|---|---|---|
| T | T | T | T | T | T | T | T | T | T | T | T | T | F | T | F | T | T | T |
| T | T | F | T | T | T | T | F | F | F | T | F | F | T | F | F | T | T | T |
| T | F | T | F | T | T | F | T | T | T | T | T | T | F | T | T | F | F | T |
| T | F | F | F | T | T | F | T | F | T | T | F | F | T | F | T | F | F | T |
| F | T | T | T | T | F | T | T | T | T | F | T | T | F | T | T | T | F | F |
| F | T | F | T | T | F | T | F | F | T | F | T | F | T | F | T | T | F | F |
| F | F | T | F | F | F | F | T | T | T | F | T | T | F | T | T | F | F | F |
| F | F | F | F | F | F | F | T | F | T | F | T | F | T | F | T | F | F | F |

The fourth and sixth rows are the only ones in which all of the set members are true; '~ (W & J)' is true in these rows as well. The following truth-table shows that {K ∨ J, ~ (K ∨ J)} ⊨ K:

| J | K | K | ↓ ∨ | J | ↓ ~ | (K | ∨ | J) | ↓ K |
|---|---|---|---|---|---|---|---|---|---|
| T | T | T | T | T | F | T | T | T | T |
| T | F | F | T | T | F | F | T | T | F |
| F | T | T | T | F | F | T | T | F | T |
| F | F | F | F | F | T | F | F | F | F |

There is no row in which 'K ∨ J' and '~ (K ∨ J)' are both true, and hence no truth-value assignment on which the set members are both true. Consequently, there is no truth-value assignment on which the members of the set are both true and 'K' is false; so the set truth-functionally entails 'K'.

On the other hand, {A, B ∨ C} does *not* truth-functionally entail 'B'. The following truth-table shows this:

| A | B | C | ↓ A | B | ↓ ∨ | C | ↓ B |
|---|---|---|---|---|---|---|---|
| T | T | T | T | T | T | T | T |
| T | T | F | T | T | T | F | T |
| T | F | T | T | F | T | T | F |
| T | F | F | T | F | F | F | F |
| F | T | T | F | T | T | T | T |
| F | T | F | F | T | T | F | T |
| F | F | T | F | F | T | T | F |
| F | F | F | F | F | F | F | F |

The circled row shows that 'A' and 'B ∨ C' are both true and 'B' is false on any truth-value assignment that assigns **T** to 'A' and 'C' and **F** to 'B'.

An *argument* of *SL* is a group of two or more sentences of *SL*, one of which is designated as the conclusion and the others as the premises.

> An argument of *SL* is *truth-functionally valid* if and only if there is no truth-value assignment on which all of the premises are true and the conclusion is false. An argument of *SL* is *truth-functionally invalid* if and only if it is not truth-functionally valid.

Thus an argument of *SL* is truth-functionally valid just in case on every truth-value assignment on which the premises are true, the conclusion is true as well. This means that an argument is truth-functionally valid if and only if the set consisting of the premises of the argument truth-functionally entails the conclusion.

The argument

F ≡ G

F ∨ G

---

F & G

is truth-functionally valid, as the following truth-table shows:

| F | G | F | ↓ ≡ | G | F | ↓ ∨ | G | F | ↓ & | G |
|---|---|---|---|---|---|---|---|---|---|---|
| T | T | T | T | T | T | T | T | T | T | T |
| T | F | T | F | F | T | T | F | T | F | F |
| F | T | F | F | T | F | T | T | F | F | T |
| F | F | F | T | F | F | F | F | F | F | F |

The first row lists the only combination of truth-values for the atomic components of these sentences for which the premises, 'F ≡ G' and 'F ∨ H', are both true; the conclusion, 'F & G', is true in this row as well. Similarly, the argument

(A & G) ∨ (B ⊃ G)

~ G ∨ B

---

~ B ∨ G

is truth-functionally valid:

| A | B | G | (A | & | G) | ↓ ∨ | (B | ⊃ | G) | ~ | G | ↓ ∨ | B | ~ | B | ↓ ∨ | G |
|---|---|---|---|---|---|---|---|---|---|---|---|---|---|---|---|---|---|
| T | T | T | T | T | T | T | T | T | T | F | T | T | T | F | T | T | T |
| T | T | F | T | F | F | F | T | F | F | T | F | T | T | F | T | F | F |
| T | F | T | T | T | T | T | F | T | T | F | T | F | F | T | F | T | T |
| T | F | F | T | F | F | T | F | T | F | T | F | T | F | T | F | T | F |
| F | T | T | F | F | T | T | T | T | T | F | T | T | T | F | T | T | T |
| F | T | F | F | F | F | F | T | F | F | T | F | T | T | F | T | F | F |
| F | F | T | F | F | T | T | F | T | T | F | T | F | F | T | F | T | T |
| F | F | F | F | F | F | T | F | T | F | T | F | T | F | T | F | T | F |

The conclusion, '~ B ∨ G', is true on every truth-value assignment on which the premises are true.

The following argument is truth-functionally invalid:

D ≡ (~ W ∨ G)

G ≡ ~ D

---

~ D

This is shown by the following truth-table:

| D | G | W | D | ↓ ≡ | (~ | W | ∨ | G) | G | ↓ ≡ | ~ | D | ↓ ~ | D |
|---|---|---|---|---|---|---|---|---|---|---|---|---|---|---|
| T | T | T | T | T | F | T | T | T | T | F | F | T | F | T |
| T | T | F | T | T | T | F | T | T | T | F | F | T | F | T |
| T | F | T | T | F | F | T | F | F | F | T | F | T | F | T |
| T | F | F | T | T | T | F | T | F | F | T | F | T | F | T |
| F | T | T | F | F | F | T | T | T | T | T | T | F | T | F |
| F | T | F | F | F | T | F | T | T | T | T | T | F | T | F |
| F | F | T | F | T | F | T | F | F | F | F | T | F | T | F |
| F | F | F | F | F | T | F | T | F | F | F | T | F | T | F |

The premises 'D ≡ (~ W ∨ G)' and 'G ≡ ~ D' are both true on every truth-value assignment that assigns **T** to 'D' and **F** to 'G' and 'W', and ' ~ D' is false on these truth-value assignments.

Where an argument is truth-functionally invalid, we can show this by constructing a shortened table that displays a row in which the premises are true and the conclusion is false. The argument

~ (B ∨ D)
~ H
―――――
B

is truth-functionally invalid, as the following shortened truth-table shows:

| B | D | H | ↓ ~ | (B | ∨ | D) | ↓ ~ | H | ↓ B |
|---|---|---|---|---|---|---|---|---|---|
| F | F | F | T | F | F | F | T | F | F |

For any argument of *SL* that has a finite number of premises, we may form a sentence called the *corresponding material conditional*, and that sentence is truth-functionally true if and only if the argument is truth-functionally valid. First, we may form an *iterated conjunction* $(\ldots(\mathscr{P}_1 \ \& \ \mathscr{P}_2) \ \& \ \ldots \ \& \ \mathscr{P}_n)$ from the sentences $\mathscr{P}_1, \ldots, \mathscr{P}_n$. The iterated conjunction for the sentences ' ~ (A ⊃ B)', 'D', and 'J ∨ H' is '((~ (A ⊃ B) & D) & (J ∨ H))'. The corresponding material conditional for an argument is then formed by constructing a material conditional with the iterated conjunction of the premises as antecedent and the conclusion of the argument as consequent. The corresponding material conditional for the argument

~ (A ⊃ B)
D
J ∨ H
―――――
~ H ∨ ~ A

is '[[~ (A ⊃ B) & D] & (J ∨ H)] ⊃ (~ H ∨ ~ A)' and the corresponding material conditional for the argument

A

A ⊃ B

---

B

is '[A & (A ⊃ B)] ⊃ B'.[4]

An argument with a finite number of premises is truth-functionally valid if and only if its corresponding material conditional is truth-functionally true (see Exercise 5). We can show that the argument

A

A ⊃ B

---

B

is truth-functionally valid by showing that the corresponding material conditional '[A & (A ⊃ B)] ⊃ B' is truth-functionally true:

| A | B | [A | & | (A | ⊃ | B)] | ↓<br>⊃ | B |
|---|---|---|---|---|---|---|---|---|
| T | T | T | T | T | T | T | T | T |
| T | F | T | F | T | F | F | T | F |
| F | T | F | F | F | T | T | T | T |
| F | F | F | F | F | T | F | T | F |

There is no truth-value assignment on which 'A & (A ⊃ B)' is true and 'B' is false, which means that there is no truth-value assignment on which 'A' and 'A ⊃ B' are both true and 'B' is false. And we can show that the argument

~ A ≡ ~ B

B ∨ A

---

~ A

is truth-functionally invalid by showing that the corresponding material conditional is not truth-functionally true:

| A | B | [(~ A | ≡ | ~ B) | & | (B | ∨ | A)] | ↓<br>⊃ | ~ A |
|---|---|---|---|---|---|---|---|---|---|---|
| T | T | F T | T | F T | T | T | T | T | F | F T |
| T | F | F T | F | T F | F | F | T | T | T | F T |
| F | T | T F | F | F T | F | T | T | F | T | T F |
| F | F | T F | T | T F | F | F | F | F | T | T F |

The first row represents truth-value assignments on which the antecedent is true

[4] Strictly speaking, an argument with more than one premise will have more than one corresponding material conditional. This is because the premises of an argument can be conjoined in more than one order. But all the corresponding material conditionals for any one argument are truth-functionally equivalent, and so we speak loosely of *the* corresponding material conditionally for a given argument.

and the consequent false. On these truth-value assignments, the premises of the argument, '$\sim A \equiv \sim B$' and '$B \vee A$', are both true and the conclusion, '$\sim A$' is false. Hence the argument is truth-functionally invalid.

### 3.5E EXERCISES

**1.** Use truth-tables to determine whether the following arguments are truth-functionally valid.

a. $A \supset (H \& J)$
$J \equiv H$
$\sim J$
―――――
$\sim A$

*b. $B \vee (A \& \sim C)$
$(C \supset A) \equiv B$
$\sim B \vee A$
―――――
$\sim (A \vee C)$

c. $(D \equiv \sim G) \& G$
$(G \vee [(A \supset D) \& A]) \supset \sim D$
―――――
$G \supset \sim D$

*d. $\sim (Y \equiv A)$
$\sim Y$
$\sim A$
―――――
$W \& \sim W$

e. $(C \supset D) \supset (D \supset E)$
$D$
―――――
$C \supset E$

*f. $B \vee B$
$[\sim B \supset (\sim D \vee \sim C)] \& [(\sim D \vee C) \vee (\sim B \vee C)]$
―――――
$C$

g. $(G \equiv H) \vee (\sim G \equiv H)$
―――――
$(\sim G \equiv \sim H) \vee \sim (G \equiv H)$

*h. $[(J \& T) \& Y] \vee (\sim J \supset \sim Y)$
$J \supset T$
$T \supset Y$
―――――
$Y \equiv T$

i. $\sim\sim F \supset \sim\sim G$
$\sim G \supset \sim F$
―――――
$G \supset F$

*j. $[A \& (B \vee C)] \equiv (A \vee B)$
$B \supset \sim B$
---
$C \vee A$

**2.** For each of the following arguments, either show that the argument is truth-functionally invalid by constructing an appropriate shortened truth-table or show that the argument is truth-functionally valid by constructing a full truth-table.

a. $(J \vee M) \supset \sim (J \& M)$
$M \equiv (M \supset J)$
---
$M \supset J$

*b. $B \& F$
$\sim (B \& G)$
---
$G$

c. $A \supset \sim A$
$(B \supset A) \supset B$
---
$A \equiv \sim B$

*d. $J \vee [M \supset (T \equiv J)]$
$(M \supset J) \& (T \supset M)$
---
$T \& \sim M$

e. $A \& \sim [(B \& C) \equiv (C \supset A)]$
$B \supset \sim B$
---
$\sim C \supset C$

**3.** Construct the corresponding material conditional for each of the following arguments. For each of the arguments either show that the argument is truth-functionally invalid by constructing an appropriate shortened truth-table for the corresponding material conditional, or show that the argument is truth-functionally valid by constructing a full truth-table for the corresponding material conditional.

a. $B \& C$
---
$B \vee C$

*b. $K \equiv L$
$L \supset J$
$\sim J$
---
$\sim K \vee L$

c. $(J \supset T) \supset J$
$(T \supset J) \supset T$
---
$\sim J \vee \sim T$

*d. $(A \vee C)\ \&\ \sim H$

$\sim C$

e. $B\ \&\ C$
$B \vee D$

$D$

*f. $\sim [A \vee \sim (B \vee \sim C)]$
$D \supset (A \supset C)$

$\sim A \equiv \sim B$

**4.** Symbolize each of the following arguments and use truth-tables to test for truth-functional validity.

a. 'Stern' means the same as 'star' if 'Nacht' means the same as 'day'. But 'Nacht' doesn't mean the same as 'day'; therefore 'Stern' means something different from 'star'.

*b. Many people believe that war is inevitable. But war is inevitable if and only if our planet's natural resources are nonrenewable. So many people believe that our natural resources are nonrenewable.

c. Thirty days hath September, April, and November. But February has forty days, since April has thirty days if and only if May doesn't, and May has thirty days if November does.

*d. The town hall is now a grocery store, and, unless I'm mistaken, the little red schoolhouse is a movie theater. No, I'm not mistaken. The old schoolbus is a boutique, and the old theater is an elementary school if the little red schoolhouse is a movie theater. So the little red schoolhouse is a movie theater.

e. Computers can think if and only if they can have emotions. If computers can have emotions, then they can have desires as well. But computers can't think if they have desires. Therefore computers can't think.

*f. If the butler murdered Devon, then the maid is lying, and if the gardener murdered Devon, then the weapon was a slingshot. The maid is lying if and only if the weapon wasn't a slingshot, and if the weapon wasn't a slingshot, then the butler murdered Devon. Therefore the butler murdered Devon.

**5.**a. Show that $(\ldots(\mathscr{P}_1\ \&\ \mathscr{P}_2)\ \&\ \ldots\ \&\ \mathscr{P}_n) \supset \mathscr{Q}$ is truth-functionally true if and only if

$\mathscr{P}_1$
$\vdots$
$\mathscr{P}_n$

$\mathscr{Q}$

is truth-functionally valid.

*b. Show that $\{\mathscr{P}\} \vDash \mathscr{Q}$ and $\{\mathscr{Q}\} \vDash \mathscr{P}$ if and only if $\mathscr{P}$ and $\mathscr{Q}$ are truth-functionally equivalent.

c. Suppose that $\{\mathscr{P}\} \vDash \mathscr{Q} \vee \mathscr{R}$. Does it follows that either $\{\mathscr{P}\} \vDash \mathscr{Q}$ or $\{\mathscr{P}\} \vDash \mathscr{R}$? Show that you are right.

*d. Show that if $\{\mathscr{P}\} \vDash \mathscr{Q}$ and $\{\mathscr{Q}\} \vDash \mathscr{R}$, then $\{\mathscr{P}\} \vDash \mathscr{R}$.

## 3.6 TRUTH-FUNCTIONAL PROPERTIES AND TRUTH-FUNCTIONAL CONSISTENCY

In Chapter One the concepts of logical truth, falsity, indeterminacy, and validity were all explicated in terms of consistency. In this chapter the truth-functional versions of these concepts have all been defined in terms of truth-value assignments. However, we could have defined all of these in terms of truth-functional consistency and inconsistency, in which case only consistency would have been defined in terms of truth-value assignments. The definitions given in this chapter will stand as the official definitions, but we shall show in this section the relations of the various truth-functional properties to truth-functional consistency and inconsistency. In Chapter Four we shall introduce an alternative test for truth-functional consistency. Since all of the other truth-functional concepts can be explicated in terms of consistency, we shall be able to use the test to determine other truth-functional properties of sentences and sets of sentences.

> A sentence $\mathscr{P}$ is truth-functionally false if and only if $\{\mathscr{P}\}$ is truth-functionally inconsistent.

(We call $\{\mathscr{P}\}$ the *unit set* of $\mathscr{P}$.) To prove that this is so, we first assume that $\mathscr{P}$ is truth-functionally false. Then, by definition, there is no truth-value assignment on which $\mathscr{P}$ is true. Consequently, as $\mathscr{P}$ is the only member of the unit set $\{\mathscr{P}\}$, there is no truth-value assignment on which every member of that set is true. So $\{\mathscr{P}\}$ is truth-functionally inconsistent. Now assume that $\{\mathscr{P}\}$ is truth-functionally inconsistent. Then, by definition, there is no truth-value assignment on which every member of $\{\mathscr{P}\}$ is true. Since $\mathscr{P}$ is the only member of its unit set, there is no truth-value assignment on which $\mathscr{P}$ is true. Hence $\mathscr{P}$ is truth-functionally false.

The corresponding relation for truth-functionally true sentences is more complicated:

> A sentence $\mathscr{P}$ is truth-functionally true if and only if $\{\sim \mathscr{P}\}$ is truth-functionally inconsistent.

We first assume that $\mathscr{P}$ is truth-functionally true. Then, by definition, $\mathscr{P}$ is true on every truth-value assignment. We know that a sentence is true on a truth-value assignment if and only if the negation of the sentence is false on that truth-value assignment. So it follows from our assumption that $\sim \mathscr{P}$ is false on every truth-value assignment; that is, there is no truth-value assignment on which $\sim \mathscr{P}$ is true. But then there is no truth-value assignment on which every member of $\{\sim \mathscr{P}\}$ is true, which means that $\{\sim \mathscr{P}\}$ is truth-functionally inconsistent. The proof of the converse, that if $\{\sim \mathscr{P}\}$ is truth-functionally inconsistent then $\mathscr{P}$ is truth-functionally true, is left as an exercise.

Since a sentence $\mathscr{P}$ is truth-functionally true if and only if $\{\sim \mathscr{P}\}$ is truth-functionally inconsistent and $\mathscr{P}$ is truth-functionally false if and only if $\{\mathscr{P}\}$ is truth-functionally inconsistent, it follows that

> A sentence $\mathscr{P}$ is truth-functionally indeterminate if and only if both $\{\sim \mathscr{P}\}$ and $\{\mathscr{P}\}$ are truth-functionally consistent.

Now we turn to truth-functional equivalence. Where $\mathscr{P}$ and $\mathscr{Q}$ are sentences of *SL*, $\mathscr{P} \equiv \mathscr{Q}$ is their *corresponding material biconditional*. $\mathscr{P}$ and $\mathscr{Q}$ are truth-functionally equivalent if and only if their corresponding material biconditional $\mathscr{P} \equiv \mathscr{Q}$ is truth-functionally true. If we assume that $\mathscr{P}$ and $\mathscr{Q}$ are truth-functionally equivalent, then, by definition, $\mathscr{P}$ and $\mathscr{Q}$ have the same truth-value on every truth-value assignment. But we know that a material biconditional has the truth-value **T** on every truth-value assignment on which its immediate sentential components have the same truth-value. So, on our assumption, $\mathscr{P} \equiv \mathscr{Q}$ is true on every truth-value assignment and hence is truth-functionally true. The converse of this, that if $\mathscr{P} \equiv \mathscr{Q}$ is truth-functionally true then $\mathscr{P}$ and $\mathscr{Q}$ are truth-functionally equivalent, is left as an exercise. It follows from these results that

> Sentences $\mathscr{P}$ and $\mathscr{Q}$ are truth-functionally equivalent if and only if $\{\sim (\mathscr{P} \equiv \mathscr{Q})\}$ is truth-functionally inconsistent.

For $\mathscr{P} \equiv \mathscr{Q}$ is truth-functionally true if and only if $\{\sim (\mathscr{P} \equiv \mathscr{Q})\}$ is truth-functionally inconsistent, by our previous result concerning truth-functional truths, and we have just shown that $\mathscr{P}$ and $\mathscr{Q}$ are truth-functionally equivalent if and only if $\mathscr{P} \equiv \mathscr{Q}$ is truth-functionally true.

To make these results more concrete, we shall consider an example. The set {~ [(A ∨ B) ≡ (~ A ⊃ B)]} is truth-functionally inconsistent, as shown by the following truth-table:

| A | B | ↓ ~ | [(A | ∨ | B) | ≡ | (~ | A | ⊃ | B)] |
|---|---|---|---|---|---|---|---|---|---|---|
| T | T | F | T | T | T | T | F | T | T | T |
| T | F | F | T | T | F | T | F | T | T | F |
| F | T | F | F | T | T | T | T | F | T | T |
| F | F | F | F | F | F | T | T | F | F | F |

The set is truth-functionally inconsistent because there is no truth-value assignment on which every member of the set (in this case there is just one member) is true. From this, we know the following:

1. '~ [(A ∨ B) ≡ (~ A ⊃ B)]' is truth-functionally false. ($\mathscr{P}$ is truth-functionally false if and only if $\{\mathscr{P}\}$ is truth-functionally inconsistent. Here {~ [(A ∨ B) ≡ (~ A ⊃ B)]} is truth-functionally inconsistent. Hence there is no truth-value assignment on which the only member of that set, '~ [(A ∨ B) ≡ (~ A ⊃ B)]', is true. That one member is thus truth-functionally false.)

2. '(A ∨ B) ≡ (~ A ⊃ B)' is truth-functionally true. ($\mathscr{P}$ is truth-functionally true if and only if $\{\sim \mathscr{P}\}$ is truth-functionally inconsistent. We have just reasoned that '~ [(A ∨ B) ≡ (~ A ⊃ B)]' is truth-functionally false. Hence the sentence of which it is the negation, '(A ∨ B) ≡ (~ A ⊃ B)', is true on every truth-value assignment—it is a truth-functionally true sentence.)

3. 'A ∨ B' and '~ A ⊃ B' are truth-functionally equivalent. ($\mathscr{P}$ and $\mathscr{Q}$ are truth-functionally equivalent if and only if $\{\sim (\mathscr{P} \equiv \mathscr{Q})\}$ is truth-functionally

inconsistent. Since '(A ∨ B) ≡ (~ A ⊃ B)' is truth-functionally true, 'A ∨ B' and '~ A ⊃ B' have the same truth-value on every truth-value assignment—they are truth-functionally equivalent.)

Of course, each of these claims can be directly verified by examining the truth-table, but our general proofs show that this is not necessary.

Next we relate the concepts of truth-functional entailment and truth-functional consistency. Where Γ is a set of sentences of *SL* and $\mathscr{P}$ is any sentence of *SL*, we may form a set which contains $\mathscr{P}$ and all of the members of Γ. This set is represented as

$$\Gamma \cup \{\mathscr{P}\}$$

which is read as

> the union of gamma and the unit set of $\mathscr{P}$

Thus, if Γ is {A, A ⊃ B}, and $\mathscr{P}$ is 'J', then $\Gamma \cup \{\mathscr{P}\}$, that is, {A, A ⊃ B} ∪ {J}, is {A, A ⊃ B, J}. Of course, if $\mathscr{P}$ is a member of Γ, then $\Gamma \cup \{\mathscr{P}\}$ is identical with Γ. So {A, A ⊃ B} ∪ {A ⊃ B} is simply {A, A ⊃ B}. In the case where Γ is ∅ (the empty set), $\Gamma \cup \{\mathscr{P}\}$ is simply $\{\mathscr{P}\}$. This follows because ∅ contains no members.

We may now prove that if $\Gamma \vDash \mathscr{P}$, for some sentence $\mathscr{P}$ and set of sentences Γ, then $\Gamma \cup \{\sim \mathscr{P}\}$ is truth-functionally inconsistent. Suppose that $\Gamma \vDash \mathscr{P}$. Then, by definition, there is no truth-value assignment on which every member of Γ is true and $\mathscr{P}$ is false. But we know that $\sim \mathscr{P}$ is true on a truth-value assignment if and only if $\mathscr{P}$ is false on that truth-value assignment. So it follows from our assumption that there is no truth-value on which every member of Γ is true and $\sim \mathscr{P}$ is true. But then there is no truth-value assignment on which every member of the set $\Gamma \cup \{\sim \mathscr{P}\}$ is true—so the set is truth-functionally inconsistent. It follows from this proof that since {J ∨ C} ⊨ ~ (~ J & ~ C), the set {J ∨ C, ~ ~ (~ J & ~ C)} is truth-functionally inconsistent. The converse, that if $\Gamma \cup \{\sim \mathscr{P}\}$ is truth-functionally inconsistent then $\Gamma \vDash \mathscr{P}$, holds as well. The proof is left as an exercise.

It follows from this result, together with the fact that an argument

$$\begin{array}{l} \mathscr{P}_1 \\ \vdots \\ \mathscr{P}_n \\ \hline \mathscr{Q} \end{array}$$

is truth-functionally valid if and only if $\{\mathscr{P}_1, \ldots, \mathscr{P}_n\} \vDash \mathscr{Q}$, that

> An argument of *SL* is truth-functionally valid if and only if the set containing as its only members the premises of the argument and the negation of the conclusion is truth-functionally inconsistent.

So the argument

$(A \supset D) \& H$

$F \vee H$

---

$D$

is truth-functionally valid if and only if $\{(A \supset D) \& H, F \vee H, \sim D\}$ is truth-functionally inconsistent.

### 3.6E EXERCISES

**1.** Prove each of the following:

a. If $\{\sim \mathscr{P}\}$ is truth-functionally inconsistent, where $\mathscr{P}$ is a sentence of *SL*, then $\mathscr{P}$ is truth-functionally true.

*b. If $\mathscr{P} \equiv \mathscr{Q}$ is truth-functionally true, where $\mathscr{P}$ and $\mathscr{Q}$ are sentences of *SL*, then $\mathscr{P}$ and $\mathscr{Q}$ are truth-functionally equivalent.

c. If $\Gamma \cup \{\sim \mathscr{P}\}$ is truth-functionally inconsistent, where $\Gamma$ is a set of sentences of *SL* and $\mathscr{P}$ is a sentence of *SL*, then $\Gamma \vDash \mathscr{P}$.

**2.** Prove each of the following:

a. A sentence $\mathscr{P}$ is truth-functionally true if and only if $\varnothing \vDash \mathscr{P}$.

*b. $\Gamma \vDash \mathscr{P} \supset \mathscr{Q}$, where $\Gamma$ is a set of sentences of *SL* and $\mathscr{P}$ and $\mathscr{Q}$ are sentences of *SL*, if and only if $\Gamma \cup \{\mathscr{P}\} \vDash \mathscr{Q}$.

c. If $\Gamma$ is truth-functionally inconsistent, where $\Gamma$ is a set of sentences of *SL*, then $\Gamma$ truth-functionally entails every sentence of *SL*.

*d. For any set $\Gamma$ of sentences of *SL* and any truth-functionally false sentence $\mathscr{P}$ of *SL*, $\Gamma \cup \{\mathscr{P}\}$ is truth-functionally inconsistent.

**3.** Prove each of the following:

a. If a set $\Gamma$ of sentences of *SL* is truth-functionally consistent and $\mathscr{P}$ is a truth-functionally true sentence of *SL*, then $\Gamma \cup \{\mathscr{P}\}$ is truth-functionally consistent.

*b. If $\Gamma \vDash \mathscr{P}$ and $\Gamma \vDash \sim \mathscr{P}$, for some sentence $\mathscr{P}$ and set $\Gamma$ of sentences of *SL*, then $\Gamma$ is truth-functionally inconsistent.

**4.** Prove each of the following:

a. If $\{\mathscr{P}\} \vDash \mathscr{Q}$ and $\{\sim \mathscr{P}\} \vDash \mathscr{R}$, where $\mathscr{P}$, $\mathscr{Q}$, and $\mathscr{R}$ are sentences of *SL*, then $\mathscr{Q} \vee \mathscr{R}$ is truth-functionally true.

*b. If $\mathscr{P}$ and $\mathscr{Q}$ are truth-functionally equivalent, where $\mathscr{P}$ and $\mathscr{Q}$ are sentences of *SL*, then for any sentence $\mathscr{R}$ of *SL*, $\{\mathscr{P}\} \vDash \mathscr{R}$ if and only if $\{\mathscr{Q}\} \vDash \mathscr{R}$.

c. If $\Gamma \vDash \mathscr{P}$ and $\Gamma' \vDash \mathscr{Q}$, where $\Gamma$ and $\Gamma'$ are sets of sentences of *SL* and $\mathscr{P}$ and $\mathscr{Q}$ are sentences of *SL*, then $\Gamma \cup \Gamma' \vDash \mathscr{P} \& \mathscr{Q}$, where $\Gamma \cup \Gamma'$ is the set that contains all of the sentences in $\Gamma$ and all of the sentences in $\Gamma'$.

## GLOSSARY

TRUTH-FUNCTIONAL TRUTH: A sentence $\mathscr{P}$ of *SL* is *truth-functionally true* if and only if $\mathscr{P}$ is true on every truth-value assignment.

TRUTH-FUNCTIONAL FALSITY: A sentence $\mathscr{P}$ of *SL* is *truth-functionally false* if and only if $\mathscr{P}$ is false on every truth-value assignment.

TRUTH-FUNCTIONAL INDETERMINACY: A sentence $\mathscr{P}$ of *SL* is *truth-functionally indeterminate* if and only if $\mathscr{P}$ is neither truth-functionally true nor truth-functionally false.

TRUTH-FUNCTIONAL EQUIVALENCE: Sentences $\mathscr{P}$ and $\mathscr{Q}$ of *SL* are *truth-functionally equivalent* if and only if there is no truth-value assignment on which $\mathscr{P}$ and $\mathscr{Q}$ have different truth-values.

TRUTH-FUNCTIONAL CONSISTENCY: A set of sentences of *SL* is *truth-functionally consistent* if and only if there is at least one truth-value assignment on which all of the members of the set are true. A set of sentences of *SL* is *truth-functionally inconsistent* if and only if the set is not truth-functionally consistent.

TRUTH-FUNCTIONAL ENTAILMENT: A set $\Gamma$ of sentences of *SL truth-functionally entails* a sentence $\mathscr{P}$ of *SL* if and only if there is no truth-value assignment on which every member of $\Gamma$ is true and $\mathscr{P}$ is false.

TRUTH-FUNCTIONAL VALIDITY: An argument of *SL* is *truth-functionally valid* if and only if there is no truth-value assignment on which all of the premises are true and the conclusion is false. An argument of *SL* is *truth-functionally invalid* if and only if it is not truth-functionally valid.

Chapter

# 4

# *SENTENTIAL LOGIC: TRUTH-TREES*

## 4.1 INTRODUCTION

In Chapter Three we used the notion of a truth-value assignment to give formal accounts of the important semantic concepts of truth-functional logic. At the end of Chapter Three we saw that, once truth-functional consistency has been explicated by means of the notion of a truth-value assignment, the remaining semantic concepts of sentential logic can be explicated in terms of truth-functional consistency. In this chapter we make use of this fact to provide an additional method, the truth-tree method, of determining whether truth-functional properties hold of sentences and sets of sentences. Truth-trees provide a systematic method of searching for truth-value assignments which are of special interest, for example, a truth-value assignment on which a given sentence of *SL* is false, or a truth-value assignment on which the premises of a given argument of *SL* are true and the conclusion false. The truth-tree method also reveals when no such truth-value assignments exist.

The truth-table method is mechanical. The truth-tree method we develop in this chapter can easily be made so. The advantage of truth-tables is that they graphically display how the truth-values of truth-functionally compound sentences are generated from the truth-values of their components. The disadvantage of truth-tables is that they become unwieldy when the number of distinct atomic components of the sentence or sentences being tested is much greater than three. Truth-trees, it must be admitted, can also become unwieldy. However, the size and complexity of truth-trees is not as direct a function of the number of distinct atomic components of the sentences being tested as is the size and complexity of truth-tables. Sets of sentences with a large number of distinct atomic components frequently have reasonably concise truth-trees.

The rules we will use in constructing truth-trees are derived directly from the characteristic truth-tables for the five truth-functional connectives. For this reason, and because truth-value assignments on which all the members of the set being tested are true can readily be recovered from truth-trees for consistent sets, we take truth-trees to constitute a second *semantic* method of determining whether the truth-functional properties defined in Chapter Three hold of sentences and sets of sentences of *SL*.

## 4.2 TRUTH-TREE RULES FOR SENTENCES CONTAINING '~', '∨', AND '&'

Recall that a set of sentences is truth-functionally consistent if and only if there is *at least one* truth-value assignment on which all the members of that set are true. Sometimes we can tell at a glance that a set is truth-functionally consistent or that it is truth-functionally inconsistent. For example, {A & ~ B, C} is fairly obviously a consistent set, and {A & ~ B, ~ A} is fairly obviously an inconsistent set. But most of us cannot tell immediately whether {(~ B & C) & (A ∨ B), A & C} is consistent or inconsistent. Truth trees provide us with a systematic method for determining, for any finite set of sentences of *SL*, whether that set is truth-functionally consistent.

We begin with some easy examples. First, we shall show that {A & ~ B, C} is indeed truth-functionally consistent. In constructing a truth-tree, the first step is to display the members of the set being tested, one above another, in a column.

A & ~ B
C

What we want to know is whether there is a truth-value assignment on which all the sentences in the column are true. The first sentence in the column is a conjunction, and we know that a conjunction is true on a truth-value assignment if and only if both its conjuncts are true on that assignment. So we can break down or decompose 'A & ~ B' into its conjuncts, adding these conjuncts, one below the other, to our column.

A & ~ B ✓
C
A
~ B

We put a check mark after 'A & ~ B' to indicate that we are finished with it. We have, in effect, replaced it in our list of sentences with two simpler sentences. This replacement is appropriate inasmuch as 'A & ~ B' is true if and only if both 'A' and ' ~ B' are true. All the sentences on the tree either have been decomposed (and checked off) or are atomic sentences or negations of atomic sentences. We shall call a sentence that is either an atomic sentence or the negation of an atomic sentence a *literal*. Once we have a tree on which the only undecomposed sentences are literals, it is easy to determine whether there is a truth-value assignment on which all the members of the set we are testing are true (i.e., whether the set is truth-functionally consistent). We try to generate the desired assignment by reading up the column of sentences, starting at the bottom. We pay attention only to the literals. If a literal is an atomic sentence, we assign the truth-value **T** to that atomic sentence. If the literal is the *negation* of an atomic sentence, we assign the truth-value **F** to the atomic sentence (not to the literal). Applying this procedure to the tree, we generate the following fragment of an assignment:

| A | B | C |
|---|---|---|
| T | F | T |

Clearly every member of the set we are testing, {A & ~ B, C}, is true on every truth-value assignment that assigns these truth-values to 'A', 'B', and 'C'. Hence the set we are testing is truth-functionally consistent.

Next we shall use the truth-tree method to show that {A & ~ B, ~ A} is truth-functionally inconsistent. We begin, as before, by listing the members of the set in a column. Next we decompose the conjunction 'A & ~ B':

```
A & ~ B✓
  ~ A

    A
  ~ B
```

All the literals on this tree must be true for the members of our set to be true. ' ~ B' occurs on the tree. To make it true, we assign 'B' the truth-value **F**. 'A' and ' ~ A' both occur on the tree. To make the former true, we must assign 'A' the truth-value **T**. To make the latter true, we must assign 'A' the truth-value **F**. But clearly there is no truth-value assignment on which 'A' is assigned both the truth-value **T** and the truth-value **F**. Hence there is no truth-value assignment on which all the literals on our tree are true. We entered the literals 'A' and ' ~ B' because they must be true if the first sentence, 'A & ~ B', is to be true. Thus it follows that there is no truth-value assignment on which 'A & ~ B' and ' ~ A', that is, the members of the set we are testing, are both true. So the set is truth-functionally inconsistent.

The truth-trees we have constructed so far both consist of single branches, that is, of single columns of sentences of *SL*. However, many trees are more complex. We can illustrate how multiple branches are formed by constructing a tree for {A & ~ B, C, ~ A ∨ ~ C}. We formed this set from the first set we tested by adding one more sentence, ' ~ A ∨ ~ C'. Thus we can use our tree for the first set as a model for the first part of our tree for this set:

```
  A & ~ B✓
     C
~ A ∨ ~ C

     A
    ~ B
```

Our tree is not yet complete; it contains a truth-functionally compound sentence, '~ A ∨ ~ C' that is not a literal and that has not been decomposed. We must decompose this sentence in such a way as to show what sentences must be true for this disjunction to be true. For a disjunction to be true only one of its disjuncts need be true. If we add both disjuncts to our list, one below the other, we shall wrongly be requiring that both those disjuncts be true. But we can represent the fact that there are *alternative* ways in which a disjunction can be made true by *branching* our tree:

```
  A & ~ B✓
     C
~ A ∨ ~ C✓

     A
    ~ B
    / \
 ~ A   ~ C
```

By displaying '~ A' and '~ C' on the same line, rather than one below the other, we show that making either of them true is sufficient to make the sentence we are decomposing true. We now have two branches, and we have to inspect each to see whether there is a way of making all the sentences we are testing true. If there is such a way, it will involve either making all the literals on the left branch true or making all the literals on the right branch true (or both, since our '∨' is inclusive). A *branch* in our sense, *consists of all the sentences that can be reached by starting with a sentence at the bottom of the tree and tracing a path up through the tree, ending with the first sentence listed in our original column.* A sentence may thus occur just once on a tree but still be on several branches. In our present example the members of the set we are testing, along with the literals 'A' and '~ B', occur on both branches of our tree.

When we inspect the branches of our tree, we immediately see that neither branch will yield a truth-value assignment on which all the members of the set we are testing are true. The left-hand branch shows us that to obtain such an assignment we would have to assign 'A' the truth-value **F** and the truth-value **T**, since both '~ A' and 'A' occur on that branch. Similarly, the right-hand branch shows us that to obtain such an assignment we would have to assign 'C' the truth-value **F** and the truth-value **T**, since both '~ C' and 'C' occur on that branch. Neither alternative is possible. So there is no truth-value assignment on which all the members of the set we are testing are true; hence that set is truth-functionally inconsistent.

In constructing truth-trees, we decompose truth-functionally compound sentences that are not literals in such a way as to display the truth-conditions for those compounds. Trees are, in effect, ways of searching out truth-value assignments on which the sentences in the set being tested are true. A branch which contains both an atomic sentence and the negation of that sentence represents a failure to find such an assignment, for no truth-value assignment assigns any atomic sentence both the truth-value **T** and the truth-value **F**. A branch which does contain both an atomic sentence and the negation of that sentence is a *closed branch*. A branch which is not closed is open. Eventually each branch will either close or become a *completed open branch*, that is, a branch such that every sentence on it is either a literal or has been decomposed, and such that no atomic sentence and its negation occur on that branch. Any truth-value assignment on which all the literals on a completed open branch are true is, by the nature of the tree rules, also an assignment on which the members of the set being tested are all true.[1] To generate such an assignment from an open branch, we assign every atomic sentence occurring on that branch **T**, every atomic sentence whose negation occurs on that branch **F**, and either **T** or **F** (it does not matter which) to every other atomic sentence.

Accordingly,

| |
|---|
| A finite set Γ of sentences of *SL* is *truth-functionally consistent* if and only if Γ has a truth-tree with at least one completed open branch. |

We will call a truth-tree each of whose branches is closed a *closed truth-tree*. Accordingly, we can also say

| |
|---|
| A set Γ of sentences of *SL* is *truth-functionally inconsistent* if and only if at least one finite subset of Γ has a closed truth-tree.[2] |

A *completed tree* is a tree each of whose branches either is closed or is a completed open branch. An *open tree* is a tree with at least one completed open branch. (Note that an open tree need not be a completed tree.) The truth-tree for the empty set is the null tree, that is, the truth-tree which has no sentences on its single null branch,

[1] These results are proven in Chapter Eleven.

[2] We here require truth-trees to be finite and to contain all the members of the set being tested. As will be proven in Chapter Six, an infinite set is truth-functionally inconsistent if and only if at least one of its finite subsets is. Hence a closed truth-tree for a finite subset of an infinite set does establish the inconsistency of the infinite set. But a completed open branch on a tree for a finite subset of an infinite set establishes only the consistency of the finite subset, not that of the infinite set. An infinite set is truth-functionally consistent if and only if it is not truth-functionally inconsistent, that is, if and only if every finite subset has a truth-tree with at least one completed open branch.

each one of which is, trivially, either a literal or has been decomposed. Hence, by the above account, the empty set is consistent, a desired result.

For the sake of clarity, we adopt the convention of numbering the lines of our truth-trees in a column on the left. We shall also include a justification column on the right. The column of line numbers and the column of justifications are not, strictly speaking, parts of truth-trees. They are notational devices we use to make the structure and logic of trees more transparent. The lines containing the members of the set we are testing for truth-functional consistency will all be justified by entering the abbreviation 'SM', for 'set member'. Later lines will be justified by entering a line number and a rule abbreviation. The two rules we have presented so far are *Conjunction Decomposition* and *Disjunction Decomposition*, abbreviated '&D' and '∨D', respectively. When these conventions are followed, our last tree will appear as follows:

| | | | |
|---|---|---|---|
| 1. | A & ~ B✓ | | SM |
| 2. | C | | SM |
| 3. | ~ A ∨ ~ C✓ | | SM |
| 4. | A | | 1 &D |
| 5. | ~ B | | 1 &D |
| 6. | ~ A | ~ C | 3 ∨D |
| | × | × | |

For the sake of clarity, no line of the justification column is allowed to contain more than one rule abbreviation or reference to more than one earlier line. The '×' under the left-hand branch of the tree indicates that that branch is closed. As with line numbers and justifications, the check marks after decomposed sentences and closed branch indicators (the occurrences of '×' at the end of closed branches) are notational conveniences and are not literally parts of truth-trees.

We noted earlier that the set {(~ B & C) & (A ∨ B), A & C} is neither obviously consistent nor obviously inconsistent. We can now use the truth-tree method to test this set for truth-functional consistency. We begin our tree in the usual way:

| | | |
|---|---|---|
| 1. | (~ B & C) & (A ∨ B)✓ | SM |
| 2. | A & C | SM |
| 3. | ~ B & C | 1 &D |
| 4. | A ∨ B | 1 &D |

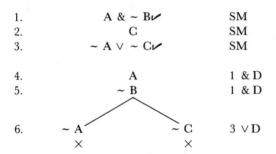

Here the results of using the rule Conjunction Decomposition are themselves truth-functionally compound sentences that will also have to be decomposed. First we decompose 'A & C'. After that we decompose ' ~ B & C' and finally 'A ∨ B'.

| | | | |
|---|---|---|---|
| 1. | (~ B & C) & (A ∨ B)✓ | | SM |
| 2. | A & C✓ | | SM |
| 3. | ~ B & C✓ | | 1 & D |
| 4. | A ∨ B✓ | | 1 & D |
| 5. | A | | 2 & D |
| 6. | C | | 2 & D |
| 7. | ~ B | | 3 & D |
| 8. | C | | 3 & D |
| 9. | A | B<br>× | 4 ∨D |

The only sentences on this tree that have not been decomposed are literals. There are no more sentences that can be decomposed. Yet we have a branch on the left that is not closed. This completed open branch displays the literals from which we can recover a truth-value assignment on which every member of our set is true. That assignment must make all those literals true, so it must assign 'A' and 'C' the truth-value **T** and 'B' the truth-value **F** (since ' ~ B' occurs on the open branch). The relevant fragment of the assignment is thus:

| A | B | C |
|---|---|---|
| **T** | **F** | **T** |

That 'A' and 'C' each occur twice on our open branch has no special significance for the truth-value assignment we are looking for. They so occur because their truth is required by two different members of the set we are testing. This tree is the first one we have encountered that has at least one completed open branch *and* at least one closed branch. An open tree will often have one or more closed branches. The process of generating a truth-value assignment from a completed open branch is called *recovering a truth-value assignment*. Since truth-value assignments are, by definition, assignments of either **T** or **F** to each of the (infinitely many) sentence letters of *SL* they are themselves infinite. Hence, when recovering truth-value assignments from truth-trees, we of course write down only the relevant (finite) fragment of the truth-value assignment. For a given sentence or set of sentences of *SL*, the relevant fragment of a truth-value assignment is that fragment which specifies the truth-values assigned to the atomic components of that sentence or set of sentences. When we talk of recovering a fragment of a truth-value assignment from a completed open branch we of course mean the relevant fragment for the set of sentences being tested, that is, the fragment which specifies the assignments made to the atomic components of the set being tested.

In the last example we decomposed the two conjunctions, '~ B & C' and 'A & C', before we decomposed the disjunction 'A ∨ B'. There is no rule that says we must do this. Any order of decomposition would have led to an open tree. Altering the order of decomposition will sometimes make a tree more or less complex, but it will never alter the final result. For a given set of sentences, if one order of decomposition generates an open tree, all orders of decomposition generate open trees, and if one order of decomposition generates a closed tree, all orders of decomposition generate closed trees. In the present case decomposing 'A ∨ B' earlier would produce the following tree:

| | | | |
|---|---|---|---|
| 1. | (~ B & C) & (A ∨ B)✓ | | SM |
| 2. | A & C✓ | | SM |
| 3. | ~ B & C✓ | | 1 &D |
| 4. | A ∨ B✓ | | 1 &D |
| 5. | A | B | 4 ∨D |
| 6. | A | A | 2 &D |
| 7. | C | C | 2 &D |
| 8. | ~ B | ~ B | 3 &D |
| 9. | C | C | 3 &D |
| | | × | |

In decomposing 'A ∨ B' before 'A & C' and '~ B & C', we produced a branching early in our tree. Consequently, the results of decomposing the remaining sentences had to be entered on both open branches, thus considerably complicating our tree. (It is important to remember that when a sentence is decomposed the results of that decomposition must be entered *on every open branch passing through the sentence being decomposed*.) But this more complex tree is also open, so the end result is the same. The '×' under the right-hand branch was not entered until both '~ B' and 'C' had been entered on that branch. The closure here occurs because the branch contains the pair of literals 'B' and '~ B', but we do not stop halfway through the application of a decomposition rule to mark the closure. Rather, we finish decomposing '~ B & C' and then place an '×' below the branch.

So far we know how to decompose conjunctions and disjunctions but not conditionals, biconditionals, or negations. To be able to do truth-trees for all finite sets of sentences of *SL*, we need to know how to decompose these truth-functionally compound sentences as well. How a negation is to be decomposed depends upon the kind of sentence being negated, and we shall have separate rules for decomposing negated conjunctions, negated disjunctions, negated material conditionals, negated material biconditional, and negated negations. Literals, that is, atomic sentences and negations of atomic sentences, are not decomposed.

We have already used the rules for decomposing conjunctions and disjunctions. Schematically, these rules are

*Conjunction Decomposition* (&D)

$$\mathscr{P} \,\&\, \mathscr{Q} \checkmark$$

$$\mathscr{P}$$
$$\mathscr{Q}$$

*Disjunction Decomposition* (∨D)

$$\mathscr{P} \vee \mathscr{Q} \checkmark$$

$$\mathscr{P} \qquad\qquad \mathscr{Q}$$

It is helpful to think of these rules in the following way. What is written below a sentence indicates what sentences must be true for that sentence to be true. That is, for $\mathscr{P} \,\&\, \mathscr{Q}$ to be true both $\mathscr{P}$ and $\mathscr{Q}$ must be true, so both $\mathscr{P}$ and $\mathscr{Q}$ are written, one under the other, beneath $\mathscr{P} \,\&\, \mathscr{Q}$. For $\mathscr{P} \vee \mathscr{Q}$ to be true, either $\mathscr{P}$ or $\mathscr{Q}$ must be true, so these alternatives are displayed below $\mathscr{P} \vee \mathscr{Q}$ but both on the same line.

The rule for decomposing negated negations is also obvious. A sentence of the form $\sim\sim\mathscr{P}$ is true if and only if $\mathscr{P}$ is true. Hence we have the rule

*Negated Negation Decomposition* (∼ ∼ D)

$$\sim\sim\mathscr{P} \checkmark$$

$$\mathscr{P}$$

Consider next the rule for negated conjunctions. A sentence of the form $\sim(\mathscr{P} \,\&\, \mathscr{Q})$ is truth-functionally equivalent to the corresponding sentence of the form $\sim\mathscr{P} \vee \sim\mathscr{Q}$, and sentences of this latter form are disjunctions. The rule for decomposing disjunctions is a branching rule, that is, a rule that increases the number of branches on a tree. Hence

*Negated Conjunction Decomposition* (∼ &D)

$$\sim(\mathscr{P} \,\&\, \mathscr{Q}) \checkmark$$

$$\sim\mathscr{P} \qquad\qquad \sim\mathscr{Q}$$

Similarly, we know that for any sentences $\mathscr{P}$ and $\mathscr{Q}$, $\sim(\mathscr{P} \vee \mathscr{Q})$ and $\sim\mathscr{P} \,\&\, \sim\mathscr{Q}$ are truth-functionally equivalent sentences, and we already know how to decompose conjunctions. So we have

*Negated Disjunction Decomposition* (~ ∨ D)

~ ($\mathscr{P}$ ∨ $\mathscr{Q}$)✓

~ $\mathscr{P}$
~ $\mathscr{Q}$

We now have all the rules we need to decompose sentences which contain only the connectives '&', '∨', and '~'. It will be useful to pause here to do a few truth-trees for sets consisting of sentences whose only connectives are those just mentioned. Consider first the set {A & ~ B, ~ (B ∨ ~ A), (B & A) ∨ (B & ~ A)}. This set is truth-functionally inconsistent, as the following truth-tree shows:

| | | | | |
|---|---|---|---|---|
| 1. | | A & ~ B✓ | | SM |
| 2. | | ~ (B ∨ ~ A)✓ | | SM |
| 3. | | (B & A) ∨ (B & ~ A)✓ | | SM |
| 4. | | A | | 1 &D |
| 5. | | ~ B | | 1 &D |
| 6. | | ~ B | | 2 ~ ∨D |
| 7. | | ~ ~ A✓ | | 2 ~ ∨D |
| 8. | | A | | 7 ~ ~ D |
| 9. | B & A✓ | | B & ~ A✓ | 3 ∨D |
| 10. | B | | B | 9 &D |
| 11. | A | | ~ A | 9 &D |
| | × | | × | |

Both branches of this tree are closed, hence the tree is closed and no truth-value assignment can be recovered from it. Hence there is no truth-value assignment on which every member of the set being tested is true. Hence that set is truth-functionally inconsistent. Note that decomposing the sentences on lines 1 and 2 does not increase the number of branches, whereas decomposing the sentence on line 3 does. Since branching makes for complexity, we decomposed the sentences on lines 1 and 2 before we decomposed the sentence on line 3. This is a use of the first of several strategies we will develop for keeping trees simple, that is,

> Stratagem 1: Give priority to decomposing sentences whose decomposition does not require branching.

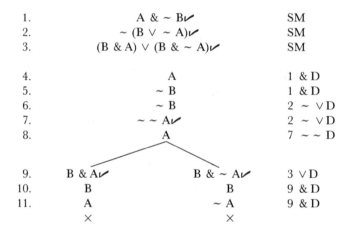

Note also that the justifications given for lines 10 and 11 actually apply to the decomposition of two sentences, 'B & A' and 'B & ~ A'. No confusion results here because both sentences occur on line 9, both are conjunctions, and both are therefore decomposed by the rule Conjunction Decomposition. For the sake of expository clarity, we will avoid writing the products of multiple decompositions on the same line except where those products are, as here, obtained by applying the same decomposition rule multiple times to sentences occurring on the same earlier line.

Consider next a set whose members contain three distinct atomic sentences: {G ∨ (H ∨ I), ~ (G ∨ H), ~ (H ∨ I), ~ (I ∨ G)}. Here is a tree for this set:

| | | |
|---|---|---|
| 1. | G ∨ (H ∨ I)✓ | SM |
| 2. | ~ (G ∨ H)✓ | SM |
| 3. | ~ (H ∨ I)✓ | SM |
| 4. | ~ (I ∨ G)✓ | SM |
| 5. | ~ G | 2 ~ ∨D |
| 6. | ~ H | 2 ~ ∨D |
| 7. | ~ H | 3 ~ ∨D |
| 8. | ~ I | 3 ~ ∨D |
| 9. | ~ I | 4 ~ ∨D |
| 10. | ~ G | 4 ~ ∨D |
| 11. | G (×)      H ∨ I✓ | 1 ∨D |
| 12. | H (×)      I (×) | 11 ∨D |

This tree has three branches, all of which are closed. Hence the set being tested is truth-functionally inconsistent.

Next we will construct a truth-tree for the set: {~ (~ S ∨ T) & ~ (T ∨ R), (T & ~ R) ∨ ~ (R & S), ~ ~ R ∨ (S & ~ T)}. Following our maxim of not using rules which produce branching until forced to do so, we obtain the following as the first part of our truth-tree for this set:

| | | |
|---|---|---|
| 1. | ~ (~ S ∨ T) & ~ (T ∨ R)✓ | SM |
| 2. | (T & ~ R) ∨ ~ (R & S) | SM |
| 3. | ~ ~ R ∨ (S & ~ T) | SM |
| 4. | ~ (~ S ∨ T)✓ | 1 &D |
| 5. | ~ (T ∨ R)✓ | 1 &D |
| 6. | ~ ~ S✓ | 4 ~ ∨D |
| 7. | ~ T | 4 ~ ∨D |
| 8. | ~ T | 5 ~ ∨D |
| 9. | ~ R | 5 ~ ∨D |
| 10. | S | 6 ~ ~ D |

Note that decomposing '~ (~ S ∨ T)' (using the rule Negated Disjunction Decomposition) yields '~ ~ S' and '~ T' on lines 6 and 7, respectively, *not* 'S' and

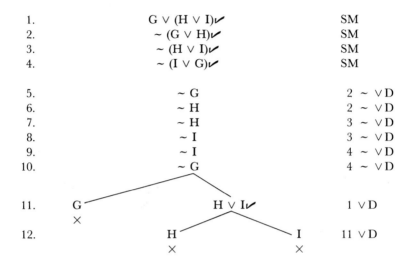

'~ T'. The tree can be completed as follows:

| | | | | | |
|---|---|---|---|---|---|
| 11. | T & ~ R✓ | ~ (R & S)✓ | | | 2 ∨D |
| 12. | T | | | | 11 &D |
| 13. | ~ R | | | | 11 &D |
| 14. | × | ~ ~ R✓ | S & ~ T✓ | | 3 ∨D |
| 15. | | R | | | 14 ~ ~ D |
| 16. | | × | S | | 14 &D |
| 17. | | | ~ T | | 14 &D |
| 18. | | | ~ R | ~ S | 11 ~ &D |
| | | | | × | |

Our tree has three closed branches and one completed open branch. The set we are testing is therefore truth-functionally consistent. Among the truth-value assignments which can be recovered from the open branch is the assignment which assigns **F** to R, **F** to T, and **T** to S, and **T** to every other sentence letter. The relevant fragment of this truth-value assignment, for the set we are testing, is

| R | S | T |
|---|---|---|
| **F** | **T** | **F** |

Obviously, although an infinite number of truth-value assignments can be recovered from this one open branch, they will all be alike in their relevant fragments, that is, in what they assign to the sentence letters 'R', 'S', and 'T'.[3]

Completed truth-trees frequently contain more than one completed open branch. Consider the tree for {~ (H & G) & ~ (H & I), G ∨ I, ~ (H ∨ ~ I)}:

[3] Note that in this tree there are two lines (11 and 14) on which two sentences occur, both of which are ultimately decomposed. But in each case, the results of the decomposition are entered on separate subsequent lines. This is because the two sentences on line 11, as well as the two sentences on line 14, are decomposed by separate rules. Hence, if we were to do the decompositions simultaneously, we could not, without engendering confusion, readily annotate what is happening in the justification column. In a pure tree, one which is not annotated with either line numbers or justifications, there would be no reason not to perform multiple decompositions, even ones using different rules, simultaneously.

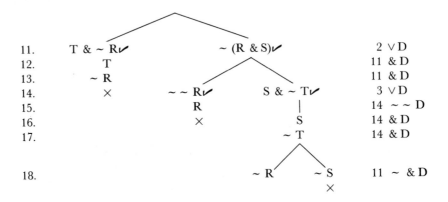

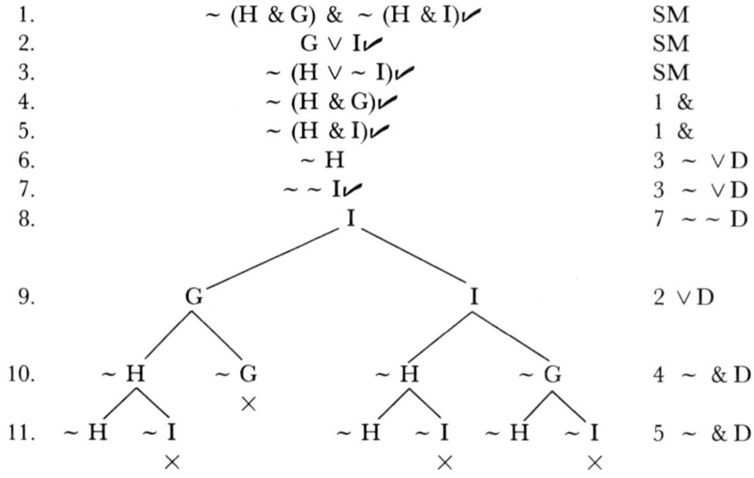
1. ~ (H & G) & ~ (H & I)✓ SM
2. G ∨ I✓ SM
3. ~ (H ∨ ~ I)✓ SM
4. ~ (H & G)✓ 1 &
5. ~ (H & I)✓ 1 &
6. ~ H 3 ~ ∨D
7. ~ ~ I✓ 3 ~ ∨D
8. I 7 ~ ~ D
9. G I 2 ∨D
10. ~ H ~ G ~ H ~ G 4 ~ &D
×
11. ~ H ~ I ~ H ~ I ~ H ~ I 5 ~ &D
× × ×

This tree has three open branches. From the left-most open branch we can recover truth-value assignments of which the following is a fragment:

| H | G | I |
|---|---|---|
| **F** | **T** | **T** |

From the middle open branch we can recover truth-values for 'H' and for 'I', but that branch is mute concerning 'G':

| H | G | I |
|---|---|---|
| **F** | | **T** |

The significance of this is that the members of the set being tested are all true on every truth-value assignment which assigns **F** to 'H' and **T** to 'I'. What is assigned to 'G', given these assignments to 'H' and 'I', does not matter. Hence we can recover *two* fragments of truth-value assignments from this branch, that is,

| H | G | I |
|---|---|---|
| **F** | **T** | **T** |
| **F** | **F** | **T** |

We complete this discussion by giving two additional sample trees. Both are closed. Hence, in each case, the set being tested is truth-functionally inconsistent.

| | | |
|---|---|---|
| 1. | ~ (~ B ∨ ~ C)✓ | SM |
| 2. | B & (~ C ∨ ~ D)✓ | SM |
| 3. | ~ (C & ~ D)✓ | SM |
| 4. | ~ ~ B✓ | 1 ~ ∨D |
| 5. | ~ ~ C✓ | 1 ~ ∨D |
| 6. | B | 2 &D |
| 7. | ~ C ∨ ~ D✓ | 2 &D |
| 8. | B | 4 ~ ~ D |
| 9. | C | 5 ~ ~ D |
| 10. | ~ C  \|  ~ ~ D✓ | 3 ~ &D |
| 11. | ×  \|  D | 10 ~ ~ D |
| 12. | ~ C  \|  ~ D (branching from D) | 7 ∨D |
| | ×  \|  × | |

| | | |
|---|---|---|
| 1. | ~ ((A ∨ B) ∨ ~ C)✓ | SM |
| 2. | C & ~ (A & B)✓ | SM |
| 3. | (A ∨ C) & (A ∨ B)✓ | SM |
| 4. | A | SM |
| 5. | ~ (A ∨ B)✓ | 1 ~ ∨D |
| 6. | ~ ~ C | 1 ~ ∨D |
| 7. | C | 2 &D |
| 8. | ~ (A & B) | 2 &D |
| 9. | A ∨ C | 3 &D |
| 10. | A ∨ B | 3 &D |
| 11. | ~ A | 5 ~ ∨D |
| 12. | ~ B | 5 ~ ∨D |
| | × | |

## 4.2E EXERCISES

Use the truth-tree method to test each of the following sets of sentences for truth-functional consistency. If a set is consistent, recover the relevant fragment of one truth-value assignment on which every member of the set is true.

a. {~ (H ∨ I), H ∨ I}
*b. {~ [(F ∨ ~ F) & G]}
c. {~ (H ∨ I), H ∨ ~ I}
*d. {~ (~ A ∨ B), A ∨ ~ B)}
e. {A & (B & C), ~ [A & (B & C)]}
*f. {A & (B & ~ C), ~ [A & (B & C)]}
g. {~ C ∨ (A & B), C, ~ (A & B)}
*h. {~ (~ A ∨ B), A ∨ ~ B, ~ (~ B & ~ A)}
i. {(~ F & ~ G) & [(G ∨ ~ I) & (I ∨ ~ H)]}
*j. {~ (~ A ∨ ~ B), ~ [A & ~ (B & C)], A ∨ (B ∨ C)}

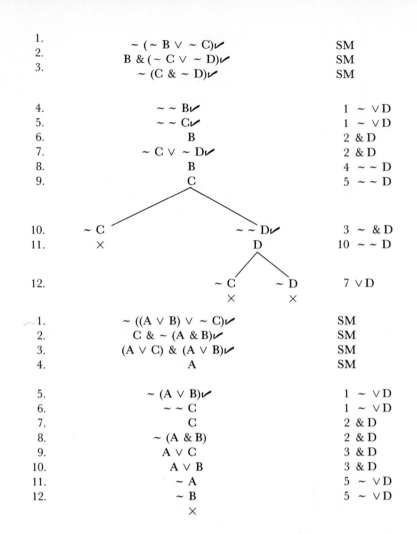

k. $\{(F \vee \sim G) \;\&\; [(G \vee \sim I) \;\&\; (I \vee \sim H)]\}$
*l. $\{\sim [A \;\&\; (\sim B \;\&\; \sim C)],\ \sim A \vee \sim C,\ \sim (\sim B \vee \sim \sim C)\}$
m. $\{A \vee (B \vee C),\ \sim (A \vee B),\ \sim (B \;\&\; C),\ \sim (A \;\&\; C)\}$
*n. $\{(H \vee \sim I) \;\&\; (I \vee \sim G),\ \sim (H \;\&\; G),\ H \vee (\sim I \;\&\; \sim G)\}$

## 4.3 RULES FOR SENTENCES CONTAINING '$\sim$', '$\supset$', AND '$\equiv$'

We now need to develop decomposition rules for material conditionals, material biconditionals, and for the negations of each. We know that, for any sentences $\mathcal{P}$ and $\mathcal{Q}$ of *SL*, $\mathcal{P} \supset \mathcal{Q}$ is equivalent to $\sim \mathcal{P} \vee \mathcal{Q}$. And we have already developed a rule for decomposing disjunctions, i.e.,

*Disjunction Decomposition* ($\vee$D)

$\mathcal{P} \vee \mathcal{Q}$ ✓

$\mathcal{P}$      $\mathcal{Q}$

Given this, and that $\mathcal{P} \supset \mathcal{Q}$ is equivalent to $\sim \mathcal{P} \vee \mathcal{Q}$, the appropriate decomposition rule for $\mathcal{P} \supset \mathcal{Q}$ is

*Conditional Decomposition* ($\supset$D)

$\mathcal{P} \supset \mathcal{Q}$ ✓

$\sim \mathcal{P}$      $\mathcal{Q}$

The negation of a material conditional, $\sim (\mathcal{P} \supset \mathcal{Q})$, is true if and only if that conditional is false, and a conditional is false if and only if its antecedent is true and its consequent is false. In other words, for any sentences $\mathcal{P}$ and $\mathcal{Q}$ of *SL*, $\sim (\mathcal{P} \supset \mathcal{Q})$ and $\mathcal{P} \;\&\; \sim \mathcal{Q}$ are truth-functionally equivalent sentences. Given the rule already developed for decomposing conjunctions, the appropriate rule for decomposing negated conditionals is clearly:

*Negated Conditional Decomposition* ($\sim \supset$D)

$\sim (\mathcal{P} \supset \mathcal{Q})$ ✓

$\mathcal{P}$
$\sim \mathcal{Q}$

The only rules we have left to present are those for material biconditionals and negated material biconditionals. A material biconditional is true if and only if either its immediate components are both true or its immediate components are both false. Alternatively put, for any sentences $\mathcal{P}$ and $\mathcal{Q}$, $\mathcal{P} \equiv \mathcal{Q}$ is truth-functionally equivalent to $(\mathcal{P} \;\&\; \mathcal{Q}) \vee (\sim \mathcal{P} \;\&\; \sim \mathcal{Q})$. The rule for material biconditionals can thus be thought of as a combination of the rule for disjunctions and the rule for conjunctions. Decomposing a material biconditional splits every open branch running through that material biconditional into two branches, and on each new branch we enter two sentences:

*Biconditional Decomposition* (≡ D)

$$\mathscr{P} \equiv \mathscr{Q} \checkmark$$

| | |
|---|---|
| $\mathscr{P}$ | $\sim \mathscr{P}$ |
| $\mathscr{Q}$ | $\sim \mathscr{Q}$ |

The rule for decomposing negations of material biconditionals is also a branching rule. Since a material biconditional is true if and only if its immediate components have the *same* truth-value, the negation of a material biconditional will be true if and only if the immediate components of the material biconditional have *different* truth-values. In other words, for $\sim (\mathscr{P} \equiv \mathscr{Q})$ to be true, either $\mathscr{P}$ must be true and $\mathscr{Q}$ false, or $\mathscr{P}$ must be false and $\mathscr{Q}$ true. So, for any sentences $\mathscr{P}$ and $\mathscr{Q}$, $\sim (\mathscr{P} \equiv \mathscr{Q})$ is truth-functionally equivalent to $(\mathscr{P}\ \&\ \sim \mathscr{Q}) \vee (\sim \mathscr{P}\ \&\ \mathscr{Q})$. Hence

*Negated Biconditional Decomposition* (~ ≡ D)

$$\sim (\mathscr{P} \equiv \mathscr{Q}) \checkmark$$

| | |
|---|---|
| $\mathscr{P}$ | $\sim \mathscr{P}$ |
| $\sim \mathscr{Q}$ | $\mathscr{Q}$ |

We list here our complete set of rules for decomposing sentences of *SL*:

*Sentential Truth-Tree Rules*

$\sim \sim \mathscr{P} \checkmark$ (~ ~ D)

$\mathscr{P}$

$\mathscr{P}\ \&\ \mathscr{Q} \checkmark$ (& D)

$\mathscr{P}$
$\mathscr{Q}$

$\sim (\mathscr{P}\ \&\ \mathscr{Q}) \checkmark$ (~ & D)

| | |
|---|---|
| $\sim \mathscr{P}$ | $\sim \mathscr{Q}$ |

$\mathscr{P} \vee \mathscr{Q} \checkmark$ (∨ D)

| | |
|---|---|
| $\mathscr{P}$ | $\mathscr{Q}$ |

$\sim (\mathscr{P} \vee \mathscr{Q}) \checkmark$ (~ ∨ D)

$\sim \mathscr{P}$
$\sim \mathscr{Q}$

$\mathscr{P} \supset \mathscr{Q} \checkmark$ (⊃ D)

| | |
|---|---|
| $\sim \mathscr{P}$ | $\mathscr{Q}$ |

$\sim (\mathscr{P} \supset \mathscr{Q}) \checkmark$ (~ ⊃ D)

$\mathscr{P}$
$\sim \mathscr{Q}$

$\mathscr{P} \equiv \mathscr{Q} \checkmark$ (≡ D)

| | |
|---|---|
| $\mathscr{P}$ | $\sim \mathscr{P}$ |
| $\mathscr{Q}$ | $\sim \mathscr{Q}$ |

$\sim (\mathscr{P} \equiv \mathscr{Q}) \checkmark$ (~ ≡ D)

| | |
|---|---|
| $\mathscr{P}$ | $\sim \mathscr{P}$ |
| $\sim \mathscr{Q}$ | $\mathscr{Q}$ |

In learning how to construct trees, the best procedure is not simply to memorize the rules. Instead, try to grasp the rationale for the rules. One way to do this, as we have tried to show, is first to understand the bases for the simple rules for conjunctions, disjunctions, and negated negations and then to see how the other rules can be viewed as applications of these three simple rules.

We begin with a few straightforward examples. Here is a tree for the set $\{A \supset B, B \supset A, \sim A\}$:

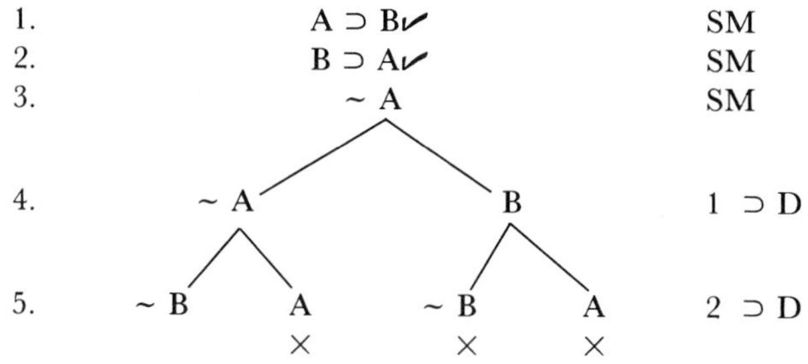


Earlier we noted that when given a choice of decomposing a sentence which will produce branching or a sentence which will not, decomposing the latter will generally produce a simpler tree. In this case we had no such choice, for the set consists of a literal and two conditionals and the rule for decomposing conditionals is a branching rule, that is, a rule which produces branches. After decomposing the first member of the set we have two open branches, one ending in '$\sim$ A', the other ending in 'B'. Decomposing the second member of the set yields four branches, but three of them close, leaving us a completed tree with one completed open branch. The set is therefore truth-functionally consistent. The one recoverable fragment of a truth-value assignment is A: **F**, B: **F**.

Here is another tree for the same set:

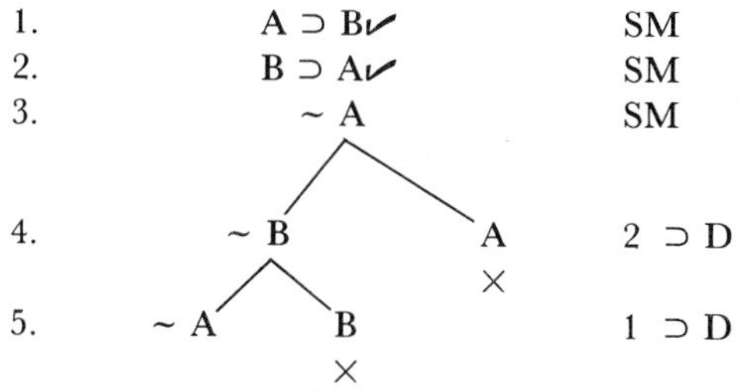


This tree is at least marginally simpler than the first; it has a total of three branches, whereas the first one had four branches. While it is true that both the sentence on line 1 and the sentence on line 2 produce multiple branches when decomposed, one of the branches produced by decomposing the sentence on line 2, the one ending in 'A', closes immediately. We can now formulate a second stratagem for keeping trees simple:

> Stratagem 2: Give priority to decomposing sentences whose decomposition results in the closing of one or more branch.

Here is a tree for {~ (A ⊃ B), B ⊃ A}:

| | | | |
|---|---|---|---|
| 1. | ~ (A ⊃ B)✓ | | SM |
| 2. | B ⊃ A✓ | | SM |
| 3. | A | | 1 ~ ⊃ D |
| 4. | ~ B | | 1 ~ ⊃ D |
| 5. | ~ B | A | 2 ⊃ D |

We decomposed the sentence on line 1 first because it does not branch. The tree has two completed open branches so the set is truth-functionally consistent. Only one relevant fragment of a truth-value assignment is recoverable: A: **T**, B: **F**.

Next we will do a tree for {H ≡ G, G ≡ I, H, ~ I}:

| | | | | |
|---|---|---|---|---|
| 1. | H ≡ G✓ | | | SM |
| 2. | G ≡ I✓ | | | SM |
| 3. | H | | | SM |
| 4. | ~ I | | | SM |
| 5. | H | | ~ H | 1 ≡ D |
| 6. | G | | ~ G | 1 ≡ D |
| | | | × | |
| 7. | G | ~ G | | 2 ≡ D |
| 8. | I | ~ I | | 2 ≡ D |
| | × | × | | |

The tree is closed, so the set is truth-functionally inconsistent. Here the order of decomposition makes no difference. Both the sentence on line 1 and the sentence on line 2 branch when decomposed; whichever is decomposed first produces one closed branch.

The set {~ (H ≡ I), I ≡ J, ~ H} yields an open tree:

| | | | | |
|---|---|---|---|---|
| 1. | ~ (H ≡ I)✓ | | | SM |
| 2. | I ≡ J✓ | | | SM |
| 3. | ~ H | | | SM |
| 4. | H | ~ H | | 1 ~ ≡ D |
| 5. | ~ I | I | | 1 ~ ≡ D |
| | × | | | |
| 6. | | I | ~ I | 2 ≡ D |
| 7. | | J | ~ J | 2 ≡ D |
| | | | × | |

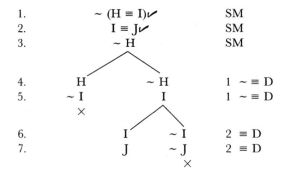

Here the order of decomposition does matter. Decomposing the sentence on line 1 first produces two branches, one of which immediately closes. Decomposing the sentence on line 2 first would produce two branches, neither of which would close immediately. The one completed open branch yields the following fragment of a truth-value assignment: H: **F**, I: **T**, J: **T**. The set is truth-functionally consistent. It is important to remember, as illustrated here, that both the rule for decomposing material biconditionals and the rule for decomposing negated material biconditionals branch, and both introduce '~'s.

Finally, consider the set {A ⊃ (B ≡ C), ~ (C ⊃ A)}. Here is a tree:

| | | | | |
|---|---|---|---|---|
| 1. | | A ⊃ (B ≡ C)✓ | | SM |
| 2. | | ~ (C ⊃ A)✓ | | SM |
| 3. | | C | | 2 ~ ⊃ D |
| 4. | | ~ A | | 2 ~ ⊃ D |
| 5. | ~ A | B ≡ C✓ | | 1 ⊃ D |
| 6. | | B | ~ B | 5 ≡ D |
| 7. | | C | ~ C | 5 ≡ D |
| | | | × | |

The tree has two completed open branches; the set is therefore truth-functionally consistent. Recoverable fragments are

| A | B | C |
|---|---|---|
| **F** | **T** | **T** |
| **F** | **F** | **T** |

What is of interest here is that the left-hand open branch becomes completed at line 5 (and the tree becomes, at that point, an open tree). When line 5 is completed we know the set is truth-functionally consistent, for one branch is now a completed open branch and will remain such, whatever happens on the rest of the tree. This suggests a third stratagem:

> Stratagem 3: Stop when a tree yields an answer to the question being asked.

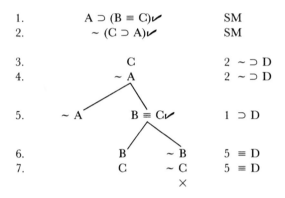

Of course, nothing less than a completed tree, with every branch closed, shows that a set is truth-functionally inconsistent. But if our only interest is in determining whether a set is consistent, and an incomplete tree for it has a completed open branch, there is no virtue in completing the tree. As soon as a branch becomes a completed open branch, we know the answer to the question we are asking: The set is consistent; we can recover a truth-value assignment which demonstrates that it is.[4] So in the present case we could just as well have stopped after line 5, that is, with the open but incomplete tree:

| | | |
|---|---|---|
| 1. | $A \supset (B \equiv C)$ ✓ | SM |
| 2. | $\sim (C \supset A)$ ✓ | SM |
| 3. | $C$ | $2 \sim\supset D$ |
| 4. | $\sim A$ | $2 \sim\supset D$ |
| 5. | $\sim A$ $\quad$ $B \equiv C$ | $1 \supset D$ |

### 4.3E EXERCISES

Use the truth-tree method to test each of the following sets of sentences for truth-functional consistency. If a set is consistent, recover one fragment of a truth-value assignment on which every member of the set is true.

a. $\{\sim (A \supset B),\ \sim (B \supset A)\}$
*b. $\{\sim [\sim A \supset (B \supset C)],\ A \supset C\}$
c. $\{\sim [(A \supset \sim B) \supset (B \supset A)],\ \sim (\sim A \supset \sim B)\}$
*d. $\{H \equiv G,\ \sim H,\ G\}$
e. $\{H \equiv G,\ \sim G\}$
*f. $\{(H \equiv G) \equiv \sim H\}$
g. $\{H \equiv G,\ \sim (H \supset G)\}$
*h. $\{H \equiv \sim G,\ H \supset G\}$
i. $\{H \equiv G,\ G \equiv I,\ \sim (H \supset I)\}$
*j. $\{A \supset \sim (A \equiv B),\ \sim (A \supset B)\}$
k. $\{A \equiv (\sim B \equiv C),\ \sim A \supset (B \supset \sim C),\ \sim (A \supset \sim C)\}$
*l. $\{\sim [A \supset (B \equiv C)],\ A \equiv \sim C,\ A \equiv B\}$
m. $\{J \supset (H \equiv \sim I),\ \sim (J \equiv H)\}$
*n. $\{J \supset K,\ K \supset J,\ \sim (J \equiv K)\}$

[4] We will continue to give completed trees in our solutions to exercise problems. This is not because there is anything virtuous about completed trees, but because alternative orders of decomposition will produce alternative trees, and the first completed open branch on one may not yield the same fragment(s) of truth-value assignments yielded by the first completed open branch on another tree.

There is another way in which truth-trees could be shortened—by defining a closed branch to be a branch which contains, for any sentence $\mathscr{P}$, both $\mathscr{P}$ and $\sim \mathscr{P}$. Exactly the same sets would have closed trees given this revised system as do on the present system, and exactly the same sets would have open trees as do on the present system. However, the revised system would presuppose (in a way the one we have developed does not) that there can be no truth-value assignment on which a sentence $\mathscr{P}$ and $\sim \mathscr{P}$ are both true. The system we have developed presupposes only that there can be no atomic sentence $\mathscr{P}$ on which both $\mathscr{P}$ and $\sim \mathscr{P}$ are true. And this does follow directly from the definition of a truth-value assignment.

## 4.4 MORE COMPLEX TRUTH-TREES

Consider the set {A ⊃ (B & ~ C), ~ (C ∨ A), C ≡ ~ A}. In constructing a truth-tree for this set we start, as always, by listing the members of the set, one below the other:

| | | |
|---|---|---|
| 1. | A ⊃ (B & ~ C) | SM |
| 2. | ~ (C ∨ A) | SM |
| 3. | C ≡ ~ A | SM |

No member of the set is a literal; hence all are candidates for decomposition. Which sentence should be decomposed first? In one sense, it does not matter. For, if any order of decomposition yields an open tree, all will; and, if any order of decomposition yields a closed tree, all will. However, as noted earlier, it is desirable to keep truth-trees as concise as possible, and one stratagem for doing this is to decompose sentences which do not branch before decomposing those that do.

The sentence on line 1, a material conditional, will branch when decomposed. So will the sentence on line 3, a material biconditional. But the sentence on line 2, a negated disjunction, will not. So we decompose it first. There are now two undecomposed sentences on our tree that are not literals, 'A ⊃ (B & ~ C)' and 'C ≡ ~ A'. Both will yield new branches when decomposed. Decomposing the material conditional will yield two open branches, one ending in '~ A', the other in 'B & ~ C'. Neither of these branches will close immediately. However, decomposing the material biconditional will yield an immediate closure.

| | | | |
|---|---|---|---|
| 1. | A ⊃ (B & ~ C) | | SM |
| 2. | ~ (C ∨ A)✓ | | SM |
| 3. | C ≡ ~ A✓ | | SM |
| 4. | ~ C | | 2 ~ ∨D |
| 5. | ~ A | | 2 ~ ∨D |
| 6. | C | ~ C | 3 ≡ D |
| 7. | ~ A | ~ ~ A | 3 ≡ D |
| | × | | |

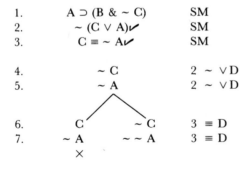

We are now left with just one open branch. There are two undecomposed nonliterals on that branch, 'A ⊃ (B & ~ C)' and '~ ~ A'. We decompose '~ ~ A', first, since negated negations do not branch when decomposed. Moreover, when we decompose '~ ~ A', we add 'A' to the one open branch of our tree and thus close that branch and the tree.

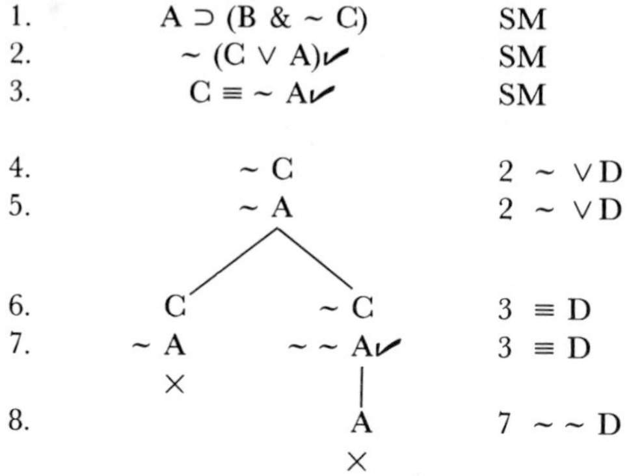


Several aspects of this tree are of interest. First, the tree is closed, and the set we are testing, {A ⊃ (B & ~ C), ~ (C ∨ A), C ≡ ~ A}, is therefore truth-functionally inconsistent. Every attempt to find a truth-value assignment on which every member of that set is true ended in failure. Second, we have shown that the set is inconsistent without decomposing every nonliteral on the tree. The sentence on line 1 was never decomposed, since decomposing the other nonliterals on the tree generated a closed tree. What this shows is that the set we are testing would be inconsistent even without its first member, 'A ⊃ (B & ~ C)'. Whenever a branch closes, we are through with that branch, even if it contains one or more undecomposed nonliterals.

This fairly concise tree was generated by following our strategies of giving priority to the decomposition of sentences whose decomposition does not require branching and to sentences whose decomposition generates one or more closed branches. Had we ignored these strategies and just worked straight down the tree, always decomposing every nonliteral on a given level before moving to a lower level, the result would have been the following more complex tree:

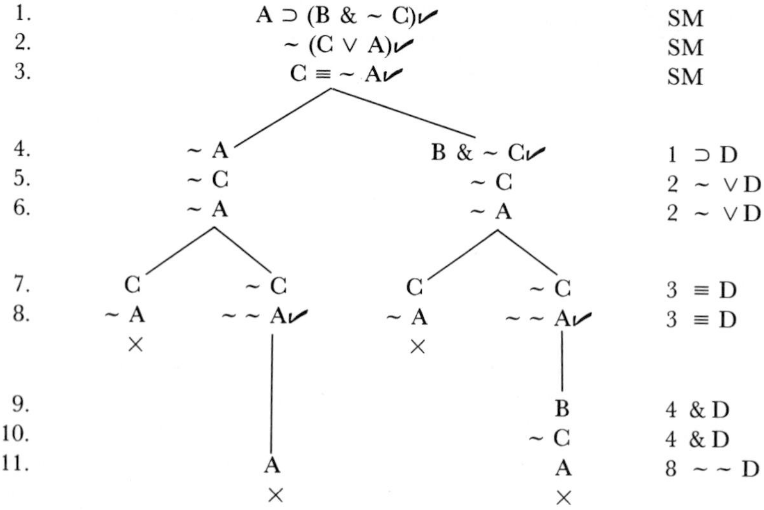

Here we have four branches, whereas in the earlier tree we had only two. Moreover, this tree takes eleven lines to construct; the earlier one took only eight. But the difference between the trees is only one of complexity. Each tree shows equally well that the set of sentences we are testing is truth-functionally inconsistent, for each tree is closed.

The more complex of the above trees can be used to illustrate several important aspects of tree construction. Note that when we decompose '~ (C ∨ A)' at lines 5 and 6, the tree already has two open branches. Hence the results of decomposing this sentence must be entered on each of these open branches. The results of decomposing a sentence must always be entered on *every open branch that runs through the sentence being decomposed.*

Consider the tree after line 8 is completed: Two branches are closed, but two are open. We next decompose 'B & ~ C' on the right-hand branch only, at lines 9 and 10 (not on the left-hand branch, because, although it is open, it does not go through 'B & ~ C'). We then decompose each occurrence of '~ ~ A' on line 8 by writing 'A' on line 11, at the end of each branch (since each branch does go through '~ ~ A'). Could we have put 'A' on the left-hand branch at line 9 at the same time that we put 'B' on the right-hand branch at line 9? We could not. The policy we follow is this: *Trees are to be so constructed that every line of the tree is fully justified either by writing* 'SM' *in the justification column or by entering the number of one and only one earlier line and one and only one rule abbreviation in the justification column.* All the entries made on line 7 come from line 3, and they are all obtained by one rule, Material Biconditional Decomposition. Had we tried to write 'A' on line 9 on the second branch from the left, we would have had two entries on that line coming from two different lines, by the use of two different rules, and thus would have been forced to enter both '8 ~ ~ D' and '4 &D' in the justification column for line 9, in clear violation of this policy.

We have so far specified three strategies for keeping truth-trees concise. We repeat them here and add a fourth:

*Stratagems for Constructing Truth-Trees*

1. Give priority to decomposing sentences whose decomposition does not require branching.
2. Give priority to decomposing sentences whose decomposition results in the closing of one or more branch.
3. Stop when a tree yields an answer to the question being asked.
4. Where stratagems 1 through 3 are not applicable, decompose the more complex sentences first.

The rationale for the first three stratagems should be clear by now. The fourth stratagem is designed to save tedious work, for a complex sentence is more work to decompose than is a less complex one. And, if a complex sentence is decomposed early in a tree, the chances are that there will be only a few open branches on which the results must be entered. But, if complex sentences are left until the end, it is likely that the results of decomposing them will have to be entered on many open branches. Roughly speaking, a sentence $\mathscr{P}$ is more complex than a sentence $\mathscr{Q}$ if decomposing $\mathscr{P}$ requires entering more sentences or longer sentences on a tree than does decomposing $\mathscr{Q}$. In this sense longer sentences are generally more complex than shorter ones, and material biconditionals and negations of material biconditionals are more complex than other sentences of approximately the same length.

The stratagems we have presented provide guidelines, not rules, for constructing truth-trees.[5] Disregarding one or more of them may produce a more complex tree than is necessary but will never yield an open tree where following them would yield a closed tree or vice versa.

As a final example we shall do a truth-tree for {(C & ~ D) ≡ A, (A & C) ⊃ ~ (D ∨ A)}.

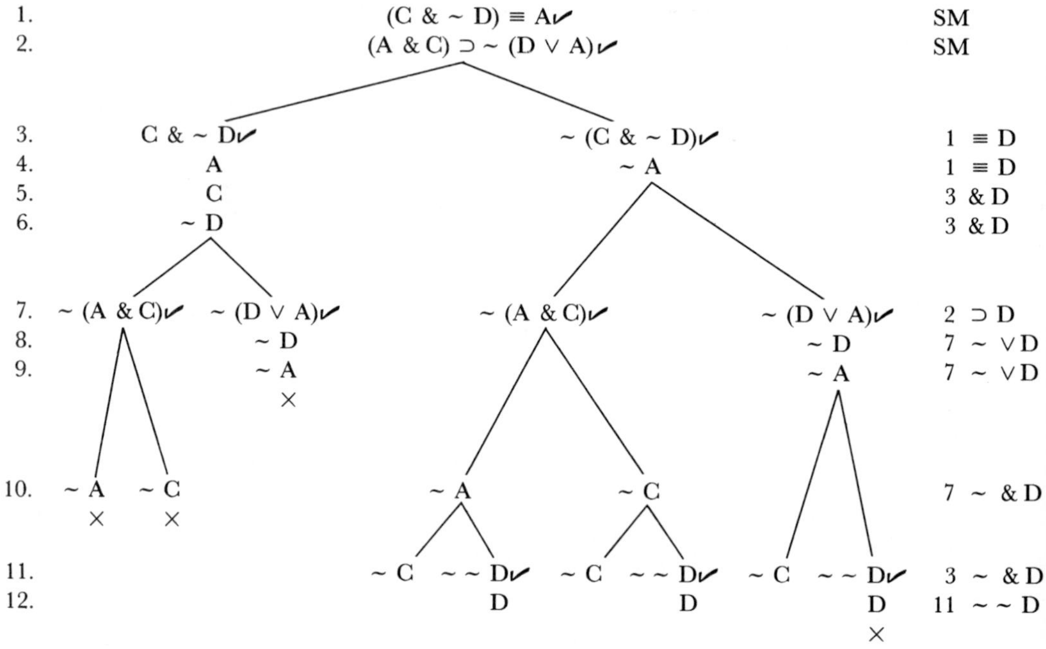


This tree has five completed open branches. The literals occurring on the left-most completed open branch are '~ C' and '~ A'. Hence this branch tells us that, to make all the sentences in the set we are testing true, it is sufficient to make '~ C' and '~ A' both true, and, to do this, we must assign the truth-value **F** to both 'A' and 'C'. But note that 'D' is an atomic component of both members of that set, and no assignment has yet been made to 'D'. This is because neither 'D' nor '~ D'

[5] We said earlier that the truth-tree method could easily be made mechanical. It could be made so by replacing our guidelines for decomposing sentences with some mandatory order of decomposition.

occurs on the open branch just examined. The significance of the nonoccurrence of both 'D' and '~ D' is this: It does not matter which truth-value we assign to 'D'; the sentences we are testing will both be true as long as we assign the truth-value **F** to 'A' and to 'C', no matter what we assign to 'D'. Of course, we must assign some truth-value to 'D', but which one we assign is of no consequence. Thus we can recover *two* fragments of truth-value assignments from the left-hand open branch:

| A | C | D |
|---|---|---|
| **F** | **F** | **T** |
| **F** | **F** | **F** |

The next open branch we come to contains the literals 'D' and '~ A'. Neither 'C' nor '~ C' occurs on this second open branch. Hence we can expect to recover two fragments of truth-value assignments from it as well. They are

| A | C | D |
|---|---|---|
| **F** | **T** | **T** |
| **F** | **F** | **T** |

In fact, only the first of these is a new fragment; the second we also obtained from the first open branch. The third open branch contains just the same literals as does the first. The fourth open branch contains the literals 'D', '~ C', and '~ A' and yields the fragment:

| A | C | D |
|---|---|---|
| **F** | **F** | **T** |

which was also yielded by all the other open branches we have examined. The last open branch contains the literals '~ C', '~ A', and '~ D', and so yields just one fragment:

| A | C | D |
|---|---|---|
| **F** | **F** | **F** |

This is also not a new fragment; it was yielded by the first and third open branches as well. In sum, we have five completed open branches on our tree, and those branches yield three distinct fragments of truth-value assignments. The number of open branches on a completed truth-tree is, again, no guide to the number of distinct fragments of truth-value assignments that can be recovered from that tree. Of course, to show that a set of sentences is consistent, we need only show that there is at least one truth-value assignment on which all the members of the set are true. And, to show that there *is* such an assignment, it suffices to recover one fragment of a truth-value assignment.

Fragments of truth-value assignments can be recovered only from completed open branches. Closed branches are unsuccessful attempts to find such fragments. Thus the branches of a truth-tree should not be thought of as corresponding to the rows of a truth-table. They do not. However, doing a truth-tree for a set of sentences does tell us a lot about what the truth-table for the same set of sentences would be like. If the tree closes, we know that there is no row in the corresponding truth-table in which every member of the set in question has **T** under its main connective. If the tree is open, we know that there is at least one row in that table in which every member of the set in question does have **T** under its main connective. And, if we count the number of distinct fragments of truth-value assignments we can recover, we know that there will be exactly that many rows in the corresponding truth-table in which every member of the set in question has a **T** under its main connective.

### 4.4E EXERCISES

**1.** Construct truth-trees to test each of the following sets of sentences for truth-functional consistency. If a set is consistent, recover one fragment of a truth-value assignment from your tree that shows this.

a. {H ∨ G, ~ G & ~ H}
*b. {K ∨ (M & ~ M), J & ~ C}
c. {~ ~ C, C & [U ∨ (~ C & B)]}
*d. {~ (M & ~ N), ~ (K ∨ M) & ~ ~ M, ~ ~ ~ K}
e. {~ [~ (E ∨ ~ C) & A], ~ (E ∨ ~ C) & A}
*f. {~ [~ (L ∨ ~ L) & (N ∨ ~ N)]}
g. {~ A ∨ ~ ~ [~ (K & ~ A) ∨ R], ~ [D ∨ (A & ~ K)], A & (R ∨ K)}
*h. {~ [~ (J ⊃ M) ≡ (J & ~ M)]}
i. {B ⊃ J, H ≡ J, ~ H ∨ B}
*j. {H & (~ K ⊃ M), ~ K, ~ (H ⊃ M)}
k. {~ [(B & J) ≡ ~ (W ∨ Z)], ~ (J & W)}
*l. {~ ~ ~ [(K ∨ M) ⊃ ~ G], G ≡ (J & U), U ⊃ (~ G & K), K & ~ U}

**2.** Which of the following claims are true? Explain your reasoning.

a. If a completed truth-tree contains at least one open branch, then at least one truth-value assignment on which all the members of the set being tested are true can be recovered from that open branch.
*b. A completed open branch of a truth-tree yields at most one fragment of a truth-value assignment on which every member of the set being tested is true.
c. If a set of sentences has an open truth-tree, then that set is truth-functionally consistent.
*d. If a truth-tree is closed, there are no open branches on the tree.
e. If a truth-tree is closed, the set of sentences being tested is truth-functionally inconsistent.
*f. If a truth-tree is closed, then every sentence on the tree either has been decomposed or is a literal.

g. If there are eight distinct atomic components of the members of a set Γ of sentences of *SL*, then a completed tree for Γ will have eight branches.

*h. A completed truth-tree with at least one open branch and at least one closed branch is an open tree.

i. If a tree has a closed branch, then there is a truth-value assignment for which all the members of the set being tested are false.

*j. If a set Γ of sentences of *SL* has an open tree, then every nonempty subset of Γ also has an open tree.

k. If no member of a set Γ of sentences of *SL* contains a tilde, then no tree for Γ will have a closed branch.

**3.** Use the truth-tree method to test symbolizations of the following passages for truth-functional consistency. If your symbolization is truth-functionally consistent, recover one fragment of a truth-value assignment from your tree that shows this.

a. Poison caused the victim's death if and only if there was a change in his blood chemistry or a residue of poison in the stomach. There was neither a change in blood chemistry nor a residue of poison in his stomach, but there were puncture marks on the body. Poison was injected by a needle only if there were puncture marks on the body. Either poison was the cause of the victim's death, or there are no puncture marks on the body.

*b. Either the bullet was fired from an intermediate distance, or it wasn't. If it wasn't, there are powder burns on the body (provided the bullet was fired at close range) or signs of a rifle bullet (provided the bullet was fired at a great distance). Although there are no powder burns on the body, there are signs of a rifle bullet. Unless the angle at which the bullet entered the body was elevated, the bullet wasn't fired from an intermediate distance, and the angle wasn't elevated.

c. The murder was committed by at least one of the staff—the butler, the maid, and the gardener—but not by all three. The butler did it only if the crime was committed indoors; and if it was not committed indoors, the gardener didn't do it. If poison was used, then the butler did it unless the maid did; but the maid didn't do it. Poison was used; and moreover, the crime was not committed indoors.

*d. Exactly two of Albert, Betty, and Christine will find employment when they graduate from law school. If Albert gets a job, Betty and Christine surely will too. Betty will not get a job unless Albert does. Christine is a first-rate lawyer and will certainly be hired by a good law firm.

## 4.5 USING TRUTH-TREES TO TEST FOR TRUTH-FUNCTIONAL TRUTH, FALSITY, AND INDETERMINACY

We know that every sentence of *SL* is either truth-functionally true, truth-functionally false, or truth-functionally indeterminate. Truth-trees can be used to determine into which of these categories a particular sentence of *SL* falls. Truth-trees test for the consistency of finite nonempty sets of sentences of *SL*. Suppose that we want to know whether a sentence $\mathcal{P}$ is truth-functionally false. Remember that if $\mathcal{P}$ is not truth-functionally false, there is some truth-value assignment on which it is true; hence the unit set of $\mathcal{P}$, $\{\mathcal{P}\}$, will be truth-functionally consistent. On the other hand, if 𝒫 is truth-functionally false, there is no truth-value assignment on which it is true; hence there is no assignment on which every member of {𝒫} is true. So

> A sentence 𝒫 of *SL* is *truth-functionally false* if and only if the set {𝒫} has a closed tree.

Here is a tree for the set {[A ⊃ (B & C] & [~ (A ⊃ B) ∨ ~ (A ⊃ C)]}.

| | | | | | |
|---|---|---|---|---|---|
| 1. | [A ⊃ (B & C)] & [~ (A ⊃ B) ∨ ~ (A ⊃ C)]✓ | | | | SM |
| 2. | A ⊃ (B & C)✓ | | | | 1 &D |
| 3. | ~ (A ⊃ B) ∨ ~ (A ⊃ C)✓ | | | | 1 &D |
| 4. | ~ (A ⊃ B)✓ | | ~ (A ⊃ C)✓ | | 3 ∨D |
| 5. | A | | A | | 4 ~ ⊃D |
| 6. | ~ B | | ~ C | | 4 ~ ⊃D |
| 7. | ~ A<br>× | B & C✓ | ~ A<br>× | B & C✓ | 2 ⊃D |
| 8. | | B | | B | 7 &D |
| 9. | | C<br>× | | C<br>× | 7 &D |

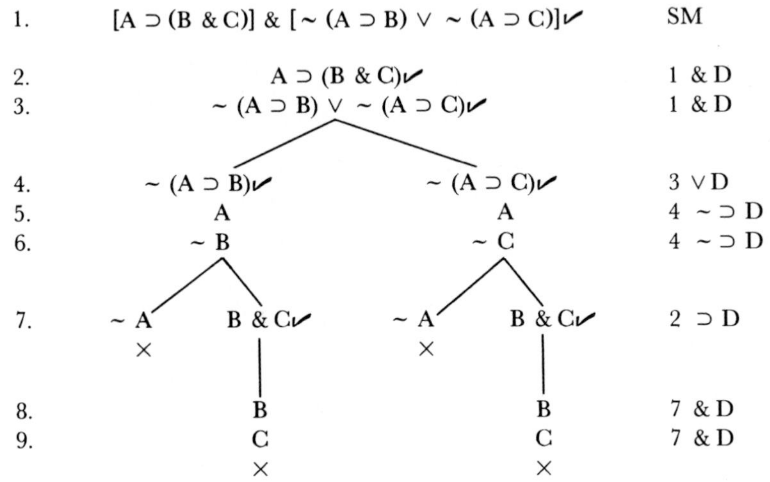

All the branches of this tree do close, so there is no truth-value assignment on which the one member of the set we are testing is true. Hence the set is truth-functionally inconsistent, and its single member is truth-functionally false. In constructing this tree we were able to save work at lines 5 and 6 by decomposing two sentences, '~ (A ⊃ B)' and '~ (A ⊃ C)', in one step. We could do so because these sentences occur on the same line, line 4, and are decomposed by the same rule, Negated Conditional Decomposition. This is acceptable because, in doing them both at once, we are not required to enter two line numbers or two rule abbreviations in our justification column. Of course, we also could have done them separately.

Next, we shall use the tree method to determine whether 'A ⊃ [B ⊃ (A ⊃ B)]' is truth-functionally false.

| | | | | | |
|---|---|---|---|---|---|
| 1. | A ⊃ [B ⊃ (A ⊃ B)]✓ | | | | SM |
| 2. | ~ A | B ⊃ (A ⊃ B)✓ | | | 1 ⊃D |
| 3. | | ~ B | A ⊃ B✓ | | 2 ⊃D |
| 4. | | | ~ A | B | 3 ⊃D |

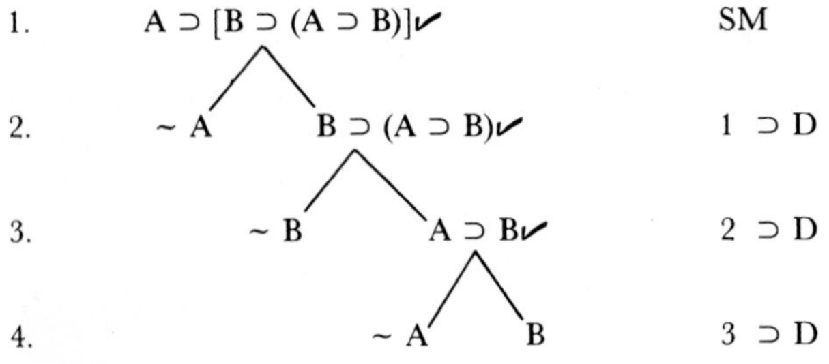

This tree is obviously open, so the unit set we are testing is truth-functionally consistent. Hence there is at least one truth-value assignment on which the one member of that set is true, and that sentence is thus not truth-functionally false.

Incidentally, if all we had wanted to known was whether 'A ⊃ [B ⊃ (A ⊃ B)]' is truth-functionally false, we could have stopped at line 2. The only unchecked sentences on the left-hand open branch are literals, so that branch is a completed open branch. Hence we know that there is a truth-value assignment on which 'A ⊃ [B ⊃ (A ⊃ B)]' is true. Although more work can be done on the right-hand branch, nothing that happens there can make the left-hand branch close.

Although we know that 'A ⊃ [B ⊃ (A ⊃ B)]' is not truth-functionally false, we do not yet know whether that sentence is truth-functionally indeterminate or truth-functionally true. We can find out by doing another tree. For suppose the sentence we are concerned with, 'A ⊃ [B ⊃ (A ⊃ B)]', is truth-functionally true. Then its negation, '~ (A ⊃ [B ⊃ (A ⊃ B)])', must be truth-functionally false. So we can determine whether the sentence is truth-functionally true by seeing if its negation is truth-functionally false, that is, by seeing if the unit set of its negation has a closed tree. Here is that tree.[6]

| | | |
|---|---|---|
| 1. | ~ (A ⊃ [B ⊃ (A ⊃ B)])✓ | SM |
| 2. | A | 1 ~⊃D |
| 3. | ~ [B ⊃ (A ⊃ B)]✓ | 1 ~⊃D |
| 4. | B | 3 ~⊃D |
| 5. | ~ (A ⊃ B)✓ | 3 ~⊃D |
| 6. | A | 5 ~⊃D |
| 7. | ~ B | 5 ~⊃D |
| | × | |

The tree is closed. So there is no truth-value assignment on which the sentence '~ (A ⊃ [B ⊃ (A ⊃ B)])', is true. Since that sentence is a negation, there is no truth-value assignment on which the sentence of which it is a negation, 'A ⊃ [B ⊃ (A ⊃ B)]', is false. That sentence is therefore truth-functionally true.

> A sentence 𝒫 of *SL* is *truth-functionally true* if and only if the set {~ 𝒫} has a closed tree.

A sentence is truth-functionally indeterminate if and only if it is neither truth-functionally true nor truth-functionally false. Therefore

> A sentence 𝒫 of *SL* is *truth-functionally indeterminate* if and only if neither the set {𝒫} nor the set {~ 𝒫} has a closed tree.

[6] Strictly speaking, there is more than one truth-tree for this set, as well as for most sets of sentences of *SL* (since there is usually more than one order of decomposition). However, since all the trees for any given set of sentences yield the same result, we sometimes speak informally of *the* tree for a set of sentences.

When we are interested in determining the truth-functional status of a sentence, the trees we do will be trees for unit sets of sentences. However, we shall allow ourselves to talk informally of doing the tree for $\mathcal{P}$ or for $\sim \mathcal{P}$. Such talk is to be understood as shorthand for talk about trees for unit sets.

When determining the truth-functional status of a sentence $\mathcal{P}$, we shall sometimes end up doing two trees, one for $\mathcal{P}$ and one for $\sim \mathcal{P}$. Of course, if we suspect that $\mathcal{P}$ is truth-functionally true, we should first do the truth-tree for $\sim \mathcal{P}$. On the other hand, if we suspect that $\mathcal{P}$ is truth-functionally false, we should first do the truth-tree for $\mathcal{P}$ itself.

Recall that our tree for 'A ⊃ [B ⊃ (A ⊃ B)]' has all open branches. One might easily think that it follows from this alone that 'A ⊃ [B ⊃ (A ⊃ B)]' is truth-functionally true, for surely, if that sentence were not truth-functionally true, the tree for it would have at least one closed branch. *This reasoning is mistaken. Many sentences that are not truth-functional truths have trees with only open branches, and many truth-functional truths have trees with some closed branches.* Consider the truth-tree for a simple disjunction, 'A ∨ B'.

| | | | |
|---|---|---|---|
| 1. | A ∨ B✓ | | SM |
| 2. | A | B | 1 ∨D |

This tree has only open branches. Yet we know that 'A ∨ B' is not a truth-functional truth. Its truth-table will mirror the characteristic truth-table for disjunctions; that is, the first three rows under its main connective will contain **T**, and the fourth row will contain **F**.

We can see that not all truth-functional truths have truth-trees with all open branches by considering the sentence '(A ∨ ~ A) ⊃ (B ⊃ B)'. This sentence is a truth-functional truth inasmuch as its consequent is a truth-functional truth (its antecedent is as well), and there is thus no truth-value assignment on which this conditional is false. But the tree for this sentence does have one closed branch:

| | | | | |
|---|---|---|---|---|
| 1. | (A ∨ ~ A) ⊃ (B ⊃ B)✓ | | | SM |
| 2. | ~ (A ∨ ~ A)✓ | B ⊃ B✓ | | 1 ⊃D |
| 3. | ~ A | | | 2 ~ ∨D |
| 4. | ~ ~ A✓ | | | 2 ~ ∨D |
| 5. | A | | | 4 ~ ~ D |
| | × | | | |
| 6. | | ~ B | B | 2 ⊃D |

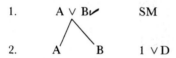

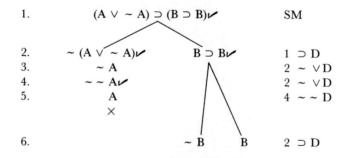

There is a way we can avoid doing two truth-trees for one sentence. Suppose we do a tree for a sentence $\mathcal{P}$, thinking it may be truth-functionally false. The tree does not close. We now know that $\mathcal{P}$ is either truth-functionally true or truth-functionally indeterminate. If it is true on all truth-value assignments it is truth-functionally true; if it is true on only some assignments, it is truth-functionally indeterminate. We can find out which is the case by counting the number of distinct fragments of truth-value assignments which are recoverable from our completed open tree—for these fragments correspond to the rows of the truth-table for the sentence being tested in which there is a **T** under that sentence's main connective. If $\mathscr{P}$ has $n$ atomic components, we shall get back $2^n$ distinct fragments of truth-value assignments from our tree if and only if $\mathscr{P}$ is truth-functionally true.

Recall our tree for 'A ∨ B'. That tree has two open and no closed branches. The only literal occurring on the left-hand branch is 'A', so from that branch we can recover two fragments, one that assigns the truth-value **T** to 'B' and one that assigns the truth-value **F** to 'B':

| A | B |
|---|---|
| **T** | **T** |
| **T** | **F** |

We can also recover two fragments from the right-hand open branch. But only one of these is a new fragment:

| A | B |
|---|---|
| **F** | **T** |

The one relevant fragment that we do not recover is that which assigns the truth-value **F** to both 'A' and 'B', and this is just what we expected. For a disjunction is false when and only when both its disjuncts are false. By recovering fragments of truth-value assignments we have shown that 'A ∨ B' is truth-functionally indeterminate without doing two trees for that sentence.

We can use this same procedure with our last truth-tree to verify that '(A ∨ ~ A) ⊃ (B ⊃ B)' is indeed truth-functionally true. This sentence has two atomic components, so we can expect to recover four distinct fragments of truth-value assignments from the tree for this sentence. The tree has two completed open branches. The only literal on the left-hand branch is '~ B', so this branch yields two fragments:

| A | B |
|---|---|
| **T** | **F** |
| **F** | **F** |

The only literal occurring on the right-hand branch is 'B', so this branch yields two new fragments:

| A | B |
|---|---|
| T | T |
| F | T |

We have recovered all the expected fragments of truth-value assignments, thus showing that the sentence being tested is true on every truth-value assignment. We have verified that it is truth-functionally true, even though the tree for that sentence has one closed branch.

Suppose we suspect that a sentence $\mathscr{P}$ is truth-functionally true and accordingly construct a tree for the negation of that sentence, $\sim \mathscr{P}$. Suppose also that our tree has at least one completed open branch. In this case our suspicions were wrong; $\mathscr{P}$ is not truth-functionally true. The standard procedure would now be to do a tree for $\mathscr{P}$, to see whether that sentence is truth-functionally false or truth-functionally indeterminate. Instead, we can see what distinct fragments of truth-value assignments can be recovered from the tree we have already done for $\sim \mathscr{P}$. The fragments we recover are fragments of truth-value assignments on which $\sim \mathscr{P}$ is true. If we recover all relevant fragments, we know that $\sim \mathscr{P}$ is true on every truth-value assignment and is thus truth-functionally true. And if $\sim \mathscr{P}$ is truth-functionally true, $\mathscr{P}$ is truth-functionally false. If we do not recover all the distinct relevant fragments from our tree, we know that there is at least one truth-value assignment on which that sentence is false, and hence on which $\mathscr{P}$ is true. In this case $\mathscr{P}$ is truth-functionally indeterminate.

The method of recovering fragments of truth-value assignments will always allow us to avoid doing a second tree. However, to use the method, we must complete the tree we are working with (rather than stopping when we have one completed open branch). As a result, when the tree is complex and the number of relevant fragments is relatively large—eight, sixteen, thirty-two, or more—it is often easier to do a second tree than to recover and count distinct relevant fragments.

## 4.5E EXERCISES

**1.** Use the truth-tree method to determine for each of the following sentences its truth-functional status (i.e., whether the sentence is truth-functionally true, truth-functionally false, or truth-functionally indeterminate).

a. $M \,\&\, \sim M$
*b. $M \vee \sim M$
c. $\sim M \vee \sim M$

*d. $(C \supset R) \supset [\sim R \supset \sim (C \& J)]$
e. $(C \supset R) \& [(C \supset \sim R) \& \sim (\sim C \vee R)]$
*f. $(K \equiv W) \vee (A \& W)$
g. $(\sim A \equiv \sim Z) \& (A \& \sim Z)$
*h. $[L \vee (J \vee \sim K)] \& (K \& [(J \vee L) \supset \sim K])$
i. $(A \vee B) \& \sim (A \vee B)$
*j. $(A \vee B) \supset \sim (A \vee B)$
k. $(A \vee B) \equiv \sim (A \vee B)$
*l. $\sim (D \vee F) \equiv \sim (D \& F)$
m. $\sim (D \vee F) \equiv (\sim D \vee \sim F)$
*n. $\sim (D \vee F) \equiv (\sim D \& \sim F)$

**2.** For each of the following sentences, use the truth-tree method to determine whether or not it is truth-functionally true. Where appropriate, give a fragment of a truth-value assignment that supports your answer.

a. $(B \supset L) \vee (L \supset B)$
*b. $(B \supset L) \& (L \supset B)$
c. $(A \equiv K) \supset (A \vee K)$
*d. $(A \equiv K) \supset (\sim A \vee K)$
e. $[(J \supset Z) \& \sim Z] \supset \sim J$
*f. $[(J \supset Z) \& \sim J] \supset \sim Z$
g. $(B \supset (M \supset H)) \equiv [(B \supset M) \supset (B \supset H)]$
*h. $M \supset [L \equiv (\sim M \equiv \sim L)]$
i. $(A \& \sim B) \supset \sim (A \vee B)$
*j. $(A \& \sim B) \supset \sim (A \& B)$
k. $[(A \& B) \supset C] \equiv [(A \supset \sim B) \vee C]$
*l. $(D \equiv \sim E) \equiv \sim (D \equiv E)$
m. $[A \supset (B \& C)] \supset [A \supset (B \supset C)]$
*n. $[A \supset (B \& C)] \equiv [A \supset (B \supset C)]$
o. $[(A \& B) \supset C] \equiv [A \supset (B \supset C)]$

**3.** Use the truth-tree method to determine for each of the following sentences its truth-functional status (i.e., whether the sentence is truth-functionally true, truth-functionally false, or truth-functionally indeterminate). In each case do only a tree for the given sentence. If the tree does not close, determine the truth-functional status of the sentence by recovering and counting relevant fragments of truth-value assignments.

a. $\sim (\sim A \supset A)$
*b. $J \supset (K \supset L)$
c. $(A \equiv \sim A) \supset \sim (A \equiv \sim A)$
*d. $(E \equiv H) \supset (\sim E \supset \sim H)$
e. $(\sim B \& \sim D) \vee \sim (B \vee D)$
*f. $([(C \supset D) \& (D \supset E)] \& C) \& \sim E$
g. $[(A \vee B) \& (A \vee C)] \supset \sim (B \& C)$
*h. $\sim ([(A \vee B) \& (B \vee C)] \& (\sim A \& \sim B))$
i. $(J \vee \sim K) \equiv \sim \sim (K \supset J)$
*j. $\sim B \supset [(B \vee D) \supset D]$

**4.** Decide which of the following claims are true and which are false. In each case explain and defend your reasoning. Use examples where appropriate.

a. If a completed tree for the unit set of $\mathcal{P}$, $\{\mathcal{P}\}$, has at least one open branch and at least one closed branch, then $\mathcal{P}$ is truth-functionally indeterminate.

*b. If $\mathcal{P}$ is truth-functionally true and has four atomic components, then the tree for $\{\mathcal{P}\}$ will have four open branches.

c. If a completed tree for $\{\mathcal{P}\}$ has all open branches, then $\mathcal{P}$ is truth-functionally true.

*d. If $\{\mathcal{P}\}$ has a closed tree and $\{\mathcal{Q}\}$ has a closed tree, then the unit set of every truth-functionally compound sentence whose immediate components are $\mathcal{P}$ and $\mathcal{Q}$ will also have a closed tree.

e. If $\{\mathcal{P}\}$ has an open tree and $\{\mathcal{Q}\}$ has an open tree, then the unit set of every truth-functionally compound sentence that has $\mathcal{P}$ and $\mathcal{Q}$ as its immediate components will have an open tree.

*f. If the completed truth-tree for $\mathcal{P}$ has exactly one open branch, then $\sim \mathcal{P}$ is truth-functionally indeterminate.

## 4.6 TRUTH-FUNCTIONAL EQUIVALENCE

Sentences $\mathcal{P}$ and $\mathcal{Q}$ of *SL* are truth-functionally equivalent if and only if there is no truth-value assignment on which $\mathcal{P}$ and $\mathcal{Q}$ have different truth-values. It follows that sentences $\mathcal{P}$ and $\mathcal{Q}$ are truth-functionally equivalent if and only if their corresponding material biconditional, $\mathcal{P} \equiv \mathcal{Q}$, is truth-functionally true. And a material biconditional $\mathcal{P} \equiv \mathcal{Q}$ is truth-functionally true just in case the tree for the negation of that biconditional is closed. That is, to determine whether a biconditional is a truth-functional truth, we simply apply the test for truth-functional truth developed in the last section. More formally,

> Sentences $\mathcal{P}$ and $\mathcal{Q}$ of *SL* are *truth-functionally equivalent* if and only if the set $\{\sim (\mathcal{P} \equiv \mathcal{Q})\}$ has a closed tree.

In discussing truth-tables, we showed that '(W & Y) ⊃ H' is truth-functionally equivalent to 'W ⊃ (Y ⊃ H)' by producing a truth-table that revealed that these two sentences have the same truth-value on every truth-value assignment. We can now use the truth-tree method to show the same result. To show that these sentences are equivalent, we need show only that their corresponding material biconditional is truth-functionally true.

W Y H   W ⊃ (Y ⊃ H)

| | | | |
|---|---|---|---|
| 1. | ~ ([(W & Y) ⊃ H] ≡ [W ⊃ (Y ⊃ H)])✓ | | SM |
| 2. | (W & Y) ⊃ H✓ | ~ [(W & Y) ⊃ H]✓ | 1 ~ ≡ D |
| 3. | ~ [W ⊃ (Y ⊃ H)]✓ | W ⊃ (Y ⊃ H)✓ | 1 ~ ≡ D |
| 4. | W | | 3 ~ ⊃ D |
| 5. | ~ (Y ⊃ H)✓ | | 3 ~ ⊃ D |
| 6. | Y | | 5 ~ ⊃ D |
| 7. | ~ H | | 5 ~ ⊃ D |
| 8. | ~ (W & Y)✓     H × 7 | | 2 ⊃ D |
| 9. | ~ W ×     ~ Y × | | 8 ~ & D |
| 10. | | W & Y✓ | 2 ~ ⊃ D |
| 11. | | ~ H | 2 ~ ⊃ D |
| 12. | | W | 10 & D |
| 13. | | Y | 10 & D |
| 14. | | ~ W ×     Y ⊃ H✓ | 3 ⊃ D |
| 15. | | ~ Y ×     H × | 14 ⊃ D |

This tree is closed. The sentence at the top of the tree is therefore false on every truth-value assignment, and the biconditional of which it is the negation is therefore true on every truth-value assignment. So the immediate components of that biconditional, '(W & Y) ⊃ H' and 'W ⊃ (Y ⊃ H)', are truth-functionally equivalent.

In our chapter on truth-tables we also showed that 'E ∨ H' and '(H ∨ J) ∨ E' are not truth-functionally equivalent. We can now show this by using the truth-tree method. These sentences are truth-functionally equivalent if and only if their corresponding material biconditional, '(E ∨ H) ≡ [(H ∨ J) ∨ E]', is truth-functionally true. And that biconditional is truth-functionally true if and only if the tree for its negation closes.

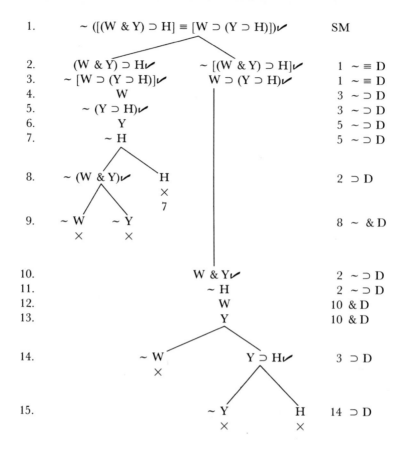

| | | | | | |
|---|---|---|---|---|---|
| 1. | ~ ((E ∨ H) ≡ [(H ∨ J) ∨ E])✓ | | | | SM |
| 2. | E ∨ H✓ | | ~ (E ∨ H)✓ | | 1 ~ ≡ D |
| 3. | ~ [(H ∨ J) ∨ E]✓ | | (H ∨ J) ∨ E✓ | | 1 ~ ≡ D |
| 4. | ~ (H ∨ J)✓ | | | | 3 ~ ∨D |
| 5. | ~ E | | | | 3 ~ ∨D |
| 6. | ~ H | | | | 4 ~ ∨D |
| 7. | ~ J | | | | 4 ~ ∨D |
| 8. | E × | H × | | | 2 ∨D |
| 9. | | | ~ E | | 2 ~ ∨D |
| 10. | | | ~ H | | 2 ~ ∨D |
| 11. | | | H ∨ J✓ | E × | 3 ∨D |
| 12. | | | H × | J | 11 ∨D |

Since this truth-tree has a completed open branch, there is at least one truth-value assignment on which the sentence at the top of the tree is true. That sentence is therefore not truth-functionally false, and the biconditional of which it is the negation is thus not truth-functionally true. It follows that the sentences that are the immediate components of that biconditional, 'E ∨ H' and '(H ∨ J) ∨ E', are not truth-functionally equivalent. They have different truth-values on every truth-value assignment of which

| E | H | J |
|---|---|---|
| **F** | **F** | **T** |

is a fragment.

### 4.6E EXERCISES

**1.** Use the truth-tree method to determine whether the following pairs of sentences are truth-functionally equivalent. For those pairs that are not truth-functionally equivalent, give a fragment of a truth-value assignment that shows this.

| | | |
|---|---|---|
| a. | ~ (Z ∨ K) | ~ Z & ~ K |
| *b. | ~ (Z ∨ K) | ~ Z ∨ ~ K |
| c. | (B & C) ⊃ R | (B ⊃ R) & (C ⊃ R) |
| *d. | (B ∨ C) ⊃ R | (B ⊃ R) & (C ⊃ R) |

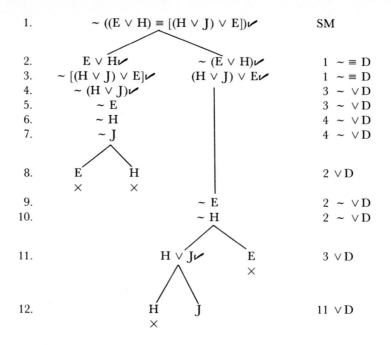

e. A & (B ∨ C) (A & B) ∨ (A & C)
*f. A ∨ (B & C) (A ∨ B) & (A ∨ C)
g. D ⊃ (L ⊃ M) (D ⊃ L) ⊃ M
*h. J ⊃ (K ≡ L) (J ⊃ K) ≡ (J ⊃ L)

**2.** Decide which of the following claims are true and which are false. In each case explain and defend your reasoning. If $\mathcal{P}$ and $\mathcal{Q}$ are truth-functionally equivalent, then

a. the truth-tree for $\{\mathcal{P} \equiv \mathcal{Q}\}$ will be open.
*b. the truth-tree for $\{\mathcal{P} \equiv \sim \mathcal{Q}\}$ will be open.
c. the truth-tree for the set $\{\mathcal{P}, \mathcal{Q}\}$ will be open.

## 4.7 TRUTH-FUNCTIONAL ENTAILMENT AND TRUTH-FUNCTIONAL VALIDITY

We can use truth-trees to test for truth-functional entailment. Recall that where $\mathcal{P}$ is a sentence and Γ is a set of sentences, Γ truth-functionally entails $\mathcal{P}$, that is, $\Gamma \models \mathcal{P}$, if and only if there is no truth-value assignment on which every member of Γ is true and $\mathcal{P}$ is false. Put another way, a set Γ of sentences truth-functionally entails a sentence $\mathcal{P}$ if and only if the set of sentences $\Gamma \cup \{\sim \mathcal{P}\}$ is truth-functionally inconsistent. Hence, to see if Γ truth-functionally entails $\mathcal{P}$, we do a tree for the members of Γ and for $\sim \mathcal{P}$. Here we have to be careful to negate the allegedly entailed sentence before doing a tree. More formally,

> A finite set Γ of sentences of *SL truth-functionally entails* a sentence $\mathcal{P}$ of *SL* if and only if the set $\Gamma \cup \{\sim \mathcal{P}\}$ has a closed truth-tree.

Does the set {B & K, N ⊃ ~ K, K ∨ ~ K} truth-functionally entail 'B ⊃ N'? We can find out by doing a tree for the members of this set and for the negation of 'B ⊃ N'.

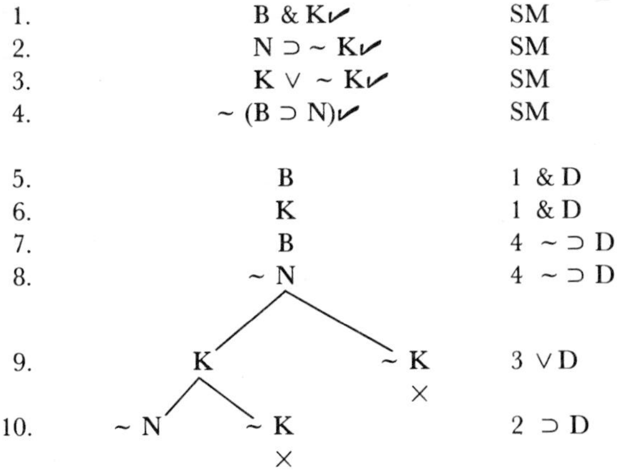

Since this truth-tree is open, there is a truth-value assignment on which all the sentences we are testing are true, hence an assignment on which the members of the set {B & K, N ⊃ ~ K, K ∨ ~ K} are all true and the allegedly entailed sentence, 'B ⊃ N', is false. So the entailment does not in fact hold. The following fragment shows this:

| B | K | N |
|---|---|---|
| T | T | F |

On the other hand, {~ J ∨ S, S ⊃ E} does truth-functionally entail 'J ⊃ E', as the following closed tree shows:

| | | |
|---|---|---|
| 1. | ~ J ∨ S✔ | SM |
| 2. | S ⊃ E✔ | SM |
| 3. | ~ (J ⊃ E)✔ | SM |
| 4. | J | 3 ~ ⊃ D |
| 5. | ~ E | 3 ~ ⊃ D |
| 6. | ~ J          S | 1 ∨ D |
| 7. | ~ S     E | 2 ⊃ D |

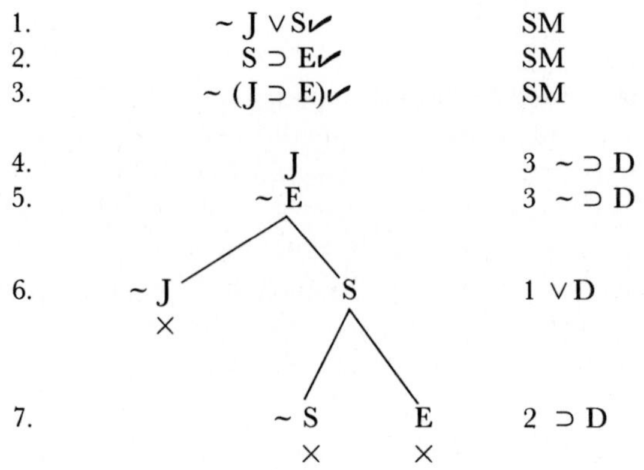

An argument is truth-functionally valid if and only if there is no truth-value assignment on which the premises are true and the conclusion false. Alternatively put, an argument is truth-functionally valid if and only if there is no truth-value assignment on which the premises and the *negation* of the conclusion are all true. Hence an argument is truth-functionally valid if and only if the set consisting of the premises and the *negation* of the conclusion is truth-functionally inconsistent.

> An argument of *SL* is *truth-functionally valid* if and only if the set consisting of the premises and the negation of the conclusion has a closed truth-tree.

In our first example, we shall use the tree method to determine whether or not the following argument is truth-functionally valid:

(~ B ∨ ~ H) ⊃ M

K & ~ M

―――――――――

B

Trees here are no different from the trees we have already constructed, but we *must* remember to do the tree for the premises and the *negation* of the conclusion, rather than for the premises and the conclusion.

| | | | |
|---|---|---|---|
| 1. | (~ B ∨ ~ H) ⊃ M✓ | | SM |
| 2. | K & ~ M✓ | | SM |
| 3. | ~ B | | SM |
| 4. | K | | 2 &D |
| 5. | ~ M | | 2 &D |
| 6. | ~ (~ B ∨ ~ H)✓ | M<br>× | 1 ⊃D |
| 7. | ~ ~ B✓ | | 6 ~ ∨D |
| 8. | ~ ~ H | | 6 ~ ∨D |
| 9. | B<br>× | | 7 ~ ~ D |

Our truth-tree is closed. So we know that the set consisting of the sentences we are testing is truth-functionally inconsistent, and hence that the argument from which the set was formed is truth-functionally valid. Our reasoning is this: The closed tree shows that there is no truth-value assignment on which the premises of our argument are all true and the negation of the conclusion is also true. Therefore there is no truth-value assignment on which those premises are true and the conclusion false, so the argument is truth-functionally valid.

Here is another argument:

~ W & ~ L
(J ⊃ ~ W) ≡ ~ L
H
________________
J & H

Our tree for this argument follows. Remember that it is the negation of the conclusion that we use along with the premises, not the conclusion itself.

| | | | | | | |
|---|---|---|---|---|---|---|
| 1. | ~ W & ~ L✓ | | | | | SM |
| 2. | (J ⊃ ~ W) ≡ ~ L✓ | | | | | SM |
| 3. | H | | | | | SM |
| 4. | ~ (J & H)✓ | | | | | SM |
| 5. | ~ W | | | | | 1 & D |
| 6. | ~ L | | | | | 1 & D |
| 7. | J ⊃ ~ W✓ | | | | ~ (J ⊃ ~ W) | 2 ≡ D |
| 8. | ~ L | | | | ~ ~ L✓ | 2 ≡ D |
| 9. | | | | | L | 8 ~ ~ D |
| | | | | | × | |
| 10. | ~ J | | ~ W | | | 7 ⊃ D |
| 12. | ~ J | ~ H | ~ J | ~ H | | 4 ~ & D |
| | | × | | × | | |

Because this tree is open, we can recover a fragment of a truth-value assignment on which the premises and the negation of the conclusion are true, and hence on which the premises are true and the conclusion false. So the argument we are testing is truth-functionally invalid. The recoverable fragment is

| H | J | L | W |
|---|---|---|---|
| **T** | **F** | **F** | **F** |

An argument is truth-functionally valid if and only if the set consisting of the premises of that argument truth-functionally entails the conclusion of that argument. Thus the procedures for constructing truth-trees to test for truth-functional validity and for truth-functional entailment are very similar. In the case of testing for truth-functional validity the conclusion is negated, and in the case of testing for truth-functional entailment the allegedly entailed sentence is negated.

### 4.7E EXERCISES

**1.** Use the truth-tree method to determine which of the following claims are true and which are false. For those that are false, give the relevant fragment of a truth-value assignment that shows this.

a. {A ⊃ (B & C), C ≡ B, ~ C} ⊨ ~ A
*b. {K ⊃ H, H ⊃ L, L ⊃ M} ⊨ K ⊃ M
c. {~ (A ≡ B), ~ A, ~ B} ⊨ C & ~ C
*d. {~ (~ A & ~ B)} ⊨ A & B
e. {~ ~ F ⊃ ~ ~ G, ~ G ⊃ ~ F} ⊨ G ⊃ F

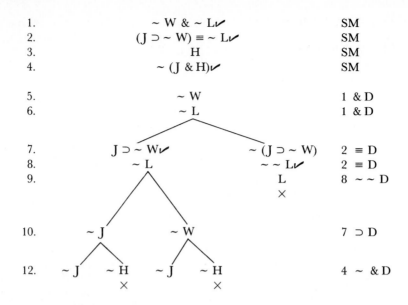

*f. $\{A \& (B \supset C)\} \vDash (A \& C) \vee (A \& B)$
g. $\{[(C \vee D) \& H] \supset A, D\} \vDash H \supset A$
*h. $\{(G \equiv H) \vee ({\sim} G \equiv H)\} \vDash ({\sim} G \equiv {\sim} H) \vee {\sim} (G \equiv H)$
i. $\{(J \vee M) \supset {\sim} (J \& M), M \equiv (M \supset J)\} \vDash M \supset J$
*j. $\vDash [A \vee ((K \supset {\sim} H) \& {\sim} A)] \vee {\sim} A$
k. $\vDash {\sim} (A \equiv B) \supset ({\sim} A \equiv {\sim} B)$
*l. $\vDash {\sim} (C \equiv C) \equiv (C \vee {\sim} C)$
m. $\vDash [(A \supset B) \supset (C \supset D)] \supset [C \supset (B \supset D)]$

**2.** Use the truth-tree method to determine which of the following arguments are truth-functionally valid and which are truth-functionally invalid. For those that are truth-functionally invalid, give the relevant fragment of a truth-value assignment that shows this.

a. $M \supset (K \supset B)$
$\sim K \supset {\sim} M$
$L \& M$
---
$B$

*b. $({\sim} J \vee K) \supset (L \& M)$
${\sim} ({\sim} J \vee K)$
---
${\sim} (L \& M)$

c. $A \& (B \vee C)$
$({\sim} C \vee H) \& (H \supset {\sim} H)$
---
$A \& B$

*d. $(D \equiv {\sim} G) \& G$
$[G \vee ((A \supset D) \& A)] \supset {\sim} D$
---
$G \supset {\sim} D$

e. $(M \equiv K) \vee {\sim} (K \& D)$
${\sim} M \supset {\sim} K$
${\sim} D \supset {\sim} (K \& D)$
---
$M$

*f. $(J \supset T) \supset J$
$(T \supset J) \supset T$
---
${\sim} J \vee {\sim} T$

g. $B \& (H \vee Z)$
${\sim} Z \supset K$
$(B \equiv Z) \supset {\sim} Z$
${\sim} K$
---
$M \& N$

*h. $A \vee \sim (B \,\&\, C)$
$\sim B$
$\sim (A \vee C)$

---

$A$

i. $A \,\&\, (B \supset C)$

---

$(A \,\&\, C) \vee (A \,\&\, \sim B)$

*j. $(G \equiv H) \vee (\sim G \equiv H)$

---

$(\sim G \equiv \sim H) \vee \sim (G \equiv H)$

k. $A \supset \sim A$
$(B \supset A) \supset B$

---

$A \equiv \sim B$

*l. $B \vee (A \,\&\, \sim C)$
$(C \vee A) \equiv B$
$\sim B \vee A$

---

$\sim (A \vee C)$

**3.** Symbolize each of the following arguments, and then use the truth-tree method to determine whether the symbolized argument is truth-functionally valid. If an argument is not truth-functionally valid, recover one fragment of a truth-value assignment that shows this.

a. The social security system will succeed if and only if more money is collected through social security taxes. Unless the social security system succeeds, many senior citizens will be in trouble. Although members of Congress claim to be sympathetic to senior citizens, more money won't be collected through social security taxes. Hence the social security system will not succeed.

*b. Either the President and the senators will support the legislation, or the President and the representatives will support it. Moreover, the representatives will support the legislation, provided that a majority of the people support it. The people don't support it. Thus the senators will support the legislation.

c. If the President acts quickly the social security system will be saved, and if the social security system is saved, senior citizens will be delighted. If the President is pressured by members of the Senate, by members of the House of Representatives, or by senior citizens, he will act quickly. However, neither members of the Senate nor members of the House will pressure the President, but senior citizens will. Therefore senior citizens will be delighted.

*d. The President won't veto the bill if Congress passes it, and Congress will pass it just in case both the Senate passes it and the House of Representatives passes it. But the House of Representatives will pass it only if a majority of Democrats will vote for it; and indeed a majority of Democrats will vote for it. Therefore the President won't veto the bill.

e. At most one of the two houses of Congress will pass the bill. If either the House of Representatives or the Senate passes it, the voters will be pleased; but if both houses of Congress pass the bill, the President will not be pleased. If the President is not pleased, not all the members of the White House will be happy. Hence some members of the White House will not be happy.

*4. Suppose that we are told that a completed tree for the premises and the conclusion (not the negation of the conclusion) of an argument is open. Give two arguments (one valid, the other invalid) that show that this information is of no use in determining whether or not the argument in question is truth-functionally valid. Now suppose we are told that a tree for the premises and conclusion of an argument is closed. Give two arguments (one valid, the other invalid) that show that this information is also of no use in determining whether or not the argument in question is truth-functionally valid.

5. Suppose we define a new connective, '|', thus:

| $\mathscr{P}$ | $\mathscr{Q}$ | $\mathscr{P} \mid \mathscr{Q}$ |
|---|---|---|
| T | T | F |
| T | F | T |
| F | T | T |
| F | F | T |

To deal with this new connective, we have to add two new rules to our truth-tree system, one for decomposing sentences of the form $\mathscr{P}|\mathscr{Q}$ and one for decomposing sentences of the form $\sim (\mathscr{P}|\mathscr{Q})$. Give these rules. Now use your new rules to test, by the truth-tree method, the following pair of sentences for truth-functional equivalence. State your result.

A|B    (A|A) ∨ (B|B)

## GLOSSARY

TRUTH-FUNCTIONAL CONSISTENCY: A finite set Γ of sentences of *SL* is *truth-functionally consistent* if and only if Γ has a truth-tree with at least one completed open branch.

TRUTH-FUNCTIONAL INCONSISTENCY: A set Γ of sentences of *SL* is *truth-functionally inconsistent* if and only if at least one finite subset of Γ has a closed truth-tree.

TRUTH-FUNCTIONAL FALSITY: A sentence $\mathscr{P}$ of *SL* is *truth-functionally false* if and only if the set $\{\mathscr{P}\}$ has a closed truth-tree.

TRUTH-FUNCTIONAL TRUTH: A sentence $\mathscr{P}$ of *SL* is *truth-functionally true* if and only if the set $\{\sim \mathscr{P}\}$ has a closed truth-tree.

TRUTH-FUNCTIONAL INDETERMINACY: A sentence $\mathscr{P}$ of *SL* is *truth-functionally indeterminate* if and only if neither the set $\{\mathscr{P}\}$ nor the set $\{\sim \mathscr{P}\}$ has a closed truth-tree.

TRUTH-FUNCTIONAL EQUIVALENCE: Sentences $\mathscr{P}$ and $\mathscr{Q}$ of *SL* are *truth-functionally equivalent* if and only if the set $\{\sim (\mathscr{P} \equiv \mathscr{Q})\}$ has a closed truth-tree.

TRUTH-FUNCTIONAL ENTAILMENT: A finite set Γ of sentences of *SL truth-functionally entails* a sentence $\mathscr{P}$ of *SL* if and only if the set $\Gamma \cup \{\sim \mathscr{P}\}$ has a closed truth-tree.

TRUTH-FUNCTIONAL VALIDITY: An argument of *SL* is *truth-functionally valid* if and only if the set consisting of the premises and the negation of the conclusion has a closed truth-tree.

Chapter

# 5

# SENTENTIAL LOGIC: DERIVATIONS

## 5.1 THE DERIVATION SYSTEM *SD*

In Chapters Three and Four we developed techniques for, among other things, determining the truth-functional validity or invalidity of arguments of *SL* and the truth-functional status of sentences of *SL*. These techniques, based on truth-tables and truth-trees, are reliable, but they can hardly be said to parallel the informal kind of reasoning we do in everyday discourse when we are interested in discovering whether an argument is valid or whether a set of beliefs is inconsistent. In this chapter we develop techniques that do parallel, at least to a considerable extent, the sort of informal reasoning we do in everyday discourse.

For example, when evaluating an argument we often try to show that its conclusion can be deduced or derived from its premises. Consider the argument

Whales breathe by lungs and whales are warm-blooded.
If whales breathe by lungs, then whales are not fish.
―――――――――――――――――――――――
Whales are warm-blooded and whales are not fish.

A way of showing that the conclusion can be derived from the premises is to proceed through a series of inferences that lead from the premises to the conclusion. From the first premise we can infer that whales breathe by lungs. From this result and the second premise we can infer that whales are not fish. Finally, since from the first premise we can infer that whales are warm-blooded and we have already inferred that whales are not fish, we conclude that whales are warm-blooded and are not fish. Here are the steps in the reasoning process:

| | | |
|---|---|---|
| 1. | Whales breathe by lungs and whales are warm-blooded. | Assumption |
| 2. | If whales breathe by lungs, then whales are not fish. | Assumption |
| 3. | Whales breathe by lungs. | from 1 |
| 4. | Whales are not fish. | from 2 and 3 |
| 5. | Whales are warm-blooded. | from 1 |
| 6. | Whales are warm-blooded and whales are not fish. | from 4 and 5 |

We have taken the premises as assumptions and proceeded through a series of inferences that lead to the conclusion of the argument. The structure of the reasoning is clearly seen when the sentences are symbolized in *SL*.

| | | |
|---|---|---|
| 1. | $L \& W$ | Assumption |
| 2. | $L \supset \sim F$ | Assumption |
| 3. | $L$ | from 1 |
| 4. | $\sim F$ | from 2 and 3 |
| 5. | $W$ | from 1 |
| 6. | $W \& \sim F$ | from 4 and 5 |

*Semantics* is concerned with the interpretation of a language, whereas *syntax* is concerned with the formal properties of a language. The reasoning in our example can be viewed as the application of a series of syntactic rules for deriving sentences. Rules are syntactic when they are applied on the basis of the forms, rather than the truth-values or truth-conditions, of sentences. Syntactic rules for deriving sentences are called *derivation rules*. For example, a derivation rule might tell us that from a sentence of the form $\mathscr{P} \& \mathscr{Q}$ we can derive $\mathscr{P}$. Another derivation rule might tell us that from $\mathscr{P}$ we can derive $\sim \mathscr{P}$. Of course, for our purposes the former would be an acceptable rule, whereas the latter would not. The first rule would be acceptable because whenever a sentence of the form $\mathscr{P} \& \mathscr{Q}$ is true, the left conjunct, $\mathscr{P}$, is true. That is, the rule is truth-preserving. On the other hand, the second rule is not truth-preserving. We shall employ only truth-preserving derivation rules, that is, derivation rules that never lead us from true sentences to false sentences.

It is important to realize that there is a connection between the derivation rules introduced in this chapter and the semantic results presented earlier, but it is equally important to realize that derivation rules can be applied without having any interpretation of the symbols in mind. In effect, a derivation rule tells us that, given a group of symbols with a certain structure, we can write down another group of symbols with a certain structure. This appeal to structure is what makes derivation rules syntactic.

Derivation rules are used to construct *derivations* that show, in a series of easily understood steps, how sentences are derived from other sentences. Systems that employ derivation rules like the ones we introduce in this chapter are called *natural deduction systems*. *SD* (for *s*entential *d*erivation) is the natural deduction system that is based on the sentential derivation rules introduced in this section.

*REITERATION*

The simplest derivation rule of *SD* is *Reiteration*.

*Reiteration* (R)

| $\mathscr{P}$
|
| $\mathscr{P}$

Reiteration allows us to derive a sentence of *SL* from itself. Here is a simple derivation that uses Reiteration.

| | | |
|---|---|---|
| 1 | (H ≡ K) & S | Assumption |
| 2 | G ∨ ~ H | Assumption |
| 3 | (H ≡ K) & S | 1 R |

In this derivation the sentences on the first two lines are taken as assumptions, and the sentence on the third line is derived. For reasons to be explained later the vertical line is called the *scope line* of the derivation. A horizontal line is drawn under the assumptions to mark them off from the derived sentences. That the sentence on line 3 is derived by Reiteration is indicated in the right-hand column of the derivation by '1R', that is, by giving the line number of the sentence to which the rule was applied and the abbreviation of the rule name.

If Reiteration were the only derivation rule available, derivations would be rather uninteresting. To make *SD* an interesting system, we need rules that allow us to introduce and to eliminate each of the five sentential connectives of *SL*. So we shall employ five pairs of derivation rules—one pair for each of the sentential connectives. One member of each pair will allow us to introduce a connective, and one will allow us to eliminate it. For this reason such derivation rules are sometimes called *intelim rules*.[1]

[1] The standard form for expressing the rules and constructing derivations is largely due to Frederic Brenton Fitch, *Symbolic Logic: An Introduction* (New York: Ronald, 1952). The derivation rules are adaptations of rules devised by Gerhard Gentzen, "Untersuchungen über das logische Schliessen," *Mathematische Zeitschrift*, 39 (1934–1935), 176–210, 405–431; and Stanislaw Jaŝkowski, "On the Rules of Suppositions in Formal Logic," *Studia Logica*, 1 (1934), 5–32.

The introduction rule for '&' is *Conjunction Introduction*.

*Conjunction Introduction* (&I)

$$\begin{array}{|l} \mathscr{P} \\ \mathscr{Q} \\ \mathscr{P} \,\&\, \mathscr{Q} \end{array}$$

This rule allows us to derive $\mathscr{P} \,\&\, \mathscr{Q}$ from sentences $\mathscr{P}$ and $\mathscr{Q}$ of *SL* which occur on earlier lines. Where several sentences are appealed to in applications of this and the other derivation rules of *SD*, then those sentences may occur in any order. Hence, if $\mathscr{P}$ occurs later than $\mathscr{Q}$, we can still derive $\mathscr{P} \,\&\, \mathscr{Q}$ by Conjunction Introduction.

The elimination rule for '&' is *Conjunction Elimination*.

*Conjunction Elimination* (&E)

$$\begin{array}{|l} \mathscr{P} \,\&\, \mathscr{Q} \\ \mathscr{P} \end{array} \quad \text{or} \quad \begin{array}{|l} \mathscr{P} \,\&\, \mathscr{Q} \\ \mathscr{Q} \end{array}$$

Conjunction Elimination allows us to derive $\mathscr{P}$ from $\mathscr{P} \,\&\, \mathscr{Q}$ and to derive $\mathscr{Q}$ from $\mathscr{P} \,\&\, \mathscr{Q}$.

To illustrate the use of these derivation rules, we consider the following argument:

> The Parthenon is being damaged by pollution and it will continue to be damaged as long as environmental standards are not imposed.
>
> The Parthenon is being damaged by tourists; each year millions of feet wear away the stone.
>
> Although the restoration efforts of the late nineteenth century were well-intentioned, the iron bars installed are cracking the stone and the Parthenon is being damaged by former restoration.
>
> ---
>
> The Parthenon is being damaged by pollution, tourists, and former restoration.

This argument can be symbolized in *SL* as

$$\begin{array}{|l} \text{P \& C} \\ \text{T \& M} \\ \text{E \& (I \& R)} \\ \hline \text{(P \& T) \& R} \end{array}$$

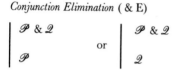

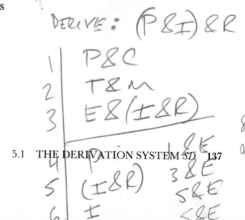

To show that the conclusion follows from the premises of the symbolized argument, we take the premises as assumptions and derive the conclusion from those assumptions. As a reminder of our goal, we list the sentence ultimately to be derived at the top of the derivation.

Derive: (P & T) & R

| | | |
|---|---|---|
| 1 | P & C | Assumption |
| 2 | T & M | Assumption |
| 3 | E & (I & R) | Assumption |
| 4 | P | 1 & E |
| 5 | T | 2 & E |
| 6 | P & T | 4, 5 & I |
| 7 | I & R | 3 & E |
| 8 | R | 7 & E |
| 9 | (P & T) & R | 6, 8 & I |

## 5.1.1E EXERCISES

Complete the following derivations:

a. Derive: Q & R

| | | |
|---|---|---|
| 1 | R & Q | Assumption |
| | R | 1 E |
| | Q | 1 (E |
| | Q & R | 2, 3 & E |

*b. Derive: (~ ~ S & ~ ~ S) & ~ ~ S

| | | |
|---|---|---|
| 1 | ~ ~ S | Assumption |

c. Derive: K

| | | |
|---|---|---|
| 1 | S & [~ T & (K & ~ F)] | Assumption |

*d. Derive: A & (B & C)

| | | |
|---|---|---|
| 1 | (C & B) & A | Assumption |

e. Derive: [(J ⊃ T) & ~ R] & (~ U ∨ G)

| | | |
|---|---|---|
| 1 | N & ~ R | Assumption |
| 2 | K & (J ⊃ T) | Assumption |
| 3 | (~ U ∨ G) & ~ J | Assumption |

The elimination rule for '⊃' is *Conditional Elimination* (sometimes called 'Modus Ponens').

*Conditional Elimination* (⊃ E)

| $\mathcal{P} \supset \mathcal{Q}$
| $\mathcal{P}$
| ▷ $\mathcal{Q}$

A sentence $\mathcal{Q}$ can be derived from sentences $\mathcal{P}$ and $\mathcal{P} \supset \mathcal{Q}$ which occur on earlier lines of a derivation. To illustrate a use of this derivation rule, we recall the earlier argument

Whales breathe by lungs and whales are warm-blooded.
If whales breathe by lungs, then whales are not fish.

---

Whales are warm-blooded and whales are not fish.

A derivation for a symbolized version of the argument is

Derive: W & ~ F

| | | |
|---|---|---|
| 1 | L & W | Assumption |
| 2 | L ⊃ ~ F | Assumption |
| 3 | L | 1 & E |
| 4 | ~ F | 2, 3 ⊃ E |
| 5 | W | 1 & E |
| 6 | W & ~ F | 4, 5 & I |

The introduction rule for '⊃' is *Conditional Introduction* (sometimes called 'Conditional Proof').

*Conditional Introduction* (⊃ I) CONDITIONAL PROOF

| | $\mathcal{P}$
| | ---
| | $\mathcal{Q}$
| ▷ $\mathcal{P} \supset \mathcal{Q}$

In deriving $\mathcal{P} \supset \mathcal{Q}$, a *subderivation* is constructed that has $\mathcal{P}$ as the assumption and

*2* as the sentence on the last line. Consider the argument

> If Wendy is on the Eiffel Tower, then she is in Paris.
>
> If she is in Paris, then she is in France.
>
> ———————————————————————
>
> If Wendy is on the Eiffel Tower, then she is in France.

To show that the conclusion follows from the premises, we might reason as follows. Assume that Wendy is on the Eiffel Tower. On the basis of this assumption and the first premise, we can infer that Wendy is in Paris. If this is so, then, on the basis of the second premise, we can infer that Wendy is in France. Of course, we have not shown that Wendy is in France on the basis of the premises alone but rather on the basis of the premises and the additional assumption that Wendy is on the Eiffel Tower. But this amounts to showing that from the premises it follows that if Wendy is on the Eiffel Tower then Wendy is in France.

A derivation for a symbolized version of the argument is given below:

Derive: E ⊃ F

| | | | |
|---|---|---|---|
| 1 | E ⊃ P | | Assumption |
| 2 | P ⊃ F | | Assumption |
| 3 | | E | Assumption  ⟵ IF you ASSUME E THAN P CAN BE DERIVED THROUGH ⊃E |
| 4 | | P | 1, 3 ⊃E |
| 5 | | F | 2, 4 ⊃E |
| 6 | E ⊃ F | | 3-5 ⊃I |

The subderivation occupies lines 3 through 5 of the derivation; this is indicated by the inner vertical line, called the scope line of the subderivation. We have shown on the basis of the primary assumptions (lines 1 and 2) that if we assume 'E' (line 3) then 'F' (line 5) can be derived. Hence we can derive 'E ⊃ F' in the main derivation. A subderivation is terminated by ending the scope line of the subderivation and moving to the next scope line on the left. When a subderivation is terminated, the assumption of the subderivation is said to be *discharged*, and none of the lines constituting that subderivation is accessible; that is, none of those lines can be appealed to later in the derivation. However, the subderivation as a whole can be appealed to; and this is done in the example, in the justification for the sentence on line 6, by using a hyphen to separate the first and last line numbers of the subderivation. In short, to derive a conditional sentence, construct a subderivation with the antecedent of the conditional as the assumption and with the consequent of the conditional as the sentence on the last line of the subderivation. Once the subderivation is terminated, the entire subderivation is cited in justifying the conditional entered below it.

WendE     (E ⊃ P)
           (P ⊃ F)

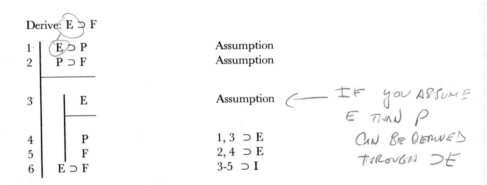

All the assumptions that occur at the top and immediately to the right of the main scope line of the derivation are called *primary assumptions*. Each subderivation begins with an assumption, called an *auxiliary assumption*, and ends with a sentence that occurs immediately to the right of the scope line of the subderivation. The scope line of the subderivation indicates the scope of the auxiliary assumption that begins the subderivation. The following illustrates how subderivations can occur within subderivations:

2 – CONDITIONALS MAKE 2 ASSUMPTIONS

Derive: G ⊃ (H ⊃ K)

| | | |
|---|---|---|
| 1 | (G & H) ⊃ K | Assumption |
| 2 | \| G | Assumption |
| 3 | \| \| H | Assumption |
| 4 | \| \| G & H | 2, 3 &I |
| 5 | \| \| K | 1, 4 ⊃E |
| 6 | \| H ⊃ K | 3-5 ⊃I |
| 7 | G ⊃ (H ⊃ K) | 2-6 ⊃I |

Each of these subderivations begins with an auxiliary assumption and ends prior to the end of the derivation. Only the primary assumption on line 1 is not discharged.

### 5.1.2E EXERCISES

Complete the following derivations:

a. Derive: U

| | | |
|---|---|---|
| 1 | H ⊃ U | Assumption |
| 2 | S & H | Assumption |

*b. Derive: E ∨ K

| | | |
|---|---|---|
| 1 | (Q & M) ⊃ (E ∨ K) | Assumption |
| 2 | M & (E ∨ C) | Assumption |
| 3 | Q & ~ N | Assumption |

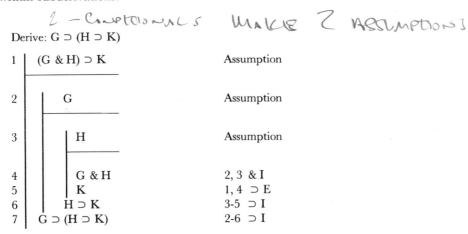

c. Derive: J ⊃ T

```
1 | J ⊃ (S & T)          Assumption
  |---------------
  |
```

*d. Derive: (Z & K) ⊃ (A & E)

```
1 | (K & Z) ⊃ (E & A)    Assumption
  |---------------
  |
```

e. Derive: (S & B) ⊃ ~ N

```
1 | S ⊃ (L & ~ N)        Assumption
  |---------------
  |
```

## *INTRODUCTION AND ELIMINATION RULES FOR '~'*

The introduction rule for '~' is *Negation Introduction*.

*Negation Introduction* (~ I)

| | $\mathcal{P}$
| |------
| |
| | $\mathcal{Q}$
| |
| | ~ $\mathcal{Q}$
|
| ~ $\mathcal{P}$

From a subderivation that has a sentence $\mathcal{P}$ as its assumption and sentences $\mathcal{Q}$ and ~ $\mathcal{Q}$ derived within it, ~ $\mathcal{P}$ can be derived. The sentences $\mathcal{Q}$ and ~ $\mathcal{Q}$ may be derived in either order, but one or the other must be the last sentence of the subderivation, and both must occur immediately to the right of the scope line of the subderivation. Consider the following argument:

> If the union votes for the contract and the management agrees to the terms of the contract, then the contract will be signed.
>
> The management agrees to the terms of the contract, but the contract will not be signed.
>
> ---
>
> The union does not vote for the contract.

Here is a derivation for a symbolized version of this argument:

Derive: ~ U

| | | |
|---|---|---|
| 1 | (U & M) ⊃ S | Assumption |
| 2 | M & ~ S | Assumption |
| 3 |     U | Assumption |
| 4 |     M | 2 &E |
| 5 |     U & M | 3, 4 &I |
| 6 |     S | 1, 5 ⊃E |
| 7 |     ~ S | 2 &E |
| 8 | ~ U | 3-7 ~I |

The elimination rule for '~' is *Negation Elimination.*

*Negation Elimination* (~ E)

```
|  | ~ 𝒫
|  |-----
|  |
|  | 𝒬
|  |
|  | ~ 𝒬
|
| 𝒫
```

We can derive $\mathscr{P}$ if we can construct a subderivation that has ~ $\mathscr{P}$ as its assumption and sentences $\mathscr{Q}$ and ~ $\mathscr{Q}$ derived within the subderivation. The sentences $\mathscr{Q}$ and ~ $\mathscr{Q}$ may be derived in either order, but one or the other must be the last sentence of the subderivation, and both must occur immediately to the right of the scope line of the subderivation. This rule is useful in constructing a derivation for the following argument:

> If the soldier will not volunteer, then his superior officer will order him to volunteer.
>
> If his superior officer orders him to volunteer, then he will volunteer.
>
> ---
>
> The soldier will volunteer.

Derive: S

| | | |
|---|---|---|
| 1 | ~ S ⊃ O | Assumption |
| 2 | O ⊃ S | Assumption |
| 3 |     ~ S | Assumption |
| 4 |     O | 1, 3 ⊃E |
| 5 |     S | 2, 4 ⊃E |
| 6 |     ~ S | 3 R |
| 7 | S | 3-6 ~E |

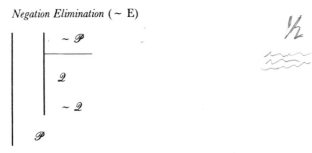

Note that when a subderivation is being constructed for use with Negation Introduction or Negation Elimination, the sentence and its negation that are derived in the subderivation may both be molecular, and one of these may be the same as the assumption. Again the sentence and its negation may be derived in any order. The following derivation illustrates these points:

Derive: $\sim\sim (J \equiv H)$

| | | |
|---|---|---|
| 1 | $\sim (J \equiv H) \supset \sim\sim (J \equiv H)$ | Assumption |
| 2 | $\quad\mid\ \sim (J \equiv H)$ | Assumption |
| 3 | $\quad\mid\ \sim\sim (J \equiv H)$ | 1, 2 $\supset$E |
| 4 | $\quad\mid\ \sim (J \equiv H)$ | 2 R |
| 5 | $\sim\sim (J \equiv H)$ | 2-4 $\sim$I |

Both Negation Introduction and Negation Elimination are akin to a strategy known as *reductio ad absurdum*. Intuitively, if we can derive both a sentence and its negation under an auxiliary assumption, the auxiliary assumption can be rejected on the grounds of leading to an absurdity. We require, for the sake of clarity, that when Negation Introduction or Negation Elimination is applied, both a sentence and its negation actually occur *under* and within the scope of the auxiliary assumption of the subderivation cited. Reiteration is often useful in obtaining the sentences needed for the application of these rules, as the following derivation illustrates:

Derive: K

| | | |
|---|---|---|
| 1 | $\sim\sim K$ | Assumption |
| 2 | $\quad\mid\ \sim K$ | Assumption |
| 3 | $\quad\mid\ \sim K$ | 2 R |
| 4 | $\quad\mid\ \sim\sim K$ | 1 R |
| 5 | $K$ | 2-4 $\sim$E |

In this case '$\sim$ K' and '$\sim\sim$ K' have been reiterated so that they occur *under* the auxiliary assumption on line 2. Negation Elimination can then be applied at line 5.

### 5.1.3E EXERCISES

Complete the following derivations:

a. Derive: $\sim G$

| | | |
|---|---|---|
| 1 | $(G \supset I)\ \&\ \sim I$ | Assumption |

*b. Derive: K

| | | |
|---|---|---|
| 1 | M & ~ M | Assumption |

c. Derive: ~ ~ R

| | | |
|---|---|---|
| 1 | ~ R ⊃ A | Assumption |
| 2 | ~ R ⊃ ~ A | Assumption |

*d. Derive: R & M

| | | |
|---|---|---|
| 1 | ~ (R & M) ⊃ (L & ~ N) | Assumption |
| 2 | N | Assumption |

e. Derive: P

| | | |
|---|---|---|
| 1 | (~ P ⊃ ~ L) & (~ L ⊃ L) | Assumption |

*INTRODUCTION AND ELIMINATION RULES FOR '∨'*

The introduction rule for '∨' is *Disjunction Introduction*.

*Disjunction Introduction* (∨I)

| | | |
|---|---|---|
| $\mathscr{P}$ | | $\mathscr{P}$ |
| | or | |
| $\mathscr{P} \vee \mathscr{Q}$ | | $\mathscr{Q} \vee \mathscr{P}$ |

This is an interesting rule, in that $\mathscr{Q}$ and all its components may be completely new to the derivation. We are not really getting something for nothing for if $\mathscr{P}$ is true, then $\mathscr{P} \vee \mathscr{Q}$ (as well as $\mathscr{Q} \vee \mathscr{P}$) is true. So Disjunction Introduction is truth-preserving. The following derivation illustrates applications of this rule.

> Business is booming, although the cost of energy is up.
>
> If either the cost of energy is up or food and clothing prices are increasing, then inflation will continue.
>
> ---
>
> Manufacturing costs will level off, or inflation will continue.

Derive: M ∨ I

| | | |
|---|---|---|
| 1 | B & E | Assumption |
| 2 | [E ∨ (F & C)] ⊃ I | Assumption |
| 3 | E | 1 &E |
| 4 | E ∨ (F & C) | 3 ∨I |
| 5 | I | 2, 4 ⊃E |
| 6 | M ∨ I | 5 ∨I |

The elimination rule for '∨' is *Disjunction Elimination*.

*Disjunction Elimination* (∨E)

$$
\begin{array}{l|l}
 & \mathcal{P} \vee \mathcal{Q} \\
 & \quad \begin{array}{|l} \mathcal{P} \\ \hline \mathcal{R} \end{array} \\
 & \quad \begin{array}{|l} \mathcal{Q} \\ \hline \mathcal{R} \end{array} \\
 & \mathcal{R}
\end{array}
$$

This rule tells us that we can derive a sentence $\mathcal{R}$ if we have a sentence of the form $\mathcal{P} \vee \mathcal{Q}$ and a subderivation that begins with the assumption $\mathcal{P}$ and ends with $\mathcal{R}$ and a subderivation that begins with the assumption $\mathcal{Q}$ and ends with $\mathcal{R}$.

Disjunction Elimination is used in our derivation for the following argument:

> The greatest painter is either Rembrandt or Van Gogh.
>
> If Rembrandt is the greatest, then Holland produced the best painter and the best painter lived during the seventeenth century.
>
> If Van Gogh is the greatest, then Holland produced the best painter and the best painter lived during the nineteenth century.
>
> ---
>
> Holland produced the best painter, and the best painter lived during the seventeenth or nineteenth century.

Derive: H & (S ∨ N)

| | | |
|---|---|---|
| 1 | R ∨ V | Assumption |
| 2 | R ⊃ (H & S) | Assumption |
| 3 | V ⊃ (H & N) | Assumption |
| 4 | \| R | Assumption |
| 5 | \| H & S | 2, 4 ⊃E |
| 6 | \| S | 5 &E |
| 7 | \| S ∨ N | 6 ∨I |
| 8 | \| H | 5 &E |
| 9 | \| H & (S ∨ N) | 8, 7 &I |
| 10 | \| V | Assumption |
| 11 | \| H & N | 3, 10 ⊃E |
| 12 | \| N | 11 &E |
| 13 | \| S ∨ N | 12 ∨I |
| 14 | \| H | 11 &E |
| 15 | \| H & (S ∨ N) | 14, 13 &I |
| 16 | H & (S ∨ N) | 1, 4-9, 10-15 ∨E |

This derivation shows that if 'R' is assumed (line 4), then 'H & (S ∨ N)' follows and if 'V' is assumed (line 10), then 'H & (S ∨ N)' follows. Therefore we can be sure that 'H & (S ∨ N)' follows from the primary assumptions, for 'R ∨ V' (line 1) assures us that either 'R' or 'V' is the case. Disjunction Elimination allows us to enter 'H & (S ∨ N)' by appealing to line 1 and the two subderivations.

## 5.1.4E EXERCISES

Complete the following derivations:

a. Derive: B ∨ (K ∨ G)

| | | |
|---|---|---|
| 1 | K | Assumption |

*b. Derive: Y

| | | |
|---|---|---|
| 1 | P ∨ C | Assumption |
| 2 | P ⊃ Y | Assumption |
| 3 | C ⊃ Y | Assumption |

c. Derive: D

| | | |
|---|---|---|
| 1 | D ∨ D | Assumption |
| | | |

*d. Derive: ~ H

| | | |
|---|---|---|
| 1 | (K ∨ P) ⊃ ~ H | Assumption |
| 2 | P | Assumption |
| | | |

e. Derive: X

| | | |
|---|---|---|
| 1 | ~ E ∨ X | Assumption |
| 2 | ~ E ⊃ X | Assumption |
| | | |

*INTRODUCTION AND ELIMINATION RULES FOR '≡'*

The introduction rule for '≡' is *Biconditional Introduction.*

*Biconditional Introduction* (≡ I)

$$\begin{array}{l|l} & \quad \mathcal{P} \\ & \quad \underline{\phantom{xx}} \\ & \quad \mathcal{Q} \\ & \\ & \quad \mathcal{Q} \\ & \quad \underline{\phantom{xx}} \\ & \quad \mathcal{P} \\ & \mathcal{P} \equiv \mathcal{Q} \end{array}$$

To derive a biconditional $\mathcal{P} \equiv \mathcal{Q}$, construct two subderivations—one that has $\mathcal{P}$ as its assumption and ends with $\mathcal{Q}$ and one that has $\mathcal{Q}$ as its assumption and ends with $\mathcal{P}$. Intuitively, it may help to think of $\mathcal{P} \equiv \mathcal{Q}$ as tantamount to $(\mathcal{P} \supset \mathcal{Q})$ & $(\mathcal{Q} \supset \mathcal{P})$. Each of these subderivations would allow us to derive one of these conjuncts. The derivation for the following argument uses Biconditional Introduction.

This solution is acidic only if it is neither basic nor neutral.
If this solution is not basic, then if it is not neutral it is acidic.

---

This solution is acidic if and only if it is neither basic nor neutral.

Derive: $A \equiv (\sim B \; \& \sim N)$

| | | |
|---|---|---|
| 1 | $A \supset (\sim B \; \& \sim N)$ | Assumption |
| 2 | $\sim B \supset (\sim N \supset A)$ | Assumption |
| 3 | $\quad A$ | Assumption |
| 4 | $\quad \sim B \; \& \sim N$ | 1, 3 $\supset$E |
| 5 | $\quad \sim B \; \& \sim N$ | Assumption |
| 6 | $\quad \sim B$ | 5 &E |
| 7 | $\quad \sim N \supset A$ | 2, 6 $\supset$E |
| 8 | $\quad \sim N$ | 5 &E |
| 9 | $\quad A$ | 7, 8 $\supset$E |
| 10 | $A \equiv (\sim B \; \& \sim N)$ | 3-4, 5-9 $\equiv$I |

The elimination rule for '$\equiv$' is *Biconditional Elimination*.

*Biconditional Elimination* ($\equiv$E)

| | | |
|---|---|---|
| $\mathscr{P} \equiv \mathscr{Q}$ | | $\mathscr{P} \equiv \mathscr{Q}$ |
| $\mathscr{P}$ | or | $\mathscr{Q}$ |
| $\mathscr{Q}$ | | $\mathscr{P}$ |

If a sentence $\mathscr{P} \equiv \mathscr{Q}$ occurs on a line and $\mathscr{P}$ occurs on another line, then we can derive $\mathscr{Q}$. Similarly, if a sentence $\mathscr{P} \equiv \mathscr{Q}$ occurs on a line and $\mathscr{Q}$ occurs on another line, then we can derive $\mathscr{P}$. Here are some applications of this rule.

> Michelle will study for the final exam; moreover, if she studies for the final exam, she will pass it.
>
> Michelle will pass the logic course if and only if she passes the final exam.
>
> Michelle will pass the logic course if and only if she graduates.
>
> ---
>
> Michelle will graduate.

Derive: G

| | | |
|---|---|---|
| 1 | $S \; \& \; (S \supset E)$ | Assumption |
| 2 | $C \equiv E$ | Assumption |
| 3 | $C \equiv G$ | Assumption |
| 4 | $S$ | 1 &E |
| 5 | $S \supset E$ | 1 &E |
| 6 | $E$ | 4, 5 $\supset$E |
| 7 | $C$ | 2, 6 $\equiv$E |
| 8 | $G$ | 3, 7 $\equiv$E |

## 5.1.5E EXERCISES

**1.** Complete the following derivations:

a. Derive: Q

| | | |
|---|---|---|
| 1 | K ≡ (~ E & Q) | Assumption |
| 2 | K | Assumption |

*b. Derive: ~ R ≡ E

| | | |
|---|---|---|
| 1 | (~ R ⊃ E) & (E ⊃ ~ R) | Assumption |

c. Derive: S & ~ A

| | | |
|---|---|---|
| 1 | (S ≡ ~ I) & N | Assumption |
| 2 | (N ≡ ~ I) & ~ A | Assumption |

*d. Derive: N

| | | |
|---|---|---|
| 1 | A ∨ L | Assumption |
| 2 | A ≡ N | Assumption |
| 3 | L ⊃ N | Assumption |

e. Derive: (E ≡ O) & (O ≡ E)

| | | |
|---|---|---|
| 1 | (E ⊃ T) & (T ⊃ O) | Assumption |
| 2 | O ⊃ E | Assumption |

**2.** Complete each of the following derivations by entering the appropriate justifications.

a. Derive: (A & C) ∨ (B & C)

| | | |
|---|---|---|
| 1 | (A ∨ B) & C | |
| 2 | A ∨ B | 1 &E |
| 3 | C | 1 &E |
| 4 | A | ASSUMP |
| 5 | A & C | 3,4 &I |
| 6 | (A & C) ∨ (B & C) | 5 ∨I |
| 7 | B | ASSUMP |
| 8 | B & C | 3-7 &I |
| 9 | (A & C) ∨ (B & C) | 8 ∨I |
| 10 | (A & C) ∨ (B & C) | 4-6, 7-9 ∨I |

*b. Derive: A ⊃ (B ⊃ C)

| Line | Derivation | Justification |
|---|---|---|
| 1 | (A & B) ⊃ C | Ass |
| 2 | \| A | Ass |
| 3 | \| \| B | Ass |
| 4 | \| \| A & B | 2,3 &I |
| 5 | \| \| C | 1,4 ⊃E |
| 6 | \| B ⊃ C | 3,5 ⊃I |
| 7 | A ⊃ (B ⊃ C) | 2,6 ⊃I |

c. Derive: ~ B

| Line | Derivation | Justification |
|---|---|---|
| 1 | B ⊃ (A & ~ B) | Ass |
| 2 | \| B | Ass |
| 3 | \| A & ~ B | 1,2 ⊃E |
| 4 | \| ~ B | 3 &E |
| 5 | \| B | 2 R |
| 6 | ~ B | 2–5 ~I |

*d. Derive: A ⊃ B

| Line | Derivation | Justification |
|---|---|---|
| 1 | (A & ~ B) ⊃ (~ B & C) | |
| 2 | C ⊃ ~ A | |
| 3 | \| A | Ass. |
| 4 | \| \| ~ B | Ass. |
| 5 | \| \| A & ~ B | 1 ⊃E |
| 6 | \| \| ~ B & C | 1 ⊃E |
| 7 | \| \| C | 6 &E |
| 8 | \| \| ~ A | 2 ⊃E |
| 9 | \| \| A | 5 &E |
| 10 | \| B | 4–8 ~E |
| 11 | A ⊃ B | 3–10 ⊃I |

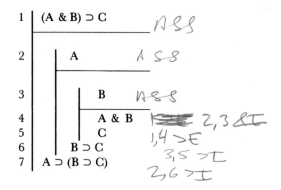

e. Derive: C ⊃ (~ A & B)

| | | |
|---|---|---|
| 1 | ~ D | |
| 2 | C ⊃ (A ≡ B) | |
| 3 | (D ∨ B) ⊃ ~ A | |
| 4 | (A ≡ B) ⊃ (D & E) | |
| 5 | ~ B ⊃ D | |
| 6 |   │ C | ASSUMP |
| 7 |   │ A ≡ B | 6,2 ⊃E |
| 8 |   │ D & E | 7,4 ⊃E |
| 9 |   │ D | 8 &E |
| 10 |   │ D ∨ B | 9 ∨I |
| 11 |   │ ~ A | 3,10 ⊃E |
| 12 |   │   │ ~ B | ASS |
| 13 |   │   │ D | 5,12 ⊃E |
| 14 |   │   │ ~ D | 1 R |
| 15 |   │ B | 12-14 ~E |
| 16 |   │ ~ A & B | 11,15 &I |
| 17 | C ⊃ (~ A & B) | 6-16 ⊃I |

*f. Derive: (A & ~ B) ∨ A

| | |
|---|---|
| 1 | C ⊃ B |
| 2 | (~ C ⊃ A) ∨ E |
| 3 | F & ~ E |
| 4 | B ⊃ (A & ~ B) |
| 5 |   │ ~ C ⊃ A |
| 6 |   │   │ C |
| 7 |   │   │ B |
| 8 |   │   │ A & ~ B |
| 9 |   │   │ ~ B |
| 10 |   │ ~ C |
| 11 |   │ A |
| 12 |   │ E |
| 13 |   │   │ ~ A |
| 14 |   │   │ E |
| 15 |   │   │ ~ E |
| 16 |   │ A |
| 17 | A |
| 18 | (A & ~ B) ∨ A |

g. Derive: A ≡ B

```
 1 | ~ A & ~ B                ASSUMP
   |----------
 2 |   | A                    ASSUMP
   |   |------
 3 |   |   | ~ B              ASSUMP
   |   |   |----
 4 |   |   | ~ A              1 &E
 5 |   |   | A                1 R
 6 |   | B                    3–5 ~E
   |
 7 |   | B                    ASSUMP
   |   |------
 8 |   |   | ~ A              ASSUMP
   |   |   |----
 9 |   |   | B                7 REP
10 |   |   | ~ B              1 &E
11 |   | A                    8–10 ~E
12 | A ≡ B                    2–6, 7–11 ≡I
```

*h. Derive: A ≡ (B ∨ C)

```
 1 | (A ≡ B) & (A ≡ C)
   |------------------
 2 |   | A
   |   |------
 3 |   | A ≡ B
 4 |   | B
 5 |   | B ∨ C
   |
 6 |   | B ∨ C
   |   |------
 7 |   |   | B
   |   |   |----
 8 |   |   | A ≡ B
 9 |   |   | A
   |   |
10 |   |   | C
   |   |   |----
11 |   |   | A ≡ C
12 |   |   | A
13 |   | A
14 | A ≡ (B ∨ C)
```

## 5.2 APPLYING THE DERIVATION RULES OF *SD*

There are several principles that should be kept in mind when using the derivation rules. First, they are rules of inference that appeal to entire sentences on earlier lines or to entire subderivations.

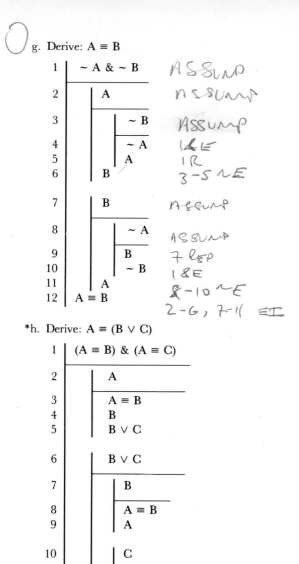

For example, in developing a derivation for the argument

(~ J & W) & Y
(N ∨ ~ B) & [~ J ⊃ (K ∨ G)]
———————————————
K ∨ G

it would be *incorrect* to use Conjunction Elimination as follows:

Derive: K ∨ G

| | | | |
|---|---|---|---|
| 1 | (~ J & W) & Y | Assumption | |
| 2 | (N ∨ ~ B) & [~ J ⊃ (K ∨ G)] | Assumption | |
| 3 | ~ J | 1 & E | **MISTAKE!** |

The mistake here is trying to derive '~ J' from '~ J & W' when the latter sentence occurs only as a component of another sentence. The sentence on line 1 is a conjunction; that is, it is a sentence of the form $\mathcal{P}$ & $\mathcal{Q}$, where $\mathcal{P}$ is '~ J & W' and $\mathcal{Q}$ is 'Y'. Conjunction Elimination only allows us to derive either of the conjuncts of a conjunction. So, though we cannot derive '~ J' from the sentence on line 1 by Conjunction Elimination, we can derive '~ J & W'. As '~ J & W' is itself a conjunction, Conjunction Elimination can be applied to it to derive '~ J'.

Derive: K ∨ G

| | | |
|---|---|---|
| 1 | (~ J & W) & Y | Assumption |
| 2 | (N ∨ ~ B) & [~ J ⊃ (K ∨ G)] | Assumption |
| 3 | ~ J & W | 1 & E |
| 4 | ~ J | 3 & E |

It is *incorrect* to continue this derivation as follows:

| | | | |
|---|---|---|---|
| 5 | K ∨ G | 2, 4 ⊃ E | **MISTAKE!** |

Again the mistake is in trying to apply a rule of inference to a component of a sentence, rather than to the entire sentence. Conditional Elimination licenses deriving $\mathcal{Q}$ from $\mathcal{P}$ and $\mathcal{P} \supset \mathcal{Q}$. Neither the sentence on line 2 nor the sentence on line 4 has '⊃' as the main connective. Hence Conditional Elimination cannot be applied to these sentences. However, the material conditional to which we want to apply the rule is a component of the sentence on line 2, and we can use Conditional Elimination if we first derive the conditional '~ J ⊃ (K ∨ G)' by Conjunction

Elimination. Therefore the completed derivation is

Derive: K ∨ G

| | | |
|---|---|---|
| 1 | (~ J & W) & Y | Assumption |
| 2 | (N ∨ ~ B) & [~ J ⊃ (K ∨ G)] | Assumption |
| 3 | ~ J & W | 1 &E |
| 4 | ~ J | 3 &E |
| 5 | ~ J ⊃ (K ∨ G) | 2 &E |
| 6 | K ∨ G | 4, 5 ⊃E |

Similarly, it is *incorrect* to cite part of a subderivation.

Derive: ~ N

| | | | |
|---|---|---|---|
| 1 | H ⊃ ~ N | Assumption | |
| 2 | (H ∨ G) & ~ M | Assumption | |
| 3 | ~ N ≡ (G ∨ B) | Assumption | |
| 4 | H ∨ G | 2 &E | |
| 5 |     H | Assumption | |
| 6 |     ~ N | 1, 5 ⊃E | |
| 7 |     ~ N ∨ H | 6 ∨I | |
| 8 |     G | Assumption | |
| 9 |     G ∨ B | 8 ∨I | |
| 10 |     ~ N | 3, 9 ≡E | |
| 11 | ~ N | 4, 5-6, 8-10 ∨E | **MISTAKE!** |

The entire subderivation must be cited; therefore the reference '5-6' on line 11 is a mistake. Line 7 can be eliminated. A proper derivation is

Derive: ~ N

| | | |
|---|---|---|
| 1 | H ⊃ ~ N | Assumption |
| 2 | (H ∨ G) & ~ M | Assumption |
| 3 | ~ N ≡ (G ∨ B) | Assumption |
| 4 | H ∨ G | 2 &E |
| 5 |     H | Assumption |
| 6 |     ~ N | 1, 5 ⊃E |
| 7 |     G | Assumption |
| 8 |     G ∨ B | 7 ∨I |
| 9 |     ~ N | 3, 8 ≡E |
| 10 | ~ N | 4, 5-6, 7-9 ∨E |

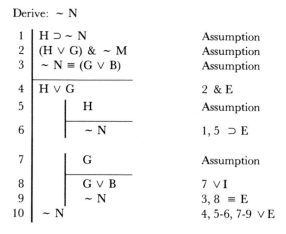

If more than one line or subderivation is appealed to when applying a derivation rule, the relevant sentences or subderivations can occur in any order. For instance, on line 10 of the last derivation appeal is made to an earlier line and to two subderivations. It would also be correct if the sentence on the line cited occurred between the subderivations or after them or if the subderivations were reversed in order. Here is an example that illustrates this flexibility in order:

Derive: ~ N

| | | | |
|---|---|---|---|
| 1 | H ⊃ ~ N | | Assumption |
| 2 | (H ∨ G) & ~ M | | Assumption |
| 3 | ~ N ≡ (G ∨ B) | | Assumption |
| 4 | | G | Assumption |
| 5 | | G ∨ B | 4 ∨I |
| 6 | | ~ N | 3, 5 ≡E |
| 7 | | H | Assumption |
| 8 | | ~ N | 1, 7 ⊃E |
| 9 | H ∨ G | | 2 &E |
| 10 | ~ N | | 9, 7-8, 4-6 ∨E |

It is essential that the lines and subderivations cited in justifying a sentence be accessible. In a derivation a sentence or subderivation is *accessible* at line ***n***, that is, it can be appealed to when justifying a sentence on line ***n***, if and only if that sentence or subderivation does not lie within the scope of an assumption that has been discharged prior to line ***n***. In other words, every scope line to the left of a cited sentence or subderivation must be to the left of the sentence on line ***n***. Some examples will make this clear. Consider the derivation

Derive: ~ U ⊃ ~ S

| | | | |
|---|---|---|---|
| 1 | ~ U ⊃ ~ W | | Assumption |
| 2 | ~ W ⊃ ~ S | | Assumption |
| 3 | | ~ U | Assumption |
| 4 | | ~ W | 1, 3 ⊃E |
| 5 | | ~ S | 2, 4 ⊃E |
| 6 | ~ U ⊃ ~ S | | 3-5 ⊃I |

Line 4 cites lines 1 and 3, which are both accessible at line 4. The sentences on lines 1 and 3 do not lie within the scope of an assumption that has been discharged prior to line 4. (Neither the sentence on line 1 nor the sentence on line 3 has a scope line to its left that is not also to the left of the sentence on line 4.) Similarly, line 5 cites lines 2 and 4, which are both accessible at line 5. Line 6 cites the subderivation from lines 3 through 5. This subderivation is accessible at line 6 because the subderivation does not lie within the scope of an assumption that has been discharged prior to line 6. (We consider the scope line of a subderivation to be part of that subderivation. Hence the scope line of a subderivation does not count as being to the left of that subderivation. In the present case every scope line to the left of the subderivation cited—there is only one—is also to the left of the sentence on line 6.)

Once an assumption has been discharged, none of the lines or subderivations *within* that subderivation is accessible for justifying sentences on later lines. In the example, once the assumption on line 3 is discharged, none of the lines within the scope of the assumption is accessible. The reason for this is that the sentences of the subderivation have been derived under the assumption of the subderivation and this assumption has been discharged. There is no guarantee that sentences that are derived on the basis of an assumption can be derived without it. For instance, it is *incorrect* to continue the derivation as follows:

```
1  | ~ U ⊃ ~ W         Assumption
2  | ~ W ⊃ ~ S         Assumption
   |-----------
3  | | ~ U             Assumption
   | |-----
4  | | ~ W             1, 3 ⊃ E
5  | | ~ S             2, 4 ⊃ E
6  | ~ U ⊃ ~ S         3-5 ⊃ I
7  | ~ S               2, 4 ⊃ E        MISTAKE!
```

The mistake at line 7 is citing line 4, which is not accessible at line 7. The sentence on line 4 does lie within the scope of an assumption (line 3) that has been discharged by line 7. (There is a scope line to the left of the sentence on line 4 that does not appear to the left of the sentence on line 7.)

Here is another example that illustrates mistakes in citing lines and subderivations that are not accessible.

```
1  | (B ⊃ A) & C           Assumption
2  | (A ⊃ C) ⊃ B           Assumption
   |-----------
3  | | A                   Assumption
   | |-----
4  | | | A                 Assumption
   | | |-----
5  | | | C                 1 &E
6  | | A ⊃ C               4-5 ⊃ I
7  | | B                   2, 6 ⊃ E

8  | | C                   Assumption
   | |-----
9  | | | B                 Assumption
   | | |-----
10 | | | B ⊃ A             1 &E
11 | | | A                 9, 10 ⊃ E
12 | | A ≡ B               3-7, 9-11 ≡ I
13 | | B                   7 R                  MISTAKE!
14 | | A                   12, 13 ≡ E
15 | A ≡ C                 4-5, 8-14 ≡ I        MISTAKE!
```

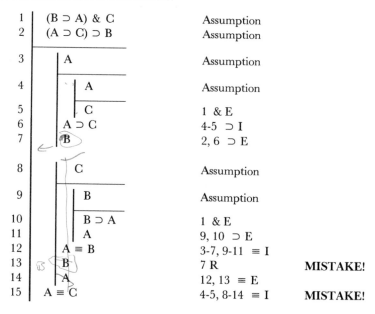

Line 13 contains a mistake because line 7, which is cited in justifying the entry of 'B' at line 13, is not accessible at line 13. The sentence on line 7 lies within the scope of an assumption (line 3) that has been discharged prior to line 13. The mistake on line 15 is citing the subderivation from lines 4 through 5. That subderivation lies within the scope of an assumption (line 3) that has been discharged prior to line 15. (There is a scope line to the left of that subderivation that ends before line 15—it ends at line 7.)

Citing a subderivation that occurs much earlier in the derivation is allowable as long as the subderivation is accessible. For instance, in the example the justification on line 12 is correct. Neither the subderivation from lines 3 through 7 nor the subderivation from lines 9 through 11 lies within the scope of an assumption that has been discharged prior to line 12. Scope lines show graphically which sentences are derived under which assumptions. Consequently, scope lines give us a handy way of checking which lines and subderivations can be properly cited in justifications for derived sentences.

---

## 5.3 BASIC CONCEPTS OF *SD*

A *derivation in SD* is a series of sentences of *SL* in which each sentence either is taken as an assumption with an indication of its scope or is justified by one of the rules of *SD*. As the previous examples illustrate, our standard derivation format is to number each line on which a sentence occurs and to state the justification for that sentence on the right-hand side of the derivation. All primary assumptions are put at the beginning of a derivation and one auxiliary assumption is put at the beginning of each subderivation. Horizontal lines are drawn below assumptions in a derivation as a way to mark off the assumptions more clearly. The main vertical derivation line serves as a scope line for all primary assumptions in a derivation, and the vertical subderivation lines serve as scope lines for auxiliary assumptions in a derivation. Scope lines show immediately which sentences and subderivations are in the scope of which assumptions. A sentence or subderivation is *in the scope of an assumption* if the scope line immediately to the left of the assumption is also to the left of the sentence or subderivation.

The concept of derivability is defined as follows:

> A sentence $\mathscr{P}$ of *SL* is *derivable in SD* from a set $\Gamma$ of sentences of *SL* if and only if there is a derivation in *SD* in which all the primary assumptions are members of $\Gamma$ and $\mathscr{P}$ occurs in the scope of only those assumptions.

The claim that $\mathscr{P}$ is derivable from $\Gamma$ is often written using the *single turnstile*, '$\vdash$':

$$\Gamma \vdash \mathscr{P}$$

We write that $\mathscr{P}$ is not derivable from $\Gamma$ as

$$\Gamma \nvdash \mathscr{P}$$

Suppose we wish to show that 'D ∨ B' is derivable from {~ F ∨ D, F, J}, that is,

{~ F ∨ D, F, J} ⊢ D ∨ B

We begin by taking members of the set as the primary assumptions and then construct a derivation such that 'D ∨ B' occurs in the scope of only those assumptions. Here is such a derivation:

```
Derive: D ∨ B
 1 | ~ F ∨ D                  Assumption
 2 | F                        Assumption
 3 | J                        Assumption
   |-------
 4 |  | ~ F                   Assumption
   |  |-------
 5 |  |  | ~ D                Assumption
   |  |  |-------
 6 |  |  | ~ F                4 R
 7 |  |  | F                  2 R
 8 |  | D                     5-7 ~ E
   |
 9 |  | D                     Assumption
   |  |-------
10 |  | D                     9 R
11 | D                        1, 4-8, 9-10 ∨E
12 | D ∨ B                    11 ∨I
```

Thus the sentence 'D ∨ B' is derivable from {~ F ∨ D, F, J}. Of course, there are many other derivations which demonstrate this claim equally well. Producing any one such derivation is sufficient to establish derivability.

Notice that, by the definition of derivability, every primary assumption must be a member of the set Γ, but not every member of the set Γ must be taken as a primary assumption. In the example, the sentence 'J' was listed as a primary assumption, but need not have been, for 'D ∨ B' can be derived from just the first two assumptions. Also, by the definition of derivability, the sentence to be derived must occur in the scope of only the primary assumptions. The following derivation would *not* demonstrate the previous derivability claim:

```
Derive: D ∨ B

 1 | ~ F ∨ D                  Assumption
 2 | F                        Assumption
 3 | J                        Assumption
   |-------
 4 |  | ~ F                   Assumption
   |  |-------
 5 |  |  | ~ D                Assumption
   |  |  |-------
 6 |  |  | ~ F                4 R
 7 |  |  | F                  2 R
 8 |  | D                     5-7 ~ E
 9 |  | D ∨ B                 8 ∨I
```

Here 'D ∨ B' lies in the scope of '~ F' (line 4) as well as in the scope of the primary assumptions, and therefore this derivation would not establish the derivability claim.

The definition for validity in *SD* is as follows:

> An argument of *SL* is *valid in SD* if and only if the conclusion of the argument is derivable in *SD* from the set consisting of the premises. An argument of *SL* is *invalid in SD* if and only if it is not valid in *SD*.

The argument

```
(~ L ∨ K) ⊃ A
A ⊃ ~ A
-------------
L & ~ K
```

is shown to be valid in *SD* by the following derivation:

Derive: L & ~ K

```
 1 | (~ L ∨ K) ⊃ A        Assumption
 2 | A ⊃ ~ A              Assumption
   |----------------
 3 |  | ~ L               Assumption
   |  |-------------
 4 |  | ~ L ∨ K           3 ∨I
 5 |  | A                 1, 4 ⊃E
 6 |  | ~ A               2, 5 ⊃E
 7 | L                    3-6 ~E
 8 |  | K                 Assumption
   |  |-------------
 9 |  | ~ L ∨ K           8 ∨I
10 |  | A                 1, 9 ⊃E
11 |  | ~ A               2, 10 ⊃E
12 | ~ K                  8-11 ~I
13 | L & ~ K              7, 12 &I
```

A special case of deriving a sentence $\mathscr{P}$ from a set Γ of sentences arises when Γ is the empty set. The following derivation demonstrates that 'B ⊃ [C ⊃ (B & C)]' is derivable from the empty set.

Derive: B ⊃ [C ⊃ (B & C)]

```
1 |  | B                     Assumption
  |  |--------------
2 |  |  | C                  Assumption
  |  |  |-----------
3 |  |  | B & C              1, 2 &I
4 |  | C ⊃ (B & C)           2-3 ⊃I
5 | B ⊃ [C ⊃ (B & C)]        1-4 ⊃I
```

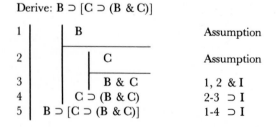

There are no primary assumptions in this derivation, and every auxiliary assumption has been discharged. The sentence 'B ⊃ [C ⊃ (B & C)]' on the last line lies in the scope of only the primary assumptions (in this case none). Hence 'B ⊃ [C ⊃ (B & C)]' is derivable from the empty set.

| A sentence $\mathscr{P}$ of *SL* is a *theorem in SD* if and only if $\mathscr{P}$ is derivable in *SD* from the empty set. |
|---|

Thus the last derivation establishes that 'B ⊃ [C ⊃ (B & C)]' is a theorem in *SD*. Because a derivation of a theorem has no primary assumptions, a main derivation line can be omitted. However, our practice will be to draw a main derivation line in such derivations to show graphically that any assumptions that are made are auxiliary assumptions. The claim that a sentence $\mathscr{P}$ of *SL* is a theorem can be expressed as

$$\vdash \mathscr{P}$$

Equivalence in *SD* is defined as follows:

| Sentences $\mathscr{P}$ and $\mathscr{Q}$ of *SL* are *equivalent in SD* if and only if $\mathscr{Q}$ is derivable in *SD* from $\{\mathscr{P}\}$ and $\mathscr{P}$ is derivable in *SD* from $\{\mathscr{Q}\}$. |
|---|

The sentences '(G & S) ∨ N' and '(G ∨ N) & (S ∨ N)' are equivalent in *SD*. We can show this with two derivations. First, '(G & S) ∨ N' is taken as an assumption, and '(G ∨ N) & (S ∨ N)' is derived.

Derive: (G ∨ N) & (S ∨ N)

```
 1 | (G & S) ∨ N                 Assumption
   |---------------
 2 |    | G & S                  Assumption
   |    |----------
 3 |    | G                      2 &E
 4 |    | G ∨ N                  3 ∨I
 5 |    | S                      2 &E
 6 |    | S ∨ N                  5 ∨I
 7 |    | (G ∨ N) & (S ∨ N)      4, 6 &I
   |
 8 |    | N                      Assumption
   |    |----------
 9 |    | G ∨ N                  8 ∨I
10 |    | S ∨ N                  8 ∨I
11 |    | (G ∨ N) & (S ∨ N)      9, 10 &I
12 | (G ∨ N) & (S ∨ N)           1, 2-7, 8-11 ∨E
```

Then the procedure is reversed. '(G ∨ N) & (S ∨ N)' is taken as an assumption, and '(G & S) ∨ N' is derived.

Derive: (G & S) ∨ N

| | | |
|---|---|---|
| 1 | (G ∨ N) & (S ∨ N) | Assumption |
| 2 | G ∨ N | 1 &E |
| 3 | S ∨ N | 1 &E |
| 4 |     N | Assumption |
| 5 |     (G & S) ∨ N | 4 ∨I |
| 6 |     G | Assumption |
| 7 |         S | Assumption |
| 8 |         G & S | 6, 7 &I |
| 9 |         (G & S) ∨ N | 8 ∨I |
| 10 |     (G & S) ∨ N | 3, 7-9, 4-5 ∨E |
| 11 | (G & S) ∨ N | 2, 6-10, 4-5 ∨E |

Inconsistency in *SD* is defined as follows:

> A set Γ of sentences of *SL* is *inconsistent in SD* if and only if both a sentence $\mathscr{P}$ of *SL* and its negation ~ $\mathscr{P}$ are derivable in *SD* from Γ. A set Γ of sentences of *SL* is *consistent in SD* if and only if it is not inconsistent in *SD*.

So we can show that the set of sentences

{(M ∨ B) ⊃ B, A ⊃ M, A & ~ B}

is inconsistent in *SD* by constructing a derivation in which the members of the set are the primary assumptions and both a sentence and its negation are derived in the scope of only the primary assumptions. Here is such a derivation:

| | | |
|---|---|---|
| 1 | (M ∨ B) ⊃ B | Assumption |
| 2 | A ⊃ M | Assumption |
| 3 | A & ~ B | Assumption |
| 4 | ~ B | 3 &E |
| 5 | A | 3 &E |
| 6 | M | 2, 5 ⊃E |
| 7 | M ∨ B | 6 ∨I |
| 8 | B | 1, 7 ⊃E |

In this derivation the sentence 'B' is derived in line 8 and its negation '~ B' is derived in line 4. Both of these sentences are in the scope of only the primary assumptions, that is, both of these sentences occur immediately to the right of the main scope line. Hence the original set is inconsistent in *SD*.

If a set of sentences of *SL* is inconsistent in *SD*, any sentence of *SL* is derivable from the set. This is easy to see. Suppose that a set of sentences is inconsistent in *SD*. Then there must be a derivation in which all of the primary assumptions are members of the set and a sentence $\mathscr{P}$ and its negation $\sim \mathscr{P}$ are derivable from them. Suppose that $\mathscr{P}$ occurs on line $i$ of this derivation and $\sim \mathscr{P}$ occurs on line $j$. Continue the derivation from a later line $n$. Now, let $\mathscr{Q}$ be any sentence of *SL*. We can proceed to derive $\mathscr{Q}$ from the set as follows:

| | | |
|---|---|---|
| $i$ | $\mathscr{P}$ | |
| $j$ | $\sim \mathscr{P}$ | |
| $n$ | \| $\sim \mathscr{Q}$ | Assumption |
| $n + 1$ | \| $\mathscr{P}$ | $i$ R |
| $n + 2$ | \| $\sim \mathscr{P}$ | $j$ R |
| $n + 3$ | $\mathscr{Q}$ | $n$ - $n + 2$ $\sim$ E |

In other words, if both $\mathscr{P}$ and $\sim \mathscr{P}$ can be derived from a set of sentences, then any sentence of *SL* can be derived in merely four more steps! This is one reason why a rational person would want to avoid beliefs which form a set which is inconsistent in *SD*. Actions cannot be guided well by a set of beliefs from which every possible belief follows.

The syntactic concepts of the system *SD* parallel the semantic concepts introduced in Chapter Three, as we prove in Chapter Six and Exercise 14 of Section 5.4E. That is,

> A sentence $\mathscr{P}$ is derivable in *SD* from a set Γ of sentences of *SL* if and only if $\mathscr{P}$ is truth-functionally entailed by Γ.
>
> An argument of *SL* is valid in *SD* if and only if the argument is truth-functionally valid.
>
> A sentence $\mathscr{P}$ of *SL* is a theorem in *SD* if and only if $\mathscr{P}$ is truth-functionally true.
>
> Sentences $\mathscr{P}$ and $\mathscr{Q}$ of *SL* are equivalent in *SD* if and only if $\mathscr{P}$ and $\mathscr{Q}$ are truth-functionally equivalent.
>
> A set Γ of sentences of *SL* is inconsistent in *SD* if and only if Γ is truth-functionally inconsistent.

Although the syntactic system *SD* has been developed with an eye to semantics, it is important to remember that *SD* as a syntactic system is independent of semantics. For example, constructing a truth-table that shows that 'A ∨ ~ A' is a truth-functional truth does not by itself show that 'A ∨ ~ A' is a theorem in *SD*.

## 5.4 STRATEGIES FOR CONSTRUCTING DERIVATIONS IN *SD*

An advantage of a natural deduction system such as *SD* is that we can show in a series of very natural steps that one sentence follows from other sentences. In this section we develop a technique for constructing derivations.[2] Of course, if we cannot construct an appropriate derivation, it does not mean that no such derivation exists. It may be that an appropriate derivation can be constructed but that we have not been ingenious enough to find it.

The first step in constructing derivations is easy. Write the sentence to be derived, the *goal sentence*, well below any primary assumptions. How should we proceed? A very tempting, though unreliable, procedure is to apply the derivation rules rather randomly to the assumptions and other derived sentences in the hope that the goal sentence eventually will emerge. This approach may work, but it often leads to mindless application of the derivation rules and eventual frustration if the goal sentence is not derived. We recommend a better approach to constructing derivations called *goal analysis*.

Goal analysis is a technique for generating a connected series of subgoals that guide the construction of derivations. Roughly put, goal analysis is a process that works backwards from the goal sentence of a derivation to its assumptions. More precisely, goal analysis, when properly done, utilizes information about the goal sentence of a derivation, the accessible sentences on earlier lines of a derivation, and the rules of *SD* to select an appropriate series of subgoals to facilitate the complete construction of a derivation. Goal analysis is not a mechanical procedure for generating derivations, but rather a system of useful guidelines. Goal analysis proceeds through a three-step cycle.

1. *Analyze the goal sentence*. Determine what kind of sentence it is. If it is not an atomic sentence, what is its main sentential connective? What kind of component sentences does it have?

2. *Analyze accessible sentences on earlier lines*. Determine what kind of sentences they are. What are their main sentential connectives? Do they have sentential components similar to the components of the goal sentence? If the goal sentence can be derived immediately, derive it. Otherwise select a subgoal sentence.

3. *Enter a subgoal sentence*. A subgoal sentence is a sentence such that if it were derived from accessible sentences on earlier lines in the derivation then it would lead directly to a derivation of the goal sentence. Select either an introduction rule subgoal or an elimination rule subgoal (discussed below). Enter this subgoal into the derivation under construction and regard that subgoal sentence as the new goal sentence. Now return to step 1 and repeat the process.

[2] We could develop a decision procedure for constructing derivations in *SD* for *finite* sets of sentences. That is, we could develop a mechanical procedure such that by following it we would always obtain a derivation of a sentence $\mathscr{P}$ from a finite set of sentences of *Sl* after a finite number of steps, if there were such a derivation. If there were no such derivation, we would know that after a finite number of steps. However, we will not develop such a decision procedure because the procedure would be cumbersome to use and would detract from the naturalness of using a natural deduction system.

If the goal sentence has a main sentential connective, then consider entering a subgoal sentence that supports the application of the rule of *SD* that *introduces* that sentential connective.

If the goal sentence has the form $\mathscr{P} \,\&\, \mathscr{Q}$, then consider entering the following subgoals:

| | | |
|---|---|---|
| Enter subgoal → | $\mathscr{P}$ | |
| Enter subgoal → | $\mathscr{Q}$ | |
| Goal sentence → | $\mathscr{P} \,\&\, \mathscr{Q}$ | _, _ &I |

Notice that these subgoals give us a new objective. We are no longer trying to derive $\mathscr{P} \,\&\, \mathscr{Q}$ but rather we are aiming at deriving $\mathscr{P}$ and deriving $\mathscr{Q}$. Once we have derived $\mathscr{P}$ and we have derived $\mathscr{Q}$, $\mathscr{P} \,\&\, \mathscr{Q}$ can be derived immediately by Conjunction Introduction. This is indicated by entering the abbreviated name, '&I', as part of the justification for $\mathscr{P} \,\&\, \mathscr{Q}$. The underlined spaces in the justification will be filled in eventually by line numbers when the rest of the derivation is completed.

If the goal sentence has the form $\mathscr{P} \vee \mathscr{Q}$, then consider entering the following subgoal:

| | | |
|---|---|---|
| Enter subgoal → | $\mathscr{P}$ | |
| Goal sentence → | $\mathscr{P} \vee \mathscr{Q}$ | _ ∨I |

Similarly, $\mathscr{Q}$ can be taken as the subgoal sentence for a later application of Disjunction Introduction.

If the goal sentence has the form $\mathscr{P} \supset \mathscr{Q}$, then consider entering the following subderivation and subgoal:

| | | |
|---|---|---|
| Enter assumption → | | $\mathscr{P}$ | Assumption |
| Enter subgoal → | | $\mathscr{Q}$ | |
| Goal sentence → | $\mathscr{P} \supset \mathscr{Q}$ | _–_ ⊃I |

If the goal sentence has the form $\mathscr{P} \equiv \mathscr{Q}$, then consider entering the following subderivations and subgoals:

| | | |
|---|---|---|
| Enter assumption → | | $\mathscr{P}$ | Assumption |
| Enter subgoal → | | $\mathscr{Q}$ | |
| Enter assumption → | | $\mathscr{Q}$ | Assumption |
| Enter subgoal → | | $\mathscr{P}$ | |
| Goal sentence → | $\mathscr{P} \equiv \mathscr{Q}$ | _–_, _–_ ≡I |

If the goal sentence has the form $\sim \mathcal{P}$, then consider entering the following subderivation:

| | | |
|---|---|---|
| Enter assumption → | $\mathcal{P}$ | Assumption |
| Subgoal? → | $\mathcal{Q}$ | |
| Subgoal? → | $\sim \mathcal{Q}$ | |
| Goal sentence → | $\sim \mathcal{P}$ | _-_ ~ I |

This introduction rule is less helpful than the others, for in this case we know only the form of the subgoals. We know we must derive some sentence $\mathcal{Q}$ and its negation. We are not given guidance about what the sentence $\mathcal{Q}$ is.

*SUBGOALS FROM THE ELIMINATION RULES*

If the goal sentence is a component of an accessible sentence on an earlier line or depends on removing a sentential connective in an accessible sentence on an earlier line, then consider entering a subgoal sentence that supports the application of the rule of *SD* that *eliminates* the relevant sentential connective.

If the goal sentence has the form $\mathcal{P}$ and a sentential component of the form $\mathcal{P}$ & $\mathcal{Q}$ occurs in an earlier accessible sentence in the derivation, then consider entering the following subgoal:

| | | |
|---|---|---|
| Enter subgoal → | $\mathcal{P}$ & $\mathcal{Q}$ | |
| Goal sentence → | $\mathcal{P}$ | _ & E |

A similar procedure applies if the goal sentence is the right conjunct of a conjunction.

If the goal sentence has the form $\mathcal{Q}$ and a sentential component of the form $\mathcal{P} \supset \mathcal{Q}$ occurs in an earlier accessible sentence in the derivation, then consider entering the following subgoals:

| | | |
|---|---|---|
| Enter subgoal → | $\mathcal{P}$ | |
| Enter subgoal → | $\mathcal{P} \supset \mathcal{Q}$ | |
| Goal sentence → | $\mathcal{Q}$ | _, _ ⊃ E |

If the goal sentence has the form $\mathcal{Q}$ and a sentential component of the form $\mathcal{P} \equiv \mathcal{Q}$ occurs in an earlier accessible sentence in the derivation, then consider entering the following subgoals:

| | | |
|---|---|---|
| Enter subgoal → | $\mathcal{P}$ | |
| Enter subgoal → | $\mathcal{P} \equiv \mathcal{Q}$ | |
| Goal sentence → | $\mathcal{Q}$ | _, _ ≡ E |

Because of the symmetry in the rule Biconditional Elimination a similar approach is possible if $\mathcal{Q} \equiv \mathcal{P}$ occurs as a sentential component rather than $\mathcal{P} \equiv \mathcal{Q}$.

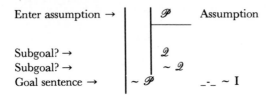

If the goal sentence has the form $\mathcal{R}$ and a sentential component of the form $\mathcal{P} \vee \mathcal{Q}$ occurs in an earlier accessible sentence in the derivation, then consider entering the following subderivations and subgoals:

| | | | |
|---|---|---|---|
| Enter subgoal → | $\mathcal{P} \vee \mathcal{Q}$ | | |
| Enter assumption → | | $\mathcal{P}$ | Assumption |
| Enter subgoal → | | $\mathcal{R}$ | |
| Enter assumption → | | $\mathcal{Q}$ | Assumption |
| Enter subgoal → | | $\mathcal{R}$ | |
| Goal sentence → | $\mathcal{R}$ | | _, _–_, _–_ ∨E |

Finally, if the goal sentence has the form $\mathcal{P}$ and a sentential component of the form $\sim \mathcal{P}$ occurs in an earlier accessible sentence in the derivation, then consider entering the following subderivation:

| | | | |
|---|---|---|---|
| Enter assumption → | | $\sim \mathcal{P}$ | Assumption |
| Subgoal? → | | $\mathcal{Q}$ | |
| Subgoal? → | | $\sim \mathcal{Q}$ | |
| Goal sentence → | $\mathcal{P}$ | | _–_ ∼E |

This approach can be used even if $\sim \mathcal{P}$ does not occur as a sentential component on an earlier line. Every goal sentence has the form $\mathcal{P}$ and we can always take $\sim \mathcal{P}$ as an assumption! In spite of the generality of Negation Elimination, this approach should be utilized only as a last resort when selecting subgoal sentences, for it hinders further goal analysis. We know we must derive some sentence $\mathcal{Q}$ and its negation, but we are not given guidance about which specific sentence $\mathcal{Q}$ to derive.

Whether an introduction rule subgoal or an elimination rule subgoal should be entered in a particular situation depends upon what the analysis of the particular goal sentence and the accessible sentences on earlier lines reveals. A strength of the *SD* rules is that they suggest the conditions for their own application. They suggest the kinds of subgoals to consider.

Some examples will help make clear how goal analysis works. Consider the argument

∼ N

(∼ N ⊃ L) & (D ≡ ∼ N)

---

(L ∨ A) & D

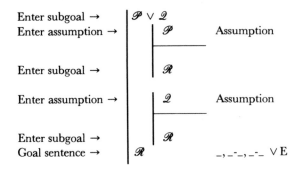

Our ultimate goal is to derive the conclusion of the argument. So we write 'Derive: (L ∨ A) & D' and then list the premises of the argument as assumptions. Since we

know what the last line of the derivation must be, we enter it farther down the page, leaving as much room as we think necessary to complete the derivation.

Derive: (L ∨ A) & D

| | | |
|---|---|---|
| 1 | ∼ N | Assumption |
| 2 | (∼ N ⊃ L) & (D ≡ ∼ N) | Assumption |
| | | |
| | (L ∨ A) & D | |

Analysis of the goal sentence '(L ∨ A) & D' and the assumptions shows that the goal sentence is not a component of any of the assumptions and cannot be derived immediately. A subgoal should be selected. Because the main connective of this goal sentence is '&', the rule Conjunction Introduction indicates the proper subgoals. After each of the conjuncts is entered into the derivation as a subgoals, the abbreviated rule name '&I' is also entered along with two underlined spaces indicating that line numbers should be filled in later.

Derive: (L ∨ A) & D

| | | |
|---|---|---|
| 1 | ∼ N | Assumption |
| 2 | (∼ N ⊃ L) & (D ≡ ∼ N) | Assumption |
| | | |
| | L ∨ A | |
| | D | |
| | (L ∨ A) & D | _, _ &I |

The two conjuncts 'L ∨ A' and 'D' become our new goal sentences. We know that once we have derived them, we can derive our original goal sentence '(L ∨ A) & D' in one step by Conjunction Introduction. 'D' occurs as one of the components of one of the assumptions. Specifically, 'D' occurs in 'D ≡ ∼ N'. Hence the sentential connective ≡ needs to be eliminated, which suggests the rule Biconditional Elimination. To apply the rule Biconditional Elimination, we need to set up two new subgoals. One of the subgoals is the sentences 'D ≡ ∼ N' and the other is the sentence '∼ N'. If we can derive both of these subgoals, then 'D' can be obtained immediately by Biconditional Elimination. As '∼ N' already occurs as an assumption, we need to enter only the subgoal 'D ≡ ∼ N'.

Derive: (L ∨ A) & D

| | | |
|---|---|---|
| 1 | ~ N | Assumption |
| 2 | (~ N ⊃ L) & (D ≡ ~ N) | Assumption |
| | | |
| | D ≡ ~ N | 2 &E |
| | L ∨ A | |
| | D | 1, _ ≡E |
| | (L ∨ A) & D | _, _ &I |

We are not finished with the derivation, for we still must derive 'L ∨ A'. This sentence cannot be derived immediately from the assumptions. However, its main connective, '∨', indicates that Disjunction Introduction is the rule to consider. We can take either 'L' or 'A' as the subgoal sentence; but because the assumptions do not contain any occurrence of 'A', it is reasonable to take 'L' as the subgoal sentence.

Derive: (L ∨ A) & D

| | | |
|---|---|---|
| 1 | ~ N | Assumption |
| 2 | (~ N ⊃ L) & (D ≡ ~ N) | Assumption |
| | | |
| | L | |
| | D ≡ ~ N | 2 &E |
| | L ∨ A | _ ∨I |
| | D | 1, _ ≡E |
| | (L ∨ A) & D | _, _ &I |

'L' becomes our new goal sentence. 'L' occurs as a component of '~ N ⊃ L' in line 2. Hence '⊃' is the connective to eliminate and Conditional Elimination is the rule to use. If we take '~ N' and '~ N ⊃ L' as subgoals, then we can derive 'L' by Conditional Elimination. '~ N' already occurs as an assumption on line 1 so we need to take only '~ N ⊃ L' as a new subgoal.

Derive: (L ∨ A) & D

| | | |
|---|---|---|
| 1 | ~ N | Assumption |
| 2 | (~ N ⊃ L) & (D ≡ ~ N) | Assumption |
| | ~ N ⊃ L | |
| | L | 1, _ ⊃E |
| | D ≡ ~ N | 2 &E |
| | L ∨ A | _ ∨I |
| | D | 1, _ ≡E |
| | (L ∨ A) & D | _, _ &I |

'~ N ⊃ L' becomes our new goal sentence. This sentence is a component of the assumption on line 2 and can be derived immediately using the rule Conjunction Elimination. We do this and follow the trail of our subgoals down the derivation filling in the line numbers as we go.

Derive: (L ∨ A) & D

| | | |
|---|---|---|
| 1 | ~ N | Assumption |
| 2 | (~ N ⊃ L) & (D ≡ ~ N) | Assumption |
| 3 | ~ N ⊃ L | 2 &E |
| 4 | L | 1, 3 ⊃E |
| 5 | D ≡ ~ N | 2 &E |
| 6 | L ∨ A | 4 ∨I |
| 7 | D | 1, 5 ≡E |
| 8 | (L ∨ A) & D | 6, 7 &I |

Suppose we wish to construct a derivation to show the following argument is valid in *SD*.

~ L ≡ [X & (~ S ∨ B)]
(E & C) ⊃ ~ L
(E & R) & C

---

X & (~ S ∨ B)

We begin the derivation thus:

Derive: X & (~ S ∨ B)

| | | |
|---|---|---|
| 1 | ~ L ≡ [X & (~ S ∨ B)] | Assumption |
| 2 | (E & C) ⊃ ~ L | Assumption |
| 3 | (E & R) & C | Assumption |
| | | |
| | X & (~ S ∨ B) | |

The goal sentence, 'X & (~ S ∨ B)', is a conjunction; this suggests using the rule Conjunction Introduction. However, a glance at the assumptions reveals that the goal sentence is a component of a biconditional on line 1. Thus a more promising strategy in this case is to use Biconditional Elimination to derive the conjunction. We can use Biconditional Elimination in this way if '~ L' can be derived first. Thus '~ L' is entered as a subgoal.

Derive: X & (~ S ∨ B)

| | | |
|---|---|---|
| 1 | ~ L ≡ [X & (~ S ∨ B) | Assumption |
| 2 | (E & C) ⊃ ~ L | Assumption |
| 3 | (E & R) & C | Assumption |
| | ~ L | |
| | X & (~ S ∨ B) | 1, _ ≡ E |

'~ L' is a component of the second assumption and can be obtained by using Conditional Elimination if 'E & C' can be derived. 'E & C' becomes our next subgoal.

Derive: X & (~ S ∨ B)

| | | |
|---|---|---|
| 1 | ~ L ≡ [X & (~ S ∨ B)] | Assumption |
| 2 | (E & C) ⊃ ~ L | Assumption |
| 3 | (E & R) & C | Assumption |
| | E & C | |
| | ~ L | 2, _ ⊃ E |
| | X & (~ S ∨ B) | 1, _ ≡ E |

Our current goal sentence is the conjunction 'E & C'. This conjunction is a component of the second assumption, but we are using that assumption, along with 'E & C', to derive '~ L'. Since 'E & C' does not occur as a component of any other assumption, using Conjunction Introduction to derive this goal sentence is a good strategy. Hence 'E' and 'C' should be entered as subgoals.

Derive: X & (~ S ∨ B)

| | | |
|---|---|---|
| 1 | ~ L ≡ [X & (~ S ∨ B)] | Assumption |
| 2 | (E & C) ⊃ ~ L | Assumption |
| 3 | (E & R) & C | Assumption |
| | E | |
| | C | |
| | E & C | _, _ & I |
| | ~ L | 2, _ ⊃ E |
| | X & (~ S ∨ B) | 1, _ ≡ E |

Deriving 'E' and deriving 'C' are the current goals, and they can be accomplished easily by using the rule Conjunction Elimination.

Derive: X & (~ S ∨ B)

| | | |
|---|---|---|
| 1 | ~ L ≡ [X & (~ S ∨ B)] | Assumption |
| 2 | (E & C) ⊃ ~ L | Assumption |
| 3 | (E & R) & C | Assumption |
| 4 | E & R | 3 & E |
| 5 | E | 4 & E |
| 6 | C | 3 & E |
| 7 | E & C | 5, 6 & I |
| 8 | ~ L | 2, 7 ⊃ E |
| 9 | X & (~ S ∨ B) | 1, 8 ≡ E |

Goal analysis is helpful in constructing subderivations in that it guides the choice of assumptions. Suppose we wish to show the following:

⊢ (U & Y) ⊃ [L ⊃ (U & L)]

To prove that '(U & Y) ⊃ [L ⊃ (U & L)]' is a theorem, we must derive it from the empty set. We enter the sentence at the bottom, leaving plenty of room to fill in the derivation above it.

Derive: (U & Y) ⊃ [L ⊃ (U & L)]

| | | |
|---|---|---|
| | (U & Y) ⊃ [L ⊃ (U & L)] | |

As our goal is a conditional sentence, using Conditional Introduction is a good strategy. We thus construct a subderivation that has as its assumption the antecedent of the conditional and as its last line the consequent of the conditional. If the consequent can be derived within the subderivation, then the subderivation can be terminated and the conditional can be derived by using Conditional Introduction.

Derive: (U & Y) ⊃ [L ⊃ (U & L)]

| | | |
|---|---|---|
| 1 | U & Y | Assumption |
| | L ⊃ (U & L) | |
| | (U & Y) ⊃ [L ⊃ (U & L)] | 1-_ ⊃ I |

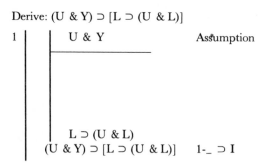

Hence our new goal is to derive 'L ⊃ (U & L)', which is itself a conditional. We should again consider using Conditional Introduction to derive it. We assume the antecedent of the conditional, and the derivation of its consequent becomes our new goal. If the consequent can be derived, then Conditional Introduction yields the desired conditional.

Derive: (U & Y) ⊃ [L ⊃ (U & L)]

| | | |
|---|---|---|
| 1 | \| \| U & Y | Assumption |
| 2 | \| \| \| L | Assumption |
| | \| \| \| | |
| | \| \| \| U & L | |
| | \| \| L ⊃ (U & L) | 2-_ ⊃I |
| | \| (U & Y) ⊃ [L ⊃ (U & L)] | 1-_ ⊃I |

Our current goal is to derive 'U & L', which is straightforward, given the assumptions. The complete derivation with the line numbers properly filled in is

Derive: (U & Y) ⊃ [L ⊃ (U & L)]

| | | |
|---|---|---|
| 1 | \| \| U & Y | Assumption |
| 2 | \| \| \| L | Assumption |
| 3 | \| \| \| U | 1 &E |
| 4 | \| \| \| U & L | 3, 2 &I |
| 5 | \| \| L ⊃ (U & L) | 2-4 ⊃I |
| 6 | \| (U & Y) ⊃ [L ⊃ (U & L)] | 1-5 ⊃I |

All the assumptions have been discharged, and now we have a derivation of the theorem.

Remember that when we use Conditional Introduction the sentence we derive will be a conditional whose antecedent is the sentence we assume. For example, if the goal sentence is of the form $(\mathcal{P} \supset \mathcal{Q}) \supset \mathcal{R}$, we assume $\mathcal{P} \supset \mathcal{Q}$, not $\mathcal{P}$, and try to derive $\mathcal{R}$.

As another example, suppose we wish to show that

⊢ [(J ⊃ [(J ∨ B) ⊃ K]) & J] ⊃ K

Our ultimate goal is to derive this sentence. Since our goal sentence is a conditional, we can plan to use Conditional Introduction in deriving it. The proper assumption is the antecedent of this conditional, and the derivation of the consequent of the conditional becomes our new goal.

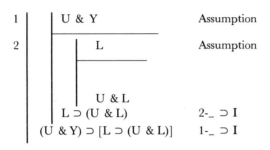

```
Derive: [(J ⊃ [(J ∨ B) ⊃ K]) & J] ⊃ K
1  | | (J ⊃ [(J ∨ B) ⊃ K]) & J      Assumption
   | |----------------------------
   | |
   | | K
   | [(J ⊃ [(J ∨ B) ⊃ K]) & J] ⊃ K   1-_ ⊃I
```

Notice that we do *not* take ‘J’ as the assumption, although ‘J’ is an antecedent of a conditional within the sentence. Nor do we take ‘J ∨ B’ as an assumption, although it too is an antecedent of a conditional within the sentence. The reason is that if we assume ‘J’ or ‘J ∨ B’, the use of Conditional Introduction to discharge the assumption would generate a conditional whose antecedent is ‘J’ or ‘J ∨ B’. But this would not accomplish our goal, for we want to derive a conditional whose antecedent is ‘(J ⊃ [(J ∨ B) ⊃ K]) & J’. Our current goal sentence is ‘K’. Because K is atomic, the introduction rules will not provide reasonable subgoals. But ‘K’ does occur in the assumption in the component ‘(J ∨ B) ⊃ K’. Therefore we need to eliminate the ‘ ⊃ ’ and Conditional Elimination indicates the subgoals ‘J ∨ B’ and ‘(J ∨ B) ⊃ K’.

```
Derive: [(J ⊃ [(J ∨ B) ⊃ K]) & J] ⊃ K
1  | | (J ⊃ [(J ∨ B) ⊃ K]) & J      Assumption
   | |----------------------------
   | |
   | | (J ∨ B) ⊃ K
   | | J ∨ B
   | | K                            _,_ ⊃E
   | [(J ⊃ [(J ∨ B) ⊃ K]) & J] ⊃ K   1-_ ⊃I
```

‘J ∨ B’ is one of the new goal sentences. Disjunction Introduction suggests either ‘J’ or ‘B’ be taken as a subgoal to introduce the ‘∨’. Because ‘J’ is easily derived from line 1 and ‘B’ is not, ‘J’ makes the better subgoal.

```
Derive: [(J ⊃ [(J ∨ B) ⊃ K]) & J] ⊃ K
1  | | (J ⊃ [(J ∨ B) ⊃ K]) & J      Assumption
   | |----------------------------
   | |
   | | J
   | | (J ∨ B) ⊃ K
   | | J ∨ B                        _ ∨I
   | | K                            _,_ ⊃E
   | [(J ⊃ [(J ∨ B) ⊃ K]) & J] ⊃ K   1-_ ⊃I
```

The goal sentences are now 'J', which is derivable immediately from line 1 by Conjunction Elimination, and '(J ∨ B) ⊃ K'. This latter goal sentence is a component of 'J ⊃ [(J ∨ B) ⊃ K]' that occurs in the first assumption. Thus 'J', which we already have, and 'J ⊃ [(J ∨ B) ⊃ K]' become the new subgoals. When 'J ⊃ [(J ∨ B) ⊃ K]' is entered as a subgoal, the derivation can be completed immediately as 'J ⊃ [(J ∨ B) ⊃ K]' can be obtained from line 1 by Conjunction Elimination.

Derive: [(J ⊃ [(J ∨ B) ⊃ K]) & J] ⊃ K

| | | |
|---|---|---|
| 1 | \| \| (J ⊃ [(J ∨ B) ⊃ K]) & J | Assumption |
| 2 | \| \| J ⊃ [(J ∨ B) ⊃ K] | 1 &E |
| 3 | \| \| J | 1 &E |
| 4 | \| \| (J ∨ B) ⊃ K | 2, 3 ⊃E |
| 5 | \| \| J ∨ B | 3 ∨I |
| 6 | \| \| K | 5, 4 ⊃E |
| 7 | \| [(J ⊃ [(J ∨ B) ⊃ K]) & J] ⊃ K | 1-6 ⊃I |

Here is another example. Suppose we wish to construct a derivation that shows

⊢ (~ A ∨ ~ B) ≡ ~ (A & B)

Since our goal sentence is a biconditional, using Biconditional Introduction is an appropriate strategy. This requires that two subderivations be constructed. One subderivation will have '~ A ∨ ~ B' as its assumption and '~ (A & B)' as its last sentence. The other will have '~ (A & B)' as its assumption and '~ A ∨ ~ B' as its last sentence.

Derive: (~ A ∨ ~ B) ≡ ~ (A & B)

| | | |
|---|---|---|
| 1 | \| \| ~ A ∨ ~ B | Assumption |
| | \| \| | |
| | \| \| ~ (A & B) | |
| | \| \| ~ (A & B) | Assumption |
| | \| \| | |
| | \| \| ~ A ∨ ~ B | |
| | \| (~ A ∨ ~ B) ≡ ~ (A & B) | 1-_, _-_ ≡I |

Goal analysis can be applied to each subderivation. In the first subderivation a negation is our goal sentence. Thus it might seem that Negation Introduction is the obvious rule to use. However, it is a mistake to think that whenever a goal sentence is a negation, Negation Introduction is the best rule to use. Since the assumption of the first subderivation is a disjunction, an alternative and in this case slightly preferable strategy is to use Disjunction Elimination to eliminate the '∨'. To follow this strategy, we set up two subderivations within the first subderivation.

Derive: (~ A ∨ ~ B) ≡ ~ (A & B)

| | | |
|---|---|---|
| 1 | ~ A ∨ ~ B | Assumption |
| 2 | ~ A | Assumption |
| | ~ (A & B) | |
| | ~ B | Assumption |
| | ~ (A & B) | |
| | ~ (A & B) | 1, 2-_, _-_ ∨E |
| | ~ (A & B) | Assumption |
| | ~ A ∨ ~ B | |
| | (~ A ∨ ~ B) ≡ ~ (A & B) | 1-_, _-_ ≡I |

If each of the two subderivations within the first subderivation can be completed, then Disjunction Elimination can be used to complete the first subderivation. Our new goal is to derive '~ (A & B)' within each of these subderivations. Negation Introduction will allow us to derive a negation if we construct a subderivation with the unnegated sentence as the assumption and derive a sentence and its negation within the subderivation. Here is the derivation so far.

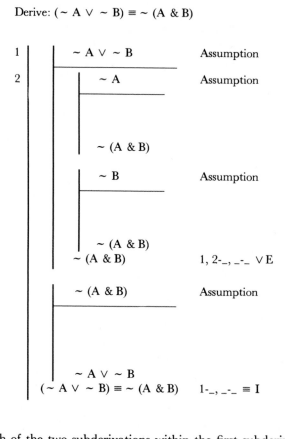

Derive: (~ A ∨ ~ B) ≡ ~ (A & B)

| | | |
|---|---|---|
| 1 | ~ A ∨ B | Assumption |
| 2 | ~ A | Assumption |
| 3 | A & B | Assumption |
| | | |
| | ~ (A & B) | 3-_ ~ I |
| | ~ B | Assumption |
| | A & B | Assumption |
| | | |
| | ~ (A & B) | _-_ ~ I |
| | ~ (A & B) | 1, 2-_, _-_ ∨E |
| | ~ (A & B) | Assumption |
| | | |
| | ~ A ∨ ~ B | |
| | (~ A ∨ ~ B) ≡ ~ (A & B) | 1-_, _-_ ≡ I |

In using the negation rules we must derive a sentence and its negation within a subderivation. It is generally wise to let a sentence that has been derived on an earlier line serve as one of these sentences, for such a sentence can easily be brought into the subderivation by Reiteration. If the sentence to be reiterated is a negation, so much the better. For example, to complete the first subderivation, we can obtain '~ A' by Reiteration from line 2 and then plan to derive 'A'. Here 'A' is easily derived by Conjunction Elimination on the assumption on line 3. Similarly, to complete the next subderivation, we can use Reiteration to obtain '~ B' and then derive 'B'.

Derive: (∼ A ∨ ∼ B) ≡ ∼ (A & B)

| | | |
|---|---|---|
| 1 | ∼ A ∨ ∼ B | Assumption |
| 2 | ∼ A | Assumption |
| 3 | A & B | Assumption |
| 4 | A | 3 &E |
| 5 | ∼ A | 2 R |
| 6 | ∼ (A & B) | 3-5 ∼ I |
| 7 | ∼ B | Assumption |
| 8 | A & B | Assumption |
| 9 | B | 8 &E |
| 10 | ∼ B | 7 R |
| 11 | ∼ (A & B) | 8-10 ∼ I |
| 12 | ∼ (A & B) | 1, 2-6, 7-11 ∨E |
| 13 | ∼ (A & B) | Assumption |
| | ∼ A ∨ ∼ B | |
| | (∼ A ∨ ∼ B) ≡ ∼ (A & B) | 1-12, 13-_ ≡ I |

The second major subderivation is still unfinished. The goal sentence for it is a disjunction '∼ A ∨ ∼ B'. A possible strategy is to use Disjunction Introduction. However, this requires that we derive one of the disjuncts of the goal sentence on a line by itself. In this case we can be sure that it is not possible, since our derivation rules are truth-preserving and the assumption '∼ (A & B)' can be true while '∼ A' is false. Similarly, '∼ (A & B)' can be true while '∼ B' is false. Therefore we reject using Disjunction Introduction as a strategy for obtaining the goal sentence. The only choice left is to assume the negation of the goal sentence in a subderivation and to derive a sentence and its negation, so that the goal sentence can be derived by Negation Elimination. Here is the relevant portion of the derivation.

| | | |
|---|---|---|
| 13 | ∼ (A & B) | Assumption |
| 14 | ∼ (∼ A ∨ ∼ B) | Assumption |
| | ∼ A ∨ ∼ B | 14-_ ∼ E |
| | (∼ A ∨ ∼ B) ≡ ∼ (A & B) | 1-12, 13-_ ≡ I |

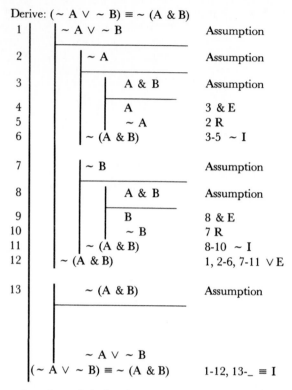

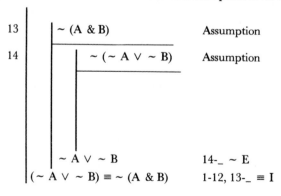

Since we have a negation as an assumption, we can try to derive the corresponding unnegated sentence 'A & B'. Thus our current goal sentence is a conjunction that can be derived by the rule Conjunction Introduction if we can first derive each of the conjuncts.

| | | |
|---|---|---|
| 13 | ~ (A & B) | Assumption |
| 14 | ~ (~ A ∨ ~ B) | Assumption |
| | A | |
| | B | |
| | A & B | _, _ & |
| | ~ (A & B) | 13 R |
| | ~ A ∨ ~ B | 14-_ ~ E |
| | (~ A ∨ ~ B) ≡ ~ (A & B) | 1-12, 13-_ ≡ I |

Since our goal sentences are atomic, they cannot be derived by any of the introduction rules. The most promising elimination rule to use is Negation Elimination. Thus we proceed by assuming the negation of each of the atomic sentences and deriving a sentence and its negation within each subderivation. This will allow us to derive the goal sentences by Negation Elimination.

| | | |
|---|---|---|
| 13 | ~ (A & B) | Assumption |
| 14 | ~ (~ A ∨ ~ B) | Assumption |
| 15 | ~ A | Assumption |
| | A | _-_ ~ E |
| | ~ B | Assumption |
| | B | _-_ ~ E |
| | A & B | _, _ & I |
| | ~ (A & B) | 13 R |
| | ~ A ∨ ~ B | 14-_ ~ E |
| | (~ A ∨ ~ B) ≡ ~ (A & B) | 1-12, 13-_ ≡ I |

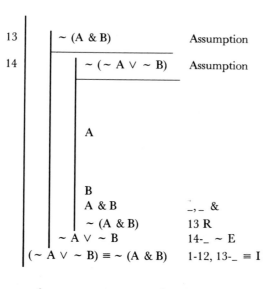

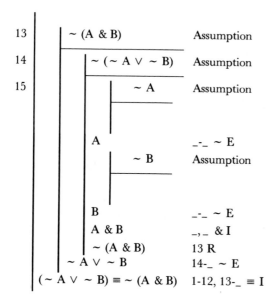

A sentence and its negation can now easily be derived within each of the subderivations by using Disjunction Introduction. The full derivation looks like this:

Derive: (~ A ∨ ~ B) ≡ ~ (A & B)

```
 1 | | ~ A ∨ ~ B                  Assumption
   | |------------
 2 | | | ~ A                      Assumption
   | | |----------
 3 | | | | A & B                  Assumption
   | | | |--------
 4 | | | | A                      3 &E
 5 | | | | ~ A                    2 R
 6 | | | ~ (A & B)                3-5 ~I
   | | |
 7 | | | ~ B                      Assumption
   | | |----------
 8 | | | | A & B                  Assumption
   | | | |--------
 9 | | | | B                      8 &E
10 | | | | ~ B                    7 R
11 | | | ~ (A & B)                8-10 ~I
12 | | ~ (A & B)                  1, 2-6, 7-11 ∨E
   |
13 | | ~ (A & B)                  Assumption
   | |------------
14 | | | ~ (~ A ∨ ~ B)            Assumption
   | | |----------
15 | | | | ~ A                    Assumption
   | | | |--------
16 | | | | ~ A ∨ ~ B              15 ∨I
17 | | | | ~ (~ A ∨ ~ B)          14 R
18 | | | A                        15-17 ~E
19 | | | | ~ B                    Assumption
   | | | |--------
20 | | | | ~ A ∨ ~ B              19 ∨I
21 | | | | ~ (~ A ∨ ~ B)          14 R
22 | | | B                        19-21 ~E
23 | | | A & B                    18, 22 &I
24 | | | ~ (A & B)                13 R
25 | | ~ A ∨ ~ B                  14-24 ~E
26 | (~ A ∨ ~ B) ≡ ~ (A & B)      1-12, 13-25 ≡I
```

This derivation is complex, but it can be constructed systematically, as we have just done, by analyzing goal sentences along the way and asking what means we have for deriving them. Of course, constructing derivations is not a spectator sport and requires practice.

*THE DERIVATION RULES OF SD*

*Reiteration* (R)

| $\mathcal{P}$
|
| $\mathcal{P}$

## '&' Introduction and Elimination Rules

*Conjunction Introduction* (&I)

| $\mathcal{P}$
| $\mathcal{Q}$
|
| $\mathcal{P}$ & $\mathcal{Q}$

*Conjunction Elimination* (&E)

| $\mathcal{P}$ & $\mathcal{Q}$
|
| $\mathcal{P}$

or

| $\mathcal{P}$ & $\mathcal{Q}$
|
| $\mathcal{Q}$

## '$\supset$' Introduction and Elimination Rules

*Conditional Introduction* ($\supset$I)

| | $\mathcal{P}$
| |---
| |
| | $\mathcal{Q}$
| $\mathcal{P} \supset \mathcal{Q}$

*Conditional Elimination* ($\supset$E)

| $\mathcal{P} \supset \mathcal{Q}$
|
| $\mathcal{P}$
|
| $\mathcal{Q}$

## '$\sim$' Introduction and Elimination Rules

*Negation Introduction* ($\sim$I)

| | $\mathcal{P}$
| |---
| |
| | $\mathcal{Q}$
| |
| | $\sim \mathcal{Q}$
|
| $\sim \mathcal{P}$

*Negation Elimination* ($\sim$E)

| | $\sim \mathcal{P}$
| |---
| |
| | $\mathcal{Q}$
| |
| | $\sim \mathcal{Q}$
|
| $\mathcal{P}$

## '$\vee$' Introduction and Elimination Rules

*Disjunction Introduction* ($\vee$I)

| $\mathcal{P}$
|
| $\mathcal{P} \vee \mathcal{Q}$

or

| $\mathcal{P}$
|
| $\mathcal{Q} \vee \mathcal{P}$

*Disjunction Elimination* ($\vee$E)

| $\mathcal{P} \vee \mathcal{Q}$
|
| | $\mathcal{P}$
| |---
| | $\mathcal{R}$
|
| | $\mathcal{Q}$
| |---
| | $\mathcal{R}$
| $\mathcal{R}$

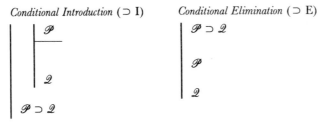

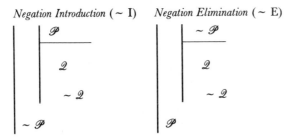

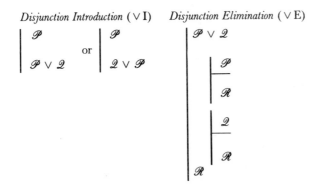

## ‘ ≡ ’ Introduction and Elimination Rules

*Biconditional Introduction* (≡ I)

$$
\begin{array}{|l}
\quad\begin{array}{|l}
\mathscr{P} \\ \hline
\\
\mathscr{Q}
\end{array} \\
\quad\begin{array}{|l}
\mathscr{Q} \\ \hline
\\
\mathscr{P}
\end{array} \\
\mathscr{P} \equiv \mathscr{Q}
\end{array}
$$

*Biconditional Elimination* (≡ E)

$$
\begin{array}{|l}
\mathscr{P} \equiv \mathscr{Q} \\
\mathscr{P} \\
\\
\mathscr{Q}
\end{array}
\quad \text{or} \quad
\begin{array}{|l}
\mathscr{P} \equiv \mathscr{Q} \\
\mathscr{Q} \\
\\
\mathscr{P}
\end{array}
$$

### 5.4E EXERCISES

**1.** Show that the following derivability claims hold in *SD*:

a. {(Z ≡ R) & H, (K ⊃ J) & ~ ~ Y, D ∨ B} ⊢ H & (K ⊃ J)
*b. {K ⊃ R, B & K} ⊢ R ∨ T
c. {A ≡ (A ⊃ B)} ⊢ A ⊃ B
*d. {(A ∨ B) ⊃ (B ≡ D), B} ⊢ B & D
e. {B & F, ~ (B & G)} ⊢ ~ G
*f. {(~ B ∨ ~ H) ⊃ M, K & ~ M} ⊢ B

**2.** Show that each of the following arguments is valid in *SD*:

a. ~ (L & E)
~ (L & E) ≡ P
―――――
L ∨ P

*b. R & (C & ~ F)
(R ∨ S) ⊃ ~ W
―――――
~ W

c. R ⊃ S
S ⊃ T
―――――
R ⊃ T

*d. (A ⊃ F) & (F ⊃ D)
[(M ∨ H) ∨ C] ⊃ A
~ (M ∨ H) & C
―――――
D

e. A ⊃ (B & C)
~ C
―――――
~ (A & D)

*f. $H$

$\overline{C \supset [A \supset (S \supset H)]}$

g. $A \equiv B$
$B \equiv C$

$\overline{A \equiv C}$

*h. $A \supset (B \supset C)$
$D \supset B$

$\overline{A \supset (D \supset C)}$

i. $F \equiv G$
$F \vee G$

$\overline{F \& G}$

*j. $\sim B \equiv Z$
$N \supset B$
$Z \& N$

$\overline{\sim H}$

3. Show that each of the following is a theorem in *SD*:

a. $A \supset (A \vee B)$
*b. $A \supset (B \supset A)$
c. $(A \equiv B) \supset (A \supset B)$
*d. $(A \& \sim A) \supset (B \& \sim B)$
e. $(A \supset B) \supset [(C \supset A) \supset (C \supset B)]$
*f. $A \vee \sim A$
g. $[(A \supset B) \& \sim B] \supset \sim A$
*h. $(A \& A) \equiv A$
i. $A \supset [B \supset (A \supset B)]$
*j. $\sim A \supset [(B \& A) \supset C]$
k. $(A \supset B) \supset [\sim B \supset \sim (A \& D)]$

4. Show that the members of each of the following pairs of sentences are equivalent in *SD*:

| | |
|---|---|
| a. $(A \vee \sim\sim B) \& C$ | $(A \vee \sim\sim B) \& C$ |
| *b. $(A \& B) \& C$ | $A \& (B \& C)$ |
| c. $A$ | $\sim\sim A$ |
| *d. $A \& A$ | $A \vee A$ |
| e. $A \supset B$ | $\sim B \supset \sim A$ |
| *f. $A \equiv B$ | $B \equiv A$ |

5. Show that each of the following sets of sentences is inconsistent in *SD*:

a. $\{A \equiv \sim (A \equiv A), A\}$
*b. $\{P \supset \sim P, \sim P \supset P\}$
c. $\{M \supset (K \supset B), \sim K \supset \sim M, (L \& M) \& \sim B\}$
*d. $\{(E \vee F) \supset (G \& \sim I), (G \vee F) \supset I, \sim F \supset E\}$
e. $\{\sim (Y \equiv A), \sim Y, \sim A\}$

*f. $\{F \supset \sim G,\ \sim F \supset \sim H,\ (\sim F \vee G) \,\&\, H\}$
g. $\{(\sim C \supset \sim D) \,\&\, (C \supset D),\ D \supset \sim C,\ \sim (B \,\&\, \sim D),\ B \equiv (\sim C \vee D)\}$

**6.** Show that the following derivability claims hold in *SD*:

a. $\{P \supset Q\} \vdash \sim Q \supset \sim P$
*b. $\{K \vee (K \vee K)\} \vdash K$
c. $\{H \supset M,\ \sim H \supset \sim M\} \vdash H \equiv M$
*d. $\{A \vee B,\ \sim B\} \vdash A$
e. $\{\sim (F \supset G),\ \sim (G \supset H)\} \vdash \sim I$
*f. $\{[E \vee (L \vee M)] \,\&\, (E \equiv F),\ L \supset D,\ D \supset \sim L\} \vdash E \vee M$
g. $\{\sim (A \equiv B)\} \vdash \sim A \equiv B$

**7.** Show that each of the following arguments is valid in *SD*:

a. $$\begin{array}{l} (H \,\&\, I) \vee (H \,\&\, S) \\ \hline H \end{array}$$

*b. $$\begin{array}{l} K \supset \sim\sim Q \\ \sim\sim K \\ \hline Q \end{array}$$

c. $$\begin{array}{l} B \equiv \sim B \\ \hline J \equiv \sim C \end{array}$$

*d. $$\begin{array}{l} F \vee H \\ \sim H \equiv (L \vee G) \\ (G \,\&\, B) \vee [G \,\&\, (K \supset G)] \\ \hline F \end{array}$$

e. $$\begin{array}{l} (\sim H \vee J) \vee K \\ K \supset \sim I \\ \hline (H \,\&\, I) \supset J \end{array}$$

*f. $$\begin{array}{l} A \equiv B \\ B \equiv \sim C \\ \hline \sim (A \equiv C) \end{array}$$

g. $$\begin{array}{l} (A \vee B) \,\&\, \sim C \\ \sim C \supset (D \,\&\, \sim A) \\ B \supset (A \vee E) \\ \hline E \vee F \end{array}$$

**8.** Show that each of the following is a theorem in *SD*:

a. $\sim [(A \,\&\, B) \,\&\, \sim (A \,\&\, B)]$
*b. $A \equiv \sim\sim A$
c. $(A \equiv \sim A) \supset \sim (A \equiv \sim A)$
*d. $[(A \supset B) \supset A] \supset A$
e. $(A \supset B) \vee (B \supset A)$

*f. $(A \equiv B) \equiv [(A \supset B) \& (B \supset A)]$
g. $[A \supset (B \supset C)] \equiv [(A \supset B) \supset (A \supset C)]$
*h. $[(A \vee B) \supset C] \equiv [(A \supset C) \& (B \supset C)]$
i. $[(A \equiv B) \supset C] \supset [\sim (A \& B) \vee C]$

**9.** Show that the members of each of the following pairs of sentences are equivalent in *SD*:

| | | |
|---|---|---|
| a. | $\sim A \vee B$ | $A \supset B$ |
| *b. | $A \& \sim A$ | $B \& \sim B$ |
| c. | $\sim (A \supset B)$ | $A \& \sim B$ |
| *d. | $A \equiv B$ | $\sim A \equiv \sim B$ |
| e. | $A \equiv B$ | $(A \& B) \vee (\sim A \& \sim B)$ |
| *f. | $\sim (A \equiv B)$ | $(A \& \sim B) \vee (\sim A \& B)$ |

**10.** Show that each of the following sets of sentences is inconsistent in *SD*:
a. $\{(A \supset B) \& (A \supset \sim B), (C \supset A) \& (\sim C \supset A)\}$
*b. $\{B \equiv (A \& \sim A), \sim B \supset (A \& \sim A)\}$
c. $\{W \vee (Z \supset Y), \sim Y \& \sim (W \vee \sim Z)\}$
*d. $\{A \& (B \vee C), (\sim C \vee H) \& (H \supset \sim H), \sim B\}$
e. $\{[(A \equiv B) \equiv (D \& \sim D)] \equiv B, A\}$

**11.** Symbolize the following arguments in *SL*, and show that the symbolized arguments are valid in *SD*:
a. Spring has sprung, and the flowers are blooming. If the flowers are blooming, the bees are happy. If the bees are happy but aren't making honey, then spring hasn't sprung. So the bees are making honey.
*b. If Luscious Food Industries goes out of business, then food processing won't be improved. And if they go out of business, canned beans will be available if and only if Brockport Company stays in business. But Brockport Company is going out of business, and canned beans will be available. Hence Luscious Food Industries is staying in business unless food processing is improved.
c. If civil disobedience is moral, then not all resistance to the law is morally prohibited, although our legal code is correct if all resistance to the law is morally prohibited. But civil disobedience is moral if and only if either civil disobedience is moral or our legal code is correct. Our judges have acted well only if all resistance to the law is morally prohibited. So our judges haven't acted well.
*d. If oranges contain citric acid so do lemons, or if lemons don't contain citric acid neither do grapefruit. Thus, if oranges and grapefruit contain citric acid, so do lemons.
e. Neither rubber nor wood is a good conductor of electricity. But either rubber is a good conductor if and only if metal is, or if metal or glass is a good conductor then wood is a good conductor if and only if metal is. So metal isn't a good conductor of electricity.
*f. If the trains stop running then airline prices will increase, and buses will reduce their fares provided that trains don't stop running. If airline prices increase, then buses won't lose their customers. Hence buses will lose their customers only if they reduce their fares.
g. If the house is built and taxes increase, Jones will go bankrupt. If Smith becomes mayor, then the tax director will quit; and Smith will become mayor unless the tax

director quits. But taxes won't increase if but only if the tax director doesn't quit and Smith becomes mayor. So if the house is built, Jones will go bankrupt.

*h. Jim is a Democrat only if Howard or Rhoda is. If Howard is a Democrat, so are Barbara and Allen. If Barbara is a Democrat, then Allen is a Democrat only if Freda is. But not both Freda and Jim are Democrats. Therefore Jim is a Democrat only if Rhoda is too.

i. If life is a carnival, then I'm a clown or a trapeze artist. But life isn't a carnival unless there are balloons, and there aren't any balloons unless I'm not a clown. So if life is a carnival, then I'm a trapeze artist.

**12.** Symbolize the following passages in *SL*, and show that the resulting sets of sentences are inconsistent in *SD*:

a. If motorcycling is dangerous sailboating is also dangerous, and if sailboating is dangerous parachuting is dangerous. Motorcycling is dangerous but parachuting is not.

*b. If the recipe doesn't call for flavoring or it doesn't call for eggs, it's not a recipe for tapioca. If the recipe calls for eggs, then it's a tapioca recipe and it doesn't call for flavoring. But this recipe calls for eggs.

c. Bach is popular only if Beethoven is ignored. If Bach is unpopular and Beethoven isn't ignored, then current musical tastes are hopeless. Current musical tastes aren't hopeless, and Beethoven isn't ignored.

*d. Historians are right just in case theologians are mistaken, if and only if Darwin's theory is correct. And if historians or philosophers are right, then Darwinian theory is correct and theologians are mistaken. Historians are right if and only if philosophers are wrong. But if Darwinian theory is correct, then historians are mistaken.

e. Either Martha Graham was commissioned to write the ballet, or if the fund-raising sale was a failure. Twyla Tharp was commissioned. Rudolf Nureyev will dance if and only if Twyla Tharp wasn't commissioned. But the fund raiser was a failure, Rudolf Nureyev will dance, and Martha Graham wasn't commissioned.

**13a.** Explain why we would not want to include the following derivation rule in *SD*:

$$\left|\begin{array}{l} \mathcal{P} \vee \mathcal{Q} \\ \\ \mathcal{P} \end{array}\right.$$

*b. Explain why Negation Introduction is a dispensable rule in *SD*.

c. Explain why Reiteration is a dispensable rule in *SD*.

*d. Why does the following not show that the set containing just 'A' and 'B ⊃ ~ A' is inconsistent in *SD*?

| | | |
|---|---|---|
| 1 | A | Assumption |
| 2 | B ⊃ ~ A | Assumption |
| 3 |     B | Assumption |
| 4 |     ~ A | 2, 3 ⊃ E |
| 5 |     A | 1 R |

e. Suppose that $\mathscr{P}$ is a theorem in *SD*. Explain why any argument of *SL* that has $\sim \mathscr{P}$ among its premises is valid in *SD*.

*f. Give a derivation that shows that there is a sentence of *SL* such that the unit set of that sentence is inconsistent in *SD*.

**14.** In Chapter Six we prove that, for any sentence $\mathscr{P}$ and set $\Gamma$ of sentences of *SL*,

* $\Gamma \vdash \mathscr{P}$ in *SD* if and only if $\Gamma \models \mathscr{P}$

Use this result to prove the following:

a. An argument of *SL* is valid in *SD* if and only if the argument is truth-functionally valid.

*b. A sentence $\mathscr{P}$ of *SL* is a theorem in *SD* if and only if $\mathscr{P}$ is truth-functionally true.

c. Sentences $\mathscr{P}$ and $\mathscr{Q}$ of *SL* are equivalent in *SD* if and only if $\mathscr{P}$ and $\mathscr{Q}$ are truth-functionally equivalent.

---

## 5.5 THE DERIVATION SYSTEM *SD* +

Although there are important theoretical advantages to having a small set of derivation rules, there are definite practical advantages to having a larger set. With a larger set of rules, derivations are often easier to construct and much shorter. In this section we introduce a new natural deduction system, *SD* + . *SD* + contains all the derivation rules of *SD* plus some more. However, *SD* + is not a stronger system than *SD* in the sense that more arguments of *SL* can be shown to be valid or that more sentences of *SL* are theorems. A sentence is derivable in *SD* + from a set of sentences of *SL* if and only if it is derivable in *SD* from the set of sentences.

### *RULES OF INFERENCE*

Suppose that prior to line $n$ of a derivation two accessible lines, $i$ and $j$, contain $\mathscr{P} \supset \mathscr{Q}$ and $\sim \mathscr{Q}$, respectively. We can derive $\sim \mathscr{P}$ as follows:

| | | |
|---|---|---|
| $i$ | $\mathscr{P} \supset \mathscr{Q}$ | |
| $j$ | $\sim \mathscr{Q}$ | |
| $n$ |     \| $\mathscr{P}$ | Assumption |
| $n + 1$ |     \| $\mathscr{Q}$ | $i$, $n$ $\supset$E |
| $n + 2$ |     \| $\sim \mathscr{Q}$ | $j$ R |
| $n + 3$ | $\sim \mathscr{P}$ | $n$ - $n + 2$ $\sim$I |

To avoid going through this routine every time such a situation arises, we introduce the rule *Modus Tollens*.

*Modus Tollens* (MT)

$$\begin{array}{|l} \mathcal{P} \supset \mathcal{Q} \\ \sim \mathcal{Q} \\ \hline \sim \mathcal{P} \end{array}$$

Now suppose that prior to line $n$ of a derivation two accessible lines, $i$ and $j$, contain $\mathcal{P} \supset \mathcal{Q}$ and $\mathcal{Q} \supset \mathcal{R}$. A routine to derive $\mathcal{P} \supset \mathcal{R}$ beginning at line $n$ is as follows.

| | | |
|---|---|---|
| $i$ | $\mathcal{P} \supset \mathcal{Q}$ | |
| $j$ | $\mathcal{Q} \supset \mathcal{R}$ | |
| $n$ | $\mid \mathcal{P}$ | Assumption |
| $n + 1$ | $\mid \mathcal{Q}$ | $i$, $n$ $\supset$E |
| $n + 2$ | $\mid \mathcal{R}$ | $j$, $n + 1$ $\supset$E |
| $n + 3$ | $\mathcal{P} \supset \mathcal{R}$ | $n$-$n + 2$ $\supset$I |

To avoid this routine, we introduce the rule *Hypothetical Syllogism*.

*Hypothetical Syllogism* (HS)

$$\begin{array}{|l} \mathcal{P} \supset \mathcal{Q} \\ \mathcal{Q} \supset \mathcal{R} \\ \hline \mathcal{P} \supset \mathcal{R} \end{array}$$

Finally, suppose that prior to the line $n$ of a derivation two accessible lines, $i$ and $j$, contain $\mathcal{P} \vee \mathcal{Q}$ and $\sim \mathcal{P}$ and that we wish to derive $\mathcal{Q}$. A routine for this is as follows:

| | | |
|---|---|---|
| $i$ | $\mathcal{P} \vee \mathcal{Q}$ | |
| $j$ | $\sim \mathcal{P}$ | |
| $n$ | $\mid \mathcal{P}$ | Assumption |
| $n + 1$ | $\mid \mid \sim \mathcal{Q}$ | Assumption |
| $n + 2$ | $\mid \mid \sim \mathcal{P}$ | $j$ R |
| $n + 3$ | $\mid \mid \mathcal{P}$ | $n$ R |
| $n + 4$ | $\mid \mathcal{Q}$ | $n + 1$ - $n + 3$ $\sim$E |
| $n + 5$ | $\mid \mathcal{Q}$ | Assumption |
| $n + 6$ | $\mid \mathcal{Q}$ | $n + 5$ R |
| $n + 7$ | $\mathcal{Q}$ | $i$, $n$ - $n + 4$, $n + 5$-$n + 6$ $\vee$E |

The rule *Disjunctive Syllogism* allows us to avoid going through this routine for this and similar cases.

*Disjunctive Syllogism* (DS)

| | | |
|---|---|---|
| $\mathscr{P} \vee \mathscr{Q}$ | | $\mathscr{P} \vee \mathscr{Q}$ |
| $\sim \mathscr{P}$ | or | $\sim \mathscr{Q}$ |
| $\mathscr{Q}$ | | $\mathscr{P}$ |

The three rules of inference just introduced can be thought of as derived rules. They are added for convenience only; whatever we can derive with them, we can derive without them, using only the rules of *SD*.

*RULES OF REPLACEMENT*

In addition to rules of inference, there are also derivation rules known as *rules of replacement*. Rules of replacement, as their name suggests, allow us to derive some sentences from other sentences by replacing sentential components. For example, from the sentence

$$G \vee (H \& K)$$

we can certainly infer

$$G \vee (\sim \sim H \& K)$$

In this instance the sentential component 'H' has been replaced with '$\sim \sim$ H'. Also from

$$G \vee (\sim \sim H \& K)$$

we can certainly infer

$$G \vee (H \& K)$$

*Double Negation* is the rule of replacement that licenses such moves within a derivation.

*Double Negation* (DN)

$$\mathscr{P} :: \sim \sim \mathscr{P}$$

That is, by using Double Negation, we can derive from a sentence $\mathscr{Q}$ which contains $\mathscr{P}$ as a sentential component another sentence that is like $\mathscr{Q}$, except that one occurrence of the sentential component $\mathscr{P}$ has been replaced with $\sim \sim \mathscr{P}$. And, by using Double Negation, we can derive from a sentence $\mathscr{Q}$ which contains $\sim \sim \mathscr{P}$ as a sentential component another sentence that is like $\mathscr{Q}$, except that one occurrence of the sentential component $\sim \sim \mathscr{P}$ has been replaced with $\mathscr{P}$.

Double Negation can be applied to any of the sentential components of a sentence. For instance, from

$$G \vee (H \& K)$$

Double Negation permits us to derive

$$G \vee \sim \sim (H \& K)$$

And from

$$G \vee \sim\sim (H \& K)$$

Double Negation allows us to derive

$$G \vee (H \& K)$$

Since every sentence is a sentential component of itself, Double Negation applies to the entire sentence as well. In a derivation Double Negation permits us to go from

$$G \vee (H \& K)$$

to

$$\sim\sim [G \vee (H \& K)]$$

and from

$$\sim\sim [G \vee (H \& K)]$$

to

$$G \vee (H \& K)$$

Here are the rules of replacement for *SD* + :

*Rules of Replacement*

*Commutation* (Com)

$\mathscr{P} \& \mathscr{Q} :: \mathscr{Q} \& \mathscr{P}$
$\mathscr{P} \vee \mathscr{Q} :: \mathscr{Q} \vee \mathscr{P}$

*Association* (Assoc)

$\mathscr{P} \& (\mathscr{Q} \& \mathscr{R}) :: (\mathscr{P} \& \mathscr{Q}) \& \mathscr{R}$
$\mathscr{P} \vee (\mathscr{Q} \vee \mathscr{R}) :: (\mathscr{P} \vee \mathscr{Q}) \vee \mathscr{R}$

*Implication* (Impl)

$\mathscr{P} \supset \mathscr{Q} :: \sim \mathscr{P} \vee \mathscr{Q}$

*Double Negation* (DN)

$\mathscr{P} :: \sim\sim \mathscr{P}$

*De Morgan* (DeM)

$\sim (\mathscr{P} \& \mathscr{Q}) :: \sim \mathscr{P} \vee \sim \mathscr{Q}$
$\sim (\mathscr{P} \vee \mathscr{Q}) :: \sim \mathscr{P} \& \sim \mathscr{Q}$

*Idempotence* (Idem)

$\mathscr{P} :: \mathscr{P} \& \mathscr{P}$
$\mathscr{P} :: \mathscr{P} \vee \mathscr{P}$

*Transposition* (Trans)

$\mathscr{P} \supset \mathscr{Q} :: \sim \mathscr{Q} \supset \sim \mathscr{P}$

*Exportation* (Exp)

$\mathscr{P} \supset (\mathscr{Q} \supset \mathscr{R}) :: (\mathscr{P} \& \mathscr{Q}) \supset \mathscr{R}$

*Distribution* (Dist)

$\mathscr{P} \& (\mathscr{Q} \vee \mathscr{R}) :: (\mathscr{P} \& \mathscr{Q}) \vee (\mathscr{P} \& \mathscr{R})$
$\mathscr{P} \vee (\mathscr{Q} \& \mathscr{R}) :: (\mathscr{P} \vee \mathscr{Q}) \& (\mathscr{P} \vee \mathscr{R})$

*Equivalence* (Equiv)

$\mathscr{P} \equiv \mathscr{Q} :: (\mathscr{P} \supset \mathscr{Q}) \& (\mathscr{Q} \supset \mathscr{P})$
$\mathscr{P} \equiv \mathscr{Q} :: (\mathscr{P} \& \mathscr{Q}) \vee (\sim \mathscr{P} \& \sim \mathscr{Q})$

Rules of replacement always allow the replacement of sentential components. In addition, all these rules of replacement are two-way rules, that is, a sentential component that has the form of the sentence on the left of ':: ' can be replaced with a sentential component that has the form of the sentence on the right of ':: ' and vice versa.

Consider the following derivation:

Derive: J ⊃ [M ∨ (G ∨ I)]

| | | |
|---|---|---|
| 1 | J ⊃ [K ∨ (L ∨ H)] | Assumption |
| 2 | [(K ∨ L) ∨ H] ⊃ [(M ∨ G) ∨ I] | Assumption |
| 3 | J ⊃ [(K ∨ L) ∨ H] | 1 Assoc |
| 4 | J ⊃ [(M ∨ G) ∨ I] | 2, 3 HS |
| 5 | J ⊃ [M ∨ (G ∨ I)] | 4 Assoc |

Here the replacement rule Association has been used twice—first to replace a sentential component of the form $\mathscr{P} \vee (\mathscr{Q} \vee \mathscr{R})$ with a sentential component of the form $(\mathscr{P} \vee \mathscr{Q}) \vee \mathscr{R}$ and second to replace a sentential component of the form $(\mathscr{P} \vee \mathscr{Q}) \vee \mathscr{R}$ with a sentential component of the form $\mathscr{P} \vee (\mathscr{Q} \vee \mathscr{R})$.

Since all the derivation rules of *SD* are derivation rules of *SD* + , the procedures for properly applying the rules of *SD* apply to *SD* + as well. The rules of inference of *SD* + , including Modus Tollens, Hypothetical Syllogism, and Disjunctive Syllogism, must be applied to entire sentences on a line. Rules of replacement, on the other hand, can be applied to sentential components. The following derivation illustrates the proper use of several of the rules of replacement:

Derive: ~ C ≡ E

| | | |
|---|---|---|
| 1 | (D ∨ B) ∨ (E ⊃ ~ C) | Assumption |
| 2 | ~ B & [~ D & (~ E ⊃ C)] | Assumption |
| 3 | (~ B & ~ D) & (~ E ⊃ C) | 2 Assoc |
| 4 | ~ (B ∨ D) & (~ E ⊃ C) | 3 DeM |
| 5 | ~ (B ∨ D) | 4 &E |
| 6 | ~ (D ∨ B) | 5 Com |
| 7 | E ⊃ ~ C | 1, 6 DS |
| 8 | ~ E ⊃ C | 3 &E |
| 9 | ~ C ⊃ ~ ~ E | 8 Trans |
| 10 | ~ C ⊃ E | 9 DN |
| 11 | (~ C ⊃ E) & (E ⊃ ~ C) | 10, 7 &I |
| 12 | ~ C ≡ E | 11 Equiv |

Notice that each application of a derivation rule requires a separate line. Moreover, care must be taken to apply each derivation rule only to sentences that have the proper form (or, in the case of rules of replacement, sentences that have components that have the proper form).

Here is an example in which these points are ignored.

Derive: ~ A ⊃ [B ⊃ (G ∨ D)]

| | | | |
|---|---|---|---|
| 1 | (A ∨ ~ B) ∨ ~ C | Assumption | |
| 2 | (D ∨ G) ∨ C | Assumption | |
| 3 | ~ (~ A & B) ∨ ~ C | 1 DeM | **MISTAKE!** |
| 4 | (~ A & B) ⊃ ~ C | 3 Impl | |
| 5 | C ∨ (G ∨ D) | 2 Com | **MISTAKE!** |
| 6 | ~ C ⊃ (G ∨ D) | 5 Impl | **MISTAKE!** |
| 7 | (~ A & B) ⊃ (G ∨ D) | 4, 6 HS | |
| 8 | ~ A ⊃ [B ⊃ (G ∨ D)] | 7 Exp | |

De Morgan does not license entering the sentence on line 3. What De Morgan does allow is the replacement of a sentential component of the form ~ $\mathscr{P}$ ∨ ~ $\mathscr{Q}$ with a sentential component of the form ~ ($\mathscr{P}$ & $\mathscr{Q}$), but the sentential component 'A ∨ ~ B' does not have the form ~ $\mathscr{P}$ ∨ ~ $\mathscr{Q}$. However, by applying Double Negation to the first assumption, we can obtain '(~ ~ A ∨ ~ B) ∨ ~ C'. And this latter sentence does have a sentential component of the form ~ $\mathscr{P}$ ∨ ~ $\mathscr{Q}$, namely, ' ~ ~ A ∨ ~ B'. Here $\mathscr{P}$ is ' ~ A', and $\mathscr{Q}$ is 'B'. Hence the derivation should begin

Derive: ~ A ⊃ [B ⊃ (G ∨ D)]

| | | |
|---|---|---|
| 1 | (A ∨ ~ B) ∨ ~ C | Assumption |
| 2 | (D ∨ G) ∨ C | Assumption |
| 3 | (~ ~ A ∨ ~ B) ∨ ~ C | 1 DN |
| 4 | ~ (~ A & B) ∨ ~ C | 3 DeM |

The second mistake above (line 5), is that Commutation is applied twice within the same line. Each application of a rule, even if it is the same rule, requires a separate line. Correctly done, the derivation proceeds:

| | | |
|---|---|---|
| 5 | (~ A & B) ⊃ ~ C | 4 Impl |
| 6 | C ∨ (D ∨ G) | 2 Com |
| 7 | C ∨ (G ∨ D) | 6 Com |

The third mistake (line 6 of the original example) also stems from our trying to apply a rule of replacement to a sentential component that does not have the form required by the rule. Implication permits the replacement of a sentential component of the form ~ $\mathscr{P}$ ∨ $\mathscr{Q}$ with a sentential component of the form $\mathscr{P}$ ⊃ $\mathscr{Q}$, but 'C ∨ (G ∨ D)' does not have the form ~ $\mathscr{P}$ ∨ $\mathscr{Q}$. However, applying Double Negation to 'C', a sentential component of 'C ∨ (G ∨ D)', generates ' ~ ~ C ∨ (G ∨ D)'. This latter sentence does have the form ~ $\mathscr{P}$ ∨ $\mathscr{Q}$, where $\mathscr{P}$ is ' ~ C' and $\mathscr{Q}$ is 'G ∨ D'. Here is the entire derivation done correctly:

Derive: $\sim A \supset [B \supset (G \vee D)]$

| | | |
|---|---|---|
| 1 | $(A \vee \sim B) \vee \sim C$ | Assumption |
| 2 | $(D \vee G) \vee C$ | Assumption |
| 3 | $(\sim\sim A \vee \sim B) \vee \sim C$ | 1 DN |
| 4 | $\sim(\sim A \,\&\, B) \vee \sim C$ | 3 DeM |
| 5 | $(\sim A \,\&\, B) \supset \sim C$ | 4 Impl |
| 6 | $C \vee (D \vee G)$ | 2 Com |
| 7 | $C \vee (G \vee D)$ | 6 Com |
| 8 | $\sim\sim C \vee (G \vee D)$ | 7 DN |
| 9 | $\sim C \supset (G \vee D)$ | 8 Impl |
| 10 | $(\sim A \,\&\, B) \supset (G \vee D)$ | 5, 9 HS |
| 11 | $\sim A \supset [B \supset (G \vee D)]$ | 10 Exp |

The definitions of the basic concepts of *SD* + are exactly like the definitions for the basic concepts of *SD*, except that '*SD*' is replaced with '*SD* + '. For example, the concept of derivability is defined as follows:

> A sentence $\mathcal{P}$ of *SL* is *derivable in SD* + from a set Γ of sentences of *SL* if and only if there is a derivation in *SD* + in which all the primary assumptions are members of Γ and $\mathcal{P}$ occurs in the scope of only those assumptions.

Consequently, tests for the various syntactic properties are carried out in the same way. To show that an argument is valid in *SD* + , we construct a derivation in *SD* + that shows that the conclusion of the argument is derivable in *SD* + from the set consisting of only the premises of the argument. To show that a sentence $\mathcal{P}$ of *SL* is a theorem in *SD* + , we show that $\mathcal{P}$ is derivable in *SD* + from the empty set. And so on for the other properties. Remember that although technically *SD* and *SD* + are different syntactic systems, they are equally strong in the sense that whatever can be derived in one can be derived in the other. The practical advantage of *SD* + is that it enables us to construct shorter derivations.

*THE DERIVATION RULES OF SD +*

All the Derivation Rules of *SD*
Plus
Rules of Inference

| *Modus Tollens* (MT) | *Hypothetical Syllogism* (HS) |
|---|---|
| $\mathcal{P} \supset \mathcal{Q}$ | $\mathcal{P} \supset \mathcal{Q}$ |
| $\sim \mathcal{Q}$ | $\mathcal{Q} \supset \mathcal{R}$ |
| $\sim \mathcal{P}$ | $\mathcal{P} \supset \mathcal{R}$ |

*Disjunctive Syllogism* (DS)

$$\begin{array}{|l} \mathcal{P} \vee \mathcal{Q} \\ \sim \mathcal{P} \\ \mathcal{Q} \end{array} \qquad \text{or} \qquad \begin{array}{|l} \mathcal{P} \vee \mathcal{Q} \\ \sim \mathcal{Q} \\ \mathcal{P} \end{array}$$

## Rules of Replacement

*Commutation* (Com)

$\mathcal{P} \,\&\, \mathcal{Q} :: \mathcal{Q} \,\&\, \mathcal{P}$
$\mathcal{P} \vee \mathcal{Q} :: \mathcal{Q} \vee \mathcal{P}$

*Association* (Assoc)

$\mathcal{P} \,\&\, (\mathcal{Q} \,\&\, \mathcal{R}) :: (\mathcal{P} \,\&\, \mathcal{Q}) \,\&\, \mathcal{R}$
$\mathcal{P} \vee (\mathcal{Q} \vee \mathcal{R}) :: (\mathcal{P} \vee \mathcal{Q}) \vee \mathcal{R}$

*Implication* (Impl)

$\mathcal{P} \supset \mathcal{Q} :: \sim \mathcal{P} \vee \mathcal{Q}$

*Double Negation* (DN)

$\mathcal{P} :: \sim \sim \mathcal{P}$

*De Morgan* (DeM)

$\sim (\mathcal{P} \,\&\, \mathcal{Q}) :: \sim \mathcal{P} \vee \sim \mathcal{Q}$
$\sim (\mathcal{P} \vee \mathcal{Q}) :: \sim \mathcal{P} \,\&\, \sim \mathcal{Q}$

*Idempotence* (Idem)

$\mathcal{P} :: \mathcal{P} \,\&\, \mathcal{P}$
$\mathcal{P} :: \mathcal{P} \vee \mathcal{P}$

*Transposition* (Trans)

$\mathcal{P} \supset \mathcal{Q} :: \sim \mathcal{Q} \supset \sim \mathcal{P}$

*Exportation* (Exp)

$\mathcal{P} \supset (\mathcal{Q} \supset \mathcal{R}) :: (\mathcal{P} \,\&\, \mathcal{Q}) \supset \mathcal{R}$

*Distribution* (Dist)

$\mathcal{P} \,\&\, (\mathcal{Q} \vee \mathcal{R}) :: (\mathcal{P} \,\&\, \mathcal{Q}) \vee (\mathcal{P} \,\&\, \mathcal{R})$
$\mathcal{P} \vee (\mathcal{Q} \,\&\, \mathcal{R}) :: (\mathcal{P} \vee \mathcal{Q}) \,\&\, (\mathcal{P} \vee \mathcal{R})$

*Equivalence* (Equiv)

$\mathcal{P} \equiv \mathcal{Q} :: (\mathcal{P} \supset \mathcal{Q}) \,\&\, (\mathcal{Q} \supset \mathcal{P})$
$\mathcal{P} \equiv \mathcal{Q} :: (\mathcal{P} \,\&\, \mathcal{Q}) \vee (\sim \mathcal{P} \,\&\, \sim \mathcal{Q})$

### 5.5E EXERCISES

**1.** Show that the following derivability claims hold in *SD* + :

a. $\{D \supset E, E \supset (Z \,\&\, W), \sim Z \vee \sim W\} \vdash \sim D$
*b. $\{(H \,\&\, G) \supset (L \vee K), G \,\&\, H\} \vdash K \vee L$
c. $\{(W \supset S) \,\&\, \sim M, (\sim W \supset H) \vee M, (\sim S \supset H) \supset K\} \vdash K$
*d. $\{[(K \,\&\, J) \vee I] \vee \sim Y, Y \,\&\, [(I \vee K) \supset F]\} \vdash F \vee N$
e. $\{(M \vee B) \vee (C \vee G), \sim B \,\&\, (\sim G \,\&\, \sim M)\} \vdash C$
*f. $\{\sim L \vee (\sim Z \vee \sim U), (U \,\&\, G) \vee H, Z\} \vdash L \supset H$

**2.** Show that each of the following is valid in *SD* + :

a. $\sim Y \supset \sim Z$
$\sim Z \supset \sim X$
$\sim X \supset \sim Y$

---
$Y \equiv Z$

*b. $(\sim A \,\&\, \sim B) \vee (\sim A \,\&\, \sim C)$
$(E \,\&\, D) \supset A$

---
$\sim E \vee \sim D$

c. $(F \,\&\, G) \vee (H \,\&\, \sim I)$
$I \supset \sim (F \,\&\, D)$

---
$I \supset \sim D$

*d. $F \supset (\sim G \vee H)$
$F \supset G$
$\sim (H \vee I)$

---
$F \supset J$

e. $F \supset (G \supset H)$
$\sim I \supset (F \vee H)$
$F \supset G$

---
$I \vee H$

*f. $G \supset (H \,\&\, \sim K)$
$H \equiv (L \,\&\, I)$
$\sim I \vee K$

---
$\sim G$

g. $[(X \,\&\, Z) \,\&\, Y] \vee (\sim X \supset \sim Y)$
$X \supset Z$
$Z \supset Y$

---
$X \equiv Y$

**3.** Show that each of the following is a theorem in *SD* + :

a. $A \vee \sim A$
*b. $\sim\sim\sim\sim\sim (A \,\&\, \sim A)$
c. $A \vee [(\sim A \vee B) \,\&\, (\sim A \vee C)]$
*d. $[(A \,\&\, B) \supset (B \,\&\, A)] \,\&\, [\sim (A \,\&\, B) \supset \sim (B \,\&\, A)]$
e. $[A \supset (B \,\&\, C)] \equiv [(\sim B \vee \sim C) \supset \sim A]$
*f. $[A \vee (B \vee C)] \equiv [C \vee (B \vee A)]$
g. $[A \supset (B \equiv C)] \equiv (A \supset [(\sim B \vee C) \,\&\, (\sim C \vee B)])$
*h. $(A \vee [B \supset (A \supset B)]) \equiv (A \vee [(\sim A \vee \sim B) \vee B])$
i. $[\sim A \supset (\sim B \supset C)] \supset [(A \vee B) \vee (\sim\sim B \vee C)]$
*j. $(\sim A \equiv \sim A) \equiv [\sim (\sim A \supset A) \equiv (A \supset \sim A)]$

**4.** Show that the members of each of the following pairs of sentences are equivalent in *SD* + :

a. $A \vee B$
$\sim (\sim A \,\&\, \sim B)$

*b. $A \,\&\, (B \vee C)$
$(B \,\&\, A) \vee (C \,\&\, A)$

c. $(A \,\&\, B) \supset C$
$\sim (A \supset C) \supset \sim B$

*d. $(A \vee B) \vee C$
$\sim A \supset (\sim B \supset C)$

e. $A \vee (B \equiv C)$
$A \vee (\sim B \equiv \sim C)$

*f. $(A \,\&\, B) \vee [(C \,\&\, D) \vee A]$
$([(C \vee A) \,\&\, (C \vee B)] \,\&\, [(D \vee A) \,\&\, (D \vee B)]) \vee A$

**5.** Show that the following sets of sentences are inconsistent in *SD* + :

a. $\{[(E \,\&\, F) \vee \sim\sim G] \supset M,\ \sim [[(G \vee E) \,\&\, (F \vee G)] \supset (M \,\&\, M)]\}$

*b. $\{\sim [(\sim C \vee \sim\sim C) \vee \sim\sim C]\}$

c. $\{M \,\&\, L,\ [L \,\&\, (M \,\&\, \sim S)] \supset K,\ \sim K \vee \sim S,\ \sim (K \equiv \sim S)\}$

*d. $\{B \,\&\, (H \vee Z),\ \sim Z \supset K,\ (B \equiv Z) \supset \sim Z,\ \sim K\}$

e. $\{\sim [W \,\&\, (Z \vee Y)],\ (Z \supset Y) \supset Z,\ (Y \supset Z) \supset W\}$

*f. $\{[(F \supset G) \vee (\sim F \supset G)] \supset H,\ (A \,\&\, H) \supset \sim A,\ A \vee \sim H\}$

**6.** Symbolize the following arguments in *SL*, and show that they are valid in *SD* + :

a. If the phone rings Ed is calling, or if the beeper beeps Ed is calling. If not both Ed and Agnes are at home today, then it's not the case that if the phone rings, Ed is calling. Ed isn't home today, and he isn't calling. So the beeper won't beep.

*b. If Monday is a bad day, then I'll lose my job provided the boss doesn't call in sick. The boss won't call in sick. So I'll lose my job—since either Monday will be a bad day, or the boss won't call in sick only if I lose my job.

c. Army coats are warm only if they're either made of wool or not made of cotton or rayon. If army coats are not made of rayon, then they're made of cotton. Hence if they're not made of wool, army coats aren't warm.

*d. If either the greenhouse is dry, or the greenhouse is sunny if and only if it's not raining, the violets will wither. But if the violets wither the greenhouse is sunny, or if the violets wither the greenhouse isn't dry. It's raining, and the greenhouse isn't sunny. So the greenhouse is dry only if the violets won't wither.

e. It's not the case that John is rich and Hugo isn't. In fact, Hugo isn't rich, unless Moe is. And if Moe just emptied his bank account, then he isn't rich. Thus, if John is rich, then it's not the case that either Moe emptied his bank account or Moe isn't rich.

*f. Neither aspirin nor gin will ease my headache, unless it's psychosomatic. If it's psychosomatic and I'm really not ill, then I'll go out to a party and drink some martinis. So if I'm not ill and don't drink any martinis, then aspirin won't ease my headache.

g. If I stay on this highway and don't slow down, I'll arrive in Montreal by 5:00. If I don't put my foot on the brake, I won't slow down. Either I won't slow down, or I'll stop for a cup of coffee at the next exit. I'll stop for a cup of coffee at the next exit only if I'm falling asleep. So if I don't arrive in Montreal by 5:00, then I'll stay on this highway only if I'm falling asleep and I put my foot on the brake.

*h. The weather is fine if and only if it's not snowing, and it's not snowing if and only if the sky is clear. So either the weather is fine, the sky is clear, and it's not snowing; or it's snowing, the sky isn't clear, and the weather is lousy.

**7.** Symbolize the following passages in *SL*, and show that the resulting sets of sentences of *SL* are inconsistent in *SD* + .

a. Unless Stowe believes that all liberals are atheists, his claims about current politics are unintelligible. But if liberals are atheists only if they're not churchgoers, then Stowe's claims about current politics are nevertheless intelligible. Liberals are in fact churchgoers if and only if Stowe doesn't believe that they're all atheists, and if liberals aren't atheists, then Stowe doesn't believe that they are atheists. Liberals aren't atheists.

*b. Either Congress won't cut taxes or the elderly and the poor will riot, if but only if big business prospers. If the elderly don't riot, then Congress won't cut taxes. It won't happen that both the poor will riot and big business will prosper, and it won't happen that the poor don't riot and big business doesn't prosper. But if big business prospers, then Congress will cut taxes.

**8a.** Suppose that we can derive $\mathscr{Q}$ from $\mathscr{P}$ by using only the rules of replacement. Why can we be sure that we can derive $\mathscr{P}$ from $\mathscr{Q}$?

*b. Why must all arguments that are valid in *SD* be valid in *SD* + as well?

c. Suppose we develop a new natural deduction system *SD**. Let *SD** contain all the derivation rules of *SD* and in addition the derivation rule Absorption.

*Absorption*

| $\mathscr{P} \supset \mathscr{Q}$
|
| $\mathscr{P} \supset (\mathscr{P} \,\&\, \mathscr{Q})$

Using only the derivation rules of *SD*, develop a routine that shows that any sentence derived by using Absorption could be derived in *SD* without using it.

## GLOSSARY[3]

DERIVABILITY IN *SD*: A sentence $\mathscr{P}$ of *SL* is *derivable in SD* from a set Γ of sentences of *SL* if and only if there is a derivation in *SD* in which all the primary assumptions are members of Γ and $\mathscr{P}$ occurs in the scope of only those assumptions.

VALIDITY IN *SD*: An argument of *SL* is *valid in SD* if and only if the conclusion of the argument is derivable in *SD* from the set consisting of the premises. An argument of *SL* is *invalid in SD* if and only if it is not valid in *SD*.

THEOREM IN *SD*: A sentence $\mathscr{P}$ of *SL* is a *theorem in SD* if and only if $\mathscr{P}$ is derivable in *SD* from the empty set.

EQUIVALENCE IN *SD*: Sentences $\mathscr{P}$ and $\mathscr{Q}$ of *SL* are *equivalent in SD* if and only if $\mathscr{Q}$ is derivable in *SD* from $\{\mathscr{P}\}$ and $\mathscr{P}$ is derivable in *SD* from $\{\mathscr{Q}\}$.

INCONSISTENCY IN *SD*: A set Γ of sentences of *SL* is *inconsistent in SD* if and only if both a sentence $\mathscr{P}$ of *SL* and its negation $\sim \mathscr{P}$ are derivable in *SD* from Γ. A set Γ of sentences of *SL* is *consistent in SD* if and only if it is not inconsistent in *SD*.

[3] Similar definitions hold for the derivation system *SD* + .

Chapter

# 6

# SENTENTIAL LOGIC: METATHEORY

## 6.1 MATHEMATICAL INDUCTION

In the three previous chapters we have concentrated on developing and using techniques of sentential logic, both semantic and syntactic. In this chapter we step back to prove some claims *about* the semantics and syntax of sentential logic. Such results constitute the *metatheory* of sentential logic.

For the language *SL*, the semantic accounts of such logical properties of sentences and sets of sentences of *SL* as validity, consistency, and equivalence given in Chapter Three are fundamental in the sense that they are the standards by which other accounts of these properties are judged. For instance, although the techniques of Chapter Five are purely syntactical—all the derivation rules appeal to the structures or forms of sentences, not to their truth-conditions—those techniques are intended to yield results paralleling those yielded by the semantic techniques of Chapter Three. One of the important metatheoretic results that we shall prove in this chapter is that this parallel does hold. We shall prove this by proving that the natural deduction system *SD* allows us to construct all and only the derivations we want to be able to construct, given the semantics of Chapter Three. Specifically, we shall prove that given any set $\Gamma$ of sentences and any sentence $\mathcal{P}$ of *SL*, $\mathcal{P}$ is derivable from $\Gamma$ in *SD* if and only if $\mathcal{P}$ is truth-functionally entailed by $\Gamma$. The results mentioned at the end of Section 5.3 follow from this. For example, all and only the truth-functionally valid arguments of *SL* are valid in *SD*, and all and only the truth-functionally true sentences of *SL* are theorems in *SD*.

Before establishing the foregoing results we introduce the method of proof known as *mathematical induction* and use that method to establish some other interesting results in the metatheory of sentential logic. We shall then use mathematical induction in later sections to prove the claims made in the previous paragraph. Mathematical induction is an extremely powerful method, in that it allows us to establish results holding of an infinite number of items.

We introduce mathematical induction with an example. It seems obvious that in each sentence of *SL* the number of left parentheses equals the number of right parentheses. How might we *prove* that this claim is true for every sentence of *SL*? We cannot show that it is true by considering the sentences of *SL* one at a time; there are infinitely many sentences of *SL* and so we would never get through all of them. Rather, we shall reason more generally about the sentences of *SL*, using the definition of those sentences that was presented in Chapter Two:

1. Every sentence letter is a sentence.
2. If $\mathscr{P}$ is a sentence, then $\sim \mathscr{P}$ is a sentence.
3. If $\mathscr{P}$ and $\mathscr{Q}$ are sentences, then $(\mathscr{P} \,\&\, \mathscr{Q})$ is a sentence.
4. If $\mathscr{P}$ and $\mathscr{Q}$ are sentences, then $(\mathscr{P} \vee \mathscr{Q})$ is a sentence.
5. If $\mathscr{P}$ and $\mathscr{Q}$ are sentences, then $(\mathscr{P} \supset \mathscr{Q})$ is a sentence.
6. If $\mathscr{P}$ and $\mathscr{Q}$ are sentences, then $(\mathscr{P} \equiv \mathscr{Q})$ is a sentence.
7. Nothing is a sentence unless it can be formed by repeated application of clauses 1–6.

It is trivial to show that every atomic sentence—that is, every sentence formed in accordance with clause 1, has an equal number of left and right parentheses, namely 0, because atomic sentences contain no parentheses. All other sentences of *SL* are formed in accordance with clauses 2–6. We note that in each of these cases, an equal number of outermost left and right parentheses are added to those already occurring in the sentence's immediate components to form the new sentence (0 of each in clause 2, 1 of each in clauses 3–6). Therefore, if we can be sure that the immediate components $\mathscr{P}$ and $\mathscr{Q}$ of sentences formed in accordance with clauses 2–6 themselves contain an equal number of parentheses, then we may conclude that the application of one of these clauses will result in a new sentence that also contains an equal number of left and right parentheses.

How can we be sure, though, that each of the immediate components of a molecular sentence *does* contain an equal number of left and right parentheses? Start with molecular sentences that contain one occurrence of a connective—sentences like '$\sim$ A', '(A $\supset$ B)', and '(A & B)'. Every sentence that contains one occurrence of a connective has one of the forms $\sim \mathscr{P}$, $(\mathscr{P} \,\&\, \mathscr{Q})$, $(\mathscr{P} \vee \mathscr{Q})$, $(\mathscr{P} \supset \mathscr{Q})$, or $(\mathscr{P} \equiv \mathscr{Q})$, in accordance with clauses 2–6. Moreover, in each case the immediate components $\mathscr{P}$ and $\mathscr{Q}$ are atomic. We have already noted that every atomic sentence contains an equal number of left and right parentheses, namely 0, and so, because clauses 2–6 each add an equal number of left and right parentheses to the ones already occurring in its immediate components, every molecular sentence with one occurrence of a connective must also have an equal number of left and right parentheses.

Now consider molecular sentences that contain two occurrences of connectives—sentences like '$\sim \sim$ A', '$\sim$ (A $\vee$ B)', '(A $\vee$ $\sim$ B)', '((A $\equiv$ B) $\supset$ C)', and

'(A ∨ (B & C))'. We may reason as we did in the previous paragraph. Every sentence that contains two occurrences of connectives has one of the forms $\sim \mathscr{P}$, $(\mathscr{P} \,\&\, \mathscr{Q})$, $(\mathscr{P} \vee \mathscr{Q})$, $(\mathscr{P} \supset \mathscr{Q})$, or $(\mathscr{P} \equiv \mathscr{Q})$, in accordance with clauses 2–6. And in each case the immediate components $\mathscr{P}$ and $\mathscr{Q}$ each contain fewer than two occurrences of connectives. We have already found that in all sentences that contain fewer than two occurrences of connectives (atomic sentences or sentences containing one occurrence of a connective), the number of left parentheses equals the number of right parentheses. Therefore, because clauses 2–6 each add an equal number of left and right parentheses to those already occurring in its immediate components, we may conclude that every molecular sentence with two occurrences of connectives also has an equal number of left and right parentheses.

If we turn to sentences that contain three occurrences of connectives, sentences like '~ ~ ~ A', '~ (~ A ∨ B)', '((A ⊃ B) & (A ∨ C))', and '(~ (A ≡ B) ≡ C)', the same pattern of reasoning emerges. In every sentence that contains three occurrences of connectives, the immediate components each contain fewer than three occurrences of connectives—either 0, 1, or 2 occurrences. We have already shown that in any sentence of *SL* that contains either 0, 1, or 2 occurrences of connectives, the number of left parentheses equals the number of right parentheses. Therefore, because clauses 2–6 each add an equal number of left and right parentheses, we may conclude that the number of left parentheses in a sentence that contains three occurrences of connectives is equal to the number of right parentheses. Having established that the claim holds true of every sentence with three or fewer occurrences of connectives, we may show that it also holds for every sentence with four occurrences, then for every sentence with five, and so on—in each case using the same reasoning that we have used for earlier cases. Generally, as soon as we have established that the claim holds for every sentence with $\mathscr{k}$ or fewer occurrences of connectives, the same pattern of reasoning shows that the claim also holds for every sentence that contains $\mathscr{k} + 1$ occurrences of connectives.

We shall now present an argument by mathematical induction that establishes that our claim is true of *every* sentence of *SL*:

> Every sentence of *SL* containing 0 occurrences of connectives, that is, every atomic sentence of *SL*, is such that the number of left parentheses in that sentence equals the number of right parentheses.
>
> If every sentence of *SL* with $\mathscr{k}$ or fewer occurrences of connectives is such that the number of left parentheses in that sentence equals the number of right parentheses, then every sentence of *SL* with $\mathscr{k} + 1$ occurrences of connectives is also such that the number of left parentheses in that sentence equals the number of right parentheses.
>
> ---
>
> Therefore every sentence of *SL* is such that the number of left parentheses in that sentence equals the number of right parentheses.

(Here we use '$\mathscr{k}$' as a variable ranging over the nonnegative integers, that is, the positive integers plus 0.) This argument is logically valid—if the premises are true, then the conclusion is true as well. The first premise is our claim about parentheses for sentences with no connectives, and the second premise says that it follows that the claim also holds for sentences containing one occurrence of a connective. Having concluded that the claim holds for all sentences containing 0 or 1 occurrences of connectives, we are assured by the second premise that the claim must also hold for sentences containing two occurrences of connectives. Having concluded that the claim holds for all sentences containing 0, 1, and 2 occurrences of connectives, we are assured by the second premise that the claim also holds for sentences containing three occurrences of connectives, and so on for any number of occurrences of connectives that a sentence may contain. Because the argument is logically valid, we can establish that its conclusion is true by showing that both premises are true. We have already shown that the first premise is true. Sentences that contain 0 occurrences of connectives are atomic sentences, and atomic sentences are simply sentence letters. The first premise is called the *basis clause* of the argument.

The second premise of the argument is called the *inductive step*. We shall prove that the inductive step is true by generalizing on the reasoning that we have already used. Assume that the antecedent of the inductive step is true for an arbitrary nonnegative integer $k$—that every sentence of *SL* that contains $k$ or fewer occurrences of connectives contains an equal number of left and right parentheses. We call this assumption (the antecedent of the inductive step) the *inductive hypothesis*. We must show that on this assumption it follows that any sentence $\mathcal{P}$ that has $k + 1$ occurrences of connectives also contains an equal number of left and right parentheses. Since $k$ is nonnegative, $k + 1$ is positive and hence such a sentence $\mathcal{P}$ contains at least one occurrence of a connective. So $\mathcal{P}$ will be a molecular sentence, having one of the forms $\sim \mathcal{Q}$, $(\mathcal{Q} \,\&\, \mathcal{R})$, $(\mathcal{Q} \vee \mathcal{R})$, $(\mathcal{Q} \supset \mathcal{R})$, $(\mathcal{Q} \equiv \mathcal{R})$. We divide these forms into two cases.

Case 1: $\mathcal{P}$ has the form $\sim \mathcal{Q}$. If $\sim \mathcal{Q}$ contains $k + 1$ occurrences of connectives, then $\mathcal{Q}$ contains $k$ occurrences of connectives. By the inductive hypothesis (that every sentence containing $k$ or fewer connectives has an equal number of left and right parentheses), the number of left parentheses in $\mathcal{Q}$ equals the number of right parentheses in $\mathcal{Q}$. But $\sim \mathcal{Q}$ contains all the parentheses occurring in $\mathcal{Q}$ and no others. So $\sim \mathcal{Q}$ contains an equal number of left and right parentheses as well.

Case 2: $\mathcal{P}$ has one of the forms $(\mathcal{Q} \,\&\, \mathcal{R})$, $(\mathcal{Q} \vee \mathcal{R})$, $(\mathcal{Q} \supset \mathcal{R})$, or $(\mathcal{Q} \equiv \mathcal{R})$. In each instance, if $\mathcal{P}$ contains $k + 1$ occurrences of connectives, then each of its immediate components, $\mathcal{Q}$ and $\mathcal{R}$, must contain $k$ or fewer occurrences of connectives. By the inductive hypothesis, then,

a. the number of left parentheses in $\mathcal{Q}$ equals the number of right parentheses in $\mathcal{Q}$,

and

b. the number of left parentheses in $\mathcal{R}$ equals the number of right parentheses in $\mathcal{R}$.

The number of left parentheses in $\mathscr{P}$ is

c. the number of left parentheses in $\mathscr{Q}$ plus the number of left parentheses in $\mathscr{R}$ plus 1—the one for the outermost left parenthesis in $\mathscr{P}$

and the number of right parentheses in $\mathscr{P}$ is

d. the number of right parentheses in $\mathscr{Q}$ plus the number of right parentheses in $\mathscr{R}$ plus 1.

By simple arithmetic, using (a) and (b), it follows that (c) equals (d)—$\mathscr{P}$ therefore has an equal number of left and right parentheses as well. This completes our proof that the second premise, the inductive step, is true. Having established that both premises are true, we may conclude that the conclusion is true as well. Every sentence of *SL* contains an equal number of left and right parentheses.

We may now generally characterize arguments by mathematical induction. In such an argument, we arrange the items about which we wish to prove some thesis in a series of groups. In our example, we arranged the sentences of *SL* into the series: all sentences containing 0 occurrences of connectives, all sentences containing 1 occurrence of connectives, all sentences containing 2 occurrences of connectives, and so on. Every sentence of *SL* appears in some group in this series—any sentence with $k$ occurrences of connectives will be part of group $k + 1$ in the series. Having arranged the items in such a series, an argument by mathematical induction will then take the following form:[1]

> The thesis holds for every member of the first group in the series.
>
> For each group in the series, if the thesis holds of every member of every prior group then the thesis holds for every member of that group as well.
>
> ---
>
> The thesis holds for every member of every group of the series.

All arguments of this form are valid. Of course, only those with true premises are sound. Hence, to establish that the thesis holds for every member of every group in the series, we must first show that the thesis does hold for every member of the first group and then that, no matter what group in the series we consider, the thesis holds for every member of that group if it holds for every member of every prior group. The first premise of such arguments is called the *basis clause*, and the second premise is called the *inductive step*. The antecedent of the second premise is called the *inductive hypothesis*.

We further illustrate mathematical induction with another example. Let $\mathscr{P}$ be a sentence that contains only '$\sim$', '$\vee$', and '&' as connectives, and let $\mathscr{P}'$ be

[1] Strictly speaking, this is the form for arguments by *strong* mathematical induction. There is another type of mathematical induction, known as *weak* induction. We shall use only the strong variety of mathematical induction in this text. There is no loss here, for every claim that can be proved by weak mathematical induction can also be proved by strong mathematical induction.

the sentence that results from

a. replacing each occurrence of '∨' in $\mathscr{P}$ with '&', and
b. replacing each occurrence of '&' in $\mathscr{P}$ with '∨', and
c. adding a '~' in front of each atomic component of $\mathscr{P}$.

We shall call a sentence that contains only '~', '∨', and '&' as connectives a *TWA* sentence (short for '*t*ilde, *w*edge, and *a*mpersand'), and we call the sentence $\mathscr{P}'$ that results from $\mathscr{P}$ by (a), (b), and (c) the *dual* of $\mathscr{P}$. Here are some examples of duals for TWA sentences:

| $\mathscr{P}$ | *Dual of* $\mathscr{P}$ |
|---|---|
| A | ~ A |
| ((A ∨ F) & G) | ((~ A & ~ F) ∨ ~ G) |
| (((B & C) & C) ∨ D) | (((~ B ∨ ~ C) ∨ ~ C) & ~ D) |
| ~ ((A ∨ ~ B) ∨ (~ A & ~ B)) | ~ ((~ A & ~ ~ B) & (~ ~ A ∨ ~ ~ B)) |

We shall use mathematical induction to establish the following thesis:

Every TWA sentence $\mathscr{P}$ is such that $\mathscr{P}$ and its dual $\mathscr{P}'$ have opposite truth-values on each truth-value assignment (i.e., if $\mathscr{P}$ true then $\mathscr{P}'$ is false and if $\mathscr{P}$ is false then $\mathscr{P}'$ is true).

As in the previous example, our series will classify sentences by the number of occurrences of connectives that they contain:

*Basis clause:* Every TWA sentence $\mathscr{P}$ of *SL* that contains 0 occurrences of connectives is such that $\mathscr{P}$ and its dual $\mathscr{P}'$ have opposite truth-values on each truth-value assignment.

*Inductive step:* If every TWA sentence $\mathscr{P}$ of *SL* with $k$ or fewer occurrences of connectives is such that $\mathscr{P}$ and its dual $\mathscr{P}'$ have opposite truth-values on each truth-value assignment, then every TWA sentence $\mathscr{P}$ of *SL* with $k + 1$ occurrences of connectives is such that $\mathscr{P}$ and its dual $\mathscr{P}'$ have opposite truth-values on each truth-value assignment.

---

*Conclusion:* Every TWA sentence $\mathscr{P}$ of *SL* is such that $\mathscr{P}$ and its dual $\mathscr{P}'$ have opposite truth-values on each truth-value assignment.

To show that the conclusion of this argument is true, we must show that the first premise, the basis clause, is true and also that the second premise, the inductive step, is true.

The basis clause is simple. A TWA sentence $\mathscr{P}$ that contains zero occurrences of connectives must be an atomic sentence, and its dual is ~ $\mathscr{P}$—because there are no connectives to replace, we simply place a tilde in front of the atomic sentence. If $\mathscr{P}$ is true on a truth-value assignment, then according to the characteristic truth-table for the tilde, ~ $\mathscr{P}$ must be false. And if $\mathscr{P}$ is false on a truth-value assignment, then $\sim \mathscr{P}$ is true. We conclude that $\mathscr{P}$ and its dual have opposite truth-values on each truth-value assignment.

We now turn to the inductive step. We assume that the inductive hypothesis is true for all sentences that contain fewer than $k + 1$ connectives—that is, that every TWA sentence that contains fewer than $k + 1$ occurrences of connectives is such that it and its dual have opposite truth-values on each truth value assignment. We must show that it follows from this assumption that the claim is also true of all TWA sentences that contain $k + 1$ occurrences of connectives. A TWA sentence $\mathscr{P}$ that contains $k + 1$ occurrences of connectives must be molecular and, because it is TWA, it will have one of the three forms $\sim \mathscr{Q}$, $(\mathscr{Q} \vee \mathscr{R})$, or $(\mathscr{Q} \& \mathscr{R})$. We will consider each form.

Case 1: $\mathscr{P}$ has the form $\sim \mathscr{Q}$. If $\mathscr{P}$ contains $k + 1$ occurrences of connectives, then $\mathscr{Q}$ contains $k$ occurrences of connectives, and $\mathscr{Q}$ is a TWA sentence (if it were not—if it contained a horseshoe or triple bar—then $\mathscr{P}$ would not be a TWA sentence either). Let $\mathscr{Q}'$ be the dual of $\mathscr{Q}$. Then the dual of $\mathscr{P}$ is $\sim \mathscr{Q}'$, the sentence that results from $\sim \mathscr{Q}$ by making the changes (a), (b), and (c) of our definition of dual sentences within $\mathscr{Q}$, and leaving the initial tilde of $\sim \mathscr{Q}$ intact.

If $\mathscr{P}$, that is, $\sim \mathscr{Q}$, is true on a truth-value assignment, then $\mathscr{Q}$ is false. Because $\mathscr{Q}$ is a TWA sentence with fewer than $k + 1$ occurrences of connectives, it follows from the inductive hypothesis that $\mathscr{Q}'$ is true. Therefore $\sim \mathscr{Q}'$—the dual of $\mathscr{P}$—is false. So if $\mathscr{P}$ is true, its dual is false. If, on the other hand, $\mathscr{P}$ is false on a truth-value assignment, then $\mathscr{Q}$ is true. It follows from the inductive hypothesis that $\mathscr{Q}'$ is false, and therefore $\sim \mathscr{Q}'$ is true. So if $\mathscr{P}$ is false, its dual is true. We conclude that $\mathscr{P}$ and its dual have opposite truth-values on each truth-value assignment.

Case 2: $\mathscr{P}$ has the form $(\mathscr{Q} \vee \mathscr{R})$. If $\mathscr{P}$ contains $k + 1$ occurrences of connectives, then $\mathscr{Q}$ and $\mathscr{R}$ each contain $k$ or fewer occurrences of connectives. $\mathscr{Q}$ and $\mathscr{R}$ are also TWA sentences. Let $\mathscr{Q}'$ be the dual of $\mathscr{Q}$ and $\mathscr{R}'$ the dual of $\mathscr{R}$. Then the dual of $\mathscr{P}$ is $(\mathscr{Q}' \& \mathscr{R}')$—the changes specified by (a), (b), and (c) must be made within $\mathscr{Q}$, yielding its dual, and within $\mathscr{R}$, yielding *its* dual, and the main connective '$\vee$' of $\mathscr{P}$ must be replaced with '&'.

If $\mathscr{P}$ is true on a truth-value assignment, then by the characteristic truth-table for the wedge, either $\mathscr{Q}$ is true or $\mathscr{R}$ is true. Because $\mathscr{Q}$ and $\mathscr{R}$ each contain $k$ or fewer occurrences of connectives, it follows from the inductive hypothesis that either $\mathscr{Q}'$ is false or $\mathscr{R}'$ is false. Either way, $(\mathscr{Q}' \& \mathscr{R}')$, the dual of $\mathscr{P}$, must be false as well. On the other hand, if $\mathscr{P}$ is false on a truth-value assignment, then both $\mathscr{Q}$ and $\mathscr{R}$ must be false. By the inductive hypothesis, both $\mathscr{Q}'$ and $\mathscr{R}'$ are true. So $(\mathscr{Q}' \& \mathscr{R}')$ is true as well. We conclude that $\mathscr{P}$ and its dual have opposite truth-values on each truth-value assignment.

Case 3: $\mathscr{P}$ has the form $(\mathscr{Q} \& \mathscr{R})$. If $\mathscr{P}$ contains $k + 1$ occurrences of connectives then $\mathscr{Q}$ and $\mathscr{R}$ each contain $k$ or fewer occurrences of connectives. And they are also TWA sentences. Let $\mathscr{Q}'$ be the dual of $\mathscr{Q}$, and $\mathscr{R}'$ the dual of $\mathscr{R}$. Then the dual of $\mathscr{P}$ is $(\mathscr{Q}' \vee \mathscr{R}')$; changes (a), (b), and (c) have to be made within each of $\mathcal{Q}$ and $\mathcal{R}$, producing their duals, and the main connective '&' has to be replaced with '∨'.

If $\mathcal{P}$ is true on a truth-value assignment, then, by the characteristic truth-table for the ampersand, both $\mathcal{Q}$ and $\mathcal{R}$ are true. Because $\mathcal{Q}$ and $\mathcal{R}$ each contain $k$ or fewer occurrences of connectives, it follows from the inductive hypothesis that $\mathcal{Q}'$ and $\mathcal{R}'$ are both false and therefore that the dual of $\mathcal{P}$, $(\mathcal{Q}' \vee \mathcal{R}')$, is false. If $\mathcal{P}$ is false on a truth-value assignment, then either $\mathcal{Q}$ is false or $\mathcal{R}$ is false. If $\mathcal{Q}$ is false, then it follows by the inductive hypothesis that $\mathcal{Q}'$ is true. If $\mathcal{R}$ is false, then it follows by the inductive hypothesis that $\mathcal{R}'$ is true. So at least one of $\mathcal{Q}'$ and $\mathcal{R}'$ is true and $(\mathcal{Q}' \vee \mathcal{R}')$, the dual of $\mathcal{P}$, must be true as well. We conclude that $\mathcal{P}$ and its dual have opposite truth-values on each truth-value assignment.

These three cases establish the inductive step of the argument by mathematical induction, and we may now conclude that its conclusion is true as well. Our argument shows that the thesis about duals is true of every TWA sentence of *SL*. The basis clause shows that the thesis is true of every TWA sentence with 0 occurrences of connectives. It follows, from the inductive step, that the thesis is also true of every TWA sentence with 1 connective. Because the thesis holds for all TWA sentences with 0 or 1 occurrences of connectives, it follows from the inductive step that the thesis is also true of every TWA sentence with 2 occurrences of connectives. And so on, for any number of occurrences of connectives that a TWA sentence may have. Together, the basis clause and the inductive step take every TWA sentence into account.

## 6.1E EXERCISES

**1.** Prove the following theses by mathematical induction:

a. No sentence of *SL* that contains only binary connectives, if any, is truth-functionally false (i.e., every truth-functionally false sentence of *SL* contains at least one '∼').

b. Every sentence of *SL* that contains no binary connectives is truth-functionally indeterminate.

c. If two truth-value assignments $\mathcal{A}'$ and $\mathcal{A}''$ assign the same truth-values to the atomic components of a sentence $\mathcal{P}$, then $\mathcal{P}$ has the same truth-value on $\mathcal{A}'$ and $\mathcal{A}''$.

d. An iterated conjunction $(\ldots(\mathcal{P}_1 \;\&\; \mathcal{P}_2) \;\&\; \ldots \;\&\; \mathcal{P}_n)$ of sentences of *SL* is true on a truth-value assignment if and only if $\mathcal{P}_1, \mathcal{P}_2, \ldots, \mathcal{P}_n$ are all true on that assignment.

e. Where $\mathcal{P}$ is a sentence of *SL* and $\mathcal{Q}$ is a sentential component of $\mathcal{P}$, let $[\mathcal{P}](\mathcal{Q}_1//\mathcal{Q})$ be a sentence that is the result of replacing at least one occurrence of $\mathcal{Q}$ in $\mathcal{P}$ with the sentence $\mathcal{Q}_1$. If $\mathcal{Q}$ and $\mathcal{Q}_1$ are truth-functionally equivalent, then $\mathcal{P}$ and $[\mathcal{P}](\mathcal{Q}_1//\mathcal{Q})$ are truth-functionally equivalent.

**2.** Consider the thesis

No sentence of *SL* that contains only binary connectives is truth-functionally true.

Show that this thesis is false by producing a sentence that contains only binary connectives and that is truth-functionally true. Explain where an attempt to prove the thesis by mathematical induction (in the manner of the answer to exercise 1.a) would fail.

## 6.2 TRUTH-FUNCTIONAL COMPLETENESS

In Chapter Two we defined the truth-functional use of sentential connectives as follows:

> A sentential connective is used *truth-functionally* if and only if it is used to generate a compound sentence from one or more sentences in such a way that the truth-value of the generated compound is wholly determined by the truth-values of those one or more sentences from which the compound is generated, no matter what those truth-values may be.

The connectives of *SL* are used only truth-functionally, since their intended interpretations are given wholly by their characteristic truth-tables. In Chapter Two we constructed truth-functional paraphrases of many English sentences and showed how to symbolize these paraphrases in *SL*. Although *SL* contains only five sentential connectives, we found that a great variety of English compounds can nevertheless be adequately symbolized by using various combinations of these connectives. For instance, an English sentence of the form

Neither $p$ nor $q$

can be appropriately symbolized either by a sentence of the form

$\sim(\mathcal{P} \vee \mathcal{Q})$

or by a sentence of the form

$\sim\mathcal{P}\ \&\ \sim\mathcal{Q}$

An interesting question now arises: Is *SL* capable of representing all the ways in which sentences can be built up from other sentences by truth-functional means? We want the answer to this question to be 'yes' because we want *SL* to be an adequate vehicle for all of truth-functional logic. If there is some way of truth-functionally compounding sentences which cannot be represented in *SL*, then there may be some truth-functionally valid arguments that do not have valid symbolizations in *SL* just because they cannot be adequately symbolized in *SL*. Similarly, there may be sets of sentences that are truth-functionally inconsistent but that cannot be shown to be inconsistent by the truth-table method, again because these sentences cannot be adequately symbolized in *SL*, and so on.

To settle this question, we might try to produce complicated examples of truth-functionally compound sentences of English and then show that each can be adequately symbolized in *SL*. But obviously we cannot in this way prove that every truth-functionally compound sentence can be adequately symbolized in *SL*. Rather, we must show that all of the possible ways of truth-functionally compounding sentences, of building up sentences from sentences by truth-functional connectives, yield sentences that can be adequately symbolized in *SL*.

We must first formulate our question somewhat more precisely: Can every truth-function be expressed by a sentence of *SL*? A *truth-function* is a mapping, for some positive integer $n$, of each combination of truth-values which $n$ sentences of *SL* may have to a truth-value. Functions are most familiar in mathematics. Addition and multiplication are, for example, both functions that map each pair of numbers to a unique number. Addition maps each pair of numbers to the sum of those numbers. Multiplication maps each pair of numbers to the product of those numbers. The members of the pairs of numbers that are mapped are the *arguments* of the function, and the number to which a pair is mapped is the *value* of the function for that pair of arguments. (Arguments in the sense of arguments of functions are not to be confused with arguments which consist of premises and conclusions.) Thus the addition function maps the pair of arguments 3 and 4 to the value 7, and the multiplication function maps that pair of arguments to the value 12.

Instead of mapping combinations of numbers to numbers, a truth-function maps each combination of truth-values that $n$ atomic sentences of *SL* may have to a truth-value. The characteristic truth-table for '$\supset$' defines the material conditional truth-function:

| $\mathcal{P}$ | $\mathcal{Q}$ | $\mathcal{P} \supset \mathcal{Q}$ |
|---|---|---|
| T | T | T |
| T | F | F |
| F | T | T |
| F | F | T |

This truth-function is a truth-function of *two* arguments. There are four distinct combinations of truth-values that two sentences may have, and the table defining the truth-function accordingly contains four rows. Each distinct combination of arguments is listed to the left of the vertical line, and the truth-value to which that combination of arguments is mapped is listed to the right of the vertical line.

The characteristic truth-table for '$\sim$' defines the negation truth-function:

| $\mathcal{P}$ | $\sim \mathcal{P}$ |
|---|---|
| T | F |
| F | T |

The negation truth-function is a truth-function of *one* argument, since it maps each combination of truth-values that one sentence of *SL* may have to a truth-value. There are only two such combinations; each consists of a single truth-value. The truth-value to which each combination is mapped is listed in the same row to the right of the vertical line.

Each truth-function is expressed in *SL* by any sentence whose truth-table contains (in the column under its main connective) exactly the column of **T**'s and **F**'s that occurs on the right-hand side of the characteristic truth-table for the truth-function in question. For example, each sentence of the form $\sim \mathscr{P}$, where $\mathscr{P}$ is an atomic sentence of *SL*, expresses the negation truth-function—for every such sentence has a two-row truth-table in which the column under the main connective contains an **F** in the first row and a **T** in the second row. This truth-function is also expressed by other sentences of *SL*, for example, by all sentences of the form $\sim \mathscr{P}$ & $\sim \mathscr{P}$, where $\mathscr{P}$ is an atomic sentence. Every such sentence has a two-row truth-table in which the column under the main connective is

**F**

**T**

The important question for us is not how many sentences of *SL* express the same truth-function, but rather whether for each truth-function there is *at least one* sentence of *SL* that expresses that truth-function. There are an infinite number of truth-functions. This is most easily seen by considering that for every positive integer $n$ there are truth-functions of $n$ arguments (truth-functions that map each combination of truth-values that $n$ sentences of *SL* may have to a truth-value), and there are infinitely many positive integers. In Chapter Two we defined one truth-function of one argument and four truth-functions of two arguments via the five characteristic truth-tables for the connectives of *SL*. There are three other truth-functions of one argument:

| $\mathscr{P}$ | |
|---|---|
| T | T |
| F | F |

| $\mathscr{P}$ | |
|---|---|
| T | T |
| F | T |

| $\mathscr{P}$ | |
|---|---|
| T | F |
| F | F |

and twelve other truth-functions of two arguments (because there are sixteen different ways of arranging **T**'s and **F**'s in a column of a four-row truth-table). Generally, where $n$ is any positive integer, there are $2^{(2^n)}$ truth-functions of $n$ arguments. So there are 256 truth-functions of three arguments, 65,536 truth-functions of four arguments, and so on. What we want to show is that, given any truth-function of any finite number of arguments, there is at least one sentence of *SL* that expresses that truth-function. In fact, we shall prove something even stronger:

> Metatheorem 6.1: Every truth-function can be expressed by a sentence of *SL* that contains no sentential connectives other than '$\sim$', '$\vee$', and '&'.

The connectives of a language in which every truth-function can be expressed form a *truth-functionally complete* set of connectives. In proving Metatheorem 6.1 we shall be proving that the set that contains the connectives '~', '&', and '∨', defined as they are defined in *SL*, is truth-functionally complete.

Characteristic truth-tables define truth-functions by giving an exhaustive list of the combinations of arguments that each truth-function takes and displaying the value to which each such combination is mapped. That is, it is the rows of **T**'s and **F**'s that serve to define truth-functions in characteristic truth-tables. It should now be clear that the following schema also specifies a truth-function:

| | | |
|---|---|---|
| T | T | F |
| T | F | F |
| F | T | F |
| F | F | T |

To the left of the vertical line the four distinct combinations of truth-values that two sentences of *SL* may have are displayed. The specified truth-function is thus a function of two arguments. The value of the function for each combination of arguments is displayed to the right of the vertical line. Since every truth-function maps only a finite number of combinations of arguments, every truth-function can be specified in a table like the above. We call such a table a *truth-function schema*. A truth-function schema is simply a truncated truth-table.

We shall now show that the set of connectives {'~', '&', '∨'} is truth-functionally complete by producing an *algorithm* for constructing, given any possible truth-function schema, a sentence of *SL* that contains no connectives other than '~', '&', and '∨' and that expresses the truth-function specified by the schema. An algorithm is an *effective* procedure for producing a desired result, that is, a mechanical procedure that, when correctly followed, will yield the desired result in a finite number of steps. Given a truth-function schema, our algorithm will produce a sentence whose truth-table contains, under its main connective, exactly the same column of **T**'s and **F**'s as occurs to the right of the vertical line in the truth-function schema. Once we produce the algorithm, Metatheorem 6.1 will be proved; the construction of such an algorithm will show that every truth-function can be expressed by a sentence of *SL* containing no connectives other than '~', '&', and '∨'.

To begin, we need a stock of atomic sentences. If the truth-function is a function of $n$ arguments, we will use the alphabetically first $n$ atomic sentences of *SL*. So for the truth-function schema

| | | |
|---|---|---|
| T | T | F |
| T | F | F |
| F | T | F |
| F | F | T |

we start with the atomic sentences 'A' and 'B'. Next we form, for each row of the truth-table, a sentence that is true if and only if its atomic components have the truth-values indicated in that row. This sentence is called the *characteristic sentence* for the row in question. The characteristic sentence for row $i$ is an iterated conjunction

$$(\ldots(\mathscr{P}_1 \,\&\, \mathscr{P}_2) \,\&\, \ldots \,\&\, \mathscr{P}_n)$$

where $\mathscr{P}_j$ is the $j$th atomic sentence if the $j$th value in row $i$ (to the left of the vertical bar) is **T**, and $\mathscr{P}_j$ is the negation of the $j$th atomic sentence if the $j$th value in row $i$ is **F**. Thus the characteristic sentences for the four rows in our sample truth-function schema are 'A & B', 'A & ~ B', '~ A & B', and '~ A & ~ B', respectively. The first sentence is true if and only if both 'A' and 'B' are true; the second sentence is true if and only if 'A' is true and 'B' is false; the third sentence is true if and only if 'A' is false and 'B' is true, and the fourth sentence is true if and only if both 'A' and 'B' are false. We leave it as an exercise to prove that the characteristic sentence for each row of a truth-function schema is true if and only if its atomic components have the truth-values presented in that row.

Finally, we identify the rows in the truth-function schema that have a **T** to the right of the vertical bar. If there is only one such row, then the characteristic sentence for that row is a sentence that expresses the truth-function specified in the schema. In our example, the fourth row is the only row that has a **T** to the right of the vertical bar; and the characteristic sentence for that row is '~ A & ~ B'. This sentence is true if and only if both 'A' and 'B' are false, and therefore this sentence expresses the truth-function specified by the truth-function schema:

| A | B | ~ A | & | ~ B |
|---|---|---|---|---|
| **T** | **T** | **F T** | **F** | **F T** |
| **T** | **F** | **F T** | **F** | **T F** |
| **F** | **T** | **T F** | **F** | **F T** |
| **F** | **F** | **T F** | **T** | **T F** |

If the truth-function schema has more than one **T** to the right of the vertical bar, as does the following,

| | | |
|---|---|---|
| **T** | **T** | **F** |
| **T** | **F** | **T** |
| **F** | **T** | **F** |
| **F** | **F** | **T** |

then we form an iterated disjunction of the characteristic sentences for the rows that have a **T** to the right of the vertical bar. In the present case, the disjunction will be '(A & ~ B) ∨ (~ A & ~ B)'—the disjunction of the characteristic sentences for the second and fourth rows. This sentence is true if and only if either 'A' is true and 'B' is false or both 'A' and 'B' are false, and it therefore expresses the truth-function specified in the schema:

| A | B | (A | & | ~ B) | ∨ | (~ A | & | ~ B) |
|---|---|---|---|---|---|---|---|---|
| T | T | T | F | F T | F | F T | F | F T |
| T | F | T | T | T F | T | F T | F | T F |
| F | T | F | F | F T | F | T F | F | F T |
| F | F | F | F | T F | T | T F | T | T F |

And if the schema is

| | | |
|---|---|---|
| T | T | F |
| T | F | T |
| F | T | T |
| F | F | T |

then the disjunction of the characteristic sentences for the last three rows, '((A & ~ B) ∨ (~ A & B)) ∨ (~ A & ~ B)', expresses the truth-function in the schema.

In general, in the case where there is more than one **T** to the right of the vertical bar in a truth-function schema, the iterated disjunction that we form from the characteristic sentences for those rows will be true if and only if at least one of its disjuncts is true, and each disjunct is true only in the row for which it is a characteristic sentence. Therefore, the iterated disjunction is true if and only if its atomic components have the truth-values specified by one of the rows that have a **T** to the right of the vertical bar, and so the disjunction expresses the truth-function specified by that schema.

If there are no **T**'s in the column to the right of the vertical bar, then we conjoin the characteristic sentence for the first row of the truth-function schema with its negation. (Any other row's characteristic sentence would have done as well.) The result will be a sentence of the form $\mathscr{P}$ & ~ $\mathscr{P}$, which is false on every truth-value assignment and hence expresses a truth-function that maps every combination of $n$ truth-values into **F**. For example, if our schema is

| | | |
|---|---|---|
| T | T | F |
| T | F | F |
| F | T | F |
| F | F | F |

then the sentence '(A & B) & ~ (A & B)' expresses the truth-function specified in the schema.

In sum, we have three cases. If a truth-function schema has exactly one row with a **T** to the right of the vertical bar, then the characteristic sentence for that row expresses the truth-function specified in the schema. If a truth-function schema has more than one row with a **T** to the right of the vertical bar, then an iterated disjunction of the characteristic sentences for all such rows will express the truth-function specified in the schema. If a truth-function schema has no T's to the right of the vertical bar, then the conjunction of the characteristic sentence for the first row and its negation will express the truth-function specified by the schema.

The algorithm tells us how to construct a sentence that expresses the truth-function indicated in a given truth-function schema, and we may use it for any truth-function schema. As a final example, consider the schema

| | | | |
|---|---|---|---|
| T | T | T | F |
| T | T | F | F |
| T | F | T | T |
| T | F | F | T |
| F | T | T | F |
| F | T | F | F |
| F | F | T | T |
| F | F | F | F |

This falls under our second case; there is more than one **T** to the right of the vertical line. We shall use the first three sentence letters of *SL*, because the truth-function is a truth-function of three arguments. We form the characteristic sentences for rows 3, 4, and 7 and then disjoin those characteristic sentences to produce

(((A & ~ B) & C) ∨ ((A & ~ B) & ~ C)) ∨ ((~ A & ~ B) & C)

This sentence is true if and only if 'A', 'B', and 'C' have one of the combinations of truth-values represented in the third, fourth, and seventh rows of the schema.

Our algorithm shows how to construct, for any truth-function, a sentence of *SL* that expresses that truth-function. It therefore shows that for each truth-function, there is *at least one* sentence of *SL* that expresses that truth-function. Moreover, because we have used only the three connectives ' ~ ', '&', and ' ∨ ', we have shown that the set of connectives {' ~ ', '&', ' ∨ '} is truth-functionally complete. This completes the proof of Metatheorem 6.1.

There is a consequence of the theorem that follows almost immediately: The smaller set {' ~ ', ' ∨ '} is also truth-functionally complete. Every conjunction $\mathscr{P}$ & $\mathscr{Q}$ is truth-functionally equivalent to ~ (~ $\mathscr{P}$ ∨ ~ $\mathscr{Q}$), and so we may rewrite each sentence produced by the algorithm using only ' ~ ' and ' ∨ '. For example, the sentence

(~ (~ A ∨ ~ ~ B) ∨ ~ (~ ~ A ∨ ~ ~ B))

expresses the same truth-function as

((A & ~ B) ∨ (~ A & ~ B))

Therefore every truth-function can be expressed by a sentence that contains only ' ~ ' and ' ∨ ' as connectives.

On the other hand, the set of connectives {' ∨ ', '&'} is *not* truth-functionally complete. To prove this, we must show that there is at least one truth-function that cannot be expressed by any sentence that contains at most the connectives '∨' and '&'. We call such a sentence a *W-A* sentence (for '*w*edge and *a*mpersand'). A little reflection suggests that no matter how many times we conjoin and disjoin, if we do not have the tilde available then we can never produce a sentence that is false from atomic components that are all true. That is, every W-A sentence is true whenever its atomic components are all true. And if this is the case, then there are many truth-functions that cannot be expressed by any W-A sentence. Take the negation truth-function as an example. This truth-function maps the argument **T** into the value **F**. If our reflection is correct, there is no W-A sentence with a single atomic component that is true when the atomic component is false.

We shall therefore show that the set of connectives {'∨', '&'} is not truth-functionally complete by proving the following thesis:

> Every W-A sentence has the truth-value **T** on every truth-value assignment on which its atomic components all have the truth-value **T**.

This is a general claim about *all* W-A sentences, and so it cannot be proved by examining W-A sentences one by one (there are infinitely many). Instead, we shall prove the thesis by mathematical induction.

The shortest W-A sentences, that is, those with 0 occurrences of connectives, are just the atomic sentences of *SL*.

> *Basis clause:* Every atomic sentence of *SL* has the truth-value **T** on every truth-value assignment on which its atomic components all have the truth-value **T**.

Since an atomic sentence is its own only component, the basis clause is obviously true.

> *Inductive step:* If every W-A sentence of *SL* with $k$ or fewer occurrences of connectives is such that it has the truth-value **T** on every truth-value assignment on which its atomic components all have the truth-value **T**, then every W-A sentence with $k+1$ occurrences of connectives has the truth-value **T** on every truth-value assignment on which its atomic components all have the truth-value **T**.

We now assume that the inductive hypothesis is true for an arbitrary nonnegative integer $k$, that is, we assume that every W-A sentence with $k$ or fewer occurrences of connectives is true whenever all of its atomic components are true. We must show that it follows that the thesis also holds for any W-A sentence $\mathscr{P}$ with $k+1$ occurrences of connectives. Since these sentences contain only '∨' and '&' as connectives, there are two cases.

Case 1: $\mathscr{P}$ has the form $\mathscr{Q} \vee \mathscr{R}$. Then $\mathscr{Q}$ and $\mathscr{R}$ each contain fewer than $k+1$ occurrences of connectives. They are also W-A sentences. So by the inductive hypothesis, each disjunct is true on every truth-value assignment on which each of its atomic components is true. So if all of the atomic components of $\mathscr{Q} \vee \mathscr{R}$ are true, then both $\mathscr{Q}$ and $\mathscr{R}$ are true, and hence $\mathscr{Q} \vee \mathscr{R}$ is itself true.

Case 2: $\mathscr{P}$ has the form $\mathscr{Q} \& \mathscr{R}$. Then each of $\mathscr{Q}$ and $\mathscr{R}$ is a W-A sentence with $k$ or fewer occurrences of connectives. Hence the inductive hypothesis holds for both $\mathscr{Q}$ and $\mathscr{R}$. Each conjunct is true on every truth-value assignment on which all of its atomic components are true. So if all the atomic components of $\mathscr{Q} \& \mathscr{R}$ are true then both $\mathscr{Q}$ and $\mathscr{R}$ are true, and $\mathscr{Q} \& \mathscr{R}$ itself is also true.

This proves the inductive step, and we can conclude that the thesis holds for every W-A sentence:

*Conclusion:* Every W-A sentence has the truth-value **T** on every truth-value assignment on which its atomic components all have the truth-value **T**.

It follows that no W-A sentence can express the negation truth-function as defined in the characteristic truth-table for the tilde, since no W-A sentence can express a truth-function that maps the truth-value **T** to the truth-value **F**. (Whenever all of the atomic components of a W-A sentence are true, the W-A sentence itself is true.)

## 6.2E EXERCISES

**1.** Show that a sentence constructed in accordance with our characteristic sentence algorithm is indeed a characteristic sentence for the row of the truth-function schema in question.

**2.** Using the algorithm in the proof of Metatheorem 6.1, construct a sentence containing at most '∼', '&', and '∨' that expresses the truth-function defined in each of the following truth-function schemata.

a.

| | | |
|---|---|---|
| T | T | F |
| T | F | T |
| F | T | F |
| F | F | T |

b.

| | |
|---|---|
| T | F |
| F | F |

*c.

| | | |
|---|---|---|
| T | T | F |
| T | F | T |
| F | T | T |
| F | F | F |

d.

| | | | |
|---|---|---|---|
| T | T | T | T |
| T | T | F | T |
| T | F | T | F |
| T | F | F | F |
| F | T | T | F |
| F | T | F | F |
| F | F | T | T |
| F | F | F | F |

3. Give an algorithm analogous to that in Metatheorem 6.1 for constructing a characteristic sentence containing only '$\sim$' and '$\vee$' for each row of a truth-function schema.

4. Using Metatheorem 6.1, prove that the sets {'$\sim$', '&'} and {'$\sim$', '$\supset$'} are truth-functionally complete.

5. Prove that the set consisting of the dagger '$\downarrow$' is truth-functionally complete, where the dagger has the following characteristic truth-table:

| $\mathscr{P}$ | $\mathscr{Q}$ | $\mathscr{P} \downarrow \mathscr{Q}$ |
|---|---|---|
| T | T | F |
| T | F | F |
| F | T | F |
| F | F | T |

*6. Prove that the set consisting of the stroke '$|$' is truth-functionally complete, where the stroke has the following characteristic truth-table:

| $\mathscr{P}$ | $\mathscr{Q}$ | $\mathscr{P} \mid \mathscr{Q}$ |
|---|---|---|
| T | T | F |
| T | F | T |
| F | T | T |
| F | F | T |

7. Using the results of Exercises 1.a and 1.b in Section 6.1E, prove that the following sets of connectives are not truth-functionally complete: {'$\sim$'}, {'&', '$\vee$', '$\supset$', '$\equiv$'}.

8. Prove that the set {'$\sim$', '$\equiv$'} is not truth-functionally complete. Hint: Show that the truth-table for any sentence $\mathscr{P}$ that contains only these two connectives and just two atomic components will have, in the column under the main connective, an even number of **T**'s and an even number of **F**'s.

9. Prove that if a truth-functionally complete set of connectives consists of exactly one binary connective, then that connective has either the characteristic truth-table for '$\downarrow$' or the characteristic truth-table for '$|$'. (That is, show that the connective must be either '$\downarrow$' or '$|$', though possibly under a different name.) Hint: In the proofs for exercises 7 and 8 above it became apparent that characteristic truth-tables for truth-functionally complete sets of connectives must have certain properties. Show that only two characteristic truth-tables with just four rows have these properties.

## 6.3 THE SOUNDNESS OF *SD* AND *SD+*

We now turn to the results announced at the beginning of this chapter. In this section we shall prove that if a sentence $\mathscr{P}$ is derivable in *SD* from a set of sentences $\Gamma$, then $\Gamma$ truth-functionally entails $\mathscr{P}$. A natural deduction system for which this result holds is said to be *sound* for sentential logic. In the next section we shall prove the converse, that if a set of sentences Γ truth-functionally entails a sentence $\mathcal{P}$, then $\mathcal{P}$ is derivable in *SD* from Γ. A natural deduction system for which this second result holds is said to be *complete* for sentential logic. Soundness and completeness are important properties for natural deduction systems. A natural deduction system that is not sound will sometimes lead us from true sentences to false ones, and a natural deduction system that is not complete will not allow us to construct all the derivations that we want to construct. In either case, the natural deduction system would not be adequate for the purposes of sentential logic.

Metatheorem 6.2 is the *Soundness Metatheorem* for *SD*. For any set Γ of sentences of *SL* and any sentence $\mathcal{P}$ of *SL*,

| |
|---|
| Metatheorem 6.2: If $\Gamma \vdash \mathcal{P}$ in *SD*, then $\Gamma \vDash \mathcal{P}$.[2] |

Recall that $\Gamma \vDash \mathcal{P}$ if and only if there is no truth-value assignment on which all the members of Γ are true and $\mathcal{P}$ is false. Metatheorem 6.2 therefore says that the derivation rules of *SD* are *truth-preserving*, that is, when correctly applied they will never take us from true sentences to a false sentence. When we constructed *SD* our intent was to pick out truth-preserving derivation rules, and we shall now prove that we were successful.

Our proof will use mathematical induction to establish that each sentence in a derivation is true if all of the undischarged assumptions in whose scope the sentence lies are true. The basis clause will show that this claim is true of the first sentence in a derivation, and the inductive step will show that if the claim is true for the first $k$ sentences in a derivation, then the claim is also true of the $k + 1$th sentence—that is, each time we apply another derivation rule in the derivation, that application is truth-preserving. We will then be able to conclude that the last sentence in any derivation, no matter how long the derivation is, is true if all of the undischarged assumptions in whose scope the sentence lies are true. And this conclusion is just what Metatheorem 6.2 says.

In the course of the proof, we shall use some set-theoretic terminology which we here explain. Let Γ and Γ′ be sets. If every member of Γ is also a member of Γ′, then Γ is said to be a *subset* of Γ′. Note that every set is a subset of itself, and the empty set is trivially a subset of every set (because the empty set has no members, it has no members that are not members of every set). As an example, the set of sentences

{A, B, C}

[2] In what follows we shall abbreviate

$\Gamma \vdash \mathcal{P}$ in *SD*

as

$\Gamma \vdash \mathcal{P}$

has eight subsets: {A, B, C}, {A, B}, {B, C}, {A, C}, {A}, {B}, {C}, and ∅. If a set Γ is a subset of a set Γ′, then Γ′ is said to be a *superset* of Γ. Thus {A, B, C} is a superset of each of its eight subsets.

Here is the argument by mathematical induction. For any derivation, let $\mathscr{P}_k$ be the $k$th sentence (the $k$th *occurrence* of a sentence—but we shall speak loosely) in the derivation, and let $\Gamma_k$ be the set of undischarged assumptions in whose scope $\mathscr{P}_k$ lies. Our induction is on the position $k$:

*Basis clause:* $\Gamma_1 \vDash \mathscr{P}_1$.

*Inductive step:* If $\Gamma_i \vDash \mathscr{P}_i$ for every positive integer $i \leq k$, then $\Gamma_{k+1} \vDash \mathscr{P}_{k+1}$.

---

*Conclusion:* For every positive integer $k$, $\Gamma_k \vDash \mathscr{P}_k$.

Once we have established that the premises of this argument are true, and hence that the conclusion is true as well, we may then conclude that in every derivation the last sentence—which is $\mathscr{P}_k$ for some positive integer $k$—is truth-functionally entailed by the primary assumptions of the derivation; these are the undischarged assumptions in whose scope the last sentence lies.

The basis clause is simple to prove. $\mathscr{P}_1$ is the first sentence in a derivation. Moreover, because every derivation in *SD* begins with one or more assumptions, $\mathscr{P}_1$ is an undischarged assumption that lies in its own scope. (We remind the reader that, by definition, every assumption of a derivation lies within its own scope.) That is, $\Gamma_1$, the set of undischarged assumptions in whose scope $\mathscr{P}_1$ lies, is $\{\mathscr{P}_1\}$. Because $\{\mathscr{P}_1\} \vDash \mathscr{P}_1$, we conclude that the basis clause is true.

We now turn to the inductive step. Let $k$ be an arbitrary positive integer, and assume the inductive hypothesis: that for every positive integer $i \leq k$, $\Gamma_i \vDash \mathscr{P}_i$. We must show that on this assumption, it follows that $\Gamma_{k+1} \vDash \mathscr{P}_{k+1}$. We shall consider each way in which $\mathscr{P}_{k+1}$ might be justified, and show that our thesis holds whichever justification is used. We now turn to cases.

Case 1: $\mathscr{P}_{k+1}$ is an Assumption. Then $\mathscr{P}_{k+1}$ is a member of $\Gamma_{k+1}$, the set of undischarged assumptions in whose scope $\mathscr{P}_{k+1}$ lies. Therefore, if every member of $\Gamma_{k+1}$ is true, $\mathscr{P}_{k+1}$, being a member of the set, is true as well. So $\Gamma_{k+1} \vDash \mathscr{P}_{k+1}$.

There is a semantic result that we shall use in the cases that follow, which we establish here:

6.3.1. If $\Gamma \vDash \mathscr{P}$, then for every superset $\Gamma'$ of $\Gamma$, $\Gamma' \vDash \mathscr{P}$.
Proof: Assume that $\Gamma \vDash \mathscr{P}$, and let $\Gamma'$ be any superset of $\Gamma$. If every member of $\Gamma'$ is true, then every member of its subset $\Gamma$ is true and so, because $\Gamma \vDash \mathscr{P}$, $\mathscr{P}$ is also true. Therefore $\Gamma' \vDash \mathscr{P}$.

Case 2: $\mathscr{P}_{k+1}$ is justified by Reiteration. Then $\mathscr{P}_{k+1}$ occurs earlier in the derivation as sentence $\mathscr{P}_i$ at some position $i$. Moreover, every assumption that is undischarged at position $i$ must remain undischarged at position $k + 1$—for if even one assumption in whose scope $\mathscr{P}_i$ lies were discharged before position $k + 1$, then $\mathscr{P}_i$ would not be accessible at position $k + 1$. Therefore $\Gamma_i$ is a subset of $\Gamma_{k+1}$; every member of $\Gamma_i$ is still an undischarged assumption at position $k + 1$. By our inductive hypothesis, $\Gamma_i \vDash \mathscr{P}_i$. Because $\Gamma_i$ is a subset of $\Gamma_{k+1}$, it follows from 6.3.1 that $\Gamma_{k+1} \vDash \mathscr{P}_i$. And because $\mathscr{P}_{k+1}$ is the same sentence as $\mathscr{P}_i$, $\Gamma_{k+1} \vDash \mathscr{P}_{k+1}$.

Case 3: $\mathscr{P}_{k+1}$ is justified by Conjunction Introduction. The conjuncts of $\mathscr{P}_{k+1}$ occur earlier in the derivation, say at positions $h$ and $j$:

$$\begin{array}{r|ll} h & \mathscr{Q} & \\ j & \mathscr{R} & \\ k+1 & \mathscr{Q} \,\&\, \mathscr{R} \ (= \mathscr{R}_{k+1}) & h, j \ \&\text{I} \end{array}$$

(There may be undischarged assumptions between positions $h$ and $j$ and between positions $j$ and $k + 1$. Moreover, it may be that $\mathscr{R}$ occurs earlier in the derivation than does $\mathscr{Q}$—the order is immaterial.) By the inductive hypothesis, $\Gamma_h \vDash \mathscr{Q}$ and $\Gamma_j \vDash \mathscr{R}$. Moreover, every member of $\Gamma_h$ is a member of $\Gamma_{k+1}$ and every member of $\Gamma_j$ is a member of $\Gamma_{k+1}$—for if this were not the case, then either $\mathscr{Q}$ or $\mathscr{R}$ would not be accessible at position $k + 1$. $\Gamma_h$ and $\Gamma_j$ are therefore subsets of $\Gamma_{k+1}$ and so, by 6.3.1, $\Gamma_{k+1} \vDash \mathscr{Q}$ and $\Gamma_{k+1} \vDash \mathscr{R}$. But whenever both $\mathscr{Q}$ and $\mathscr{R}$ are true, $\mathscr{P}_{k+1}$, which is $\mathscr{Q} \,\&\, \mathscr{R}$, is also true. So $\Gamma_{k+1} \vDash \mathscr{P}_{k+1}$ as well.

Case 4: $\mathscr{P}_{k+1}$ is justified by Conjunction Elimination:

$$\begin{array}{r|ll} h & \mathscr{Q} \,\&\, \mathscr{P}_{k+1} & \\ & & \\ k+1 & \mathscr{P}_{k+1} & h \ \&\text{E} \end{array} \qquad \text{or} \qquad \begin{array}{r|ll} h & \mathscr{P}_{k+1} \,\&\, \mathscr{Q} & \\ & & \\ k+1 & \mathscr{P}_{k+1} & h \ \&\text{E} \end{array}$$

By the inductive hypothesis, $\Gamma_h$ truth-functionally entails the conjunction at position $h$. And whenever the conjunction is true, both conjuncts must be true. So $\Gamma_h \vDash \mathscr{P}_{k+1}$. $\Gamma_h$ is a subset of $\Gamma_{k+1}$—all assumptions that have not been discharged by position $h$ must remain undischarged at position $k + 1$. It follows, by 6.3.1, that $\Gamma_{k+1} \vDash \mathscr{P}_{k+1}$.

Case 5: $\mathscr{P}_{k+1}$ is justified by Disjunction Introduction:

$$\begin{array}{r|ll} h & \mathscr{Q} & \\ & & \\ k+1 & \mathscr{Q} \vee \mathscr{R} \ (= \mathscr{P}_{k+1}) & h \ \vee\text{I} \end{array} \qquad \text{or} \qquad \begin{array}{r|ll} h & \mathscr{R} & \\ & & \\ k+1 & \mathscr{Q} \vee \mathscr{R} \ (= \mathscr{P}_{k+1}) & h \ \vee\text{I} \end{array}$$

By the inductive hypothesis, $\Gamma_h$ truth-functionally entails the sentence at position $h$. That sentence is one of the disjuncts of $\mathscr{Q} \vee \mathscr{R}$, so whenever it is true so is $\mathscr{Q} \vee \mathscr{R}$. Thus $\Gamma_h \vDash \mathscr{P}_{k+1}$. $\Gamma_h$ must be a subset of $\Gamma_{k+1}$ if the sentence at position $h$ is accessible at position $k + 1$ and so, by 6.3.1, $\Gamma_{k+1} \vDash \mathscr{P}_{k+1}$.

Case 6: $\mathscr{P}_{k+1}$ is justified by Conditional Elimination:

$$\begin{array}{r|ll} h & \mathscr{Q} & \\ j & \mathscr{Q} \supset \mathscr{P}_{k+1} & \\ k+1 & \mathscr{P}_{k+1} & h, j \supset\text{E} \end{array}$$

By the inductive hypothesis, $\Gamma_h \vDash \mathscr{Q}$ and $\Gamma_j \vDash \mathscr{Q} \supset \mathscr{P}_{k+1}$. Both $\Gamma_h$ and $\Gamma_j$ must be subsets of $\Gamma_{k+1}$, if the sentences at positions $h$ and $j$ are accessible at position $k + 1$. By 6.3.1, then, $\Gamma_{k+1} \vDash \mathscr{Q}$ and $\Gamma_{k+1} \vDash \mathscr{Q} \supset \mathscr{P}_{k+1}$. Because $\mathscr{P}_{k+1}$ must be true whenever both $\mathscr{Q}$ and $\mathscr{Q} \supset \mathscr{P}_{k+1}$ are true, $\Gamma_{k+1} \vDash \mathscr{P}_{k+1}$ as well.

Case 7: $\mathscr{P}_{k+1}$ is justified by Biconditional Elimination:

| | | | | | | |
|---|---|---|---|---|---|---|
| $h$ | $\mathscr{Q}$ | | | $h$ | $\mathscr{Q}$ | |
| $j$ | $\mathscr{Q} \equiv \mathscr{P}_{k+1}$ | | or | $j$ | $\mathscr{P}_{k+1} \equiv \mathscr{Q}$ | |
| $k + 1$ | $\mathscr{P}_{k+1}$ | $h, j \equiv \mathrm{E}$ | | $k + 1$ | $\mathscr{P}_{k+1}$ | $h, j \equiv \mathrm{E}$ |

By the inductive hypothesis, $\Gamma_h \vDash \mathscr{Q}$ and $\Gamma_j$ truth-functionally entails the biconditional at position $j$. $\Gamma_h$ and $\Gamma_j$ must be subsets of $\Gamma_{k+1}$, if the sentences at positions $h$ and $j$ are accessible at position $k + 1$. By 6.3.1, then, $\Gamma_{k+1}$ truth-functionally entails both $\mathscr{Q}$ and the biconditional at position $j$. Because the sentence $\mathscr{P}_{k+1}$ must be true whenever both $\mathscr{Q}$ and the biconditional at position $j$ are true, $\Gamma_{k+1} \vDash \mathscr{P}_{k+1}$ as well.

Case 8: $\mathscr{P}_{k+1}$ is justified by Conditional Introduction:

| | | |
|---|---|---|
| $h$ | \| $\mathscr{Q}$ | |
| | \| ——— | |
| $j$ | \| $\mathscr{R}$ | |
| $k + 1$ | $\mathscr{Q} \supset \mathscr{R}$ $(= \mathscr{P}_{k+1})$ | $h$–$j$ $\supset$I |

By the inductive hypothesis, $\Gamma_j \vDash \mathscr{R}$. Because the subderivation in which $\mathscr{R}$ is derived from $\mathscr{Q}$ is accessible at position $k + 1$, every assumption that is undischarged at position $j$ is undischarged at position $k + 1$, except for the assumption $\mathscr{Q}$ that begins the subderivation. So the set of undischarged assumptions $\Gamma_j$ is a subset of $\Gamma_{k+1} \cup \{\mathscr{Q}\}$. Because $\Gamma_j \vDash \mathscr{R}$, it follows, by 6.3.1, that $\Gamma_{k+1} \cup \{\mathscr{Q}\} \vDash \mathscr{R}$. And because it can be proved that

> 6.3.2. If $\Gamma \cup \{\mathscr{Q}\} \vDash \mathscr{R}$, then $\Gamma \vDash \mathscr{Q} \supset \mathscr{R}$ (see Exercise 2.b of Section 3.6E)

it follows that $\Gamma_{k+1} \vDash \mathscr{Q} \supset \mathscr{R}$.

Case 9: $\mathscr{P}_{k+1}$ is justified by Negation Introduction:

| | | |
|---|---|---|
| $h$ | \| $\mathscr{Q}$ | |
| | \| ——— | |
| $j$ | \| $\mathscr{R}$ | |
| $m$ | \| $\sim \mathscr{R}$ | |
| $k + 1$ | $\sim \mathscr{Q}$ $(= \mathscr{P}_{k+1})$ | $h$–$m$ $\sim$I |

By the inductive hypothesis, $\Gamma_j \vDash \mathscr{R}$ and $\Gamma_m \vDash \sim \mathscr{R}$. Because the subderivation that derives $\mathscr{R}$ from $\mathscr{Q}$ is accessible at position $k + 1$, every assumption that is undischarged at position $j$ is undischarged at position $k + 1$, except for the assumption $\mathcal{Q}$ that begins the subderivation. That is, the set of undischarged assumptions $\Gamma_j$ is a subset of $\Gamma_{k+1} \cup \{\mathcal{Q}\}$. By similar reasoning, $\Gamma_m$ must be a subset of $\Gamma_{k+1} \cup \{\mathcal{Q}\}$. Therefore, by 6.3.1, $\Gamma_{k+1} \cup \{\mathcal{Q}\} \vDash \mathcal{R}$ and $\Gamma_{k+1} \cup \{\mathcal{Q}\} \vDash \sim \mathcal{R}$. Because it can be proved that

> 6.3.3. If $\Gamma \vDash \mathcal{Q}$ and $\Gamma \vDash \sim \mathcal{Q}$ for some sentence $\mathcal{Q}$, then $\Gamma$ is truth-functionally inconsistent (see Exercise 3.b of Section 3.6E)

we conclude that $\Gamma_{k+1} \cup \{\mathcal{Q}\}$ is truth-functionally inconsistent. We can also prove that

> 6.3.4. If $\Gamma \cup \{\mathcal{Q}\}$ is truth-functionally inconsistent, then $\Gamma \vDash \sim \mathcal{Q}$.
> Proof: Assume that $\Gamma \cup \{\mathcal{Q}\}$ is truth-functionally inconsistent. Then there is no truth-value assignment on which every member of $\Gamma \cup \{\mathcal{Q}\}$ is true. Therefore, if every member of $\Gamma$ is true on some truth-value assignment, $\mathcal{Q}$ must be false on that assignment, and $\sim \mathcal{Q}$ will be true. So $\Gamma \vDash \sim \mathcal{Q}$.

It follows, from the fact that $\Gamma_{k+1} \cup \{\mathcal{Q}\}$ is truth-functionally inconsistent, that $\Gamma_{k+1} \vDash \sim \mathcal{Q}$.

Case 10: $\mathcal{P}_{k+1}$ is justified by Negation Elimination. See Exercise 3.

Case 11: $\mathcal{P}_{k+1}$ is justified by Disjunction Elimination:

| | | | |
|---|---|---|---|
| $h$ | $\mathcal{Q} \vee \mathcal{R}$ | | |
| $j$ | | $\mathcal{Q}$ | |
| $m$ | | $\mathcal{P}_{k+1}$ | |
| $n$ | | $\mathcal{R}$ | |
| $p$ | | $\mathcal{P}_{k+1}$ | |
| $k+1$ | $\mathcal{P}_{k+1}$ | | $h$, $j$–$m$, $n$–$p$ $\vee$E |

By the inductive hypothesis, $\Gamma_h \vDash \mathcal{Q} \vee \mathcal{R}$, $\Gamma_m \vDash \mathcal{P}_{k+1}$, and $\Gamma_p \vDash \mathcal{P}_{k+1}$. Because the two subderivations are accessible at position $k+1$, the undischarged assumptions $\Gamma_m$ form a subset of $\Gamma_{k+1} \cup \{\mathcal{Q}\}$, and the undischarged assumptions $\Gamma_p$ form a subset of $\Gamma_{k+1} \cup \{\mathcal{R}\}$. By 6.3.1, then, $\Gamma_{k+1} \cup \{\mathcal{Q}\} \vDash \mathcal{P}_{k+1}$ and $\Gamma_{k+1} \cup \{\mathcal{R}\} \vDash \mathcal{P}_{k+1}$. Moreover, because $\mathcal{Q} \vee \mathcal{R}$ at position $h$ is accessible at position $k+1$, $\Gamma_h$ is a subset of $\Gamma_{k+1}$. So, because $\Gamma_h \vDash \mathcal{Q} \vee \mathcal{R}$, it follows, by 6.3.1, that $\Gamma_{k+1} \vDash \mathcal{Q} \vee \mathcal{R}$. Now consider any truth-value assignment on which every member of $\Gamma_{k+1}$ is true. Because $\Gamma_{k+1} \vDash \mathcal{Q} \vee \mathcal{R}$, $\mathcal{Q} \vee \mathcal{R}$ is also true on this assignment. So either $\mathcal{Q}$ or $\mathcal{R}$ is true. If $\mathcal{Q}$ is true, then every member of $\Gamma_{k+1} \cup \{\mathcal{Q}\}$ is true and hence $\mathcal{P}_{k+1}$ is true as well, because $\Gamma_{k+1} \cup \{\mathcal{Q}\} \vDash \mathcal{P}_{k+1}$. Similarly, if $\mathcal{R}$ is true then every member of $\Gamma_{k+1} \cup \{\mathcal{R}\}$ is true and hence $\mathcal{P}_{k+1}$ is true as well, because $\Gamma_{k+1} \cup \{\mathcal{R}\} \vDash \mathcal{P}_{k+1}$. Either way it follows that $\mathcal{P}_{k+1}$ must be true on any truth-value assignment on which every member of $\Gamma_{k+1}$ is true. So $\Gamma_{k+1} \vDash \mathcal{P}_{k+1}$.

Case 12: $\mathscr{P}_{k+1}$ is justified by Biconditional Introduction:

| | | |
|---|---|---|
| $h$ | $\mathscr{Q}$ | |
| | | |
| $j$ | $\mathscr{R}$ | |
| $m$ | $\mathscr{R}$ | |
| | | |
| $n$ | $\mathscr{Q}$ | |
| $k + 1$ | $\mathscr{Q} \equiv \mathscr{R}$ $(= \mathscr{P}_{k+1})$ | $h$–$j$, $m$–$n$ $\equiv$I |

By the inductive hypothesis, $\Gamma_j \vDash \mathscr{R}$ and $\Gamma_n \vDash \mathscr{Q}$. Because the two subderivations are accessible at position $k + 1$, $\Gamma_j$ is a subset of $\Gamma_{k+1} \cup \{\mathscr{Q}\}$ and $\Gamma_n$ is a subset of $\Gamma_{k+1} \cup \{\mathscr{R}\}$. By 6.3.1, then, $\Gamma_{k+1} \cup \{\mathscr{Q}\} \vDash \mathscr{R}$ and $\Gamma_{k+1} \cup \{\mathscr{R}\} \vDash \mathscr{Q}$. Now consider any truth-value assignment on which every member of $\Gamma_{k+1}$ is true. If $\mathscr{R}$ is also true on that assignment, then so is $\mathscr{Q}$ because $\Gamma_{k+1} \cup \{\mathscr{R}\} \vDash \mathscr{Q}$. If $\mathscr{R}$ is false on that assignment, then $\mathscr{Q}$ must also be false—if $\mathscr{Q}$ were true, then $\mathscr{R}$ would have to be true as well because $\Gamma_{k+1} \cup \{\mathscr{Q}\} \vDash \mathscr{R}$. Either way, $\mathscr{Q}$ and $\mathscr{R}$ have the same truth-value and so $\mathscr{Q} \equiv \mathscr{R}$ is true on every truth-value assignment on which every member of $\Gamma_{k+1}$ is true. So $\Gamma_{k+1} \vDash \mathscr{P}_{k+1}$.

This completes the proof of the inductive step; we have considered every way in which the sentence at position $k + 1$ of a derivation might be justified and have shown that in each case $\Gamma_{k+1} \vDash \mathscr{P}_{k+1}$ if the same is true of all earlier positions in the derivation. We have therefore established that the conclusion of the argument by mathematical induction is also true: For any position in a derivation, the sentence at that position is truth-functionally entailed by the set of undischarged assumptions in whose scope it lies. In particular, this thesis is true of the last position in any derivation—the sentence that has been derived is truth-functionally entailed by the undischarged assumptions in whose scope it lies, and these are the primary assumptions of the derivation. So the Soundness Metatheorem for *SD* has been established: If $\Gamma \vdash \mathscr{P}$ in *SD*, then $\Gamma \vDash \mathscr{P}$. It follows from Metatheorem 6.2 that every sentence of *SL* that is a theorem in *SD* is truth-functionally true and that every argument that is valid in *SD* is truth-functionally valid (see Exercise 14 of Section 5.4E).

## 6.3E EXERCISES

**1.** List all of the subsets of each of the following sets.

a. {A ⊃ B, C ⊃ D}
b. {C ∨ ~D, ~D ∨ C, C ∨ C}
c. {(B & A) ≡ K}
d. ∅

**2.** Of which of the following sets is $\{A \supset B, C \& D, D \supset A\}$ a superset?

a. $\{A \supset B\}$
b. $\{D \supset A, A \supset B\}$
c. $\{A \supset D, C \& D\}$
d. $\varnothing$
e. $\{C \& D, D \supset A, A \supset B\}$

***3.** Prove case 10 of the inductive step in the proof of Metatheorem 6.2.

**4.a.** Suppose that system *SD** is just like *SD* except that it also contains a new rule of inference:

*Negated Biconditional Introduction* ($\sim \equiv$ I)

$$\begin{array}{|l} \mathscr{P} \\ \\ \sim \mathscr{Q} \\ \\ \sim (\mathscr{P} \equiv \mathscr{Q}) \end{array}$$

Prove that system *SD** is a sound system for sentential logic; that is, prove that if $\Gamma \vdash \mathscr{P}$ in *SD** then $\Gamma \vDash \mathscr{P}$. (You may use Metatheorem 6.2.)

*b. Suppose that system *SD** is just like *SD*, except that it also contains a new rule of inference:

*Backwards Conditional Introduction* (B $\supset$ I)

$$\begin{array}{|l} \begin{array}{|l} \sim \mathscr{Q} \\ \hline \\ \sim \mathscr{P} \end{array} \\ \mathscr{P} \supset \mathscr{Q} \end{array}$$

Prove that system *SD** is sound for sentential logic.

c. Suppose that system *SD** is just like *SD* except that it also contains a new rule of inference:

*Crazy Disjunction Elimination* (C $\vee$ E)

$$\begin{array}{|l} \mathscr{P} \vee \mathscr{Q} \\ \\ \mathscr{P} \\ \mathscr{Q} \end{array}$$

Prove that *SD** is not a sound system for sentential logic.

*d. Suppose that system *SD** is just like *SD*, except that it also contains a new rule of inference:

*Crazy Conditional Introduction* (C $\supset$ I)

$$
\begin{array}{l|l}
 & \quad \sim \mathscr{P} \\
 & \quad \mathscr{Q} \\
 & \mathscr{P} \supset \mathscr{Q}
\end{array}
$$

Prove that *SD** is not a sound system for sentential logic.

e. Suppose that the rules of a system *SD** form a subset of the rules of *SD*. Is *SD** a sound system for sentential logic? Explain.

**5.** Suppose that in our semantics for *SL* the characteristic truth-table for '&' was

| $\mathscr{P}$ | $\mathscr{Q}$ | $\mathscr{P}$ & $\mathscr{Q}$ |
|---|---|---|
| T | T | T |
| T | F | T |
| F | T | F |
| F | F | F |

while the characteristic truth-tables for the other sentential connectives remained the same. Would *SD* still be a sound system for sentential logic? Explain.

**6.** Using Metatheorem 6.2 and Exercise 1.e of Section 6.1E, prove that *SD+* is sound for sentential logic.

## 6.4 THE COMPLETENESS OF *SD* AND *SD+*

We proved in the last section that derivations in *SD* never lead from true premises to a false conclusion, so every derivation in *SD* is semantically acceptable. This fact alone does not establish that *SD* is an adequate natural deduction system for sentential logic. In addition, it is to be hoped that if an argument is truth-functionally valid then we can derive its conclusion from its premises in *SD*, that every sentence that is truth-functionally true can be derived in *SD* from the empty set, in short, that everything that we want to derive in *SD can* be derived in *SD*. If there is even one argument that is truth-functionally valid but for which no derivation can be constructed in *SD*, then *SD* is not adequate to sentential logic. Our final metatheorem assures us that we can derive all that we want to derive in *SD*; it is called the Completeness Metatheorem:

> Metatheorem 6.3: If $\Gamma \vDash \mathscr{P}$, then $\Gamma \vdash \mathscr{P}$ in *SD*.

That is, if a set Γ truth-functionally entails a sentence $\mathscr{P}$, then $\mathscr{P}$ may be derived from Γ in *SD*. It follows from this metatheorem that every argument of *SL* that is truth-functionally valid is valid in *SD* and that every sentence of *SL* that is truth-functionally true is a theorem in *SD* (see Exercise 14 of Section 5.4E). A system for which Metatheorem 6.3 holds is said to be *complete* for sentential logic.

There are several well-known ways to establish a completeness metatheorem. Some of these are said to be *constructive*—they show, for any set Γ and sentence $\mathscr{P}$ such that $\Gamma \vDash \mathscr{P}$, how to construct a derivation of $\mathscr{P}$ from Γ. We shall present a *nonconstructive* proof of completeness.[3] The proof will establish that, for every truth-functional entailment, there is at least one corresponding derivation in *SD*. It will not, however, show how to construct such a derivation.

As preliminaries, we note that

6.4.1. For any set of sentences Γ and any sentence $\mathscr{P}$, $\Gamma \vDash \mathscr{P}$ if and only if $\Gamma \cup \{\sim \mathscr{P}\}$ is truth-functionally inconsistent. (See 6.3.4 and Exercise 1c of Section 3.6E.)

6.4.2. For any set of sentences Γ and any sentence $\mathscr{P}$, $\Gamma \vdash \mathscr{P}$ in *SD* if and only if $\Gamma \cup \{\sim \mathscr{P}\}$ is inconsistent in *SD*. (See Exercise 1.)

Because of 6.4.1, the Completeness Metatheorem is equivalent to the claim

If $\Gamma \cup \{\sim \mathscr{P}\}$ is truth-functionally inconsistent, then $\Gamma \vdash \mathscr{P}$ in *SD*.

Because of 6.4.2, this claim is equivalent to

If $\Gamma \cup \{\sim \mathscr{P}\}$ is truth-functionally inconsistent, then $\Gamma \cup \{\sim \mathscr{P}\}$ is inconsistent in *SD*.

The last claim will follow immediately from the Inconsistency Lemma:

| Lemma 6.1: If a set Γ of sentences of *SL* is truth-functionally inconsistent, then Γ is also inconsistent in *SD*. |
|---|

So if we can show that Lemma 6.1 is true, it will follow that the Completeness Metatheorem is true. For if a set Γ truth-functionally entails a sentence $\mathscr{P}$, by 6.4.1 we know that $\Gamma \cup \{\sim \mathscr{P}\}$ is truth-functionally inconsistent, by Lemma 6.1 it follows that $\Gamma \cup \{\sim \mathscr{P}\}$ is inconsistent in *SD*, and by 6.4.2 it follows that $\Gamma \vDash \mathscr{P}$ in *SD*.

Lemma 6.1 is, like other results that we have presented in this chapter, a sweeping claim—it is a claim about *all* sets of sentences that are truth-functionally

[3] The method that we use to prove completeness is due to Leon Henkin, "The Completeness of the First-Order Functional Calculus," *Journal of Symbolic Logic*, 14 (1949), 159–166.

inconsistent. We shall establish Lemma 6.1 by showing that

> If Γ is *consistent* in *SD*, then Γ is truth-functionally consistent.

(For then, if Γ is truth-functionally *inconsistent*, Γ must also be *inconsistent* in *SD*.) Our strategy will be to show, for any set Γ that is consistent in *SD*, how to construct a truth-value assignment on which every member of Γ is true. We shall construct the truth-value assignment in two steps. First, we shall form a superset of Γ (a set that includes all of the members of Γ and possibly other sentences) that is *maximally consistent in SD*. A maximally consistent set is, intuitively, a consistent set that contains as many sentences as it can without being inconsistent in *SD*:

> A set Γ of sentences of *SL* is *maximally consistent in SD* if and only if Γ is consistent in *SD* and, for every sentence $\mathscr{P}$ of *SL* that is not a member of Γ, $\Gamma \cup \{\mathscr{P}\}$ is inconsistent in *SD*.

If a set is maximally consistent in *SD*, then if we add to the set any sentence that is not already a member, it will be possible to derive some sentence and its negation from the augmented set.

Having constructed a maximally consistent superset of Γ, we shall then construct a truth-value assignment on which every member of the maximally consistent superset is true. We use a superset of Γ that is maximally consistent in *SD*, rather than simply using the original set Γ, because there is a straightforward way to construct a truth-value assignment on which every member of a maximally consistent set is true. Of course, because every member of Γ will be in the maximally consistent superset, it follows that every member of Γ will be true on the truth-value assignment that we have constructed and therefore that Γ is truth-functionally consistent.

Our construction of the superset will show that Lemma 6.2, the Maximal Consistency Lemma, is true:

> Lemma 6.2: If Γ is a set of sentences of *SL* that is consistent in *SD*, then Γ is a subset of at least one set of sentences that is maximally consistent in *SD*.

This lemma is important, for we are then going to show how to construct the desired truth-value assignment for a maximally consistent set. If there were any sets of sentences that were consistent in *SD* but that were not subsets of any set that is *maximally* consistent in *SD*, our construction would fail to show that Lemma 6.1 is true of these sets. At most, we would be able to conclude that some sets of sentences that are consistent in *SD*—those that can be expanded to maximally consistent supersets—are also truth-functionally consistent.

In proving Lemma 6.2, we shall make use of the fact that the sentences of *SL* can be *enumerated*, that is, placed in a definite order in one-to-one correspondence with the positive integers so that there is a first sentence, a second sentence, and so on for each positive integer. Here is a method of enumerating the sentences of *SL*. First we associate with each symbol of *SL* the two-digit numeral occurring to its right:

| *Symbol* | *Numeral* | *Symbol* | *Numeral* |
|---|---|---|---|
| ~ | 10 | A | 30 |
| ∨ | 11 | B | 31 |
| & | 12 | C | 32 |
| ⊃ | 13 | D | 33 |
| ≡ | 14 | E | 34 |
| ( | 15 | F | 35 |
| ) | 16 | G | 36 |
| 0 | 20 | H | 37 |
| 1 | 21 | I | 38 |
| ⋮ | ⋮ | ⋮ | ⋮ |
| 9 | 29 | Z | 55 |

(The ellipses mean to assign the next two-digit numeral to the next digit or letter of the alphabet.) Next we associate with each sentence of *SL*, atomic or molecular, the number designated by the numeral that consists of the numerals associated with the symbols in the sentence, in the order in which those symbols occur. As an example, the numbers associated with the sentences

$(A \vee C_2)$ $\quad\quad$ $\sim\sim (A \supset (B \;\&\; \sim C))$

are, respectively,

153011322216 $\quad\quad$ 10101530131531121032161

It is obvious that each sentence of *SL* will thus have a distinct number associated with it. Finally, we enumerate all the sentences of *SL* by taking them in the order of their associated numbers: The first sentence in the enumeration is the sentence with the smallest associated number, the second sentence is the sentence with the next smallest associated number, and so on. In effect, we have imposed an alphabetical order on the sentences of *SL* so that we may freely talk of the first sentence of *SL* (which turns out to be 'A'—because only atomic sentences will have two-digit associated numbers, and the number for 'A' is the smallest of these), the second sentence of *SL* (which turns out to be 'B'), and so on.

We shall now start with a set Γ of sentences that is consistent in *SD* and construct a superset of Γ that is maximally consistent in *SD*. The construction considers in turn each sentence in the enumeration we have just described, and adds it to the set if and only if the resulting set is consistent in *SD*. In the end, the construction will have added as many sentences as can be added to the original set without producing a set that is inconsistent in *SD*. As the construction goes through the sentences of *SL*, deciding whether or not to add each sentence, it will be producing an infinite sequence $\Gamma_1, \Gamma_2, \Gamma_3, \ldots$ of sets of sentences of *SL*:

1. $\Gamma_1$ is $\Gamma$, the original set.
2. If $\mathscr{P}_i$ is the $i$th sentence in the enumeration, then $\Gamma_{i+1}$ is $\Gamma_i \cup \{\mathscr{P}_i\}$ if $\Gamma_i \cup \{\mathscr{P}_i\}$ is consistent in *SD*; otherwise $\Gamma_{i+1}$ is $\Gamma_i$.

As an example, if $\Gamma_i$ is $\{\sim B, \ \sim C \vee \sim B\}$ and $\mathscr{P}_i$ is 'A', then $\Gamma_i \cup \{\mathscr{P}_i\}$, which is $\{\sim B, \ \sim C \vee \sim B, A\}$, is consistent in *SD*. In this case $\Gamma_{i+1}$ will be the expanded set $\Gamma_i \cup \{\mathscr{P}_i\}$. On the other hand, if $\Gamma_i$ is $\{A, \ \sim B, \ \sim C \vee \sim B\}$ and $\mathscr{P}_i$ is 'B', then $\Gamma_i \cup \{\mathscr{P}_i\}$, which is $\{A, \ \sim B, \ \sim C \vee \sim B, B\}$, is inconsistent in *SD* (this is readily verified). In this case $\mathscr{P}_i$ does not get added to the set—$\Gamma_{i+1}$ is just the set $\{A, \ \sim B, \ \sim C \vee \sim B\}$.

Because we have an infinite sequence of sets, we cannot take the last member of the series as the maximally consistent set desired—there is no last member. Instead, we form a set $\Gamma^*$ that is the union of all the sets in the series: $\Gamma^*$ is defined to contain every sentence that is a member of at least one set in the series and no other sentences. $\Gamma^*$ is a superset of $\Gamma$, because it follows from the definition of $\Gamma^*$ that every sentence in $\Gamma_1$ (as well as $\Gamma_2, \Gamma_3, \ldots$) is a member of $\Gamma^*$, and $\Gamma_1$ is the original set $\Gamma$. It remains to be proved that $\Gamma^*$ is consistent in *SD*, and that it is *maximally* consistent in *SD*. To prove the first claim, we note that every set in the sequence $\Gamma_1, \Gamma_2, \Gamma_3, \ldots$ is consistent in *SD*. This is easily established by mathematical induction:

> *Basis clause:* The first member of the sequence, $\Gamma_1$, is consistent in *SD*.
> Proof: $\Gamma_1$ is defined to be the original set $\Gamma$, which is consistent in *SD*.
>
> *Inductive step:* If every set in the sequence prior to $\Gamma_{k+1}$ is consistent in *SD*, then $\Gamma_{k+1}$ is consistent in *SD*.
> Proof: $\Gamma_{k+1}$ was defined to be $\Gamma_k \cup \{\mathscr{P}_k\}$ if the latter set was consistent in *SD*, and to be $\Gamma_k$ otherwise. In the first case $\Gamma_{k+1}$ is obviously consistent in *SD*. In the second case $\Gamma_{k+1}$ is consistent because, by the inductive hypothesis, $\Gamma_k$ is consistent in *SD*.
>
> ---
>
> *Conclusion:* Every member of the series $\Gamma_1, \Gamma_2, \Gamma_3, \ldots$ is consistent in *SD*.

Now suppose, contrary to what we wish to prove, that $\Gamma^*$ is *inconsistent* in *SD*. Then, by

> 6.4.3 If $\Gamma$ is inconsistent in *SD*, then some finite subset of $\Gamma$ is inconsistent in *SD* (see Exercise 2)

it follows that there is a finite subset $\Gamma'$ of $\Gamma^*$ that is inconsistent in *SD*. $\Gamma'$ must be nonempty, for the empty set is consistent in *SD* (see Exercise 3). Moreover, because $\Gamma'$ is finite, there is a sentence in $\Gamma'$ that comes after all the other members of $\Gamma'$ in our enumeration—call this sentence $\mathscr{P}_j$. (That is, any other member of $\Gamma'$ is $\mathscr{P}_h$

for some $h < j$.) Then every member of $\Gamma'$ is a member of $\Gamma_{j+1}$, by the way we constructed the series $\Gamma_1, \Gamma_2, \Gamma_3, \ldots$ . (This is because we have constructed the sets in such a way that, if a sentence that is the $i$th sentence in our enumeration is a member of *any* set in the sequence—and hence of $\Gamma^*$—it must be in the set $\Gamma_{i+1}$ and every set thereafter. After the construction of $\Gamma_{i+1}$ the only sentences that get added are sentences at position $i + 1$ in the enumeration or later.) But if $\Gamma'$ is inconsistent in *SD*, and every member of $\Gamma'$ is a member of $\Gamma_{j+1}$, then $\Gamma_{j+1}$ is inconsistent in *SD* as well, by 6.4.4:

> 6.4.4. If $\Gamma$ is inconsistent in *SD*, then every superset of $\Gamma$ is inconsistent in *SD*.
>
> Proof: Assume that $\Gamma$ is inconsistent in *SD*. Then for some sentence $\mathscr{P}$, there is a derivation in *SD* in which all the primary assumptions are members of $\Gamma$ and a derivation of $\sim \mathscr{P}$ in *SD* in which all the primary assumptions are members of $\Gamma$ and in which both $\mathscr{P}$ and $\sim \mathscr{P}$ are derived. The primary assumptions of the derivation are members of any superset of $\Gamma$, so $\mathscr{P}$ and $\sim \mathscr{P}$ are both derivable from any superset of $\Gamma$. Therefore every superset of $\Gamma$ is also inconsistent in *SD*.

But we have already proved by mathematical induction that every set in the infinite sequence is consistent in *SD*. So $\Gamma_{j+1}$ *cannot* be inconsistent in *SD*, and our supposition that led to this conclusion is wrong—we may conclude that $\Gamma^*$ is consistent in *SD*.

Now we shall prove that $\Gamma^*$ is not only consistent in *SD*; it is *maximally* consistent. For suppose that $\Gamma^*$ is not maximally consistent in *SD*, then there is at least one sentence $\mathscr{P}_k$ of *SL* that is not a member of $\Gamma^*$ and is such that $\Gamma^* \cup \{\mathscr{P}_k\}$ is consistent in *SD*. We showed, in 6.4.3, that every superset of a set that is inconsistent in *SD* is itself inconsistent, so every subset of a set that is *consistent* in *SD* must itself be consistent in *SD*. In particular, the subset $\Gamma_k \cup \{\mathscr{P}_k\}$ of $\Gamma^* \cup \{\mathscr{P}_k\}$ must be consistent in *SD*. But then, by step 2 of the construction of the sequence of sets, $\Gamma_{k+1}$ is defined to be $\Gamma_k \cup \{\mathscr{P}_k\}$—$\mathscr{P}_k$ is a member of $\Gamma_{k+1}$. $\mathscr{P}_k$ is therefore a member of $\Gamma^*$, contradicting our supposition that it is not a member of $\Gamma^*$. Therefore $\Gamma^*$ must be maximally consistent in *SD*—every sentence that can be consistently added to $\Gamma^*$ is already a member of $\Gamma^*$. This and the result of the previous paragraph establish Lemma 6.2; we have shown that given any set of sentences that is consistent in *SD*, we can construct a superset that is maximally consistent in *SD*.

It remains to be shown that for every set that is maximally consistent in *SD*, we can construct a truth-value assignment on which all the sentences in the set are true; this will establish the Consistency Lemma:

| |
|---|
| Lemma 6.3: Every set of sentences of *SL* that is maximally consistent in *SD* is truth-functionally consistent. |

In Establishing Lemma 6.3, we shall appeal to the following important facts about sets that are maximally consistent in *SD*:

6.4.5 If $\Gamma \vdash \mathscr{P}$ and $\Gamma^*$ is a maximally consistent superset of $\Gamma$, then $\mathscr{P}$ is a member of $\Gamma^*$.
Proof: Assume that $\Gamma \vdash \mathscr{P}$ and let $\Gamma^*$ be a maximally consistent superset of $\Gamma$. Suppose, contrary to what we wish to prove, that $\mathscr{P}$ is *not* a member of $\Gamma^*$. Then, by the definition of maximal consistency, $\Gamma^* \cup \{\mathscr{P}\}$ is inconsistent in *SD*. By 6.4.3, some finite subset $\Gamma'$ of $\Gamma^* \cup \{\mathscr{P}\}$ is therefore inconsistent in *SD*. By 6.4.4, $\Gamma' \cup \{\mathscr{P}\}$ is also inconsistent in *SD*. Therefore, by

6.4.6. If $\Gamma \cup \{\mathscr{P}\}$ is inconsistent in *SD*, then $\Gamma \vdash \sim \mathscr{P}$ (see Exercise 1) it follows that $\Gamma' \vdash \sim \mathscr{P}$. But then, because $\Gamma \vdash \mathscr{P}$, $\Gamma \cup \Gamma' \vdash \mathscr{P}$ and $\Gamma \cup \Gamma' \vdash \sim \mathscr{P}$, so $\Gamma \cup \Gamma'$ is inconsistent in *SD*. $\Gamma^*$ is a superset of $\Gamma \cup \Gamma'$, so it follows, by 6.4.4, that $\Gamma^*$ is inconsistent in *SD*. But $\Gamma^*$ is maximally consistent in *SD*, so it cannot be inconsistent in *SD*. We conclude that our supposition about $\mathscr{P}$, that it is not a member of $\Gamma^*$, is wrong—$\mathscr{P}$ *is* a member of $\Gamma^*$.

In what follows, we will use the standard notation

$\mathscr{P} \in \Gamma$

to mean

$\mathscr{P}$ is a member of $\Gamma$

and the standard notation

$\mathscr{P} \notin \Gamma$

to mean

$\mathscr{P}$ is not a member of $\Gamma$.

6.4.7. If $\Gamma^*$ is maximally consistent in *SD* and $\mathscr{P}$ and $\mathscr{Q}$ are sentences of *SL*, then

a. $\mathscr{P} \in \Gamma^*$ if and only if $\sim \mathscr{P} \notin \Gamma^*$.
b. $\mathscr{P} \& \mathscr{Q} \in \Gamma^*$ if and only if both $\mathscr{P} \in \Gamma^*$ and $\mathscr{Q} \in \Gamma^*$.
c. $\mathscr{P} \vee \mathscr{Q} \in \Gamma^*$ if and only if either $\mathscr{P} \in \Gamma^*$ or $\mathscr{Q} \in \Gamma^*$.
d. $\mathscr{P} \supset \mathscr{Q} \in \Gamma^*$ if and only if either $\mathscr{P} \notin \Gamma^*$ or $\mathscr{Q} \in \Gamma^*$.
e. $\mathscr{P} \equiv \mathscr{Q} \in \Gamma^*$ if and only if either $\mathscr{P} \in \Gamma^*$ and $\mathscr{Q} \in \Gamma^*$ or $\mathscr{P} \notin \Gamma^*$ and $\mathscr{Q} \notin \Gamma^*$.

Proof of a: Assume that $\mathscr{P} \in \Gamma^*$. Then $\sim \mathscr{P} \notin \Gamma^*$ for, if it were a member, then $\Gamma^*$ would have a finite subset that is inconsistent in *SD*, namely, $\{\mathscr{P}, \sim\mathscr{P}\}$, and according to 6.4.4 this is impossible if $\Gamma^*$ is consistent in *SD*. Now assume that $\sim\mathscr{P} \notin \Gamma^*$. Then, by the definition of maximal consistency in *SD*, $\Gamma^* \cup \{\sim\mathscr{P}\}$ is inconsistent in *SD*. So, by reasoning similar to that used in proving 6.4.5, some finite subset $\Gamma'$ of $\Gamma^*$ is such that $\Gamma' \cup \{\sim\mathscr{P}\}$ is inconsistent in *SD*, and therefore such that $\Gamma' \vdash \mathscr{P}$, by 6.4.2. It follows, by 6.4.5, that $\mathscr{P} \in \Gamma^*$.

Proof of b: Assume that $\mathscr{P} \& \mathscr{Q} \in \Gamma^*$. Then $\{\mathscr{P} \& \mathscr{Q}\}$ is a subset of $\Gamma^*$. Because $\{\mathscr{P} \& \mathscr{Q}\} \vdash \mathscr{P}$ and $\{\mathscr{P} \& \mathscr{Q}\} \vdash \mathscr{Q}$ (both by Conjunction Elimination), it follows, by 6.4.5, that $\mathscr{P} \in \Gamma^*$ and $\mathscr{Q} \in \Gamma^*$. Now suppose that $\mathscr{P} \in \Gamma^*$ and $\mathscr{Q} \in \Gamma^*$. Then $\{\mathscr{P}, \mathscr{Q}\}$ is a subset of $\Gamma^*$ and, because $\{\mathscr{P}, \mathscr{Q}\} \vdash \mathscr{P} \& \mathscr{Q}$ (by Conjunction Introduction), it follows, by 6.4.5, that $\mathscr{P} \& \mathscr{Q} \in \Gamma^*$.

Proof of c: See Exercise 5.

Proof of d: Assume that $\mathscr{P} \supset \mathscr{Q} \in \Gamma^*$. If $\mathscr{P} \notin \Gamma^*$, then it follows trivially that either $\mathscr{P} \notin \Gamma^*$ or $\mathscr{Q} \in \Gamma^*$. If $\mathscr{P} \in \Gamma^*$, then $\{\mathscr{P}, \mathscr{P} \supset \mathscr{Q}\}$ is a subset of $\Gamma^*$. Because $\{\mathscr{P}, \mathscr{P} \supset \mathscr{Q}\} \vdash \mathscr{Q}$ (by Conditional Elimination), it follows, by 6.4.5, that $\mathscr{Q} \in \Gamma^*$. So, if $\mathscr{P} \supset \mathscr{Q} \in \Gamma^*$, then either $\mathscr{P} \notin \Gamma'$ or $\mathscr{Q} \in \Gamma^*$. Now assume that either $\mathscr{P} \notin \Gamma^*$ or $\mathscr{Q} \in \Gamma^*$. In the former case, by (a), $\sim\mathscr{P} \in \Gamma^*$. So either $\{\sim\mathscr{P}\}$ is a subset of $\Gamma^*$ or $\{\mathscr{Q}\}$ is a subset of $\Gamma^*$. $\mathscr{P} \supset \mathscr{Q}$ is derivable from either subset:

| | | |
|---|---|---|
| 1 | $\sim\mathscr{P}$ | Assumption |
| 2 | $\quad\mathscr{P}$ | Assumption |
| 3 | $\quad\quad\sim\mathscr{Q}$ | Assumption |
| 4 | $\quad\quad\mathscr{P}$ | 2 R |
| 5 | $\quad\quad\sim\mathscr{P}$ | 1 R |
| 6 | $\quad\mathscr{Q}$ | 3-5 $\sim$E |
| 7 | $\mathscr{P} \supset \mathscr{Q}$ | 2-6 $\supset$I |

| | | |
|---|---|---|
| 1 | $\mathscr{Q}$ | Assumption |
| 2 | $\quad\mathscr{P}$ | Assumption |
| 3 | $\quad\mathscr{Q}$ | 1 R |
| 4 | $\mathscr{P} \supset \mathscr{Q}$ | 2-4 $\supset$I |

Either way, there is a finite subset of $\Gamma^*$ from which $\mathscr{P} \supset \mathscr{Q}$ is derivable; so, by 6.4.5, it follows that $\mathscr{P} \supset \mathscr{Q} \in \Gamma^*$.

Proof of e: See Exercise 5.

Turning now to Lemma 6.3, let $\Gamma$ be a set of sentences that is maximally consistent in *SD*. We said earlier that it is easy to construct a truth-value assignment on which every member of a maximally consistent set is true, and it is: We need only consider the atomic sentences in the set. Let $\mathscr{A}^*$ be the truth-value assignment that assigns the truth-value **T** to every atomic sentence of *SL* that is a member of $\Gamma^*$ and that assigns the truth-value **F** to every other atomic sentence of *SL*. We shall prove by mathematical induction that each sentence of *SL* is true on the truth-value assignment $\mathscr{A}^*$ if and only if it is a member of $\Gamma^*$—from which it follows that every member of $\Gamma^*$ is true on $\mathscr{A}^*$, thus establishing truth-functional consistency. The induction will be based on the number of occurrences of connectives in the sentences of *RL*:

> *Basic clause:* Each atomic sentence of *SL* is true on $\mathcal{A}^*$ if and only if it is a member of $\Gamma^*$.
>
> *Inductive step:* If every sentence of *SL* with $k$ or fewer occurrences of connectives is such that it is true on $\mathcal{A}^*$ if and only if it is a member of $\Gamma^*$, then every sentence of *SL* with $k + 1$ occurrences of connectives is such that it is true on $\mathcal{A}^*$ if and only if it is a member of $\Gamma^*$.
>
> ---
>
> *Conclusion:* Every sentence of *SL* is such that it is true on $\mathcal{A}^*$ if and only if it is a member of $\Gamma^*$.

The basis clause is obviously true; we defined $\mathcal{A}^*$ to be an assignment that assigns **T** to all and only the atomic sentences of *SL* that are members of $\Gamma^*$. To prove the inductive step, we will assume that the inductive hypothesis holds for an arbitrary integer $k$: That each sentence containing $k$ or fewer occurrences of connectives is true on $\mathcal{A}^*$ if and only if it is a member of $\Gamma^*$. We must now show that the same holds true of every sentence $\mathcal{P}$ containing $k + 1$ occurrences of connectives. We consider five cases, reflecting the five forms that a molecular sentence of *SL* might have.

Case 1: $\mathcal{P}$ has the form $\sim \mathcal{Q}$. If $\sim \mathcal{Q}$ is true on $\mathcal{A}^*$, then $\mathcal{Q}$ is false on $\mathcal{A}^*$. Because $\mathcal{Q}$ contains fewer than $k + 1$ occurrences of connectives, it follows by the inductive hypothesis that $\mathcal{Q} \notin \Gamma^*$. Therefore, by 6.4.7(a), $\sim \mathcal{Q} \in \Gamma^*$. If $\sim \mathcal{Q}$ is false on $\mathcal{A}^*$, then $\mathcal{Q}$ is true on $\mathcal{A}^*$. It follows by the inductive hypothesis that $\mathcal{Q} \in \Gamma^*$. Therefore, by 6.4.7(a), $\sim \mathcal{Q} \notin \Gamma^*$.

Case 2: $\mathcal{P}$ has the form $\mathcal{Q} \& \mathcal{R}$. If $\mathcal{Q} \& \mathcal{R}$ is true on $\mathcal{A}^*$, then both $\mathcal{Q}$ and $\mathcal{R}$ are true on $\mathcal{A}^*$. Because $\mathcal{Q}$ and $\mathcal{R}$ each contain fewer than $k + 1$ occurrences of connectives, it follows by the inductive hypothesis that $\mathcal{Q} \in \Gamma^*$ and $\mathcal{R} \in \Gamma^*$. Therefore, by 6.4.7(b), $\mathcal{Q} \& \mathcal{R} \in \Gamma^*$. If $\mathcal{Q} \& \mathcal{R}$ is false on $\mathcal{A}^*$, then either $\mathcal{Q}$ is false on $\mathcal{A}^*$ or $\mathcal{R}$ is false on $\mathcal{A}^*$. Therefore, by the inductive hypothesis, either $\mathcal{Q} \notin \Gamma^*$ or $\mathcal{R} \notin \Gamma^*$ and so, by 6.4.7(b), $\mathcal{Q} \& \mathcal{R} \notin \Gamma^*$.

Case 3: $\mathcal{P}$ has the form $\mathcal{Q} \vee \mathcal{R}$. See Exercise 6.

Case 4: $\mathcal{P}$ has the form $\mathcal{Q} \supset \mathcal{R}$. If $\mathcal{Q} \supset \mathcal{R}$ is true on $\mathcal{A}^*$, then either $\mathcal{Q}$ is false on $\mathcal{A}^*$ or $\mathcal{R}$ is true on $\mathcal{A}^*$. Because $\mathcal{Q}$ and $\mathcal{R}$ each contain fewer than $k + 1$ occurrences of connectives, it follows from the inductive hypothesis that either $\mathcal{Q} \notin \Gamma^*$ or $\mathcal{R} \in \Gamma^*$. By 6.4.7(d), then, $\mathcal{Q} \supset \mathcal{R} \in \Gamma^*$. If $\mathcal{Q} \supset \mathcal{R}$ is false on $\mathcal{A}^*$, then $\mathcal{Q}$ is true on $\mathcal{A}^*$ and $\mathcal{R}$ is false on $\mathcal{A}^*$. By the inductive hypothesis, then, $\mathcal{Q} \in \Gamma^*$ and $\mathcal{R} \notin \Gamma^*$. And by 6.4.7(d), it follows that $\mathcal{Q} \supset \mathcal{R} \notin \Gamma^*$.

Case 5: See Exercise 6.

This completes the proof of the inductive step. Hence we may conclude that each sentence of *SL* is such that it is a member of $\Gamma^*$ if and only if it is true on $\mathcal{A}^*$. So every member of a set $\Gamma^*$ that is maximally consistent in *SD* is true on $\mathcal{A}^*$, and the set $\Gamma^*$ is therefore truth-functionally inconsistent. This establishes Lemma 6.3.

We now know that Lemma 6.1 is true. Because every set of sentences $\Gamma$ that is consistent in *SD* is a subset of a set of sentences that is maximally consistent in *SD* (Lemma 6.2), and because every set of sentences that is maximally consistent in *SD* is truth-functionally consistent (Lemma 6.3), it follows that every set of sentences that is consistent in *SD* is a subset of a truth-functionally consistent set and is therefore itself truth-functionally consistent. So if a set is truth-functionally *inconsistent*, it must be inconsistent in *SD*.

It now follows that Metatheorem 6.3:

$$\text{If } \Gamma \vDash \mathscr{P}\text{, then } \Gamma \vdash \mathscr{P}$$

is true. For if $\Gamma \vDash \mathscr{P}$, then $\Gamma \cup \{\sim \mathscr{P}\}$ is truth-functionally inconsistent. Then, by Lemma 6.1, $\Gamma \cup \{\sim \mathscr{P}\}$ is inconsistent in *SD*. And if $\Gamma \cup \{\sim \mathscr{P}\}$ is inconsistent in *SD*, then, by 6.4.2, $\Gamma \vdash \mathscr{P}$ in *SD*. So *SD* is complete for sentential logic—for every truth-functional entailment there is at least one corresponding derivation that can be constructed in *SD*. This, together with the proof of the Soundness Metatheorem in Section 6.3, shows that *SD* is an adequate system for sentential logic.

## 6.4E EXERCISES

**1.** Prove 6.4.2 and 6.4.6.

**2.** Prove 6.4.3.

***3.** Prove that the empty set is consistent in *SD*.

**4.** Using Metatheorem 6.3, prove that *SD*+ is complete for sentential logic.

***5.** Prove that every set that is maximally consistent in *SD* has the following properties:

c. $\mathscr{P} \vee \mathscr{Q} \in \Gamma^*$ if and only if either $\mathscr{P} \in \Gamma^*$ or $\mathscr{Q} \in \Gamma^*$.
e. $\mathscr{P} \equiv \mathscr{Q} \in \Gamma^*$ if and only if either $\mathscr{P} \in \Gamma^*$ and $\mathscr{Q} \in \Gamma^*$, or $\mathscr{P} \notin \Gamma^*$ and $\mathscr{Q} \notin \Gamma^*$.

***6.** Establish cases 3 and 5 of the inductive step in the proof of Lemma 6.3.

**7.a.** Suppose that *SD** is like *SD* except that it lacks Reiteration. Show that *SD** is complete for sentential logic.
***b.** Suppose that *SD** is like *SD* except that it lacks Negation Introduction. Show that *SD* is complete for sentential logic.

**8.** Suppose that *SD** is like *SD* except that it lacks Conjunction Elimination. Show where our completeness proof for *SD* will fail as a completeness proof for *SD**.

**9.** Using Lemma 6.1 and Metatheorem 6.2, prove the following metatheorem (known as the *Compactness Theorem* for sentential logic):

| |
|---|
| Metatheorem 6.4: A set $\Gamma$ of sentences of *SL* is truth-functionally consistent if and only if every finite subset of $\Gamma$ is truth-functionally consistent. |

Chapter

# 7

# PREDICATE LOGIC: SYMBOLIZATION AND SYNTAX

## 7.1 INTRODUCTION

One of the goals of logic has been to develop tools which allow us to understand (and test for the holding of) various logical properties of sentences and sets of sentences *of natural languages*. Until well into the twentieth century many, if not most, logicians assumed that to meet this goal they had to accomplish two projects, the first being the development of formal languages and systems in which all, or at least all "important",[1] natural language discourse can be represented, the second being the development of test procedures for these formal languages. It was expected that the test procedures would be such that each of the logical properties defined for a formal system would be *decidable*, that is, that the associated test procedure would always yield, after a finite number of steps, a yes or no answer to the question 'does this logical property hold in this case'.

In Chapter Two we introduced the language *SL* and techniques for symbolizing sentences of English in *SL*. In subsequent chapters we presented various semantic and syntactic methods for testing sentences and sets of sentences of *SL* for the logical properties defined for that language, including validity, consistency, and logical truth. One of the test procedures we developed, that based on truth-tables, is entirely mechanical and another, that based on truth-trees, can readily be made so. (A procedure is 'mechanical' in this sense if each step is

[1] The only sometimes expressed view driving this research effort was that scientific discourse is the important part of natural language discourse and that mathematics, or perhaps mathematics and physics, constitute the core of science.

dictated by some rule, given prior steps—a procedure for which a computer program can be written is a mechanical procedure.)

The interesting question to ask now is "To what extent does *SL* and its associated test procedures meet the goal of the first paragraph of this section?" *SL* is a *decidable* system. That is, if we restrict ourselves to finite sets of sentences and use, for example, the truth-table method, it is always possible to determine, in a finite number of steps, whether one of the logical properties defined for *SL* (truth-functional truth, falsity, indeterminacy, validity, equivalence, entailment, consistency) holds in a given case. But *SL* is far from powerful enough to allow the representation, within *SL*, of all, or even "all the important parts of", natural language discourse. To see this, we need only recall that the results obtained for sentences and sets of sentences of *SL* do not necessarily carry over to the sentences and sets of sentences of English from which they were obtained by the symbolization process.

It is true that, for example, any English language argument which has an acceptable symbolization in *SL* that is truth-functionally valid is itself logically valid. So too a sentence of English which can be fairly symbolized as a sentence of *SL* which is truth-functionally true (or truth-functionally false) is itself logically true (or logically false); similarly for equivalence and entailment. And if a set of English sentences can be fairly symbolized as a set of sentences of *SL* which is truth-functionally *inconsistent*, then that set of English sentences is itself logically *inconsistent*.

Unfortunately, the converse of the above relationships do not hold. If an argument of English has a symbolization in *SL* which is truth-functionally invalid, *it does not follow* that the English argument is invalid. If a sentence of *SL* is not truth-functionally true, *it does not follow* that the English sentence it symbolizes is not logically true. If a sentence of *SL* is not truth-functionally false *it does not follow* that the English sentence it symbolizes is not logically false; so too for equivalence and entailment. And if a set of sentences of *SL* is truth-functionally consistent, *it does not follow* that the set of English sentences we are trying to evaluate is logically consistent.

The problem is not that we have no test for determining when a sentence or group of sentences of *SL* constitute a *fair* symbolization of a sentence or group of sentences of English, although this is true. The problem is rather that the language *SL* is itself not sophisticated enough to allow the adequate symbolization of a great deal of natural language discourse. Put another way, even a *correct* symbolization of an English sentence by a sentence of *SL* frequently fails to capture much of the content of the English sentence. The syntactic structure of English, and of every natural language, is much more complex than the structure of a purely truth-functional language such as *SL*. No truth-functional language can mirror all of the syntactic relationships which hold between sentences and sets of sentences of a natural language.

For example, while the sentence

Each citizen will either vote or pay a fine

might form part of a recommendation for rather dramatic reforms in our political system, the sentence

Each citizen will either vote or not vote

is not similarly controversial. Rather, it smacks of being a logical truth. Each citizen, for example, Cynthia, obviously either will vote or will not vote. Indeed, the claim about Cynthia, or any other specified citizen, can be symbolized as a truth-functional truth of *SL*. Where 'C' abbreviates 'Cynthia will vote', '$C \vee \sim C$' says of Cynthia what the general claim says of each citizen. But there is, barring heroic measures, no symbolization of the general claim in *SL* which is truth-functionally true.[2]

Similarly, the following argument should strike the reader as being logically valid, although it has no symbolization in *SL* which is truth-functionally valid:

> None of David's friends supports Republicans. Sarah supports Breitlow, and Breitlow is a Republican. So Sarah is no friend of David's.

One attempt at a symbolization of this argument in *SL* is

$$\begin{array}{l} N \\ S \& B \\ \hline \sim F \end{array}$$

Here 'S' abbreviates 'Sarah supports Breitlow', 'B' abbreviates 'Breitlow is a Republican', and 'F' abbreviates 'Sarah is a friend of David's'. 'None of David's friends supports Republicans' is treated as an atomic sentence and symbolized as 'N'. This argument of *SL* is truth-functionally invalid. We could have treated 'None of David's friends supports Republicans' as the negation of 'Some of David's friends support Republicans' and symbolized it as '$\sim S$', but the result would still be truth-functionally invalid.

The problem is that we cannot show, via the syntax of *SL*, that there is a relation between supporting Breitlow, Breitlow's being a Republican, and supporting Republicans. This is because *SL*, in taking sentences to be the smallest linguistic units (other than sentential connectives), makes all *subsentential* relationships invisible.

In this chapter we will develop a new language, *PL* (for *p*redicate *l*ogic). *PL* will allow us to express many subsentential relationships.[3] It will turn out that

[2] Since there are presumably only finitely many citizens we could construct a very long extended conjunction with as many conjuncts of the sort '$C \vee \sim C$' as there are citizens. But even such heroic measures will fail when the items about which we wish to talk (e.g., the positive integers) constitute an infinite, not just an exceedingly large, collection. See Section 7.2.

[3] There are, as one might expect, arguments that are logically valid but whose symbolizations in *PL* are not valid, sentences which are logically true, but whose symbolizations in *PL* do not reflect this, and so on. To deal with natural language discourse which cannot be represented in *PL* even more powerful formal systems are available, for example, tense logic and modal logic. A discussion of these systems is beyond the scope of this text.

the above argument has a valid symbolization in *PL*, and that 'Each citizen will either vote or not vote' has a symbolization in *PL* which is logically true. However, it will also turn out that *PL* and its associated test procedures do not constitute a *decidable* system. That is, there is no mechanical test procedure which will always yield, in a finite number of steps, a 'yes or no' answer to such questions as 'Is this argument of *PL* valid?' In fact, we now know that there can be no formal system which is both decidable and has a vocabulary, syntax, and semantics powerful enough to allow the expression of even moderately complex natural language discourse, including the claims of mathematics and physics.[4]

### *PREDICATES, INDIVIDUAL CONSTANTS, AND QUANTITY TERMS OF ENGLISH*

A distinction between singular terms and predicates is central to understanding the subsentential structure of English discourse. A singular term is any word or phrase that designates or purports to designate (or denote, or refer to) some one thing. Singular terms are of two sorts, proper names and definite descriptions. Examples of proper names include 'George Washington', 'Marie Curie', 'Sherlock Holmes', 'Rhonda', and 'Henry'. Generally speaking, proper names are attached to the things they name by simple convention. Definite descriptions, for example 'the discoverer of radium', 'the person Henry is talking to', 'Mary's best friend', and 'James' only brother', on the other hand, pick out or purport to pick out a thing by providing a unique description of that thing. A definite description just is a description which, by its grammatical structure, purports to describe exactly one thing. Thus 'James' only brother' is a definite description, whereas 'James' brother' is not—the latter could accurately describe many persons, the former can describe at most one.

In English not every singular term does designate. In its normal use, 'Sherlock Holmes' fails to designate because there is no such person as Sherlock Holmes. Similarly, a definite description fails to designate if nothing satisfies or is uniquely described by that description. Both 'the largest prime number' and 'the present Prime Minister of the United States' are definite descriptions that for this reason fail to designate.

What thing, if any, a name or definite description designates clearly depends upon the context of use. In its most familiar use 'George Washington' designates the first President of the United States. But a historian may have named her dog after the first President, and if so there will be contexts in which she and her friends use the term 'George Washington' to designate a dog, not a figure from American history. In the same way, 'the person Henry is talking to' may designate one person on one occasion, another on another occasion, and (Henry being a taciturn fellow) very often no one at all. *Hereafter, when we use a sentence of English as an example, or in an exercise set, we shall, unless otherwise noted, be assuming that a context is available for that sentence such that in that context all the singular terms in the sentence do designate.* Moreover, when we are working with a group of sentences, the context

[4] See Chapter Eight, Section 2, for a further discussion of this point.

that is assumed must be the same for all the sentences in the group. That is, we assume that a singular term that occurs several times in the piece of English discourse under discussion designates the same thing in each of its occurrences.

In English pronouns are often used in place of proper names and definite descriptions. When they are so used their references are determined by the proper names or definite descriptions for which they are going proxy. For example, in the most straightforward reading of the conditional

If Sue has read Darwin, she's no creationist

the reference of 'she' is established by the use of 'Sue' in the antecedent of that conditional. So it is clearly appropriate to paraphrase this sentence as

If Sue has read Darwin, Sue's no creationist.

But not every pronoun can be replaced by a singular term. Replacing 'her or his' in

This test is so easy that if anyone fails the test it's her or his own fault

with a singular term, any singular term, will create a nonequivalent sentence, for example,

This test is so easy that if anyone fails the test it's Cynthia's own fault.

The former claim places responsibility for failure on the test taker, the latter places it, no matter who the test taker is, on Cynthia. We will return below to uses of pronouns which cannot be replaced with singular terms.

Obviously, a sentence can contain more than one singular term. For example,

New York is between Philadelphia and Boston

contains three singular terms: 'New York', 'Philadelphia', and 'Boston'.[5] *Predicates* of English are parts of English sentences which can be obtained by deleting one or more singular terms from an English sentence. Alternatively, a predicate is a string of words with one or more holes or blanks in it such that when the holes are filled with singular terms, a sentence of English results. From the above example, all of

[5] We are here concerned only with isolating singular terms that do not occur as constituents of other singular terms. That is, we here take

The Roman general who defeated Pompey invaded both Gaul and Germany

to contain just three singular terms: 'The Roman general who defeated Pompey', 'Gaul', and 'Germany'. In Section 7.6 we will introduce techniques which allow us to recognize and symbolize singular terms which are themselves constituents of singular terms, for example, 'Pompey' as it occurs in 'The Roman general who defeated Pompey'.

the following predicates can be obtained:

_______ is between Philadelphia and Boston.

New York is between _______ and Boston.

New York is between Philadelphia and _______.

_______ is between _______ and Boston.

_______ is between Philadelphia and _______.

New York is between _______ and _______.

_______ is between _______ and _______.

A predicate with just one blank is a *one-place* predicate. A predicate with more than one blank is a *many-place* predicate. (A predicate with exactly two blanks is a *two-place* predicate, a predicate with exactly three blanks is a *three-place* predicate, and so on. Generally, where $n$ is a positive integer, a predicate with $n$ blanks is an $n$-place predicate.)

One way of generating a sentence from a predicate is to fill the blanks in the predicate with singular terms. Any singular term can be put in any blank, and the same singular term can be put in more than one blank. So from the two-place predicate '_______ works for _______' and the singular terms 'Pat', 'Tom', '3M', 'IBM', and 'the smallest prime number' we can generate the following sentences:

Tom works for 3M

Pat works for 3M

Tom works for Pat

Pat works for Tom

Pat works for Pat

3M works for Tom

IBM works for 3M

The smallest prime number works for IBM

and so on. Note that all of the above are sentences of English by the standard grammatical rules of English. When a sentence which consists of an $n$-place predicate with the holes filled with $n$ singular terms is true, we will say that that predicate is true of the $n$ things designated by those $n$ singular terms. As it happens, '_______ works for _______' is true of the pair consisting of Tom and 3M, but false of the pair consisting of 3M and Tom (pairs, and triples, etc., have an order built in). The Tom we have in mind does work for 3M, but 3M does not work for Tom.

It may be objected that not all of the above sentences "make sense"—what would it be for the smallest prime number (2) to work for anything or anyone? One approach here would be to declare such sentences as the last listed semantically deviant and therefore not a candidate for truth, that is, neither true nor false. We, however, will take the simpler approach of counting such sentences meaningful but false. After all, on any normal understanding, the smallest prime number is not the sort of thing that works for anyone or anything. Hence the claim that it works for IBM is false. (The predicate '_______ works for _______' is not true of the pair consisting of the smallest prime number and IBM.) By this move we will gain an overall simplicity and generality when we come to develop the formal syntax and semantics for *PL*.

So far in displaying predicates we have been marking the blanks into which singular terms can be placed by underscoring those blanks. It is time to adopt a more standard notation. Hereafter, in displaying predicates we shall use the lower-case letters 'w', 'x', 'y', and 'z' (with numerical subscripts where necessary) to mark the holes in those predicates. Using this convention, the three-place predicate of English discussed above can be displayed as

x is between y and z

Given a stock of predicates, singular terms, and the sentential connectives 'and', 'or', 'if ... then', 'if and only if', and 'not', we can generate a wide variety of sentences of English. For example, from the just enumerated sentential connectives, the singular terms 'Henry', 'Sue', 'Rita', and 'Michael' and the predicates 'x likes lying on the beach', 'x likes y', and 'x is taller than y' we can generate:

Michael likes lying on the beach.

Sue likes lying on the beach.

Michael is taller than Sue and Sue is taller than Henry.

Sue likes Henry and Michael likes Rita.

If Rita likes Henry, then Rita is taller than Henry.

If Michael likes lying on the beach then Rita doesn't like lying on the beach.

but we cannot, with these limited resources, generate such simple but powerful claims as

Everyone likes lying on the beach.

No one likes Michael.

Michael likes everyone.

Michael does not like anyone.

Michael doesn't like everyone.

Someone likes Sue.

No one is taller than her or himself.

What is missing is an account of such *quantity* terms as 'every', 'all', 'each', 'some', and 'none'.

The first thing to note is that quantity terms are not singular terms. 'Everyone' is neither a proper name nor a definite description—there is no thing which is either named or described by the term 'everyone'. So too for 'everything', 'no one', 'nothing', 'anyone', 'anything', 'someone', and 'something'. These and other quantity terms serve to indicate how many of the persons or things under discussion are thus-and-so, not to name or refer to some single entity. Hence quantity claims should not be analyzed as being of the subject/predicate form.

Consider the simple claim 'Someone likes lying on the beach'. We can see this sentence as being composed of the one-place predicate 'x likes lying on the beach' and the expression 'someone'. If this claim is true, then there is some person who likes lying on the beach, that is, someone of whom the predicate 'x likes lying on the beach' is true. But his or her name is not 'someone', nor is 'someone' a description of that person.

Similarly,

Everyone likes lying on the beach

is true if and only if 'x likes lying on the beach' is true of every person, and

No one likes lying on the beach

is true if and only if there is no person of whom the predicate 'x likes lying on the beach' is true.[6]

### *INTRODUCTION TO PL*

It is time to introduce the basic elements of the formal language *PL*. We will need the sentential connectives of *SL*, and analogues to the singular terms, predicates, and quantity terms of English. The sentential connectives are, to review, the five truth-functional connectives '&', '$\vee$', '$\supset$', '$\equiv$' and '$\sim$'. As analogues to denoting singular terms of English, that is, to singular terms which actually do, on the occasion of use in question, denote, *PL* contains *individual constants*, the lower-case Roman letters 'a' through 'v', with or without numerical subscripts. The predicates of *PL* are the upper-case Roman letters 'A' through 'Z', with or without numerical subscripts, followed by one or more primes. Predicates of *PL*, like predicates of English, come with holes or blanks, the number of holes officially indicated by the number of primes. A predicate with one hole is called a 'one-place predicate', a predicate with two holes a 'two-place predicate', and so on. Hence

F′

is a one-place predicate of *PL*,

F″

is a two-place predicate of *PL*. In specifying predicates we will, in practice, generally omit the primes and indicate that the predicate in question is an *n*-place predicate by writing *n* of the letters 'w', 'x', 'y', and 'z' (with subscripts if

[6] Instead of talking of a predicate's being true or false of a thing or an ordered collection of things, we will hereafter frequently talk instead of a thing or ordered collection of things *satisfying* or *failing to satisfy* a predicate. Thus all and only red things *satisfy* the predicate 'x is red'. This notion of satisfaction will be used in the semantics for *PL*.

necessary) after the predicate letter. (For example, the predicate in 'Fx' is a one-place predicate and the predicate in 'Fxy' is a two-place predicate.) These letters, 'w' through 'z' with and without subscripts, are called the *variables* of *PL* and will have more than a hole-marking use.

In *SL* a single sentence letter can be used to symbolize or abbreviate different English sentences on different occasions. Analogously in *PL*, we might use the two-place predicate 'Lxy' to symbolize 'x likes y' on one occasion; on another we might use it to symbolize 'x loves y', on another 'x loathes y', on another 'x is less than y', and so on. Of course, we could use 'Fxy' to symbolize 'x likes y', but that would be harder to remember. Similarly, on one occasion we might use the individual constant 'a' to designate Alfred, on another Adrian, on another the number 1.

It will be useful to have a way of specifying how predicates and constants of *PL* are being used on a particular occasion, as well as what group of things is being talked about. We call the collection of things being talked about on a given occasion the *universe of discourse* for that occasion, and use the abbreviation 'U.D.' to specify a universe of discourse.[7] For this purpose we introduce the notion of a *symbolization key*. The following is an example of a symbolization key. We will use it in symbolizing the English sentences discussed above concerning Henry, Michael, Rita, and Sue.

U.D.: people in Michael's office
Lxy: x likes y
Bx: x likes lying on the beach
Txy: x is taller than y
h: Henry
m: Michael
r: Rita
s: Sue

Note that whereas in English proper names are capitalized and predicates written with lower-case letters, in *PL* lower-case letters are used to symbolize singular terms of English, including proper names, and upper-case letters are used to symbolize predicates. In English sentences can be generated from predicates by filling the holes with singular terms. Similarly, in *PL* sentences can be generated from predicates by filling the holes (replacing the variables which mark the holes) with individual constants.

For example,

Lsh

[7] By stipulation, in *PL* universes of discourse must be nonempty, that is, discourses must always be about at least one thing. This is not a *very* restrictive stipulation, as there is very little to say about nothing and *no one* to say it.

symbolizes, given the above symbolization key, 'Sue likes Henry'. 'Henry likes Sue' is symbolized as 'Lhs'. And 'Michael likes lying on the beach' is symbolized as 'Bm'.

Still using the above symbolization key, the sentences

Sue likes lying on the beach.

Michael is taller than Sue and Sue is taller than Henry.

Sue likes Henry and Michael likes Rita.

If Rita likes Henry, then Rita is taller than Henry.

If Michael likes lying on the beach then Rita doesn't like lying on the beach.

can be symbolized as follows in *PL*:

Bs

Tms & Tsh

Lsh & Lmr

Lrh ⊃ Trh

Bm ⊃ ~ Br

In *PL*, as in *SL*, when a binary connective is used to join sentences the result must be enclosed within parentheses. So the official versions of the last two sentences of *PL* are '(Lrh ⊃ Trh)' and '(Bm ⊃ ~ Br)'. But with *PL*, as with *SL*, we will informally omit the outermost parentheses of a sentence whose main logical operator is a binary connective. (Also as in *SL*, we will informally allow the use of square brackets in place of parentheses.)

We can use the above symbolization key to give English readings for the following sentences of *PL*:

Lhr & ~ Lrh

Lrh ⊃ Lrm

Trh & ~ Trs

Tsh ⊃ Lhs

(Lmh ∨ Lms) ⊃ (Lmh & Lms)

In English these become, respectively,

Henry likes Rita and Rita does not like Henry.

If Rita likes Henry then Rita likes Michael.

Rita is taller than Henry and Rita is not taller than Sue.

If Sue is taller than Henry, then Henry likes Sue.

If Michael likes Henry or Michael likes Sue, then Michael likes Henry and Michael likes Sue.

We can, of course, improve on the English. For example, the last sentence can be more colloquially paraphrased as

If Michael likes either Henry or Sue he likes both of them.

There is a way we can symbolize some English sentences involving quantity terms using only the resources of *PL* so far available to us. If we are talking just about the people in Michael's office, that is, just about Michael, Sue, Rita, and Henry, then one way to symbolize 'Michael likes everyone' in *PL* is

(Lms & Lmh) & (Lmr & Lmm)

Note that we are here taking the scope or range of application of 'everyone' in 'Michael likes everyone' to be all and only those persons in Michael's office (one of whom is Michael himself). We could use the same strategy to symbolize 'Michael likes someone' as

(Lms $\vee$ Lmh) $\vee$ (Lmr $\vee$ Lmm)

### 7.1E EXERCISES

**1.** Symbolize the following sentences in *PL*, using the indicated symbolization key:

U.D.: Alfy, Barbara, Clyde, Dawn, Euston, and the cities Houston, Indianapolis, Kalamazoo, Newark, Philadelphia, San Francisco, and Tulsa
Bxy: x was born in y
Lxy: x lives in y
Axy: x is larger than y
Txy: x is taller than y
a: Alfy
b: Barbara
c: Clyde
d: Dawn
e: Euston
h: Houston
i: Indianapolis
k: Kalamazoo
n: Newark
p: Philadelphia
s: San Francisco
t: Tulsa

a. Alfy was born in Indianapolis.
*b. Clyde was born in Tulsa.
c. Barbara was born in Newark.
*d. Dawn was born in San Francisco.
e. Euston was born in Houston.
*f. No one was born in Kalamazoo.

g. Philadelphia is larger than Houston, Houston is larger than Newark, and Newark is larger than Kalamazoo.
*h. Tulsa isn't larger than either Philadelphia or Houston.
i. Indianapolis is larger than Houston if and only if it is larger than Philadelphia.
*j. Barbara lives in Philadelphia only if Dawn does.
k. Everyone lives in Philadelphia, but no one was born there.
*l. Barbara is taller than Clyde and Clyde is taller than Alfy, but neither Barbara nor Clyde is taller than Euston.
m. Dawn is the tallest person in the office.
*n. Alfy isn't taller than everyone else in the office.
o. Alfy isn't taller than anyone in the office, but he is larger than everyone else in the office.
*p. If Clyde is taller than Barbara, he's also larger than Alfy.

**2.** Symbolize the following sentences in *PL*, using the indicated symbolization key:

U.D.: Agatha, Bertram, Charles, and Desdemona
Bx: x is beautiful
Ix: x is intelligent
Rx: x is rich
Axy: x is attracted to y
Dxy: x despises y
Lxy: x loves y
Sxy: x is shorter than y
a: Agatha
b: Bertram
c: Charles
d: Desdemona

a. Agatha is both intelligent and beautiful, but she is not rich.
*b. Charles is rich and beautiful, but not intelligent.
c. Desdemona is beautiful, rich, and intelligent.
*d. Bertram is neither rich, nor beautiful, nor intelligent.
e. If Bertram is intelligent, so are both Desdemona and Agatha.
*f. Agatha is beautiful and intelligent, Bertram is intelligent but not beautiful, and neither is rich.
g. Agatha loves Bertram but despises Charles.
*h. Agatha loves both herself and Charles, and despises both Bertram and Desdemona.
i. Charles neither loves nor despises Agatha, but he both loves and despises Desdemona.
*j. Neither Desdemona nor Bertram is attracted to Charles, but Charles is attracted to both of them.
k. Charles is attracted to Bertram if and only if Bertram is both shorter than he is and rich.
*l. Agatha is attracted to both Bertram and Desdemona, but she doesn't love either of them.
m. If Desdemona is shorter than Charles and Charles is shorter than Agatha, then Desdemona is shorter than Agatha.
*n. If Bertram is attracted to Desdemona and she is attracted to him, then they love each other.

o. If Charles loves Bertram and Bertram loves Agatha, then Charles both despises and is shorter than Agatha.
*p. If Charles is neither rich nor beautiful nor intelligent, then no one loves him.
q. Only Desdemona is rich.
*r. Only Desdemona is both rich and intelligent.

**3.** For each of the following passages, provide a symbolization key and then use it to symbolize the passage in *PL*.

a. Margaret and Todd both like skateboarding, but neither is good at it. Charles is good at skateboarding but he doesn't like it. Sarah is both good at skateboarding and likes it. All of them wear head gear but Charles and Sarah are the only ones who wear knee pads. Sarah is more reckless than the rest, and Charles is more skillful than the rest.
*b. Charles is a sailor but not a tennis player, while Linda is both. Linda is a yuppie and while Charles wants to be one, he isn't. Everyone likes Charles, but everyone also likes someone else more. Stan is a yuppie, and although Linda likes Charles she likes Stan more. Stan is a sailor, a tennis player, a squash player, and he likes himself more than he likes either of the other two.
(Hint: Take the universe of discourse to consist of just Charles, Linda, and Stan.)

## 7.2 QUANTIFIERS

In the preceding section we saw how quantity claims can sometimes be symbolized using conjunctions and/or disjunctions of predicates. For example, we symbolized 'Michael likes someone in his office' as '(Lms ∨ Lmh) ∨ (Lmr ∨ Lmm)'. But this is a bit awkward. And this strategy will not, in practice, work if we want to symbolize 'Michael likes everyone he has ever met', where Michael has met a lot of people. And what if Michael is a born-again Christian and at least believes himself to like literally everyone, everyone everywhere in the world? To express this view using the above strategy would require, first, knowing just how many people there are in the world, and then constructing a sentence of *PL* containing over three billion components of the form 'Lmx' with the 'x' replaced by distinct individual constants. Finally, what if Michael is a mathematician and likes prime numbers, all infinitely many of them? It is true that through the use of numerical subscripts we have an infinite number of individual constants available to us (e.g., $a_1, a_2, a_3, \ldots$) but since we will not allow infinitely long sentences in *PL*, there is no way, even in theory, to express this claim in *PL* with just the resources so far available to us. A better strategy is needed.[8]

Instead of quantity terms *PL* contains quantifier symbols and variables. There are two quantifier symbols, '∀' and '∃'. The variables of *PL* are the letters 'w' through 'z', with or without subscripts. A *quantifier* of *PL* consists of a quantifier symbol followed by a variable, both enclosed in parentheses. Thus '(∀x)' and '(∃y)' are both quantifiers.

[8] The problem is even more serious than is here suggested, for Michael might like all real numbers, and there are more real numbers than individual constants of *PL*.

Returning to our discussion of Michael and his co-workers, we can now abandon the use of iterated conjunctions for a straightforward symbolization of 'Michael likes everyone':

(∀x)Lmx

Here we have a predicate with one hole filled by an individual constant and one filled by a variable. The predicate is prefaced with a quantifier built from the same variable that fills the second hole. Quantifiers formed from '∀' are called *universal quantifiers* and are used to claim that *each and every one of the things being talked about is of the sort specified by the expression following the quantifier*. The things being talked about, the members of the current universe of discourse, are called the *values* of the variables—because they are the things the variables are used to talk about. Here the claim being made is that each thing being talked about, that is, each person in Michael's office (each value of the variable 'x'), is of the sort Lmx, that is, is such that Michael likes it.

To symbolize 'Michael likes someone', still talking exclusively about the people in Michael's office, we can use an *existential quantifier*, that is, a quantifier built from '∃'.

(∃x)Lmx

says there is at least one x (i.e., at least one value of the variable 'x') which is such that Michael likes that x. Since we are talking exclusively of the people in Michael's office, this amounts to

There is at least one person Michael likes

or

Michael likes someone.

Note that we interpret 'some' to mean 'at least one'.[9] Variables of *PL* serve some of the functions of English pronouns and of such place-holder terms as 'thing', 'body', 'one' (in 'something', 'somebody', 'someone'). 'Something is out of place' means at least one of the things, whatever they may be, that we are currently discussing is out of place. 'Everything is out of place' means that each one of the things we are currently discussing is out of place. It is more stilted, but still acceptable English, to paraphrase these claims as, respectively,

At least one of the things under discussion is such that it is out of place

and

Each of the things under discussion is such that it is out of place.

[9] This is certainly appropriate for such English locutions as 'Someone is in the house' and 'John knows someone in the Bursar's Office'. But 'There are some cookies in the cookie jar' suggests to many that there are *at least two* cookies in that vessel. Nonetheless, we will always take the existential quantifier to mean 'at least one'. We will later introduce a way of saying 'at least two' when it is important to distinguish between 'at least one' and 'at least two'.

These paraphrases have a syntax that closely mirrors that of *PL*. Using 'Ox' to express 'x is out of place', we can write

(∃x)Ox

and

(∀x)Ox

Note that in each the variable 'x' occurs twice; the first occurrence corresponds to 'thing' of the stilted English version, the second occurrence to 'it'. We can paraphrase these sentences of *PL* into quasi-English as 'At least one x is such that x is out of place' and 'Each x is such that x is out of place', respectively.

We can now return to the English sentences listed above and provide *PL* symbolizations for them, using the symbolization key given in Section 7.1.

U.D.: people in Michael's office
Lxy: x likes y
Bx: x likes lying on the beach
Txy: x is taller than y
h: Henry
m: Michael
r: Rita
s: Sue

The sentences to be symbolized are

Everyone likes lying on the beach.
No one likes Michael.
Michael likes everyone.
Michael doesn't like anyone.
Michael doesn't like everyone.
Someone likes Sue.
No one is taller than her or himself.

These can be symbolized in *PL* as, respectively:

(∀x)Bx
~ (∃x)Lxm
(∀x)Lmx
~ (∃x)Lmx
~ (∀x)Lmx
(∃x)Lxs
~ (∃x)Txx

Several points need to be noted before proceeding. First, there is nothing sacrosanct about our choice of variables. In each of the above cases, every occurrence of 'x' can be uniformly replaced with any other variable. '(∃y)Lys' says 'Someone likes Sue' just as well as does '(∃x)Lxs'. Nor is there anything sacrosanct about the variables used in specifying predicates in symbolization keys. The above symbolization key included

Bx: x likes lying on the beach.

Any other variable would have done as well in specifying how the one-place predicate in question is to be interpreted. And whatever variables are used in specifying predicates in symbolization keys need not be used in constructing symbolizations based on those keys. Given the above symbolization key, we are perfectly free to symbolize 'Everyone likes lying on the beach' as '(∀z)Bz'.

Second, there is a very important difference between 'Michael doesn't like everyone' and 'Michael doesn't like anyone'. If Michael is like most of us, he likes some people and not others, so it is true that he doesn't like everyone (he doesn't, for example, like Kathy at all), but false that he doesn't like anyone (he likes Leann very much). The difference between 'doesn't like every' and 'doesn't like any' is very clearly marked by the syntax of *PL*: The first can be expressed by a' ~ ' followed by a *universal* quantifier, the second by a ' ~ ' followed by an *existential* quantifier.

Finally, we do not really need both existential and universal quantifiers. Instead of saying 'Everything is thus-and-so' ('Everyone likes Michael', or '(∀x)Lxm'), we can say 'It is *not* the case that something is *not* thus-and-so' ('It is not the case that someone does not like Michael', or ' ~ (∃x) ~ Lxm'). And instead of saying 'Something is thus-and-so' ('Someone likes Michael', or '(∃x)Lxm'), we can say 'It is *not* the case that everything is *not* thus-and-so' ('It is not the case that everyone does not like Michael', or ' ~ (∀x) ~ Lxm'). However, having both quantifiers available does make symbolization somewhat easier and more natural.

### 7.2E EXERCISES

**1.** Symbolize the following sentences in *PL*, using the indicated symbolization key:

U.D.: the jellybeans in the jar on Ronny's desk
Bx: x is black
Rx: x is red

a. All the jellybeans are black.
*b. Some of the jellybeans are black.
c. None of the jellybeans are black.
*d. Some of the jellybeans are not black.
e. Some of the jellybeans are black and some are red.
*f. If all the jellybeans are black then none are red.
g. If some are red some are black.

*h. If none are black all are red.
 i. All are black if and only if none are red.
*j. Either all are black or all are red.

**2.** Symbolize the following sentences in *PL*, using the indicated symbolization key:

> U.D.: the students in a logic class
> Px: x will pass
> Sx: x will study
> j: Jamie
> r: Rhoda

 a. If Jamie will pass everyone will pass.
*b. No one will pass unless Jamie does.
 c. If anyone passes both Jamie and Rhoda will.
*d. Not everyone will pass, but Rhoda will.
 e. If Rhoda doesn't pass no one will.
*f. Some, but not all, of the students will pass.
 g. Rhoda will pass if Jamie does, and if Rhoda will pass everyone will pass.
*h. No one will pass unless Jamie does, and if he does everyone will.
 i. Everyone will study but not everyone will pass.
*j. If everyone studies everyone will pass.
 k. If everyone studies some will pass.

$$P_j > (\forall x)Px$$

$$(\exists x)Px > (P_j \& Pr)$$

---

## 7.3   FORMAL SYNTAX OF *PL*

Before attempting more complex symbolizations it will be useful to acquire a fuller understanding of the syntax of *PL*. To this end, we now pause to present the formal syntax for the language *PL* and to introduce some important syntactical concepts. While this material may at first seem difficult, it can be readily mastered and doing so will make mastering the rest of this chapter immensely easier.

The *vocabulary* of *PL* consists of:

*Sentence letters of PL:* The capital Roman letters 'A' through 'Z', with or without positive integer subscripts (these are just the sentence letters of *SL*).

*Predicates of PL:* The capital Roman letters 'A' through 'Z' with or without positive integer subscripts followed by one or more prime. (An *n*-place predicate is indicated by the presence of exactly *n* primes.[10])

*Individual terms of PL:*

> *Individual constants of PL:* The lower-case Roman letters 'a' through 'v' with or without positive integer subscripts.

> *Individual variables of PL:* The lower-case Roman letters 'w' through 'z' with or without positive integer subscripts.

---

[10] We will continue to informally omit the primes where no confusion results from doing so.

*Truth-functional connectives:* The five connectives

$\sim \quad \& \quad \vee \quad \supset \quad \equiv$

*Quantifier symbols:* The two symbols

$\forall \quad \exists$

*Punctuation marks:* The left and right parentheses

( )

We define an *expression of PL* to be a sequence of not necessarily distinct elements of the vocabulary of *PL*. The following are expressions of *PL*:

(((()(((A ⊃ BBA ≡)
(A ⊃ Bab))
(∀x)(∃x)Fxx

but

(({ABA)
(A ⊃ 3)
A#Bab
(∀@)(Cab)

are not, since '{', '3', '#', and '@' are not elements of the vocabulary of *PL*.

In what follows we will use the boldfaced script letters

$\boldsymbol{\mathcal{P}} \quad \boldsymbol{\mathcal{Q}} \quad \boldsymbol{\mathcal{R}} \quad \boldsymbol{\mathcal{S}}$

as metavariables ranging over expressions of *PL*. We will use boldfaced script '$\boldsymbol{a}$' as a metavariable ranging over individual constants of *PL*; and a boldfaced script '$\boldsymbol{x}$' as a metavariable ranging over individual variables of *PL*.

*Quantifier of PL:* A quantifier of *PL* is an expression of *PL* of the form $(\forall \boldsymbol{x})$ or $(\exists \boldsymbol{x})$. An expression of the first form is a *universal* quantifier, one of the second form is an *existential* quantifier.

We will say that a quantifier *contains* a variable. Thus '(∀y)' and '(∃y)' both contain the variable 'y' (and are 'y-quantifiers'); '(∀z)' and '(∃z)' both contain the variable 'z' (and are 'z-quantifiers').

*Atomic formulas of PL:* Every expression of *PL* which is either a sentence letter of *PL* or an $\boldsymbol{n}$-place predicate of *PL* followed by $\boldsymbol{n}$ individual terms of *PL* is an atomic formula of *PL*.

We are now ready to give a recursive definition of 'formula of *PL*':

*Formula of PL:*

1. Every atomic formula of *PL* is a formula of *PL*.
2. If $\mathcal{P}$ is a formula of *PL*, so is $\sim \mathcal{P}$.
3. If $\mathcal{P}$ and $\mathcal{Q}$ are formulas of *PL*, so are $(\mathcal{P} \,\&\, \mathcal{Q})$, $(\mathcal{P} \vee \mathcal{Q})$, $(\mathcal{P} \supset \mathcal{Q})$, and $(\mathcal{P} \equiv \mathcal{Q})$.
4. If $\mathcal{P}$ is a formula of *PL* that contains at least one occurrence of $x$ and no $x$-quantifier, then $(\forall x)\mathcal{P}$ and $(\exists x)\mathcal{P}$ are both formulas of *PL*.
5. Nothing is a formula of *PL* unless it can be formed by repeated applications of clauses 1–4.

Last, we specify the logical operators of *PL*:

*Logical operator of PL:* An expression of *PL* that is either a quantifier or a truth-functional connective.

Consider the following expressions of *PL*:

Rabz

~ (Rabz & Hxy)

(~ Rabz & Hxy)

(Hab ⊃ (∀z)(Fz ⊃ Gza))

(Haz ⊃ ~ (∀z)(Fz ⊃ Gza))

(∀z)(Haz ⊃ (∀z)(Fz ⊃ Gza))

(∀x)(Haz ⊃ (∀z)(Fz ⊃ Gza))

(∀y)(Hay ⊃ (Fy ⊃ Gya))

The first expression consists of a three-place predicate followed by three individual terms, the first two being individual constants, the third an individual variable. Hence it is an atomic formula of *PL* and, by clause 1 of the recursive definiton of 'formula of *PL*' a formula of *PL*. The second expression consists of a tilde, ' ~ ', followed by '(Rabz & Hxy)', so it is a formula of *PL* by clause 2 *if* '(Rabz & Hxy)' is a formula of *PL*. And since 'Rabz' and 'Hxy' are both atomic formulas of *PL*, and hence formulas of *PL*, '(Rabz & Hxy)' is a formula of *PL* by clause 3 of the recursive definition of 'formula of *PL*'.

'(~ Rabz & Hxy)' is a formula of *PL* by clause 3 if ' ~ Rabz' and 'Hxy' are both formulas of *PL*. They are. 'Hxy' is an atomic formula and hence a formula; 'Rabz' is an atomic formula and hence a formula, so ' ~ Rabz' is a formula by clause 2.

'(Hab ⊃ (∀z)(Fz ⊃ Gza))' is a formula of *PL* by clause 3 if 'Hab' and '(∀z)(Fz ⊃ Gza)' are both formulas of *PL*. The first is an atomic formula, a two-place predicate followed by two individual terms (both constants), and hence a formula of *PL* (by clause 1). The second is a formula of *PL* by clause 4 *if* '(Fz ⊃ Gza)' is a formula containing at least one occurrence of 'z' and no z-quantifier. It clearly satisfies the last two conditions, and since 'Fz' and 'Gza' are both atomic formulas of *PL* and hence formulas of *PL*, '(Fz ⊃ Gza)' is a formula of *PL* by clause 3 of the recursive definition. So the whole expression is a formula of *PL*.

For reasons parallel to those outlined above, '(Haz ⊃ ~ (∀z)(Fz ⊃ Gza))' is also a formula of *PL*. The differences are that the antecedent of the conditional, 'Haz' is an atomic formula containing one constant and one variable, instead of two constants, and the consequent is a negation, ' ~ (∀z)(Fz ⊃ Gza)'. Since '(∀z)(Fz ⊃ Gza)' is a formula, so is ' ~ (∀z)(Fz ⊃ Gza)' by clause 2 of the recursive definition.

The sixth expression displayed above, '(∀z)(Haz ⊃ (∀z)(Fz ⊃ Gza))', is not a formula of *PL*. It would be a formula, by clause 4, if '(Haz ⊃ (∀z)(Fz ⊃ Gza))' were a formula containing at least one occurrence of 'z' and no z-quantifier. The first two conditions are satisfied but the third is not. '(Haz ⊃ (∀z)(Fz ⊃ Gza))' does contain a z-quantifier in '(∀z)(Fz ⊃ Gza)'.

The seventh expression, '(∀x)(Hay ⊃ (∀y)(Fy ⊃ Gya))', is also not a formula. As we saw above, '(Hay ⊃ (∀y)(Fy ⊃ Gya))' is a formula. But since it contains no occurrence of the variable 'x', prefixing it with an x-quantifier does not produce a formula of *PL*. The last expression, '(∀y)(Hay ⊃ (Fy ⊃ Gya))', is a formula. While it looks rather similar to the two expressions just considered, it is built up in rather different ways. Note first that 'Fy' and 'Gya' are formulas of *PL*. So '(Fy ⊃ Gya)' is also a formula of *PL*. And since 'Hay' is an atomic formula, and therefore a formula of *PL*, '(Hay ⊃ (Fy ⊃ Gya))' is also a formula of *PL*. Since this formula contains at least one occurrence of the variable 'y' and no y-quantifier, prefixing it with a y-quantifier, here '(∀y)', produces a formula of *PL*, that is, '(∀y)(Hay ⊃ (Fy ⊃ Gya))'.

Not all formulas of *PL* qualify as sentences of *PL*. But before we can explicitly state the relationship between formulas and sentences we need to introduce some more terminology. We introduce the notions of a *subformula* and of a *main logical* operator by cases:

1. If $\mathcal{P}$ is an atomic formula of *PL*, then $\mathcal{P}$ contains no logical operator, and hence no main logical operation, and $\mathcal{P}$ is the only subformula of $\mathcal{P}$.
2. If $\mathcal{P}$ is a formula of *PL* of the form $\sim \mathcal{Q}$, then the tilde (' ~ ') which precedes $\mathcal{Q}$ is the main logical operator of $\mathcal{P}$, and $\mathcal{Q}$ is a subformula of $\mathcal{P}$.
3. If $\mathcal{P}$ is a formula of *PL* of the form $(\mathcal{Q} \mathbin{\&} \mathcal{R})$, $(\mathcal{Q} \vee \mathcal{R})$, $(\mathcal{Q} \supset \mathcal{R})$, or $(\mathcal{Q} \equiv \mathcal{R})$, then the binary connective between $\mathcal{Q}$ and $\mathcal{R}$ is the main logical operator of $\mathcal{P}$, and $\mathcal{Q}$ and $\mathcal{R}$ are subformulas of $\mathcal{P}$.
4. If $\mathcal{P}$ is a formula of *PL* of the form $(\forall x)\mathcal{Q}$ or of the form $(\exists x)\mathcal{Q}$, then the quantifier which occurs before $\mathcal{Q}$ is the main logical operator of $\mathcal{P}$, and $\mathcal{Q}$ is a subformula of $\mathcal{P}$.
5. If $\mathcal{P}$ is a formula of *PL*, then every subformula of a subformula of $\mathcal{P}$ is a subformula of $\mathcal{P}$, and $\mathcal{P}$ is a subformula of itself.

A *subformula* $\mathcal{Q}$ of $\mathcal{P}$ is a *proper subformula* of $\mathcal{P}$ just in case $\mathcal{Q}$ is not $\mathcal{P}$. (No formula is a proper subformula of itself.)

We can classify formulas of *PL* (and later sentences) by their main logical operator. Atomic formulas have no main logical operator. Quantified formulas have a quantifier as their main logical operator. Truth-functional compounds have a truth-functional connective as their main logical operator.

Consider again the eight expressions of *PL* displayed above. The sixth and seventh are not formulas of *PL*, and hence the notions of 'main logical operator' and 'subformula' do not apply to them. For each of the rest we display its subformulas, identify the main logical operator of each (if any), and classify each subformula as either atomic, quantified, or a truth-functional compound:

| *Formula* | *Subformula* | *Main Logical Operator* | *Type* |
|---|---|---|---|
| Rabz | Rabz | None | Atomic |
| ~ (Rabz & Hxy) | | | |
| | ~ (Rabz & Hxy) | ~ | Truth-functional |
| | (Rabz & Hxy) | & | Truth-functional |
| | Rabz | None | Atomic |
| | Hxy | None | Atomic |
| (~ Rabz & Hxy) | | | |
| | (~ Rabz & Hxy) | & | Truth-functional |
| | ~ Rabz | ~ | Truth-functional |
| | Hxy | None | Atomic |
| | Rabz | None | Atomic |
| (Hab ⊃ (∀z)(Fz ⊃ Gza)) | | | |
| | (Hab ⊃ (∀z)(Fz ⊃ Gza)) | ⊃ | Truth-functional |
| | Hab | None | Atomic |
| | (∀z)(Fz ⊃ Gza) | (∀z) | Quantified |
| | (Fz ⊃ Gza) | ⊃ | Truth-functional |
| | Fz | None | Atomic |
| | Gza | None | Atomic |
| (Haz ⊃ ~ (∀z)(Fz ⊃ Gza)) | | | |
| | (Haz ⊃ ~ (∀z)(Fz ⊃ Gza)) | ⊃ | Truth-functional |
| | Haz | None | Atomic |
| | ~ (∀z)(Fz ⊃ Gza) | ~ | Truth-functional |
| | (∀z)(Fz ⊃ Gza) | (∀z) | Quantified |
| | (Fz ⊃ Gza) | ⊃ | Truth-functional |
| | Fz | None | Atomic |
| | Gza | None | Atomic |
| (∀y)(Hay ⊃ (Fy ⊃ Gya)) | | | |
| | (∀y)(Hay ⊃ (Fy ⊃ Gya)) | (∀y) | Quantified |
| | (Hay ⊃ (Fy ⊃ Gya)) | ⊃ | Truth-functional |
| | Hay | None | Atomic |
| | (Fy ⊃ Gya) | ⊃ | Truth-functional |
| | Fy | None | Atomic |
| | Gya | None | Atomic |

Earlier we talked informally of quantifiers serving to interpret variables. We can now make that notion explicit. The interpretive range of a quantifier is its scope.

> *Scope of a quantifier:* The scope of a quantifier in a formula $\mathscr{P}$ of *PL* is the subformula $\mathscr{Q}$ of $\mathscr{P}$ of which that quantifier is the main logical operator.

Recall, from the recursive definition of 'formula of *PL*' that the only way quantifiers get into formulas is by clause 4, which specifies the conditions under which a quantifier may be attached to a formula. So attaching a quantifier to a formula produces a new formula, of which the quantifier is the main logical operator. The scope of that quantifier is all of the new formula, that is, is the quantifier itself and the formula to which it is being attached. For example, '(∀x)Fxy' is a quantified formula of which '(∀x)' is the main logical operator. The scope of that quantifier is all of '(∀x)Fxy', that is, the scope includes the quantifier, '(∀x)' and the formula immediately following the quantifier, 'Fxy'.

Consider the formula '(Hx ⊃ (∀y)Fxy)'. This expression is a formula (by clause 3 of the recursive definition of 'formula of *PL*') inasmuch as 'Hx' is a formula (an atomic formula) and '(∀y)Fxy' is a formula by clause 4 ('Fxy' is a formula of *PL* in which 'x' occurs and in which no x-quantifier occurs). The formula contains two distinct variables, 'x' and 'y', and a total of four occurrences of variables ('x' and 'y' each occur twice). The scope of '(∀y)' includes the occurrence of 'y' from which it is formed and the occurrences of 'x' and 'y' in 'Fxy', for the subformula of which '(∀y)' is the main logical operator is '(∀y)Fxy'. But the first occurrence of 'x', that in 'Hx', does not fall within the scope of '(∀y)', for it is not in the subformula '(∀y)Fxy'. In '((∀z)Gz ⊃ ~ Hz)' the scope of the quantifier '(∀z)' is '(∀z)Gz', hence the first two occurrences of 'z' in this formula fall within its scope but the last occurrence, that in ' ~ Hz', does not.

We can now introduce the notions of *free* and *bound* variables of *PL*.

> *Bound variable:* An occurrence of a variable $x$ in a formula $\mathscr{P}$ of *PL* is *bound* if and only if that occurrence is within the scope of an $x$-quantifier.
>
> *Free variable:* An occurrence of a variable $x$ in a formula $\mathscr{P}$ of *PL* is free if and only if it is not bound.

At long last we are ready to formally introduce the notion of a *sentence of PL*:

> *Sentence of PL:* A formula $\mathscr{P}$ of *PL* is a sentence of *PL* if and only if no occurrence of a variable in $\mathscr{P}$ is free.

We will speak of a formula of *PL* which is not a sentence of *PL* as an *open sentence* of *PL*.

We can now see that '(Hx ⊃ (∀y)Fxy)' is not a sentence of *PL* for two reasons; the first occurrence of 'x' does not fall within the scope of any quantifier, and is therefore free, and the second occurrence of 'x', while falling within the scope of a quantifier, does not fall within the scope of an x-quantifier. And '((∀z)Gz ⊃ ~ Hz)' is not a sentence because the third occurrence of 'z' does not fall within the scope of a z-quantifier. The scope of '(∀z)' is limited to the subformula of which it is the main logical operator, that is, to '(∀z)Gz'.

Earlier we considered the following eight expressions of *PL*:

Rabz

~ (Rabz & Hxy)

(~ Rabz & Hxy)

(Hab ⊃ (∀z)(Fz ⊃ Gza))

(Haz ⊃ ~ (∀z)(Fz ⊃ Gza))

(∀z)(Haz ⊃ (∀z)(Fz ⊃ Gza))

(∀x)(Hab ⊃ (∀z)(Fz ⊃ Gza))

(∀y)(Hay ⊃ (Fy ⊃ Gya))

The first is not a sentence because it contains a free occurrence of 'z'. However, this formula can be made a sentence by prefacing it with a z-quantifier, that is, both '(∀z)Rabz' and '(∃z)Rabz' are sentences of *PL*. Note that formulas which contain no variables, for example, 'Rabc', 'Hab', and '(Gd & Fab)' are sentences of *PL*; they contain no occurrences of variables and hence no free occurrences of variables. It is individual variables, *not individual constants*, that need to be interpreted by quantifiers.

The second formula listed above contains three free occurrences of variables, one each of 'z', 'x', and 'y', and so is not a sentence of *PL*. We would have to add three quantifiers to this formula to make it a sentence, a z-quantifier, an x-quantifier, and a y-quantifier, in any order. So too for the third formula. The fourth formula is a sentence since the only variable it contains is 'z' and all occurrences of 'z' fall within the scope of '(∀z)'. (The scope of that quantifier is '(∀z)(Fz ⊃ Gza)'.)

The fifth formula is not a sentence of *PL* since it does contain a free variable, the first occurrence of 'z' (in 'Haz'). The sixth expression is not even a formula, as noted earlier. It is not a formula because the initial z-quantifier is attached to an expression which, while it is a formula, already contains a z-quantifier. We can now see why this prohibition is appropriate. If we allowed this expression to be a formula we would have two z-quantifiers with overlapping scopes, and we would need some further rule to determine which quantifier interprets the last two occurrences of 'z'.

The seventh expression is also not a formula, and hence not a sentence, of *PL*.[11] The x-quantifier '(∀x)' is doing no work, since there are no occurrences of 'x' in the formula following the quantifier. The eighth expression is a formula and a sentence of *PL*.

Since sentences of *PL* are formulas of *PL*, we can speak of sentences as being either quantified (sentences whose main logical operator is a quantifier),

[11] We could change the recursive definition and allow it to be a sentence, but there is nothing to be gained by this complication.

truth-functional (sentences whose main logical operator is a truth-functional connective), or atomic (sentences which have no main logical operator).

We have been omitting the primes which, by the formal requirements of *PL*, are parts of the predicates of *PL*. We will continue to do so. We will also frequently omit the outermost parentheses of a formula of *PL*. On our usage, outermost parentheses are a pair of left and right parentheses which are, respectively, the first symbol and the last symbol of a formula of *PL* and are added, as a pair, when a binary connective is inserted between two formulas of *PL*. Thus we will frequently write 'Fa & ~ (∀x)Fx' instead of '(Fa & ~ (∀x)Fx)'. Note that while ' ~ (Fa & (∃x) ~ Fx)' is a truth-functionally compound formula (and sentence) it has no outermost parentheses. So too, '(∀x)(Fx ⊃ Gx)' has as its first symbol a left parentheses and as its last a right parentheses, but these are not 'outermost parentheses', for the first and last symbols of this sentence were not added as a pair when formulas were joined by a binary connective.

The omission of outermost parentheses should cause no confusion. Note, however, that when outer parentheses are customarily dropped it is not safe to assume that every sentence which begins with a quantifier is a quantified sentence. Consider

(∀x)(Fx ⊃ Ga)

and

(∀x)Fx ⊃ Ga

Both begin with quantifiers but only the first is a quantified sentence. The scope of the x-quantifier in this sentence is the whole formula. The second sentence is a truth-functional compound; the scope of the x-quantifier is just '(∀x)Fx'. It will turn out that the above sentences are not just syntactically distinct, but also that they say very different things.

To make complicated formulas of *PL* easier to read, we will hereafter also allow the use of square brackets, '[' and ']', in place of the parentheses which are required by clause 3 of the recursive definition of 'formula of *PL*', that is, by the use of truth-functional connectives. But we will not allow square brackets in place of parentheses in quantifiers. So instead of

~ (∀y)((∃z)Fzy ⊃ (∃x)Gxy)

we can write

~ (∀y)[(∃z)Fzy ⊃ (∃x)Gxy]

In later chapters we will require one further syntactic concept, that of a *substitution instance* of a quantified sentence. We use the notation

$\mathscr{P}(\boldsymbol{a}/\boldsymbol{x})$

to specify the formula of *PL* that is like $\mathscr{P}$ except that it contains the individual constant $\boldsymbol{a}$ wherever $\mathscr{P}$ contains the individual variable $\boldsymbol{x}$. Thus, if $\mathscr{P}$ is

(Fza ∨ ~ Gz)

$\mathscr{P}$(c/z) is

(Fca ∨ ~ Gc)

*Substitution instance of* $\mathscr{P}$: If $\mathscr{P}$ is a sentence of *PL* of the form $(\forall \boldsymbol{x})\mathscr{Q}$ or $(\exists \boldsymbol{x})\mathscr{Q}$ and $\boldsymbol{a}$ an individual constant, then $\mathscr{Q}(\boldsymbol{a}/\boldsymbol{x})$ is a *substitution instance* of $\mathscr{P}$. The constant $\boldsymbol{a}$ is the *instantiating constant*.

For example, 'Fab', 'Fbb', and 'Fcb' are all substitution instances of '(∀z)Fzb'. In the first case 'a' has been substituted for 'z' in 'Fzb'. In the second case 'b' has been substituted for 'z'; and in the third case 'c' has been substituted for 'z'.

In forming a substitution instance of a quantified sentence, we drop the initial quantifier and replace all remaining occurrences of the variable that that quantifier contains with some one constant. Thus '(∃y)Hay' and '(∃y)Hgy' are both substitution instances of '(∀x)(∃y)Hxy', but 'Hab' is not. (In forming substitution instances *only* the initial quantifier is dropped and every occurrence of the variable which becomes free when that quantifier is dropped is replaced by the *same* constant.) All of the following are substitution instances of '(∃w)[Fw ⊃ (∀y)(~ Dwy ≡ Ry)]':

Fd ⊃ (∀y)(~ Ddy ≡ Ry)
Fa ⊃ (∀y)(~ Day ≡ Ry)
Fn ⊃ (∀y)(~ Dny ≡ Ry)

but

Fd ⊃ (∀y)(~ Dny ≡ Ry)

is not—for here we used one constant to replace the first occurrence of 'w', a different constant to replace the second occurrence of 'w'. Again, in generating substitution instances each occurrence of the variable being replaced must be replaced by the same individual constant.

## 7.3E EXERCISES

**1.** Which of the following are formulas of *PL*? (You may assume that we are making use of our stated conventions for writing down formulas.) For those that are not, explain why they are not. For those that are, state whether they are sentences or open sentences.

a. B & Z
*b. (x)Px ∨ Py
c. (∃y) ~ Hyy & Ga
*d. (∀z)(Ex)(Fzx & Fxz)
e. (∀z)((∃x)Fzx & Fxz)

*f. (∀x)A
g. (∃z)(Fz & Bgz) ≡ (∃z)Gzb
*h. (∃x)[Fx & (∀x)(Px ⊃ Gx)]
i. (~ ∃x)(Fx ∨ Gx)
*j. ~ (∀x)(G ≡ (∃z)Fzx)
k. (∃x)(∃y)Lxx
*l. (∀x)[(∃y)Fyx ⊃ (∃y)Fxy]
m. (B & ~ Faa) ⊃ (∀w) ~ Fww
*n. (∃a)Fa
o. Fw ⊃ (∃w)Gww
*p. (∀z)(Hza ⊃ (∃z)Gaz)

**2.** For each of the following formulas,
i. Indicate whether it is a sentence. If it is not a sentence, explain.
ii. List all its subformulas, identifying the main logical operator of each.
a. (∃x)(∀y)Byx
*b. (∃x) ~ (∀y)Byx
c. (∀x)(~ Fx & Gx) ≡ (Bg ⊃ Fx)
*d. (∀y)[(∀z) ~ Byz ∨ Byy]
e. ~ (∃x)Px & Rab
*f. Rax ⊃ ~ (∀y)Ryx
g. ~ (~ (∀x)Fx ≡ (∃w) ~ Gw) ⊃ Maa
*h. (∀x)(∀y)(∀z)Mxyz & (∀z)(∀x)(∀y)Myzx
i. ~ ~ ~ (∃x)(∀z)(Gxaz ∨ ~ Hazb)
*j. (∀z)[Fz ⊃ (∃w)(~ Fw & Gwaz)]
k. (∃x)Fx ⊃ (∀w)(~ Gx ⊃ ~ Hwx)
*l. ~ [(∀x)Fx ∨ (∀x) ~ Fx]
m. (H ∨ Fa) ≡ (∃z)(~ Fz & Gza)
*n. (∃w)(Fw & ~ Fw) ≡ (H & ~ H)

**3.** Indicate, for each of the following sentences, whether it is an atomic sentence, a truth-functional compound, or a quantified sentence.
a. (∀x)(Fx ⊃ Ga)
*b. (∀x) ~ (Fx ⊃ Ga)
c. ~ (∀x)(Fx ⊃ Ga)
*d. (∃w)Raw ∨ (∃w)Rwa
e. ~ (∃x)Hx
*f. Habc
g. (∀x)(Fx ≡ (∃w)Gw)
*h. (∀x)Fx ≡ (∃w)Gw
i. (∃w)(Pw ⊃ (∀y)(Hy ≡ ~ Kyw))
*j. ~ (∃w)(Jw ∨ Nw) ∨ (∃w)(Mw ∨ Lw)
k. ~ [(∃w)(Jw ∨ Nw) ∨ (∃w)(Mw ∨ Lw)]
*l. D
m. (∀z)Gza ⊃ (∃z)Fz
*n. ~ (∃x)(Fx & ~ Gxa)
o. (∃z) ~ Hza
*p. (∀w)(~ Hw ⊃ (∃y)Gwy)
q. (∀x) ~ Fx ≡ (∀z) ~ Hza

**4.** For each of the following sentences, give the substitution instance in which ‘a’ is the instantiating term.

a. (∀w)(Mww & Fw)
*b. (∃y)(Mby ⊃ Mya)
c. (∃z) ~ (Cz ≡ ~ Cz)
*d. (∀x)((Laa & Lab) ⊃ Lax)
e. (∃z)[(Fz & ~ Gb) ⊃ (Bzb ∨ Bbz)]
*f. (∃w)[Fw & (∀y)(Cyw ⊃ Cwa)]
g. (∀y)[~ (∃z)Nyz ≡ (∀w)(Mww & Nyw)]
*h. (∀y)[(Fy & Hy) ⊃ [(∃z)(Fz & Gz) ⊃ Gy]]
i. (∃x)(Fxb ≡ Gbx)
*j. (∀x)(∀y)[(∃z)Hzx ⊃ (∃z)Hzy]
k. (∀x) ~ (∃y)(Hxy & Hyx)
*l. (∀z)[Fz ⊃ (∃w)(~ Fw & Gwaz)]
m. (∀w)(∀y)[(Hwy & Hyw) ⊃ (∃z)Gzw]
*n. (∃z)(∃w)(∃y)[(Fzwy ≡ Fwzy) ≡ Fyzw]

**5.** Which of the following are substitution instances of the sentence ‘(∃w)(∀y)(Rwy ⊃ Byy)’?

a. (∀y)Ray ⊃ Byy
*b. (∀y)(Ray ⊃ Byy)
c. (∀y)(Rwy ⊃ Byy)
*d. (∀y)(Rcy ⊃ Byy)
e. (∀y)(Ryy ⊃ Byy)
*f. (∃y)(Ray ⊃ Byy)
g. (Ray ⊃ Byy)
*h. (∀y)(Ray ⊃ Baa)
i. Rab ⊃ Bbb

**6.** Which of the following are substitution instances of the sentence ‘(∀x)[(∀y) ~ Rxy ≡ Pxa]’?

a. (∀y) ~ Ray ≡ Paa
*b. (∀y) ~ Raa ≡ Paa
c. (∀y) ~ Ray ≡ Pba
*d. (∀y) ~ Rpy ≡ Ppa
e. (∀y)(~ Ray ≡ Paa)
*f. (∀y) ~ Ray ≡ Pya
g. (∀w) ~ Raw ≡ Paa
*h. (∀y) ~ Rcy ≡ Pca

## 7.4 SYMBOLIZATION TECHNIQUES

In symbolizing sentences of English we have, up to this point, used quantifiers only in sentences with single predicates, sometimes preceded by a tilde. This is fine so long as we want only to say that everything, at least one thing, or nothing, is thus-and-so (or, is not thus-and-so), where the ‘thus-and-so’ is expressed by a single predicate. But we often need to make more sophisticated claims—we want to say, not that all the things we are talking about, all the things in our present universe of discourse, are of the sort specified by one predicate (if they are, this is likely to be obvious and not merit remarking upon), but rather that a certain subset of the things we are talking about are of a particular sort.

For example, if we are doing elementary biology and talking about all living things, we will want to say, not that all of those things are warm-blooded, but rather that all of those which are mammals are warm-blooded. This claim can be expressed in various ways in English, the following among them:

All mammals are warm-blooded.

Every mammal is warm-blooded.

Each mammal is warm-blooded.

Mammals are warm-blooded.

The same claim can be expressed as

A mammal is warm-blooded[12]

and somewhat more stiltedly, but still intelligibly, as

If a living thing is a mammal, then it is warm-blooded.

We will use the following symbolization key in seeking an adequate symbolization of the above sentences:

U.D.: living things
Mx: x is a mammal
Wx: x is warm-blooded

Note that because the sentence we want to symbolize does not single out any particular living thing for special comment the symbolization key does not include the assignment of individual constants to particular members of the universe of discourse (to this or that particular living thing). The following sentences of *PL do not* accomplish the task at hand:

$(\forall z)Mz \ \& \ (\forall z)Wz$
$(\forall y)My \supset (\forall y)Wy$

Both sentences are truth-functional compounds. The first, a conjunction, says both that every living creature is such that it is a mammal and that every living creature is such that it is warm-blooded. Both conjuncts of the conjunction are false, whereas the English sentence we are trying to symbolize is true (a sure sign something is very wrong). The second sentence of *PL*, a conditional, says 'If *every* living thing is a mammal, then *every* living thing is warm-blooded' (or, equivalently, 'If *each* living thing is a mammal, then *each* living thing is warm-blooded'). The antecedent

[12] We frequently use the singular articles 'a' and 'an' to mean 'all'. Consider 'A vacation is a good thing', 'An accident incurred while at work is covered by the employee insurance plan', and 'An unexcused absence on an examination day will result in a failure'.

of this claim is false, as is the consequent, so the whole claim is, on truth-functional grounds, true (truth-functional conditionals with false antecedents are true, remember the truth-table for '$\supset$'). Although this sentence of *PL* is true, it does not say what we want to say.

Suppose a biology professor points to a closed box, saying that it contains a living thing. Do we want to say of the thing in the box, not knowing what sort of a living thing it is, that it is warm-blooded? Certainly not. The thing in question may, after all, turn out to be a fish, or an insect, or a bacterium. Is there anything we are willing to say of the inhabitant of the box, vis-a-vis its being warm-blooded? Well, we can certainly say that if that thing is a mammal, then it is warm-blooded. And this conditional claim is true of the inhabitant of the box, be it a snake or a koala bear.

To put the point another way, if what we want to say is that all mammals are warm-blooded, then we should also be prepared to say, of each and every living thing, that if it is a mammal, then it is warm-blooded. This suggests the following *quantified* sentence of *PL*.

$$(\forall x)(Mx \supset Wx)$$

In quasi-English: 'Each x is such that if x is a mammal then x is warm-blooded'.

The English sentence 'All mammals are warm-blooded' might seem to be of the subject/predicate form, the subject being 'All mammals', the predicate being 'are warm-blooded'. But, for our purposes at least, this is not a useful analysis. Quantity terms do not generally pick out entities about which the rest of the sentences asserts something. (Consider 'Nothing is in the box'. Here there is not even a temptation to say that 'Nothing' denotes something which is then said to be in the box.) 'All mammals are warm-blooded' does not identify a thing or collection of things (all mammals) and claim that that thing (the collection itself) is warm-blooded. The predicate 'is warm-blooded' is satisfied by individuals, not by collections thereof.

Universal claims of the sort we have been discussing, claims that all things of this sort (animals) are also of that sort (warm-blooded), do not pick out or refer to a group of things and then predicate something of that group. Such claims are better analyzed as deriving from conditionals which apply to each thing in the given universe of discourse. They say of *each* thing under discussion that if it is of such-and-such a sort then it is also thus-and-so. Each living thing is such that if it is a mammal then it is warm-blooded. This is, again, true as much of a given reptile as it is of a given koala bear.[13]

Similarly, 'Some mammals are carnivorous' does not say of some particular mammal that it is carnivorous. Rather, it says that there is some living thing

[13] But consider 'Insects are more numerous than mammals'. This is not a disguised conditional claim about each living thing—its force is not 'Each living thing is such that if it is an insect it is more numerous than . . .'. The correct analysis here is rather something like 'The set consisting of all insects is larger than the set consisting of all mammals', that is, as a claim about a relation between two things, the set of insects and the set of mammals.

(assuming still that our universe of discourse is living things) which is both a mammal and carnivorous. The correct symbolization in *PL*, using obvious predicates, is thus

(∃x)(Mx & Cx)

a quantified sentence of *PL*, and *not* either of the following:

(∃x)Mx & (∃x)Cx

(∃x)(Mx ⊃ Cx)

The first of the above sentences is a truth-functional compound. It says that there is something which is a mammal and there is something (not necessarily the same thing) which is carnivorous. The second says that there is some living thing such that if it is a mammal it is carnivorous. While this is true, it is a much weaker claim than is intended. It would, for example, be true even if the universe of discourse were limited to reptiles. For every reptile (and hence at least one) is such that if it is a mammal (which it is not) then it is warm-blooded. Remember that material conditionals with false antecedents are true.

Note that in neither '(∀x)(Mx ⊃ Wx)' nor '(∃x)(Mx & Cx)' are there outermost parentheses. The formulas to which the quantifiers attach, '(Mx ⊃ Wx)' and '(Mx & Cx)' respectively, do contain outer parentheses, but these are not 'outer' once the quantifiers are attached. '(∀x)Mx ⊃ Wx' is *not* an informal version of '(∀x)(Mx ⊃ Wx)'. Rather, it is a formula which is not a sentence of *PL*, a formula whose main logical operator is ' ⊃ ', not '(∀x)'.

We are now ready to symbolize the following sentences about the people in Michael's office:

Everyone who likes Michael likes lying on the beach.

Everyone who is taller than Rita is taller than Henry.

No one who likes Henry doesn't like Michael.

We will use the symbolization key given in Section 7.1:

U.D.: People in Michael's office
Lxy: x likes y
Bx: x likes lying on the beach
Txy: x is taller than y
h: Henry
m: Michael
r: Rita
s: Sue

The first two of these claims can reasonably be understood as making claims of the form 'Each thing which is of this sort is also of that sort'. So in each case we can use a conditional formula preceded by a universal quantifier:

$(\forall z)(Lzm \supset Bz)$

$(\forall y)(Tyr \supset Tyh)$

The last of the above English sentences, 'No one who likes Henry doesn't like Michael' may seem difficult to symbolize in *PL*. But once we see that it can be rephrased in the 'each thing which is of this sort is also of that sort' idiom, that is, as

Each person who likes Henry likes Michael

the appropriate symbolization is obvious:

$(\forall x)(Lxh \supset Lxm)$

The grammatical structure of English sentences is often a good guide as to what the structure of its symbolization in *PL* should be. Compare

Every integer is either odd or even.

Every integer is odd or every integer is even.

In the second sentence there are two quantity terms. Each falls within a disjunct of the overall sentence, which is clearly a disjunction. But in the first sentence, the disjunction-indicating terms 'either' and 'or' both fall within the scope of the quantity term 'every'. This suggests, correctly, that the first sentence can be symbolized as a quantified sentence, the second as a truth-functional compound of quantified sentences. If we restrict our universe of discourse to integers, appropriate paraphrases are

Each integer y is such that either y is odd or y is even

and

Either each integer y is such that y is odd or each integer y is such that y is even.

Using obvious predicates, we can now produce *PL* symbolizations:

$(\forall y)(Oy \vee Ey)$

$(\forall y)Oy \vee (\forall y)Ey$

There is a world of difference here. The first sentence of *PL* is clearly true; each integer is either odd or even. The second is just as clearly false. It is not the case that all integers are odd, and it is not the case that all integers are even. The great importance of the placement of quantifiers in relation to truth-functional connectives is here illustrated.

The use of 'and' in such sentences as 'All whales and dolphins are mammals' is, at least at first glance, a less clear guide in constructing a *PL* symbolization. This English sentence employs only one quantity term. Taking the universe of discourse to be living things and using obvious predicates, one might be led to offer the following symbolization:

$$(\forall x)[(Wx \ \& \ Dx) \supset Mx]$$

That this is a mistake can be seen by reading the *PL* sentence into quasi-English:

Each x is such that if x is a whale *and* x is a dolphin, then x is a mammal.

This is a very strange claim—we set out to say something about whales and dolphins and have ended up talking about things which are both whales and dolphins, of which there are none. The problem is that the 'and' in the original sentence really signals, not a conjunction of predicates, but collapse of a longer conjunction, viz.:

All whales are mammals *and* all dolphins are mammals.

If we had started from this conjunction we would have ended up with the following *PL* conjunction:

$$(\forall x)(Wx \supset Mx) \ \& \ (\forall x)(Dx \supset Mx)$$

Just as the English conjunction can be collapsed into a claim employing only one quantity term, so too the above *PL* truth-functional compound can be collapsed into a quantified sentence:

$$(\forall x)[(Wx \vee Dx) \supset Mx]$$

This sentence does correctly symbolize 'All whales and dolphins are mammals', for it says of each thing in the universe of discourse that if it is either a whale or a dolphin, then it is a mammal. The important point to notice is that in the *PL* collapsed version we need to join the predicates with a '$\vee$', whereas in English 'and' is used.

Care must be taken when symbolizing English sentences using the quantity term 'any'. Consider these examples:

1. Anyone who likes Sue likes Rita.
2. Everyone who likes Sue likes Rita.
3. If anyone likes Sue Michael does.
4. If everyone likes Sue Michael does.
5. If anyone likes Sue, he or she likes Rita.

Assuming we restrict our universe of discourse to people, it is probably apparent that the first two of these sentences can each appropriately be symbolized as '$(\forall x)(Lxs \supset Lxr)$'. So in the first sentence the 'any' of 'anyone' has the force of 'every'. But in the third sentence 'anyone' does not have the force of 'everyone', for the third and fourth sentences clearly make different claims. (Sentence 3 may be very informative—we might have suspected that someone likes Sue, but have had no idea that Michael did. But sentence 4 is not at all informative. Of course, Michael likes Sue if everyone does, for Michael is one of *every*one.) Appropriate symbolizations for sentences 3 and 4 are, respectively:

$$(\exists x)Lxs \supset Lms$$

and

$$(\forall x)\, Lxs \supset Lms$$

Note that both of the above sentences of *PL* are truth-functional compounds. It might be tempting to conclude that 'any' means 'every' except when it is used in the antecedent of an explicit conditional, in which case it means 'some'. But this rule is too simplistic, as sentence 5 above makes clear. In 'If anyone likes Sue, he or she likes Rita' 'any' does appear in the antecedent of an explicit English conditional but here the force of 'any' cannot be captured by an existential quantifier, nor can the English sentence be symbolized as a conditional sentence of *PL*. Attempting to do so will generate

$$(\exists x)Lxs \supset Lxr$$

which is a formula but not a sentence of *PL* (the third occurrence of 'x' is free). Changing the scope of the existential quantifier will not help either, for while

$$(\exists x)(Lxs \supset Lxr)$$

is a sentence of *PL* (albeit not a conditional), it says that there is *someone* such that if that person likes Sue then that person likes Rita. It is sufficient for the truth of this claim that there be someone who does not like Rita, for if a person does not like Rita, then '$(Lxs \supset Lxr)$' is true of that person—remember the weakness of the material conditional. To say what we want to say, we need a universally quantified sentence, that is, we need the symbolization we used for sentences 1 and 2:

$$(\forall x)(Lxs \supset Lxr)$$

This sentence of *PL* will be true if and only if all those who like Sue like Rita. That we end up with this symbolization should not be surprising, for the force of sentence 5 ('If anyone likes Sue, he or she likes Rita') is, upon reflection, clearly the same as that of sentence 1 ('Anyone who likes Sue likes Rita').

A better rule can be formulated by appealing to the notion of *pronominal cross reference*. In 'Sarah will deliver the lumber if she gets her truck fixed' the reference of 'she' is established by the earlier use of the noun 'Sarah'—there is pronominal cross reference from the pronoun back to the noun 'Sarah'. Pronominal cross reference can be to quantity terms as well as to nouns. In sentence 5, 'If anyone likes Sue, he or she likes Rita', the reference of 'he or she' is fixed by 'anyone who likes Sue'.

In sentence 3, 'If anyone likes Sue Michael does', there is no pronominal cross reference from the consequent of the English conditional back to the 'any' term in the antecedent. 'Michael does' in the consequent expands to 'Michael likes Sue', a complete sentence which does not need further interpretation. But in 'If anyone likes Sue he or she likes Rita' the consequent, 'he or she likes Rita', cannot be understood in isolation. This allows us to state the following rule:

> Where a quantity term is used in the antecedent of an English conditional and there is, in the consequent of that conditional, pronominal cross reference to that quantity term, a universal quantifier is called for.

We can, with a little stretching, use this rule in dealing with such sentences as

> Anyone who fails the final examination flunks the course.

This sentence is not a conditional, and there is no obvious pronominal cross reference. But, since the person who will flunk the course is the one who fails the final examination, we can construct a paraphrase of this sentence which is a conditional and in which there is pronominal cross reference:

> If a person fails the final examination then he or she flunks the course.

This is a sentence to which the above rule applies. Taking our universe of discourse to be students in the class and using 'Fx' for 'x fails the final examination' and 'Cx' for 'x flunks the course', we can, following the above rule, offer

$$(\forall x)(Fx \supset Cx)$$

as an appropriate symbolization.

'Any' also functions differently from 'all', 'every', and 'each' when combined with a negation expression. For example, as noted in Section 7.2,

> Michael doesn't like everyone

and

> Michael doesn't like anyone

are very different claims. In general, 'not any' can be symbolized as the negations of existential quantifiers (not at least one), whereas 'not every', 'not all', and 'not each' call for the negation of a universal quantifier. In the present case, taking the people in Michael's office as our universe of discourse, 'm' as designating Michael, and 'Lxy' as 'x likes y', we can use '$\sim (\forall x)Lmx$' as a symbolization of the first of the above sentences and '$\sim (\exists x)Lmx$' as a symbolization of the second.

Quantity constructions built from 'some' usually call for an existential quantifier. But some uses of 'some' constructions call for universal quantifiers, and the rule developed above will help in identifying them. Consider these two sentences:

If someone likes Sue then he or she likes Rita.

If someone likes Sue then someone likes Rita.

The first of these is a conditional with a quantity construction in the antecedent to which the 'he or she' in the consequent bears pronominal cross reference. So a universal quantifier is called for, even though 'someone' usually signals an existential quantifier. A correct symbolization is '$(\forall x)(Lxs \supset Lxr)$'. That this symbolization is correct becomes apparent when we reflect that the force of 'someone' in the first sentence is clearly that of 'anyone'. There is, in the second sentence, no pronominal cross reference from the consequent back to the antecedent. The claim is not that if someone likes Sue then that very person likes Rita, but rather that if someone likes Sue then *someone*, quite possibly someone different, likes Rita. Here two existential quantifiers are called for:

$$(\exists x)Lxs \supset (\exists x)Lxr$$

Since the time of Aristotle many logicians have tried to classify *quantity* claims of both natural and symbolic languages, claims to the effect that all or some things are, or are not, thus-and-so, into four groups, traditionally called A-, E-, I-, and O-sentences. Using '$\mathscr{P}$' and '$\mathscr{Q}$' as dummy predicates, we can use the following schema to present this traditional classification as it applies to sentences of *PL*:

A: $(\forall x)(\mathscr{P} \supset \mathscr{Q})$
E: $(\forall x)(\mathscr{P} \supset \sim \mathscr{Q})$
I: $(\exists x)(\mathscr{P} \,\&\, \mathscr{Q})$
O: $(\exists x)(\mathscr{P} \,\&\, \sim \mathscr{Q})$

A-sentences say each thing of this sort is a thing of that sort, for example,

Each cat is a mouser.

All cats are mousers.

Every cat is a mouser.

Cats are mousers.

A cat is a mouser.

All of these are universal claims, each says of each thing in the universe of discourse that if it is a cat then it is a mouser.

E-sentences (sentences with *PL* symbolizations of the form $(\forall x)(\mathscr{P} \supset \sim \mathscr{Q})$) say each thing of this sort is *not* a thing of that sort, for example,

Each cat is a non-mouser.

All cats are non-mousers.

Every cat is a non-mouser.

Cats are non-mousers.

No cat is a mouser.

E-sentences are also universal claims. Each says of each thing that if it is of this sort it is not of that sort.

I-sentences (sentences with *PL* symbolizations of the form $(\exists x)(\mathscr{P} \& \mathscr{Q})$) say that there are some things of this sort that are also of that sort, for example,

Some cats are mousers.

There are cats that are mousers.

Cats include some mousers.

Each of these is, on our account, an *existential* claim; each says that there is at least one thing in the universe of discourse which is both a cat and a mouser.

O-sentences (sentences with *PL* symbolizations of the form $(\exists x)(\mathscr{P} \& \sim \mathscr{Q})$) are also *existential* sentences. Each says that there are some things of this sort that are not of that sort, for example,

Some cats are not mousers.

There are cats that are not mousers.

Each of these says, on our account, that there is at least one thing in the universe of discourse which is a cat and is not a mouser.

In symbolizing sentences of English in *PL* it will frequently be useful to start by determining whether the English sentence we are seeking to symbolize can plausibly be seen as of one of the four kinds, A-, E-, I-, or O-. If it can, then we have a model for the overall structure of the sentence of *PL* we are trying to construct.

Above we gave as an example of an E-sentence 'All cats are non-mousers' rather than 'All cats are not mousers'. We did this because in English we often fail to distinguish between, for example,

Not all cats are mousers

and

All cats are not mousers.

The former is properly seen as the negation of an A-sentence. It denies that all cats are mousers, and hence asserts that there are some cats that are not mousers. The latter is often used to make the same claim, that is, that there are some cats that are not mousers. But what it literally says is that *all* cats are not mousers, that is, that each and every cat is not a mouser. That is, it is literally an E-sentence.

In practice we must rely on the context to determine whether what is literally an E-sentence is being used as an E-sentence or as the negation of an A-sentence. For example, if, in a conversation about professions someone provocatively asserts

All lawyers are scoundrels

and someone else responds

Oh come now, all lawyers are not scoundrels,

the second remark is probably correctly taken as denying that all lawyers are scoundrels, not as asserting that no lawyers are scoundrels. It was to avoid the need to appeal to a specific context that we previously used the 'non-mouser' locution. 'All cats are non-mousers' is unambiguous. It clearly means that each and every cat is not a mouser.

In this text, whenever we do use a sentence of the sort 'All $\mathscr{P}$s are not $\mathscr{Q}$s', and no context is provided, we mean the sentence to be interpreted literally, as saying each and every $\mathscr{P}$ thing is not a $\mathscr{Q}$ thing.

The following relations hold between pairs of A-, E-, I-, and O-sentences. If an A-sentence is true, the corresponding O-sentence is false, and vice versa. If an E-sentence is true, the corresponding I-sentence is false, and vice versa. This is to say A- and O-sentences are contradictories. Each is equivalent to the negation of the other. So too for E- and I-sentences. 'All cats are mousers' is true if and only if 'Some cats are non-mousers' is false, and vice versa. 'No cats are mousers' is true if and only if 'Some cats are mousers' is false, and vice versa.

These relations between A-, E-, I-, and O-sentences are sometimes presented through a *square of opposition*:

A-sentence
$(\forall x)(\mathscr{P} \supset \mathscr{Q})$

E-sentence
$(\forall x)(\mathscr{P} \supset \sim \mathscr{Q})$

$(\exists x)(\mathscr{P} \,\&\, \mathscr{Q})$
I-sentence

$(\exists x)(\mathscr{P} \,\&\, \sim \mathscr{Q})$
O-sentence

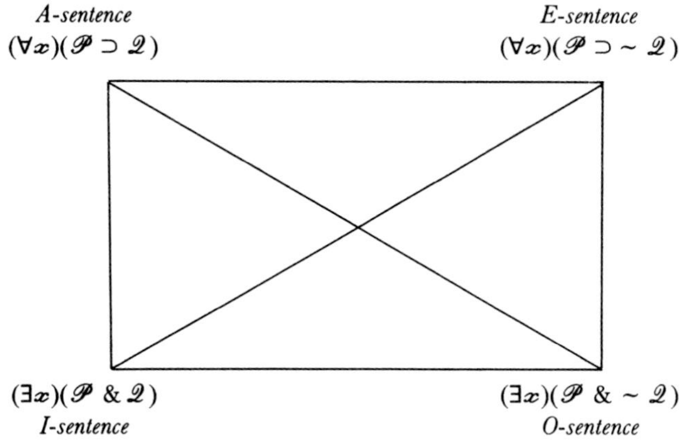

The important equivalencies to remember here are the following:

| | | |
|---|---|---|
| $(\forall x)(\mathcal{P} \supset \mathcal{Q})$ | and | $\sim (\exists x)(\mathcal{P} \,\&\, \sim \mathcal{Q})$ |
| $(\forall x)(\mathcal{P} \supset \sim \mathcal{Q})$ | and | $\sim (\exists x)(\mathcal{P} \,\&\, \mathcal{Q})$ |
| $(\exists x)(\mathcal{P} \,\&\, \mathcal{Q})$ | and | $\sim (\forall x)(\mathcal{P} \supset \sim \mathcal{Q})$ |
| $(\exists x)(\mathcal{P} \,\&\, \sim \mathcal{Q})$ | and | $\sim (\forall x)(\mathcal{P} \supset \mathcal{Q})$ |

In some systems of logic, if an A-sentence is true then so is the corresponding I-sentence, and if an E-sentence is true then so is the corresponding O-sentence. These relationships do not hold in *PL*. This may seem counter intuitive, for it is very tempting to believe that if 'All rabbits are mammals' is true, then so must be 'Some rabbits are mammals' and that if 'No rabbits are cold-blooded' is true, then so must be 'Some rabbits are not cold-blooded'. The reason these relationships do not hold for A- and I- and for E- and O-sentences is that in *PL* we allow predicates which are not satisfied by any member of the universe of discourse.

Given that we treat universal claims as saying of each thing that if it is of this sort it is also of that sort, this is obviously a sensible policy. For example, when working with a culture of unknown bacteria, we might reasonably say, after having placed the culture in an hermetically sealed container for an appropriate length of time,

All the aerobic (air-dependent) bacteria in the culture are dead.

This is true even if there are no such bacteria in the culture, for we will paraphrase it as saying of each bacterium, of whatever sort, that if it is aerobic it is dead. Since there may be no aerobic bacteria in the culture, dead or alive, we clearly do not want the corresponding I-sentence,

Some aerobic bacteria in the culture are dead

to follow, for it says that there are bacteria in the culture which are both aerobic and dead. Again, in the system we are developing A-sentences do not entail I-sentences, and E-sentences do not entail O-sentences.

We will next work through a series of symbolizations concerning the marbles being used in a marble game.

U.D.: The marbles being used by Ashley, Clarence, Rhoda, and Terry
Bx: x is a blue marble
Gx: x is a green marble
Rx: x is a red marble
Sx: x is a shooter
Cx: x is a cat's-eye
Tx: x is a steely

We will symbolize:

1. All the marbles are blue.
2. None of the marbles are blue.
3. Some of the marbles are blue.
4. Some of the marbles are not blue.
5. Some but not all of the marbles are blue.
6. All of the marbles are blue or all the marbles are green.
7. All the marbles are either blue or green.
8. Some of the marbles are blue and some are green, but none are red.
9. If any marble is blue they all are.
10. If any marble is blue it's a cat's-eye.
11. There are only red, green, and blue marbles.
12. All the shooters are red.
13. All the shooters except the steelies are red.

These sentences can be symbolized in *PL*, as, respectively:

1′. $(\forall y)By$
2′. $\sim (\exists y)By$
3′. $(\exists y)By$
4′. $(\exists y) \sim By$
5′. $(\exists y)By \ \& \ \sim (\forall y)By$
6′. $(\forall z)Bz \vee (\forall y)Gy$
7′. $(\forall z)(Bz \vee Gz)$
8′. $[(\exists x)Bx \ \& \ (\exists x)Gx] \ \& \ \sim (\exists x)Rx$
9′. $(\exists w)Bw \supset (\forall x)Bx$
10′. $(\forall x)(Bx \supset Cx)$
11′. $(\forall x)[(Rx \vee Gx) \vee Bx]$
12′. $(\forall y)(Sy \supset Ry)$
13′. $(\forall y)[(Sy \ \& \ \sim Ty) \supset Ry]$

It is here easy to see how the choice of a universe of discourse affects the symbolization process. The universe we have selected consists exclusively of the marbles being used in the game. Hence we were able to symbolize sentence 1 as '$(\forall y)By$'. If, as is usually the case, our universe of discourse were more heterogeneous (e.g., if it contained the players as well as their marbles), we would have to here use a more complex symbolization, for example, '$(\forall y)(My \supset By)$', where '$Mx$' is a new predicate interpreted as '$x$ is a marble'.

Generally, where the universe of discourse is severely restricted A-, E-, I-, and O-sentences have a simpler form than that specified above, that is,

A: $(\forall \mathscr{x})\mathscr{P}$

E: $(\forall \mathscr{x}) \sim \mathscr{P}$

I: $(\exists \mathscr{x})\mathscr{P}$

O: $(\exists \mathscr{x}) \sim \mathscr{P}$

Our symbolization 1′ is thus an A-sentence, and 6′ is a disjunction of A-sentences. The symbolization of 2, 2′, is the negation of an I-sentence, but we could equally well have used an E-sentence, '$(\forall y) \sim By$'. Similarly, 3′ is an I-sentence and 4′ an O-sentence. Sentence 5′ is the conjunction of an I-sentence and the negation of an A-sentence, 8′ is a conjunction of two I-sentences with the negation of an I-sentence. Sentence 9′ is a conditional whose antecedent is an I-sentence and whose consequent is an A-sentence.

Sentences 7′ and 9′–13′ are more complicated, for here quantifiers attach not to a single predicate but to groups of predicates linked with truth-functional operators. In other words, what is being attributed or denied of some or all the things in the universe of discourse is specified not by a single predicate but by a combination of predicates. Sentence 7′ is an A-sentence; it says each and everything in the universe of discourse is of the sort $Bz \vee Gz$, that is, is of the sort 'either blue or green'. The 'any' of sentence 10 has the force of 'every'. Hence 10′, which says that each thing in the universe of discourse is such that if it is blue it is a cat's-eye. Sentence 11 utilizes a 'There are' construction, but followed immediately by 'only'. 'There are only such-and-such kinds of things' means that there are no other kinds of things. Hence sentence 11 has the force of 'Each marble is either red, green, or blue', that is, of an A-sentence. Hence 11′, which says of each thing in the universe of discourse that it is of the sort 'either red or green or blue'. Sentence 12′ is an A-sentence of the sort discussed earlier, it says of each thing in the universe of discourse that if it is of this sort (satisfies '$Sx$') then it is also of that sort (satisfies '$Rx$'). Sentence 13′ is like 12′ except that the condition it specifies is itself conjunctive. That is, it is equivalent to 'Everything which is a shooter and is not a steely is red'.

Note the difference between sentences 6 and 7, and their symbolizations 6′ and 7′. Sentence 6 is a disjunction which will be true if and only if all the marbles are the same color, and that color is either blue or green. Sentence 7, on the other hand, makes a weaker claim. It will of course be true if all of the marbles are blue, and it will be true if all of the marbles are green. But it will also be true if the marbles are not all the same color but none is a color other than blue or green (each is either blue or green).

Alternative, equally correct, symbolizations are possible for each of the above English sentences. For example, 2 can be translated as an E-sentence ('$(\forall y) \sim By$') as well as the negation of an I-sentence. And sentence 13 could be translated as either '$(\forall y)[Sy \supset (\sim Ty \supset Ry)]$' or '$(\forall y)[Sy \supset (Ty \vee Ry)]$'. The notion of there being a single correct, or even "most intuitive" symbolization for each English sentence is even more inappropriate here than it was when working in *SL*.

For our next set of examples we modify the symbolization key used above so as to include the players as well as their marbles, and we add assignments for four individual constants and several new predicates, as indicated below:

U.D.: Ashley, Clarence, Rhoda, Terry, and their marbles

a: Ashley

c: Clarence

r: Rhoda
t: Terry
Bx: x is a blue marble
Gx: x is a green marble
Rx: x is a red marble
Sx: x is a shooter
Cx: x is a cat's-eye
Tx: x is a steely
Px: x is a person
Mx: x is a marble
Bxy: x belongs to y
Wxy: x wins y
Gxyz: x gives y to z

We will use this expanded symbolization key to symbolize the following:

14. All the cat's-eyes belong to Rhoda.
15. All the marbles except the shooters are cat's-eyes.
16. Some, but not all, of the cat's-eyes are green.
17. None of the steelies are red, green, or blue.
18. All of the shooters that are steelies belong to Terry.
19. Some green marbles and some blue marbles but no red ones belong to Clarence.
20. Ashley wins all of Clarence's marbles.
21. Terry doesn't have any marbles.
22. Rhoda wins all of Terry's cat's-eyes and shooters.
23. Terry loses all of his marbles.
24. Terry wins everyone else's marbles.
25. Rhoda gives all the red marbles she wins to Clarence.
26. Clarence gives all his green marbles to Ashley and all his blue marbles to Terry.

We now give one correct symbolization of each of these sentences. Below we will discuss some of the noteworthy aspects of these examples.

14′. $(\forall y)(Cy \supset Byr)$
15′. $(\forall x)[(Mx \,\&\, \sim Sx) \supset Cx]$
16′. $(\exists x)(Cx \,\&\, Gx) \,\&\, \sim (\forall x)(Cx \supset Gx)$
17′. $(\forall w)[Tw \supset \sim (Rw \vee (Gw \vee Bw))]$
18′. $(\forall z)[(Sz \,\&\, Tz) \supset Bzt]$

19′. $[(\exists y)((My \,\&\, Gy) \,\&\, Byc) \,\&\, (\exists y)((My \,\&\, By) \,\&\, Byc)] \,\&\, \sim (\exists y)((My \,\&\, Ry) \,\&\, Byc)$

20′. $(\forall x)[(Mx \,\&\, Bxc) \supset Wax]$

21′. $\sim (\exists z)(Mz \,\&\, Bzt)$

22′. $(\forall x)([(Cx \vee Sx) \,\&\, Bxt] \supset Wrx)$

23′. $(\forall x)[(Mx \,\&\, Bxt) \supset (\exists y)(Py \,\&\, Wyx)]$

24′. $(\forall y)[(My \,\&\, \sim Byt) \supset Wty]$

25′. $(\forall x)[((Mx \,\&\, Rx) \,\&\, Wrx) \supset Grxc]$

26′. $(\forall z)[(Mz \,\&\, Bzc) \supset ((Gz \supset Gcza) \,\&\, (Bz \supset Gczt))]$

Sentence 14 is unproblematic and 14′ an obvious symbolization. Sentence 15 is not quite so straightforward. It does not claim that all the marbles are cat's-eyes (which could be symbolized as '$(\forall x)(Mx \supset Cx)$'), but that all the marbles *except the shooters* are cat's-eyes. Note that literally speaking no claim is being made about the shooters, either that they are or that they are not cat's-eyes. What is being said is merely that when the shooters are excluded the rest are cat's-eyes. Analogously, 'Everyone except Tom passed the test' does not *mean* that Tom did not pass. Tom's test may not yet be graded; the speaker may not know how Tom fared, or may simply not want to reveal whether Tom passed. In general 'All except such-and-such' does not mean 'All and not such-and-such'. Rather, it means 'All excluding such-and-such', with no claim being made about such-and-such.

Example 16 is also straightforward. An alternative and perhaps more intuitive, although longer, symbolization for 17 is '$(\forall x)(Tx \supset \sim Rx) \,\&\, [(\forall x)(Tx \supset \sim Gx) \,\&\, (\forall x)(Tx \supset \sim Bx)]$'. But note that we really do not need three quantifiers. We can, as in 17′, single out the group of things being talked about (steelies) just once and then in one swoop deny that any member of that group is either red, green, or blue. Example 18 asserts, not that all of the shooters belong to Terry, but that all those which are steelies do. So the group we need to single out consists of those things which are both shooters and steelies, and this is what we do in the antecedent of the conditional in 18′.

We needed only one quantifier to symbolize 17, but this is not so with 19. Indeed, even two quantifiers are not enough. For example, the force of '$(\exists x)[(Mx \,\&\, Gx) \,\&\, (Bx \,\&\, Bxc)] \,\&\, \sim (\exists x)[(Mx \,\&\, Rx) \,\&\, Bxc]$' is that Clarence possesses at least one marble which is both green and blue and no red marbles, which is not what is intended.

Example 20 is easy enough once we realize that Clarence's marbles are just the marbles which belong to Clarence. Similarly, to say, as in 21, that Terry has no marbles is to say there are no marbles which belong to Terry. What is of interest in 22 is that it can be symbolized using only one quantifier, although Terry's cat's-eyes and his shooters may be mutually exclusive groups. That is, while we could use a conjunction, for example, '$(\forall x)[(Cx \,\&\, Bxt) \supset Wrx] \,\&\, (\forall x)[(Sx \,\&\, Bxt) \supset Wrx]$' this is being unnecessarily verbose. '$Cx \,\&\, Bxt$' applies to things which are cat's-eyes and belong to Terry. '$(Cx \vee Sx) \,\&\, Bxt$' picks out those things which are either cat's-eyes or shooters and which belong to Terry, that is, it picks out all the cat's-eyes and all the shooters that belong to Terry. In English we can pick out a possibly heterogeneous group by an 'or' construction:

> Animals that are either members of endangered species or that constitute a public danger cannot be sold as pets

picks out all members of endangered species and all animals that constitute a public danger. But we can also use an 'and' construction:

> Members of endangered species and animals constituting a public danger cannot be sold as pets.

In *PL*, unless we use two quantifiers, we must use a disjunctive expression to pick out a group which contains all of the things of this sort *and* all of the things of that sort, as in '(Cx ∨ Sx)'.

Example 23 asserts that Terry loses all of his marbles, and given our symbolization key, the only way to say something is lost is to say someone wins it. But 23 does not assert that Terry loses all of his marbles to the same person. Hence '(∃x)[Px & (∀y)[My & Byt) ⊃ Wxy])' is not a correct symbolization of 23, for it does say that some *one* person wins all of Terry's marbles. Note that the 'Py' in the '(∃y)(Py & Wyx)' clause of 23′ makes explicit what is presumably intended in 23 —that Terry loses his marbles to persons (not to marbles)—remember that our universe of discourse includes both.

'Terry wins all the marbles' could be symbolized as '(∀x)(Mx ⊃ Wtx)'. But to win all the marbles Terry presumably started with zero marbles. Example 24, somewhat literalistically, makes it clear that Terry wins all the marbles which do not already belong to him. Hence the '∼ Byt' part of 24′.

Example 25 is straightforward. What is of interest in 26 is that it can be symbolized using a single quantifier. We could also have used two quantifiers, viz.,

(∀x)[((Mx & Gx) & Bxc) ⊃ Gcxa] & (∀x)[((Mx & Bx) & Bxc) ⊃ Gcxt]

But if we first single out those things which are marbles and belong to Clarence, as we do in 26′, and then say that if such a thing is green then Clarence gives it to Ashley, and if it is blue then Clarence gives it to Terry, we can get by with one quantifier.

Before ending this section we issue some cautionary notes about symbolizing sentences in *PL*. The first concerns the selection of predicates of *PL* for use in symbolizing English sentences. Frequently, but not always, English descriptions which consist of "stacked-up" adjectives, as in 'A second-hand, broken-down, uncomfortable, tan recliner is in the corner' can be captured by conjoining appropriate predicates of *PL*. Taking the furniture in the room to constitute the universe of discourse and using obvious predicates, we can symbolize the foregoing as

(∃z)([(Sz & Bz) & (Uz & Tz)] & (Rz & Cz))

This symbolization is appropriate because the recliner in question is second-hand, is broken-down, is uncomfortable, is tan, is a recliner, and is in the corner. On the other hand, a bloody fool is presumably a very foolish person, but not necessarily a person covered with blood. So too a counterfeit dollar is not something which both is counterfeit *and* is a dollar (because it is *not* a dollar), and while the animal in the corner may be a large mouse, it is not clear there is something in the corner which is large, is an animal, and is a mouse—even large mice are not large as animals go. And a second-rate mathematician who is also a first-rate drama critic is not a second-rate person and a first-rate person. Rather 'second-rate mathematician' and 'first-rate drama critic' should each normally be symbolized by a single predicate of *PL*, as should 'bloody fool', 'counterfeit dollar' and 'large mouse'.

This practice will cause problems in some contexts. For example, from 'Sue is a first-rate drama critic' we will not be able to infer 'Sue is a drama critic'. We can save such inferences by the admittedly *ad hoc* device of using one predicate for 'first-rate drama critic' and another for 'drama critic'. That is, using the following symbolization key

U.D.: People
Fx: x is a first-rate drama critic
Dx: x is a drama critic

we can symbolize these two sentences, respectively, as

Fs & Ds

and

Ds

And we will be able to show that the second of these *PL* sentences follows from the first.

As the above case illustrates, the appropriate selection of predicates commonly depends upon the context. For example, given just that the universe of discourse is living things and the sentence

Rabid bats are dangerous

and no context, it is impossible to tell whether we should treat 'x is a rabid bat' by one predicate, 'Rx', and symbolize the whole sentence as

$(\forall y)(Ry \supset Dy)$

where 'Dx' is interpreted as 'x is dangerous', or treat 'x is rabid' and 'x is a bat' as two predicates (rabid bats are things which are both rabid and bats) and symbolize the given sentence as

$(\forall y)[(Ry \ \& \ By) \supset Dy]$

Taken in isolation, there is no correct answer to this question. But suppose that, instead of the foregoing single sentence, we are given a complete argument:

> Some bats are rabid. Rabid animals are dangerous. Therefore some bats are dangerous.

Here we want our symbolization to reveal as much as possible of what is common to the premises and the conclusion. To do this, we clearly need to use separate predicates of *PL* for 'x is a bat' and 'x is rabid'. Where animals constitute the universe of discourse, an appropriate symbolization is

$$\begin{array}{l} (\exists y)(Ry \ \& \ By) \\ (\forall z)(Rz \supset Dz) \\ \hline (\exists y)(By \ \& \ Dy) \end{array}$$

We will be able to show that this is a valid argument of *PL*. But had we chosen to use a single predicate, say 'Rx', to symbolize being a rabid bat we would have had to use a different predicate to symbolize being a rabid animal, say 'Ax':

$$\begin{array}{l} (\exists x)Rx \\ (\forall y)(Ay \supset Dy) \\ \hline (\exists y)(By \ \& \ Dy) \end{array}$$

In this second symbolization we have made opaque the obvious fact that rabid bats are rabid animals as well as the fact that rabid bats are bats. As a result, although the English language argument is valid, as is our first symbolization of it, the second symbolization is not valid.

There is a further complication in the selection of predicates. Consider the sentence

Ponce de Leon is searching for the fountain of youth.

We cannot symbolize this sentence as

Spf

where 'Sxy' is interpreted as 'x is searching for y', 'p' designates 'Ponce de Leon', and 'f' the fountain of youth, for there is no such thing as the fountain of youth. We can interpret 'Sx' as 'x is searching for the fountain of youth' and symbolize the sentence as

Sp

Although things that do not exist cannot be found, it is unfortunately all too easy to search for them. For this reason

Ponce de Leon is hunting for mermaids

is also problematic. There is no problem about interpreting 'Mx' as 'x is a mermaid' and 'Hxy' as 'x is hunting for y'; nonetheless neither of the following is an acceptable symbolization of the foregoing claim concerning Ponce de Leon:

$(\exists x)(Mx \ \& \ Hpx)$

$(\forall x)(Mx \supset Hpx)$

The first of these sentences asserts that there is at least one thing that is a mermaid, which is false. But the nonexistence of mermaids does not keep people from hunting for them. That is, it might well be true that Ponce de Leon is hunting for mermaids. The second sentence of *PL* says that each thing is such that, if it is a mermaid, Ponce de Leon is hunting for it. But, since there are no mermaids, this sentence is true no matter what Ponce de Leon is doing, for it says only that if a thing is a mermaid (and nothing is), then Ponce de Leon is hunting it. The way out of the present difficulty is to use a one-place predicate, for example, to interpret 'Mx' as 'x is hunting for mermaids' and to symbolize

Ponce de Leon is hunting for mermaids

as

Mp

The difficulty we are encountering in symbolizing sentences concerned with such activities as hunting, searching, looking for, and desiring arise even when what is being sought does exist. Suppose the sentence we want to symbolize is

Ponce de Leon is searching for a good harbor.

It might be thought that, if we interpret 'Sxy' as 'x is searching for y' and 'Gx' as 'x is a good harbor', a proper symbolization of this sentence would be

(∃x)(Gx & Spx)

This symbolization might be acceptable if Ponce de Leon is looking for a particular harbor, say the harbor at Vera Cruz. But, if he is prowling the Florida coast and merely wants a haven from an impending storm, any good harbor, it is false to say that there is a good harbor such that he is looking for *that* harbor. Imagine that there are three good harbors in his vicinity. Ponce de Leon will be glad to reach any one of them, and he is not interested in reaching more than one (so '(∀x)(Gx ⊃ Spx)' is clearly not the right symbolization). Which good harbor is it that he is searching for? Since he does not know of the existence of any of the three and each will fulfill his desires for a good harbor equally well, the only answer can be that there is no good harbor such that Ponce de Leon is looking for *it*. So here too we should use a one-place predicate. If we interpret 'Sx' as 'x is searching for a good harbor', the proper symbolization is

Sp

Generally, unless what is being sought, hunted, searched for, hoped for, or desired is a particular thing, as opposed to a *kind* of thing, a one-place rather than a two-place predicate of *PL* should be used.[15]

[15] There are logics, known as intensional logics, in which problematic sentences of the sort we have just been discussing can be further analyzed.

## 7.4E EXERCISES

**1.** Symbolize the following sentences in *PL*:

*Symbolization Key*

U.D.: Persons
Dx: x is at the door
Hx: x is honest
Ix: x is an influence-peddler
Lx: x is likeable
Px: x is a politician
Rx: x is a registered lobbyist
h: Harrington

a. All politicians are honest.
*b. No politicians are honest.
c. Some politicians are honest.
*d. Some politicians are not honest.
e. An honest politician is not an influence-peddler.
*f. An honest politician is at the door.
g. Politicians and influence-peddlers are not all honest.
*h. Honest influence-peddlers are nonexistent.
i. An influence-peddler is honest only if he or she is a registered lobbyist.
*j. Some but not all registered lobbyists are honest.
k. If anyone is an influence-peddler, Harrington is.
*l. If anyone is an influence-peddler, he or she is either a politician or a registered lobbyist.
m. If anyone is an influence-peddler, every registered lobbyist is.
*n. Harrington is no influence-peddler, but he is an honest politician.
o. No one is honest, a politician, and an influence-peddler.
*p. Everyone's a politician, but not everyone is honest.
q. If every politician is an influence-peddler, then no politician is honest.
*r. Some politicians who are influence-peddlers are honest, but none are likeable.
s. Registered lobbyists are likeable influence peddlers, but they are not honest.

**2.** Symbolize the following sentences in *PL*:

*Symbolization Key*

U.D.: People
Ex: x is a real estate agent
Lx: x is a lawyer
Px: x is a professor
Nx: x lives next door
Rx: x is rich
Sx: x can sell to yuppies
Yx: x is a yuppie
Sxy: x respects y
f: Fred

a. All real estate agents are yuppies.
*b. No real estate agents are yuppies.
c. Some but not all real estate agents are yuppies.
*d. Some real estate agents are yuppies and some are not.
e. If any real estate agent is a yuppie all lawyers are.
*f. Any real estate agent who isn't a yuppie isn't rich.
g. If any real estate agent can sell to yuppies, he or she is a yuppie.
*h. If any real estate agent can sell to yuppies, Fred can.
i. Anyone who is a lawyer and a real estate agent is a yuppie and rich.
*j. Yuppies who aren't rich don't exist.
k. Real estate agents and lawyers are rich if they are yuppies.
*l. If Fred is a yuppie he's not a professor, and if he's a professor he's not rich.
m. No professor who isn't rich is a yuppie.
*n. No professor who is self-respecting is a yuppie.
o. Every self-respecting real estate agent is a yuppie.
*p. Real estate agents and lawyers who are rich are self-respecting.
q. Real estate agents and lawyers who are either rich or yuppies are self-respecting.
*r. A yuppie who is either a real estate agent or a lawyer is self-respecting.
s. A yuppie who is both a lawyer and a real estate agent is self-respecting.
*t. A yuppie who is both a lawyer and a real estate agent lives next door.

**3.** Symbolize the following sentences in *PL*:

*Symbolization Key*

U.D.: Mammals
Cxy: x is chasing y
Lx: x is a lion
Ax: x is a formidable animal
Fx: x is ferocious
Tx: x is a tiger
Bx: x is best avoided
t: Tom Selleck

a. A lion is a formidable animal.
*b. Lions are ferocious.
c. Lions are ferocious, but tigers are not.
*d. A lion is chasing Tom Selleck.
e. Tom Selleck is chasing a ferocious lion.
*f. Ferocious lions are best avoided.
g. Lions and tigers are ferocious.
*h. Lions and tigers are chasing Tom Selleck.
i. Some, but not all, tigers are ferocious.
*j. Ferocious lions and tigers are best avoided.
k. Any lion Tom Selleck is chasing is a formidable animal but is not ferocious.
*l. Tom Selleck and ferocious lions and tigers are all best avoided.
m. If any lion is ferocious, all tigers are.
*n. A lion is ferocious if and only if Tom Selleck is chasing it.
o. Tom Selleck is not ferocious, but he is best avoided.
*p. If Tom Selleck is ferocious, all lions are tigers.

4. Symbolize the following sentences in *PL*:

*Symbolization Key*

U.D.: People
Ax: x is an administrator
Px: x is a professor
Ux: x is underpaid
Ox: x is overworked
Sx: x is a secretary

a. Professors are underpaid and overworked.
*b. Overworked professors are underpaid.
c. Administrators are neither overworked nor underpaid.
*d. Administrators are neither overworked nor underpaid, but professors are both.
e. A person is overworked if and only if he or she is underpaid.
*f. If any administrator is underpaid, all professors are; and if any professor is underpaid, all secretaries are.
g. Some professors are underpaid, but those who are administrators are not.
*h. Administrators are overworked but not underpaid; secretaries are both underpaid and overworked, and professors are neither overworked nor underpaid.
i. Some professors are overworked and underpaid, and all secretaries are.
*j. Some underpaid professors are also secretaries, and some overworked administrators are also professors, but no administrator is a secretary.
k. Some secretaries and some professors are underpaid, but no administrator is.

5. The square of opposition:
a. Can an I-sentence of *PL* and the corresponding O-sentence both be true? Can two such sentences both be false? Explain.
*b. Can an A-sentence of *PL* and the corresponding E-sentence both be false? Can two such sentences both be true? Explain.

## 7.5 MULTIPLE QUANTIFICATION

In symbolizing sentences of English as sentences of *PL* we have frequently encountered sentences of *PL* which contain more than one quantifier. But these have all been truth-functional compounds. In none of these sentences has one quantifier fallen within the scope of another quantifier. It is time to consider sentences of English whose *PL* symbolizations do contain multiple quantifiers *with* overlapping scope.

Consider again our early examples concerning the people in Michael's office. We there gave a symbolization of 'Michael likes everyone' as '(∀x)Lmx' but we did not attempt a symbolization of

Everyone likes everyone.

To symbolize 'Everyone likes everyone' we need to say of each person what '(∀x)Lmx' says of Michael. To accomplish this we replace the constant 'm' with a second variable and add a second universal quantifier:

$(\forall y)(\forall x)Lyx$

In quasi-English this says 'Each person y is such that for each person x, y likes x', or, 'Each person y is such that y likes everyone', or 'Everyone likes everyone'.

Similarly, as '$(\exists x)Lmx$' symbolizes 'Michael likes someone'

$(\exists y)(\exists x)Lyx$

symbolizes 'Someone likes someone'. In each of these sentences of *PL* the scope of the second quantifier falls within that of the first quantifier. It is also possible to mix universal and existential quantifiers. Consider

$(\forall x)(\exists y)Lxy$

$(\exists y)(\forall x)Lyx$

$(\exists y)(\forall x)Lxy$

$(\forall x)(\exists y)Lyx$

The first of the above sentences can be paraphrased as 'Each person x is such that x likes at least one person y', or 'Everyone likes someone'. The second can be paraphrased as 'There is at least one person y such that y likes every person x', or 'Someone likes everyone'. Note that these are *very* different claims. For 'Everyone likes someone' to be true it is sufficient that each person like at least one person. Perhaps Michael likes Rita, Rita likes Henry, Henry likes Sue, and Sue likes Michael. But for 'Someone likes everyone' to be true there has to be at least *one* person who likes *everyone*, including him- or herself. If we extend the universe of discourse to include all persons, it is at least plausible to think that everyone does like someone, that is, someone or other. It is, on the other hand, an act of complete naivete to suggest that there is someone who likes everyone. (There may indeed be some persons who believe they like everyone, but given that they obviously do not even know everyone, it is hard to see how they could like everyone.) The moral here is that in *mixed multiple quantification* the order of the quantifiers does make a world of difference.

The third sentence looks very much like the second—only the order of the variables occurring after the two-place predicate is different. The third sentence says, not that someone likes everyone, but that someone *is liked by* everyone. If we limit our universe of discourse to the people in Michael's office, or any other reasonably small group, there may be such a lucky person. But if the universe of discourse is all people, there is no such person, again because there is no person who is even known to everyone, far less liked by everyone. The fourth sentence says that everyone *is liked by* at least one person. The moral here is that we need to pay attention both to the order of quantifiers in mixed quantification and to the order in which individual terms follow predicates.

Note that while 'Everyone likes everyone' and 'Everyone is liked by everyone' are clearly different English sentences, and can be symbolized as different sentences of *PL*, for example, as '$(\forall x)(\forall y)Lxy$' and '$(\forall x)(\forall y)Lyx$', respectively, there is no difference in the truth-conditions for the two sentences of English (nor in those for the sentences of *PL*). If everyone likes everyone, then each person gets liked by everyone, that is, everyone is liked by everyone, and vice versa. Generally, when we have two universal quantifiers, the order in which they occur does not matter, nor does the order in which variables bound by those quantifiers follow two-place predicates. Similarly, when we have two existential quantifiers, the order in which they occur, and the order in which the variables they bind follow two-place predicates, does not matter. If someone likes someone, then someone is liked by someone, and vice versa. More generally, when we have a series of quantifiers, all existential or all universal, the order in which they occur does not matter. But this is, again, not true where we have mixed quantification, that is, some existential and some universal quantifiers.

There are four combinations in which pairs of quantifiers can occur. We display them here along with useful quasi-English paraphrases:

| | |
|---|---|
| $(\exists x)(\exists y)\ldots$ | There is an x and there is a y such that ... |
| $(\forall x)(\forall y)\ldots$ | For each x and for each y ... |
| $(\forall x)(\exists y)\ldots$ | For each x there is a y such that ... |
| $(\exists x)(\forall y)\ldots$ | There is an x such that for each y ... |

So far we have been assuming that our universe of discourse is limited to persons, either just the persons in Michael's office or all persons. Suppose we now allow our universe of discourse to be more heterogeneous, including, say, all living things. To be able to say that, for example, every*one* (as opposed to every*thing*) loves some*one* (as opposed to some*thing*) we need a predicate which singles out persons. We will use 'Px', here interpreted as 'x is a person'. Appropriate symbolizations of

1. Everyone likes everyone.
2. Someone likes someone.
3. Everyone likes someone.
4. Someone likes everyone.
5. Everyone is liked by someone.
6. Someone is liked by everyone.

are, respectively,

1′. $(\forall x)(\forall y)[(Px \ \& \ Py) \supset Lxy]$
2′. $(\exists x)(\exists y)[(Px \ \& \ Py) \ \& \ Lxy]$
3′. $(\forall x)[Px \supset (\exists y)(Py \ \& \ Lxy)]$
4′. $(\exists x)[Px \ \& \ (\forall y)(Py \supset Lxy)]$
5′. $(\forall x)[Px \supset (\exists y)(Py \ \& \ Lyx)]$
6′. $(\exists x)[Px \ \& \ (\forall y)(Py \supset Lyx)]$

Note that in 1′ and 2′ the quantifiers occur at the beginning of the sentence, whereas in 3′–6′ the second quantifier occurs later in the sentences. We can move the y-quantifier closer to the first predicate containing 'y' in symbolizing 1 and 2. That is, '(∀x)[Px ⊃ (∀y)(Py ⊃ Lxy)]' is also an appropriate symbolization of 1, as is '(∃x)[Px & (∃y)(Py & Lxy)]' of sentence 2. Similarly, in symbolizing 3–6 the second quantifier can be brought closer to the front of the sentence. That is, '(∀x)(∃y)[Px ⊃ (Py & Lxy)]' is an appropriate symbolization of sentence 3, '(∃x)(∀y)[Px & (Py ⊃ Lxy)]' of 4, '(∀x)(∃y)[Px ⊃ (Py & Lyx)]' of 5 and '(∃x)(∀y)[Px & (Py ⊃ Lyx)]' of 6. There is no "most natural" placement of quantifiers. Some prefer to move quantifiers to the front of a sentence, at least when the quantifiers are either all universal or all existential. Others prefer to place a quantifier as close as possible to the first predicate containing a variable bound by that quantifier. In any event, care must be taken in moving quantifiers around. While '(∀x)(∀y)[(Px & Py) ⊃ Lxy]' and '(∀x)[Px ⊃ (∀y)(Py ⊃ Lxy)]' both say 'Everyone loves everyone', '(∀x)[(Px & (∀y)Py) ⊃ Lxy]', which might be the result of carelessly moving a universal quantifier into the middle of a sentence, is a formula but not a *sentence* of *PL*, this because the occurrence of 'y' in 'Lxy' is free. Attempting to remedy this by altering the placement of parentheses might produce '(∀x)[Px & (∀y)(Py ⊃ Lxy)]'. While this expression is a sentence of *PL*, it does not say what we intend, for it says 'Each x is such that it is a person *and* each y is such that if y is a person x likes y'. That is, it says, in part, that everything is a person, which is false in a universe of discourse not restricted to persons (as our present universe is not). In constructing complex symbolizations it is a good practice to inspect the expression one constructs, see if it is a sentence of *PL*, and, if it is, try to read it back into English.

In Section 7.1 we presented a valid English language argument that cannot be shown to be valid by the techniques associated with *SL*:

> None of David's friends support Republicans. Sarah supports Breitlow, and Breitlow is a Republican. So Sarah is no friend of David's.

We are now able to symbolize this argument in *PL*. An appropriate symbolization key is:

U.D.: People
Fxy: x is a friend of y
Sxy: x supports y
Rx: x is a Republican
d: David
b: Breitlow
s: Sarah

The second premise, a conjunction, is readily symbolized as 'Ssb & Rb'. The conclusion is also easy to symbolize, once we see that it simply amounts to the claim that Sarah is not a friend of David's: ' ~ Fsd'. It is only the first premise that seems to pose difficulties. That premise is of the general form

> No thing of such-and-such a sort is a thing of such-and-such a sort.

That is, it is an E-sentence. In Section 7.4 we saw that E-sentences can be symbolized either as universally quantified sentences or as negations of existentially quantified sentences. If we opt for the former, an appropriate first step toward a symbolization is

> Each x is such that if x is a friend of David's then x does not support Republicans.

This quasi-English locution readily becomes

> (∀x)(Fxd ⊃ it is not the case that x supports Republicans).

What remains is to find a symbolization for 'it is not the case that x supports Republicans'. A quasi-English first step is

> it is not the case that there is a y such that y is a Republican and x supports y

which can be symbolized as ' ~ (∃y)(Ry & Sxy)'. The full symbolization of the first premise is thus

> (∀x)(Fxd ⊃ ~ (∃y)(Ry & Sxy))

The resulting argument of *PL* is

> (∀x)(Fxd ⊃ ~ (∃y)(Ry & Sxy))
> Ssb & Rb
> ―――――――――――――
> ~ Fsd

This argument is, as we will see in later chapters, both semantically and syntactically valid.

Note that while we chose to treat the embedded clause 'it is not the case that x supports Republicans' as the negation of an I-claim, we could equally well have treated it as an E-claim, symbolizing it as '(∀y)(Ry ⊃ ~ Sxy)'. So doing would yield the following alternative symbolization of the first premise:

> (∀x)(Fxd ⊃ (∀y)(Ry ⊃ ~ Sxy))

Moving the second quantifier yields

> (∀x)(∀y)(Fxd ⊃ (Ry ⊃ ~ Sxy))

an equivalent sentence of *PL*. A final rewrite yields the following equivalent sentence:

> (∀x)(∀y)((Fxd & Ry) ⊃ ~ Sxy)

All of these symbolizations of the first premise, and many others we have not given, are equally acceptable. In constructing symbolizations it is often useful to start, as we did here, by determining whether the sentence to be symbolized fits one of the four patterns provided by the A-, E-, I-, O-sentence classification, if it does, next picking the overall structure to be used (e.g., universal quantification of a conditional formula), laying out that structure, and then filling in the missing pieces—successively replacing bits of English with formulas of *PL*.

Here is a somewhat more interesting argument:

> Anyone who is proud of anyone is proud of Sam. Rhoda isn't proud of anyone who's proud of him or herself, but she is proud of everyone who has mastered calculus. Therefore if Art has mastered calculus Sam isn't proud of himself.

We will use the following symbolization key:

U.D.: People in Sam's class
Pxy: x is proud of y
Mx: x has mastered calculus
a: Art
r: Rhoda
s: Sam

The first occurrence of 'anyone' in the first premise will clearly go over to a universal quantifier in *PL*, as becomes apparent when we try to paraphrase the sentence:

...(y is proud of anyone ⊃ y is proud of Sam)

Here there is clear pronominal cross reference, the y that is proud of Sam is the y that is proud of anyone. So as a next step we have

(∀y)(y is proud of anyone ⊃ Pys)

an A-sentence. What remains is to determine whether the second 'anyone' should go over to a universal or an existential quantifier in *PL*. Note that there is no pronominal cross reference from the consequent of 'y is proud of anyone ⊃ Pys' back to 'anyone'. So we can use an existential quantifier. That a universal quantifier is not called for is also apparent when we consider that

(∀y)(y is proud of everyone ⊃ Pys)

is clearly an inappropriate paraphrase of the first premise while

(∀y)(y is proud of someone ⊃ Pys)

is an appropriate paraphrase. To be proud of someone is for there to be someone of whom one is proud. So the missing formula is '$(\exists x)Pyx$'. The complete symbolization of the first premise is thus:

$$(\forall y)[(\exists x)Pyx \supset Pys]$$

The second premise is a conjunction, and should be symbolized as a conjunction of *PL*. The left conjunct will be a symbolization of 'Rhoda isn't proud of anyone who is proud of him- or herself', which can be treated as an E-sentence (as 'No person who is proud of him- or herself is a person of whom Rhoda is proud'). So an appropriate left conjunct for our *PL* symbolization is '$(\forall z)(Pzz \supset \sim Prz)$'. The right conjunct of the second premise can be treated as an A-sentence (as 'Everyone who has mastered calculus is a person of whom Rhoda is proud') and symbolized as '$(\forall z)(Mz \supset Prz)$'. The second premise of our symbolized argument is thus

$$(\forall z)(Pzz \supset \sim Prz) \ \& \ (\forall z)(Mz \supset Prz)$$

The conclusion of our English language argument is a conditional and can be symbolized as '$Ma \supset \sim Pss$'. The complete argument of *PL* is

$$(\forall y)[(\exists x)Pyx \supset Pys]$$
$$(\forall z)(Pzz \supset \sim Prz) \ \& \ (\forall z)(Mz \supset Prz)$$
$$\overline{Ma \supset \sim Pss}$$

This is also a syntactically and semantically valid argument of *PL*.

We just symbolized 'Anyone who is proud of anyone is proud of Sam' as '$(\forall y)[(\exists x)Pyx \supset Pys]$'. An alternative symbolization is

$$(\forall y)(\forall x)(Pyx \supset Pys)$$

A quasi-English reading of this second symbolization is

Each y and each x is such that if y is proud of x then y is proud of Sam.

The obvious difference between these two sentences of *PL* is that in the second the x-quantifier is a universal quantifier whose scope extends to the end of the sentence.

A simpler example may be helpful here. Consider the sentences:

If any student passes, Donna will pass.

Each student is such that if that student passes, Donna will pass.

If we restrict our universe of discourse to students in the class in question, interpret '$Px$' as '$x$ will pass', and let '$d$' designate Donna, these sentences can be symbolized as

1. $(\exists x)Px \supset Pd$
2. $(\forall x)(Px \supset Pd)$

The first of these sentences can be read

If there is at least one student x such that x passes, then Donna passes.

Now suppose that some student, say Art, does pass. Then, according to sentence 1, Donna also passes. Sentence 2 can be read

Each student x is such that if x passes, then Donna passes.

Now, if each student is of this sort, then Art is of this sort. So, if sentence 2 holds and Art passes, Donna passes. Sentences 1 and 2 are also false under just the same circumstances. The first will be false only if some student passes and Donna does not. Suppose, for example, that Bud passes but that Donna does not. Then sentence 1 is false, and so is sentence 2. For the second sentence says that each student, including Bud, is such that if he or she passes Donna passes. And this is false if Bud passes and Donna does not.

The general rule is this: When an existential quantifier has only the antecedent of a conditional within its scope and its scope is then broadened to include the consequent of that conditional, the quantifier becomes a universal quantifier. That is, where $\mathscr{P}$ is a predicate in which $x$ does not occur,

$$(\exists x)\mathscr{A}x \supset \mathscr{P}$$

and

$$(\forall x)(\mathscr{A}x \supset \mathscr{P})$$

are equivalent sentence forms.

An analogous though less common case occurs when a universal quantifier has only the antecedent of a conditional within its scope and its scope is broadened to include the entire conditional. When this happens, the universal quantifier becomes an existential quantifier. That is, where $x$ does not occur in $\mathscr{P}$, the following sentence forms are equivalent:

$$(\forall x)\mathscr{A}x \supset \mathscr{P} \qquad (\exists x)(\mathscr{A}x \supset \mathscr{P})$$

The cases to watch out for, then, are cases where the consequent of a conditional does not lie within the scope of a quantifier and is then brought within that scope, or vice versa. In these cases the quantifier in question must change. If it was universal it becomes existential, and if it was existential it becomes universal.

Fortunately, there are many cases in which quantifiers do not change when their scopes are broadened or narrowed. If the scope of a quantifier extends over only one disjunct of a disjunction or over only one conjunct of a conjunction and that scope is broadened to include the entire disjunction or conjunction, the quantifier does not change. Similarly, when a quantifier has scope only over the consequent of a conditional and its scope is broadened, the quantifier does not change. So, where $x$ does not occur in $\mathscr{P}$, the following are all pairs of equivalent sentence forms:

| | | |
|---|---|---|
| $(\exists x)\mathscr{A}x \supset \mathscr{P}$ | and | $(\forall x)(\mathscr{A}x \supset \mathscr{P})$ |
| $(\forall x)\mathscr{A}x \supset \mathscr{P}$ | and | $(\exists x)(\mathscr{A}x \supset \mathscr{P})$ |
| $\mathscr{P} \supset (\exists x)\mathscr{A}x$ | and | $(\exists x)(\mathscr{P} \supset \mathscr{A}x)$ |
| $\mathscr{P} \supset (\forall x)\mathscr{A}x$ | and | $(\forall x)(\mathscr{P} \supset \mathscr{A}x)$ |
| $(\exists x)\mathscr{A}x \vee \mathscr{P}$ | and | $(\exists x)(\mathscr{A}x \vee \mathscr{P})$ |
| $(\forall x)\mathscr{A}x \vee \mathscr{P}$ | and | $(\forall x)(\mathscr{A}x \vee \mathscr{P})$ |
| $\mathscr{P} \vee (\exists x)\mathscr{A}x$ | and | $(\exists x)(\mathscr{P} \vee \mathscr{A}x)$ |
| $\mathscr{P} \vee (\forall x)\mathscr{A}x$ | and | $(\forall x)(\mathscr{P} \vee \mathscr{A}x)$ |
| $(\exists x)\mathscr{A}x \,\&\, \mathscr{P}$ | and | $(\exists x)(\mathscr{A}x \,\&\, \mathscr{P})$ |
| $(\forall x)\mathscr{A}x \,\&\, \mathscr{P}$ | and | $(\forall x)(\mathscr{A}x \,\&\, \mathscr{P})$ |
| $\mathscr{P} \,\&\, (\exists x)\mathscr{A}x$ | and | $(\exists x)(\mathscr{P} \,\&\, \mathscr{A}x)$ |
| $\mathscr{P} \,\&\, (\forall x)\mathscr{A}x$ | and | $(\forall x)(\mathscr{P} \,\&\, \mathscr{A}x)$ |

Biconditionals are a special case. $(\forall x)\mathscr{A}x \equiv \mathscr{P}$ is not equivalent either to

$$(\forall x)(\mathscr{A}x \equiv \mathscr{P})$$

or to

$$(\exists x)(\mathscr{A}x \equiv \mathscr{P})$$

That is, the scope of a quantifier that does not extend over both sides of a biconditional *cannot* be broadened to cover both sides, nor can the scope of a quantifier that does cover both sides of a biconditional be narrowed to cover only one side.

*FURTHER SYMBOLIZATIONS*

Next we shall symbolize a group of sentences of increasing complexity:

1. Everyone who understands either Bertrand Russell's *Principia Mathematica* or Lewis Carroll's *Alice in Wonderland* understands this text.
2. No one understands everything.
3. No one understands anything.

U.D.: everything
Exy: x envies y
Uxy: x understands y
Px: x is a person
a: Lewis Carroll's *Alice in Wonderland*
p: Bertrand Russell's *Principia Mathematica*
t: this text

In symbolizing these sentences, we shall again use the procedure of moving gradually from English to symbols.

Sentence 1 is an A-sentence. So it will be symbolized as a universally quantified sentence. Hence we can start with

> Each x is such that if x is a person and x understands either Bertrand Russell's *Principia Mathematica* or Lewis Carroll's *Alice in Wonderland*, then x understands this text

and then

> (∀x)(if both Px and x understands either Bertrand Russell's *Principia Mathematica* or Lewis Carroll's *Alice in Wonderland*, then x understands this text).

We can now see that we can complete our symbolization without using any more quantifiers. The complete symbolization is

> (∀x)([Px & (Uxp ∨ Uxa)] ⊃ Uxt)

Sentence 2 is a E-sentence. So we shall symbolize it as a universal quantification that says of each thing that if it is a person, then it doesn't understand everything. That is,

> Each y is such that if y is a person, then y doesn't understand everything.

Next we move to

> (∀y)(Py ⊃ it is not the case that y understands everything).

The remaining bit of English obviously goes over to '~ (∀z)Uyz', so the entire sentence of *PL* is

> (∀y)(Py ⊃ ~ (∀z)Uyz)

'No one understands everything' and 'No one understands anything' are very different claims. The former is certainly true, for it simply denies that anyone is omniscient. But, though no one understands everything, presumably some people do understand some things; that is, sentence 3, 'No one understands anything', is false. As before, we can obtain the appropriate symbolization in stages:

> Each x is such that if x is a person, then x doesn't understand anything
>
> (∀x)(Px ⊃ it is not the case that x understands anything).

The phrase 'it is not the case that x understands anything' can be paraphrased as

> it is not the case that there is a y such that x understands y

and symbolized as

> ~ (∃y)Uxy

The complete symbolization is

$$(\forall x)(Px \supset \sim (\exists y)Uxy)$$

The expression 'it is not the case that x understands anything' can also be symbolized as

$$(\forall y) \sim Uxy$$

This is equivalent to our earlier symbolization, for an existential quantifier can always be replaced by a tilde followed by the corresponding universal quantifier followed by another tilde. Performing this replacement on '$\sim (\exists y)Uxy$' yields

$$\sim \sim (\forall y) \sim Uxy$$

which is of course equivalent to '$(\forall y) \sim Uxy$'.

4. If someone understands Bertrand Russell's *Principia Mathematica*, that person understands Lewis Carroll's *Alice in Wonderland.*

This sentence is one of those rare cases in which 'someone' is used to mean everyone. This becomes apparent when we realize that there is pronominal cross reference here from the consequent of this English conditional (from the pronominal phrase 'that person') back to the quantity term in the antecedent ('someone'). Once we see this, the symbolization is trivial:

$$(\forall z)[(Pz \,\&\, Uzp) \supset Uza]$$

5. Only people who understand either Bertrand Russell's *Principia Mathematica* or Lewis Carroll's *Alice in Wonderland* understand this text.

This sentence is an interesting example in that it is a quantificational analogue to an 'only if' claim of sentential logic. That is, we are not told here that all those persons who understand either Bertrand Russell's *Principia Mathematica* or Lewis Carroll's *Alice in Wonderland* understand this text, but rather that understanding one of those two books is a prerequisite for understanding this text. An appropriate start is therefore

> Each y is such that if y is a person and y doesn't understand either Bertrand Russell's *Principia Mathematica* or Lewis Carroll's *Alice in Wonderland*, then y doesn't understand this text.

A correct symbolization is

$$(\forall y)([Py \,\&\, \sim (Uyp \vee Uya)] \supset \sim Uyt)$$

This is equivalent to

$$(\forall y)[(Py \,\&\, Uyt) \supset (Uyp \vee Uya)]$$

but *not* to

$$(\forall y)([Py \,\&\, (Uyp \vee Uya)] \supset Uyt)$$

6. Anyone who understands anything is envied by someone.

Sentence 6 contains two occurrences of the quantity term 'any', one of which will go to a universal quantifier in *PL* and one of which will go to an existential quantifier. That the first occurrence of 'any' (in 'anyone') must be replaced by a universal quantifier becomes apparent when we note that there is a pronominal cross reference from 'is envied by someone' back to 'anyone'. That is, the person who is envied is clearly the very same person who does the understanding. On the other hand, there is no pronominal cross reference back to the second 'any' (in 'anything'). That is, the example is equivalent to 'Anyone who understands something is envied by someone'. A start at a paraphrase is

> Each x such that if (x is a person and x understands something), then x is envied by someone.

Next we move to

$$(\forall x)[(Px \text{ and } x \text{ understands something}) \supset x \text{ is envied by someone}].$$

The second part of the antecedent of our conditional of *PL* will be

$$(\exists y)Uxy$$

And clearly 'x is envied by someone' will go over into 'someone envies x'. That is, since 'Exy' is being interpreted as 'x envies y', we must here transform the passive 'is envied by someone' into the active 'someone envies'. And 'someone envies x' will become

$$(\exists z)(Pz \ \& \ Ezx)$$

We can now put all the parts together:

$$(\forall x)[(Px \ \& \ (\exists y)Uxy) \supset (\exists z)(Pz \ \& \ Ezx)]$$

It is perhaps time to make explicit a practice we have been implicitly following when selecting variables for use in symbolizations. Variables function as pronouns that help us to keep pronominal cross references clear. We do not interpret them in symbolization keys, and which variables we use is arbitrary, with this exception: When we have quantifiers with overlapping scopes, that is, one quantifier embedded within the scope of another quantifier, those quantifiers must be formed from distinct variables. We are, that is to say, disallowing

$$(\forall x)(Px \supset (\exists x)Uxx)$$

The reason for this restriction should be obvious. A great part of the value of individual variables is that they make pronominal cross references crystal clear. But this would cease to be the case if we were to allow expressions such as the one noted as sentences of *PL*. To what quantifier, for example, do the variables in 'Uxx' in this expression have pronominal cross reference? We could establish a convention for interpreting such cases, but it is far simpler just to disallow them.

7. Anyone who envies him- or herself doesn't understand anyone.

Symbolizing this sentence will require two quantifiers. That the first quantifier must be a universal quantifier is easy enough to see, for we have pronominal cross reference here. The person who is said not to understand anyone is the very person who envies him- or herself. Hence

> Each x is such that if x is a person and x envies x, then x doesn't understand anyone

and

$$(\forall x)[(Px \ \& \ Exx) \supset x \text{ doesn't understand anyone}].$$

How do we convert this last bit of English into symbols? Well, here we have an 'any' construction falling within the scope of a negation-forming expression. So we can use either a tilde followed by an existential quantifier, or a universal quantifier followed by a tilde. This becomes clear when we realize that 'it is not the case that x understands anyone' can be equally appropriately paraphrased as either

> each y is such that if y is a person, then it is not the case that x understands y

or

> there is no y such that y is a person and x understands y.

In symbols the first becomes

$$(\forall y)(Py \supset \sim Uxy)$$

while the second becomes

$$\sim (\exists y)(Py \ \& \ Uxy)$$

These are in fact equivalent expressions. Recall that $\mathcal{P} \supset \sim \mathcal{Q}$ is equivalent to $\sim \mathcal{P} \vee \sim \mathcal{Q}$, which in turn is equivalent to $\sim (\mathcal{P} \ \& \ \mathcal{Q})$. So too, '$(\forall y)(Py \supset \sim Uxy)$' is equivalent to '$(\forall y) \sim (Py \ \& \ Uxy)$', which is equivalent to '$\sim (\exists y)(Py \ \& \ Uxy)$'. Hence, for complete symbolizations of sentence 7, we have our choice between

$$(\forall x)[(Px \ \& \ Exx) \supset (\forall y)(Py \supset \sim Uxy)]$$

and

$$(\forall x)[(Px \ \& \ Exx) \supset \sim (\exists y)(Py \ \& \ Uxy)]$$

8. Anyone who understands everything is envied by everyone.

Although sentence 8 contains three quantity terms, it is straightforward. They will all become universal quantifiers in *PL*. A start at a symbolization is

> Each x is such that if (x is a person and x understands everything) then every y is such that if y is a person, y envies x.

Putting this much in quasi-symbols, we have

(∀x)[(Px & x understands everything) ⊃ (∀y)(Py ⊃ Eyx)].

Since 'x understands everything' becomes '(∀z)Uxz', the final result is

(∀x)[(Px & (∀z)Uxz) ⊃ (∀y)(Py ⊃ Eyx)]

9. If no one understands Bertrand Russell's *Principia Mathematica*, no one understands anything.

This is a sentence that should be symbolized as a truth-functional compound. The English sentence is clearly a conditional, and there is no pronominal cross reference connecting the antecedent and consequent. So the paraphrase might start

> If each w is such that if w is a person, then w doesn't understand Bertrand Russell's *Principia Mathematica*, then each y is such that if y is a person, y doesn't understand anything.

From this we move to

> (∀w)(Pw ⊃ w doesn't understand Bertrand Russell's *Principia Mathematica*) ⊃ (∀y)(Py ⊃ y doesn't understand anything).

The obvious next step is

(∀w)(Pw ⊃ ~ Uwp) ⊃ (∀y)(Py ⊃ y doesn't understand anything).

We are now faced with another case of an 'any' construction falling within the scope of a negation-forming expression. This time, for the sake of variety, we shall use an existential quantifier preceded by a tilde

~ (∃x)Uyx

and the entire symbolization is

(∀w)(Pw ⊃ ~ Uwp) ⊃ (∀y)(Py ⊃ ~ (∃x)Uyx)

Sentence 10, unlike sentence 9, will be symbolized as a quantified sentence —for here there is pronominal cross reference:

10. Anyone who doesn't understand Bertrand Russell's *Principia Mathematica* doesn't understand anything.

A proper symbolization can be obtained in the following stages:

> Each x is such that if x is a person and x doesn't understand Bertrand Russell's *Principia Mathematica*, then x doesn't understand anything.
>
> (∀x)[(Px & ~ Uxp) ⊃ x doesn't understand anything].
>
> (∀x)[(Px & ~ Uxp) ⊃ ~ (∃y)Uxy]

11. Everyone envies whatever anyone understands.

In this sentence we have a quantity term we have not seen before, 'whatever'. Here that term will go over to a universal quantifier of *PL*, for to envy whatever anyone understands is to envy everything anyone understands. The first step is

> Each x is such that if x is a person, then x envies whatever anyone understands.

Next we have

> (∀x)(Px ⊃ x envies whatever anyone understands).

The claim 'x envies whatever anyone understands' is tantamount to 'if someone understands a thing then x envies that thing', that is, to

> (∀z)(if someone understands z then x envies z).

Since we have no pronominal cross reference to 'someone' here, we can use an existential quantifier:

> (∀z)[(∃y)(Py & Uyz) ⊃ Exz]

The entire sentence is

> (∀x)(Px ⊃ (∀z)[(∃y)(Py & Uyz) ⊃ Exz])

Sentence 11 could also have been paraphrased and symbolized either as

> Each thing x and each thing y and each thing z is such that if x and y are persons, and y understands z, then x envies z

and

> (∀x)(∀y)(∀z)([Px & Py) & Uyz] ⊃ Exz)

or as

> Each x and z is such that if x is a person and there is a y such that y is a person and y understands z, then x envies z

and

> (∀x)(∀z)([Px & (∃y)(Py & Uyz)] ⊃ Exz)

We hope that by this time these three symbolizations do seem equivalent. In the shift from the second to the third symbolization a quantifier, '(∀y)', whose scope covered an entire conditional has had its scope narrowed to include only part of the antecedent of that conditional and has thus become an existential quantifier.

## 7.5E EXERCISES

**1.** Symbolize the following sentences in *PL*, using the symbolization key:

U.D.: People
Sx: x is a sailor
Lx: x is lucky
Cx: x is careless
Dx: x dies young
Sxy: x is a son of y
Dxy: x is a daughter of y
Wx: x is a Wilcox
d: Daniel Wilcox
j: Jacob Wilcox
r: Rebecca Wilcox

a. Some sailors are both careless and lucky.
*b. Some careless sailors aren't lucky.
c. Not all lucky sailors are careless.
*d. All careless sailors, except the lucky ones, die young.
e. Not all sons of sailors are sailors.
*f. Not all daughters of sailors are sailors.
g. Not all sons and daughters of sailors are sailors.
*h. Sailors who aren't lucky and are careless have neither daughters nor sons.
i. Sailors who have either sons or daughters are lucky.
*j. Sailors who have both daughters and sons are lucky.
k. Rebecca Wilcox is either a sailor or the daughter of a sailor.
*l. Every Wilcox is either a sailor or the offspring of a sailor.
m. Either Rebecca Wilcox and all her children are sailors, or Jacob Wilcox and all his children are sailors.

**2.** Symbolize the following sentences in *PL*, using the symbolization key:

U.D.: The employees of this college
Exy: x earns more than y
Dxy: x distrusts y
Fx: x is a faculty member
Ax: x is an administrator
Cx: x is a coach
Ux: x is a union member
Rx: x should be fired
Mx: x is an M.D.
Px: x is paranoid
Ox: x is a union officer
p: the president
j: Jones

a. Every administrator earns more than some faculty member, and every faculty member earns more than some administrator.
*b. If any administrator earns more than every faculty member, Jones does.
c. No faculty member earns more than the president.
*d. Any administrator who earns more than every faculty member should be fired.
e. No faculty member earns more than the president, but some coaches do.

*f. Not all faculty members are union members, but all union members are faculty members.

g. No administrator is a union member, but some are faculty members.

*h. Every faculty member who is an administrator earns more than some faculty members who are not administrators.

i. Some administrator who is not a faculty member earns more than every faculty member who is an administrator.

*j. Every faculty member who is an M.D. earns more than every faculty member who is not an M.D.

k. Some faculty members distrust every administrator and some administrators distrust every faculty member.

*l. There is an administrator who is a faculty member and distrusts all administrators who are not faculty members.

m. Anyone who distrusts everyone is either paranoid or an administrator or a union officer.

*n. Everyone distrusts someone, but only administrators who are not faculty members distrust everyone.

**3.** Symbolize the following sentences in *PL*, using the symbolization key:

U.D.: Everything
Uxyz: x understands y as well as does z
Bxy: x bores y
Gxy: x gives a low grade to y
Lxy: x listens to y
Sxy: x is a student of y
Uxy: x understands y
Dx: x deserves to be fired
Px: x is a professor
Ux: x is unpopular
Wx: x is wasting x's time
t: this text

a. Every professor bores some of his or her students.

*b. Any professor who bores all of his or her students deserves to be fired.

c. Any professor who is bored by everything bores all his or her students.

*d. Professors bore all and only those of their students they are bored by.

e. If all students are bored by all their professors, then every professor is wasting his or her time.

*f. If a professor bores a student, then both are wasting their time.

g. Professors don't understand the students they bore, and students don't listen to the professors they are bored by.

*h. No professor understands everything.

i. Some professors bore all professors.

*j. An unpopular professor either bores or gives a low grade to each of his or her students.

k. Unpopular professors either bore all of their students or give all of their students low grades.

*l. If a professor doesn't listen to a student, then that student is wasting his or her time.

m. If a student and his or her professor bore each other, then both are wasting their time.

*n. Some professors don't understand this text.

o. Some professors don't understand this text as well as do some of their students.

*p. No professor who understands this text bores any of his or her students.

q. Any student who doesn't listen to his or her professor doesn't understand that professor and bores that professor.

**4.** Construct fluent English readings for the following sentences of *PL*, using the symbolization key:

U.D.: Everything (including times)
Lxyz: x loves y at z
Px: x is a person
Tx: x is a time
h: Hildegard
m: Manfred
s: Siegfried

a. (∃x)(Tx & Lhmx)
*b. (∀y)[(Ty & Lmhy) ⊃ Lhmy]
c. (∃w)(Tw & Lmhw) & (∀z)(Tz ⊃ Lmsz)
*d. (∀x)(Tx ⊃ Lshx)
e. (∃x)(Tx & Lmmx) ⊃ (∀x)[(Tx & Lhmx) ⊃ Lmmx]
*f. (∀x)[Px ⊃ (∃y)(Ty & ~ (∃z)(Pz & Lzxy))]
g. (∃x)[Px & ~ (∃y)(∃z)(Ty & (Pz & Lzxy))]
*h. (∀x)[Tx ⊃ (∃y)(Py & ~ (∃z)(Pz & Lzyx))]
i. (∃x)[Tx & (∃y)(Py & (∀z)(Pz ⊃ Lyzx))]
*j. (∀x)[Tx ⊃ (∃y)(∃z)((Py & Pz) & Lyzx)]
k. (∀x)[Tx ⊃ (∃y)(Py & (∀z)(Pz ⊃ Lyzx))]
*l. (∀x)[Px ⊃ (∃y)(∃z)((Py & Tz) & Lxyz)]
m. ~ (∃x)[Px & (∃y)(Py & (∀z)(Tz ⊃ Lxyz))]
*n. (∃x)[Px & (∀y)(∀z)((Ty & Pz) ⊃ Lxzy)]
o. (∀x)[Px ⊃ (∃y)(Ty & Lxxy)]

## 7.6 IDENTITY, DEFINITE DESCRIPTIONS, AND PROPERTIES OF RELATIONS

Our standard reading of 'some' is 'at least one'. Some may object that this is not an accurate reading, that 'some' sometimes means something like 'at least two'. It is alleged, for example, that to say

There are still some apples in the basket

when there is only one apple in the basket is at best misleading and at worst false. In any event, we clearly do want a means of symbolizing such claims as

There are at least two apples in the basket.

We can do this by interpreting one of the two-place predicates of *PL* as expressing the identity relation. For example, we could interpret 'Ixy' as 'x is identical with y'. Given the symbolization key:

U.D.: Everything
Nxy: x is in y
Ixy: x is identical with y
Ax: x is an apple
b: the basket

both

(∃x)(Ax & Nxb)

and

(∃x)[(Ax & Nxb) & (∃y)(Ay & Nyb)]

say 'There is at least one apple in the basket'. The latter merely says it twice, so to speak. But

(∃x)(∃y)([(Ax & Ay) & (Nxb & Nyb)] & ~ Ixy)

does say 'There are at least two apples in the basket', for it says, in quasi-English, 'There is an x and there is a y, x and y are both apples, x and y are both in the basket, and x and y are not identical'. This last clause is not redundant, because *using different variables does not commit us to there being more than one thing of the specified sort*.

An alternative to interpreting one of the two-place predicates of *PL* as expressing identity is to introduce a special two-place predicate and specify that it always be interpreted as expressing the identity relation. This is the course we shall follow. In adding this predicate to *PL* we generate a new language, *PLI*. The syntax of *PLI* is exactly like that of *PL* except that we add that '= ″' is a two-place predicate of *PLI*. Officially, formulas are generated from '= ″' by writing two individual terms after that predicate. By informal convention we drop the two primes and instead of writing the individual terms after '=' we write '=' between the individual terms, for example, instead of '= ab', '= xy', and '= aa' we write 'a = b', 'x = y', and 'a = a'. And in place of, for example, '~ = ab' we will write '~ a = b'. Since the interpretation of '=' is fixed, we never have to include it in symbolization keys.

We can now symbolize 'There are at least two apples in the basket' in *PLI*, using the above symbolization key (less the interpretation for 'Ixy'), as

(∃x)(∃y)([Ax & Ay) & (Nxb & Nyb)] & ~ x = y)

In *PLI* we can also say that there are just so many apples in the basket and no more, for example that there is exactly one apple in the basket. An appropriate paraphrase is

> There is a y such that y is an apple and y is in the basket, and each thing z is such that if z is an apple and is in the basket then z is identical with y.

A full symbolization is

$$(\exists y)[(Ay \ \& \ Nyb) \ \& \ (\forall z)[(Az \ \& \ Nzb) \supset z = y]]$$

What we are saying is that there is at least one apple in the basket and that anything which is an apple and is in the basket *is that very apple*.

Consider next

> Henry hasn't read *Alice in Wonderland* but everyone else in the class has.

If we limit our universe of discourse to the students in the class in question, let 'h' designate Henry, and interpret 'Ax' as 'x has read *Alice in Wonderland*', we can symbolize this claim as

$$\sim Ah \ \& \ (\forall y)[\sim y = h \supset Ay]$$

And, using 'b' to designate Bob, we can symbolize 'Only Henry and Bob have not read *Alice in Wonderland*' as

$$\sim (Ah \vee Ab) \ \& \ (\forall x)[\sim (x = h \vee x = b) \supset Ax]$$

This says that neither Henry nor Bob has read *Alice in Wonderland* and everyone else, that is, each person in the class who is neither identical to Henry nor identical to Bob, has read it.

We can also use the identity predicate to symbolize the following sentences in *PLI*:

1. There are apples and pears in the basket.
2. The only pear in the basket is rotten.
3. There are at least two apples in the basket.
4. There are two (and only two) apples in the basket.
5. There are no more than two pears in the basket.
6. There are at least three apples in the basket.

U.D.: everything
Ax: x is an apple
Nxy: x is in y
Px: x is a pear
Rx: x is rotten
b: the basket

If we paraphrase sentence 1 as 'There is at least one apple and at least one pear in the basket' we can symbolize it without using the identity predicate:

$$(\exists x)(\exists y)[(Ax \mathbin{\&} Py) \mathbin{\&} (Nxb \mathbin{\&} Nyb)]$$

However, if we take 1 to be asserting that there are at least two apples and at least two pears in the basket we do need the identity predicate

$$(\exists x)(\exists y)[((Ax \mathbin{\&} Ay) \mathbin{\&} (Nxb \mathbin{\&} Nyb)) \mathbin{\&} \sim x = y] \mathbin{\&} (\exists x)(\exists y)[((Px \mathbin{\&} Py) \mathbin{\&} (Nxb \mathbin{\&} Nyb)) \mathbin{\&} \sim x = y]$$

Sentence 2 says there is one and only one pear in the basket, and that that one pear is rotten:

$$(\exists x)[((Px \mathbin{\&} Nxb) \mathbin{\&} Rx) \mathbin{\&} (\forall y)[(Py \mathbin{\&} Nyb) \supset y = x]]$$

Sentence 3 says only that there are at least two apples in the basket, not that there are exactly two. Hence

$$(\exists x)(\exists y)[((Ax \mathbin{\&} Ay) \mathbin{\&} (Nxb \mathbin{\&} Nyb)) \mathbin{\&} \sim x = y]$$

To symbolize sentence 4, we start with the symbolization for sentence 3 and add a clause that says there are no additional apples in the basket:

$$(\exists x)(\exists y)([((Ax \mathbin{\&} Ay) \mathbin{\&} (Nxb \mathbin{\&} Nyb)) \mathbin{\&} \sim x = y] \mathbin{\&} (\forall z)[(Az \mathbin{\&} Nzb) \supset (z = x \vee z = y)])$$

The added clause says, in effect, 'and anything which is an apple and is in the basket is either x or y'. Sentence 5 does not say that there are two pears in the basket, it says, more modestly, that there are at most two pears in the basket. We can express this in *PLI* by saying that of any pears x, y, and z that are in the basket, these are really at most two, that is, either x is identical to y or x is identical to z.

$$(\forall x)(\forall y)(\forall z)[([(Px \mathbin{\&} Py) \mathbin{\&} Pz] \mathbin{\&} [(Nxb \mathbin{\&} Nyb) \mathbin{\&} Nzb]) \supset (x = y \vee x = z)]$$

Sentence 6 can be symbolized by building on the symbolization for sentence 3:

$$(\exists x)(\exists y)(\exists z)(([(Ax \mathbin{\&} Ay) \mathbin{\&} Az] \mathbin{\&} [(Nxb \mathbin{\&} Nyb) \mathbin{\&} Nzb]) \mathbin{\&} [(\sim x = y \mathbin{\&} \sim y = z) \mathbin{\&} \sim x = z])$$

As a final set of examples where the identity predicate is useful we consider the following claims concerning the positive integers:

1. There is no largest positive integer.
2. There is a smallest positive integer.
3. Two is the only even prime.
4. There are exactly two primes between ten and fourteen.
5. Every positive integer has exactly one successor.
6. Two is the only prime whose successor is prime.

We will symbolize these sentences in *PLI* using the symbolization key

U.D.: Positive integers
Bxyz: x is between y and z
Lxy: x is larger than y
Sxy: x is a successor of y
Ex: x is even
Px: x is prime
a: 1
b: 2
c: 10
d: 14

A good start at a paraphrase of sentence 1 is

It is not the case that there is an x such that x is the largest integer.

To say that x is the largest integer is to say that x is larger than each integer *other than x*, that is,

$$(\forall y)(\sim y = x \supset Lxy)$$

So our completed symbolization of sentence 1 is

$$\sim (\exists x)(\forall y)(\sim y = x \supset Lxy)$$

We can also say that there is no largest integer without using the identity predicate by saying that for each integer there is a larger integer, that is,

$$(\forall x)(\exists y)Lyx$$

Sentence 2, 'There is a smallest positive integer', says that there is a positive integer such that every *other* integer is larger than it. Our paraphrase is

There is a z such that for each y, if y is not identical with z, then y is larger than z.

Our symbolization is

$$(\exists z)(\forall y)(\sim y = z \supset Lyz)$$

The same claim can be made without using the identity predicate by saying there is some integer that is not larger than any integer

$$(\exists x)(\forall y) \sim Lxy$$

Sentence 3, 'Two is the only even prime', says that two is prime and is even and that all other primes are not even:

Two is prime and two is even, and each z is such that if z is prime and z is not identical with two, then z is not even.

In *PLI*

$$(Pb \,\&\, Eb) \,\&\, (\forall z)[(Pz \,\&\, \sim z = b) \supset \sim Ez]$$

This is equivalent to

$$(Pb \,\&\, Eb) \,\&\, (\forall z)[(Pz \,\&\, Ez) \supset z = b]$$

Notice that we could equally well have paraphrased and symbolized sentence 3 as

> Two is prime and two is even, and it is not the case that there is a z such that z is prime, z is even, and z is not identical with two

and

$$(Pb \,\&\, Eb) \,\&\, \sim (\exists z)[(Pz \,\&\, Ez) \,\&\, \sim z = b]$$

Notice too that all three symbolic versions of sentence 3 are truth-functional compounds, not quantified sentences.

To symbolize sentence 4, 'There are exactly two primes between ten and fourteen', we must say that there are at least two such primes and there are no additional ones. So our paraphrase will start

> There is an x and there is a y such that x and y are prime, x and y are between ten and fourteen, and x is not identical with y, . . .

This much can be symbolized as

$$(\exists x)(\exists y)((Px \,\&\, Py) \,\&\, [(Bxcd \,\&\, Bycd) \,\&\, \sim x = y])$$

What we now need to add is that any prime that is between ten and fourteen is one of these two primes:

> Each z is such that if z is prime and z is between ten and fourteen, then z is either x or y.

That is,

$$(\forall z)[(Pz \,\&\, Bzcd) \supset (z = x \vee z = y)]$$

In joining the two fragments of our symbolization, we must be sure to extend the scope of our two existential quantifiers over the entire sentence, for we want to bind the occurrences of 'x' and 'y' in the last half of the sentence.

$$(\exists x)(\exists y)[((Px \,\&\, Py) \,\&\, [(Bxcd \,\&\, Bycd) \,\&\, \sim x = y]) \,\&\,$$
$$(\forall z)[(Pz \,\&\, Bzcd) \supset (z = x \vee z = y)]]$$

A successor of an integer is that integer plus one. Sentence 5, 'Every positive integer has exactly one successor' can be symbolized as

$$(\forall x)(\exists y)[Syx \,\&\, (\forall z)(Szx \supset z = y)]$$

This says that each positive integer x has a successor y and that any integer which is a successor of x is identical to y, that is, that there is one and only one successor.

Sentence 6, 'Two is the only prime whose successor is prime' can be paraphrased as

> Two is prime, it has one (and only one) successor, that successor is prime, and any successor of any prime other than two is not prime.

The first conjunct can be symbolized as:

$$Pb \ \& \ (\exists x)[(Sxb \ \& \ (\forall y)(Syb \supset y = x)) \ \& \ Px]$$

The second conjunct can be symbolized as

$$(\forall x)(\forall y)[(Sxy \ \& \ (Py \ \& \ \sim y = b)) \supset \sim Px]$$

*IDENTITY AND DEFINITE DESCRIPTIONS*

In Section 7.1 we noted that there are two kinds of singular terms in English, proper names and definite descriptions. We subsequently noted that individual constants of *PL* should be used to symbolize both kinds of singular terms of English. This of course means that the internal structure of definite descriptions is not represented in *PL*. Consider, by way of illustration, the argument:

> The Roman general who defeated Pompey invaded both Gaul and Germany. Therefore Pompey was defeated by someone who invaded both Gaul and Germany.

This is fairly obviously a valid argument. But its symbolization in *PL* will not be valid:

U.D.: People and countries
Ixy: x invaded y
Dxy: x defeated y
r: the Roman general who defeated Pompey
p: Pompey
g: Gaul
e: Germany

Treating 'The Roman general who defeated Pompey' as an unanalyzable unit, to be symbolized by 'r', and paraphrasing the conclusion as 'there is an x such that x defeated Pompey and invaded Gaul and invaded Germany', yields

$$Irg \ \& \ Ire$$

---

$$(\exists x)[Dxp \ \& \ (Ixg \ \& \ Ixe)]$$

The techniques we will develop for testing arguments of *PL* will show that this argument of *PL* is invalid. This should not be surprising, for the premise tells us only that the thing designated by 'r' invaded both Gaul and Germany, it does not tell us that that thing is a thing that defeated Pompey, as the conclusion claims.

By using the identity predicate we can capture the structure of definite descriptions within *PLI*. Suppose we paraphrase the first premise of the above argument as

> There is exactly one thing which is a Roman general and defeated Pompey, and that thing invaded both Gaul and Germany.

Definite descriptions are, after all, descriptions which purport to specify conditions which are satisfied by exactly one thing. Using the above symbolization key, plus 'Rx' for 'x is a Roman general', we can symbolize the first premise as

$$(\exists x)[[(Rx \ \& \ Dxp) \ \& \ (\forall y)[(Ry \ \& \ Dyp) \supset y = x]] \ \& \ (Ixg \ \& \ Ixe)]$$

We will be able to show that in *PLI* the conclusion, '$(\exists x)[Dxp \ \& \ (Ixg \ \& \ Ixe)]$' follows from this premise.

By transforming definite descriptions into unique existence claims, that is, claims that there is exactly one object of such-and-such a sort, we gain the further benefit of being able to symbolize English language definite descriptions which may in fact not designate anything. For example, taking the U.D. to be persons, using 'Dxy' for 'x is a daughter of y', 'Bx' for 'x is a biochemist', and 'j' to designate John, we might symbolize 'John's only daughter is a biochemist' as

$$(\exists x)[(Dxj \ \& \ (\forall y)(Dyj \supset y = x)) \ \& \ Bx]$$

If it turns out that John has no, or more than one, daughter the above sentence of *PLI* will thus be shown to be false, not meaningless or truth-valueless. This is an acceptable result.

*PROPERTIES OF RELATIONS*

Identity is a relation with three rather special properties. First, identity is a *transitive* relation. That is, if an object x is identical with an object y and y is identical with an object z, then x is identical with z. The following sentence of *PLI* says, in effect, that identity is transitive:

$$(\forall x)(\forall y)(\forall z)[(x = y \ \& \ y = z) \supset x = z]$$

Many relations other than identity are also transitive relations. The predicates

x is larger than y

x is taller than y

x is an ancestor of y

x is heavier than y

x occurs before y

all represent transitive relations. On the other hand, 'x is a friend of y' does not represent a transitive relation. That is, 'any friend of a friend of mine is a friend of mine' is a substantive claim and one that is generally false. Where $x$, $y$, and $z$, are all variables of *PL* or *PLI* and $\mathcal{A}$ is a two-place predicate of *PL* or *PLI*, the following says that $\mathcal{A}$ represents a transitive relation:

$$(\forall x)(\forall y)(\forall z)[(\mathcal{A}xy \ \& \ \mathcal{A}yz) \supset \mathcal{A}xz]$$

Identity is also a *symmetric* relation; that is, if an object x is identical with an object y, then y is identical with x. The following says that $\mathcal{A}$ represents a symmetric relation

$$(\forall x)(\forall y)(\mathcal{A}xy \supset \mathcal{A}yx)$$

The following predicates also represent symmetric relations:

x is a sibling of y

x is a classmate of y

x is a relative of y

x has the same father as does y

Note that neither 'x is a sister of y' nor 'x loves y' represents a symmetric relation. Jane Fonda is a sister of Peter Fonda, but Peter Fonda is not a sister of Jane Fonda. And, alas, it may be that Hildegard loves Manfred, even though Manfred doesn't love Hildegard.

A relation is *reflexive* if and only if each object stands in that relation to itself. In *PL* and *PLI* the following says that $\mathcal{A}$ represents a reflexive relation:

$$(\forall x)\mathcal{A}xx$$

Identity is, of course, a reflexive relation. In an unrestricted universe of discourse it is rather hard to find other reflexive relations. For example, a little thought should show that none of the following represents a reflexive relation in an unrestricted universe of discourse:

x is the same age as y

x is the same color as y

x is in the same place as y

Since the number 48 is not of any age, it is not the same age as itself, nor the same color as itself. Numbers have neither age nor color, though inscriptions of *numerals* usually have both. So too, neither the number 93 nor the set of human beings is in any place. Numbers and sets do not have spatial positions. Hence neither is in the same place as itself. However, the relations just discussed are reflexive relations in suitably restricted universes of discourse. For example, if the universe of discourse consists exclusively of people, then

x is the same age as y

represents a reflexive relation (it is also transitive and symmetric). Every person is the same age as him- or herself. In this restricted universe 'x is the same color as y' and 'x is in the same place as y' also represent reflexive relations. Each person is the same color as him- or herself and is in the same place as him- or herself. And, if the universe of discourse is restricted to the positive integers, then

x is evenly divisible by y

represents a reflexive relation, for every positive integer is evenly divisible by itself. This relation is not, of course, symmetric (not every positive integer evenly divides all the positive integers it is evenly divisible by). However, 'x is evenly divisible by y' does represent a transitive relation.

### 7.6E EXERCISES

**1.** Symbolize the following sentences in *PLI*, using the symbolization key given in Exercise 1 of Section 7.5E.

a. Every Wilcox except Daniel is a sailor.
*b. Every Wilcox except Daniel is the offspring of a sailor.
c. Every Wilcox except Daniel is either a sailor or the offspring of a sailor.
*d. Daniel is the only son of Jacob.
e. Daniel is the only child of Jacob.
*f. All the Wilcoxes except Daniel are sailors.
g. Rebecca's only son is Jacob's only son.
*h. Rebecca Wilcox has only one son who is a sailor.
i. Rebecca Wilcox has at least two daughters who are sailors.
*j. There are two and only two sailors in the Wilcox family.
k. Jacob Wilcox has one son and two daughters, and they are all sailors.

**2.** Give fluent English readings for the following sentences of *PLI*, using the symbolization key:

U.D.: Positive integers
Pxyz: x is the product of y times z
Lxy: x is less than y
Gxy: x is greater than y
Ex: x is even
Ox: x is odd
Px: x is prime
t: two
f: five
n: nine

a. $(\forall x)(\exists y)Lxy$
*b. $(\exists x) \sim (\exists y)Lyx$
c. $(\exists x)(\forall y)(\sim y = x \supset Lxy)$ or $\sim (\forall x)(\exists y)Lyx$

*d. ~ (∃x)(∀y)(~ y = x ⊃ Lyx) or (∀x)(∃y)Lxy
e. (Pt & Et) & (∀x)[(Px & Ex) ⊃ x = t]
*f. ~ (∃x)(∃y)(∃z)[(Py & Pz) & (Pxyz & Px)]
g. (∀x)(∀y)(∀z)[(Oy & Oz) ⊃ (Pxyz ⊃ Ox)]
*h. (∀x)(∀y)(∀z)[(Ey & Ez) ⊃ (Pxyz ⊃ Ex)]
i. (∀x)(∀y)(∀z)[(Oy & Ez) ⊃ (Pxyz ⊃ Ex)]
*j. (∀x)[Ex ⊃ (∃y)(Oy & Gxy)] & ~ (∀x)[Ox ⊃ (∃y)(Ey & Gxy)]
k. (∃x)[[Px & (Gxf & Lxn)] & (∀y)([Py & (Gyf & Lyn)] ⊃ y = x)]

**3.** For a–p, decide whether the specified relation is reflexive (in a suitably restricted universe of discourse), whether it is symmetric, and whether it is transitive. In each case give the sentences of *PL* that assert the appropriate properties of the relation in question. If the relation is reflexive in a restricted universe of discourse, specify what that universe is.

a. Nxy: x is a neighbor of y
*b. Mxy: x is married to y
c. Axy: x admires y
*d. Nxy: x is north of y
e. Rxy: x is a relative of y
*f. Sxy: x is the same size as y
g. Txy: x is at least as tall as y
*h. Cxy: x coauthors a book with y
i. Exy: x enrolls in the same course as y
*j. Fxy: x fights y
k. Wxy: x weighs the same as y
*l. Cxy: x contracts with y
m. Axy: x is an ancestor of y
*n. Cxy: x is a cousin of y
o. Lxy: x and y have the same taste in food
*p. Rxy: x respects y

**4.** Symbolize the following sentences in *PLI*, using the symbolization key:

U.D.: People in Doreen's home town
Dxy: x is a daughter of y
Sxy: x is a son of y
Bxy: x is a brother of y
Oxy: x is older than y
Mxy: x is married to y
Txy: x is taller than y
Px: x is a physician
Bx: x is a baseball player
Mx: x is a marine biologist
d: Doreen
c: Cory
j: Jeremy
h: Hal

a. Jeremy is Cory's son.
*b. Jeremy is Cory's only son.

c. Jeremy is Cory's oldest son.
*d. Doreen's only daughter is a physician.
e. Doreen's eldest daughter is a physician.
*f. Doreen is a physician and so is her eldest daughter.
g. Cory is Doreen's eldest daughter.
*h. Cory is married to Hal's only son.
i. Cory is married to Hal's tallest son.
*j. Doreen's eldest daughter is married to Hal's only son.
k. The only baseball player in town is the only marine biologist in town.
*l. The only baseball player in town is married to one of Jeremy's daughters.
m. Cory's husband is Jeremy's only brother.

# Chapter 8

# *PREDICATE LOGIC: SEMANTICS*

## 8.1 INFORMAL SEMANTICS FOR *PL*

The basic semantic concept for the language of sentential logic, *SL*, is that of a truth-value assignment. The semantics for *PL* is more complex than truth-functional semantics. One source of the added complexity is this: Whereas the atomic sentences of *SL* are not analyzable in terms of more basic linguistic units of *SL*, the same does not hold for all atomic sentences of *PL*. Some atomic sentences of *PL*, such as 'Fa', are themselves complex expressions composed of predicates and individual constants. Consequently, we do not directly assign truth-values to all the atomic sentences of *PL*; only the sentence letters are directly assigned truth-values. The truth-values of complex atomic sentences like 'Fa' depend on the interpretations of the predicates and individual constants that constitute such sentences. The basic semantic concept of *PL*, in terms of which other semantic concepts are defined, is that of an *interpretation*. Just as truth-value assignments for *SL* assign truth-values to every sentence of *SL*, an interpretation interprets *every* individual constant, predicate, and sentence letter of *PL*. Usually, however, we shall only be interested in that part of an interpretation that affects the truth-value of a particular sentence or set of sentences that we are looking at.

We can view the symbolization keys for sentences presented in Chapter Seven as embodying interpretations for those sentences. That is, the truth-conditions of sentences of *PL* are dependent upon the choice of universe of discourse and upon how each of the predicates and individual constants in the sentences is interpreted. In this section we shall discuss in an informal manner how interpretations determine the truth-conditions of sentences, appealing to the readings of sentences of *PL* that were used in Chapter Seven.

Let us start with an example of an atomic sentence of *PL*: 'Fa'. Whether or not this sentence is true depends on how we interpret the predicate 'F' and the individual constant 'a'. If we interpret them as follows:

Fx: x is human

a: Socrates

then 'Fa' is true, for Socrates was human. But if we interpret them as:

Fx: x is a potato

a: Socrates

then 'Fa' is false, for Socrates was not a potato. Similarly, the truth-value of the sentence 'Bdc' depends upon the interpretation of the expressions that constitute the sentence. If we interpret them as:

Bxy: x is bigger than y

c: the Statue of Liberty

d: the Empire State Building

then 'Bdc', which may be read as 'The Empire State Building is bigger than the Statue of Liberty', is true. But with the following interpretations:

Bxy: x is bigger than y

c: the moon

d: the Empire State Building

'Bdc' is false. The Empire State Building is not bigger than the moon.

Predicates are interpreted relative to a *universe of discourse*. A universe of discourse (U.D.) is simply a nonempty set. We may choose the set of natural numbers, the set of all people, the set of words in this chapter, the set of all the objects in the world, the set containing only Mark Twain, or any other nonempty set as the U.D. when we specify an interpretation. The U.D. that we choose includes all and only those things that we want to interpret sentences of *PL* as being about. Once we specify the U.D., our interpretations of predicates are interpretations relative to that U.D. For example, if an interpretation includes

U.D.: set of living creatures

Fx: x is human

then 'F' picks out all the living creatures in the U.D. that are human. We call the set of those things that the predicate picks out the *extension* of the predicate for the interpretation. If an interpretation includes

U.D.: set of living creatures in San Francisco

Fx: x is human

then the predicate 'F' picks out all those living creatures in San Francisco that are human. The set of such creatures is the extension of the predicate 'F'. And if an interpretation includes

U.D.: set of living creatures
Fx: x is an automobile

then the predicate 'F' picks out nothing—no member of the U.D. is an automobile. In this case, the extension of the predicate 'F' is the empty set.

Now let us consider two-place predicates. Suppose that an interpretation includes the following:

U.D.: set of positive integers
Gxy: x is greater than y

In this case, we cannot simply say that the predicate 'G' picks out members of the U.D. We are interpreting 'G' as a *relational* predicate, so the extension of the predicate in this case is a set of *pairs* of objects, rather than simply a set of objects. One of the pairs of positive integers that is in the extension of the predicate is the pair consisting of the number 5 and the number 2, in that order, since 5 is greater than 2. We must think of these pairs as ordered because, although the predicate picks out the pair whose first member is 5 and whose second member is 2, it does not pick out the pair whose first member is 2 and whose second member is 5—2 is not greater than 5. The extension of 'G' includes all and only those pairs of objects in the U.D. (pairs of positive integers) of which the first member is greater than the second.

On some interpretations, the extension of a two-place predicate will include pairs in which the first and second member are the same. For example, on an interpretation that includes

U.D.: set of positive integers
Lxy: x is less than or equal to y

the extension of 'L' includes the pair consisting of 1 and 1, the pair consisting of 2 and 2, the pair consisting of 3 and 3, and so on—because each positive integer is less than or equal to itself. (The extension includes other pairs as well—any pair of positive integers in which the first member is less than or equal to the second.)

Three-place predicates, four-place predicates, and all other many-place predicates are interpreted similarly. A three-place predicate has as its extension a set of ordered triples of objects in the U.D. A four-place predicate has as its extension a set of ordered quadruples of members of the U.D., and so on.

An individual constant is interpreted by assigning to the constant some member of the selected U.D. So, if we choose as our U.D. the set of living creatures, then we may assign to 'a', as its interpretation, some specific living creature. Here are two examples of interpretations for the sentence 'Fa':

1. U.D.: set of positive integers
Fx: x is a prime number
a: the number 4

2. U.D.: set of animals in the Bronx Zoo

   Fx: x is a giraffe

   a: the oldest giraffe in the Bronx Zoo

Once we have given interpretations of the expressions in the sentence 'Fa', we may determine the truth-value of 'Fa' on that interpretation. The sentence 'Fa' is true on an interpretation just in case the object that the constant 'a' designates is a member of the set that is the extension of the predicate 'F' for that interpretation. The sentence 'Fa' is false on interpretation 1 and true on interpretation 2. (Actually, neither 1 nor 2 is a full interpretation; a full interpretation interprets every constant, predicate, and sentence letter of *PL*. For example, 1 represents infinitely many interpretations. It represents all interpretations that have the specified U.D. and that interpret 'F' and 'a' as indicated, and that interpret all other predicates, constants, and sentence letters as they please. However, we shall continue to talk informally of our partial interpretations simply as interpretations.)

Here is an interpretation for 'Gab':

3. U.D.: set of positive integers

   Gxy: x is greater than y

   a: the number 2

   b: the number 16

The sentence 'Gab' is false on interpretation 3, for on this interpretation 'Gab' says that 2 is greater than 16, which is not the case. On the other hand, 'Gba', which may be read as 'The number 16 is greater than the number 2', is true on this interpretation because the pair of numbers whose first member is 16 and whose second member is 2 *is* in the extension of the predicate 'G'.

An interpretation may assign the same member of the U.D. to more than one constant. The following is a legitimate interpretation for 'Jln':

4. U.D.: set of planets in the solar system

   Jxy: x is closer to the sun than is y

   l: Jupiter

   n: Jupiter

Here both 'l' and 'n' have been interpreted as designating Jupiter. The sentence is false on this interpretation, since Jupiter is not closer to the sun than itself. Usually, when we *symbolize* English sentences in *PL*, we use different constants to designate different individuals. But, if we want to use different constants to designate the same individual, we may do so. This is similar to the case in which an object is referred to by more than one expression in the English language. For instance, 'the first U.S. President' and 'George Washington' designate the same person. But note that whereas in English one name may stand for more than one object (in which case it is *ambiguous*), we do not allow this in *PL*. Two names may designate the same object, but *no one name may designate more than one object*.

The truth-conditions for compound sentences of *PL* that do not contain quantifiers are determined in accordance with the truth-functional reading of the connectives; so we use the information in the characteristic truth-tables for the truth-functional connectives to determine the truth-values of such sentences. Consider the sentence '(B ∨ ~ Fh) & Gsh'. This sentence contains a sentence letter, so an interpretation for the sentence must interpret the sentence letter as well as the predicates and constants that occur in the sentence. We interpret a sentence letter by assigning to it one of the two truth-values. Here is an interpretation for the sentence:

5. U.D.: set of all things
   B: T
   Fx: x is an animal
   Gxy: x owns y
   h: the Liberty Bell
   s: Norman Mailer

The sentence 'Fh' is false on this interpretation, since the Liberty Bell is not an animal. So ' ~ Fh' is true. Since 'B' and ' ~ Fh' are both true, the sentence 'B ∨ ~ Fh' is true. Norman Mailer does not own the Liberty Bell, so 'Gsh' is false on this interpretation. Consequently, '(B ∨ ~ Fh) & Gsh' has one false conjunct and is false on interpretation 5. Another interpretation may make the same sentence true:

6. U.D.: set of all people
   B: F
   Fx: x is a negative integer
   Gxy: x is the mother of y
   h: Jay Doe
   s: Jane Doe (who is the mother of Jay Doe)

On this interpretation, 'Fh' is false. As we have interpreted the predicate 'F', its extension is the empty set. The predicate picks out nothing in the U.D. since no person is a negative integer. So ' ~ Fh' is true. Although 'B' is false, 'B ∨ ~ Fh' is true—a disjunction with one true disjunct is itself true. Since Jane Doe is Jay Doe's mother, 'Gsh' is true. The sentence '(B ∨ ~ Fh) & Gsh' thus has two true conjuncts and is true on interpretation 6.

We have yet to consider interpretations for the *quantified* sentences of *PL*. Quantified sentences are not atomic, and they are not truth-functions of smaller sentences of *PL* either. The quantified sentence

(∀x)(Fx ⊃ Gx)

is not truth-functionally compound; indeed, it contains no proper subformula that is itself a sentence. To give an interpretation for this sentence, we must specify a

U.D. and interpret the predicate letters 'F' and 'G'. *We do not interpret individual variables.* As noted in Chapter Seven, individual variables function in *PL* much as pronouns do in English. They are not names; consequently, interpretations do not assign to them members of the U.D.

We may read '(∀x)(Fx ⊃ Gx)' as 'Each x is such that if x is F then x is G' or 'Everything that is F is G'. When we specify a U.D. for interpreting the sentence, we thereby specify what 'everything' is—namely, everything in the U.D. Here is an interpretation for '(∀x)(Fx ⊃ Gx)':

7. U.D.: set of people
   Fx: x is a politician
   Gx: x is honest

With this interpretation, we may read the sentence as 'Every person who is a politician is honest'. Unfortunately, some politicians are not honest; the sentence is therefore false on interpretation 7. The part of the sentence that follows the universal quantifier, the open sentence '(Fx ⊃ Gx)', specifies a condition that may or may not hold for the individual members of the U.D.; the function of the universal quantifier is to state that this condition holds for *each* member of the U.D. Consequently, the sentence is true if and only if every member of the U.D. meets that condition.

Consider the following interpretation for the sentence

(∀x)(Ax ≡ ~ Bx)

8. U.D.: set of positive integers
   Ax: x is evenly divisible by 2
   Bx: x is an odd number

The universal quantifier states that the condition specified by 'Ax ≡ ~ Bx' holds for every member of the U.D. The sentence, which we may read as 'Each positive integer is evenly divisible by 2 if and only if it is not an odd number', is true on this interpretation. On the other hand, the interpretation

9. U.D.: set of positive integers
   Ax: x is evenly divisible by 4
   Bx: x is an odd number

makes the same sentence false. A universally quantified sentence is false if there is at least one member of the U.D. for which the condition specified after the quantifier does not hold. The number 6 is one member for which the condition specified by 'Ax ≡ ~ Bx' does not hold. The number 6 is not evenly divisible by 4 and it is not an odd number—so 6 does not meet the condition that it *is* evenly divisible by 4 if and only if it is not an odd number.

In determining the truth-conditions for universally quantified sentences, then, we should keep two points in mind. First, individual variables are *not* interpreted. The function of these variables is to range over the members of the U.D.; consequently, it is the specification of the U.D. for an interpretation that is relevant in determining the contribution that individual variables and quantifiers make to the truth-conditions of sentences of *PL*. Second, the role of the universal quantifier in a sentence of *PL* is to indicate that *every* member of the U.D. satisfies a certain condition. The condition is, of course, specified by that part of the sentence that lies within the scope of the quantifier.

Existential quantifiers function in sentences of *PL* to indicate that at least one member of the U.D. satisfies a certain condition. Here is an interpretation for the existentially quantified sentence

(∃y)(Cy & By)

10. U.D.: set of all things
    Cx: x is a car
    Bx: x is brown

The sentence is true on this interpretation. It may be read as: 'At least one object (in the universe) is a brown car'. Because it is existentially quantified, the sentence is true just in case at least one object in the universe is a car and is brown, that is, just in case at least one object in the universe satisfies the condition specified by 'Cy & By'. Since there is at least one such object, '(∃y)(Cy & By)' is true on this interpretation. However, the same sentence is false on the following interpretation:

11. U.D.: set of all things
    Cx: x is a car
    Bx: x has a brain

Marvelous as technology is, it has not yet produced cars with brains. Hence no object satisifes the condition specified by 'Cy & By', and so '(∃y)(Cy & By)' is false on the present interpretation.

The different sentence

(∃y)Cy & (∃y)By

is true on interpretation 11. This is because both '(∃y)Cy' and '(∃y)By' are true—there is an object that is a car, and there is an object that has a brain. It is not one and the same object that has both these properties, of course. That is why the sentence '(∃y)(Cy & By)' is false on this interpretation. Although 'y' occurs in both 'Cy' and 'By' of '(∃y)Cy & (∃y)By', these two occurrences of the variable are not in the scope of a single occurrence of the quantifier '(∃y)'. So the predicates 'is a car' and 'has a brain' do not have to hold for the same object for the sentence '(∃y)Cy & (∃y)By' to be true. In '(∃y)(Cy & By)', however, all occurrences of 'y' *are* within the scope of one occurrence of '(∃y)'; so for '(∃y)(Cy & By)' to be true on interpretation 11, a single member of the U.D. must both be a car and have a brain.

Now we shall consider an interpretation for a sentence containing a two-place predicate and two quantifiers:

$(\exists x)(\forall y)Fxy$

12. U.D.: set of people
    Fxy: x is acquainted with y

Since the whole sentence is existentially quantified, it is true on interpretation 12 if at least one person satisfies the condition specified by the rest of the sentence, that is, if at least one person is acquainted with every member of the U.D. Obviously, there is no such person, so '$(\exists x)(\forall y)Fxy$' is false on interpretation 12. Using the same interpretation, let us look at the sentence that is formed by reversing the order of the quantifiers:

$(\forall y)(\exists x)Fxy$

Prefixed with the universal quantifier, the sentence says that *each* member of the U.D. satisfies a certain condition. For this sentence to be true, each person y must be such that at least one person is acquainted with y. This is true (since every person is at least self-acquainted), so '$(\forall y)(\exists x)Fxy$' is true on interpretation 12. Note that the difference that accounts for the diverging truth-values of '$(\exists x)(\forall y)Fxy$' and '$(\forall y)(\exists x)Fxy$' is that in the first case it is one and the same person who must be acquainted with everyone. Another sentence that we may interpret using interpretation 12 is

$(\exists x)(\exists y)Fxy$

This sentence is true on interpretation 12 since there is at least one person who is acquainted with at least one person.

The following is an interpretation for the sentence

$(\forall x)(Fx \supset (\exists y) \sim Gyy)$

13. U.D.: set of houses in the world
    Fx: x is made of brick
    Gxy: x is larger than y

Given this interpretation, the sentence may be read as 'For any brick house, there is at least one house that is not larger than itself.' This sentence is universally quantified and hence is true just in case every house x in the world satisfies the condition that if x is made of brick then at least one house is not larger than itself. Any house that is not made of brick trivially satisfies the condition, since it does not fulfill the condition of being made of brick. That is, a house x that is not made of brick is such that if x is made of brick (which it is not) then some house is not larger than itself. Brick houses also satisfy the condition specified in the sentence. For, since it is true that at least one house is not larger than itself, it is true of any brick house x that if x is made of brick (which it is) then some house is not larger than itself (which is true).

The sentence

$(\forall y)(\forall x)(Fyx \supset Fxy)$

is false on the following interpretation:

14. U.D.: set of integers

Fxy: x is smaller than y

No integer y satisfies the condition specified by '$(\forall x)(Fyx \supset Fxy)$', which is that every integer than which y is smaller is in turn smaller than y. For any integer y, there are (infinitely many) integers x than which y is smaller, but not even one of these integers is in turn smaller than y. On the other hand, the sentence

$(\forall y)(\forall x)(Fyy \supset Fxy)$

is true on interpretation 14. Every integer y trivially satisfies the condition specified by '$(\forall x)(Fyy \supset Fxy)$', which is that every integer x is such that <u>if</u> y is smaller than itself (it is not) <u>then</u> x is also smaller than y.

Now we shall consider sentences that contain individual constants and sentence letters as well as quantifiers. Consider

$(\exists x)(Fx \;\&\; (\forall y)Gxy) \supset {\sim} Gsl$

and this interpretation:

15. U.D.: set of people

Fx: x is female

Gxy: x is the sister of y

l: Michael Jackson

s: Janet Jackson

On this interpretation, the sentence may be read as 'If some person is a female and is everybody's sister (including her own), then Janet Jackson is not Michael Jackson's sister.' The consequent of this sentence, '${\sim}$Gsl', is false, because Janet *is* Michael's sister. But the antecedent is also false; there is no female person who is everybody's sister. So the sentence '$(\exists x)(Fx \;\&\; (\forall y)Gxy) \supset {\sim} Gsl$' is true on this interpretation.

Here are two interpretations for the sentence

${\sim} D \vee (\forall x)(\exists y)(Bx \supset Cyx)$

16. U.D.: set of people

D: T

Bx: x is bald

Cxy: x has seen y on television

17. U.D.: set of people

D: F

Bx: x is a banana

Cxy: x will hire y to wash windows

The sentence is false on interpretation 16, since both disjuncts are false on that interpretation. The disjunct '$\sim$D' is false since 'D' is true; and '(∀x)(∃y)(Bx ⊃ Cyx)', which may be read as 'Every bald person has been seen on television by someone', is false. At least one bald person has not been seen on television by anyone. Interpretation 17 makes the sentence true because both disjuncts are true. Since 'D' is false, '$\sim$D' is true. And since no person is a banana, it follows trivially that each person x satisfies the condition that if x is a banana (which x is not) then x will be hired by someone to wash windows. On interpretation 17, the sentence '(∀x)(∃y)(Bx ⊃ Cyx)' may be read as 'Everybody who is a banana will be hired by someone to wash windows.'

As a final example, here is an interpretation for the four sentences

(∃x)(Nx ⊃ (∃y)Lyx)

(∀x)(Nx ⊃ (∃y)Lyx)

(∃x)Nx ⊃ (∃y)Lya

(∀x)Nx ⊃ (∃y)Lya

18. U.D.: set of positive integers
 Nx: x is odd
 Lxy: x is smaller than y
 a: the number 1

The first sentence, '(∃x)(Nx ⊃ (∃y)Lyx)', is true on this interpretation. It is existentially quantified, and there *is* at least one positive integer x such that if it is odd then some positive integer is smaller than x. Every even positive integer trivially satisfies this condition (because every even positive integer fails to satisfy the antecedent) and every odd positive integer except for 1 satisfies it. Because the number 1 does not satisfy the condition specified by 'Nx ⊃ (∃y)Lyx', the second sentence is false. The positive integer 1 is odd, but there is no positive integer that is smaller than 1. So it is not true of every positive integer x that if x is odd then there is a positive integer that is smaller than x.

The third sentence, '(∃x)Nx ⊃ (∃y)Lya', is false on interpretation 18 because its antecedent, '(∃x)Nx', is true, whereas the consequent, '(∃y)Lya', is false. There is at least one odd positive integer, but there is no positive integer that is smaller than the integer 1. On the other hand, '(∀x)Nx ⊃ (∃y)Lya' is true because its antecedent is false—some positive integers are not odd.

In summary, the truth-conditions for sentences of *PL* are determined by *interpretations*. Officially, an interpretation consists in the specification of a U.D. and the interpretation of each sentence letter, predicate, and individual constant in the language *PL*. (This parallels the definition of truth-value assignments for *SL*, where a truth-value assignment assigns a truth-value to *every* atomic sentence of *SL*.) But for most purposes, we can ignore most of the interpreting that each interpretation does. In *SL* we were able to determine the truth-value of a sentence on a truth-value assignment by considering only the relevant part of that assignment, that is, the truth-values assigned to the atomic components of the sentence in question. Similarly, in order to determine the truth-value of a sentence of *PL* on an interpretation we need only consider the U.D. and the interpretation of those sentence letters, predicates, and constants that occur in the sentence in question. In what follows, we shall continue the practice of displaying only the relevant parts of interpretations and of informally referring to such partial interpretations simply as *interpretations*.

## 8.1E EXERCISES

**1.** Determine the truth-value of the following sentences on the interpretation:

U.D.: set of integers
C: T
D: F
Ax: x is a positive number
Bxy: x is a square root of y
a: 0
b: 39
c: −4

a. C & (Ac ∨ Bca)
*b. Ab ⊃ Ab
c. ~Bcb ⊃ (Bba ∨ ~Ac)
*d. D ≡ (~Ab ≡ Ac)
e. (D & C) & ~Baa
*f. ~(~Ab ∨ D) ⊃ Baa
g. Baa ≡ [Bca ⊃ (D ∨ ~Ab)]
*h. ~(Ab ∨ Bcc) & (C ⊃ ~Ac)

**2.** Determine the truth-value of the following sentences on the interpretation:

U.D.: set of countries, cities, and people
G: T
Bxyz: x is between y and z
Dxy: x lives in y
Fx: x is a large city
a: West Germany
b: The United States
c: Italy
d: The U.S. President
e: Tokyo
f: Rome

a. Fa ⊃ Dda
*b. Ff ⊃ Ddb
c. (~Babc ∨ ~Bbac) ∨ ~Bcab
*d. (G ≡ Fe) ⊃ Dde
e. (~G ∨ Ddf) & (G ∨ Fb)
*f. Baaa ⊃ Bfff

g. (Dda ∨ Ddc) ∨ (Dde ∨ Ddf)
*h. (Fa ≡ Dda) & ~(Ddb ⊃ Bccc)

**3.** For each of the following sentences, construct an interpretation on which the sentence is true:
a. Nad ⊃ ~Nda
*b. D ≡ ~(Fb ∨ Gc)
c. (Lm & ~Lm) ∨ Chm
*d. ~(Wab ⊃ (Wbb & Eb))
e. (Ma ∨ Na) ∨ (Mb ∨ Nb)
*f. ~Fc & [(Fa ⊃ Na) & (Fb ⊃ Nb)]

**4.** For each of the following sentences, construct an interpretation on which the sentence is false:
a. (Crs ∨ Csr) ∨ (Css ∨ Crr)
*b. (K ≡ ~Ma) ≡ Gh
c. (Li ∨ Lj) ∨ Lm
*d. Iap ⊃ (Ipa ⊃ Iaa)
e. (~Ja ≡ Jb) & (~Jc ≡ ~Jd)
*f. (Ha ∨ ~Ha) ⊃ (Fbb ⊃ Fba)

**5.** For each pair, construct an interpretation on which one sentence is true and the other false:
a. Fab ⊃ Fba, Fba ⊃ Fab
*b. (Caa & Cab) ∨ D, ~D ≡ ~(Caa & Cab)
c. ~Ma ∨ Cpqr, Capq ∨ ~Mr
*d. Kac ∨ Kad, Kac & Kad
e. ~Ljk ≡ (Mjk ∨ Mkj), (Mjk & Mkj) & Ljk

6a. Explain why there is no interpretation on which 'Ba ∨ ~Ba' is false.
*b. Can the sentence 'Eab & ~Eba' be true on an interpretation for which the U.D. contains exactly one member? Explain.

**7.** Determine the truth-value of the following sentences on the interpretation:

U.D.: set of people
N: T
Bx: x is a child
Cx: x is over forty years old
Dxy: x and y are sisters
Fxy: x and y are brothers

a. (∀w)(Cw ⊃ (∃x)Dxx)
*b. (∃x)(∃y)(Fxy & N)
c. (∃x)(∀y)(By ∨ Fxy)
*d. (∀x)(∀y)(Dxy ≡ Fxy)
e. (∃x)Cx ⊃ (N ⊃ (∃y)By)
*f. ~(∀w)(Cw ∨ Bw)
g. (∀x)Bx ⊃ (∀x)Cx
*h. (∀x)[(∃y)(Dxy ∨ Fxy) ⊃ Bx]
i. (∃x)[Cx ∨ (∃y)(Dxy & Cy)]

**8.** Determine the truth-value of each of the following sentences on the interpretation:

U.D.: set of U.S. presidents
K: F
Ax: x was the first U.S. President
Bx: x is a female
Ux: x is a U.S. Citizen
Dxy: x held office after y's first term of office
g: George Washington

a. (∀w)Dwg
*b. (∀x)(∀y)((Bx & Ay) ⊃ Dyx)
c. (∃x)(Ax & (∃y)Dyx)
*d. ((∃x)Ax & ~(∃z)Bz) & (K ⊃ (∀y)Uy)
e. (∀y)(Uy ⊃ (∃x)(Dyx ∨ Dxy))
*f. (∀w)(Bw ≡ ~Uw)
g. (∀x)(Dxg ⊃ (∃y)(~Uy & Dxy))
*h. (∃x)(Ax & Bx) ≡ (∀y)(Ay ⊃ Uy)
i. ~(K ∨ (∃x)(∀y)Dxy)

**9.** Determine the truth-value of each of the following sentences on the interpretation:

U.D.: set of positive integers
Bx: x is an even number
Gxy: x is greater than y
Exy: x equals y
Mxyz: x minus y equals z
a: 1
b: 2
c: 3

a. Bb & (∀w)(Gwb ⊃ ~Ewb)
*b. (∀x)(∀z)(~Exz ≡ Gxz)
c. (∀x)(∀z)(Gxz ⊃ ~Exz)
*d. (∀x)(∃w)(Gwx & (∃z)Mzxw)
e. ~(∀w)(∀y)Gwy ⊃ Mcba
*f. (∀y)(Eya ∨ Gya)
g. (∀z)(Bz ⊃ ~(∃y)(By & Mzay))
*h. (∀y)[(Bb & (∃x)Exb) ⊃ Mcby]
i. (∀x)(Exx ≡ ~(∃y)(∃z)Myzx)

## 8.2 QUANTIFICATIONAL TRUTH, FALSEHOOD, AND INDETERMINACY

Using the concept of an interpretation, we may now specify the quantificational counterparts of various truth-functional concepts. Here are the relevant properties that individual sentences of *PL* may have:

| |
|---|
| A sentence 𝒫 of *PL* is *quantificationally true* if and only if 𝒫 is true on every interpretation. |

A sentence $\mathscr{P}$ of *PL* is *quantificationally false* if and only if $\mathscr{P}$ is false on every interpretation.

A sentence $\mathscr{P}$ of *PL* is *quantificationally indeterminate* if and only if $\mathscr{P}$ is neither quantificationally true nor quantificationally false.

These are the quantificational analogues of truth-functional truth, falsehood, and indeterminacy. The definitions here, however, are stated in terms of interpretations rather than truth-value assignments.

A sentence $\mathscr{P}$ is quantificationally true if and only if it is true on every interpretation. The sentence '(∃x)(Gx ∨ ~ Gx)' is quantificationally true. We cannot hope to show this by going through each of the interpretations of the sentence, since there are infinitely many. (To see this, it suffices to note that there are infinitely many possible universes of discourse for the sentence. We can, for instance, choose as our U.D. a set containing exactly one positive integer. Because there are an infinite number of positive integers, there are an infinite number of such universes of discourse.)

However, we may reason about the sentence as follows. Because the sentence is existentially quantified, it is true on an interpretation just in case at least one member of the U.D. satisfies the condition specified by 'Gx ∨ ~ Gx', that is, just in case at least one member of the U.D. either is G or is not G. Without knowing what the interpretation of 'G' is, we know that every member of a U.D. will satisfy this condition, for every member is either in or not in the extension of 'G'. And, since by definition every interpretation has a nonempty set as its U.D., we know that the U.D. for any interpretation has at least one member and hence at least one member that satisfies the condition specified by the open sentence 'Gx ∨ ~ Gx'. Therefore '(∃x)(Gx ∨ ~ Gx)' is true on every interpretation.

In general, to show that a sentence of *PL* is quantificationally true, we must use reasoning that shows that no matter what the U.D. is, and no matter how the sentence letters, predicates, and individual constants in the sentence are interpreted, the sentence always turns out to be true. Here is another example. The sentence

(∃x)(∃y)(Gxy ⊃ (∀z)(∀w)Gzw)

is quantificationally true. That is, given any U.D. and any interpretation of 'G', there will always be members x and y of the U.D. that satisfy the condition specified by '(Gxy ⊃ (∀z)(∀w)Gzw)'. The sentence claims that there is a pair of members of the U.D. such that if they stand in the relation G then all members of the U.D. stand in the relation G. We will consider two possibilities for the interpretation of the predicate: Either every pair of members of the U.D. is in its extension, or not every pair is in its extension.

If every pair *is* in the extension of 'G', then every pair x and y (and hence at least one pair) satisfies the condition specified by '(Gxy ⊃ (∀z)(∀w)Gzw)', because the consequent is true in this case. Now consider the other possibility—that some (at least one) pair is not in the extension of 'G'. In this case, that pair satisfies the condition specified by '(Gxy ⊃ (∀z)(∀w)Gzw)' because that pair *fails* to satisfy the antecedent 'Gxy'. Because either the interpretation of 'G' includes every pair of members of U.D. in its extension or it does not (there are no other possibilities), we have just shown that whatever the interpretation of 'G' may be there will always be at least one pair of members of the U.D. that satisfy '(Gxy ⊃ (∀z)(∀w)Gzw)'. This being so, the sentence '(∃x)(∃y)(Gxy ⊃ (∀z)(∀w)Gzw)' will be true on every interpretation. The sentence is therefore quantificationally true.

The sentence

(∀y)By & (∃z) ~ Bz

is quantificationally false. If an interpretation makes the first conjunct true, then every member of the U.D. will be in the extension of 'B'. But if this is so, then no member of the U.D. satisfies the condition specified by ' ~ Bz' and so the existentially quantified second conjunct is false. So on any interpretation on which the first conjunct is true, the entire sentence will be false. The sentence will also be false on any interpretation on which the first conjunct is false, just because that conjunct is false. Since any interpretation will either make the first conjunct true or make the first conjunct false, it follows that on every interpretation the sentence '(∀y)By & (∃z) ~ Bz' is false.

The sentence

(∀x)(∃y)(Fx ⊃ Gy) ≡ ((∃x)Fx & (∀y) ~ Gy)

is also quantificationally false. Because the sentence is a biconditional it will be false on any interpretation on which its immediate components have different truth-values, and we can show that this will be the case for every interpretation. Consider first an interpretation on which the immediate component '(∀x)(∃y)(Fx ⊃ Gy)' is true. For this to be true, every member x of the U.D. must satisfy the condition specified by '(∃y)(Fx ⊃ Gy)'. That is, every member x must be such that if it is in the extension of 'F' then there is some member y of the U.D. that is in the extension of 'G'. It follows that the second immediate component of the biconditional, '((∃x)Fx & (∀y) ~ Gy)' cannot be true. If it *were* true, then some member of the U.D. would be in the extension of 'F' (to satisfy the first conjunct) and no member of the U.D. would be in the extension of 'G'. But the truth of '(∀x)(∃y)(Fx ⊃ Gy)', as we have seen, requires that if any object is in the extension of 'F' then at least one object must be in the extension of 'G'. It follows that if '(∀x)(∃y)(Fx ⊃ Gy)' is true on an interpretation, then '((∃x)Fx & (∀y) ~ Gy)' is false on that interpretation.

Now let us consider an interpretation on which '(∀x)(∃y)(Fx ⊃ Gy)' is false. In this case, some member x of the U.D. must fail to satisfy the condition specified by '(∃y)(Fx ⊃ Gy)'—x must be in the extension of 'F' (to satisfy the antecedent of the conditional) and the extension of 'G' must be empty (so the consequent will not be satisfied). But in this case '((∃x)Fx & (∀y) ~ Gy)' must be true because both conjuncts will be true. '(∃x)Fx' will be true because some member of the U.D. is in the extension of 'F', and '(∀y) ~ Gy' will be true because the extension of 'G' is empty. So any interpretation that makes '(∀x)(∃y)(Fx ⊃ Gy)' false will make '((∃x)Fx & (∀y) ~ Gy)' true. Combined with the results of the last paragraph, this establishes that on any interpretation, the immediate components of '(∀x)(∃y)(Fx ⊃ Gy) ≡ ((∃x)Fx & (∀y) ~ Gy)' will have different truth-values. So the biconditional must be false on every interpretation and therefore is quantificationally false.

Unfortunately, it is not always so easy to show that a sentence is quantificationally true or that it is quantificationally false. However, because a quantificationally true sentence must be true on every interpretation, we can show that a sentence is *not* quantificationally true by showing that it is false on at least one interpretation. Take as an example the sentence

(G & (∃z)Bz) ⊃ (∀x)Bx

This sentence is not quantificationally true. To show this, we shall construct an interpretation on which the sentence is false. The sentence is a material conditional, and so our interpretation must make its antecedent true and its consequent false. For the antecedent to be true, 'G' must be true and at least one member of the U.D. must be in the extension of 'B'. For the consequent to be false, at least one member of the U.D. must fail to be in the extension of 'B'. So we shall choose a U.D. with at least two members and an interpretation for 'B' that includes at least one member of the U.D., but not all, in its extension, and we shall make 'G' true. The following interpretation will do the trick:

19. U.D.: set of people
    G: T
    Bx: x is a boy

The antecedent 'G & (∃z)Bz' is true because 'G' is true and at least one person is a boy, but '(∀x)Bx' is false because not all people are boys.

As a second example, '(∀x)[(Fx ∨ Gx) ∨ (∃y)Hxy]' is not quantificationally true. We shall show this by constructing an interpretation on which the sentence is false. Because the sentence is universally quantified, the U.D. must have at least one member that fails to satisfy the condition specified by '(Fx ∨ Gx) ∨ (∃y)Hxy'. We shall choose the set of positive integers as our U.D., and choose 2 as the member of the U.D. that will not satisfy the condition. (There is no particular reason for using 2, but choosing a number will help us develop the rest of the interpretation). We will interpret 'F' and 'G' so that the number 2 has neither property (otherwise it would satisfy either 'Fx' or 'Gx'). We must also interpret 'H' so that the number 2 does not stand in the relation H to any positive integer:

20. U.D.: set of positive integers
    Fx: x is odd
    Gx: x is greater than 4
    Hxy: x is equal to y squared

Because 2 is neither odd nor greater than 4, and it is not the square of any positive integer, it fails to satisfy the condition specified by '(Fx ∨ Gx) ∨ (∃y)Hxy'. Therefore the universally quantified sentence is false on interpretation 20. Having shown that there is at least one interpretation on which the sentence is false, we may conclude that it is not quantificationally true.

We may show that a sentence is not quantificationally *false* by constructing an interpretation on which it is true. The sentence

~(~Ga & (∃y)Gy)

is not quantificationally false. To construct an interpretation on which it is true, we must make '~Ga & (∃y)Gy' false. To do so, we must make one or both conjuncts false. We will choose the first, and interpret 'G' and 'a' so that '~Ga' is false:

21. U.D.: set consisting of Martha Graham
    Gx: x is female
    a: Martha Graham

Because Martha Graham is female, 'Ga' is true. Hence '~Ga' is false and so is '~Ga & (∃y)Gy'. (The fact that the second conjunct turns out to be true on our interpretation is irrelevant—the conjunction as a whole is still false.) Therefore the negation of the conjunction is true on interpretation 21, and we may conclude that the sentence is not quantificationally false.

Note that we cannot show that a sentence *is* quantificationally true or that it *is* quantificationally false by constructing a single interpretation. To show that a sentence is quantificationally true, we must demonstrate that it is true on every interpretation, and to show that a sentence is quantificationally false, we must show that it is false on every interpretation.

A quantificationally indeterminate sentence is one that is neither quantificationally true nor quantificationally false. We may show that a sentence is quantificationally indeterminate by constructing two interpretations: one on which it is true (to show that the sentence is not quantificationally false) and one on which it is false (to show that the sentence is not quantificationally true). The sentence

~(~Ga & (∃y)Gy)

is quantificationally indeterminate. We have already constructed an interpretation (interpretation 21) on which it is true; all that is left is to construct an interpretation on which it is false. For the sentence to be false, '~Ga & (∃y)Gy' must be true. To make '~Ga' true, our U.D. must contain at least one member that is not in the extension of 'G', and 'a' will designate this member. But the U.D. must also contain another member that is in the extension of 'G', to make '(∃y)Gy' true:

22. U.D.: set of people
    Gx: x is Japanese
    a: Albert Einstein

Albert Einstein was not Japanese, but at least one person *is* Japanese, so '~Ga & (∃y)Gy' is true and '~(~Ga & (∃y)Gy)' is false on interpretation 22.

The sentence is therefore not quantificationally true. Having shown that the sentence is neither quantificationally true nor quantificationally false, we may conclude that it is quantificationally indeterminate.

Sometimes it takes ingenuity to find either an interpretation on which a sentence is true or an interpretation on which a sentence is false. Examine the sentence itself for guidelines, as we have just done. If it is a truth-functional compound, then use your knowledge of the truth-conditions for that type of compound. If the sentence is universally quantified, then the sentence will be true if and only if the condition specified after the quantifier is satisfied by all members of the U.D. you choose. If the sentence is existentially quantified, then it will be true if and only if the condition specified after the quantifier is satisfied by at least one member of the U.D. As you examine the components of the sentence you may reason in the same way—are they truth-functional compounds or quantified? Sometimes, of course, the desired interpretation cannot be obtained. For example, a quantificationally true sentence is not false on any interpretation; therefore any attempt to construct an interpretation that makes the sentence false will fail.

Two theoretical points are of interest here. The first is that if a sentence of predicate logic without identity is true on at least one interpretation, then it is true on some interpretation that has the set of positive integers as its U.D. This result is known as the *Löwenheim Theorem* (it will be proved in the exercises to Chapter Eleven). It follows from this result that if a sentence of *PL* is true on some interpretation with a finite U.D., then it is true on some interpretation that has the set of positive integers as its U.D. And if a sentence of *PL* is true on some interpretation for which the U.D. is *larger* then the set of positive integers (for example, the set of real numbers), then it is true on at least one interpretation that has the set of positive integers as its U.D.

Note that this result means that the set of positive integers is always a good choice for your U.D. as you construct interpretations. In fact, there are sentences of *PL* that are not quantificationally true but that are nevertheless true on every interpretation with a finite U.D., and there are sentences of *PL* that are not quantificationally false but are false on every interpretation with a finite U.D. For instance, the following sentence is not quantificationally false:

$$(\forall x)(\forall y)(\forall z)[(Bxy \;\&\; Byz) \supset Bxz] \;\&\; [(\forall x)(\exists y)Bxy \;\&\; (\forall z) \sim Bzz]$$

But it is false on every interpretation with a finite U.D. To show that it is not quantificationally false, then, you must choose a U.D. that has infinitely many members—and the set of positive integers is a good choice.

The second point is that there is no decision procedure for deciding, for each sentence of *PL*, whether that sentence is quantificationally true, quantificationally false, or quantificationally indeterminate. (We shall not prove the result here.) This is a very important way in which the semantics for *PL* differs from the semantics for *SL*. For *SL* the construction of truth-tables gives a decision procedure for whether a sentence is truth-functionally true, false, or indeterminate. That is, in a finite number of mechanical steps we can always correctly answer the questions 'Is this sentence truth-functionally true?', 'Is this sentence truth-functionally false?', and 'Is this sentence truth-functionally indeterminate?' The present result, due to Church, is that there is no analogous method for predicate logic—we have no such general method now and no such general method will ever be found. This result does not mean that we cannot ever show that some sentences of *PL* are quantificationally true, false, or indeterminate; rather, it shows that there is no decision procedure (mechanical, certain, and requiring only a finite number of steps) for determining the quantificational status of *every* sentence of *PL*. However, it is interesting to note that there *is* such a procedure for determining the quantificational status of sentences of *PL* which contain no many-place predicates, that is, in which the predicates are all one-place predicates. This follows from a result by the logicians Bernays and Schönfinkel.[1]

### 8.2E EXERCISES

**1.** Show that each of the following sentences is not quantificationally true by constructing an interpretation on which it is false.

a. (∀x)(Fx ⊃ Gx) ⊃ (∀x)Gx
*b. (∃x)(Fx ∨ Gx) ⊃ ((∃x)Fx ⊃ (∃x) ~ Gx)
c. (∀x)(∃y)Bxy ⊃ (∃y)(∀x)Bxy
*d. (∀x)(Fxb ∨ Gx) ⊃ [(∀x)Fxb ∨ (∀x)Gx]
e. [(∀x)Fx ⊃ (∀w)Gw] ⊃ (∀z)(Fz ⊃ Gz)
*f. (∀x)(Ax ⊃ (∀y)By) ⊃ (∀y)(By ⊃ (∀x)Ax)
g. ~ (∃x)Gx ⊃ (∀y)(Fyy ⊃ Gy)
*h. (∀x)(Bx ≡ Hx) ⊃ (∃x)(Bx & Hx)

**2.** Show that each of the following sentences is not quantificationally false by constructing an interpretation on which it is true.

a. ~ (∀w)(∀y)Bwy ≡ (∀z)Bzz
*b. (∃x)Fx & (∃x) ~ Fx
c. ((∃x)Fx & (∃x)Gx) & ~ (∃x)(Fx & Gx)
*d. (∃x)((∃y)Fy ⊃ ~ Fx)
e. (∀x)(Fx ⊃ Gx) & (∀x)(Gx ⊃ ~ Fx)
*f. (∃x)(∀y)(Dyx ⊃ ~ Dxy)
g. (∀x)(Bx ≡ Hx) ⊃ (∃x)(Bx & Hx)
*h. (∃x)(∀y)Dxy ∨ ~ (∀y)(∃x)Dxy
i. (∀x)(∀y)(∀z)[(Bxy & Byz) ⊃ Bxz] & [(∀x)(∃y)Bxy & (∀z) ~ Bzz]

**3.** Show that each of the following sentences is quantificationally indeterminate, by constructing an interpretation on which it is true and an interpretation on which it is false.

a. (∃x)(Fx & Gx) ⊃ (∃x) ~ (Fx ∨ Gx)
*b. (∃x)Fx ⊃ (∀w)(Cw ⊃ Fw)
c. (∀x)Bnx ⊃ (∀x) ~ Bnx
*d. (∃x)(Fx ⊃ Gx) ⊃ (∃x)(Fx & Gx)

[1] "Zum Entscheidungsproblem der mathematischen Logik," *Mathematische Annalen*, 99 (1928), 342–372. The result mentioned in the previous paragraph is from Alonzo Church, "A Note on the Entscheidungsproblem," *Journal of Symbolic Logic*, 1 (1936), 40–41, 101–102.

e. (∀x)(∀w)[(Nwx ∨ Nxw) ⊃ Nww]
*f. (Ma & Mb) & (∃x) ~ Mx
g. (∀x)(Cx ∨ Dx) ≡ (∃y)(Cy & Dy)
*h. [~ (∃x)Hx ∨ ~ (∃x)Gx] ∨ (∀x)(Hx & Gx)

**4.** Each of the following sentences is quantificationally true. Explain why.
a. (∃x)(∀y)Bxy ⊃ (∀y)(∃x)Bxy
*b. [(∀x)Fx ∨ (∀x)Gx] ⊃ (∀x)(Fx ∨ Gx)
c. Fa ∨ [(∀x)Fx ⊃ Ga]
*d. (∀x)(∃y)Mxy ⊃ (∃x)(∃y)Mxy
e. (∃x)Hx ∨ (∀x)(Hx ⊃ Jx)

**5.** Each of the following sentences is quantificationally false. Explain why.
a. (∃w)(Bw ≡ ~ Bw)
*b. (∀w)(Fw ⊃ Gw) & [(∀w)(Fw ⊃ ~ Gw) & (∃w)Fw]
c. [(∀x)Fx ⊃ (∃y)Gy] & [~ (∃x)Gx & ~ (∃x) ~ Fx]
*d. (∃x)(Fx & ~ Gx) & (∀x)(Fx ⊃ Gx)

## 8.3 QUANTIFICATIONAL EQUIVALENCE AND CONSISTENCY

The next concept to be introduced is that of quantificational equivalence:

> Sentences 𝒫 and 𝒬 of *PL* are *quantificationally equivalent* if and only if there is no interpretation on which 𝒫 and 𝒬 have different truth-values.

The sentences

(∃x)Fx ⊃ Ga

and

(∀x)(Fx ⊃ Ga)

are quantificationally equivalent. We may reason as follows. First suppose that '(∃x)Fx ⊃ Ga' is true on some interpretation. Then '(∃x)Fx' is either true or false on this interpretation. If it is true, then so is 'Ga' (by our assumption that '(∃x)Fx ⊃ Ga' is true). But then, since 'Ga' is true, every object x in the U.D. is such that if x is F then a is G. So '(∀x)(Fx ⊃ Ga)' is true. If '(∃x)Fx' is false, on the other hand, then every object x in the U.D. is such that if x is F (which, on our assumption, it is not) then a is G. Again, '(∀x)(Fx ⊃ Ga)' is true. Hence, if '(∃x)Fx ⊃ Ga' is true on an interpretation, '(∀x)(Fx ⊃ Ga)' is also true on that interpretation.

Now suppose that '(∃x)Fx ⊃ Ga' is false on some interpretation. Since the sentence is a conditional, it follows that '(∃x)Fx' is true and 'Ga' is false. But if '(∃x)Fx' is true, then some object x in the U.D. is in the extension of 'F'. This object then does not satisfy the condition that if it is F (which it is) then a is G (which is false on our present assumption). So '$(\forall x)(Fx \supset Ga)$' is false if '$(\exists x)Fx \supset Ga$' is. Taken together with our previous result, this demonstrates that the two sentences are quantificationally equivalent.

The sentences

$$\sim (\exists x)(\forall y)(Gxy \vee Gyx)$$

and

$$(\forall x)(\exists y)(\sim Gxy \ \& \ \sim Gyx)$$

are also quantificationally equivalent. As in the previous example, we will show that if the first sentence is true on an interpretation, so is the second sentence, and that if the first sentence is false on an interpretation, so is the second sentence. First consider an interpretation on which '$\sim (\exists x)(\forall y)(Gxy \vee Gyx)$' is true. '$(\exists x)(\forall y)(Gxy \vee Gyx)$' must be false on this interpretation, so no member x of the U.D. satisfies the condition specified by '$(\forall y)(Gxy \vee Gyx)$'. That is, no member x of the U.D. is such that for every object y, either the pair x and y or the pair y and x is in the extension of 'G'. Put another way, for each member x of the U.D., there is at least one object y such that both '$\sim Gxy$' and '$\sim Gyx$' hold. And that is exactly what the second sentence says, so it is true as well.

Now consider an interpretation on which the first sentence is false; '$(\exists x)(\forall y)(Gxy \vee Gyx)$' will be true on such an interpretation. So there is at least one member x of the U.D. such that for every object y, either 'Gxy' or 'Gyx' holds. Such a member x therefore does *not* satisfy the condition specified by '$(\exists y)(\sim Gxy \ \& \ \sim Gyx)$' (there is *no* y such that neither 'Gxy' nor 'Gyx' holds). And so the universally quantified sentence '$(\forall x)(\exists y)(\sim Gxy \ \& \ \sim Gyx)$' is also false. From this and the result of the preceding paragraph, we conclude that the two sentences are quantificationally equivalent.

If we want to establish that two sentences are *not* quantificationally equivalent, we may construct an interpretation to show this. The interpretation must make one of the two sentences true and the other sentence false. For example, the sentences

$$(\forall x)(Fx \supset Ga)$$

and

$$(\forall x)Fx \supset Ga$$

are not quantificationally equivalent. We shall construct an interpretation on which the first sentence is false and the second sentence is true. To make the first sentence false, 'Ga' will have to be false and there must be at least one object in the extension of 'F'—for then this object will fall to satisfy '$(Fx \supset Ga)$'. On the other hand, we can still make '$(\forall x)Fx \supset Ga$' true on our interpretation if the extension of 'F' does not include the entire U.D.—because then the antecedent '$(\forall x)Fx$' will be false. Here is our interpretation:

23. U.D.: set of U.S. states
    Fx: x is in the Midwest
    Gx: x is on the East Coast
    a: California

Illinois (as one example) does not satisfy the condition that if it is in the Midwest (which it is) then California is on the East Coast (which is false). So '(∀x)(Fx ⊃ Ga)' is false on the interpretation. On the other hand, '(∀x)Fx ⊃ Ga' is true, because its antecedent '(∀x)Fx' is false—not every U.S. state is in the Midwest. Once again, we see that the scope of quantifiers is very important in determining the truth-conditions of sentences of *PL*.

The sentences

(∀x)(∃y)(Hy ⊃ Lx)

and

(∀x)[(∃y)Hy ⊃ Lx]

are also not quantificationally equivalent. We shall show this by constructing an interpretation on which the first sentence is true and the second sentence is false. To make '(∀x)[(∃y)Hy ⊃ Lx]' false, some member of the U.D. must fail to satisfy '(∃y)Hy ⊃ Lx'. Therefore the U.D. must contain at least one object in the extension of 'H' (so that '(∃y)Hy' is satisfied) and at least one object x that is not in the extension of 'L' (so that this object will not satisfy 'Lx'). To make '(∀x)(∃y)(Hy ⊃ Lx)' true, every member of the U.D. must satisfy '(∃y)(Hy ⊃ Lx)' —for every member x of the U.D. there must be an object y such that if y is H then x is L. We have already decided that at least one object x will not be in the extension of 'L'. So, if x (along with all other members of the U.D.) is to satisfy '(∃y)(Hy ⊃ Lx)', then at least one member y of the U.D. must not be in the extension of 'H'—for then y will be such if it is H (it is not), then x is L. To sum up, we need at least one object that is in the extension of 'H', at least one object that is not in the extension of 'L', and at least one object that is not in the extension of 'H'. Here is our interpretation:

24. U.D.: set of people
    Hx: x is Hungarian
    Lx: x is Lithuanian

The sentence '(∀x)[(∃y)Hy ⊃ Lx]' is false—every person x who is not Lithuanian fails to satisfy the condition that if someone is Hungarian (which at least one person is) then x is Lithuanian. The sentence '(∀x)(∃y)(Hy ⊃ Lx)' is true because at least one person is not Hungarian. For any person x, there is at least one person y who is not Hungarian, and hence at least one person y such that if y is Hungarian (which y is not) then x is Lithuanian.

While we may construct single interpretations to show that two sentences are not quantificationally equivalent, we may not use the same method to show that sentences *are* quantificationally equivalent. In the latter case, we must reason about every interpretation as we did in the examples at the beginning of this section.

Quantificational consistency is our next concept:

> A set of sentences of *PL* is *quantificationally consistent* if and only if there is at least one interpretation on which all of the members of the set are true.
> A set of sentences of *PL* is *quantificationally inconsistent* if and only if the set is not quantificationally consistent.

The set of sentences

$$\{(\forall x)Gax,\ \sim Gba \vee (\exists x) \sim Gax\}$$

is quantificationally consistent. The following interpretation shows this:

25. U.D.: set of positive integers
    Gxy: x is less than or equal to y
    a: the number 1
    b: the number 2

On this interpretation '$(\forall x)Gax$' is true, since 1 is less than or equal to every positive integer. The sentence '$\sim Gba$' is true, since 2 is neither less than nor equal to 1; so '$\sim Gba \vee (\exists x) \sim Gax$' is true. Since both members of the set are true on this interpretation, the set is quantificationally consistent.

The set

$$\{(\forall w)(Fw \supset Gw),\ (\forall w)(Fw \supset \sim Gw)\}$$

is also quantificationally consistent. This may seem surprising, since the first sentence says that everything that is F is G and the second sentence says that everything that is F is not G. But the set is consistent because if no object in the U.D. of an interpretation is in the extension of 'F', then every object w in the U.D. will be such that <u>if</u> w is F (which w is not) <u>then</u> w is both G and not G. The following interpretation illustrates this.

26. U.D.: set of people
    Fx: x is an amphibian
    Gx: x has three eyes

No person is an amphibian, so each person w is such that if w is an amphibian (which w is not), then w does and does not have three eyes. Both '$(\forall w)(Fw \supset Gw)$' and '$(\forall w)(Fw \supset \sim Gw)$' are true on this interpretation.

Note that while a single interpretation may be produced to show that a set of sentences is quantificationally consistent, a single interpretation *cannot* be used to show that a set of sentences is quantificationally *in*consistent. To show that a set is quantificationally inconsistent, we must show that on every interpretation, at least one sentence in the set is false. In some cases, simple reasoning will show that a set of sentences is quantificationally inconsistent. The set

{(∃y)(Fy & ~ Ny), (∀y)(Fy ⊃ Ny)}

is quantificationally inconsistent. For suppose that '(∃y)(Fy & ~ Ny)' is true on some interpretation, then some member y of the U.D. is F and is not N. But then that member is *not* such that if it is F (which it is) then it is N (which it is not). Hence the universally quantified sentence '(∀y)(Fy ⊃ Ny)' is false on such an interpretation. So there is no interpretation on which both set members are true; the set is quantificationally inconsistent.

## 8.3E EXERCISES

**1.** Show that the sentences in each of the following pairs are not quantificationally equivalent by constructing an interpretation on which one of the sentences is true and the other is false.

a. (∃x)Fx ⊃ Ga, (∃x)(Fx ⊃ Ga)
*b. (∃x)Fx & (∃x)Gx, (∃x)(Fx & Gx)
c. (∀x)Fx ∨ (∀x)Gx, (∀x)(Fx ∨ Gx)
*d. (∃x)(Fx ∨ Ga), (∃x)(Fx ∨ Gb)
e. (∀x)(Fx ≡ Gx), (∃x)Fx ≡ (∃x)Gx
*f. (∀x)(Fx ⊃ Gx), (∀y)((∀x)Fx ⊃ Gy)
g. (∃x)(Bx & (∀y)Dyx), (∀x)(Bx ⊃ (∀y)Dyx)
*h. (∃y)(My ≡ Ny), (∃y)My ≡ (∃y)Ny
i. (∀x)(∃y)(Fx ⊃ Kyx), (∃x)(∃y)(Fx ⊃ Kyx)

**2.** In each of the following pairs the sentences are quantificationally equivalent. Explain why.

a. (∀x)Fx ⊃ Ga, (∃x)(Fx ⊃ Ga)
*b. (∀x)(Fx ⊃ Gx), ~ (∃x)(Fx & ~ Gx)
c. (∃x)(Fx ∨ Gx), ~ (∀y)(~ Fy & ~ Gy)
*d. (∀x)(∀y)(Mxy & Myx), ~ (∃x)(∃y)(~ Mxy ∨ ~ Myx)

**3.** Show that each of the following sets of sentences is quantificationally consistent by constructing an interpretation on which every member of the set is true.

a. {(∃x)Bx, (∃x)Cx, ~ (∀x)(Bx ∨ Cx)}
*b. {(∃x)Fx ∨ (∃x)Gx, (∃x) ~ Fx, (∃x) ~ Gx}
c. {(∀x)(Fx ⊃ Gx), (∀x)(Nx ⊃ Mx), (∀x)(Gx ⊃ ~ Mx)}
*d. {(∀x)(Dax ≡ Bax), ~ Dab, ~ Bba}
e. {(∀w)(Nw ⊃ (∃z)(Mz & Cwz), (∀z)(∀w)(Mz ⊃ ~ Cwz)}
*f. {(∃w)Fw, (∀w)(Fw ⊃ (∃x)Bxw), (∀x) ~ Bxx}
g. {~ (∀y)(Ny ⊃ My), ~ (∀y) ~ (Ny ⊃ My)}
*h. {(∀x)(Bx ≡ (∀y)Cxy), (∃x) ~ Bx, (∃x)(∃y)Cxy}
i. {(∃y)Fay, (∃y) ~ Gay, (∀y)(Fay ∨ Gay)}

4. Each of the following sets of sentences is quantificationally inconsistent. Explain why.
   a. {(∃x)(Bx & Cx), (∀x) ~ (Bx ∨ Cx)}
   *b. {(∃x)(∃y)(Bxy ∨ Byx), ~ (∃x)(∃y)Bxy}
   c. {(∀x)(∀y)(Byx ∨ Bxy), (∃y) ~ Byy}
   *d. {Ba, (∃y)Day, (∀x)(Bx ⊃ (∀y) ~ Dxy)}

5. Explain why sentences $\mathscr{P}$ and $\mathscr{Q}$ of *PL* are quantificationally equivalent if and only if $\mathscr{P} \equiv \mathscr{Q}$ is quantificationally true.

---

## 8.4 QUANTIFICATIONAL ENTAILMENT AND VALIDITY

Our last two semantic concepts for the language *PL* are the concepts of quantificational entailment and quantificational validity:

> A set Γ of sentences of *PL* quantificationally entails a sentence $\mathscr{P}$ of *PL* if and only if there is no interpretation on which every member of Γ is true and $\mathscr{P}$ is false.

> An argument of *PL* is *quantificationally valid* if and only if there is no interpretation on which every premise is true and the conclusion is false. An argument of *PL* is *quantificationally invalid* if and only if the argument is not quantificationally valid.

The set

{(∀x)(Bx ⊃ Ga), (∃x)Bx}

quantificationally entails the sentence 'Ga'. As in *SL* we may use the double turnstile and write this as

{(∀x)(Bx ⊃ Ga), (∃x)Bx} ⊨ Ga

Suppose that '(∀x)(Bx ⊃ Ga)' and '(∃x)Bx' are both true on some interpretation. Since '(∀x)(Bx ⊃ Ga)' is true we know that every object x in the U.D. is such that if x is B then a is G. Since '(∃x)Bx' is true we know that at least one object x in the U.D. of the interpretation is in the extension of 'B'. Since it is true that if that object is B (which it is) then a is G, 'Ga' must therefore be true. So, on any interpretation on which '(∀x)(Bx ⊃ Ga)' and '(∃x)Bx' are both true, 'Ga' is also true. So the entailment does hold.

The set

{(∀y)( ~ Jy ∨ (∃z)Kz), (∃y)Jy}

quantificationally entails the sentence

(∃z)Kz

We shall show that any interpretation that makes the two sentences in the set true will also make '$(\exists z)Kz$' true. If an interpretation makes the first sentence in the set true, then every member y of the U.D. satisfies the condition specified by '$(\sim Jy \vee (\exists z)Kz)$'. Every member is such that either it is not J or some member of the U.D. is K. If the second sentence is also true on the interpretation, then some member of the U.D. is J. Because this member must satisfy the disjunction '$\sim Jy \vee (\exists z)Kz$' and, being J, it does not satisfy the disjunct '$\sim Jy$', the second disjunct must be true. And the second disjunct is '$(\exists z)Kz$', so it is true whenever the two set members are true.

The argument

$$(\exists x)(Fx \vee Gx)$$
$$(\forall x) \sim Fx$$
$$\overline{(\exists x)Gx}$$

is quantificationally valid. Suppose that on some interpretation both premises are true. If the first premise is true, then some member x of the U.D. is either F or G. If the premise '$(\forall x) \sim Fx$' is true, then no member of the U.D. is F. Therefore, because the member that is either F or G is not F, it must be G. Thus '$(\exists x)Gx$' will also be true on such an interpretation.

We can show that a set of sentences does *not* quantificationally entail a sentence by constructing an interpretation. For example, the set

$$\{\sim (\forall x)(Gx \equiv Fx), \ \sim Fb\}$$

does not quantificationally entail the sentence

$$(\forall x) \sim Gx$$

We will construct an interpretation on which the members of the set are true and '$(\forall x) \sim Gx$' is false. For the sentence '$\sim (\forall x)(Gx \equiv Fx)$' to be true, the U.D. must contain at least one member that fails to satisfy '$Gx \equiv Fx$'—the member must be in the extension of one of the two predicates but not in the extension of the other. For '$\sim Fb$' to be true, 'b' must designate an object that is not in the extension of 'F'. And '$(\forall x) \sim Gx$', which claims that everything is not G, will be false if at least one object in the U.D. is in the extension of 'G'. Here is an interpretation that satisfies these conditions:

27. U.D.: set of positive integers
    Fx: x is greater than 5
    Gx: x is prime
    b: the number 3

Not all positive integers are prime if and only if they are greater than 5—take 2 as an example—and 3 is not greater than 5. Therefore the set members are both true on this interpretation. On the other hand, '$(\forall x) \sim Gx$' is false. Some positive integers are prime.

To show that an argument is quantificationally invalid, we can construct an interpretation on which its premises are true and its conclusion is false. The argument

$$(\exists x)[(\exists y)Fy \supset Fx]$$
$$(\exists y) \sim Fy$$
$$\overline{\sim (\exists x)Fx}$$

is quantificationally invalid. We can make the first premise true by interpreting 'F' so that at least one member of the U.D. is in its extension—for then that object will satisfy the condition specified by '$(\exists y)Fy \supset Fx$' because it will satisfy its consequent. The second premise will be true if at least one member of the U.D. is not in the extension of 'F'. So 'F' will have some, but not all, of the members of the U.D. in its extension. Because some members will be in the extension, the conclusion will turn out to be false. Here is an interpretation:

28. U.D.: set of people
    Fx: x is fifty years old

Some person x is such that if there is a person who is fifty years old, then x is fifty years old, and some person is not fifty years old, but it is false that no person is fifty years old.

Note that we cannot prove that a quantificational entailment *does* hold or that an argument *is* quantificationally valid by constructing a single interpretation. Proving either of these involves proving something about the truth-value of sentences on every interpretation, not just a select few.

And, once again, there are limitations on deciding questions of quantificational equivalence, consistency, entailment, and validity. Owing to Church's result, mentioned at the end of Section 8.2, we know that there is no decision procedure for deciding these questions for every group of sentences of *PL*.[2] However, our method of producing interpretations to establish quantificational consistency, nonequivalence, nonentailment, and invalidity, although not a decision procedure, often produce the desired result. We have, for instance, just used this method to show that an argument is quantificationally invalid. Ingenuity in choosing an appropriate interpretation for sentences containing quantifiers is once again generally required.

[2] Moreover, some arguments can be proved quantificationally invalid and some sets quantificationally consistent only by means of interpretations with universes of discourse containing an infinite number of members. However, there is a result for sets of sentences analogous to the Löwenheim Theorem (mentioned in Section 8.2), which says that if a set of sentences is quantificationally consistent—or an argument quantificationally invalid—then this can be shown by means of interpretations with the set of positive integers as the U.D. It is not necessary in any case to check interpretations with larger universes of discourse. This result is known as the *Löwenheim-Skolem Theorem* and is assigned as an exercise in Chapter Eleven.

## 8.4E EXERCISES

**1.** Establish each of the following by constructing an appropriate interpretation.

a. $\{(\forall x)(Fx \supset Gx), (\forall x)(Hx \supset Gx)\} \not\models (\exists x)(Hx \ \& \ Fx)$
*b. $\{(\forall y)(Fy \equiv D), Fa\} \not\models \sim Fb$
c. $\{(\exists x)Fx\} \not\models Fa$
*d. $\{(\forall x)(Bx \supset Cx), (\exists x)Bx\} \not\models (\forall x)Cx$
e. $\{(\exists x)(Bx \supset Cx), (\exists x)Cx\} \not\models (\exists x)Bx$
*f. $\{(\forall x)(Fx \supset Gx), (\forall x)(Hx \supset \sim Fx)\} \not\models (\forall x)(Hx \supset Gx)$
g. $\{(\forall x)(\exists y) \sim Lxy\} \not\models (\forall x) \sim Lxx$
*h. $\{(\exists x)(\forall y\}(Hxy \vee Jxy), (\exists x)(\forall y) \sim Hxy\} \not\models (\exists x)(\forall y)Jxy$

**2.** Show that each of the following arguments is quantificationally invalid by constructing an appropriate interpretation.

a. $(\forall x)(Fx \supset Gx) \supset (\exists x)Nx$
$(\forall x)(Nx \supset Gx)$
__________
$(\forall x)(\sim Fx \vee Gx)$

*b. $(\sim (\exists y)Fy \supset (\exists y)Fy) \vee \sim Fa$
__________
$(\exists z)Fz$

c. $(\exists x)(Fx \ \& \ Gx)$
$(\exists x)(Fx \ \& \ Hx)$
__________
$(\exists x)(Gx \ \& \ Hx)$

*d. $(\forall x)(Fx \supset Gx)$
$Ga$
__________
$Fa$

e. $(\forall x)(Fx \supset Gx)$
$\sim (\exists x)Fx$
__________
$\sim (\exists x)Gx$

*f. $(\forall x)(\forall y)(Mxy \supset Nxy)$
__________
$(\forall x)(\forall y)(Mxy \supset (Nxy \ \& \ Nyx))$

g. $(\exists x)Gx$
$(\forall x)(Gx \supset Dxx)$
__________
$(\exists x)(\forall y)(Gx \ \& \ Dxy)$

*h. $Fa \vee (\exists y)Gya$
$Fb \vee (\exists y) \sim Gyb$
__________
$(\exists y)Gya$

i. $(\forall x)(Fx \supset Gx)$
$(\forall x)(Hx \supset Gx)$
__________
$(\forall x)(Fx \vee Hx)$

3. Using the given symbolization keys, symbolize the following arguments in *PL*. Then show that the first symbolized argument in each pair is quantificationally valid while the second is not.

a. U.D.: set consisting of all things

Bx: x is beautiful
Px: x is a person

Everything is beautiful. Therefore something is beautiful.

Everyone is beautiful. Therefore someone is beautiful.

*b. U.D.: set of people

Rx: x roller skates
Dx: x can dance

Not everyone can dance. Therefore someone can't dance.

No one who roller skates can dance. Therefore some roller skater can't dance.

c. U.D.: set of people

Lxy: x loves y

There is a person who loves everyone. Therefore everyone is loved by someone.

Everyone is loved by someone. Therefore there is a person who loves everyone.

*d. U.D.: set of numbers

Ex: x is even
Dx: x is divisible by 2

Some numbers are even and some numbers are divisible by 2. Therefore some numbers are even if and only if some numbers are divisible by 2.

A number is even if and only if it is divisible by 2. Therefore some number is even.

e. U.D.: set of people

Tx: x is a student
Sx: x is smart
Hx: x is happy

Some students are smart, and some students are not happy. Therefore there is a student who is smart or not happy.

All students are smart, and no student is happy. Therefore there is a student who is smart or not happy.

*f. U.D.: set of people

Sx: x is a senator
Rx: x is a Republican
Dx: x is a Democrat

Any senator who is not a Republican is a Democrat. There is a senator who is not a Republican. Therefore some senator is a Democrat.

There is a senator who is not a Republican. Therefore some senator is a Democrat.

g. U.D.: set of people

Ax: x likes asparagus
Sx: x likes spinach
Cx: x is crazy

Anyone who likes asparagus is crazy, and anyone who is crazy likes spinach. Therefore anyone who likes asparagus also likes spinach.

Anyone who likes spinach is crazy, and anyone who is crazy likes asparagus. Therefore anyone who likes asparagus also likes spinach.

## 8.5 TRUTH-FUNCTIONAL EXPANSIONS

In the preceding sections we have constructed interpretations for sentences of *PL* to establish various semantic results: A sentence is not quantificationally true, a set of sentences is quantificationally consistent, and so on. When we give an interpretation for a sentence or a set of sentences of *PL*, the U.D. we select may be very large or even infinite. However, when we ask whether certain sentences have various semantic properties, we can often find the answer by considering only interpretations with a relatively small U.D. *Truth-functional expansions* enable us to reason about the truth-values of sentences for interpretations with small U.D.'s.

We shall introduce truth-functional expansions with an example. Consider the sentence

$(\forall x)(Wx \supset (\exists y)Cxy)$

and the interpretation

29. U.D.: set consisting of the numbers 1 and 2

Wx: x is even

Cxy: x is greater than y

The sentence is true on this interpretation; every even member of the U.D. (in this case, the number 2) is greater than some member of the U.D. If we designate each member of the U.D. with a constant, for example,

a: 1

b: 2

then we can use these constants to produce a sentence without quantifiers that says the same thing about our U.D. as the sentence above. We can eliminate the universal quantifier and use a conjunction instead to say that each member of the U.D. is such that if it is even, then it is greater than some member of the U.D.:

$(Wa \supset (\exists y)Cay) \ \& \ (Wb \supset (\exists y)Cby)$

We can now eliminate the existential quantifier in '(∃y)Cay' and use a disjunction instead to say that 1 is greater than some member of the U.D.:

(Wa ⊃ (Caa ∨ Cab)) & (Wb ⊃ (∃y)Cby)

Because 'a' and 'b' designate the two objects in the U.D., '(Caa ∨ Cab)' makes the same claim about the U.D. as does '(∃y)Cay'—the claim that 1 is greater than at least one member of the U.D. We can eliminate the remaining existential quantifier in a similar way:

(Wa ⊃ (Caa ∨ Cab)) & (Wb ⊃ (Cba ∨ Cbb))

The sentence that we have just produced says the same thing about our U.D. as the original sentence. It is called a *truth-functional expansion* of the original sentence for the set of constants {'a', 'b'}.

Although we introduced interpretation 29 for illustration, we may generalize what we have just said about the quantified sentence and its truth-functional expansion. On *any* interpretation in which each member of the U.D. is designated by one of the constants 'a' and 'b', the quantified sentence will have the same truth-value as its truth-functional expansion using those constants.

The principles behind truth-functional expansions are simple. A universally quantified sentence says something about each member of the U.D. If we have a finite U.D. and a set of constants such that each member of the U.D. is designated by at least one of these constants, then we can reexpress a universally quantified sentence as a conjunction of its substitution instances formed from the constants. As long as every member of the U.D. is designated by at least one of the constants, the conjunction will end up saying the same thing as the universally quantified sentence—that every member of the U.D. satisfies some condition. An existentially quantified sentence says that there is at least one member of the U.D. of which such-and-such is true, and can be reexpressed as a disjunction of its substitution instances: The sentence says that such-and-such is true of *this* object or of *that* object or. . . . As long as every member of the U.D. is designated by at least one of the constants, the disjunction of substitution instances will make the same claim about the U.D. as did the existentially quantified sentence.

In constructing a truth-functional expansion we first choose a set of individual constants. If the sentence contains any constants, they must be among the constants chosen. To expand a universally quantified sentence $(\forall \mathbf{x})\mathscr{P}$, we remove the initial quantifier from the sentence and replace the resulting open sentence with the iterated conjunction

$$(\ldots(\mathscr{P}(\mathbf{a}_1/\mathbf{x}) \;\&\; \mathscr{P}(\mathbf{a}_2/\mathbf{x})) \;\&\; \ldots \;\&\; \mathscr{P}(\mathbf{a}_n/\mathbf{x}))$$

where $\mathbf{a}_1, \ldots, \mathbf{a}_n$ are the chosen constants and $\mathscr{P}(\mathbf{a}_i/\mathbf{x})$ is a substitution instance of $(\forall \mathbf{x})\mathscr{P}$. Each of the conjuncts is a substitution instance of $(\forall \mathbf{x})\mathscr{P}$, differing from one another only in that each is formed from a different constant, and there is one substitution instance for each of the individual constants.

We shall expand the sentence '(∀x)Nx' for the set of constants {'a', 'b'}, Removing the quantifier gives us the open sentence 'Nx', and we replace 'Nx' by the conjunction 'Na & Nb'. We can expand '(∀y)(My ⊃ Jyy)' for the same set of constants by first dropping the quantifier and then replacing 'My ⊃ Jyy' by an iterated conjunction. In the first conjunct, 'a' replaces the free variable 'y', and in the second conjunct, 'b' replaces that variable:

(Ma ⊃ Jaa) & (Mb ⊃ Jbb)

This truth-functional expansion will have the same truth-value as the unexpanded sentence on every interpretation in which each member of the U.D. is named by at least one of the two constants. If we have an interpretation with a two-member U.D., for example, in which 'a' designates one member and 'b' designates the other, then '(Ma ⊃ Jaa) & (Mb ⊃ Jbb)' makes the same claim about the U.D. as '(∀y)(My ⊃ Jyy)'—namely, that each of the two members is such that if it is M, then it stands in the relation J to itself.

We have claimed that a truth-functional expansion will have the same truth-value as the unexpanded sentence on any interpretation on which each member of the U.D. is named *by at least one* of the constants used in the expansion. We note two points about this claim, using the previous example to illustrate. The first is that the interpretations in question may assign the same object to several of the constants, as long as each object in the U.D. is named by at least one of them. So if we have an interpretation with a one-member U.D., both 'a' and 'b' must refer to that one member. In this case, every object in the U.D. is named by at least one of the two constants. The expanded sentence above says twice that the one member of the U.D. is such that if it is M, then it stands in the relation J to itself, and this is equivalent to the universal claim that every member of the U.D. satisfies that condition.

The second point is that if a U.D. for an interpretation has even one member that is not designated by one of the two constants, then the two sentences may fail to have the same truth-value. The following interpretation shows this:

30. U.D.: set consisting of the numbers 1 and 2
Mx: x is positive
Jxy: x equals y squared
a: 1
b: 1

The expanded sentence '(Ma ⊃ Jaa) & (Mb ⊃ Jbb)', which says twice that if one is positive then it equals itself squared, is true on this interpretation. But the universally quantified sentence '(∀y)(My ⊃ Jyy)' is false on this interpretation because 2, which was not mentioned in the expansion, does not satisfy the condition specified after the quantifier. If, on the other hand, interpretation 30 had interpreted 'b' to designate 2 (leaving 'a' to designate 1), our requirement that each member of the U.D. be designated by at least one of the constants would have been met; and in this case the two sentences would have had the same truth-value (false).

Now we shall expand the sentence

(∀x)(Gac ∨ Fx)

We have stipulated that the set of constants that we use for an expansion must include all the individual constants that occur in the sentence being expanded. So any set of constants for which we expand the sentence must include 'a' and 'c'. We can expand the sentence for the set containing just those constants, in which case removing the initial quantifier and replacing 'x' with each constant in turn results in the expansion

(Gac ∨ Fa) & (Gac ∨ Fc)

If we expand the sentence for the larger set {'a', 'c', 'e'} we obtain

((Gac ∨ Fa) & (Gac ∨ Fc)) & (Gac ∨ Fe)

If the sentence we want to expand contains more than one universal quantifier, we can start with the left-most one and remove each in turn. To expand

(∀y)(Ly & (∀z)Bzy)

for the set of constants {'a', 'b'}, we first eliminate the quantifier '(∀y)' and expand the resulting open sentence, '(Ly & (∀x)Bzy)', to obtain

[La & (∀z)Bza] & [Lb & (∀z)Bzb]

The expanded sentence now contains two occurrences of the quantifier '(∀z)'; this is because '(∀z)Bzy' was part of the open sentence obtained by removing the quantifier '(∀y)' and hence became part of each conjunct. We now expand each of the universally quantified sentences that are components of '[La & (∀z)Bza] & [Lb & (∀z)Bzb]' by eliminating each occurrence of '(∀z)' and expanding the resulting open sentences, first to obtain

[La & (Baa & Bba)] & [Lb & (∀z)Bzb]

and then

[La & (Baa & Bba)] & [Lb & (Bab & Bbb)]

Here we replaced '(∀z)Bza' with '(Baa & Bba)' and '(∀z)Bzb' with '(Bab & Bbb)'. Note that when we expand a quantified sentence that is a component of another sentence—as with '(∀z)Bza' and '(∀z)Bzb'—we replace that component exactly where it occurred in the sentence being expanded.

We may expand existentially quantified sentences just as we expand universally quantified sentences, except in this case we construct an iterated *disjunction*, rather than an iterated conjunction. A sentence of the form $(\exists \boldsymbol{x})\mathscr{P}$ expands to the disjunction

$$(\ldots(\mathscr{P}(\boldsymbol{a}_1/\boldsymbol{x}) \vee \mathscr{P}(\boldsymbol{a}_2/\boldsymbol{x})) \vee \ldots \vee \mathscr{P}(\boldsymbol{a}_n/\boldsymbol{x}))$$

where $\boldsymbol{a}_1, \ldots, \boldsymbol{a}_n$ are the constants in the chosen set and $\mathscr{P}(\boldsymbol{a}_i/\boldsymbol{x})$ is a substitution instance of $(\forall \boldsymbol{x})\mathscr{P}$. We construct an iterated disjunction because an existential quantification indicates that at least one member of the U.D. satisfies the specified condition: *This* member satisfies the condition, or *that* member satisfies the condition, and so on.

We can expand the sentence

$(\exists x)(Fx \supset Gx)$

for the set of constants {'a', 'b', 'c'} as

$[(Fa \supset Ga) \vee (Fb \supset Gb)] \vee (Fc \supset Gc)$

On any interpretation on which all the members of the U.D. are named by at least one of 'a', 'b', and 'c', the expanded sentence will have the same truth-value as the existentially quantified sentence. If the existentially quantified sentence is true, for example, then some member of the U.D. is such that if it is F then it is G. As long as at least one of 'a', 'b', or 'c' designates this object, the disjunct that contains that constant will be true as well. If the existentially quantified sentence is false, then no object in the U.D. satisfies the condition and hence none of the disjuncts will be true.

As with universally quantified sentences, our claims require that *each* member of the U.D. be designated by at least one of the constants. For example, '$(\exists x)(Fx \supset Gx)$' is true but its expansion '$[(Fa \supset Ga) \vee (Fb \supset Gb)] \vee (Fc \supset Gc)$' is false on interpretation 31:

31. U.D.: set consisting of the numbers 1 and 2
    Fx: x is prime
    Gx: x is odd
    a: 2
    b: 2
    c: 2

The number 1 satisfies the condition that if it is prime then it is odd, so the existentially quantified sentence is true. However, the expansion only mentions the number 2 on interpretation 31; it is false because 2 does not satisfy the condition that if it is prime (it is) then it is odd. The existentially quantified sentence and its expansion will have the same truth-value on an interpretation *only if* every member of the U.D. is named by at least one of the constants used in the expansion.

We expand the sentence

$(\exists x)(\exists w)Zwx$

for the set of constants {'a', 'b'} as follows. First, we eliminate '$(\exists x)$' and replace '$(\exists w)Zwx$' with an iterated disjunction:

$(\exists w)Zwa \vee (\exists w)Zwb$

Then we eliminate '$(\exists w)$' in each of its occurrences, first to obtain

$(Zaa \vee Zba) \vee (\exists w)Zwb$

then to obtain

(Zaa ∨ Zba) ∨ (Zab ∨ Zbb)

To expand the sentence

(∃w)[G ⊃ ∼(Fw ∨ (∃z)Bz)]

for the set of constants {'a', 'b'} we first eliminate '(∃w)' to obtain

[G ⊃ ∼(Fa ∨ (∃z)Bz)] ∨ [G ⊃ ∼(Fb ∨ (∃z)Bz)]

and then we eliminate both occurrences of '(∃z)' to obtain

[G ⊃ ∼(Fa ∨ (Ba ∨ Bb))] ∨ [G ⊃ ∼(Fb ∨ (Ba ∨ Bb))]

The sentence

(∀x)(Fx ∨ (∃z)[Fz & ∼Izx])

can also be expanded by systematic elimination of its quantifiers. We shall expand it for the set of constants {'b', 'f'}. First, the universal quantifier is eliminated to obtain the conjunction

[Fb ∨ (∃z)[Fz & ∼Izb]) & (Ff ∨ (∃z)[Fz & ∼Izf])

Next we eliminate the first occurrence of '(∃z)' to obtain

(Fb ∨ [(Fb & ∼Ibb) ∨ (Ff & ∼Ifb)]) & (Ff ∨ (∃z)[Fz & ∼Izf])

Now we eliminate the second occurrence of '(∃z)', again using a disjunction since we are eliminating an existential quantifier:

(Fb ∨ [(Fb & ∼Ibb) ∨ (Ff & ∼Ifb)])
& (Ff ∨ [(Fb & ∼Ibf) ∨ (Ff & ∼Iff)])

When we expand a sentence, we may choose a set containing only one constant for the expansion. In this case, we simply remove the quantifier and replace the free variable in the resulting open sentence with that constant. '(∀x)Fx' is expanded for the set of constants {'a'} as 'Fa', and '(∃x)Fx' is also expanded as 'Fa'. With the same set of constants, '(∃y)Gyy' is expanded as 'Gaa' and '(∀x)(Fx ∨ (∃y)Gyy)' is expanded first to obtain 'Fa ∨ (∃y)Gyy' and then to obtain '(Fa ∨ Gaa)'.

As a final example, we expand the sentence

Dg ∨ (∀y)(∃x)Cyx

for the set of constants {'a', 'g'} (we must include 'g' in the set because it occurs in the sentence to be expanded). We first replace '(∀y)(∃x)Cyx' with its expansion to obtain

Dg ∨ [(∃x)Cax & (∃x)Cgx]

Then we replace '(∃x)Cax' with its expansion to obtain

Dg ∨ [(Caa ∨ Cag) & (∃x)Cgx]

Finally, we replace '(∃x)Cgx' with its expansion to obtain

Dg ∨ [(Caa ∨ Cag) & (Cga ∨ Cgg)]

When we have expanded a sentence of *PL* to eliminate every quantifier, the truth-functional expansion that results will always be an atomic sentence or a truth-functional compound of atomic sentences of *PL*. Because of this, we can construct truth-tables for truth-functional expansions. And the truth-tables in turn will tell us something about the truth-conditions of the sentences that have been expanded. As an example, the truth-functional expansion of the sentence '(∀x) (Fx & ~ Bx)' for the set of constants {'a', 'b'} is '(Fa & ~ Ba) & (Fb & ~ Bb)'. Here is a truth-table for the expansion:

| Ba | Bb | Fa | Fb | (Fa | & | ~ Ba) | ↓<br>& | (Fb | & | ~ Bb) |
|---|---|---|---|---|---|---|---|---|---|---|
| T | T | T | T | T | F | F T | F | T | F | F T |
| T | T | T | F | T | F | F T | F | F | F | F T |
| T | T | F | T | F | F | F T | F | T | F | F T |
| T | T | F | F | F | F | F T | F | F | F | F T |
| T | F | T | T | T | F | F T | F | T | T | T F |
| T | F | T | F | T | F | F T | F | F | F | T F |
| T | F | F | T | F | F | F T | F | T | T | T F |
| T | F | F | F | F | F | F T | F | F | F | T F |
| F | T | T | T | T | T | T F | F | T | F | F T |
| F | T | T | F | T | T | T F | F | F | F | F T |
| F | T | F | T | F | F | T F | F | T | F | F T |
| F | T | F | F | F | F | T F | F | F | F | F T |
| F | F | T | T | T | T | T F | T | T | T | T F |
| F | F | T | F | T | T | T F | F | F | F | T F |
| F | F | F | T | F | F | T F | F | T | T | T F |
| F | F | F | F | F | F | T F | F | F | F | T F |

This truth-table tells us that the quantified sentence is true on some interpretations with one- or two-member U.D.'s and false on some interpretations with one- or two-member U.D.'s. We shall now explain why.

If each object in a U.D. is designated by either 'a' or 'b', then each of the combinations of truth-values to the left of the vertical line represents an interpretation of 'B' and 'F'. (This assumption means, of course, that we are restricting our attention to U.D.'s with at most two members, because the number of constants is not enough for naming more than two members.) For example, the first row represents interpretations with one- or two-member U.D.'s in which all objects are in the extension of 'B' and also are in the extension of 'F'. If all objects are named by either 'a' or 'b', then the assignment of **T** to both 'Ba' and 'Bb' means that all objects are in the extension of 'B', and the assignment of **T** to both 'Fa' and 'Fb' means that all objects are in the extension of 'F'. The second row represents interpretations with two-member U.D.'s in which both objects are in the extension of 'B' (because both 'Ba' and 'Bb' are true), one object is in the extension of 'F' (because 'Fa' is true), and one object is not in the extension of 'F' (because 'Fb' is false). Note that because one object is in the extension of 'F' and one is not, the U.D. for any interpretation represented by this row cannot have just one member —the single object in a one-member U.D. cannot both be in the extension of 'F' and not be in the extension of 'F'.

In fact, the sixteen rows between them represent all the combinations of extensions that the two predicates may have for a one- or two-member U.D. For example, we have the following possibilities for a one-member U.D.: The one object is in the extension of both 'B' and 'F' (row 1), the one object is in the extension of 'B' but not of 'F' (row 4), the one object is in the extension of 'F' but not of 'B' (row 13), or the one object is not in the extension of either predicate (row 16). For a two-member U.D. we have the following possibilities: Both members are in the extensions of both 'B' and 'F' (row 1), both members are in the extension of 'B' but only one is in the extension of 'F' (rows 2 and 3), both members are in the extension of 'B' but neither is in the extension of 'F' (row 4), and so on.

The truth-value assigned to the truth-functional expansion in each row is the truth-value that '(∀x)(Fx & ~ Bx)' will receive for the interpretations of 'B' and 'F' represented by that row. The expansion has the truth-value **F** in the first row, from which we may conclude that on every interpretation with a one- or two-member U.D. in which every member is in the extension of 'B' and also in the extension of 'F', '(∀x)(Fx & ~ Bx)' is false. The expansion also has the truth-value **F** in the second row, from which we may conclude that, on every interpretation with a two-member U.D. (remember, this row cannot represent interpretations with one-member U.D.'s) in which both members are in the extension of 'B' but only one member is in the extension of 'F', the sentence '(∀x)(Fx & ~ Bx)' is false.

The thirteenth row is the only one on which the expansion is true. From this we may conclude that every interpretation with a one- or two-member U.D. in which every member is in the extension of 'B' and no member is in the extension of 'F' will make '(∀x)(Fx & ~ Bx)' true, and that every other interpretation with a one- or two-member U.D. will make the sentence false.

We can use the information in the thirteenth row to construct an interpretation on which the unexpanded quantified sentence is true. Because neither 'a' nor 'b' appears in the quantified sentence, we need only specify a U.D. (we will choose one with two members rather than one), an interpretation of 'B' which holds for neither member of the U.D. (because 'Ba' and 'Bb' are both false), and an interpretation of 'F' which holds for both members of the U.D. (because 'Fa' and 'Fb' are both true). Here is a candidate:

32. U.D.: the set containing the numbers 3 and 5

    Bx: x is an even integer

    Fx: x is a positive integer

Both objects in the U.D. satisfy the condition of being positive and not even, so '(∀x)(Fx & ~ Bx)' is true on this interpretation.

We can use the information in the first row to construct an interpretation on which the sentence is false. We will choose a two-member U.D. again, and interpret 'B' and 'F' so that both members are in the extension of both predicates —because the four atomic sentences in that row are all true:

33. U.D.: the set containing Enrico Caruso and Paul Robeson
    Bx: x was a singer
    Fx: x was male

Any row in the truth-table in which 'Ba' has the same truth-value as 'Bb' and 'Fa' has the same truth-value as 'Fb' can be used to construct an interpretation with a one-member U.D. For example, using the first row, we can construct an interpretation on which our quantified sentence is false by making sure that the one object in the U.D. is in the extension of both 'B' and 'F':

34. U.D.: the set consisting of Enrico Caruso
    Bx: x was a singer
    Fx: x was a male

A truth-functional expansion of the sentence '(∃x)(∀y)Nyx' for the set of constants {'a', 'b'} is '(Naa & Nba) ∨ (Nab & Nbb)'. We may show that the sentence '(∃x)(∀y)Nyx' is true on at least one interpretation with a two-member U.D. by producing a shortened truth-table in which the expansion is true:

| Naa | Nab | Nba | Nbb | (Naa | & | Nba) | ↓<br>∨ | (Nab | & | Nbb) |
|---|---|---|---|---|---|---|---|---|---|---|
| T | T | F | T | T | F | F | T | T | T | T |

(The table in this case gives us information only about two-member U.D.'s, because if there were only one member in the U.D. then it would be named by both 'a' and 'b' and hence the four atomic sentences would have to have the same truth-value, since each would in that case make the same claim—that the one object stands in the relation N to itself.) We do not have to give an actual interpretation on which the sentence is true; the shortened truth-table suffices to show that there is such an interpretation. It shows that the quantified sentence is true on any interpretation with a two-member U.D. in which both members stand in the relation N to themselves and one stands in the relation N to the other, but not vice versa. And the following shortened truth-table shows that the quantified sentence is false on at least one interpretation with a one- or two-member U.D.:

| Naa | Nab | Nba | Nbb | (Naa | & | Nba) | ↓<br>∨ | (Nab | & | Nbb) |
|---|---|---|---|---|---|---|---|---|---|---|
| F | F | F | F | F | F | F | F | F | F | F |

(Because the four atomic sentences have the same truth-value in this table, the row of assignments may represent an interpretation with a one-member U.D.) From these two shortened truth-tables, we may conclude that '(∃x)(∀y)Nyx' is quantificationally indeterminate. The tables show that the sentence is true on at least one interpretation and false on at least one interpretation.

We may use truth-functional expansions and truth-tables to demonstrate that sentences of *PL* have, or fail to have, some other semantic properties as well. For example, to show that a sentence is not quantificationally true, we must show that the sentence is false on at least one interpretation. And we can show this by producing a shortened truth-table in which a truth-functional expansion of the sentence is false. We will have to choose a set of constants first, ideally a small set to save us work. An expansion of the sentence '(G & (∃z)Bz) ⊃ (∀x)Bx' for the set of constants {'a', 'b'} is '(G & (Ba ∨ Bb)) ⊃ (Ba & Bb)', and the expansion is false in the following shortened truth-table:

| Ba | Bb | G | (G | & | (Ba | ∨ | Bb)) | ↓ ⊃ | (Ba | & | Bb) |
|---|---|---|---|---|---|---|---|---|---|---|---|
| T | F | T | T | T | T | T | F | F | T | F | F |

The table shows that there is at least one interpretation on which the sentence '(G & (∃z)Bz) ⊃ (∀x)Bx)' is false. This sentence is therefore not quantificationally true.

Note that we cannot in general use truth-functional expansions to show that a sentence *is* quantificationally true. Even if we construct a full truth-table for a truth-functional expansion and find that the expansion is true in every row of the truth-table, all that we may generally conclude is that the sentence is true on every interpretation with a U.D. that is the same size as or smaller than the number of constants in the set that was used for the expansion. (An exception will be noted at the end of this section.)

The sentence '~(~Ga & (∃y)Gy)' is not quantificationally false. The truth-functional expansion of this sentence for the set of constants {'a'} ('a' must be in this set because it occurs in the sentence) is '~(~Ga & Ga)' and this expansion is true in the following shortened truth-table:

| Ga | ↓ ~ | (~Ga | & | Ga) |
|---|---|---|---|---|
| T | T | F T | F | T |

This shows that the sentence '~(~Ga & (∃y)(Gy)' is true on at least one interpretation and hence that the sentence is not quantificationally false. As with quantificational truth, we cannot in general use truth-functional expansions to show that a sentence is quantificationally false, for that would involve showing that the sentence is false on every interpretation, not just those with a particular size U.D.

The sentences

$(\forall x)(Fx \supset Ga)$

and

$(\forall x)Fx \supset Ga$

are not quantificationally equivalent. To show this, we shall expand both sentences for the same set of constants (which must include 'a') and produce a shortened truth-table in which the expansions have different truth-values. Expanding the sentences for the set {'a', 'b'}, we obtain

$(Fa \supset Ga) \& (Fb \supset Ga)$

and

$(Fa \& Fb) \supset Ga$

The first sentence is false and the second true in the following shortened truth-table:

| Fa | Fb | Ga | (Fa | ⊃ | Ga) | ↓ & | (Fb | ⊃ | Ga) | (Fa | & | Fb) | ↓ ⊃ | Ga |
|---|---|---|---|---|---|---|---|---|---|---|---|---|---|---|
| T | F | F | T | F | F | F | F | T | F | T | F | F | T | F |

This shows that there is at least one interpretation on which '$(\forall x)(Fx \supset Ga)$' is false and '$(\forall x)Fx \supset Ga$' is true.

The set of sentences

$\{(\forall x)Gax, \ \sim Gba \vee (\exists x) \sim Gax\}$

is quantificationally consistent. The truth-functional expansions of these sentences for the set {'a', 'b'} are 'Gaa & Gab' and '$\sim Gba \vee (\sim Gaa \vee \sim Gab)$'. Both expansions are true in the following shortened truth-table, and so we may conclude that there is at least one interpretation on which both members of the set are true:

| Gaa | Gab | Gba | Gaa | ↓ & | Gab | ~ Gba | ↓ ∨ | (~ Gaa | ∨ | ~ Gab) |
|---|---|---|---|---|---|---|---|---|---|---|
| T | T | F | T | T | T | T F | T | F T | F | F T |

The set of sentences

$\{\sim(\forall x)(Ga \equiv Fx), \ \sim Fb\}$

does not quantificationally entail the sentence

$(\forall x) \sim Gx$

We shall expand the sentences for the set of constants {'a', 'b'} to obtain

~ [(Ga ≡ Fa) & (Gb ≡ Fb)]

and

~ Fb

for the set members (' ~ Fb' expands to itself because it contains no quantifiers), and

~ Ga & ~ Gb

for the sentence '(∀x) ~ Gx'. Here is a shortened truth-table in which the expanded set members are true and the expansion of '(∀x) ~ Gx' is false:

| | | | | ↓ | | | | | | | | ↓ | | | | ↓ | | |
|---|---|---|---|---|---|---|---|---|---|---|---|---|---|---|---|---|---|---|
| Fa | Fb | Ga | Gb | ~ | [(Ga | ≡ | Fa) | & | (Gb | ≡ | Fb)] | ~ | Fb | ~ | Ga | & | ~ | Gb |
| F | F | F | T | T | F | T | F | F | T | F | F | T | F | T | F | F | F | T |

We thus know that there is at least one interpretation on which the set members are both true and '(∀x) ~ Gx' is false, so '(∀x) ~ Gx' is not quantificationally entailed by the set.

Finally, we may use truth-functional expansions to show that some arguments are not quantificationally valid. The expansions of the premises and conclusion of the argument

(∃x)[(∃y)Fy ⊃ Fx]
(∃y) ~ Fy
―――――――――
~ (∃x)Fx

for the set of constants {'a', 'b'} are

[(Fa ∨ Fb) ⊃ Fa] ∨ [(Fa ∨ Fb) ⊃ Fb]
~ Fa ∨ ~ Fb
―――――――――
~ (Fa ∨ Fb)

The premises of this expanded argument are true and the conclusion false in the following shortened truth-table:

| | | | | | | | ↓ | | | | | | | | ↓ | | | | | |
|---|---|---|---|---|---|---|---|---|---|---|---|---|---|---|---|---|---|---|---|---|
| Fa | Fb | [(Fa | ∨ | Fb) | ⊃ | Fa] | ∨ | [(Fa | ∨ | Fb) | ⊃ | Fb] | ~ | Fa | ∨ | ~ | Fb | ~ | (Fa | ∨ | Fb) |
| T | F | T | T | F | T | T | T | T | T | F | F | F | F | T | T | T | F | F | T | T | F |

There is thus an interpretation on which the premises of the original argument are true and the conclusion is false.

Note once again that truth-functional expansions cannot generally be used to show that a set of sentences of *PL* *is* quantificationally inconsistent, that a set of sentences *does* quantificationally entail some sentence, or that an argument of *PL is* quantificationally valid. In each of these cases we must prove something about every interpretation, not just those represented in the truth-table for a particular set of expansions.

However, there is an exception to our claims about the limitations of using truth-functional expansions to test for semantic properties. We noted at the end of Section 8.2 that there is a decision procedure (based on a result by Bernays and Schönfinkel) for determining the quantificational status of sentences of *PL* that contain no many-place predicates, that is, in which the predicates are all one-place predicates. A decision procedure will allow us to answer correctly in a finite number of mechanical steps the question 'Is this sentence quantificationally true?', and hence also questions like 'Is this sentence quantificationally false?' (it is if its negation is quantificationally true) and 'Is this finite set of sentences quantificationally consistent?' (it is if the conjunction of the sentences in the set is not quantificationally false). It will allow us to answer correctly these questions for sentences that do not contain many-place predicates.

Bernays and Schönfinkel's result is that a sentence that contains no many-place predicates and that contains $k$ distinct one-place predicates is quantificationally true if and only if the sentence is true on every interpretation with a U.D. containing exactly $2^k$ members. This being the case, we can truth-functionally expand the sentence for a set of at least $2^k$ constants, produce a truth-table for the expanded sentence, and determine whether it is quantificationally true by examining the truth-table. If the expanded sentence is true in every row of the truth-table, we may conclude that the sentence is true on every interpretation with a U.D. that is the same size as the set of constants or smaller. In particular, we may conclude that the sentence is true on every interpretation with a U.D. that contains exactly $2^k$ members. And, by Bernays and Schönfinkel's result, we may finally conclude that the sentence is quantificationally true.

## 8.5E EXERCISES

**1.** Give a truth-functional expansion of each of the sentences in Exercise 7 of Section 8.1E for a set containing one constant.

**2.** Give a truth-functional expansion of each of the sentences in Exercise 8 of Section 8.1E for a set containing two constants.

**3.** Give a truth-functional expansion of each of the sentences in Exercise 9 of Section 8.1E for a set containing two constants.

**4.** Give a truth-functional expansion of each of the following sentences for the set {'a', 'b', 'c'}.

a. (∀w)(Gw ⊃ Nww)
*b. (N ∨ (∃z)Bz)
c. (∃z)(N ≡ Bz)
*d. (∀w)Bw ∨ ~(∃w)Bw

5. Construct truth-functional expansions of the sentence

'((∃x)Fx & (∃y) ~ Fy) ⊃ (∀x) ~ Fx'

for the sets {'a'} and {'a', 'b'}. Construct a truth-table for each expansion. What information does the first truth-table give you about this sentence? What information does the second truth-table give you?

6. For each of the following sentences, construct a truth-functional expansion for the set of constants {'a', 'n'}. Show that the expansion is true on at least one truth-value assignment. Then use the information in the truth-table to construct an interpretation on which the original sentence is true.

a. (∀x)(Nxx ∨ (∃y)Nxy)
*b. (∃x)Fx ≡ (∀x)Fx
c. (∀y)Syyn

7. Show that each of the sentences in Exercise 1 of Section 8.2E is not quantificationally true by producing a shortened truth-table in which a truth-functional expansion of the sentence is false.

8. Show that each of the sentences in Exercise 2 of Section 8.2E is not quantificationally false by producing a shortened truth-table in which a truth-functional expansion of the sentence is true.

9. Show that each of the sentences in Exercise 3 of Section 8.2E is quantificationally indeterminate by producing a shortened truth-table in which a truth-functional expansion of the sentence is true and a shortened truth-table in which a truth-functional expansion of the sentence is false.

*10. In this section it was claimed that in general a sentence of *PL* that contains quantifiers cannot be shown to be quantificationally true by producing truth-tables for truth-functional expansions. Does the claim hold for sentences of *PL* that do not contain quantifiers, such as 'Fa ⊃ (Gb ⊃ Fa)'? Explain.

11. The truth-functional expansion of the sentence '(∃y)Gy & (∃y) ~ Gy' for the set {'a'} is 'Ga & ~ Ga'. The expanded sentence is quantificationally false. Explain this, and then explain why this does *not* show that the original sentence '(∃y)Gy & (∃y) ~ Gy' is quantificationally false.

12. Show that the sentences in each pair in Exercise 1 of Section 8.3E are not quantificationally equivalent by producing a shortened truth-table in which a truth-functional expansion of one sentence of the pair is true and a truth-functional expansion of the other sentence (for the same set of constants) is false.

13. Show that each set of sentences in Exercise 3 of Section 8.3E is quantificationally consistent by producing a shortened truth-table in which a truth-functional expansion of each sentence in the set (for the same set of constants) is true.

*14.a. Is the set {Ba, Bb, Bc, Bd, Be, Bf, Bg, ~ (∀x)Bx} quantificationally consistent? Explain.

b. For the set in exercise 14.a, what is the minimum size set of constants for which the sentences in the set must be expanded in order to show that the set is quantificationally consistent? Explain.

c. Can all the sentences in the set of exercise 14.a be true on an interpretation with a U.D. smaller than the set of constants indicated in the answer to exercise 14.b? Explain.

**15.** Show that each argument in Exercise 2 of Section 8.4E is quantificationally invalid by producing a shortened truth-table in which truth-functional expansions of the premises are true and a truth-functional expansion of the conclusion for the same set of constants is false.

## 8.6 SEMANTICS FOR PREDICATE LOGIC WITH IDENTITY

Interpretations for the language *PLI* are the same as interpretations for *PL*. The *identity* predicate, ' = ', is *not* explicitly given an interpretation. This is because we always want its extension to be the set of ordered pairs of members of the U.D. in which the first member is identical to the second, no matter what the U.D. is. The extension of the identity predicate is determined once the U.D. has been determined. If the U.D. is the set of positive integers, for example, then the extension of the identity predicate will include the pair whose first and second member are 1, the pair whose first and second member are 2, and so on for each positive integer—and no other pairs.

Every atomic sentence of the form $\boldsymbol{a} = \boldsymbol{a}$, where $\boldsymbol{a}$ is an arbitrary individual constant, will be true on every interpretation. This is because $\boldsymbol{a}$ will designate exactly one member of the U.D. on a given interpretation, and the identity predicate must include the pair consisting of that object and itself in its extension. On the other hand, the truth-value of an atomic sentence of the form $\boldsymbol{a} = \boldsymbol{b}$, where $\boldsymbol{a}$ and $\boldsymbol{b}$ are different individual constants, will depend on the interpretations of $\boldsymbol{a}$ and $\boldsymbol{b}$. Interpretation 35 makes the sentence 'g = k' true, while interpretation 36 makes the sentence false:

35. U.D.: set of U.S. presidents
    g: George Washington
    k: George Washington
36. U.D.: set of U.S. presidents
    g: George Washington
    k: Abraham Lincoln

The sentence '(∀x)(∀y)(~x = y ⊃ Gxy)' is true on interpretation 37 and false on interpretation 38:

37. U.D.: set of positive integers
    Gxy: the sum of x and y is positive
38. U.D.: set of positive integers
    Gxy: x is greater than y

On interpretation 37, the sentence may be read as 'The sum of any pair of nonidentical positive integers is a positive integer'—which is true. On interpretation 38, the sentence claims that for any pair of nonidentical positive integers, the first is greater than the second. This is false—1 and 2 are nonidentical positive integers, for example, but 1 is not greater than 2.

We may show that various sentences and sets of sentences in the language *PLI* have, or fail to have, semantic properties much as we did for *PL*. We will give a few examples for the semantic properties of quantificational truth and quantificational validity. We may show that the sentence

$$(\forall x)(\forall y)({\sim}\, x = y \lor (Fx \supset Fy))$$

is quantificationally true by reasoning generally about interpretations, showing that on every interpretation the sentence will turn out to be true. The sentence is universally quantified, and is true on an interpretation just in case for every pair x and y of members of the U.D., either they satisfy the condition specified by '$\sim x = y$' or they satisfy the condition specified by '$Fx \supset Fy$'. So let us consider two members x and y of an arbitrary U.D. If x and y are not the same member, then the first disjunct '$\sim x = y$' is satisfied, because the extension of the identity predicate includes only pairs in which the first and second member are the same. If, on the other hand, x and y *are* the same member of the U.D. (and hence will not satisfy the first disjunct), they will satisfy the second disjunct. If x is in the extension of 'F', then so is y—because y is identical to x, and so x and y will satisfy the condition '$Fx \supset Fy$'. Because x and y either are or are not the same member of the U.D., we have shown that each pair of members of any U.D. will satisfy the condition '$\sim x = y \lor (Fx \supset Fy)$', no matter what the interpretation of 'F' may be. Therefore the sentence '$(\forall x)(\forall y)({\sim}\, x = y \lor (Fx \supset Fy))$' must be true on any interpretation; it is quantificationally true.

On the other hand, the sentence

$$(\forall x)(\forall y)(x = y \lor (Fx \supset Fy))$$

is not quantificationally true. To show this, we construct an interpretation on which the sentence is false. The sentence claims that every pair of members of the U.D. x and y satisfies '$x = y \lor (Fx \supset Fy)$', that is, that either x and y are the same member or if x is F then so is y. If we choose a two-member U.D., then a pair consisting of the two members will not satisfy the condition '$x = y$'. If the first member is F but the other is not, then this pair also will not satisfy '$Fx \supset Fy$'. Here is our interpretation:

39. U.D.: set consisting of Margaret Thatcher and Jimmy Carter
    Fx: x is a former U.S. President

The pair consisting of Jimmy Carter and Margaret Thatcher does not satisfy '$x = y \lor (Fx \supset Fy)$'. The two people are not identical, and it is not true that if Jimmy Carter is a former U.S. President (which he is) then Margaret Thatcher is a former U.S. President (she is not).

The argument

$(\forall x)(Fx \equiv Gx)$
$(\forall x)(\forall y)x = y$
Ga
―――――――――
$(\forall x)Fx$

is quantificationally valid. We shall show that any interpretation that makes the three premises true will also make '$(\forall x)Fx$' true. If '$(\forall x)(Fx \equiv Gx)$' is true, then every member of the U.D. that is F is also G, and every member of the U.D. that is G is also F. If '$(\forall x)(\forall y)x = y$' is also true, then there is exactly one object in the U.D. The sentence says that for any object x and any object y, x and y are identical —and this cannot be the case if there is more than one member of the U.D. If 'Ga' is also true then, because there is exactly one object in the U.D., this object must be designated by 'a' and must therefore be in the extension of 'G'. It follows, from the truth of the first sentence, that this object is also in the extension of 'F'. Therefore it follows that '$(\forall x)Fx$' is true—every object in our single-member U.D. is F.

On the other hand, the argument

$(\forall x)(\exists y)x = y$
―――――――――
$a = b$

is not quantificationally valid. The premise, it turns out, is quantificationally true —every member of any U.D. is identical to something (namely, itself). But the conclusion will be false on any interpretation on which 'a' and 'b' designate different objects, such as the following:

40. U.D.: set of positive integers
 a: 6
 b: 7

It is true that every positive integer is identical to some positive integer, but it is false that 6 is identical to 7.

Readers who have worked through the section on truth-functional expansions may wonder whether sentences containing the identity predicate may be expanded and truth-tables used to check for various semantic properties. The answer is yes, although we shall see that there is a complication. Sentences that contain the identity predicate are expanded in the same way as sentences without the identity predicate: Quantifiers are eliminated in favor of iterated conjunctions or disjunctions. The sentence '$(\forall x)(\exists y)x = y$' can be expanded for the set of constants {'a', 'b'} first to obtain

$(\exists y)a = y \;\&\; (\exists y)b = y$

and then to obtain

$$(a = a \lor a = b) \ \& \ (b = a \lor b = b)$$

But if we freely assign truth-values to the atomic components of this sentence, we end up with the truth-table:

| a = a | a = b | b = a | b = b | (a = a | ∨ | a = b) | ↓ & | (b = a | ∨ | b = b) |
|---|---|---|---|---|---|---|---|---|---|---|
| T | T | T | T | T | T | T | T | T | T | T |
| T | T | T | F | T | T | T | T | T | T | F |
| T | T | F | T | T | T | T | T | F | T | T |
| T | T | F | F | T | T | T | F | F | F | F |
| T | F | T | T | T | T | F | T | T | T | T |
| T | F | T | F | T | T | F | T | T | T | F |
| T | F | F | T | T | T | F | T | F | T | T |
| T | F | F | F | T | T | F | F | F | F | F |
| F | T | T | T | F | T | T | T | T | T | T |
| F | T | T | F | F | T | T | T | T | T | F |
| F | T | F | T | F | T | T | T | F | T | T |
| F | T | F | F | F | T | T | F | F | F | F |
| F | F | T | T | F | F | F | F | T | T | T |
| F | F | T | F | F | F | F | F | T | T | F |
| F | F | F | T | F | F | F | F | F | T | T |
| F | F | F | F | F | F | F | F | F | F | F |

There is something wrong with this truth-table! The sentence '$(\forall x)(\exists y)x = y$' is quantificationally true, and yet we have assigned its expansion the truth-value **F** in seven rows. Let us look at the first row where this happened: row 4. In this row, we have assigned **T** to 'a = b' and **F** to 'b = a', and that is the problem. If an interpretation makes 'a = b' true then it must make 'b = a' true as well; a and b are the same object. So row 4 does not correspond to any interpretation at all. By the same reasoning, we find that none of rows 3–6 or 11–14 correspond to interpretations, for each of these rows assigns different truth-values to 'a = b' and 'b = a'. However, this still leaves us with problematic rows 8, 15, and 16—all of which make the expanded sentence false. The problem with each of these rows is that the truth-value **F** has been assigned to one or both of 'a = a' and 'b = b'—thus claiming that some object is not the same as itself. Because every interpretation makes every sentence of the form a = a true, rows 8, 15, and 16, as well as all other rows which make one or both of 'a = a' and 'b = b' false, do not correspond to interpretations. In fact, we have just ruled out all rows in the truth-table except rows 1 and 7. These are the only rows in which 'a = a' and 'b = b' are both true and in which 'a = b' and 'b = a' have the same truth-value—and, as we should have expected for a quantificationally true sentence, the expanded sentence is true in both rows.

The rows of a truth-table that do not correspond to any interpretation cannot be used to establish semantic properties of the sentence that has been expanded. We therefore require that each row in the truth-table that we construct for an expansion of a sentence containing the identity predicate must meet two conditions:

1. Every sentence of the form $\boldsymbol{a} = \boldsymbol{a}$ has the truth-value **T**.

2. If a sentence of the form $\boldsymbol{a} = \boldsymbol{b}$ has the truth-value **T**, then for each atomic sentence $\mathscr{P}$ that contains $\boldsymbol{a}$, every atomic sentence $\mathscr{P}(\boldsymbol{a}//\boldsymbol{b})$ that results from replacing one or more occurrences of $\boldsymbol{a}$ in $\mathscr{P}$ with $\boldsymbol{b}$ must have the same truth-value as $\mathscr{P}$.

If conditions 1 and 2 are met, then if a sentence containing $\boldsymbol{a} = \boldsymbol{b}$ has the truth-value **T** in a row, $\boldsymbol{b} = \boldsymbol{a}$ will also have the truth-value **T**. Condition 1 requires that $\boldsymbol{a} = \boldsymbol{a}$ have the truth-value **T**, and, because $\boldsymbol{b} = \boldsymbol{a}$ can be obtained from $\boldsymbol{a} = \boldsymbol{a}$ by replacing the first occurrence of $\boldsymbol{a}$ with $\boldsymbol{b}$, condition 2 requires that $\boldsymbol{b} = \boldsymbol{a}$ is true since $\boldsymbol{a} = \boldsymbol{b}$ and $\boldsymbol{a} = \boldsymbol{a}$ are. Condition 2 will also rule out rows like the one in the following shortened truth-table for the expansion

[(a = a ⊃ (Fa ⊃ Fa)) & (a = b ⊃ (Fa ⊃ Fb))]
& [(b = a ⊃ (Fb ⊃ Fa)) & (b = b ⊃ (Fb ⊃ Fb))]

of the sentence

(∀x)(∀y)(x = y ⊃ (Fx ⊃ Fy)

for the set of constants {'a', 'b'}:

| a = a | a = b | b = a | b = b | Fa | Fb | [(a = a | ⊃ | (Fa | ⊃ | Fa)) | & | (a = b | ⊃ | (Fa | ⊃ | Fb))] |
|---|---|---|---|---|---|---|---|---|---|---|---|---|---|---|---|---|
| T | T | T | T | T | F | T | T | T | T | T | F | T | F | T | F | F |

↓

| & | [(b = a | ⊃ | (Fb | ⊃ | Fa)) | & | (b = b | ⊃ | (Fb | ⊃ | Fb))] |
|---|---|---|---|---|---|---|---|---|---|---|---|
| F | T | T | F | T | T | T | T | T | F | T | F |

Once again, we have expanded a quantificationally true sentence and produced a row of a truth-table in which the truth-functional expansion is false. We have ensured that both sentences 'a = a' and 'b = b' are true, and that 'a = b' and 'b = a' have the same truth-value. The problem is that we have assigned 'Fa' and 'Fb' different truth-values, although 'a = b' is true. Condition 2 rules out this combination: 'Fb' results from replacing 'a' in 'Fa' with 'b' and so, because 'a = b' is true, 'Fb' must have the same truth-value as 'Fa'. Our second condition reflects the fact that when the identity predicate occurs in a truth-functional expansion, the atomic sentences that are components of the expansion may not be truth-functionally independent. Once a sentence of the form $a = b$, where $a$ and $b$ are different constants, has been made true, certain other atomic sentences must agree in truth-value.

The following truth-table shows the only combinations of truth-values for the atomic components of our sentence that correspond to interpretations with one- or two-member U.D.'s:

| a = a | a = b | b = a | b = b | Fa | Fb | [(a = a | ⊃ | (Fa | ⊃ | Fa)) | & | (a = b | ⊃ | (Fa | ⊃ | Fb))] |
|---|---|---|---|---|---|---|---|---|---|---|---|---|---|---|---|---|
| T | T | T | T | T | T | T | T | T | T | T | T | T | T | T | T | T |
| T | T | T | T | F | F | T | T | F | T | F | T | T | T | F | T | F |
| T | F | F | T | T | T | T | T | T | T | T | T | F | T | T | T | T |
| T | F | F | T | T | F | T | F | T | T | T | T | F | T | T | F | F |
| T | F | F | T | F | T | T | T | F | T | F | T | F | T | F | T | T |
| T | F | F | T | F | F | T | T | F | T | F | T | F | T | F | T | F |

↓

| & | [(b = a | ⊃ | (Fb | ⊃ | Fa)) | & | (b = b | ⊃ | (Fb | ⊃ | Fb))] |
|---|---|---|---|---|---|---|---|---|---|---|---|
| T | T | T | T | T | T | T | T | T | T | T | T |
| T | T | T | F | T | F | T | T | T | F | T | F |
| T | F | T | T | T | T | T | T | T | T | T | T |
| T | F | T | F | T | T | T | T | T | F | T | F |
| T | F | T | T | F | F | T | T | T | T | T | T |
| T | F | T | F | T | F | T | T | T | F | T | F |

All other rows are excluded by one or both of our conditions. And again, we find that the expanded sentence is true in all six rows—we have shown that there are no interpretations with one- or two-member U.D.'s on which the sentence is false.

Adhering to our two conditions, we now produce a shortened truth-table that shows that the sentence

$$(\forall z)((Fz \ \& \ (\exists y)z = y) \supset (\forall x)Fx)$$

is not quantificationally true. The sentence claims that for each member of the U.D., if it is F and is identical to something, then everything is F. Certainly the sentence will be true if the U.D. contains exactly one object—but for larger U.D.'s it will be true only if either no member is F or all members are. We will expand the sentence for the set of constants {'a', 'b'}, and produce a shortened truth-table in which the expansion is false:

| a = a | a = b | b = a | b = b | Fa | Fb | [(Fa | & | (a = a | ∨ | a = b)) | ⊃ | (Fa | & | Fb)] |
|---|---|---|---|---|---|---|---|---|---|---|---|---|---|---|
| T | F | F | T | T | F | T | T | T | T | F | F | T | F | F |

↓

| & | [(Fb | & | (b = a | ∨ | b = b)) | ⊃ | (Fa | & | Fb)] |
|---|---|---|---|---|---|---|---|---|---|
| F | F | F | F | T | T | T | T | F | F |

Condition 1 has been met—both 'a = a' and 'b = b' are true. Condition 2 has also been met, trivially. The two identity statements that are true are 'a = a' and 'b = b', and the result of substituting 'a' for 'a' in any sentence is just that sentence itself and the same holds for 'b'. Here is an interpretation that has been constructed using the truth-values in the truth-table as a guide:

41. U.D.: the set {2, 3}
 Fx: x is even

We have chosen a U.D. with two members because the identity statements 'a = b' and 'b = a' are false in the shortened table, and so 'a' and 'b' must designate different objects. We have interpreted 'F' so that one member of the U.D., but not the other, is in its extension.

## 8.6E EXERCISES

**1.** Determine the truth-values of the following sentences on the interpretation:

U.D.: set of positive integers
Ex: x is even
Gxy: x is greater than y
Ox: x is odd
Pxyz: x plus y equals z

a. $(\exists x)(\forall y)(x = y \supset Gxy)$
*b. $(\forall x)(\forall y) \sim x = y$
c. $(\forall x)(\exists y)Oy \supset Gyx)$
*d. $(\forall x)(\forall y)(\forall z)[(Gxy \ \& \ Gyz) \supset \sim x = z]$
e. $(\exists w)[Ew \ \& \ (\forall y)(Oy \supset \sim w = y)]$
*f. $(\forall y)(\forall z)[(Oy \ \& \ y = z) \supset \sim Ez)]$
g. $(\exists z)(\exists w)(z = w \ \& \ Gzw)$
*h. $(\forall x)(\forall y)(\exists z)[(Pxyz \ \& \ \sim x = z) \ \& \ \sim y = z]$
i. $(\forall x)(\forall y)(Pxyy \lor \sim x = y)$

**2.** Show that each of the following sentences is not quantificationally true by producing an interpretation on which it is false:
a. $(\exists x)(\forall y)x = y$
*b. $(\forall w)(w = b \supset Fw)$
c. $(\forall x)(\forall y)(\forall z)[(x = y \lor y = z) \lor x = z]$
*d. $(\exists w)[Gw \ \& \ (\forall z)(\sim Hzw \supset z = w)]$
e. $(\exists x)(\exists y)(\sim x = y \lor Gxy)$
*f. $(\forall x)(\forall y)(\exists z)(x = y \supset \sim x = z)$

**3.** Each of the following sentences is quantificationally true. Explain why.
a. $(\forall x)(\forall y)(\forall z)[(x = y \ \& \ y = z) \supset x = z]$
*b. $(\forall z)(\forall y)(\exists z)(x = z \lor y = z)$
c. $(\forall x)(\forall y)[x = y \supset (Gxy \equiv Gyx)]$

**4.** Show that the sentences in each of the following pairs are not quantificationally equivalent by constructing an interpretation on which one sentence is true and the other is false.

a. $(\forall x)(\exists y)x = y$, $(\forall x)(\forall y)x = y$

*b. $(\forall x)(\forall y)[x = y \supset (Fx \equiv Fy)]$, $(\forall x)(\forall y)[(Fx \equiv Fy) \supset x = y]$

c. $(a = b \vee a = c) \supset a = d$, $a = c \supset (a = b \vee a = d)$

*d. $(\exists x)(\forall y)({\sim} x = y \supset Gy)$, $(\exists x)(\forall y)(Gy \supset {\sim} x = y)$

**5.** Show that each of the following sets of sentences is quantificationally consistent by constructing an interpretation on which each sentence in the set is true.

a. $\{a = b,\ a = c,\ {\sim} a = d\}$

*b. $\{(\forall x)(\forall y)x = y,\ (\exists x)Fx,\ (\forall y)Gy\}$

c. $\{(\exists x)(\exists z) {\sim} x = z,\ (\forall x)(\exists z)(\exists w)(x = z \vee x = w)\}$

*d. $\{(\forall x)(Gx \supset (\forall y)({\sim} y = x \supset Gy)),\ (\forall x)(Hx \supset Gx),\ (\exists z)Hz\}$

**6.** Establish each of the following by producing an interpretation on which the set members are true and the sentence after the double turnstile is false.

a. $\{(\forall x)(\forall y)(\forall z)[(x = y \vee x = z) \vee y = z]\} \nvDash (\forall x)(\forall y)(x = y)$

*b. $\{(\exists w)(\exists z) {\sim} w = z,\ (\exists w)Hw\} \nvDash (\exists w) {\sim} Hw$

c. $\{(\exists w)(\forall y)Gwy,\ (\exists w)(\forall y)({\sim} w = y \supset {\sim} Gwy)\} \nvDash (\exists z) {\sim} Gzz$

*d. $\{(\forall x)(\forall y)[(Fx \equiv Fy) \equiv x = y],\ (\exists z)Fz\} \nvDash (\exists x)(\exists y)[{\sim} x = y \ \&\ (Fx \ \&\ {\sim} Fy)]$

**7.** Using the given symbolization key, symbolize each of the following arguments in *PLI*. Then, for each symbolized argument, decide whether it is quantificationally valid and defend your answer.

U.D.: set of all people
Fx: x is female
Mx: x is male
Lxy: x loves y
Pxy: x is a parent of y

a. Every male loves someone other than himself, and every male loves his children. Therefore no male is his own parent.

*b. Everyone loves her or his parents, and everyone has two parents. Therefore everyone loves at least two people.

c. A female who loves her children loves herself as well. Therefore every female loves at least two people.

*d. Everybody has exactly two parents. Therefore everybody has exactly four grandparents.

e. Nobody has three parents. Everybody has more than one parent. Therefore everybody has two parents.

**8.** Use truth-functional expansions to establish each of the following claims. Be sure that the truth-value assignments you produce meet the two conditions discussed in this section.

a. The sentence '$(\exists x)(\exists y) {\sim} x = y$' is quantificationally indeterminate.

*b. The sentence '$(\forall w)(Fw \supset (\exists y) {\sim} y = w)\ \&\ (\exists w)Fw$' is quantificationally indeterminate.

c. The sentences '$(\forall y)(\forall z)[(Gyz \vee Gzy) \vee y = z]$' and '$(\forall y)(\exists z)Gyz$' are not quantificationally equivalent.

*d. The set of sentences $\{(\forall y)(\forall z)[(Gxy \vee Gyz) \vee x = z], (\forall y)(\exists z)Gyz\}$ is quantificationally consistent.

e. The set of sentences $\{(\forall y)y = y, (\exists z)(\exists w) \sim w = z\}$ does not quantificationally entail the sentence '$(\exists z)(\forall w) \sim z = w$'.

*f. The argument

$(\forall y)(\forall z)(Gyz \supset y = z)$

---

$(\forall y)(\forall z)(y = z \supset Gyz)$

is quantificationally invalid.

## 8.7 FORMAL SEMANTICS OF *PL* AND *PLI*

The semantics for *PL* and *PLI* used so far in this chapter have been informal, in the sense that strict definitions of truth on an interpretation and falsehood on an interpretation have not been specified. For example, we explained the truth-conditions for quantified sentences by saying that all or some of the members of the U.D. in question must satisfy the condition specified by that part of the sentence following the quantifier. But we have not as yet given a formalized account of how we determine what that condition is or how we determine whether it is satisfied as required. In this section we specify the formal semantics for *PL* and then for *PLI*.

To do so, we first need to regiment the definition of an interpretation. Every interpretation must have a nonempty set as its U.D. Interpreting an individual constant consists in the assignment of a member of the U.D. to that constant, and interpreting a sentence letter consists in the assignment of a truth-value to that sentence letter.

In the first section of this chapter we pointed out that when we give an English reading for an *n*-place predicate of *PL*, that reading determines the *extension* of the predicate. The extension of an *n*-place predicate is a set of *n-tuples* of members of the U.D. that are picked out by the predicate. An *n*-tuple is an ordered set containing *n* members—it is ordered in the sense that one member is designated as the first, one as the second, and so on. A 2-tuple is an ordered pair, a 3-tuple is an ordered triple, a 4-tuple is an ordered quadruple, and so on.

For instance, if we take the set of positive integers as our U.D. and interpret 'Gxy' as 'x is greater than y' then the *extension* of 'G' is the set of ordered pairs (2-tuples) of positive integers such that the first member of each pair is greater than the second. A sentence containing the predicate 'G'—say, the sentence 'Gab'—will then be true just in case the ordered pair of positive integers whose first member is designated by 'a' and whose second member is designated by 'b' is a member of the extension of 'G'. It is possible to give 'G' a different English reading which determines the same extension; for example, we might interpret 'Gxy' to mean 'x plus 1 is greater than y plus 1'. Since for any numbers x and y, x plus 1 is greater than y plus 1 just in case x is greater than y, it follows that the extension of

'G' for these two English readings of the predicate is the same. And, since the extension is the same in each case, the truth-conditions of 'Gab' for the latter interpretation of 'G' coincide with the truth-conditions of 'Gab' for the former interpretation. It is thus the *extension* of the predicate, not the particular English reading we use to specify the extension, that is important for determining the truth-conditions of any sentence in which the predicate occurs. So, in our formal account, we take the interpretation of a predicate of *PL* to be the set that is the extension of that predicate.[3]

An interpretation of an *n*-place predicate in a U.D. will thus consist in the assignment of a set of *n*-tuples (ordered sets containing *n* members) of members of the U.D. to that predicate. In the U.D. that consists of all people, years, and cities, we may wish to interpret the four-place predicate 'D' so that 'Dwxyz' reads 'w marries x in the year y in the city z'. We would then have the interpretation assign to 'D' the set of 4-tuples of members of the U.D. such that the first two members are people who marry each other, the third member is the year in which they marry, and the fourth member is the city in which they marry. If John Doe and Jane Doe marry in 1975 in Kansas City, then one of the 4-tuples that the interpretation assigns to 'D' is

⟨John Doe, Jane Doe, 1975, Kansas City⟩

(the *n*-tuple whose first, second, third, and fourth members, respectively, are John Doe, Jane Doe, 1975, Kansas City.)

Note that we designate an *n*-tuple by listing names of the members of the *n*-tuple, in the order in which the members occur in the *n*-tuple, between the angle brackets '⟨' and '⟩'. Thus we may designate the 3-tuple whose first member is the number 1, whose second member is Arthur Conan Doyle, and whose third member is Yankee Stadium as

⟨1, Arthur Conan Doyle, Yankee Stadium⟩

and the 5-tuple all of whose members are the fraction $\frac{1}{2}$ as

$$\left\langle \tfrac{1}{2}, \tfrac{1}{2}, \tfrac{1}{2}, \tfrac{1}{2}, \tfrac{1}{2} \right\rangle$$

A special case of the interpretation of predicates deserves attention here. The interpretation of a one-place predicate will assign to that predicate a set of 1-tuples of members of the U.D. A 1-tuple is an ordered set containing exactly one member. It might seem more natural simply to assign to a one-place predicate a set of members of the U.D.—namely those members we want the predicate to pick out. But, for the sake of generality in our definition of truth on an interpretation, it is convenient to assign to a one-place predicate a set of 1-tuples of members of the

[3] And when we assign an extension, which is simply a set, to a predicate we need not have any natural English reading in mind. It is important to realize this, for when we say, for example, that a quantificationally true sentence is true on *every* interpretation, we include those interpretations that have no obvious English language renderings.

U.D. We may designate the 1-tuple of John Doe by

⟨John Doe⟩

We may now formally define the concept of an interpretation:

An *interpretation* for *PL* consists in the specification of a U.D. and the assignment of a truth-value to each sentence letter of *PL*, a member of the U.D. to each individual constant of *PL*, and a set of *n*-tuples of members of the U.D. to each *n*-place predicate of *PL*.

The next concept we need is that of a variable assignment. This concept will play an important role in the specification of truth-conditions for the sentences of *PL*, and the idea is this. We are going to explain the truth-conditions of sentences like '(∀x)(Fx ∨ Gx)' in terms of the semantics of their subformulas. But 'Fx ∨ Gx' is an open sentence, and for us open sentences are neither true nor false—because free variables are not names. We have noted several times that variables function as pronouns do. Here we exploit that feature of variables in order to determine the truth-conditions of quantified sentences. That is, we determine the truth-conditions of quantified sentences by exploring whether the things to which a variable in its role as pronoun can refer satisfy the condition specified by the formula in which the variable occurs. Our concept of variable assignments will be used to regiment the informal notion of satisfaction that we have used throughout this chapter.

A *variable assignment for an interpretation* **I** assigns to each individual variable of *PL* a member of the U.D. Intuitively, a variable assignment captures one way in which the variables of *PL*, in their role as pronouns, can refer to objects in the U.D. If an interpretation has a one-member U.D., there is exactly one variable assignment for that interpretation, the variable assignment that assigns the one member of the U.D. to each individual variable of *PL*. If an interpretation has more than one member in its U.D., there will be infinitely many different variable assignments. For a two-member U.D. consisting of the integers 1 and 2, for example, there is a variable assignment that assigns the integer 1 to every individual variable and there is a variable assignment that assigns the integer 2 to every individual variable, and there are infinitely many variable assignments that will assign the integer 1 to only some of the individual variables and the integer 2 to the remaining variables (there are infinitely many ways of choosing which of the infinite number of variables of *PL* will designate 1 and which will designate 2). Note that it is not required that distinct variables be assigned different members of the U.D.; some variable assignments will assign the same member to two or more variables—in fact, every variable assignment for an interpretation with a finite U.D. must do so. Nor is it required that every member of the U.D. be assigned to a variable; some variable assignments will leave some members unnamed.

We will use the letter '**d**' to range over variable assignments (think of '**d**' as shorthand for 'designates'). If **d** is a variable assignment and $\mathbf{x}$ is an individual variable of *PL*, then $\mathbf{d}(\mathbf{x})$ designates the member of the U.D. that **d** assigns to $\mathbf{x}$. So $\mathbf{d}(\mathbf{x})$ is 2 just in case **d** assigns 2 to $\mathbf{x}$. We need some additional notation that will be used in regimenting our informal notion of satisfaction. If **d** is a variable assignment for an interpretation, **u** is a member of the interpretation's U.D., and $x$ is an individual variable of *PL*, then $\mathbf{d}[\mathbf{u}/x]$ is a variable assignment that assigns the same value to each variable as does **d** *except that* it assigns **u** to $x$. $\mathbf{d}[\mathbf{u}/x]$ is called a *variant* of the assignment **d**. More generally, if **d** is a variable assignment for an interpretation, $\mathbf{u}_1, \mathbf{u}_2, \ldots, \mathbf{u}_n$ are (not necessarily distinct) members of the interpretation's U.D., and $x_1, x_2, \ldots, x_n$ are (not necessarily distinct) individual variables of *PL*, then $\mathbf{d}[\mathbf{u}_1/x_1, \mathbf{u}_2/x_2, \ldots, \mathbf{u}_n/x_n]$ is shorthand for the variable assignment $\mathbf{d}[\mathbf{u}_1/x_1][\mathbf{u}_2/x_2]\ldots[\mathbf{u}_n/x_n]$—the variable assignment that starts out like **d**, and results from successive stipulations that $\mathbf{u}_1$ will be assigned to $x_1$, $\mathbf{u}_2$ to $x_2, \ldots,$ and $\mathbf{u}_n$ to $x_n$.

As an example, let us assume that an interpretation has the set of positive integers as its U.D. and that the variable assignment **d** assigns 1 to every individual variable of *PL*. Then **d**[5/'x', 8/'z'] is the variable assignment that assigns 5 to 'x' and 8 to 'z' and that assigns 1 to all other individual variables of *PL*. It assigns 1 to all other individual variables because aside from the assignments it makes to 'x' and 'z', our definition requires that **d**[5/'x', 8/'z'] assign the same values to variables as does **d**. Note that **d**[1/'x', 1/'y'] is the same variable assignment as **d**, because the values that we specified for the variables 'x' and 'y' are the same values that **d** assigns to them. Also note that if a variable occurs more than once between the square brackets, then the value it receives on $\mathbf{d}[\mathbf{u}_1/x_1, \mathbf{u}_2/x_2, \ldots, \mathbf{u}_n/x_n]$ is the last value that appears for the variable in that list. For example, where **d** is as above, **d**[1/'x', 2/'y', 3/'x'] assigns 3, not 1, to 'x'. For notational convenience, we shall drop the single quotes around names of individual variables when they appear between the square brackets; **d**[5/'x', 8/'z'] may be written as **d**[5/x, 8/z].

Truth and falsehood of sentences on an interpretation are not defined directly; rather, they are defined in terms of *satisfaction* by variable assignments. We shall first define the concept of satisfaction, then define truth and falsehood, and afterward illustrate through examples the role of the intermediate step. Here, as in Chapter Seven, we use '$\mathcal{P}$', '$\mathcal{Q}$', and '$\mathcal{R}$' as metavariables ranging over formulas of *PL*, '$\mathcal{A}$' as a metavariable ranging over predicates of *PL*, '$t$' with or without subscripts as a metavariable ranging over individual terms (individual constants and individual variables of *PL*), and '$x$' as a metavariable ranging over individual variables of *PL*. We shall use $\mathbf{I}(\mathcal{X})$ to mean the value that the interpretation **I** assigns to the symbol $\mathcal{X}$.

Let **I** be an interpretation, **d** a variable assignment for **I**, and $\mathcal{P}$ a formula of *PL*. Then

1. If $\mathcal{P}$ is a sentence letter, then **d** satisfies $\mathcal{P}$ on interpretation **I** if and only if $\mathbf{I}(\mathcal{P}) = \mathbf{T}$.

Note that the values that **d** assigns to variables play no role in this case.

2. If $\mathcal{P}$ is an atomic formula of the form $\mathcal{A}t_1 \ldots t_n$ (where $\mathcal{A}$ is an $n$-place predicate), then **d** satisfies $\mathcal{P}$ on interpretation **I** if and only if

$\langle \mathbf{u}_1, \mathbf{u}_2, \ldots, \mathbf{u}_n \rangle$ is a member of $\mathbf{I}(\mathscr{A})$, where $\mathbf{u}_i$ is $\mathbf{I}(t_i)$ if $t_i$ is an constant and $\mathbf{u}_i$ is $\mathbf{d}(t_i)$ if $t_i$ is a variable.

So **d** satisfies 'Gxa', for example, if ⟨**d**('x'), **I**('a')⟩—the 2-tuple whose first member is the object that **d** assigns to the variable 'x' and whose second member is the object that **I** assigns to the constant 'a'—is a member of the extension that **I** assigns to 'G'.

3. If $\mathscr{P}$ is of the form $\sim \mathscr{Q}$, then **d** satisfies $\mathscr{P}$ on interpretation **I** if and only if **d** does not satisfy $\mathscr{Q}$ on interpretation **I**.

4. If $\mathscr{P}$ is of the form $\mathscr{Q}$ & $\mathscr{R}$, then **d** satisfies $\mathscr{P}$ on interpretation **I** if and only if **d** satisfies $\mathscr{Q}$ on interpretation **I** and **d** satisfies $\mathscr{R}$ on interpretation **I**.

5. If $\mathscr{P}$ is of the form $\mathscr{Q} \vee \mathscr{R}$, then **d** satisfies $\mathscr{P}$ on interpretation **I** if and only if either **d** satisfies $\mathscr{Q}$ on interpretation **I** or **d** satisfies $\mathscr{R}$ on interpretation **I**.

6. If $\mathscr{P}$ is of the form $\mathscr{Q} \supset \mathscr{R}$, then **d** satisfies $\mathscr{P}$ on interpretation **I** if and only if either **d** does not satisfy $\mathscr{Q}$ on interpretation **I** or **d** satisfies $\mathscr{R}$ on interpretation **I**.

7. If $\mathscr{P}$ is of the form $\mathscr{Q} \equiv \mathscr{R}$, then **d** satisfies $\mathscr{P}$ on interpretation **I** if and only if either **d** satisfies $\mathscr{Q}$ on interpretation **I** and **d** satisfies $\mathscr{R}$ on interpretation **I**, or **d** does not satisfy $\mathscr{Q}$ on interpretation **I** and **d** does not satisfy $\mathscr{R}$ on interpretation **I**.

8. If $\mathscr{P}$ is of the form $(\forall x)\mathscr{Q}$, then **d** satisfies $\mathscr{P}$ on interpretation **I** if and only if for every member **u** of the U.D., $\mathbf{d}[\mathbf{u}/x]$ satisfies $\mathscr{Q}$ on interpretation **I**.

9. If $\mathscr{P}$ is of the form $(\exists x)\mathscr{Q}$, then **d** satisfies $\mathscr{P}$ on interpretation **I** if and only if there is at least one member **u** of the U.D. such that $\mathbf{d}[\mathbf{u}/x]$ satisfies $\mathscr{Q}$ on interpretation **I**.

Finally, the definitions of truth and falsehood are:

> A sentence $\mathscr{P}$ of *PL* is *true on an interpretation* **I** if and only if every variable assignment **d** (for **I**) satisfies $\mathscr{P}$ on **I**.
>
> A sentence $\mathscr{P}$ of *PL* is *false on an interpretation* **I** if and only if no variable assignment **d** (for **I**) satisfies $\mathscr{P}$ on **I**.

In Chapter Eleven we shall prove that for each sentence $\mathscr{P}$ and interpretation **I**, either all variable assignments for **I** will satisfy $\mathscr{P}$ or none will. (This is not generally true for *open* formulas.) This being the case, each sentence will be true or false on any interpretation according to our definitions.

Our definitions have been long, so we shall look at some examples. Consider the sentence

$$(\forall y)(By \supset \sim (\exists z)Dyz)$$

and an interpretation that makes the following assignments:

42. U.D.: set of positive integers
  Bx: x is prime
  Dxy: x is greater than y

The interpretation must assign values to all other predicates, individual constants, and sentence letters of *PL* as well, but as we shall see only the values assigned to 'B' and 'D' are used in determining the truth-value of the sentence. As we apply our definitions, it may be helpful to keep in mind the reading of the sentence on this interpretation: 'Every positive integer y is such that if it is prime, then there is no positive integer than which it is greater'. The sentence is obviously false on this interpretation; what we shall now show is that we come to exactly this conclusion by using our definitions.

To show that the sentence is false, we must show that no variable assignment **d** (for **I**) satisfies the sentence Let **d** be any variable assignment for **I**. According to clause 8 of the definition of satisfaction,

a. **d** satisfies '(∀y)(By ⊃ ~ (∃z)Dyz)' if and only if for every member **u** of the U.D., **d**[**u**/y] satisfies '(By ⊃ ~ (∃z)Dyz)'.

So **d**[1/y] must satisfy the open sentence, **d**[2/y] must satisfy the open sentence, **d**[3/y] must satisfy the open sentence, and so on for every positive integer. Intuitively, this means that no matter *what* we may take y to be, y must satisfy the condition specified by that open sentence. We must consider all possible values that might be assigned to 'y', rather than just the value that **d** itself assigns to 'y'—that is, all values that variants of **d** might assign to 'y', because the variable 'y' is universally quantified.

But not every member **u** of the U.D. is such that **d**[**u**/y] satisfies '(By ⊃ ~ (∃z)Dyz)'—for example, 2 is not such that if it is prime then there is no positive integer than which it is greater. We shall show formally that **d**[2/y] does not satisfy '(By ⊃ ~ (∃z)Dyz)'. According to clause 6,

b. **d**[2/y] satisfies '(By ⊃ ~ (∃z)Dyz)' if and only if either **d**[2/y] does not satisfy 'By' or **d**[2/y] does satisfy ' ~ (∃z)Dyz'.

According to clause 2,

c. **d**[2/y] satisfies 'By' if and only if ⟨**d**[2/y](y)⟩ is a member of **I**(B).

The 1-tuple ⟨**d**[2/y](y)⟩ is ⟨2⟩—the set consisting of the integer that the variant assignment **d**[2/y] assigns to 'y', and **I**(B) is the set of 1-tuples of positive integers that are prime. Because ⟨2⟩ is a member of this set, **d**[2/y] does satisfy 'By'. We now turn to ' ~ (∃z)Dyz'. According to clause 3,

d. **d**[2/y] satisfies ' ~ (∃z)Dyz' if and only if it does not satisfy '(∃z)Dyz'.

And clause 9 tells us that

e. **d**[2/y] satisfies '(∃z)Dyz' if and only if there is at least one member **u** of the U.D. such that **d**[2/y, **u**/z], the variable assignment that is just like **d**[2/y] except that it assigns **u** to 'z', satisfies 'Dyz'

that is, if and only if there is a member **u** of the U.D. that is smaller than 2. There is such a member—the integer 1. Let us consider the variable assignment **d**[2/y, 1/z]. By clause 2,

f. **d**[2/y, 1/z] satisfies 'Dyz' if and only if the 2-tuple ⟨2, 1⟩ (this is the pair ⟨**d**[2/y, 1/z](y), **d**[2/y, 1/z](z)⟩) is a member of **I**(D).

**I**(D) is the set of 2-tuples of positive integers in which the first member is greater than the second—and ⟨2, 1⟩ is indeed a member of this set. Therefore **d**[2/y, 1/z] satisfies 'Dyz'. Returning to step (e), this shows that **d**[2/y] satisfies '(∃z)Dyz' and so, by (d), **d**[2/y] does not satisfy ' ~ (∃z)Dyz'. We now have a variable assignment, **d**[2/y], that satisfies 'By' but does not satisfy ' ~ (∃z)Dyz'. Therefore, by (b), **d**[2/y] does not satisfy '(By ⊃ ~ (∃z)Dyz)'. The number 2 is *not* such that if it is prime, then it is not larger than any positive integer. We may conclude from (a) that **d** does not satisfy '(∀y)(By ⊃ ~ (∃z)Dyz)', because we have found a variant of **d** that does not satisfy the open sentence following the universal quantifier.

We may also conclude that the sentence is *false* on interpretation 41, because we have just shown that every variable assignment for **I** will fail to satisfy '(∀y)(By ⊃ ~ (∃z)Dyz)'. The value that the original assignment **d** assigned to 'y' did not come into play in our proof, for when we removed the universal quantifier in step (a) we considered all values that might be assigned to 'y' by variants of **d**. The universally quantified sentence is satisfied by a variable assignment **d** if and only if the open sentence following the quantifier is satisfied no matter *what* value is assigned to 'y'. Similarly, when we removed the existential quantifier in step (e) we considered all values that might be assigned to 'z'—not just the value assigned by **d** or its variant **d**[2/y]. The values that **d** itself assigned to the variables 'y' and 'z' therefore played no role in showing that **d** did not satisfy the sentence. Moreover, because no other individual variables appear in the sentence, the values that **d** assigned to the other individual variables of *PL* also played no role. In sum, it does not matter which variable assignment we started with, because when we removed the quantifiers we had to consider variants that explicitly assigned values to the variables thus freed. We conclude that no matter which variable assignment **d** we choose, **d** will fail to satisfy the sentence.

The sentence '(∀y)(By ⊃ ~ (∃z)Dyz)' is true, however, on interpretation 43:

43. U.D.: the set {2, 4}
Bx: x is prime
Dxy: x is greater than y

Consider any variable assignment **d** for this interpretation. By clause 8, **d** satisfies the sentence if and only if for every member **u** of the U.D., **d**[**u**/y] satisfies '(By ⊃ ~ (∃z)Dyz)'—that is, if and only if both **d**[2/y] and **d**[4/y] satisfy the open sentence, because 2 and 4 are the only members of the U.D. We will examine each variant. **d**[2/y] satisfies the consequent of the open sentence (in addition to its antecedent)—because it fails to satisfy '(∃z)Dyz'. There is no member **u** of the set {2, 4} such that **d**[2/y, **u**/z] satisfies 'Dyz'. **d**[2/y, 2/z] does not satisfy 'Dyz', because ⟨**d**[2/y, 2/z](y), **d**[2/y, 2/z](z)⟩, which is ⟨2, 2⟩, is not in the extension of 'D'. **d**[2/y, 4/z] does not satisfy 'Dyz', because ⟨2, 4⟩ is not in the extension of 'D'. We have exhausted the possible values for 'z', so there is no member **u** of the U.D. such that **d**[2/y, **u**/z] satisfies 'Dyz'. Hence '(∃z)Dyz' is not satisfied by **d**[2/y] and its negation is satisfied. This establishes that **d**[2/y] satisfies '(By ⊃ ~ (∃z)Dyz)'. The variant **d**[4/y] also satisfies '(By ⊃ (∃z)Dyz)', because it fails to satisfy the antecedent (in addition, it satisfies the consequent). The 1-tuple ⟨**d**[4/y](y)⟩ is just ⟨4⟩, and this 1-tuple is not a member of **I**(B), which is the set of 1-tuples of prime positive integers. So **d**[4/y] fails to satisfy 'By' and therefore does satisfy '(By ⊃ ~ (∃z)Dyz)'. Having shown that both **d**[2/y] and **d**[4/y] satisfy '(By ⊃ ~ (∃z)Dyz)', we have established that for every member **u** of the U.D., **d**[**u**/y] satisfies the conditional open sentence, and we may conclude that **d** satisfies '(∀y)(By ⊃ (∃z)Dyz)'. Once again, because we used no specific values assigned to variables by our original variable assignment **d**, we have shown that every variable assignment for **I** will satisfy the sentence. It is therefore true on interpretation 43.

As another example, we may use our definitions to prove that the sentence '(∀x)(Bx ≡ ~ Bx)' is quantificationally false. We will begin by assuming that there is an interpretation on which the sentence is true and then show that this is impossible. Suppose that **I** is an interpretation on which '(∀x)(Bx ≡ ~ Bx)' is true. By definition, every variable assignment **d** for **I** must therefore satisfy '(∀x)(Bx ≡ ~ Bx)'. And because the sentence is universally quantified, for every member **u** of **I**'s U.D., the variant **d**[**u**/x] for each variable assignment **d** must satisfy '(Bx ≡ ~ Bx)' (by clause 8). We shall show that not even one variant of one variable assignment can do so. Suppose that **u** is a member of the U.D. such that ⟨**u**⟩ is in the extension of 'B'. Then, no matter which variable assignment **d** we started with, **d**[**u**/x] satisfies 'Bx' according to clause 2, because ⟨**d**[**u**/x](x)⟩ is a member of **I**(B). But then, by clause 3, **d**[**u**/x] does not satisfy ' ~ Bx', and hence, by clause 7, it does not satisfy '(Bx ≡ ~ Bx)'. Suppose on the other hand that **u** is a member of the U.D. such that ⟨**u**⟩ is not in the extension of 'B'. In this case **d**[**u**/x] does not satisfy 'Bx', because ⟨**d**[**u**/x](x)⟩ is not a member of **I**(B), and therefore does satisfy ' ~ Bx'. So, once again, '(Bx ≡ ~ Bx)' will not be satisfied. Because each member of the U.D. either is or is not in the extension of 'B', we conclude that there is no member **u** such that **d**[**u**/x] satisfies '(Bx ≡ ~ Bx)'. This being the case, no variable assignment for any interpretation **I** will satisfy '(∀x)(Bx ≡ ~ Bx)'. The sentence is false on every interpretation and is therefore quantificationally false.

It should now be clear why the definition of truth was given in terms of the concept of satisfaction, rather than directly in terms of interpretations. For the language *SL*, we were able to define the truth-conditions of a sentence directly in terms of the truth-conditions of its atomic components, for the atomic components were themselves sentences and so had truth-values on truth-value assignments. But consider the sentence of *PL* '(∀y)(By ⊃ ~ (∃z)Dyz)', which we used as an example in this section. There is no proper subformula of this sentence that is itself a sentence. The largest proper subformula is '(By ⊃ ~ (∃z)Dyz)', which is an *open sentence*. We do not consider open sentences to be true or false on interpretations, because their free variables are not given values on interpretations. So we cannot define the truth-conditions of '(∀y)(By ⊃ ~ (∃z)Dyz)' in terms of the truth or falsehood of its subformula '(By ⊃ ~ (∃z)Dyz)'. But variable assignments, which do assign values to variables, can satisfy or fail to satisfy open formulas for interpretations, and so we have defined the truth-conditions of sentences in terms of the satisfaction conditions of their subformulas.[4]

Finally, we shall have a full formal semantics for *PLI* if we add the following clause to our definition of satisfaction:

10. If $\mathscr{P}$ is an atomic formula of the form $t_1 = t_2$, then **d** satisfies $\mathscr{P}$ on interpretation **I** if and only if $\mathbf{u}_1 = \mathbf{u}_2$, where $\mathbf{u}_i$ is $\mathbf{I}(t_i)$ if $t_i$ is a constant and $\mathbf{u}_i$ is $\mathbf{d}(t_i)$ if $t_i$ is a variable.

This clause implicitly defines an extension for the identity predicate: The extension includes ⟨**u**, **u**⟩ for each member **u** of the U.D. and that is all that it includes. We can use clause 10, along with others, to show that the sentence

(∃x)(Fx & (∀y)(Fy ⊃ y = x))

is false on interpretation 44:

44. U.D.: set of positive integers
 Fx: x is odd

On this interpretation, the sentence may be read as: 'Exactly one positive integer is odd'. To show that the sentence is false, we must show that no variable assignment for **I** satisfies it. Let **d** be a variable assignment. Then, by clause 9, **d** satisfies the sentence if and only if there is some member **u** of the U.D. such that **d**[**u**/x] satisfies '(Fx & (∀y)(Fy ⊃ y = x)'. Because at least one positive integer is odd, there is at least one member **u** such that **d**[**u**/x] does satisfy the first conjunct 'Fx' —for example, ⟨**d**[3/x](x)⟩, which is ⟨3⟩, is a member of **I**(F). However, no matter which odd integer **u** may be, **d**[**u**/x] cannot satisfy '(∀y)(Fy ⊃ y = x)'. If **d**[**u**/x]

[4] Some authors allow all open sentences to be true or false on interpretations, so the concept of satisfaction is not needed in their truth definitions. Other authors use a type of semantics for quantificational languages known as *substitution semantics*; in this type of semantics the concept of satisfaction is also unnecessary. For obvious reasons, the semantics we have presented is known as *satisfaction semantics* (or sometimes as *referential* or *objectual* semantics). Satisfaction semantics was first presented by Alfred Tarski in "Der Wahrheitsbegriff in den formalisierten Sprachen," *Studia Philosophica*, 1 (1936), 261–405.

*did* satisfy this formula, then, according to clause 8, it would do so because for every positive integer $\mathbf{u}_1$, $\mathbf{d}[\mathbf{u}/x, \mathbf{u}_1/y]$ satisfies '(Fy ⊃ y = x)'. But for any odd positive integer **u**, there is at least one positive integer $\mathbf{u}_1$ such that $\mathbf{d}[\mathbf{u}/x, \mathbf{u}_1/y]$ does *not* satisfy '(Fy ⊃ y = x)'—let $\mathbf{u}_1$ be any odd integer other than **u**. In this case $\mathbf{d}[\mathbf{u}/x, \mathbf{u}_1/y]$ will satisfy 'Fy', because $\langle \mathbf{u}_1 \rangle$ is in the extension of 'F', but according to clause 10 it will not satisfy 'y = x' because $\mathbf{d}[\mathbf{u}/x, \mathbf{u}_1/y](x)$—which is **u**—and $\mathbf{d}[\mathbf{u}/x, \mathbf{u}_1/y](y)$—which is $\mathbf{u}_1$—are different integers. It follows that no positive integer **u** is such that $\mathbf{d}[\mathbf{u}/x]$ satisfies '(∀y)(Fy ⊃ y = x)', and so **d** does not satisfy the existentially quantified sentence '(∃x)(∀y)(Fy ⊃ y = x)'. The sentence is therefore false on interpretation 44.

### 8.7E EXERCISES

**1.** Using the definitions of this section, determine the truth-value of each of the following sentences on an interpretation that makes the following assignments:

U.D.: set of positive integers
K: F
Ex: x is even
Lxy: x is less than y
o: 1

a. ~(∀x)Ex ⊃ (∃y)Lyo
*b. ~Loo & ~(∀y) ~Loy
c. (∃x)(K ∨ Ex)
*d. (∀x)(Lox ⊃ (∀y)Lxy)
e. (K ≡ (∀x)Ex) ⊃ (∃y)(∃z)Lyz
*f. (∀x)[Ex ⊃ (∃y)(Lyx ∨ Lyo)]

**2.** Using the definitions of this section, determine the truth-value of each of the following sentences on an interpretation which makes the following assignments:

U.D.: the set {1, 3}
Ex: x is even
Gxy: x is greater than y
Tx: x is less than 2
t: 3

a. (∃x)(Ex ⊃ (∀y)Ey)
*b. (∀x)(∀y)(Gxy ∨ Gyx)
c. (∀x)(Tx ⊃ (∃y)Gyx)
*d. (∀x)(Et ⊃ Ex)
e. (∀x)[(∀y)Gxy ∨ (∃y)Gxy]
*f. (∀y)[Ty ∨ (∀x)(Ex ⊃ Gxy)]

**3.** Using the definitions in this section, determine the truth-value of each of the following sentences on an interpretation that makes the following assignments:

U.D.: set of positive integers
Mxyz: x minus y equals z
Pxyz: x plus y equals z
o: 1

a. Mooo ≡ Pooo
*b. (∀x)(∀y)(Mxyo ≡ Pyox)
c. (∀x)(∀y)(∀z)(Mxyz ≡ Pxyz)
*d. (∃x)(∀y)(∀z)(Mxyz ∨ Pzyx)
e. (∀y)(∃z)(Pyoz ⊃ Pooo)

***4.** Using the definitions in this section, explain why the following two sentences are quantificationally equivalent:

(∀x)Fx
~(∃x) ~ Fx

**5.** Using the definitions in this section, explain why the following sentence is quantificationally true:

(∀x)((∀y)Fy ⊃ Fx)

***6.** Using the definitions in this section, explain why {(∀x)Fx} quantificationally entails every substitution instance of '(∀x)Fx'.

**7.** Using the definitions in this section, explain why 'Fa' quantificationally entails '(∃x)Fx'.

***8.** Using the definitions in this section, explain why '(∃x)Fx & (∀x) ~ Fx' is quantificationally false.

**9.** Using the definitions in this section, determine the truth-value of each of the following sentences on an interpretation that makes the following assignments:

U.D.: set of positive integers
Ex: x is even
Gxy: x is greater than y

a. (∀x)(∀y)[~x = y ⊃ (Ex ⊃ Gxy)]
*b. (∀x)(∀y)(x = y ∨ ~Ey)
c. (∀x)[Ex ⊃ (∃y)(~x = y & ~Gxy)]

**10a.** Using the definitions in this section, explain why every sentence of the form $(\forall \mathcal{x})\mathcal{x} = \mathcal{x}$ is quantificationally true.
*b. Using the definitions in this section, explain why

'(∀x)(∀y)(x = y ⊃ Fxy) ⊃ (∀x)Fxx'

is quantificationally true.

## GLOSSARY

QUANTIFICATIONAL TRUTH: A sentence $\mathcal{P}$ of *PL/PLI* is *quantificationally true* if and only if $\mathcal{P}$ is true on every interpretation.
QUANTIFICATIONAL FALSITY: A sentence $\mathcal{P}$ of *PL/PLI* is *quantificationally false* if and only if $\mathcal{P}$ is false on every interpretation.

QUANTIFICATIONAL INDETERMINACY: A sentence $\mathcal{P}$ of *PL/PLI* is *quantificationally indeterminate* if and only if $\mathcal{P}$ is neither quantificationally true nor quantificationally false.

QUANTIFICATIONAL EQUIVALENCE: Sentences $\mathcal{P}$ and $\mathcal{Q}$ of *PL/PLI* are *quantificationally equivalent* if and only if there is no interpretation on which $\mathcal{P}$ and $\mathcal{Q}$ have different truth-values.

QUANTIFICATIONAL CONSISTENCY: A set of sentences of *PL/PLI* is *quantificationally consistent* if and only if there is at least one interpretation on which all of the members of the set are true.

A set of sentences of *PL/PLI* is *quantificationally inconsistent* if and only if the set is not quantificationally consistent.

QUANTIFICATIONAL ENTAILMENT: A set $\Gamma$ of sentences of *PL/PLI* *quantificationally entails* a sentence $\mathcal{P}$ of *PL/PLI* if and only if there is no interpretation on which every member of $\Gamma$ is true and $\mathcal{P}$ is false.

QUANTIFICATIONAL VALIDITY: An argument of *PL/PLI* is *quantificationally valid* if and only if there is no interpretation on which all of the premises are true and the conclusion is false.

An argument of *PL/PLI* is *quantificationally invalid* if and only if the argument is not quantificationally valid.

Chapter 9

# PREDICATE LOGIC: TRUTH-TREES

## 9.1 EXPANDING THE RULES FOR TRUTH-TREES

Truth-trees, as developed in Chapter Four, provide the basis for an effective method of testing for truth-functional consistency and thus for all the properties of sentences and groups of sentences that can be explicated in terms of truth-functional consistency (e.g., truth-functional validity, truth-functional truth, and truth-functional equivalence). In this chapter we extend the truth-tree method to make it applicable to sets of sentences of *PL*. The result will be a method of testing for quantificational consistency and thus for those properties of sentences and groups of sentences that can be explicated in terms of quantificational consistency.

Some sets of sentences of *PL* consist exclusively of sentences whose only logical operators are truth-functional connectives. We can, of course, test these sets for consistency by using the truth-tree rules of Chapter Four. For the set

$$\{\text{Fab, Gac \& Rab, Fab} \supset (\sim \text{Gac} \vee \sim \text{Rab})\}$$

we can construct the following tree:

| 1. | Fab | SM |
| 2. | Gac & Rab✔ | SM |
| 3. | Fab ⊃ (~Gac ∨ ~Rab)✔ | SM |
| 4. | Gac | 2 & D |
| 5. | Rab | 2 & D |
| 6. | ~Fab        ~Gac ∨ ~Rab✔ | 3 ⊃ D |
|    | ×                                  |        |
| 7. | ~Gac      ~Rab | 6 ∨ D |
|    | ×            × |        |

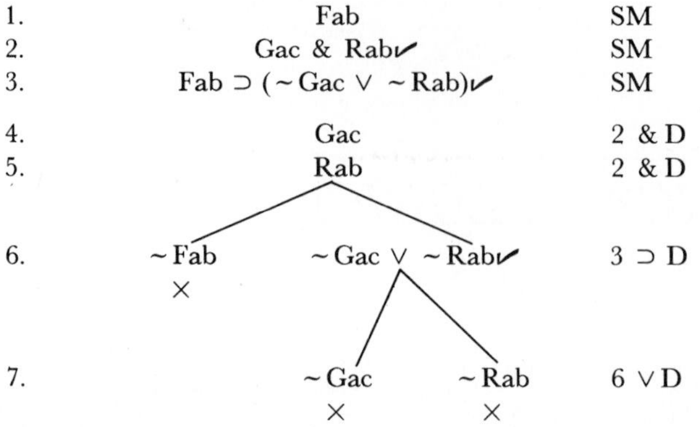

The various branches represent abortive attempts to discover a way in which all the members of the set being tested might come to be true. There is an interpretation on which all the members of the set being tested are true if and only if there is a completed open branch and an interpretation on which all the literals on that branch are true. Each branch of this tree contains an atomic sentence and the negation of that sentence. We know that there is no interpretation on which both a sentence and its negation are true. Hence there is no interpretation on which the truth-functional compounds composing the set being tested are all true. So this set is, on truth-functional grounds, quantificationally inconsistent.

However, many sets that are quantificationally inconsistent are not inconsistent on truth-functional grounds. The rules we presently have for constructing truth-trees do not allow us to construct closed trees for such sets. For example, using the decomposition rules we presently have, we can obtain only the following tree for the set {(∀x)(Fxc ⊃ Gxb), Fac & ~Gab}.

| 1. | (∀x)(Fxc ⊃ Gxb) | SM |
| 2. | Fac & ~Gab✔ | SM |
| 3. | Fac | 2 & D |
| 4. | ~Gab | 2 & D |

We cannot decompose the quantified sentence '(∀x)(Fxc ⊃ Gxb)' using only the truth-tree rules given in Chapter Four. In fact, there are four varieties of nonatomic sentences of *PL* that cannot be decomposed by those rules. These are sentences of the forms:

$$(\forall x)\mathscr{P}$$
$$(\exists x)\mathscr{P}$$
$$\sim(\forall x)\mathscr{P}$$
$$\sim(\exists x)\mathscr{P}$$

In this section we introduce one new tree rule for each of these kinds of sentence.

We begin with the rules for negations of quantified sentences. Both are nonbranching rules.

| *Negated Existential Decomposition* ($\sim\exists$D) | *Negated Universal Decomposition* ($\sim\forall$D) |
| --- | --- |
| $\sim(\exists x)\mathscr{P}$ ✓ | $\sim(\forall x)\mathscr{P}$ ✓ |
| $(\forall x) \sim \mathscr{P}$ | $(\exists x) \sim \mathscr{P}$ |

In each case the sentence entered is equivalent to the sentence being decomposed. ('It is not the case that something is so-and-so' is equivalent to 'each thing is such that it is not so-and-so', and 'it is not the case that each thing is so-and-so' is equivalent to 'something is not so-and-so'.) Note that negations of quantified sentences are truth-functionally compound sentences. Hence Negated Existential Decomposition and Negated Universal Decomposition count as rules for decomposing truth-functionally compound sentences.

If a universally quantified sentence $(\forall x)\mathscr{P}$ is true, then so is each substitution instance $\mathscr{P}(a/x)$ of that sentence. We want a rule that allows us to "decompose" a universally quantified sentence into the appropriate substitution instances of that sentence. Recall the tree we started for the set {(∀x)(Fxc ⊃ Gxb), Fac & ~ Gab}. The only sentence on that tree remaining to be decomposed is '(∀x)(Fxc ⊃ Gxb)'. Since that sentence is true on an interpretation only if all its substitution instances are true on that interpretation, we are justified in entering on line 5 *any* substitution instance of that sentence we may choose. So we add the following to our set of tree rules.

*Universal Decomposition* ($\forall$D)

$(\forall x)\mathscr{P}$

$\mathscr{P}(a/x)$

At any point in the construction of a tree any universally quantified sentence $(\forall x)\mathscr{P}$ may be decomposed by entering *any* substitution instance of that sentence on *one or more* open branches passing through $(\forall x)\mathscr{P}$. Because a universally quantified sentence has an infinite number of substitution instances, we can never "finish" decomposing it. (Consequently, universally quantified sentences are never checked off.)

Universal Decomposition does *not* require that the selected substitution instance be entered on every open branch passing through the universally quantified sentence being decomposed. This is appropriate because a substitution instance will often be of use on one open branch passing through the sentence being decomposed but not on another. And, as universally quantified sentences are never checked off, we can always later add, to any open branch on which a universally quantified sentence occurs, any substitution instance of that sentence.

The tree started for the set {(∀x)(Fxc ⊃ Gxb), Fac & ~Gab} can now be completed:

| | | | |
|---|---|---|---|
| 1. | (∀x)(Fxc ⊃ Gxb) | | SM |
| 2. | Fac & ~Gab ✓ | | SM |
| 3. | Fac | | 2 &D |
| 4. | ~Gab | | 2 &D |
| 5. | Fac ⊃ Gab ✓ | | 1 ∀D |
| 6. | ~Fac | Gab | 5 ⊃D |
| | × | × | |

At line 5 we entered 'Fac ⊃ Gab' by Universal Decomposition. We could have entered any substitution instance of '(∀x)(Fxc ⊃ Gxb)', but only the one we did enter is of use in producing a closed tree.

The last tree rule is that for decomposing existentially quantified sentences:

*Existential Decomposition* (∃D)

$(\exists \mathbf{x})\mathscr{P}$ ✓

$\mathscr{P}(\mathbf{a}/\mathbf{x})$

where $\mathbf{a}$ is a constant foreign to the branch. A constant is foreign to a branch of a tree if and only if it does not occur in any sentence on that branch. (Existentially quantified sentences, unlike universally quantified sentences, are checked off when they are decomposed. This is because we know that if an existentially quantified sentence $(\exists \mathbf{x})\mathscr{P}$ is true, then there is something that is of the sort specified by $\mathscr{P}$, but there need not be more than one such thing.) In picking an individual constant foreign to a branch we are, so to speak, decreeing that on the current branch that individual constant designates the thing that is of the sort specified by $\mathscr{P}$. We can do this because $\mathbf{a}$, the selected constant, is foreign to the branch. If $\mathbf{a}$ were not foreign to the branch it would already have a role on that branch and quite possibly a conflicting role (e.g., as the name of something that is not of the sort specified by $\mathscr{P}$).

For example, 'Some cars are yellow' and 'Some cars are not yellow' are both true. Hence a set consisting of symbolizations of these sentences, {(∃x)(Cx & Yx), (∃x)(Cx & ~Yx)}, should be quantificationally consistent and accordingly should have only open truth-trees. However, if we were to drop the restriction on

Existential Decomposition just discussed, we could produce a closed tree for this set:

| | | | |
|---|---|---|---|
| 1. | (∃x)(Cx & Yx)✓ | SM | |
| 2. | (∃x)(Cx & ~Yx)✓ | SM | |
| 3. | Ca & Ya✓ | 1 ∃D | |
| 4. | Ca | 3 & D | |
| 5. | Ya | 3 & D | |
| 6. | Ca & ~Ya✓ | 2 ∃D | **MISTAKE!** |
| 7. | Ca | 6 & D | |
| 8. | ~Ya | 6 & D | |
| | × | | |

The individual constant 'a', used in existential decomposition at line 6, is not, at the time 'Ca & ~Ya' is entered, foreign to the single branch of the tree. Hence line 6 is a mistake.

The following tree contains three uses of Existential Decomposition.

| | | | |
|---|---|---|---|
| 1. | (∀x)Fx ⊃ (∃x) ~Gx✓ | | SM |
| 2. | (∃x) ~Fx✓ | | SM |
| 3. | ~Fa | | 2 ∃D |
| 4. | ~(∀x)Fx✓ | (∃x) ~ Gx✓ | 1 ⊃ D |
| 5. | (∃x) ~Fx✓ | | 4 ~ ∀D |
| 6. | ~Fb | | 5 ∃D |
| 7. | | ~ Gb | 4 ∃D |

At line 3 Existential Decomposition is used for the first time. Since no constant occurs on the single branch which constitutes the tree at that point, 'a' is used as the instantiating constant. The next use of Existential Decomposition is at line 6 on the left-hand branch. At that point 'a' does already occur on the branch (at line 3, remember the sentences on lines 1–3 occur on both branches of this tree). So a new instantiating constant, 'b', is used. The final use of Existential Decomposition is at line 7 on the right-hand branch. The constant 'a' cannot be used because it occurs on line 3. But 'b' can be used, for although it already occurs on the left-hand branch, it does not occur, before '~Gb' is entered, on the right-hand branch.

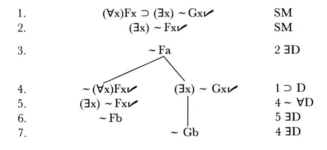

The above tree contains two open branches, each of which contains only literals and decomposed nonliterals. The complexities of predicate logic will force us to complicate the accounts of 'completed open branch' and 'open tree' given in Chapter Four. However, on those revised accounts, as on the accounts of Chapter Four, an open branch which contains only literals and decomposed nonliterals is a completed open branch and a tree with at least one completed open branch is an open tree. Hence both branches of the above tree are completed open branches and that tree is, accordingly, an open tree. (It will turn out that from a completed open branch an interpretation is recoverable on which every member of the set being tested is true, and hence that the above tree demonstrates that the set {(∀x)Fx ⊃ (∃x) ~ Gx, (∃x) ~ Fx, ~ Fa} is quantificationally consistent.)

Except for Universal Decomposition, the tree rules introduced in this section are like the tree rules of Chapter Four in that the results of applying one of them must be entered on *every* open branch running through the sentence being decomposed. Also as in Chapter Four, it is generally wise to apply decomposition rules that do not produce new branches before applying those that do. In using Universal Decomposition it is a good idea to try to select a substitution instance in which the instantiating constant is a constant already occurring on the open branch in question. It is also wise to try to use Existential Decomposition before using Universal Decomposition, for the former but not the latter includes a restriction on the individual constant that can be used in forming the substitution instance to be entered on the tree. We illustrate these last two points by doing a tree for {(∀x)(∀y) ~ Mxy, (∃x)Mxb}:

| | | |
|---|---|---|
| 1. | (∀x)(∀y) ~ Mxy | SM |
| 2. | (∃x)Mxb✓ | SM |
| 3. | Mab | 2 ∃D |
| 4. | (∀y) ~ May | 1 ∀D |
| 5. | ~ Mab | 4 ∀D |
| | × | |

Note that we did use Existential Decomposition before Universal Decomposition. At line 4 we entered '(∀y) ~ May', rather than, say, '(∀y) ~ Mgy', because 'a' does occur earlier on the tree. And we entered '(∀y) ~ May', rather than '(∀y) ~ Mby', because the former but *not* the latter will yield, when appropriately decomposed, the negation of the sentence on line 3. Here using Universal Decomposition before Existential Decomposition, that is, decomposing the sentence on line 1 before the sentence on line 2, also produces a closed tree, but such a tree is more complex:

| | | |
|---|---|---|
| 1. | (∀x)(∀y) ~ Mxy | SM |
| 2. | (∃x)Mxb✓ | SM |
| 3. | (∀y) ~ Mby | 1 ∀D |
| 4. | ~ Mbb | 3 ∀D |
| 5. | Mab | 2 ∃D |
| 6. | (∀y) ~ May | 1 ∀D |
| 7. | ~ Mab | 6 ∀D |
| | × | |

In this tree we had to enter 'Mab', rather than 'Mbb', at line 5 because Existential Decomposition requires that we enter a substitution instance of the sentence being decomposed in which the instantiating constant is foreign to the branch. The constant 'b' is not, at line 5, foreign to the branch. Having entered 'Mab' at line 5, we were able to close the tree only by reapplying Universal Decomposition to the sentence on line 1. Lines 3 and 4 of the tree are thus superfluous.

In Chapter Three we developed four stratagems for keeping truth-trees for sets of sentences of *SL* as concise as possible. Those stratagems are also applicable here. We repeat them below, along with the two new stratagems just discussed (suitably rearranged).

> Stratagems for Constructing Truth-Trees
>
> 1. Give priority to decomposing sentences whose decomposition does not require branching.
> 2. Give priority to decomposing sentences whose decomposition results in the closing of one or more branch.
> 3. Give priority to decomposing existentially quantified sentences over universally quantified sentences.
> 4. When using Universal Decomposition, try to use a substitution instance in which the instantiating constant already occurs on the branch in question.
> 5. Stop when a tree yields an answer to the question being asked.
> 6. Where stratagems 1–5 are not applicable, decompose the more complex sentences first.

Stratagem 1 should be used with care when dealing with universally quantified sentences. Consider the following tree, in which Universal Decomposition is used before Conditional Decomposition:

| | | |
|---|---|---|
| 1. | $(\forall x)(Fxa \supset Fax)$ | SM |
| 2. | $(\forall y)(Hy \supset Fya)$ | SM |
| 3. | $(\exists x)(Hx \ \& \ {\sim} Fax)$ ✓ | SM |
| 4. | $Hb \ \& \ {\sim} Fab$ ✓ | 3 ∃D |
| 5. | $Hb$ | 4 & D |
| 6. | ${\sim} Fab$ | 4 & D |
| 7. | $Faa \supset Faa$ | 1 ∀D |
| 8. | $Fba \supset Fab$ ✓ | 1 ∀D |
| 9. | $Ha \supset Faa$ | 2 ∀D |
| 10. | $Hb \supset Fba$ ✓ | 2 ∀D |
| 11. | ${\sim} Hb$ ×  \|  $Fba$ | 10 ⊃ D |
| 12. | (under $Fba$:) ${\sim} Fba$ ×  \|  $Fab$ × | 8 ⊃ D |

At line 7 we used Universal Decomposition and continued using it until each universally quantified sentence (there are two) has been decomposed to every substitution instance that can be formed from a constant already on the branch. The idea is that these are the substitution instances which may be useful later on. As it turns out, lines 7 and 9 are unnecessary, but this is not completely obvious at the point where we had a choice between applying Universal Decomposition and Conditional Decomposition. An alternative stratagem would be to use Universal Decomposition only when no other rule can be applied. But this stratagem produces the following considerably more complex tree:

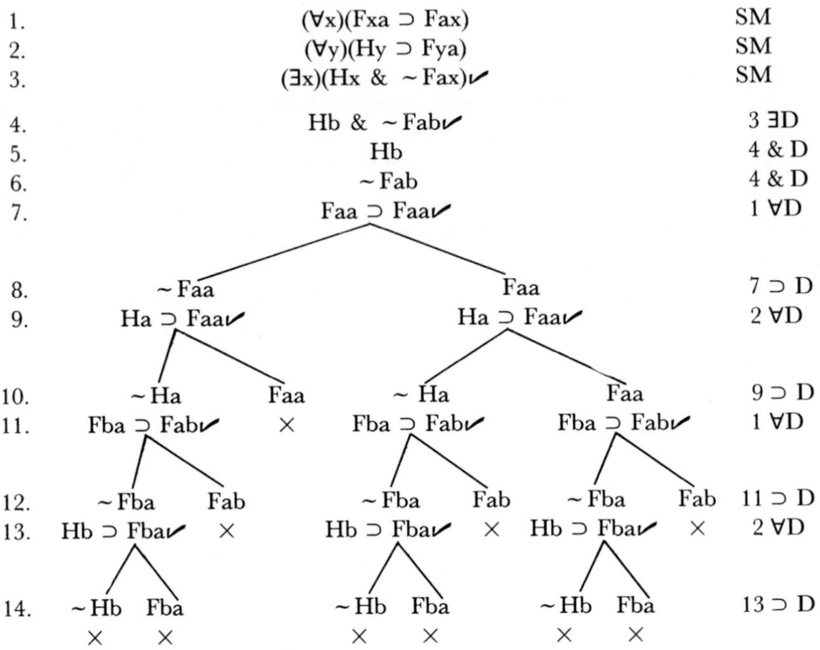


The best policy appears to be to stick with stratagem 1, but with the caveat that when a shorter route to a closed tree is apparent it should be pursued.[1]

### 9.1E EXERCISES

Construct truth-trees for the following sets of sentences. For each, note whether the tree is open or closed by the accounts of 'open tree' and 'closed tree' given in Chapter Four.

a. {(∃x)Fx, (∃x) ~ Fx}
*b. {(∃x)Fx, (∀x) ~ Fx}
c. {(∃x)(Fx & ~Gx), (∀x)(Fx ⊃ Gx)}

[1] A further caveat will be required when we introduce systematic trees in Section 9.5, for the routine for constructing such trees requires abandoning stratagem 1 altogether as it applies to universally quantified sentences.

*d. {(∃x)(Fx & ~Gx), (∀x)Fx ⊃ (∀x)Gx}
e. {~(∀x)(Fx ⊃ Gx), ~(∃x)Fx, ~(∃x)Gx}
*f. {~(∀x)(Fx & Gx), (∃y)(Fy & Gy)}
g. {(∃x)Fx, (∃y)Gy, (∃z)(Fz & Gz)}
*h. {(∀x)(Fx ⊃ Gx), (∀x)(Gx ⊃ Hx), (∃x)(Fx & ~Hx)}
i. {(∀x)(∀y)(Fxy ⊃ Fyx), (∃x)(∃y)(Fxy & ~ Fyx)}
*j. {(∀x)(∃y)Lxy, Lta & ~Lat, ~ (∃y)Lay}
k. {(∃x)Fx ⊃ (∀x)Fx, ~(∀x)[Fx ⊃ (∀y)Fy]}
*l. {(∀x)(Fx ⊃ Gx), ~(∀x) ~Fx, (∀x) ~ Gx}
m. {(∀x)[Fx ⊃ (∃y)Gyx], ~(∀x) ~ Fx, (∀x)(∀y) ~Gxy}
*n. {(∃x)Gx ⊃ (∀x)Gx, (∃z)Gz & (∃y) ~ Gy}
o. {(∃x)Lxx, ~(∃x)(∃y)(Lxy & Lyx)}
*p. {(∃y)(Fy ∨ Gy), ~(∀y)Fy & ~(∀y)Gy, ~(∀x)(Fx & Gx)}
q. {(∃x)(Fx ∨ Gx), (∀x)(Fx ⊃ ~Gx), (∀x)(Gx ⊃ ~Fx), ~(∃x)(~Fx ∨ ~Gx)}

## 9.2 TRUTH-TREES AND QUANTIFICATIONAL CONSISTENCY

So far we have seen a variety of truth-trees for sets of sentences of *PL*. Some have been closed, others open, by the accounts of Chapter Four. The trees which are open trees by the account of Chapter Four are so in virtue of having at least one branch such that no new sentence can be added to it (every sentence on the branch is either a literal or has been decomposed). But not all open trees for sets of sentences of *PL* are of this sort.

Consider a tree for {(∃y)Gy ⊃ (∀x)Fxb, (∃z) ~ Fzb}:

| | | | |
|---|---|---|---|
| 1. | (∃y)Gy ⊃ (∀x)Fxb ✓ | | SM |
| 2. | (∃z) ~ Fzb ✓ | | SM |
| 3. | ~ Fab | | 2 ∃D |
| 4. | ~ (∃y)Gy ✓ | (∀x)Fxb | 1 ⊃ D |
| 5. | | Fab | 4 ∀D |
| | | × | |
| 6. | (∀y) ~ Gy | | 4 ~∃D |
| 7. | ~ Ga | | 6 ∀D |
| 8. | ~ Gb | | 6 ∀D |

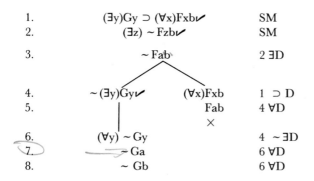

This tree has one closed branch and one open branch. Further sentences could be added to the open branch, for one of the sentences on that branch, '(∀y) ~ Gy', is a universally quantified sentence and there is no limit to the number of times a universally quantified sentence can be decomposed. (Such sentences are never checked off.) In the present example we began adding substitution instances of '(∀y) ~ Gy' at line 7, and it is clear that there is no limit to the number of such instances that can be added. However, it is also clear that adding more such instances will not close the open branch. We have already added all the instances that can be formed from individual constants appearing earlier on the open branch. Substitution instances formed from individual constants not already on the open branch will be such that their truth or falsity does not bear on the truth of literals already on the branch, so there is no point in entering '~ Gh', for example.

In light of the existence of such trees, we modify our account of a completed open branch as follows. A branch of a truth-tree for a set of sentences of *PL* is a *completed open branch* if and only if it is a finite open branch, that is, an open branch with a finite number of entries, and each sentence occurring on that branch is one of the following:

1. a literal (an atomic sentence or the negation of an atomic sentence)
2. not a universally quantified sentence and has been decomposed
3. a universally quantified sentence $(\forall \mathcal{x})\mathcal{P}$ such that $\mathcal{P}(\mathcal{a}/\mathcal{x})$ also occurs on that branch *for each constant* $\mathcal{a}$ occurring on the branch and at least one instance $\mathcal{P}(\mathcal{a}/\mathcal{x})$ does occur on the branch.

By this revised account, the tree does contain a completed open branch.

We summarize here the important properties of truth-trees for sets of sentences of *PL*. With the exception of the notion of a completed open branch, these accounts strictly parallel those given in Chapter Four:

*Closed branch:* a branch on which some atomic sentence and its negation both occur

*Open branch:* a branch which is not closed

*Completed open branch:* a finite open branch on which each sentence is of one of the sorts specified in clauses 1–3 in the preceding paragraph

*Completed tree:* a tree on which each branch either is closed or is a completed open branch

*Closed tree*: a tree on which every branch is closed

We also note that all trees containing at least one completed open branch are *open trees*.[2] Note that an open tree need not be a completed tree.

To see why we require that a completed open branch on which a universally quantified sentence occurs contain at least one substitution instance of that sentence, consider the unit set {~(∃x)(Fx ∨ ~ Fx)}. The sole member of this set says that it is not the case that there is an x such that either x is F or x is not F. But each thing x either is F or is not F. So this sentence is false and indeed quantificationally false (since every U.D. is nonempty). Hence we want the trees

[2] This is not a definition of 'open tree', for some trees are open although they contain no completed open branches. See p. 383 and Section 9.5.

for the unit set of this sentence to close. One tree is as follows:

| | | |
|---|---|---|
| 1. | ~(∃x)(Fx ∨ ~ Fx)✓ | SM |
| 2. | (∀x) ~ (Fx ∨ ~Fx) | 1 ~∃D |
| 3. | ~(Fa ∨ ~Fa)✓ | 2 ∀D |
| 4. | ~Fa | 3 ~∨D |
| 5. | ~~Fa✓ | 3 ~∨D |
| 6. | Fa | 5 ~~D |
| | × | |

At line 2 we replaced the negated existentially quantified sentence on line 1 with a universally quantified sentence by Negated Existential Decomposition. If we did not require that a completed open branch contain at least one substitution instance of every universally quantified sentence occurring on that branch, we would have, at line 2, a completed open branch and thus an open tree. But we do make this requirement, and the branch is therefore not completed. We must continue the branch, and the only way to do so is by entering a substitution instance of '(∀x) ~ (Fx ∨ ~Fx)' at line 3. The result is a tree that closes three lines later. Note that this tree would close no matter what substitution instance of '(∀x) ~ (Fx ∨ ~Fx)' were entered at line 3.

In *PL*, as in *SL*, a closed tree signifies inconsistency. To allow for infinite sets we make the following our official account:

> A set Γ of sentences of *PL* is *quantificationally inconsistent* if and only if at least one finite subset of Γ has a closed truth-tree.

A set Γ of sentences of *PL* is quantificationally consistent if and only if Γ is not quantificationally inconsistent, that is, if and only if no finite subset of Γ has a closed tree.[3]

If a finite set Γ of sentences of *PL* has a tree with a completed open branch, then Γ is quantificationally consistent. However, in *PL*, unlike *SL*, some finite consistent sets have truth-trees with no completed open branches (because all their open branches are infinite and we require a completed open branch to be finite). In Section 9.5 we explicate the notion of an *open tree* in a way that allows such trees to count as open trees.

The following tree for the unit set {(∃x)Fx} illustrates another complexity that characterizes quantificational but not sentential truth-trees:

| | | |
|---|---|---|
| 1. | (∃x)Fx✓ | SM |
| 2. | Fa | 1 ∃D |

The tree for this unit set has only one open branch. But we cannot argue, as we could if it were the tree for the unit set of a sentence of *SL*, that the one member of the set in question is true if and only if every sentence on at least one open branch

[3] The proof of this result is very similar to the proof of the parallel result for sentential logic given in Chapter Six.

is true. Suppose '(∃x)Fx' symbolizes the true sentence 'Someone is fat'. This sentence is true even if the person designated by 'a', say Albert, is not fat, that is, even if 'Fa' is in fact false. Of course we can make the weak claim that if the sentence to which an existentially quantified sentence is decomposed is true, so is that existentially quantified sentence. And this weak claim does justify our taking the preceding tree as establishing the quantificational consistency of the unit set {(∃x)Fx}.

Since a sentence obtained by Existential Decomposition need not be true for the decomposed sentence to be true, how can we justify taking the following tree as showing that {(∃x)(Fx & ~Fx)} is quantificationally inconsistent?

| | | |
|---|---|---|
| 1. | (∃x)(Fx & ~Fx)✓ | SM |
| 2. | Fa & ~Fa✓ | 1 ∃D |
| 3. | Fa | 2 &D |
| 4. | ~Fa | 2 &D |
| | × | |

Here we must reason as follows. If there is indeed something that both is and is not F, then there is an interpretation that assigns that thing to 'a', and 'Fa & ~Fa' will have to be true on that interpretation. But our tree shows that if 'Fa & ~Fa' is true on an interpretation, so are both 'Fa' and '~Fa'. And we know there is no interpretation on which an atomic sentence and its negation are both true. Hence we can conclude that there is no interpretation on which '(∃x)(Fx & ~Fx)' is true.

We prove in Chapter Eleven that an interpretation on which every member of the set being tested is true can always be constructed from a completed open branch. Here we illustrate how interpretations are constructed from completed open branches. Consider a tree for the set {(∀x)(Gx ⊃ Hxx), ~(∀y)Hyy, (∃z)Gz}:

| | | | | |
|---|---|---|---|---|
| 1. | | (∀x)(Gx ⊃ Hxx) | | SM |
| 2. | | ~(∀y)Hyy✓ | | SM |
| 3. | | (∃z)Gz✓ | | SM |
| 4. | | (∃y)~Hyy✓ | | 2 ~∀D |
| 5. | | ~Haa | | 4 ∃D |
| 6. | | Gb | | 3 ∃D |
| 7. | | Ga ⊃ Haa✓ | | 1 ∀D |
| 8. | | Gb ⊃ Hbb✓ | | 1 ∀D |
| 9. | ~Gb | | Hbb | 8 ⊃D |
| | × | | | |
| 10. | | ~Ga | Haa | 7 ⊃D |
| | | | × | |

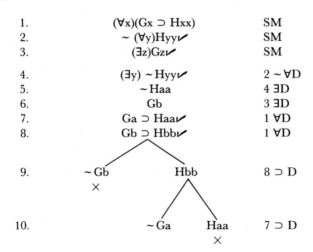

This tree has two closed branches and one completed open branch. Our strategy is to construct an interpretation on which all the literals on that open branch are true. That branch contains just two individual constants, 'a' and 'b'. So we shall take as our U.D. the set consisting of the positive integers 1 and 2 and assign 1 to 'a' and 2 to 'b'. We now have to interpret the predicates 'G' and 'H' in such a way that 'Gb' and 'Hbb' are true (since those literals occur on the open branch) and 'Ga' and 'Haa' are false on the resulting interpretation (since '~Ga' and '~Haa' occur on the open branch). One way to do this is to interpret 'Gx' as 'x is 2' and 'Hxy' as 'x is an even number equal to y'. This gives us the following interpretation:

U.D.: {1, 2}
a: 1
b: 2
Gx: x is 2
Hxy: x is an even number equal to y

Note that when an interpretation is constructed in this way, each individual constant on the open branch is assigned a distinct member of the U.D., and each member of the U.D. is assigned to some constant or other. All the members of the set {(∀x)(Gx ⊃ Hxx), ~(∀y)Hyy, (∃z)Gz} are true on this interpretation. This establishes that the set consisting of those three sentences is quantificationally consistent.

Since an interpretation *can* always be constructed from a completed open branch, there is no need actually to do so each time we construct an open tree. Rather, we shall take the presence of a completed open branch as itself guaranteeing that the set being tested is quantificationally consistent.

## 9.2E EXERCISES

Use the truth-tree method to test the following sets of sentences for quantificational consistency. State your result *and* what it is about the tree that establishes this result.

a. {(∀x)Fx ∨ (∃y)Gy, (∃x)(Fx & Gb)}
*b. {(∀x)Fx ∨ (∃y)Gy, (∃x)(~Fx & Gx)}
c. {(∀x)(Fx ⊃ Gxa), (∃x)Fx, (∀y) ~ Gya}
*d. {(∀x)(Fx ⊃ Gxa), (∃x)Fx}
e. {(∀x)(Fx ⊃ Gxa), (∃x)Fx, (∀y)Gya}
*f. {(∀x)(Fx ⊃ Gxa), (∃x)Fx, (∀x)(∀y)Gxy}
g. {(∀x)(Fx ∨ Gx), ~(∃y)(Fy ∨ Gy)}
*h. {(∀x)(Fx ∨ Gx), ~(∃y)(Fy ∨ Gy), Fa & ~Gb)}
i. {(∀z)Hz, (∃x)Hx ⊃ (∀y)Fy}
*j. {(∀z) ~Hzb, (∃y)Fy ⊃ (∃x)Hxc}
k. {(∀x)(∀y)Lxy, (∃z) ~Lza ⊃ (∀y) ~Lza}

*l. {(∀x)(∀y)Lxy, (∃z) ~ Lza ⊃ (∀z) ~ Lzb}
m. {(∀x)(Rx ≡ ~ Hxa), ~ (∀y) ~ Hby, Ra}
*n. {(∀x)Fxa ≡ ~ (∀x)Gxb, (∃x)(Fxa & ~ Gxb)}

## 9.3 TRUTH-TREES AND OTHER SEMANTIC PROPERTIES

To use truth-trees to test sentences and sets of sentences for properties other than consistency, we must specify those other properties in terms of open and closed truth-trees. We begin by so specifying quantificational falsity, quantificational truth, and quantificational indeterminacy.

> A sentence 𝒫 of *PL* is *quantificationally false* if and only if the set {𝒫} has a closed truth-tree.

> A sentence 𝒫 of *PL* is *quantificationally true* if and only if the set {~ 𝒫} has a closed truth-tree.

> A sentence 𝒫 of *PL* is *quantificationally indeterminate* if and only if neither the set {𝒫} nor the set {~ 𝒫} has a closed truth-tree.

Quantificational equivalence, quantificational entailment, and quantificational validity are specified analogously:

> Sentences 𝒫 and 𝒬 of *PL* are *quantificationally equivalent* if and only if {~ (𝒫 ≡ 𝒬)} has a closed truth-tree.

> A finite set Γ of sentences of *PL quantificationally entails* a sentence 𝒫 of *PL* if and only if Γ ∪ {~ 𝒫} has a closed truth-tree.

> An argument of *PL* is *quantificationally valid* if and only if the set consisting of the premises and the negation of the conclusion has a closed truth-tree.

We will illustrate how truth-trees can be used to test for each of these semantic properties. We begin with quantificational truth, quantificational falsity, and quantificational indeterminacy. Consider the sentence '(∀x)(Fx & (∃y) ~ Fy)'. This says, 'Each thing is F and at least one thing is not F', a claim for which we should not hold out much hope. To verify that this sentence is quantificationally false, we do a tree for the unit set of this sentence, expecting the tree to close, which it does:

$$(\exists) \quad \text{AT LEAST ONE}$$

| 1. | (∀x)(Fx & (∃y) ~ Fy) | SM |
|---|---|---|
| 2. | Fa & (∃y) ~ Fy✓ | 1 ∀D |
| 3. | Fa | 2 & D |
| 4. | (∃y) ~ Fy✓ | 2 & D |
| 5. | ~ Fb | 4 ∃D |
| 6. | Fb & (∃y) ~ Fy✓ | 1 ∀D |
| 7. | Fb | 6 & D |
| 8. | (∃y) ~ Fy | 6 & D |
| | × | |

Since the tree closes, the set being tested is quantificationally inconsistent. There-fore there is no interpretation on which every member of the set is true. Since there is only one member of that set, there is no interpretation on which that sentence, '(∀x)(Fx & (∃y) ~ Fy)' is true. Hence that sentence is indeed quantificationally false. Note that we used Universal Decomposition on the sentence on line 1 twice, once to obtain the sentence on line 2 and once to obtain the sentence on line 6. This was necessary because by the time we had reached line 5, we had introduced a new constant by means of which the universally quantified sentence on line 1 had not yet been instantiated.

Now consider the sentence '(∃x) ~ Fx ⊃ ~ (∀x)Fx', which says 'If there is something which is not F, then not everything is F', and is fairly obviously quantificationally true. To verify that this sentence is quantificationally true, we do a tree for the unit set of its negation, that is, for { ~ [(∃x) ~ Fx ⊃ ~ (∀x)Fx]}. (Note that in forming the negation of this truth-functionally compound sentence we were careful to reinstate the outer brackets which had been omitted.)

| 1. | ~ [(∃x) ~ Fx ⊃ ~ (∀x)Fx] | SM |
|---|---|---|
| 2. | (∃x) ~ Fx | 1 ~⊃ D |
| 3. | ~ ~ (∀x)Fx | 1 ~⊃ D |
| 4. | (∀x)Fx | 3 ~~ D |
| 5. | ~ Fa | 2 ∃D |
| 6. | Fa | 4 ∀D |
| | × | |

This tree is closed, so the set being tested is quantificationally inconsistent, so there is no interpretation on which the one member of that set, '~ [(∃x) ~ Fx ⊃ ~ (∀x)Fx]', is true. Hence there is no interpretation on which the sentence of which it is the negation, '(∃x) ~ Fx ⊃ ~ (∀x)Fx', is false. So that latter sentence is quantificationally true.

Of course one does not always have a clear intuition about a sentence's status, that is, about whether it is quantificationally true, quantificationally false, or quantificationally indeterminate. Consider, for example, '(∃x)(Fx ⊃ (∀y)Fy)'. The uninitiated at least may think this sentence is clearly quantificationally indeterminate. It is if and only if both the tree for it and the tree for its negation are open. We begin with a tree for the sentence itself:

| | | | |
|---|---|---|---|
| 1. | (∃x)(Fx ⊃ (∀y)Fy)✓ | | SM |
| 2. | Fa ⊃ (∀y)Fy✓ | | 1 ∃D |
| 3. | ~Fa | (∀y)Fy | 2 ⊃ D |
| 4. | | Fa | 3 ∀D |

As expected, the tree is open (it has two completed open branches). So the sentence is not quantificationally false. We next do a tree for the negation of the sentence:

| | | |
|---|---|---|
| 1. | ~ (∃x)(Fx ⊃ (∀y)Fy)✓ | SM |
| 2. | (∀x) ~ (Fx ⊃ (∀y)Fy) | 1 ~ ∃D |
| 3. | ~ (Fa ⊃ (∀y)Fy)✓ | 2 ∀D |
| 4. | Fa | 3 ~⊃ D |
| 5. | ~ (∀y)Fy✓ | 3 ~⊃ D |
| 6. | (∃y) ~ Fy✓ | 5 ~ ∀D |
| 7. | ~ Fb | 6 ∃D |
| 8. | ~ (Fb ⊃ (∀y)Fy)✓ | 2 ∀D |
| 9. | Fb | 8 ~⊃ D |
| 10. | ~ (∀y)Fy | 8 ~⊃ D |
| | × | |

Perhaps surprisingly, this tree is closed. So the negation being tested is quantificationally false and the original sentence in which we were interested, '(∃x)(Fx ⊃ (∀y)Fy)', is in fact quantificationally true.

Insufficient attention to the importance of the scope of quantifiers might lead one to think that '(∃x)(Fx & Gx)' and '(∃x)Fx & (∃x)Gx' are quantificationally equivalent, and hence that

(∃x)(Fx & Gx) ≡ [(∃x)Fx & (∃x)Gx]

is quantificationally true. To test this supposition, we do a tree for the negation of the above sentence:

| | | | | | | |
|---|---|---|---|---|---|---|
| 1. | ~((∃x)(Fx & Gx) ≡ ((∃x)Fx & (∃x)Gx))✓ | | | | | SM |
| 2. | (∃x)(Fx & Gx)✓ | | | ~(∃x)(Fx & Gx)✓ | | 1 ~≡ D |
| 3. | ~((∃x)Fx & (∃x)Gx)✓ | | | (∃x)Fx & (∃x)Gx✓ | | 1 ~≡ D |
| 4. | Fa & Ga✓ | | | | | 2 ∃D |
| 5. | Fa | | | | | 4 & D |
| 6. | Ga | | | | | 4 & D |
| 7. | ~(∃x)Fx✓ | ~(∃x)Gx✓ | | | | 3 ~ & D |
| 8. | (∀x) ~Fx | (∀x) ~ Gx | | | | 7 ~∃D |
| 9. | ~Fa | ~Ga | | | | 8 ∀D |
| 10. | × | × | | (∃x)Fx✓ | | 3 & D |
| 11. | | | | (∃x)Gx✓ | | 3 & D |
| 12. | | | | (∀x) ~ (Fx & Gx) | | 2 ~ ∃D |
| 13. | | | | Fa | | 10 ∃D |
| 14. | | | | Gb | | 11 ∃D |
| 15. | | | | ~(Fa & Ga)✓ | | 12 ∀D |
| 16. | | | | ~(Fb & Gb)✓ | | 12 ∀D |
| 17. | | | ~Fa | ~Ga | | 15 ~ & D |
| | | | × | | | |
| 18. | | | | ~Fb | ~Gb | 16 ~ & D |
| | | | | ↑ | × | |

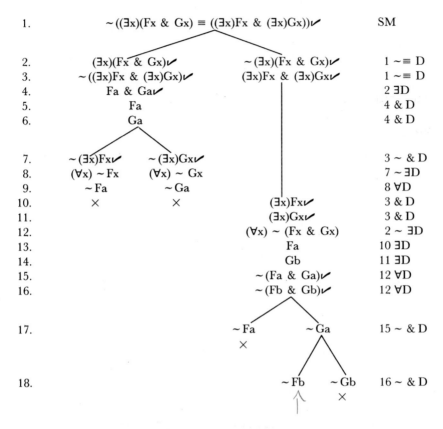

The tree is open, not closed. So the negation we are testing is not quantificationally false, the biconditional of which it is a negation is therefore not quantificationally true, and the immediate components of that biconditional, '(∃x)(Fx & Gx)' and '(∃x)Fx & (∃x)Gx' are not quantificationally equivalent. If we are interested in establishing, by the tree method, that this biconditional is quantificationally indeterminate (and not quantificationally false) we must do a tree for this biconditional:

| | | | |
|---|---|---|---|
| 1. | (∃x)(Fx & Gx) ≡ ((∃x)Fx & (∃x)Gx)✓ | | SM |
| 2. | (∃x)(Fx & Gx)✓ | ~(∃x)(Fx & Gx)✓ | 1 ≡ D |
| 3. | (∃x)Fx & (∃x)Gx✓ | ~((∃x)Fx & (∃x)Gx)✓ | 1 ≡ D |
| 4. | | (∀x) ~(Fx & Gx) | 2 ~∃D |
| 5. | | ~(Fa & Ga)✓ | 4 ∀D |
| 6. | | ~(∃x)Fx✓    ~(∃x)Gx✓ | 3 ~ & D |
| 7. | | (∀x) ~Fx    (∀x) ~ Gx | 6 ~∃D |
| 8. | | ~Fa    ~ Ga | 7 ∀D |
| 9. | | ~Fa   ~Ga    ~Fa   ~Ga | 5 ~ & D |
| 10. | (∃x)Fx✓ | | 3 & D |
| 11. | (∃x)Gx✓ | | 3 & D |
| 12. | Fa & Ga✓ | | 2 ∃D |
| 13. | Fa | | 12 & D |
| 14. | Ga | | 12 & D |
| 15. | Fb | | 10 ∃D |
| 16. | Gc | | 11 ∃D |

It is surely not surprising that this tree is open. That it is establishes that the biconditional being tested is not quantificationally false and is, given the previous open tree, quantificationally indeterminate.

The sentences '(∀x)(Fx ⊃ (∃y)Gya)' and '(∃x)Fx ⊃ (∃y)Gya' are quantificationally equivalent, as the following closed tree for the negation of their corresponding material biconditional establishes.

| | | | | | |
|---|---|---|---|---|---|
| 1. | ~((∀x)(Fx ⊃ (∃y)(Gya) ≡ ((∃x)Fx ⊃ (∃y)Gya))✓ | | | | SM |
| 2. | (∀x)(Fx ⊃ (∃y)Gya) | | ~(∀x)(Fx ⊃ (∃y)Gya)✓ | | 1 ~≡ D |
| 3. | ~((∃x)Fx ⊃ (∃y)Gya)✓ | | (∃x)Fx ⊃ (∃y)Gya✓ | | 1 ~≡ D |
| 4. | (∃x)Fx✓ | | | | 3 ~⊃ D |
| 5. | ~(∃y)Gya✓ | | | | 3 ~⊃ D |
| 6. | (∀y) ~Gya | | | | 5 ~∃D |
| 7. | Fb | | | | 4 ∃D |
| 8. | Fb ⊃ (∃y)Gya✓ | | | | 2 ∀D |
| 9. | ~Fb | (∃y)Gya✓ | | | 8 ⊃ D |
| 10. | × | Gca | | | 9 ∃D |
| 11. | | ~Gca | | | 6 ∀D |
| 12. | | × | (∃x) ~(Fx ⊃ (∃y)Gya)✓ | | 2 ~∀D |
| 13. | | | ~(Fb ⊃ (∃y)Gya)✓ | | 12 ∃D |
| 14. | | | Fb | | 13 ~⊃ D |
| 15. | | | ~(∃y)Gya✓ | | 13 ~⊃ D |
| 16. | | | (∀y) ~Gya | | 15 ~∃D |
| 17. | | | ~(∃x)Fx✓ | (∃y)Gya✓ | 3 ⊃ D |
| 18. | | | (∀x) ~Fx | | 17 ~∃D |
| 19. | | | ~Fb | | 18 ∀D |
| 20. | | | × | Gca | 17 ∃D |
| 21. | | | | ~Gca | 16 ∀D |
| | | | | × | |

To use the tree method to test for quantificational validity, we construct a tree for the premises and the *negation* of the argument in question. Here is a tree for the argument

(∀w) ~ Gww
~ (∀x)Hx ⊃ (∃y)Gya
―――――――――――
(∃z)(Hz & ~ Gzz)

| | | | | | |
|---|---|---|---|---|---|
| 1. | | (∀w) ~ Gww | | | SM |
| 2. | | ~ (∀x)Hx ⊃ (∃y)Gya✓ | | | SM |
| 3. | | ~ (∃z)(Hz & ~ Gzz)✓ | | | SM |
| 4. | | (∀z) ~ (Hz & ~ Gzz) | | | 3 ~ ∃D |
| 5. | ~ ~ (∀x)Hx✓ | | (∃y)Gya✓ | | 2 ⊃ D |
| 6. | \| | | Gba | | 5 ∃D |
| 7. | (∀x)Hx | | \| | | 5 ~ ~ D |
| 8. | ~ Gaa | | ~ Gaa | | 1 ∀D |
| 9. | ~ (Ha & ~ Gaa)✓ | | ~ (Ha & ~ Gaa)✓ | | 4 ∀D |
| 10. | ~ Ha | ~ ~ Gaa✓ | ~ Ha | ~ ~ Gaa | 9 ~ & D |
| 11. | Ha | \| | \| | | 7 ∀D |
| 12. | × | Gaa | \| | Gaa | 10 ~ ~ D |
| 13. | | × | ~ Gbb | × | 1 ∀D |
| 14. | | | ~ (Hb & ~ Gbb)✓ | | 4 ∀D |
| 15. | | | ~ Hb    ~ ~ Gbb | | 14 ~ & D |
| 16. | | | Gbb | | 15 ~ ~ D |

~Hb ~Gbb ~Ha (~Gaa) Gba

The tree has a completed open branch, so the argument is quantificationally invalid. (There is an interpretation on which the premises and the negation of the conclusion are all true, i.e., on which the premises are true and the conclusion is false.)

As with truth-trees for sentential logic, the procedure for testing alleged entailments parallels that for testing for validity. Consider the claim

{(∀x)(Hx ≡ ~ Ix), ~ (∃x) ~ Ix} ⊨ (∀x) ~ Hx

If this claim is true, there is no interpretation on which the members of the above set are both true and the allegedly entailed sentence false, that is, there is no interpretation on which all the members of

{(∀x)(Hx ≡ ~ Ix), ~ (∃x) ~ Ix, ~ (∀x) ~ Hx}

are true. So we will test the latter set for quantificational consistency:

| | | | |
|---|---|---|---|
| 1. | (∀x)(Hx ≡ ~ Ix) | | SM |
| 2. | ~ (∃x) ~ Ix✓ | | SM |
| 3. | ~ (∀x) ~ Hx✓ | | SM |
| 4. | (∀x) ~ ~ Ix | | 2 ~ ∃D |
| 5. | (∃x) ~ ~ Hx✓ | | 3 ~ ∀D |
| 6. | ~ ~ Ha✓ | | 5 ∃D |
| 7. | Ha | | 6 ~ ~ D |
| 8. | Ha ≡ ~ Ia✓ | | 1 ∀D |
| 9. | Ha | ~ Ha | 8 ≡ D |
| 10. | ~ Ia | ~ ~ Ia | 8 ≡ D |
| 11. | ~ ~ Ia✓ | × | 4 ∀D |
| 12. | Ia | | 11 ~ ~ D |
| | × | | |

The tree is closed, so the set consisting of the members of the original set and the negation of the allegedly entailed sentence is quantificationally inconsistent. Therefore there is no interpretation on which all the members of that original set are true and the allegedly entailed sentence false. So the entailment does hold.

## 9.3E EXERCISES

Construct truth-trees as necessary to provide the requested information. In each case state your result and what it is about your tree that establishes this result.

**1.** Which of the following sentences are quantificationally true?

a. (∃x)Fx ∨ ~ (∃x)Fx
*b. (∃x)Fx ∨ (∃x) ~ Fx
c. (∀x)Fx ∨ (∀x) ~ Fx
*d. (∀x)Fx ∨ ~ (∀x)Fx
e. (∀x)Fx ∨ (∃x) ~ Fx
*f. (∀x)(Fx ∨ Gx) ⊃ [(∃x)Fx ∨ (∃x)Gx]
g. (∀x)(Fx ∨ Gx) ⊃ [(∃x) ~ Fx ⊃ (∃x)Gx]
*h. (∀x)(Fx ∨ Gx) ⊃ [(∃x)Fx ∨ (∀x)Gx]
i. [(∀x)Fx ∨ (∀x)Gx] ⊃ (∀x)(Fx ∨ Gx)
*j. (∀x)(Fx ∨ Gx) ⊃ [(∀x)Fx ∨ (∀x)Gx]
k. (∃x)(Fx & Gx) ⊃ [(∃x)Fx & (∃x)Gx]
*l. [(∃x)Fx & (∃x)Gx] ⊃ (∃x)(Fx & Gx)
m. ~ (∃x)Fx ∨ (∀x) ~ Fx
*n. (∀x)[Fx ⊃ (Gx & Hx)] ⊃ (∀x)[(Fx & Gx) ⊃ Hx]
o. (∀x)[(Fx & Gx) ⊃ Hx] ⊃ (∀x)[Fx ⊃ (Gx & Hx)]
*p. (∀x)(Fx & ~ Gx) ∨ (∃x)( ~ Fx ∨ Gx)
q. (∀x)(Fx ⊃ Gx) ⊃ (∀x)(Fx ⊃ (∀y)Gy)
*r. (∀x)(∀y)Gxy ⊃ (∀x)Gxx

s. $(\forall x)Gxx \supset (\forall x)(\forall y)Gxy$
*t. $(\forall x)Fxx \supset (\forall x)(\exists y)Fxy$
u. $(\exists x)(\forall y)Gxy \supset (\forall x)(\exists y)Gyx$
*v. $(\exists x)(\exists y)(Lxy \equiv Lyx)$
w. $((\exists x)Lxx \supset (\forall y)Lyy) \supset (Laa \supset Lgg)$

**2.** Which of the following sentences are quantificationally false?
a. $(\forall x)Fx \;\&\; (\exists x) \sim Fx$
*b. $(\forall x)Fx \;\&\; \sim(\exists x)Fx$
c. $(\exists x)Fx \;\&\; (\exists x) \sim Fx$
*d. $(\exists x)Fx \;\&\; \sim(\forall x)Fx$
e. $(\forall x)(Fx \supset (\forall y) \sim Fy)$
*f. $(\forall x)(Fx \supset \sim Fx)$
g. $(\forall x)(Fx \equiv \sim Fx)$
*h. $(\exists x)Fx \supset (\forall x) \sim Fx$
i. $(\exists x)(\exists y)(Fxy \;\&\; \sim Fyx)$
*j. $(\exists x)Fx \;\&\; \sim(\exists y)Fy$
k. $(\forall x)(\forall y)(Fxy \supset \sim Fyx)$
*l. $(\forall x)(Gx \equiv \sim Fx) \;\&\; \sim (\forall x) \sim (Gx \equiv Fx)$
m. $(\exists x)(\forall y)Gxy \;\&\; \sim(\forall y)(\exists x)Gxy$

**3.** What is the quantificational status (quantificationally true, quantificationally false, or quantificationally indeterminate) of each of the following sentences?
a. $(\exists x)Fxx \supset (\exists x)(\exists y)Fxy$
*b. $(\exists x)(\exists y)Fxy \supset (\exists x)Fxx$
c. $(\exists x)(\forall y)Lxy \supset (\exists x)Lxx$
*d. $(\forall x)(Fx \supset (\exists y)Gyx) \supset ((\exists x)Fx \supset (\exists x)(\exists y)Gxy)$
e. $(\forall x)(Fx \supset (\exists y)Gya) \supset (Fb \supset (\exists y)Gya)$
*f. $((\exists x)Lxx \supset (\forall y)Lyy) \supset (Laa \supset Lgg)$
g. $(\forall x)(Fx \supset (\forall y)Gxy) \supset (\exists x)(Fx \supset \sim(\forall y)Gxy)$

**4.** Which of the following pairs of sentences are quantificationally equivalent?

| | | |
|---|---|---|
| a. | $(\forall x)Mxx$ | $\sim(\exists x) \sim Mxx$ |
| *b. | $(\exists x)(Fx \supset Ga)$ | $(\exists x)Fx \supset Ga$ |
| c. | $(\forall x)(Fa \supset Gx)$ | $Fa \supset (\forall x)Gx$ |
| *d. | $Ls \equiv (\forall x)Lx$ | $(\exists x)Lx$ |
| e. | $(\exists x)Fx \supset Ga$ | $(\exists x)(Fx \supset Ga)$ |
| *f. | $(\forall x)(Fx \vee Gx)$ | $(\forall x)Fx \vee (\forall x)Gx$ |
| g. | $(\forall x)Fx \supset Ga$ | $(\exists x)(Fx \supset Ga)$ |
| *h. | $(\exists x)(Ax \;\&\; Bx)$ | $(\exists x)Ax \;\&\; (\exists x)Bx$ |
| i. | $(\forall x)(\forall y)(Fx \supset Gy)$ | $(\forall x)(Fx \supset (\forall y)Gy)$ |
| *j. | $(\forall x)(Fx \equiv \sim Gx)$ | $(\forall x) \sim (Fx \equiv Gx)$ |
| k. | $(\forall x)(Fa \equiv Gx)$ | $Fa \equiv (\forall x)Gx$ |
| *l. | $(\forall x)(Fx \vee (\exists y)Gy)$ | $(\forall x)(\exists y)(Fx \vee Gy)$ |
| m. | $(\forall x)(Fx \supset (\forall y)Gy)$ | $(\forall x)(\forall y)(Fx \supset Gy)$ |

**5.** Which of the following arguments are quantificationally valid?

a. $(\forall x)(Fx \supset Gx)$
Ga
__________
Fa

*b. $(\forall x)(Tx \supset Lx)$
$\sim Lb$
———
$\sim Tb$

c. $(\forall x)(Kx \supset Lx)$
$(\forall x)(Lx \supset Mx)$
———
$(\forall x)(Kx \supset Mx)$

*d. $(\forall x)(Fx \supset Gx)$
$(\forall x)(Hx \supset Gx)$
———
$(\forall x)((Fx \vee Hx) \supset Gx)$

e. $(\forall x)(Fx \supset Gx) \supset (\exists x)Nx$
$(\forall x)(Nx \supset Gx)$
———
$(\forall x)(\sim Fx \vee Gx)$

*f. $(\sim (\exists y)Fy \supset (\exists y)Fy) \vee \sim Fa$
———
$(\exists z)Fz$

g. $(\forall x)(\sim Ax \supset Kx)$
$(\exists y) \sim Ky$
———
$(\exists w)(Aw \vee \sim Lwf)$

*h. $(\forall y)(Hy \ \& \ (Jyy \ \& \ My))$
———
$(\exists x)Jxb \ \& \ (\forall x)Mx$

i. $(\forall x)(\forall y)Cxy$
———
$(Caa \ \& \ Cab) \ \& \ (Cba \ \& \ Cbb)$

*j. $(\exists x)(Fx \ \& \ Gx)$
$(\exists x)(Fx \ \& \ Hx)$
———
$(\exists x)(Gx \ \& \ Hx)$

k. $(\forall x)(Fx \supset Gx)$
$\sim (\exists x)Fx$
———
$\sim (\exists x)Gx$

*l. $(\exists z)Bzz$
$(\forall x)(Sx \supset Bxx)$
———
$\sim Sg$

m. $(\exists x)Cx \supset Ch$
———
$(\exists x)Cx \equiv Ch$

*n. $Fa \vee (\exists y)Gya$
$Fb \vee (\exists y) \sim Gyb$
———
$(\exists y)Gya$

6. Which of the following alleged entailments hold?

a. $\{(\forall x) \sim Jx, (\exists y)(Hby \vee Ryy) \supset (\exists x)Jx\} \vDash (\forall y) \sim (Hby \vee Ryy)$

*b. $\{(\forall x)(\forall y)(Mxy \supset Nxy)\} \vDash (\forall x)(\forall y)(Mxy \supset (Nxy \; \& \; Nyx))$

c. $\{(\forall y)((Hy \; \& \; Fy) \supset Gy), (\forall z)Fz \; \& \; \sim(\forall x)Kxb\} \vDash (\forall x)(Hx \supset Gx)$

*d. $\{(\forall x)(Fx \supset Gx), (\forall x)(Hx \supset Gx)\} \vDash (\forall x)(Fx \vee Hx)$

e. $\{(\forall z)(Lz \equiv Hz), (\forall x) \sim (Hx \vee \sim Bx)\} \vDash \sim Lb$

## 9.4 TREES FOR *PLI*

To apply the tree method to the language *PLI*, we must modify the tree system developed in the preceding sections so as to accommodate sentences containing the identity predicate. We will accomplish this by introducing one new decomposition rule and by modifying the definitions of a closed branch and of a completed open branch. The modified tree system we here develop applies to *PLI*. The system developed in earlier sections remains intact and is adequate as it now stands for the language *PL*.

We begin with the new rule.

$\boldsymbol{a} = \boldsymbol{b}$ = D

$\mathcal{P}$

$\mathcal{P}(\boldsymbol{a}//\boldsymbol{b})$

The rule, Identity Decomposition, is to be understood in the following way. Where a branch contains a sentence of the form $\boldsymbol{a} = \boldsymbol{b}$, $\mathcal{P}(\boldsymbol{a}//\boldsymbol{b})$ may be entered on any open branch passing through $\boldsymbol{a} = \boldsymbol{b}$, where $\mathcal{P}$ is a literal containing $\boldsymbol{b}$ and $\mathcal{P}(\boldsymbol{a}//\boldsymbol{b})$ is like $\mathcal{P}$ except that it contains $\boldsymbol{a}$ *in at least one place* where $\mathcal{P}$ contains $\boldsymbol{b}$. Sentences of the form $\boldsymbol{a} = \boldsymbol{b}$ are not checked off because they can be decomposed again and again. The idea behind this rule is that if $\boldsymbol{a}$ and $\boldsymbol{b}$ are identical, are one and the same thing, then whatever is true of one is true of the other. So whatever is claimed of $\boldsymbol{b}$ can be claimed of $\boldsymbol{a}$. Identity Decomposition is used in the following tree:

| | | | |
|---|---|---|---|
| 1. | $(\forall x)(Fx \supset Gx)$ | | SM |
| 2. | Fc | | SM |
| 3. | $\sim$Gd | | SM |
| 4. | c = d | | SM |
| 5. | $Fc \supset Gc$ ✓ | | 1 $\forall$D |
| 6. | $\sim$ Fc | Gc | 5 $\supset$D |
| 7. | × | $\sim$Gc | 4, 3 = D |
| | | × | |

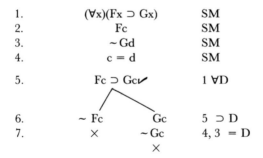

Identity Decomposition is used at line 7. Here $\boldsymbol{a} = \boldsymbol{b}$ is 'c = d', $\mathcal{P}$ is '$\sim$Gd', and $\mathcal{P}(\boldsymbol{a}//\boldsymbol{b})$ is '$\sim$Gd'(c//d), that is, '$\sim$Gc', the sentence entered on line 7. Note that the justification column for line 7 contains two line numbers. This is because Identity Decomposition licenses the entry of a sentence on a branch based on the presence of two other sentences. In this respect it is unlike the other decomposition rules.

Consider the sentence '(∃y) ~ y = y'. This sentence says 'There is something which is not identical with itself', and is clearly quantificationally false. So we want the tree for the unit set of this sentence to close:

| | | |
|---|---|---|
| 1. | (∃y) ~ y = y ✓ | SM |
| 2. | ~ a = a | 1 ∃D |

The one branch on this tree does not contain an atomic sentence and its negation. So it is not, by our present account, a closed branch. What is perhaps worse, it is, by the account given in Section 9.2, a completed open branch—the sentence on line one has been decomposed and the sentence on line two is a literal. We cannot countenance this result. Two alternatives present themselves: We can modify our account of a closed branch so as to make this branch a closed branch, or we can modify our account of a completed open branch so as to make this branch *not* a completed open branch. Pursuing the latter course will require subsequent further alterations, for our goal is to generate a closed tree for the present sentence, not just to fail to generate an open tree.

The latter alternative could be accomplished by requiring that a sentence of the form $(\forall \boldsymbol{x})\boldsymbol{x} = \boldsymbol{x}$ be entered on every branch on which a sentence of the form $\boldsymbol{a} = \boldsymbol{b}$ occurs. Since sentences of the former sort are all quantificationally true, adding them to trees will never produce unwanted results. In the present case we would get the following closed tree:

| | | |
|---|---|---|
| 1. | (∃y) ~ y = y | SM |
| 2. | ~ a = a | 1 ∃D |
| 3. | (∀y)y = y | New Identity Rule |
| 4. | a = a | 3 ∀D |
| | × | |

At line 3 we enter '(∀y)y = y'. Universal Decomposition yields 'a = a' at line 4, an atomic sentence whose negation appears on line 2. So the tree is closed. On this approach, we retain the notion that a branch is closed if and only if it contains an atomic sentence and its negation. But the cost is that of introducing a second identity rule, one which is not remotely a "decomposition" rule.

The other approach, that of suitably revising our account of a closed branch, is more simply accomplished, and is the one we choose. The rationale for declaring a branch on which an atomic sentence and its negation both occur a closed branch is that there is no interpretation on which an atomic sentence and its negation are both true. Almost as obviously, there is no interpretation on which a sentence of the form $\sim \boldsymbol{a} = \boldsymbol{a}$ is true, this by the fixed interpretation of the identity predicate. So we can modify our account of a closed branch as follows:

> *Closed branch:* A branch on which some atomic sentence and its negation both occur, or on which a sentence of the form $\sim \boldsymbol{a} = \boldsymbol{a}$ occurs.

Given this revised account, we need only one identity rule, Identity Decomposition.

Just as we want the tree method to yield a closed tree for $\{(\exists y) \sim y = y\}$ we want it to yield an open tree for $\{Fa,\ a = b,\ \sim Gb\}$. Here is a start of such a tree

| | | |
|---|---|---|
| 1. | Fa | SM |
| 2. | a = b | SM |
| 3. | ~Gb | SM |

Our present account of a completed open branch speaks to literals, decomposed sentences, and universally quantified sentences, requiring that each sentence on such a branch be one of the three, that is,

1. a literal
2. not a universally quantified sentence and decomposed
3. a universally quantified sentence $(\forall \boldsymbol{x})\mathscr{P}$ such that $\mathscr{P}(\boldsymbol{a}/\boldsymbol{x})$ occur on that branch *for each constant* $\boldsymbol{a}$ occurring on the branch and at least one instance $\mathscr{P}(\boldsymbol{a}/\boldsymbol{x})$ does occur on the branch.

Clause 2 was intended to deal with sentences which are decomposed only once (and are checked off). Since Identity Decomposition, like Universal Decomposition, can be applied more than once to a single sentence, we need to add a clause dealing specifically with Identity Decomposition. It is

4. a sentence of the form $\boldsymbol{a} = \boldsymbol{b}$ where the branch also contains, for every literal $\mathscr{P}$ containing $\boldsymbol{b}$ on that branch, every sentence $\mathscr{P}(\boldsymbol{a}//\boldsymbol{b})$ which can be obtained from $\mathscr{P}$ by Identity Decomposition and which is *not* of the form $\boldsymbol{a} = \boldsymbol{a}$.

Clause 4 requires that we add a further sentence to the single branch of the above tree to make that branch a completed open branch, the sentence '~Ga'. This because 'a = b', which is a sentence of the form $\boldsymbol{a} = \boldsymbol{b}$, occurs on line 2, '~Gb', which occurs on line 3, is a literal containing 'b', and from these two sentences we can obtain, by Identity Decomposition, '~Ga'. ('~Ga' is '~Gb(a//b)'.) The completed tree is thus:

| | | |
|---|---|---|
| 1. | Fa | SM |
| 2. | a = b | SM |
| 3. | ~Gb | SM |
| 4. | ~Ga | 2, 3 ID |

The one branch on the above tree is a completed open branch and that tree is therefore an open tree.

The force of the last phrase of clause 4, "and which is *not* of the form $\boldsymbol{a} = \boldsymbol{a}$", is to alleviate the need to enter sentences which cannot close a branch. No sentence of the form $\boldsymbol{a} = \boldsymbol{a}$ can close a branch because were the needed matching sentence also present, $\sim \boldsymbol{a} = \boldsymbol{a}$, that sentence by itself would close the branch. Hence while Identity Decomposition does license, for example, the adding of both 'c = c' and 'd = d' to a branch which contains 'c = d' and 'd = c', the above account of a completed open branch does not require that they be added.

Given our expanded set of rules and revised notions of closed and completed open branches, the explications developed in Sections 9.2 and 9.3 of semantic properties in terms of open and closed trees also hold for *PLI*. We therefore adopt them for *PLI* without here repeating them.

The set {a = b, (∀x)(Fbx & ~ Fxa)} is quantificationally inconsistent, as the following tree shows:

| | | |
|---|---|---|
| 1. | a = b | SM |
| 2. | (∀x)(Fbx & ~ Fax) | SM |
| 3. | Fbb & ~ Fab✓ | 2 ∀D |
| 4. | Fbb | 3 & D |
| 5. | ~ Fab | 3 & D |
| 6. | Fab | 1, 4 = D |
| | × | |

What is interesting here is the use of Identity Decomposition at line 6. We generated 'Fab' from 'a = b' and 'Fbb' by replacing only the first occurrence of 'b' in the latter with 'a'. (When generating $\mathscr{P}(\boldsymbol{a}//\boldsymbol{b})$ from $\mathscr{P}$, given $\boldsymbol{a} = \boldsymbol{b}$, it is not required that *every* occurrence of $\boldsymbol{b}$ in $\mathscr{P}$ be replaced with $\boldsymbol{a}$, but only that at least one occurrence be so replaced. Of course we could also have closed the tree by entering 'Faa' at line 6 (replacing both occurrences of 'b' in 'Fbb' with 'a') and then entering '~ Faa' at line 7, both by Identity Decomposition.

Consider now a quantificationally consistent set: (c = b, (∀x)(Fxc ⊃ ~ Gxb), (∀x)Gxc}. Here is a tree for this set:

| | | | | |
|---|---|---|---|---|
| 1. | | c = b | | SM |
| 2. | | (∀x)(Fxc ⊃ ~ Gxb) | | SM |
| 3. | | (∀x)Gxc | | SM |
| 4. | | Gcc | | 3 ∀D |
| 5. | | Gbc | | 3 ∀D |
| 6. | | Fcc ⊃ ~ Gcb✓ | | 2 ∀D |
| 7. | | Fbc ⊃ ~ Gbb✓ | | 2 ∀D |
| 8. | ~ Fcc | | ~ Gcb | 6 ⊃ D |
| 9. | | | ~ Gcc | 1, 8 = D |
| | | | × | |
| 10. | ~ Fbc | ~ Gbb | | 7 ⊃ D |
| 11. | | ~ Gbc | | 1, 10 = D |
| | | × | | |

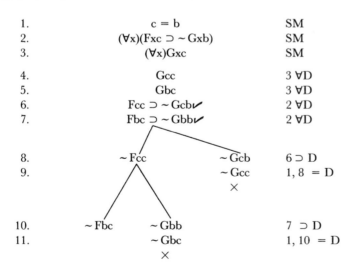

The left-hand branch of this tree is a completed open branch and hence establishes that this set is quantificationally consistent. The left-hand branch does contain every required sentence which can be generated from the identity on line 1 and a literal containing 'c'. (We could generate 'Gcc' from lines 1 and 5, but it already occurs on line 4. Similarly, we could generate '∼Fcc' from lines 1 and 10, but it already occurs at line 8.) Note also that while Identity Decomposition allows, given an identity sentence $\boldsymbol{a} = \boldsymbol{b}$, the generation of literals in which one or more occurrence of $\boldsymbol{b}$ in an existing literal has been replaced with $\boldsymbol{a}$, it does not license the generation of literals in which one or more occurrence of $\boldsymbol{a}$ has been replaced with $\boldsymbol{b}$. We could rewrite Identity Decomposition so as to allow this, but so doing, given our account of a completed open branch for trees for *PLI*, would frequently require adding more literals to trees. In the present case, it would require adding 'Gbb', '∼Fbb', and '∼Fcb' to that branch.[4]

As noted in Chapter Seven, identity is a relation which is transitive; symmetrical, and fully reflexive. Accordingly, we expect the following sentences of *PLI*, which assert, respectively, the transitivity, symmetry, and reflexivity, of identity to be quantificationally true:

$$(\forall x)(\forall y)(\forall z)[(x = y \,\&\, y = z) \supset x = z]$$
$$(\forall x)(\forall y)(x = y \supset y = x)$$
$$(\forall x)x = x$$

As we might expect, the truth-tree method will produce a closed tree for the negations of these sentences. Here is the relevant tree for the claim that identity is reflexive

| | | |
|---|---|---|
| 1. | $\sim(\forall x)x = x$ ✓ | SM |
| 2. | $(\exists x) \sim x = x$ ✓ | 1 $\sim\forall$D |
| 3. | $\sim a = a$ | 2 $\exists$D |
| | × | |

The tree is closed, so the tree method yields, as desired, the result that the sentence '$\sim(\forall x)x = x$' is quantificationally false, and '$(\forall x)x = x$' quantificationally true, that is, identity is fully reflexive. It should be noted that when we earlier modified the definition of a closed branch so as to count every branch containing a sentence of the form '$\sim \boldsymbol{a} = \boldsymbol{a}$' as a closed branch we were, in effect, presupposing the reflexivity of identity. The present result is therefore neither surprising nor an independent proof of the reflexivity of identity.

[4] We have not, of course, demonstrated either that the expanded set of tree rules and modified accounts of open and closed branches introduced in this section are adequate to their intended task, nor that the original tree rules and definitions introduced in earlier sections are adequate to the task assigned them for testing sentences and sets of sentences of *PL*. We shall demonstrate this in Chapter Eleven.

Symmetry is next. The relevant tree is

| | | |
|---|---|---|
| 1. | $\sim (\forall x)(\forall y)(x = y \supset y = x) \checkmark$ | SM |
| 2. | $(\exists x) \sim (\forall y)(x = y \supset y = x) \checkmark$ | $1 \sim\forall D$ |
| 3. | $\sim (\forall y)(a = y \supset y = a) \checkmark$ | $2\ \exists D$ |
| 4. | $(\exists y) \sim (a = y \supset y = a) \checkmark$ | $3 \sim\forall D$ |
| 5. | $\sim (a = b \supset b = a) \checkmark$ | $4\ \exists D$ |
| 6. | $a = b$ | $5 \sim\supset D$ |
| 7. | $\sim b = a$ | $5 \sim\supset D$ |
| 8. | $\sim a = a$ | $6, 7\ = D$ |
| | $\times$ | |

The tree is closed; also a desired result since the sentence '$\sim (\forall x)(\forall y)(x = y \supset y = x)$' is quantificationally false and the sentence '$(\forall x)(\forall y)(x = y \supset y = x)$' is quantificationally true, that is, identity is symmetrical.

Finally, we consider transitivity. The relevant tree is

| | | |
|---|---|---|
| 1. | $\sim (\forall x)(\forall y)(\forall z)[(x = y \ \& \ y = z) \supset x = z] \checkmark$ | SM |
| 2. | $(\exists x) \sim (\forall y)(\forall z)[(x = y \ \& \ y = z) \supset x = z] \checkmark$ | $1 \sim\forall D$ |
| 3. | $\sim (\forall y)(\forall z)[(a = y \ \& \ y = z) \supset a = z] \checkmark$ | $2\ \exists D$ |
| 4. | $(\exists y) \sim (\forall z)[(a = y \ \& \ y = z) \supset a = z] \checkmark$ | $3 \sim\forall D$ |
| 5. | $\sim (\forall z)[(a = b \ \& \ b = z) \supset a = z] \checkmark$ | $4\ \exists D$ |
| 6. | $(\exists z) \sim [(a = b \ \& \ b = z) \supset a = z] \checkmark$ | $5 \sim\forall D$ |
| 7. | $\sim [(a = b \ \& \ b = c) \supset a = c] \checkmark$ | $6\ \exists D$ |
| 8. | $(a = b \ \& \ b = c) \checkmark$ | $7 \sim\supset D$ |
| 9. | $\sim a = c$ | $7 \sim\supset D$ |
| 10. | $a = b$ | $8\ \& D$ |
| 11. | $b = c$ | $8\ \& D$ |
| 12. | $a = c$ | $10, 11\ = D$ |
| | $\times$ | |

This tree, as expected, is closed, reflecting the fact that the sentence on line 1 is quantificationally false, and '$(\forall x)(\forall y)(\forall z)[(x = y \ \& \ y = z) \supset x = z]$' quantificationally true, that is, identity is transitive. Here we closed the tree by applying Identity Decomposition to lines 10 and 11, taking '$a = b$' as $\mathbf{a} = \mathbf{b}$, '$b = c$' as $\mathscr{P}$, producing '$a = c$' as $\mathscr{P}(\mathbf{a}//\mathbf{b})$. Since '$\sim a = c$' occurs on line 9, the one branch of the tree contains an atomic sentence, '$a = c$', and its negation, '$\sim a = c$', and is therefore closed.

Consider now the sentence '$(\forall x)(\forall y)[(Fxx \ \& \sim Fyy) \supset \sim x = y]$'. We expect this sentence to be quantificationally true (if a thing x and a thing y were identical, then it could not be the case that x but not y bears a relation F to itself).

The following truth-tree confirms this expectation:

| | | |
|---|---|---|
| 1. | ∼(∀x)(∀y)[(Fxx & ∼Fyy) ⊃ ∼x = y]✓ | SM |
| 2. | (∃x) ∼(∀y)[(Fxx & ∼Fyy) ⊃ ∼x = y]✓ | 1 ∼∀D |
| 3. | ∼(∀y)[(Faa & ∼Fyy) ⊃ ∼a = y]✓ | 2 ∃D |
| 4. | (∃y) ∼ [(Faa & ∼Fyy) ⊃ ∼a = y]✓ | 3 ∼∀D |
| 5. | ∼[(Faa & ∼Fbb) ⊃ ∼a = b]✓ | 4 ∃D |
| 6. | Faa & ∼Fbb✓ | 5 ∼⊃ D |
| 7. | ∼∼a = b✓ | 5 ∼⊃ D |
| 8. | a = b | 7 ∼∼D |
| 9. | Faa | 6 & D |
| 10. | ∼Fbb | 6 & D |
| 11. | ∼Faa | 8, 10 = D |
| | × | |

At line 11 we replaced both occurrences of 'b' in '∼Fbb' to generate '∼Faa'. Replacing just one occurrence, while allowed, would not here have produced a closed tree.

Here is a final example:

(∃x)Gxa & ∼(∃x)Gax
(∀x)(Gxb ⊃ x = b)
―――――――――――
∼a = b

To test this argument for quantificationally validity, we do a tree for the premises and the negation of the conclusion.

| | | | |
|---|---|---|---|
| 1. | (∃x)Gxa & ∼(∃x)Gax✓ | | SM |
| 2. | (∀x)(Gxb ⊃ x = b) | | SM |
| 3. | ∼∼a = b✓ | | SM |
| 4. | a = b | | 3 ∼∼ D |
| 5. | (∃x)Gxa✓ | | 1 & D |
| 6. | ∼(∃x)Gax✓ | | 1 & D |
| 7. | (∀x) ∼Gax | | 6 ∼∃D |
| 8. | Gca | | 5 ∃D |
| 9. | Gab ⊃ a = b | | 2 ∀D |
| 10. | Gbb ⊃ b = b | | 2 ∀D |
| 11. | Gcb ⊃ c = b✓ | | 2 ∀D |
| 12. | ∼Gaa | | 7 ∀D |
| 13. | ∼Gab | | 7 ∀D |
| 14. | ∼Gac | | 7 ∀D |
| 15. | ∼Gcb | c = b | 11 ⊃ D |
| 16. | ∼Gca | \| | 4, 15 = D |
| 17. | × | a = c | 15, 4 = D |
| 18. | | Gaa | 17, 8 = D |
| | | × | |

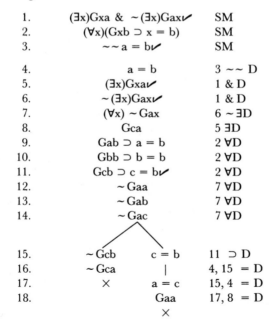

This tree is closed. Therefore, the argument we are testing is quantificationally valid. The secret to keeping this tree reasonably concise was to carefully study the sentences on lines 9–11 to determine which should be decomposed first. The identity on line 4 licenses replacing 'b' with 'a' in literals, and line 11 yields '~Gcb' on the left branch when decomposed. Replacing the 'b' with 'a' in that literal yielded '~Gca' at line 17, which closed the left branch. At line 15 the right branch is open and contains 'c = b'. That branch contains, at that point, two identity claims, 'a = b' and 'c = b'. From these and the other literals on the branch ('Gca', ~'Gaa', '~Gab', and '~ Gac') a host of sentences could be obtained by Identity Decomposition. Careful study reveals that any of 'Gac', 'Gab', and 'Gaa' would close the branch. But only the latter will come from 'Gca' on line 8 in one step. ('Gaa' can be obtained by replacing 'c' with 'a' in 'Gca'.) But to do so we first had to obtain 'a = c'. The latter was obtained from lines 15 and 4 by Identity Decomposition. (The sentence 'c = b' on line 15 allows us to replace one or more occurrence of 'b' with 'c' in any literal containing 'b'. The sentence 'a = b' on line 4 is such a literal. So we applied Identity Decomposition to these sentences to yield 'a = c' at line 17.) At line 18 we obtained 'Gaa', also by Identity Decomposition, and closed the branch and the tree.

## 9.4E EXERCISES

Construct truth-trees as necessary to provide the requested information. In each case state your result and what it is about your tree which establishes this result.

**1.** Determine, for each of the following sets, whether the set is quantificationally consistent.

a. {(∀x)Fxx, (∃x)(∃y) ~ Fxy, (∀x)x = a}
*b. {(∀x)(Fxc ⊃ x = a), ~c = a, (∃x)Fxc}
c. {(∀x)(x = a ⊃ Gxb), ~(∃x)Gxx, a = b}
*d. {(∃x)(∃y) ~ x = y, (∀x)(Gxx ⊃ x = b), Gaa}
e. {(∀x)((Fx & ~Gx) ⊃ ~ x = a), Fa & ~ Ga}
*f. {(∃y)(∀x)Fxy, ~ (∀x)(∀y)x = y, Fab & ~Fba}

**2.** Determine, for each of the following sentences, whether it is quantificationally true, quantificationally false, or quantificationally indeterminate.

a. a = b ≡ b = a
*b. (~a = b & ~b = c) ⊃ ~a = c
c. (Gab & ~ Gba) ⊃ ~a = b
*d. (∀x)(∃y)x = y
e. Fa ≡ (∃x)(Fx & x = a)
*f. ~ (∃x)x = a
g. (∀x)x = a ⊃ [(∃x)Fx ⊃ (∀x)Fx]
*h. (∀x)(∀y)x = y
i. (∀x)(∀y) ~x = y
*j. (∃x)(∃y)x = y

k. $(\exists x)(\exists y) \sim x = y$
*l. $(\forall x)(\forall y)[x = y \supset (Fx \equiv Fy)]$
m. $(\forall x)(\forall y)[(Fx \equiv Fy) \supset x = y]$
*n. $(\forall x)(\forall y)[x = y \supset (\forall z)(Fxz \equiv Fyz)]$
o. $[(\exists x)Gax \ \& \ \sim (\exists x)Gxa] \supset (\forall x)(Gxa \supset \sim x = a)$

**3.** Determine which of the following pairs of sentences are quantificationally equivalent.

| | | |
|---|---|---|
| a. | $\sim a = b$ | $\sim b = a$ |
| *b. | $(\exists x) \sim x = a$ | $(\exists x) \sim x = b$ |
| c. | $(\forall x)x = a$ | $(\forall x)x = b$ |
| *d. | $a = b \ \& \ b = c$ | $a = c \ \& \ b = c$ |
| e. | $(\forall x)(\forall y)x = y$ | $(\forall x)x = a$ |
| *f. | $(\forall x)(\exists y)x = y$ | $(\forall y)(\exists x)x = y$ |
| g. | $(\forall x)(Fx \supset x = a)$ | $(\forall x)(Fa \supset x = a)$ |
| *h. | $(\forall x)(x = a \vee x = b)$ | $(\forall x)x = a \vee (\forall x)x = b$ |
| i. | $(\forall x)Fx \vee (\forall x) \sim Fx$ | $(\forall y)(Fy \supset y = b)$ |
| *j. | $a = b$ | $(\forall y)(y = a \supset y = b)$ |
| k. | $(\exists x)(x = a \ \& \ x = b)$ | $a = b$ |

**4.** Determine which of the following arguments are quantificationally valid.

a. $a = b \ \& \sim Bab$
____________
$\sim (\forall x)Bxx$

*b. $Ge \supset d = e$
$Ge \supset He$
____________
$Ge \supset Hd$

c. $(\forall z)(Gz \supset (\forall y)(Ky \supset Hzy))$
$(Ki \ \& \ Gj) \ \& \ i = j$
____________
$Hii$

*d. $(\exists x)(Hx \ \& \ Mx)$
$Ms \ \& \sim Hs$
____________
$(\exists x)((Hx \ \& \ Mx) \ \& \sim x = s)$

e. $a = b$
____________
$Ka \vee \sim Kb$

*f. $(\exists x) \sim Pxx \supset \sim a = a$
$a = c$
____________
$Pac$

g. $(\forall x)(x = a \vee x = b)$
$(\exists x)(Fxa \ \& \ Fbx)$
____________
$(\exists x)Fxx$

*h. $(\exists x)Fxa$
$(\forall y)(y = a \supset y = b)$

---

$(\exists y)Fyy$

i. $(\forall x)(\forall y)(Fxy \lor Fyx)$
$a = b$

---

$(\forall x)(Fxa \lor Fbx)$

*j. $(\exists x)Fxa \ \& \ (\exists x)Fxb$
$\sim a = b$

---

$(\forall x)(\forall y)((Fxa \ \& \ Fyb) \supset \sim x = y)$

k. $(\forall x)(Fx \equiv \sim Gx)$
$Fa$
$Gb$

---

$\sim a = b$

*l. $\sim (\exists x)Fxx$

---

$(\forall x)(\forall y)(Fxy \supset \sim x = y)$

m. $(\forall x)(\forall y)x = y$

---

$\sim (\exists x)(\exists y)(Fx \ \& \ \sim Fy)$

*n. $(\forall x)(\sim x = a \equiv (\exists y)Gyx)$
$Gbc$

---

$\sim c = a$

**5.** Determine which of the following claims are true.
a. $\{(\forall x)(Fx \supset (\exists y)(Gyx \ \& \ \sim y = x)), (\exists x)Fx\} \vDash (\exists x)(\exists y) \sim x = y$
*b. $\{\sim (\exists x)(Fxa \lor Fxb), (\forall x)(\forall y)(Fxy \supset \sim x = y)\} \vDash \sim a = b$
c. $\{(\forall x)(Fx \supset \sim x = a), (\exists x)Fx\} \vDash (\exists x)(\exists y) \sim x = y$
*d. $\{(\forall x)(\exists y)(Fxy \ \& \ \sim x = y), a = b, Fab\} \vDash (\exists y)(Fay \ \& \ y = b)$
e. $\{(\exists w)(\exists z) \sim w = z, (\exists w)Hw\} \vDash (\exists w) \sim Hw$
*f. $\{(\exists w)(\forall y)Gwy, (\exists w)(\forall y)(\sim w = y \supset \sim Gwy)\} \vDash (\exists z) \sim Gzz$
g. $\{(\forall x)(\forall y)((Fx \equiv Fy) \equiv x = y), (\exists z)Fz\} \vDash (\exists x)(\exists y)(\sim x = y \ \& \ (Fx \ \& \ \sim Fy))$

## 9.5 FINE TUNING THE TREE METHOD

When we introduced the language *PL* in Chapter Seven we cautioned "that *PL* and its associated test procedures do not constitute a *decidable* system. That is, there is no mechanical test procedure which will always yield, in a finite number of steps, a yes or no answer to such questions as 'Is this argument of *PL* valid?'" Let a *finite truth-tree* be a truth-tree which is either closed or has a completed open branch. Given the above caveat it should come as no surprise that not every finite set of sentences of *PL* has a finite truth-tree.

Here is the start of a tree for {(∀y)(∃z)Fyz}, a set which, given the tree system we have developed, has no finite truth-tree:

| | | |
|---|---|---|
| 1. | (∀y)(∃z)Fyz | SM |
| 2. | (∃z)Fazr✓ | 1 ∀D |
| 3. | Fab | 2 ∃D |
| 4. | (∃z)Fbz✓ | 1 ∀D |
| 5. | Fbc | 4 ∃D |
| 6. | (∃z)Fcz✓ | 1 ∀D |
| 7. | Fcd | 6 ∃D |

There is no hope of closing the one open branch on this tree. At every other step after the first, a new atomic sentence is added to the open branch, and, since every atomic sentence is quantificationally consistent with every other atomic sentence, continuing to add more atomic sentences will never close the tree. This branch will also never become a completed open branch. Every time Universal Decomposition is applied to the sentence '(∀y)(∃z)Fyz' on line 1 a new existentially quantified sentence is added to the branch. And decomposing that sentence adds a new individual constant to the branch, necessitating a further application of Universal Decomposition to '(∀y)(∃z)Fyz', resuming the cycle. We call an open branch that cannot be completed—one that will never close and cannot, in a finite number of steps, be made into a completed open branch—*a nonterminating branch.*

Not every finite set of sentences of *PL/PLI* has a finite tree. This is an unavoidable result. There are, however, two ways in which the tree method we have developed can be improved. First, we would like assurances that when a set does have a finite tree we will eventually find it. The tree rules we have presented do not guarantee this, for they allow the construction of trees such as the following:

| | | |
|---|---|---|
| 1. | (∀x)Fx | SM |
| 2. | (∀x) ~ Fx | SM |
| 3. | Fa | 1 ∀D |
| 4. | Fb | 1 ∀D |
| 5. | Fc | 1 ∀D |
| 6. | Fd | 1 ∀D |
| | ⋮ | |

The dots indicate that the tree is continued indefinitely by adding one substituting instance after another of the sentence on line 1. Continuing in this way does not involve misusing any tree rule but will never produce a closed tree or a completed open branch. A closed tree for the above set can be produced in just four lines:

| | | |
|---|---|---|
| 1. | (∀x)Fx | SM |
| 2. | (∀x) ~ Fx | SM |
| 3. | Fa | 1 ∀D |
| 4. | ~ Fa | 2 ∀D |
| | × | |

What we need is a procedure for applying the decomposition rules that will always yield a finite tree where one exists.

The second problem with the tree method as we have presented it is that some sets which we would like to have finite trees do not have them. To help understand this problem, we introduce the notion of a model. A model for a set of sentences of *PL/PLI* is an interpretation on which all the members of the set are true. (So all the only consistent sets have models.) A finite model is an interpretation with a finite U.D., an infinite model an interpretation with an infinite U.D. There are finite sets of sentences of *PL* that have only infinite models. That is, there are finite quantificationally consistent sets such that every interpretation on which all the members of the set are true is an interpretation with an infinite U.D. For example, {(∀x)(∀y)(Fxy ⊃ ~ Fyx), ~ (∃x)Fxx, (∀x)(∃y)Fxy} has only infinite models.

We would like to have a tree system such that every finite inconsistent set has a closed tree *and* every finite set with a finite model has a finite tree. The tree system we have developed *is* such that every finite inconsistent set has a closed tree. Unfortunately, it *is not* such that every finite set with a finite model has a finite tree. Above we saw that the set {(∀x)(∃y)Fxy} does not have a finite tree. Yet it does have a finite model, for example:

U.D.: {1}
Fxy: x = y

Each thing in this restricted universe of discourse, namely the positive integer 1, is equal to something, namely itself.

We have, then, two tasks in this section: to devise a procedure that will guarantee the construction of a finite tree where one exists, and to revise the tree rules so that every finite set with a finite model has a finite tree. We begin with the latter task. Our strategy is to modify the rule Existential Decomposition. Recall that the Existential Decomposition rule requires that a sentence of the form $(\exists \boldsymbol{x})\mathscr{P}$ be decomposed to a substitution instance $\mathscr{P}(\boldsymbol{a}/\boldsymbol{x})$, where $\boldsymbol{a}$ is foreign to the branch in question. Recall also that trees are attempts to find interpretations on which all the members of the set being tested are true. To use a substitution instance formed from a constant already on the branch in question would be to narrow the range of interpretations we are willing to consider. As an example, consider the clearly consistent set {(∃x)Fx, (∃x) ~ Fx} and a tree for this set which misuses the current Existential Decomposition rule:

| | | | |
|---|---|---|---|
| 1. | (∃x)Fx | SM | |
| 2. | (∃x) ~ Fx | SM | |
| 3. | Fb | 1 ∃D | |
| 4. | ~ Fb | 2 ∃D | **MISTAKE!** |
| | × | | |

There is no interpretation on which something is of the sort F and that very same thing is of the sort not-F, and in using ‘b’ at line 4 as well as line 3 we are, in effect, looking for such an interpretation. It is no surprise that the search fails. So we cannot simply drop the present restriction on Existential Decomposition—doing so will sometimes, as here, produce closed trees for consistent sets. But consider next a tree for {(∃x)Fx, (∃x)Gx} which similarly misuses Existential Decomposition:

| | | | |
|---|---|---|---|
| 1. | (∃x)Fx✓ | SM | |
| 2. | (∃x)Gx✓ | SM | |
| 3. | Fa | 1 ∃D | |
| 4. | Ga | 2 ∃D | **MISTAKE!** |

This tree is open and from it *we can* construct an interpretation on which all the members of {(∃x)Fx, (∃x)Gx} are true, for example:

U.D.: {San Francisco}
Fx: x is a city
Gx: x is in California

The point is that trees are intended to give us information about the existence or nonexistence of interpretations on which all the members of the set being tested are true. In applying existential decomposition it is not, it is true (witness the first of the above two trees), safe to use only a substitution instance formed from a constant already on the branch in question. But we also should not assume that the only viable interpretations are those we will be led to by using a constant foreign to that branch, witness the second of the above trees. This suggests that we need a branching existential decomposition rule (we will call it ‘Existential Decomposition-2’, abbreviated as ‘∃D2’), for we need to consider both substitution instances formed from constants already on the branch and one formed from a new constant. Pursuing this line of reasoning, we can redo the above two trees as follows:

```
1.          (∃x)Fx✓           SM
2.        (∃x) ~ Fx✓          SM

3.             Fa             1 ∃D2
              /  \
             /    \
4.       ~ Fa      ~ Fb       2 ∃D2
           ×
```

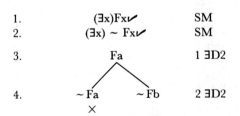

The closed left-hand branch shows that there is no interpretation on which ‘(∃x)Fx’ and ‘(∃x) ~ Fx’ are both true *and* some one thing is of the sort F and of the sort not-F. The right-hand branch is open and shows that there is an interpretation, whose U.D. need not be of a size greater than two, on which both these two sentences are true.

| | | | |
|---|---|---|---|
| 1. | (∃x)Fx | | SM |
| 2. | (∃x)Gx | | SM |
| 3. | Fa | | 2 ∃D2 |
| 4. | Ga | Gb | 3 ∃D2 |

Both branches of this tree are open. The left-hand branch, on which only one constant occurs, reveals that there is an interpretation on which both '(∃x)Fx' and '(∃x)Gx' are true and whose U.D. need not be of size greater than one. The right-hand branch reveals that there is such an interpretation whose U.D. need not be of size greater than two.

We are devising an existential decomposition rule which is a branching rule. But it is unlike other branching rules. First, it does not always produce additional branches. If there are no constants already on the branch in question, there is only one case to consider, that where a new constant is used. (See line 3 of each of the above two trees.) Second, if there is already more than one constant on a branch, the new existential decomposition rule will produce more than two branches. Consider a tree for the set {~Fa, (∃x)(Fx & Gx), (∃x) ~Gx}:

| | | | | | |
|---|---|---|---|---|---|
| 1. | | ~Fa | | | SM |
| 2. | | (∃x)(Fx & Gx) | | | SM |
| 3. | | (∃x) ~ Gx | | | SM |
| 4. | Fa & Ga | | Fb & Gb | | 2 ∃D2 |
| 5. | Fa | | Fb | | 4 & D |
| 6. | Ga | | Gb | | 4 & D |
| | × | | | | |
| 7. | | ~Ga | ~Gb | ~Gc | 3 ∃D2 |
| | | | × | | |

The rule we are developing can be schematically presented as

*Existential Decomposition-2* (∃D2)

$$(\exists x)\mathscr{P} \checkmark$$

$$\mathscr{P}(a/x) \quad \ldots \quad \mathscr{P}(m/x) \quad \mathscr{P}(n/x)$$

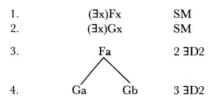

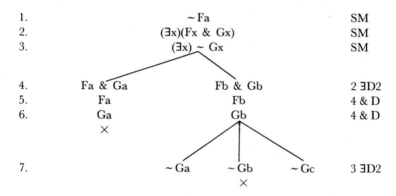

This rule is to be interpreted as requiring that in decomposing an existentially quantified sentence $(\exists x)\mathscr{P}$ appropriate substitution instances of that sentence be entered on every open branch passing through it. The schema specifies, for any such branch, which instances are to be entered on *that* branch. Specifically, substitution instances formed from the constants $\boldsymbol{a}$ through $\boldsymbol{m}$, where $\boldsymbol{a}$ is the alphabetically earliest constant (if any) on that branch and $\boldsymbol{m}$ is the alphabetically last constant on that branch, are to be entered, each on a distinct branch. And $\mathscr{P}(\boldsymbol{n}/x)$ is to be entered on a further branch where $\boldsymbol{n}$ is any constant not already occurring on the branch. Hence each existing open branch passing through $(\exists x)\mathscr{P}$ will generate $\boldsymbol{m} + 1$ branches where $\boldsymbol{m}$ is the number of constants already on that branch. Existential Decomposition-2 is a branching rule, but a rule which produces a varying number of new branches.[5]

For example, here is a tree for {(∀y)(∃z)Fyz} which uses Existential Decomposition-2 instead of Existential Decomposition:

| | | | |
|---|---|---|---|
| 1. | (∀y)(∃z)Fyz | | SM |
| 2. | (∃z)Faz | | 1 ∀D |
| 3. | Faa | Fab | 2 ∃D2 |

Think of this tree this way: Line 2 says there is something to which a bears F. To find an interpretation on which this sentence is true, we consider both the case where that thing is a itself—this is the left-hand branch, and the case where it might be something else—this is the right-hand branch. If both branches close we will know there is neither sort of interpretation. But if *either* becomes a completed open branch we will have a finite open tree, and a branch from which we can construct a finite model for the set being tested. Here the left-hand branch is completed, and from it we can recover an interpretation with a U.D. of size one (for there is only one constant on that branch), for example, the interpretation given above (U.D.: {1}, Fxy: x = y). The right-hand branch is open but is *not* a completed open branch: The universally quantified sentence on line 1 has not been decomposed to a substitution instance formed from 'b'. In Chapter Eleven we will prove that when we replace Existential Decomposition with Existential Decomposition-2 the resulting tree method is such that every finite set of sentences of *PL/PLI* with a finite model has a finite truth-tree, and such that every finite set of sentences of *PL/PLI* which is quantificationally inconsistent has a closed truth-tree.

Nonterminating branches are, again, branches which will never close and cannot become completed open branches. Consistent sets which have only infinite models have trees whose only open branches are nonterminating branches. We need to allow for this case in our specification of what constitutes an open tree.

[5] This Existential Decomposition rule is due to George Boolos. See "Trees and Finite Satisfiability: Proof of a Conjecture of Burgess," *Notre Dame Journal of Formal Logic*, 25(3), 1984, 193–197.

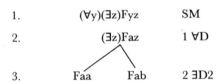

Accordingly, we adopt the following:

> *Open tree:* A tree containing either at least one completed open branch or at least one nonterminating branch.

And:

> A finite set Γ of sentences of *PL/PLI* is *quantificationally consistent* if and only if Γ has an open tree.

An infinite set is quantificationally consistent if and only if each of its finite subsets has an open tree.

Our original tree rules and our revised tree rules, with Existential Decomposition-2 in place of Existential Decomposition, are equivalent in this sense: On both sets of rules a finite set of sentences of *PL/PLI* has a closed tree if and only if it is quantificationally inconsistent, and an open tree if and only if it is quantificationally consistent. The difference is, again, that, given the original tree rules, some consistent sets with finite models will not have finite trees—they will have trees whose only open branches are nonterminating branches.

As might be anticipated, trees constructed using the Existential Decomposition-2 rule are frequently considerably more complicated than those constructed using Experimental Decomposition. It is for this reason that we did not introduce Existential Decomposition-2 as the only existential decomposition rule. Our overall strategy is this: Where it seems likely that a finite tree can be produced using Existential Decomposition, we will attempt to do so. If this does not seem likely, or if the attempt fails to produce a finite tree in a "reasonable" number of steps, we will do a tree using Existential Decomposition-2. It is even permissible to use both existential decomposition rules in the same tree.

Before turning to the second task of this section, that of developing a tree construction procedure which will yield a finite tree wherever one exists, we present three more trees using Existential Decomposition-2. Consider first a tree for the set {(∀x)(Fx ⊃ (∃y)Gyx), (∃x)Fx}:

```
1.                 (∀x)(Fx ⊃ (∃y)Gyx)          SM
2.                      (∃x)Fx✓                 SM

3.                         Fa                   2 ∃D2
4.                   Fa ⊃ (∃y)Gya✓              1 ∀D
                        /      \
5.             ~Fa             (∃y)Gya✓         4 ⊃ D
                ×               /    \
6.                           Gaa      Gba       5 ∃D2
```

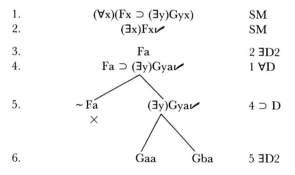

This tree has one completed open branch, the middle branch. The one universally quantified sentence on the branch (the one on line 1) has been decomposed to every constant on the branch, namely 'a'. Every other sentence on the branch is either a literal or has been decomposed. So the set is quantificationally consistent. Had we used Existential Decomposition at line 6, the tree would have only two branches, the right-hand one being a nonterminating branch.

Consider next a tree for the set {~[(∀x)(∃y)Fxy ≡ (∀x)[Fxa]}:

```
1.                      ~[(∀x)(∃y)Fxy ≡ (∀x)Fxa]✓                          SM
                       /                          \
2.             (∀x)(∃y)Fxy                     ~(∀x)(∃y)Fxy✓               1 ~≡ D
3.             ~(∀x)Fxa✓                          (∀x)Fxa                  1 ~≡ D
4.                 |                          (∃x) ~(∃y)Fxy✓               2 ~∀D
5.                 |                                Faa                    3 ∀D
                   |                              /     \
6.                 |                   ~(∃y)Fay✓     ~(∃y)Fby✓             4∃D2
7.                 |                   (∀y) ~Fay     (∀y) ~Fby             6 ~∃D
8.                 |                     ~Faa          ~Fba                7 ∀D
9.                 |                       ×            Fba                3 ∀D
10.            (∃x) ~Fxa✓                                ×
11.            (∃y)Fay✓                                                    3 ~∀D
                /      \                                                   2 ∀D
12.         ~Faa        ~Fba                                               10 ∃D2
           /    \      /  |  \
13.  Faa     Fab      Faa      Fab      Fac                                11 ∃D2
14.   ×  (∃y)Fby✓ (∃y)Fby (∃y)Fby (∃y)Fby                                  2 ∀D
                                         (∃y)Fcy                           2 ∀D
          /  |  \
15.  Fba   Fbb   Fbc                                                       14 ∃D2
```

At line 15 Existential Decomposition-2 produces three branches from the left-most open branch of line 14. Although the tree is not now complete, it does have two completed open branches, one ending in 'Fba' and one ending in 'Fbb'. The branch ending in 'Fbc' is not complete, as '(∀x)(∃y)Fxy' has not been decomposed to '(∃y)Fcy'. The branches ending in undecomposed existentially quantified sentences are also, for that reason, not complete.

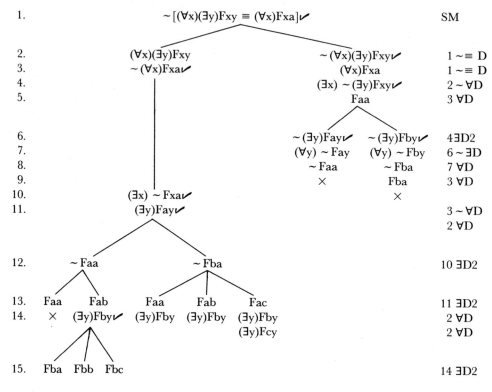

One finite set which has only infinite models is $\{(\forall x)(\exists y)Fxy,\ \sim(\exists x)Fxx,$ $(\forall x)(\forall y)(Fxy \supset \sim Fyx)\}$. Here is a start of a tree for this set:

| | | |
|---|---|---|
| 1. | $(\forall x)(\exists y)Fxy$ | SM |
| 2. | $\sim(\exists x)Fxx$✔ | SM |
| 3. | $(\forall x)(\forall y)(Fxy \supset \sim Fyx)$ | SM |
| 4. | $(\forall x) \sim Fxx$ | $2 \sim \exists D$ |
| 5. | $(\exists y)Fay$✔ | $1\ \forall D$ |
| 6. | $(\forall y)(Fay \supset \sim Fya)$ | $3\ \forall D$ |
| 7. | $Faa \supset \sim Faa$✔ | $6\ \forall D$ |
| 8. | $\sim Faa$ | $4\ \forall D$ |

```
9.              Faa                    Fab                          5 ∃D2
                 ×

10.      ~ Faa                    ~ Faa                             7 ⊃ D
11.      (∃y)Fby✔                 (∃y)Fby✔                          1 ∀D
12.      (∀y)(Fby ⊃ ~ Fyb)        (∀y)(Fby ⊃ ~ Fyb)                 3 ∀D
13.      Fab ⊃ ~ Fba✔             Fab ⊃ ~ Fba✔                      6 ∀D
14.      Fbb ⊃ ~ Fbb✔             Fbb ⊃ ~ Fbb                       12 ∀D
15.      Fba ⊃ ~ Fab✔             Fba ⊃ ~ Fab✔                      12 ∀D
16.         ~ Fbb                    ~ Fbb                          4 ∀D

17. ~ Fab          ~ Fba      ~ Fab          ~ Fba                  13 ⊃ D
     ×                          ×

18.           ~ Fba   ~ Fab         ~ Fba      ~ Fab               15 ⊃ D
                        ×                        ×

19.        ~ Fbb   ~ Fbb        ~ Fbb      ~ Fbb                    14 ⊃ D

20.   Fba Fbb Fbc Fba Fbb Fbc  Fba Fbb Fbc Fba Fbb Fbc  11 ∃D2
       ×   ×       ×   ×         ×   ×       ×   ×
```

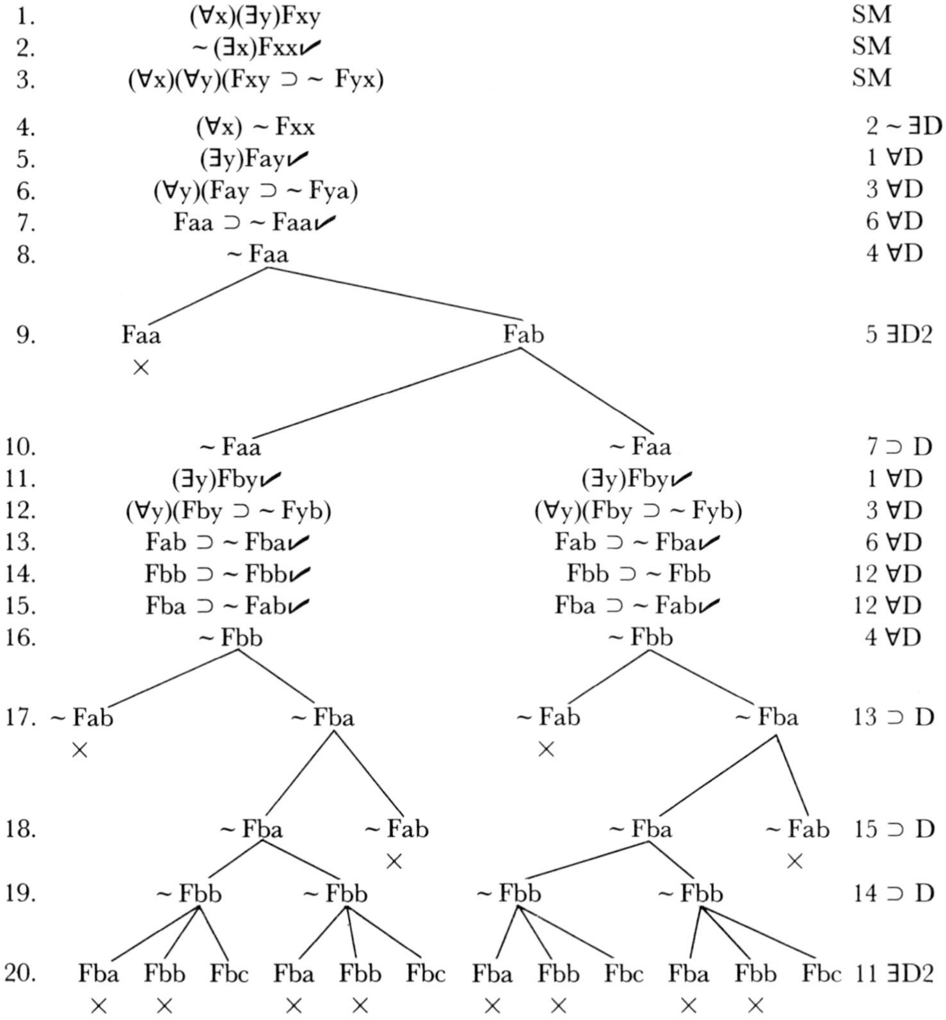

There are four open branches on this tree, none of which is a completed open branch. Continuing the tree will produce more branches, some but not all of which will close, and eventually the introduction of a new constant, 'd', the next time Existential Decomposition-2 is used.

The above example should make it clear that truth-trees can become very complex. It can happen that one or more of the branches on a tree are nonterminating but that others, if pursued, will become completed open branches. In such cases unless care is taken one can work continuously on a branch which is in fact nonterminating while ignoring a branch which, if continued, will become a completed open branch. To prevent this, to guarantee that all possibilities are pursued so that if a finite branch exists it will be found, we introduce a procedure for constructing trees in a systematic fashion. We call the procedure simply *The System*. For *PL* The System is

*The System*

List the members of the set to be tested

Exit conditions: Stop if

a. The tree closes.
b. An open branch becomes a completed open branch.

Construction Procedures:

Stage 1: Decompose all truth-functionally compound and existentially quantified sentences and each resulting sentence which is itself either a truth-functional compound or an existentially quantified sentence.

Stage 2: For each universally quantified sentence $(\forall x)\mathcal{P}$ on the tree, on each open branch passing through $(\forall x)\mathcal{P}$.

If no constant occurs on that branch, add $\mathcal{P}(a/x)$ to that branch, where 'a' is the instantiating constant.

If one or more constants do occur on that branch, add $\mathcal{P}(a/x)$ for every such constant $a$ to that branch.

Repeat this process until every universally quantified sentence on the tree, including those added as a result of this process, has been so decomposed.

Return to stage 1.

The System for *PLI* includes an added stage, stage 3:

Stage 3: Repeatedly apply Identity Decomposition until every sentence of the form $a = b$ on the tree is such that every open branch passing through it also contains, for every literal $\mathcal{P}$ containing $b$ on that branch, every sentence $\mathcal{P}(a//b)$ which can be obtained from $\mathcal{P}$ by Identity Decomposition and is not of the form $a = a$.

Stage 3 ensures that after passing through that stage every sentence of the form $a = b$ on every open branch meets the requirements of clause 4 of the definition of a completed open branch for *PLI*. That is, if the branch is not completed it is *not* because Identity Decomposition has not been applied the required number of times.

We call trees that have been constructed in accordance with The System *systematic trees*. In all systematic trees Existential Decomposition-2 is used rather than Existential Decomposition. To construct a systematic tree, follow the directions given in the order in which they are given. That is, first the members of the set being tested are listed; next all truth-functionally compound and all existentially quantified sentences are decomposed. At this stage it is, of course, wise to apply nonbranching rules before applying branching rules. When and only when the tree contains no undecomposed truth-functional compounds and no undecomposed existentially quantified sentences, do we proceed to stage 2. At stage 2 each universally quantified sentence on the tree is decomposed by entering one or more substitution instances of that sentence on every open branch passing through that sentence. Which substitution instances are entered on a particular open branch passing through a universally quantified sentence is determined by the constants already occurring on that branch. If no constants occur, only the substitution instance formed from 'a' is entered; if constants do occur, all the substitution instances which can be formed by using those constants as instantiating constants are entered. It is important to note that work at stage 2 is not complete until every universally quantified sentence on the tree has been decomposed in the required manner, including universally quantified sentences that are entered as a result of work at stage 2, as well as those that were on the tree when we passed from stage 1 to stage 2. After completion of stage 2, we either return to stage 1 (for *PL*) or proceed to stage 3 (for *PLI*) and then return to stage 1.

Systematic trees differ from nonsystematic trees in two important respects. First, Existential Decomposition-2 is always used rather than Existential Decomposition. This alone will frequently make systematic trees more complex than nonsystematic trees. Second, The System does not allow work on one branch to be continued to the point of excluding work on another open branch. This is the advantage of The System. The disadvantage is that for this reason systematic trees are often much larger than the kinds of trees constructed in the first four sections of this chapter.

The start of a tree for {(∀x)(∃y)Fxy, ~(∃x)Fxx, (∀x)(∀y)(Fxy ⊃ ~Fyx)} displayed above was constructed in accordance with The System. As the set contains two universally quantified sentences and one truth-functional compound, work starts (after listing the members of the set) at stage 1. After '~(∃x)Fxx' is decomposed to '(∀x) ~Fxx' every truth-functional compound (the sentence on line 2) and every existentially quantified sentence on the tree (there are none) has been decomposed. We proceed to stage 2. Since there are, at this point, no constants on the tree, we decompose each universally quantified sentence on the tree to a substitution instance formed from 'a'. This takes us through line 8. We now return to stage 1. There are two sentences to be decomposed, the existentially quantified sentence on line 5 and the truth-functional compound on line 7. The former will branch when decomposed because there is already one constant, 'a', on the one branch of the tree; the latter will branch because the sentence is a material conditional. We choose to decompose the former first, as it will yield one closed branch (the left branch), at line 9. Next we decompose the material conditional at line 8. It yields two open branches. As it happens these are identical, that is, exactly the same sentences occur on each branch. Nonetheless, The System requires us to pursue both branches. We do so by proceeding to stage 2. All the universally quantified sentences on the tree have already been decomposed to substitution instances formed from 'a'. But 'b' now also occurs on the tree, in 'Fab' at line 9, and both open branches pass through that sentence. So the universally quantified sentences must all be decomposed to substitution instances formed from 'b'. We do this on lines 11–16. At line 17 we return to stage 1. On each branch we have three truth-functional compounds, all material conditionals, and one existentially quantified sentence to decompose. We decompose the material conditionals first, at lines 17–19. Some branches do close. At line 20 we decompose the existentially quantified sentence, '(∃y)Fby' which occurs on both open branches at line 11. Because each branch already contains two constants, 'a' and 'b', Existential Decomposition-2 produces three branches on each of the open branches. Again, some branches close. Were we to continue, we would now return to stage 2 and decompose every universally quantified sentence on each of the open branches to substitution instances formed from 'c'. (They have already been decomposed to substitution instances formed from 'a' and from 'b'.)

We have not demonstrated that this tree will never close and will never have a completed open branch, but this is the case. The only way to demonstrate this is to show, independently of the tree method, that the above set is quantificationally consistent, that it has only infinite models, and that no set which has only infinite models has a finite tree. The last claim will be established in Chapter Eleven. Here the point is that the tree method cannot be used to show that sets such as the above are quantificationally consistent. We abandon the above tree, we do not complete it. And an abandoned tree is a failure to establish that the set being tested is consistent and a failure to establish that it is inconsistent. However, having used The System, we can be sure that we have not, as far as we have gone, missed a completed open branch or a chance to close the tree.

Although The System has not been presented as a mechanical method and will not yield any result if a set has only infinite models, it does place restrictions on how trees can be constructed and will prevent us from failing to find closed trees and completed open branches, where they exist, provided we persevere long enough (a finite tree can be indefinitely large). Consider again the tree presented earlier for {(∀x)Fx, (∀x) ~ Fx}:

| | | |
|---|---|---|
| 1. | (∀x)Fx | SM |
| 2. | (∀x) ~ Fx | SM |
| 3. | Fa | 1 ∀D |
| 4. | Fb | 1 ∀D |
| 5. | Fc | 1 ∀D |
| 6. | Fd | 1 ∀D |
| | ⋮ | |

As noted earlier, a tree constructed in this fashion can be continued indefinitely, for there is an infinite supply of substitution instances of '(∀x)Fx', and no tree rule is being misused. So long as '(∀x) ~ Fx' is not decomposed the tree will never close. Clearly, the above tree is, while allowed, a silly tree, for the inconsistency of the set being tested is due to the incompatibility of the two sentences composing the set. The System prevents the construction of such trees, as the following tree, constructed in accordance with The System, illustrates:

| | | |
|---|---|---|
| 1. | (∀x)Fx | SM |
| 2. | (∀x) ~ Fx | SM |
| 3. | Fa | 1 ∀D |
| 4. | ~ Fa | 2 ∀D |
| | × | |

An advantage of The System is that it prevents us from endlessly and pointlessly decomposing one universally quantified sentence while ignoring other sentences on the branch. That is, stage 2 places a restriction on how many instances of a universally quantified sentence can be entered before going on to work on other sentences. Moreover, stage 2 guarantees that we choose the *right* constants in doing Universal Decomposition. That is, stage 2 prevents us from constructing trees such as the following:

| | | |
|---|---|---|
| 1. | (∀x)Fx | SM |
| 2. | (∀x) ~ Fx | SM |
| 3. | Fa | 1 ∀D |
| 4. | ~ Fb | 2 ∀D |
| 5. | Fc | 1 ∀D |
| 6. | ~ Fd | 2 ∀D |
| | ⋮ | |

This tree could also be continued indefinitely without closing. But it is not a systematic tree. Were we to use The System, stage 2 would prevent us from constructing such a tree by requiring that at line 4 '(∀x)Fx' be decomposed to a substitution instance formed from a constant already on the branch. The only such constant is 'a', and entering ' ~ Fa' at line 4 would close the tree. Here is a systematic tree for the set {(∀x)(∃y)Fxy, Ga & ~ (∃y)Fay}.

| | | | |
|---|---|---|---|
| 1. | (∀x)(∃y)Fxy | | SM |
| 2. | Ga & ~ (∃y)Fay ✓ | | SM |
| 3. | Ga | | 2 & D |
| 4. | ~ (∃y)Fay ✓ | | 2 & D |
| 5. | (∀y) ~ Fay | | 4 ~ ∃D |
| 6. | (∃y)Fay ✓ | | 1 ∀D |
| 7. | ~ Faa | | 5 ∀D |
| 8. | Faa | ~ Fab | 6 ∃D2 |
| 9. | × | ~ Fab | 5 ∀D |
| | | × | |

The tree closes the second time we pass through stage 2.

Though The System is not a mechanical method, it does, as these examples illustrate, yield either closed or finite completed open branches when such are forthcoming. And, since The System is reliable in the aforementioned sense, it should be used when one does not see how to close a branch or produce a completed open branch without using The System. This will, of course, usually not be so in cases as simple as the ones we have just considered. It should, moreover, be remembered that The System is not as economical as it is reliable. Frequently, strict adherence to it produces more complex trees than are necessary to establish the desired result.

We have not given instructions for identifying a systematic tree that is caught in an endless cycle of decompositions and is such that it has only nonterminating branches. It is precisely because trees do not and cannot provide an effective test for quantificational consistency that we cannot here give such instructions. We can only say that if one has cycled through the stages of The System several times and there are still open branches, one should consider the possibility that the set has only infinite models, and consider abandoning the tree. Abandoning a tree is abandoning the tree method without obtaining a result. One can, of course, try to establish the consistency of the set in question by trying to find an interpretation on which all the members of the set are true.

## 9.5E EXERCISES

**1.** Construct systematic trees to determine, for each of the following sets, whether that set is quantificationally consistent. State your result. If you abandon a tree, explain why you abandon it.

a. {(∀x)Jx, (∀x)(Jx ≡ (∃y)(Gyx ∨ Ky))}
*b. {(∀x)(Fx ⊃ Cx), ~(∀x)(Fx & Cx)}
c. {(∃x)Fx, (∃x) ~ Fx}
*d. {~(∀x) ~Hx, (∀x)(Hx ⊃ Kx), ~(∃x)(Kx & Hx)}
e. {(∃x)Fx & (∃x) ~Fx, (∃x)Fx ⊃ (∀x) ~Fx}
*f. {(∃x)Fx & (∃x) ~ Fx, (∀x)Fx ⊃ (∀x) ~Fx}
g. {(∀x)(∃y)Fxy, (∃y)(∀x) ~ Fyx}
*h. {(∀x)(~Gx ⊃ Fx), (∃x)(Fx & ~Gx), Fa ⊃ ~Ga}
i. {(∃x)Hx, ~ (∀x)Hx, (∀x)(Hx ⊃ Kx), (∃x)(Kx & Hx)}
*j. {(∃x)(∀y)Lxy, (∃x)(∀y) ~Lxy}
k. {(∀x)(∃y)Lxy, (∀x)(∃y) ~ Lxy}
*l. {(∀x) ~(∃y)Lxy, (∀w)(∀y)(Swy ∨ ~Lwy), ~(∃x) ~(∃z)Sxz}
m. {(∀x)(∃y)Fxy, (∃x)(∃y) ~Fxy}
*n. {(∀x)(∀y)(∀z)((Hxy & Hyz) ⊃ Hxz), (∀x)(∀y)(Hxy ⊃ Hyx), (∃x) ~Hxx}
o. {~(∀x)(Kx ⊃ (∀y)(Ky ∨ Lxy)), (∀y)(Ky ⊃ (∀x)(Rx ⊃ Lyx)), (∀x)Rx}

**2.** Construct systematic trees to determine, for each of the following sentences, whether that sentence is quantificationally true, quantificationally false, or quantificationally indeterminate. In each case state your result. If you abandon a tree, explain why you do so.

a. (∀x)(Fax ⊃ (∃y)Fya)

*b. (∃x) ∼ Fx ⊃ (Fa ⊃ ∼ Fb)
c. (∀x)[Fx ⊃ (∀y)(Hy ⊃ Fy)]
*d. (∃y)(∀x)Fxy ⊃ (∀x)(∃y)Fxy
e. (∃x)(Fx ∨ ∼ Fx) ≡ ((∃x)Fx ∨ (∃x) ∼ Fx)
*f. (∀x)(Fx ≡ [(∃y)Gyx ⊃ H]) ⊃ (∀x)[Fx ⊃ (∃y)(Gyx ⊃ H)]
g. (∀x)(Fx ⊃ [(∃y)Gyx ⊃ H]) ⊃ (∀x)[Fx ⊃ (∃y)(Gyx ⊃ H)]

**3.** Construct systematic trees to determine which of the following arguments are quantificationally valid. In each case, state your result. If you abandon a tree, explain why you abandon it.

a. Fa
(∀x)(Fx ⊃ Cx)

(∀x)(Fx & Cx)

*b. (∀x)(Jx ∨ Ixb) ∨ (∀x)(∃y)(Hxy ⊃ Mx)

Iab

c. Fa
(∀x)(Fx ⊃ Cx)

(∃x)(Fx & Cx)

*d. ∼ (∀y)Kyy ∨ (∀x)Hxx

(∃x)(∼ Hxx ⊃ ∼ Kxx)

e. (∀x)(∀y)(∀z)[(Lxy & Lyz) ⊃ Lxz]
(∀x)(∀y)(Lxy ⊃ Lyx)

(∀x)Lxx

*f. (∀x)(∀y)(Fx ∨ Gxy)
(∃x)Fx

(∃x)(∃y)Gxy

g. (∃x)[(Lx ∨ Sx) ∨ Kx]
(∀y) ∼ (Ly ∨ Ky)

(∃x)Sx

*h. (∃x)((Lx ∨ Sx) ∨ Kx)
(∀y) ∼ (Ly ∨ Ky)

(∀x)Sx

i. (∀x)(Hx ⊃ Kcx)
(∀x)(Lx ⊃ ∼ Kcx)
Ld

(∃y) ∼ Hy

**4.** Construct systematic trees to determine which of the following pairs of sentences are quantificationally equivalent. In each case, state your result. If you abandon a tree, explain why you do so.

| | | |
|---|---|---|
| a. | $(\forall x)(\forall y) \sim Sxy$ | $\sim(\exists x)(\exists y)Sxy$ |
| *b. | $(\forall x)(\exists y)Lxy$ | $(\exists y)(\forall x)Lyx$ |
| c. | $(\exists x)(Ax \supset B)$ | $(\forall x)Ax \supset B$ |
| *d. | $(\forall x)(Ax \supset B)$ | $(\forall x)Ax \supset B$ |
| e. | $(\forall x)(Ax \supset B)$ | $(\exists x)Ax \supset B$ |
| *f. | $(\exists x)(Ax \supset B)$ | $(\exists x)Ax \supset B$ |
| g. | $(\exists x)(\exists y)Hxy$ | $(\exists y)(\exists x)Hxy$ |

**5.** Construct systematic trees to determine which of the following alleged entailments hold. In each case, state your result. If you abandon a tree, explain why you do so.

a. $\{(\forall x)(Fax \supset Fxa)\} \vDash Fab \vee Fba$
*b. $\{(\forall x)(\forall y)(Fx \vee Gxy), (\exists x)Fx\} \vDash (\exists x)(\exists y)Gxy$
c. $\{\sim Fa, (\forall x)(Fa \supset (\exists y)Gxy)\} \vDash \sim(\exists y)Gay$
*d. $\{(\exists x)(\forall y)Gxy\} \vDash (\forall y)(\exists x)Gxy$
e. $\{(\exists x)Gx, (\forall x)(Gx \supset Dxx)\} \vDash (\exists x)(Gx \;\&\; (\forall y)Dxy)$
*f. $\{(\forall y)(\exists x)Gxy\} \vDash (\exists x)(\forall y)Gxy$

***6.** Show that if the members of a set $\Gamma$ of sentences of *PL* contain only '$\sim$' and universal and existential quantifiers as logical operators, then $\Gamma$ has no tree with more than one branch if the rule $\exists$D is used, but may have a tree with more than open branch if $\exists$D2 is used.

**7.** Show that no closed truth-tree can have an infinite branch.

***8.** Could we replace Universal Decomposition and Existential Decomposition with the following two rules? Explain.

| | |
|---|---|
| $(\forall \boldsymbol{x})\mathscr{P}$ | $(\exists \boldsymbol{x})\mathscr{P}$ |
| $\sim(\exists \boldsymbol{x}) \sim \mathscr{P}$ | $\sim(\forall \boldsymbol{x}) \sim \mathscr{P}$ |

**9.** Let $\mathscr{P}(\boldsymbol{a}/\boldsymbol{x})$ be a substitution instance of some sentence $(\exists \boldsymbol{x})\mathscr{P}$ such that $\{\mathscr{P}(\boldsymbol{a}/\boldsymbol{x})\}$ has a closed tree. Does it follow that $\{(\exists \boldsymbol{x})\mathscr{P}\}$ has a closed tree? Explain.

***10.** Let $(\forall \boldsymbol{x})\mathscr{P}$ be a sentence such that for *every* substitution instance $\mathscr{P}(\boldsymbol{a}/\boldsymbol{x})$, $\{\mathscr{P}(\boldsymbol{a}/\boldsymbol{x})\}$ has a closed tree. Does it follow that a systematic tree for $\{(\forall \boldsymbol{x})\mathscr{P}\}$ will close? Explain.

**11.** What would have to be done to make The System a mechanical procedure?

***12.** Suppose a tree for a set $\Gamma$ of sentences of *PL* is abandoned without either closing or having a completed open branch. Suppose also that we find a model on which all the members of $\Gamma$ are true. Suppose the model is an infinite model. Does it follow that all the open branches on the abandoned tree are nonterminating branches? Suppose the model is finite. Does anything follow about the abandoned tree?

QUANTIFICATIONAL CONSISTENCY: A finite set Γ of sentences of *PL/PLI* is *quantificationally consistent* if and only if Γ has an open tree.

QUANTIFICATIONAL INCONSISTENCY: A set Γ of sentences of *PL/PLI* is *quantificationally inconsistent* if and only if at least one finite subset of Γ has a closed truth-tree.

QUANTIFICATIONAL FALSITY: A sentence $\mathcal{P}$ of *PL/PLI* is *quantificationally false* if and only if the set $\{\mathcal{P}\}$ has a closed truth-tree.

QUANTIFICATIONAL TRUTH: A sentence $\mathcal{P}$ of *PL/PLI* is *quantificationally true* if and only if the set $\{\sim \mathcal{P}\}$ has a closed truth-tree.

QUANTIFICATIONAL INDETERMINACY: A sentence $\mathcal{P}$ of *PL/PLI* is *quantificationally indeterminate* if and only if neither the set $\{\mathcal{P}\}$ nor the set $\{\sim \mathcal{P}\}$ has a closed truth-tree.

QUANTIFICATIONAL EQUIVALENCE: Sentences $\mathcal{P}$ and $\mathcal{Q}$ of *PL/PLI* are *quantificationally equivalent* if and only if $\{\sim(\mathcal{P} \equiv \mathcal{Q})\}$ has a closed truth-tree.

QUANTIFICATIONAL ENTAILMENT: A finite set Γ of sentences of *PL/PLI* *quantificationally entails* a sentence $\mathcal{P}$ of *PL/PLI* if and only if $\Gamma \cup \{\sim \mathcal{P}\}$ has a closed truth-tree.

QUANTIFICATIONAL VALIDITY: An argument of *PL/PLI* is *quantificationally valid* if and only if the set consisting of the premises and the negation of the conclusion has a closed truth-tree.

*Chapter* **10**

# *PREDICATE LOGIC: DERIVATIONS*

## 10.1 THE DERIVATION SYSTEM *PD*

A natural deduction system for predicate logic is developed in this chapter. The system is called *PD* (for *p*redicate *d*erivations), and it provides syntactic methods for evaluating sentences and sets of sentences of *PL*, just as the natural deduction system *SD* provides methods for evaluating sentences and sets of sentences of *SL*. The derivation rules of *PD* allow us to derive sentences on the basis of the *forms* of sentences. Although the derivation rules can be applied without having in mind any interpretation of the sentences in question, the derivation rules of *PD* were chosen with an eye to semantics. The derivation rules of *PD*, like the derivation rules of *SD*, are truth-preserving. Given the semantics developed for *PL*, the derivation rules of *PD* will never lead us from true sentences to false ones.

The derivation rules of *PD* include all the derivation rules of *SD*, with the understanding that they apply to sentences of *PL*. For example, the following is a derivation in *PD*:

Derive: (∀x)(∃y)Hxy ⊃ (∃y)Ky

| | | |
|---|---|---|
| 1 | (∀x)(∃y)Hxy ⊃ Cb | Assumption |
| 2 | (Cb ∨ ~(∀z)(∀x)Bxaz) ⊃ (∃y)Ky | Assumption |
| 3 |     (∀x)(∃y)Hxy | Assumption |
| 4 |     Cb | 1, 3 ⊃E |
| 5 |     Cb ∨ ~(∀z)(∀x)Bxaz | 4 ∨I |
| 6 |     (∃y)Ky | 2, 5 ⊃E |
| 7 | (∀x)(∃y)Hxy ⊃ (∃y)Ky | 3-6 ⊃I |

*PD* has four additional derivation rules. These additional rules allow us to introduce and eliminate quantifiers.

*ELIMINATION RULE FOR UNIVERSAL QUANTIFIERS*

The elimination rule for universal quantifiers is *Universal Elimination* (sometimes called Universal Instantiation). To understand the basis for this rule, consider some informal reasoning which shows that the conclusion of the following argument is a consequence of its premises.

All philosophers are somewhat strange.
Socrates is a philosopher.

---

Socrates is somewhat strange.

The first premise makes a universal claim. Each thing is such that if it is a philosopher, then it is somewhat strange. It follows from this premise that if David Hume is a philosopher, then David Hume is somewhat strange; and if Isaac Newton is a philosopher, then Isaac Newton is somewhat strange; and if the Milky Way is a philosopher, then the Milky Way is somewhat strange; and so forth. In this case we are interested in Socrates. It follows from the first premise that if Socrates is a philosopher, then Socrates is somewhat strange. Since we have from the second premise the information that Socrates is a philosopher, we can conclude that Socrates is somewhat strange. The inference from a universal claim to a specific instance of it is captured in *PD* by the rule Universal Elimination (∀E). Here is a derivation for a symbolized version of the preceding argument in which the rule Universal Elimination is used.

Derive: Ss

| | | |
|---|---|---|
| 1 | (∀y)(Py ⊃ Sy) | Assumption |
| 2 | Ps | Assumption |
| 3 | Ps ⊃ Ss | 1 ∀E |
| 4 | Ss | 2, 3 ⊃ E |

Recall that a *substitution instance* of a quantified sentence is generated by removing the initial quantifier and replacing each occurrence of the free variable in the resulting open sentence with some one individual constant. Where

$$(\forall \boldsymbol{x})\mathscr{P}$$

is a sentence of *PL*,

$$\mathscr{P}(\boldsymbol{a}/\boldsymbol{x})$$

is used to designate a substitution instance of $(\forall \boldsymbol{x})\mathscr{P}$. The expression '$\mathscr{P}(\boldsymbol{a}/\boldsymbol{x})$' is read as '$\mathscr{P}$ with $\boldsymbol{a}$ (everywhere) in place of $\boldsymbol{x}$'. Notice that $\boldsymbol{x}$ must occur in $\mathscr{P}$, for $(\forall \boldsymbol{x})\mathscr{P}$ is a sentence. The individual constant $\boldsymbol{a}$ in this case is called the *instantiating constant*. Thus the universally quantified sentence

(∀y)(Py ⊃ Sy)

has as a substitution instance

Ps ⊃ Ss

where 's' is the instantiating constant.

The derivation rule Universal Elimination permits us to derive a substitution instance of a universally quantified sentence from the universally quantified sentence. This rule is

*Universal Elimination* (∀E)

| (∀$x$)$\mathscr{P}$
|
| $\mathscr{P}(a/x)$

The individual constant employed in using Universal Elimination may or may not already occur in the quantified sentence. In the following case 't' does not occur in the universally quantified sentence, and it is proper to derive a substitution instance where 't' is the instantiating constant:

| | | |
|---|---|---|
| 1 | (∀x)Lxa | Assumption |
| 2 | Lta | 1 ∀E |

If everyone loves Alice, then it follows that Tom loves Alice. On the other hand, 'a' does occur in the universally quantified sentence '(∀x)Lxa', and it is equally proper to derive a substitution instance where 'a' is the instantiating constant:

| | | |
|---|---|---|
| 1 | (∀x)Lxa | Assumption |
| 2 | Laa | 1 ∀E |

If everyone loves Alice, then it follows that Alice loves herself.

### 10.1.1E EXERCISES

Complete the following derivations:

a. Derive: Fa & Fb

| | | |
|---|---|---|
| 1 | (∀x)Fx | Assumption |

*b. Derive: Kg

| | | |
|---|---|---|
| 1 | (∀x)(∀y)Hxy | Assumption |
| 2 | Hcf ⊃ Kg | Assumption |

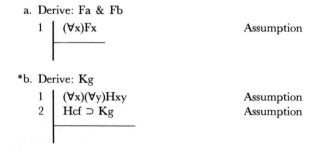

c. Derive: $\sim$ Qe

| | | |
|---|---|---|
| 1 | (∀z)Mz | Assumption |
| 2 | (∀z) $\sim$ Mz | Assumption |
| | | |

*d. Derive: Pi ⊃ Ai

| | | |
|---|---|---|
| 1 | (∀x)(Px ≡ Tx) | Assumption |
| 2 | (∀z)(Tz ≡ Az) | Assumption |
| | | |

*INTRODUCTION RULE FOR EXISTENTIAL QUANTIFIERS*

The introduction rule for existential quantifiers is *Existential Introduction* (sometimes called Existential Generalization). Consider the following:

Gold is a metal that is precious.

---

There is a metal that is precious.

The conclusion follows from the premise, for it is a generalization from a specific instance. This kind of inference is reflected in *PD* by Existential Introduction (∃I). Existential Introduction permits us to derive an existentially quantified sentence from a substitution instance of that sentence. Here is a derivation for a symbolized version of the preceding argument that uses Existential Introduction:

| | | |
|---|---|---|
| 1 | Mg & Pg | Assumption |
| 2 | (∃z)(Mz & Pz) | 1 ∃I |

More formally, where

$(\exists x)\mathscr{P}$

is a sentence of *PL*,

$\mathscr{P}(a/x)$

is used to designate a substitution instance of $(\exists x)\mathscr{P}$. Hence the rule Existential Introduction is

*Existential Introduction* (∃I)

$\mathscr{P}(a/x)$

$(\exists x)\mathscr{P}$

This rule does not require that every occurrence of a given individual constant be generalized. For instance, the following derivations illustrate three proper uses of

Existential Introduction:

| | | |
|---|---|---|
| 1 | Rmm | Assumption |
| 2 | (∃x)Rxx | 1 ∃I |

If Mt. McKinley resembles Mt. McKinley, then it follows that something resembles itself.

| | | |
|---|---|---|
| 1 | Rmm | Assumption |
| 2 | (∃x)Rxm | 1 ∃I |

If Mt. McKinley resembles Mt. McKinley, then it follows that something resembles Mt. McKinley. And

| | | |
|---|---|---|
| 1 | Rmm | Assumption |
| 2 | (∃x)Rmx | 1 ∃I |

If Mt. McKinley resembles Mt. McKinley, then it follows that Mt. McKinley resembles something. Notice that 'Rmm' is a substitution instance of '(∃x)Rxx', of '(∃x)Rxm', and of '(∃x)Rmx'. In each of these three cases 'Rmm' is the result of dropping the quantifier '(∃x)' and rewriting the rest with the instantiating constant 'm' replacing every occurrence of the individual variable 'x'. Of course, the inference is not from the existentially quantified sentence to its substitution instance but the other way around, *from* the substitution instance *to* the existentially quantified sentence.

### **10.1.2E** EXERCISES

Complete the following derivations:

a. Derive: (∃x)(Ax & Jx)

| | | |
|---|---|---|
| 1 | Jc | Assumption |
| 2 | Ac | Assumption |
| 3 | Ac & Jc | 1,2 &I |
| 4 | (∃x)Ax & Jx | 3 (∃I) |

*b. Derive: (∃x)Fxax

| | | |
|---|---|---|
| 1 | Faaa | Assumption |

c. Derive: (∃y)(∃z)Cyz

| | | |
|---|---|---|
| 1 | (∀w)(∀z)Cwz | Assumption |

*d. Derive: Wf

| | | |
|---|---|---|
| 1 | (∀x)Sx | Assumption |
| 2 | (∃z)Sz ⊃ (∀z)Wz | Assumption |

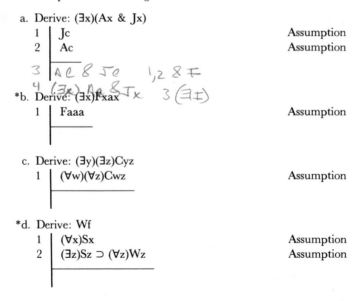

*INTRODUCTION RULE FOR UNIVERSAL QUANTIFIERS*

The introduction rule for universal quantifiers is *Universal Introduction* (sometimes called Universal Generalization). To understand the basis for this rule, consider the reasoning we might use to show that the conclusion of this argument follows from its premises:

> Anybody who has run the distance of a marathon has run over twenty miles.
>
> Anybody who has run over twenty miles has great stamina.
>
> ---
>
> Anybody who has run the distance of a marathon has great stamina.

Informally, we can show that the conclusion of the argument follows from the premises by reasoning about a specific individual, say Kerry. From the first premise we can infer that if Kerry has run the distance of a marathon, then Kerry has run over twenty miles. From the second premise we can infer that if Kerry has run over twenty miles, then Kerry has great stamina. Hence it follows that if Kerry has run the distance of a marathon, then Kerry has great stamina. So far our reasoning has been about Kerry. However, Kerry was arbitrarily selected. Any other individual could have been chosen and the reasoning carried out in an analogous manner. For example, if Sam had been selected, then our reasoning would have led to the result that if Sam has run the distance of a marathon, then Sam has great stamina. If we had picked Sir Walter Raleigh, then our reasoning would have led to the result that if Sir Walter Raleigh has run the distance of a marathon, then Sir Walter Raleigh has great stamina. In short, although we have reasoned about a specific individual, the result is completely general in that it holds for every individual. No special information about Kerry was used. Therefore we can generalize to the claim that each individual is such that if he or she has run the distance of a marathon, then he or she has great stamina.

Universal Introduction ($\forall$I) is a rule of inference that permits the derivation of a universally quantified sentence from a substitution instance of that sentence. Here is a derivation for a symbolized version of the preceding argument that uses Universal Introduction:

Derive: $(\forall x)(Dx \supset Sx)$

| | | |
|---|---|---|
| 1 | $(\forall x)(Dx \supset Ox)$ | Assumption |
| 2 | $(\forall x)(Ox \supset Sx)$ | Assumption |
| 3 | $Dk \supset Ok$ | 1 $\forall$E |
| 4 | $Ok \supset Sk$ | 2 $\forall$E |
| 5 |     $Dk$ | Assumption |
| 6 |     $Ok$ | 3, 5 $\supset$E |
| 7 |     $Sk$ | 4, 6 $\supset$E |
| 8 | $Dk \supset Sk$ | 5-7 $\supset$I |
| 9 | $(\forall x)(Dx \supset Sx)$ | 8 $\forall$I |

In this derivation 'k' is the instantiating constant on lines 3 and 4. The constant 'k' has been *arbitrarily selected*, in the sense that any other individual constant could have been selected to produce an analogous result on line 8. Since 'k' does not occur in any undischarged assumption of the derivation, we did not use any special information about any individual that 'k' may designate. So the result obtained on line 8 can be generalized. Universal Introduction allows us to derive the universally quantified sentence of which the sentence on line 8 is a substitution instance.

Now let us examine a case in which the result obtained cannot be generalized.

> Phidippides, a Greek messenger, has run the distance of a marathon and has announced the Greek victory to the Athenians.
>
> Anybody who has run the distance of a marathon has run over twenty miles.
>
> Anybody who has run over twenty miles has great stamina.

From the first sentence we infer that Phidippides has run the distance of a marathon. From the second sentence we infer that if Phidippides has run the distance of a marathon, then Phidippides has run over twenty miles. Hence it follows that Phidippides has run over twenty miles. From the third sentence we infer that if Phidippides has run over twenty miles, then Phidippides has great stamina. Hence we conclude that Phidippides has great stamina. This conclusion certainly follows from the sentences. However, suppose we now generalize from the result that Phidippides has great stamina to the claim that everyone has great stamina. This generalization is *not* justified. In this case the individual is *not* arbitrarily selected, for analogous results cannot be obtained for every other individual. For instance, we cannot infer that Kerry has great stamina because the sentences do not contain the information that Kerry is a runner who has run the distance of a marathon. We cannot use the sentences to obtain this result about Sam or Sir Walter Raleigh or any individual except Phidippides. Consequently, to generalize from this result would be a mistake. A derivation that formalizes our reasoning about Phidippides is

| | | |
|---|---|---|
| 1 | Gp & (Dp & Ap) | Assumption |
| 2 | (∀x)(Dx ⊃ Ox) | Assumption |
| 3 | (∀x)(Ox ⊃ Sx) | Assumption |
| 4 | Dp & Ap | 1 &E |
| 5 | Dp | 4 &E |
| 6 | Dp ⊃ Op | 2 ∀E |
| 7 | Op | 5, 6 ⊃E |
| 8 | Op ⊃ Sp | 3 ∀E |
| 9 | Sp | 7, 8 ⊃E |

Because in this derivation 'p' is not an arbitrarily selected constant, Universal Introduction cannot be applied to 'Sp' on line 9 to obtain '(∀x)Sx'. The constant 'p' is not arbitrarily selected, for it occurs in the first assumption, and this information is used to derive 'Sp' on line 9. Notice that given these assumptions, similar derivations for 'Sk', 'Ss', and 'Sr' are not possible.

The rule Universal Introduction is

*Universal Introduction* (∀I)

| |
|---|
| $\mathscr{P}(a/x)$ |
| $(\forall x)\mathscr{P}$ |

provided that

(i) $a$ does not occur in an undischarged assumption.
(ii) $a$ does not occur in $(\forall x)\mathscr{P}$.

The restrictions placed on the rule are important, for, if followed, they ensure that the constant is arbitrarily selected. For instance, in the last derivation Universal Introduction cannot be applied to the sentence on line 9 because 'p' occurs in an undischarged assumption on line 1. Applying the rule in this case would violate the first restriction. Here are two simple examples of what can happen if the restrictions on Universal Introduction are not observed. The first restriction decrees that the relevant individual constant not occur in any currently undischarged assumption. The following move is therefore mistaken:

| | | | |
|---|---|---|---|
| 1 | Et | Assumption | |
| 2 | (∀x)Ex | 1 ∀I | **MISTAKE!** |

It does not follow from the fact that 2 is even that all numbers are even.

The second restriction tells us that the relevant individual constant cannot occur in the resulting universally quantified sentence. Here is what can happen if it does:

| | | | |
|---|---|---|---|
| 1 | (∀x)Exx | Assumption | |
| 2 | Ess | 1 ∀E | |
| 3 | (∀x)Exs | 2 ∀I | **MISTAKE!** |

Every number is equal to itself. But it does not follow that every number is equal to 7.

For a further illustration of the use of Universal Introduction and the other derivation rules introduced so far, recall an earlier argument:

Everyone loves a lover.
Tom loves Alice.
―――――――――――
Everyone loves everyone.

A derivation for a symbolized version of this argument, where we restrict the universe of discourse to persons, is given here:

Derive: (∀x)(∀y)Lxy

| | | |
|---|---|---|
| 1 | (∀z)(∀y)((∃w)Lyw ⊃ Lzy) | Assumption |
| 2 | Lta | Assumption |
| 3 | (∃w)Ltw | 2 ∃I |
| 4 | (∀y)((∃w)Lyw ⊃ Ljy) | 1 ∀E |
| 5 | (∃w)Ltw ⊃ Ljt | 4 ∀E |
| 6 | Ljt | 3, 5 ⊃E |
| 7 | (∃w)Ljw | 6 ∃I |
| 8 | (∀y)((∃w)Lyw ⊃ Lky) | 1 ∀E |
| 9 | (∃w)Ljw ⊃ Lkj | 8 ∀E |
| 10 | Lkj | 7, 9 ⊃E |
| 11 | (∀y)Lky | 10 ∀I |
| 12 | (∀x)(∀y)Lxy | 11 ∀I |

Notice that Universal Introduction cannot be applied to 'Lta' on line 2 to derive '(∀y)Lty', for 'a' occurs in an undischarged assumption, namely the one on line 2. Moreover, Universal Introduction cannot be applied to 'Ljt' on line 6 to derive '(∀y)Ljy', since 't' occurs in an undischarged assumption, again on line 2. To derive '(∀x)(∀y)Lxy', we need first to derive an atomic sentence with the predicate 'L' and two individual constants that do not occur in any undischarged assumption. The expression 'Lkj' is such a sentence, and it is derived on line 10. The sentence 'Lkj' can be used to derive '(∀y)Lky' by Universal Introduction, since 'j' does not occur in an undischarged assumption and does not occur in '(∀y)Lky'. Finally, Universal Introduction is applied to '(∀y)Lky' to derive '(∀x)(∀y)Lxy' on line 12. This is allowed since 'k' does not occur in an undischarged assumption or in the derived sentence on line 12.

The kind of reasoning suggested by Universal Introduction occurs in mathematics. A mathematician might arbitrarily select a prime number and show that there is a larger prime number. The mathematician can then generalize this result; that is, he or she can assert that for every prime number, there is a larger prime number. However, in order to generalize properly, the mathematician must be careful that the prime number is indeed arbitrarily selected, in the sense that no special properties of that number other than the fact that it is prime are appealed to. If the mathematician chooses the number 5 and notes that 5 is less than 7, it would clearly be incorrect for him or her to generalize that all prime numbers are less than 7. Generalization is legitimate only if any prime number could have been chosen and an analogous result obtained for it. Similarly, in using Universal Introduction we must be sure that the instantiating constant is arbitrarily selected. If the restrictions on the rule are not violated, we can be sure that the constant is arbitrarily chosen.

### 10.1.3E EXERCISES

Complete the following derivations:

a. Derive: (∀y)Hy

| | | |
|---|---|---|
| 1 | (∀x)Hx | Assumption |

*b. Derive: (∀y)(Hyy & By)

| | | |
|---|---|---|
| 1 | (∀y)Hyy | Assumption |
| 2 | (∀z)Bz | Assumption |

c. Derive: (∀x)(Ex ⊃ Kx)

| | | |
|---|---|---|
| 1 | (∀x)(Ex ⊃ Sx) | Assumption |
| 2 | (∀x)(Sx ⊃ Kx) | Assumption |

*d. Derive: (∀w) ~ Bw

| | | |
|---|---|---|
| 1 | (∀z)(∀y)Lzy | Assumption |
| 2 | (∀x)(∀y)(Lxy ⊃ ~ Bx) | Assumption |

*ELIMINATION RULE FOR EXISTENTIAL QUANTIFIERS*

The elimination rule for existential quantifiers is *Existential Elimination* (sometimes called Existential Instantiation). To introduce this rule, we consider the following argument:

If anybody is a genius, then Einstein is.
Somebody is a genius.

---

Einstein is a genius.

The derivation for a standard symbolization of this argument is quite simple.

Derive: Ge

| | | |
|---|---|---|
| 1 | (∃x)Gx ⊃ Ge | Assumption |
| 2 | (∃x)Gx | Assumption |
| 3 | Ge | 1, 2 ⊃ E |

But, as we noted in Chapter Seven, a sentence like

If anybody is a genius, then Einstein is a genius

can also be symbolized as

$(\forall x)(Gx \supset Ge)$

The derivation for the argument using this symbolization is somewhat more difficult. To understand it, consider how we might informally reason that the English version of the argument is valid. The second premise tells us that there is somebody who is a genius but not who he or she is. Let us suppose Smith is a genius. From the first premise we can infer that if Smith is a genius, then Einstein is a genius. Since we are assuming that Smith is a genius, we can conclude that Einstein is a genius. Of course, this conclusion is reached on the basis of an assumption that Smith is a genius, which may be false. But notice that reference to Smith played only an intermediary role. Any individual would have done, and the reasoning would have gone through just as well. Since the second premise guarantees that there is some individual who is a genius, we are sure that the conclusion follows and does not depend upon the assumption that it is Smith who is a genius. In *PD* Existential Elimination is the derivation rule that captures this kind of reasoning. Here is a derivation of a symbolized version of this argument that uses Existential Elimination (∃E):

Derive: Ge

| | | |
|---|---|---|
| 1 | $(\forall x)(Gx \supset Ge)$ | Assumption |
| 2 | $(\exists x)Gx$ | Assumption |
| 3 |     Gs | Assumption |
| 4 |     $Gs \supset Ge$ | 1 ∀E |
| 5 |     Ge | 3, 4 ⊃E |
| 6 | Ge | 2, 3-5 ∃E |

The derivation formalizes our previous reasoning. On line 3 a substitution instance of the existentially quantified sentence on line 2 is assumed. The conclusion, 'Ge', has been reached on line 5 but only under the assumption on line 3. The instantiating constant, 's', does not occur in 'Ge'. The instantiating constant plays only an intermediary role; that is, any individual constant could have been used in place of 's' to reach the result on line 5. On the basis of our assumption at line 2, '(∃x)Gx', we know that some individual is G. Hence Existential Elimination can be used to derive 'Ge' on line 6 by appealing to line 2 and the subderivation from line 3 to line 5.

The rule Existential Elimination is

*Existential Elimination* (∃E)

$$\begin{array}{l|l} & (\exists x)\mathscr{P} \\ & \quad \mathscr{P}(a/x) \\ & \quad \overline{\quad\quad\quad} \\ & \quad \mathscr{Q} \\ & \mathscr{Q} \end{array}$$

provided that

(i) $\boldsymbol{a}$ does not occur in an undischarged assumption.
(ii) $\boldsymbol{a}$ does not occur in $(\exists \boldsymbol{x})\mathscr{P}$.
(iii) $\boldsymbol{a}$ does not occur in $\mathscr{Q}$.

Notice that the sentence $\mathscr{Q}$ can be any sentence of *PL* as long as it does not contain the instantiating constant $\boldsymbol{a}$. The sentence $\mathscr{Q}$ must occur as the last sentence of the subderivation immediately next to the scope line of the subderivation.

The restrictions for the rule Existential Elimination are important because they ensure that the instantiating constant employed in the assumption plays only an intermediary role. The following illustrates a violation of the first restriction:

| | | | |
|---|---|---|---|
| 1 | Ef | Assumption | |
| 2 | (∃x)Ox | Assumption | |
| 3 |     Of | Assumption | |
| 4 |     Ef & Of | 1, 3 &I | |
| 5 |     (∃x)(Ex & Ox) | 4 ∃I | |
| 6 | (∃x)(Ex & Ox) | 2, 3-5 ∃E | **MISTAKE!** |

It is true that 4 is even (first assumption) and that some number is odd (second assumption). It does not follow that some number is even and odd. The mistake is in using the individual constant 'f' in the assumption on line 3 when it already occurs in an assumption on line 1. Notice that a similar derivation of the sentence on line 5 is not possible if the instantiating constant is other than 'f'. Thus 'f' is playing more than an intermediary role in deriving the sentence on line 5.

Here is a violation of the second restriction:

| | | | |
|---|---|---|---|
| 1 | (∀x)(∃y)Lyx | Assumption | |
| 2 | (∃y)Lyk | 1 ∀E | |
| 3 |     Lkk | Assumption | |
| 4 |     (∃x)Lxx | 3 ∃I | |
| 5 | (∃x)Lxx | 2, 3-4 ∃E | **MISTAKE!** |

It is true that for every number, there is a larger number, but it does not follow that some number is larger than itself. The existentially quantified sentence on line 2 indicates that there is a number larger than k. But the assumption on line 3 is that it is k that is larger than k. Here again the instantiating constant 'k' plays more than an intermediary role in deriving the sentence on line 4. A similar derivation of '(∃x)Lxx' is not possible if 'm', for example, is used as the instantiating constant.

If the third restriction is violated, the attempted derivation can go astray as follows:

| | | | |
|---|---|---|---|
| 1 | (∃x)Nx | Assumption | |
| 2 | Nt | Assumption | |
| 3 | Nt | 2 R | |
| 4 | Nt | 1, 2-3 ∃E | **MISTAKE!** |

It is true that some number is negative, but it does not follow that 2 is a negative number. The instantiating constant plays more than an intermediary role in deriving the sentence on line 3. A similar derivation of 'Nt' is not possible if any constant other than 't' is used as the instantiating constant. As long as the restrictions for Existential Elimination are not violated, we can be sure that the instantiating constant plays only an intermediary role.

Consider the application of Existential Elimination in the derivation for a more complex argument.

France is a country that is bigger than Luxembourg.

Some country is bigger than France.

If one thing is bigger than a second and the second is bigger than a third, then the first is bigger than the third.

---

Some country is bigger than France and bigger than Luxembourg.

A symbolization and derivation for this argument are given here:

Derive: (∃z)[Cz & (Bzf & Bzl)]

| | | |
|---|---|---|
| 1 | Cf & Bfl | Assumption |
| 2 | (∃x)(Cx & Bxf) | Assumption |
| 3 | (∀x)(∀y)(∀z)[(Bxy & Byz) ⊃ Bxz] | Assumption |
| 4 | Cr & Brf | Assumption |
| 5 | Brf | 4 & E |
| 6 | Bfl | 1 & E |
| 7 | Brf & Bfl | 5, 6 & I |
| 8 | (∀y)(∀z)[(Bry & Byz) ⊃ Brz] | 3 ∀E |
| 9 | (∀z)[(Brf & Bfz) ⊃ Brz] | 8 ∀E |
| 10 | (Brf & Bfl) ⊃ Brl | 9 ∀E |
| 11 | Brl | 7, 10 ⊃ E |
| 12 | Brf & Brl | 5, 11 & I |
| 13 | Cr | 4 & E |
| 14 | Cr & (Brf & Brl) | 13, 12 & I |
| 15 | (∃z)[Cz & (Bzf & Bzl)] | 14 ∃I |
| 16 | (∃z)[Cz & (Bzf & Bzl)] | 2, 4-15 ∃E |

The second assumption is an existentially quantified sentence. A substitution instance of this existentially quantified sentence is assumed on line 4. The instantiating constant 'r' is new to the derivation. From this assumption the sentence on line 15, which does not contain an occurrence of 'r', is derived. Notice that 'r' plays only an intermediary role. Any other individual constant could have been used in place of 'r' and the sentence on line 15 derived. The assumption on line 4 is discharged by moving to the left at line 16, and Existential Elimination is then used to derive the sentence entered on line 16 by appeal to line 2 and the subderivation from line 4 to line 15.

### 10.1.4E EXERCISES

**1.** Complete the following derivations:

**a.** Derive: (∃y)(Zy ∨ Hy)

| | | |
|---|---|---|
| 1 | (∃x)Zx | Assumption |

*b. Derive: (∃x)Lx

| | | |
|---|---|---|
| 1 | (∀x)(Fx ⊃ Lx) | Assumption |
| 2 | (∃x)Fx | Assumption |

c. Derive: (∀x)(∃y)Bxy

| | | |
|---|---|---|
| 1 | (∃y)(∀x)Bxy | Assumption |

*d. Derive: (∃y)(∃x)Gxy

| | | |
|---|---|---|
| 1 | (∃x)(∃y)Gxy | Assumption |

**2.** Given the following start of a derivation

| | | |
|---|---|---|
| 1 | (∀x)Saaxx | Assumption |
| 2 | Saabb | 1 ∀E |
| 3 | | |

which of the following sentences could be derived on line 3 by one of the quantifier introduction or elimination rules?

| | |
|---|---|
| a. Saacc | g. (∃w)Swwbb |
| *b. Saaaa | *h. (∃x)Sxaxb |
| c. Saaab | i. (∀x)Sxxbb |
| *d. (∃x)Saxbb | *j. (∀x)Saaxx |
| e. (∃x)Sxabb | k. (∀x)Saxxb |
| *f. (∃y)Saayb | *l. (∀z)Saabz |

**3.** Complete the following derivations by entering the appropriate justification for each sentence:

a. Derive: (Mk & Gh) & Md

| | |
|---|---|
| 1 | (∀x)(Mx & Gx) |
| 2 | Mk & Gk |
| 3 | Mk |
| 4 | Mh & Gh |
| 5 | Gh |
| 6 | Mk & Gh |
| 7 | Md & Gd |
| 8 | Md |
| 9 | (Mk & Gh) & Md |

*b. Derive: ~(Jb & Qb)

| | | |
|---|---|---|
| 1 | (∀z)(Jz ⊃ Lz) | |
| 2 | (∀w)(~Qw ≡ Lw) | |
| 3 | | Jb & Qb |
| 4 | | Jb |
| 5 | | Jb ⊃ Lb |
| 6 | | Lb |
| 7 | | ~Qb ≡ Lb |
| 8 | | ~Qb |
| 9 | | Qb |
| 10 | ~(Jb & Qb) | |

c. Derive: (∃x)(~Bxx ⊃ (∀z)Msz)

```
 1 | Bnn ∨ (Kn & Lj)
 2 | ~(∀z)Msz ⊃ ~Kn
   |------------------
 3 |  | ~Bnn
   |  |---------------
 4 |  |  | Bnn
   |  |  |------------
 5 |  |  |  | ~Kn
   |  |  |  |---------
 6 |  |  |  | Bnn
 7 |  |  |  | ~Bnn
 8 |  |  | Kn
   |  |
 9 |  |  | Kn & Lj
   |  |  |------------
10 |  |  | Kn
11 |  | Kn
12 |  |  | ~(∀z)Msz
   |  |  |------------
13 |  |  | ~Kn
14 |  |  | Kn
15 |  | (∀z)Msz
16 | ~Bnn ⊃ (∀z)Msz
17 | (∃x)(~Bxx ⊃ (∀z)Msz)
```

*d. Derive: Jaa

```
 1 | Kmm & ~Cmr
 2 | (∃y) ~(Kmy ⊃ Cyr) ⊃ (∀x)Jxx
   |------------------------------
 3 |  | Kmm ⊃ Cmr
   |  |------------
 4 |  | Kmm
 5 |  | Cmr
 6 |  | ~Cmr
 7 | ~(Kmm ⊃ Cmr)
 8 | (∃y) ~(Kmy ⊃ Cyr)
 9 | (∀x)Jxx
10 | Jaa
```

e. Derive: ((∀x)Hxg ∨ Rg) ∨ Lg

| | |
|---|---|
| 1 | (∀z)[(Rz ∨ (∀x)Hxz) ≡ Kzzz] |
| 2 | Kggg |
| 3 | (Rg ∨ (∀x)Hxg) ≡ Kggg |
| 4 | Rg ∨ (∀x)Hxg |
| 5 | │ Rg |
| 6 | │ (∀x)Hxg ∨ Rg |
| 7 | │ (∀x)Hxg |
| 8 | │ (∀x)Hxg ∨ Rg |
| 9 | (∀x)Hxg ∨ Rg |
| 10 | ((∀x)Hxg ∨ Rg) ∨ Lg |

*f. Derive: (∀w)(Lwg ∨ Jw)

| | |
|---|---|
| 1 | (∀x)(Dxx ∨ Px) |
| 2 | (∀y) ~ Dyy |
| 3 | (∀z)(Pz ⊃ Jz) |
| 4 | ~ Daa |
| 5 | Daa ∨ Pa |
| 6 | Pa ⊃ Ja |
| 7 | │ Daa |
| 8 | │ │ ~ Ja |
| 9 | │ │ Daa |
| 10 | │ │ ~ Daa |
| 11 | │ Ja |
| 12 | │ Pa |
| 13 | │ Ja |
| 14 | Ja |
| 15 | Lag ∨ Ja |
| 16 | (∀w)(Lwg ∨ Jw) |

g. Derive: (∀w)(∃z) ~(Hz & Rzw)

```
 1 | (∀z)[Hz ⊃ (Rzz ⊃ Gz)]
 2 | (∀z)(Gz ⊃ Bz) & (∀z) ~Bz
   |-------------------------
 3 | Ha ⊃ (Raa ⊃ Ga)
 4 | (∀z)(Gz ⊃ Bz)
 5 | Ga ⊃ Ba
 6 | (∀z) ~Bz
 7 |   | Ha & Raa
   |   |----------
 8 |   | Ha
 9 |   | Raa ⊃ Ga
10 |   | Raa
11 |   | Ga
12 |   | Ba
13 |   | ~Ba
14 | ~(Ha & Raa)
15 | (∃z) ~(Hz & Rza)
16 | (∀w)(∃z) ~(Hz & Rzw)
```

*h. Derive: (∃w) ~Lwn

```
 1 | (∃y)(My & Ry)
 2 | (∀y)[Lyn ⊃ ~(Ry ∨ Cy)]
   |-----------------------
 3 |   | Ma & Ra
   |   |----------
 4 |   | Lan ⊃ ~(Ra ∨ Ca)
 5 |   |   | Lan
   |   |   |----------
 6 |   |   | ~(Ra ∨ Ca)
 7 |   |   | Ra
 8 |   |   | Ra ∨ Ca
 9 |   | ~Lan
10 |   | (∃w) ~Lwn
11 | (∃w) ~Lwn
```

i. Derive: Sc

```
 1 | (∃x)Px ⊃ Sc
 2 | (∃x)[Txx & (∃y)(Py & ~Jy)]
   |---------------------------
 3 |   | Taa & (∃y)(Py & ~Jy)
   |   |----------------------
 4 |   | (∃y)(Py & ~Jy)
 5 |   |   | Pb & ~Jb
   |   |   |----------
 6 |   |   | Pb
 7 |   |   | (∃x)Px
 8 |   |   | Sc
 9 |   | Sc
10 | Sc
```

*j. Derive: (∃y)(∀w)(∃x)Hxxwyxx

| | | |
|---|---|---|
| 1 | (∀x)(∀y)(∃w)(∀z)Hwwxyzz | |
| 2 | (∀y)(∃w)(∀z)Hwwayzz | |
| 3 | (∃w)(∀z)Hwwabzz | |
| 4 | | (∀z)Hccabzz |
| 5 | | Hccabcc |
| 6 | | (∃x)Hxxabxx |
| 7 | (∃x)Hxxabxx | |
| 8 | (∀w)(∃x)Hxxwbxx | |
| 9 | (∃y)(∀w)(∃x)Hxxwyxx | |

## 10.2 APPLYING THE DERIVATION RULES OF *PD*

Universal Introduction, Existential Introduction, Existential Elimination, and Universal Elimination are rules of inference that must be applied to entire sentences on earlier lines and, in the case of Existential Elimination, to entire subderivations as well. A common error is illustrated by the following:

| | | | |
|---|---|---|---|
| 1 | (∀y)Cym ⊃ Em | Assumption | |
| 2 | Crm ⊃ Em | 1 ∀E | **MISTAKE!** |

It may be true that if everybody casts his or her ballot for Marty, then Marty is elected. But it does not follow that if Robinson casts her vote for Marty, Marty is elected. The mistake here was in trying to apply the rule Universal Elimination to the antecedent of the sentence on line 1. Since the sentence on line 1 is not a universally quantified sentence, Universal Elimination cannot be used.

A similar error is illustrated by the following:

| | | | |
|---|---|---|---|
| 1 | ~ (∀x)Px | Assumption | |
| 2 | ~ Pk | 1 ∀E | **MISTAKE!** |

It does not follow from the fact that not everyone has been President that John Kennedy has not been President. The sentence on line 1 is not a universally quantified sentence but the negation of a universally quantified sentence. Hence Universal Elimination cannot be applied to it.

## 10.3 BASIC CONCEPTS OF *PD*

The basic concepts for the system *PD* are analogous to the basic concepts for the system *SD* introduced in Chapter Five. A *derivation in PD* is a series of sentences of *PL* in which each sentence either is taken as an assumption with an indication of its scope or is justified by one of the rules of *PD*. As illustrated in the previous sections, derivations in *PD* are constructed in the same format as derivations in *SD*, that is, with line numbers, justifications, scope lines, and so on. The concept of derivability is also defined in a similar way.

> A sentence 𝒫 of *PL* is *derivable in PD* from a set Γ of sentences of *PL* if and only if there is a derivation in *PD* in which all the primary assumptions are members of Γ and 𝒫 occurs in the scope of only those assumptions.

Suppose we wish to show that

(∃z)Mz

is derivable in *PD* from the set of sentences

{(∀x)((∃y)Lxy ⊃ (∃y) ∼ Jy), (∃y)(∃z)Lyz, (∀x)( ∼ Jx ≡ Mx)}

That is, expressed in terms of the turnstile notation, we wish to show that

{(∀x)(∃y)Lxy ⊃ (∃y) ∼ Jy), (∃y)(∃z)Lyz, (∀x)( ∼ Jx ≡ Mx)} ⊢ (∃z)Mz

We begin by taking the members of the set as assumptions and proceed to derive '(∃z)Mz'.

Derive: (∃z)Mz

| | | |
|---|---|---|
| 1 | │ (∀x)((∃y)Lxy ⊃ (∃y) ∼ Jy) | Assumption |
| 2 | │ (∃y)(∃z)Lyz | Assumption |
| 3 | │ (∀x)( ∼ Jx ≡ Mx) | Assumption |
| 4 | │ │ (∃z)Lmz | Assumption |
| 5 | │ │ │ Lmn | Assumption |
| 6 | │ │ │ (∃y)Lmy ⊃ (∃y) ∼ Jy | 1 ∀E |
| 7 | │ │ │ (∃y)Lmy | 5 ∃I |
| 8 | │ │ │ (∃y) ∼ Jy | 6, 7 ⊃E |
| 9 | │ │ │ │ ∼ Ji | Assumption |
| 10 | │ │ │ │ ∼ Ji ≡ Mi | 3 ∀E |
| 11 | │ │ │ │ Mi | 9, 10 ≡E |
| 12 | │ │ │ │ (∃z)Mz | 11 ∃I |
| 13 | │ │ │ (∃z)Mz | 8, 9-12 ∃E |
| 14 | │ │ (∃z)Mz | 4, 5-13 ∃E |
| 15 | │ (∃z)Mz | 2, 4-14 ∃E |

Although additional assumptions have been made in the derivation, they have all been discharged by the end of the derivation so that '(∃z)Mz' on line 15 lies in the scope of only the primary assumptions. Hence '(∃z)Mz' is derivable in *PD* from the given set of sentences.

The definition of validity in *PD* is as follows:

> An argument of *PL* is *valid in PD* if and only if the conclusion of the argument is derivable in *PD* from the set consisting of the premises. An argument of *PL* is *invalid in PD* if and only if it is not valid in *PD*.

This definition simply formalizes a concept we have been using informally. To show that an argument is valid in *PD*, we take its premises as primary assumptions and derive its conclusion so that the only undischarged assumptions are primary assumptions. Consider the argument

Only people who are neither wealthy nor famous are logicians.
Anybody who doesn't need to ask the price of anything is wealthy.

---

Logicians need to ask the price of something.

This argument can be symbolized as

(∀x)(Lx ⊃ [Px & (~Wx & ~Fx)])
(∀x)[(Px & ~(∃y)Nxy) ⊃ Wx]

---

(∀x)(Lx ⊃ (∃y)Nxy)

The symbolized argument is shown to be valid in *PD* by the following derivation:

Derive: (∀x)(Lx ⊃ (∃y)Nxy)

| | | |
|---|---|---|
| 1 | (∀x)(Lx ⊃ [Px & (~Wx & ~Fx)]) | Assumption |
| 2 | (∀x)[(Px & ~(∃y)Nxy) ⊃ Wx] | Assumption |
| 3 | Lb | Assumption |
| 4 | ~(∃y)Nby | Assumption |
| 5 | Lb ⊃ [Pb & (~Wb & ~Fb)] | 1 ∀E |
| 6 | Pb & (~Wb & ~Fb) | 3, 5 ⊃E |
| 7 | ~Wb & ~Fb | 6 &E |
| 8 | ~Wb | 7 &E |
| 9 | Pb | 6 &E |
| 10 | Pb & ~(∃y)Nby | 9, 4 &I |
| 11 | (Pb & ~(∃y)Nby) ⊃ Wb | 2 ∀E |
| 12 | Wb | 10, 11 ⊃E |
| 13 | (∃y)Nby | 4-12 ~E |
| 14 | Lb ⊃ (∃y)Nby | 3-13 ⊃I |
| 15 | (∀x)(Lx ⊃ (∃y)Nxy) | 14 ∀I |

Although auxiliary assumptions are made in the derivation, they are discharged by the end of the derivation. The conclusion of the argument on the last line of the derivation lies in the scope of only primary assumptions which are the premises of the argument.

A special case of deriving a sentence from a set of sentences occurs when the set is the empty set.

> A sentence $\mathscr{P}$ of *PL* is a *theorem in PD* if and only if $\mathscr{P}$ is derivable in *PD* from the empty set.

So to demonstrate that

$$(\forall x)(Hxx \supset (\exists y)Gy) \equiv ((\exists x)Hxx \supset (\exists y)Gy)$$

is a theorem, that is, to show that

$$\vdash (\forall x)(Hxx \supset (\exists y)Gy) \equiv ((\exists x)Hxx \supset (\exists y)Gy)$$

we might construct the following derivation:

Derive: $(\forall x)(Hxx \supset (\exists y)Gy) \equiv ((\exists x)Hxx \supset (\exists y)Gy)$

| | | |
|---|---|---|
| 1 | $(\forall x)(Hxx \supset (\exists y)Gy)$ | Assumption |
| 2 | $(\exists x)Hxx$ | Assumption |
| 3 | $Hkk$ | Assumption |
| 4 | $Hkk \supset (\exists y)Gy$ | 1 $\forall$E |
| 5 | $(\exists y)Gy$ | 3, 4 $\supset$ E |
| 6 | $(\exists y)Gy$ | 2, 3-5 $\exists$E |
| 7 | $(\exists x)Hxx \supset (\exists y)Gy$ | 2-6 $\supset$ I |
| 8 | $(\exists x)Hxx \supset (\exists y)Gy$ | Assumption |
| 9 | $Hkk$ | Assumption |
| 10 | $(\exists x)Hxx$ | 9 $\exists$I |
| 11 | $(\exists y)Gy$ | 8, 10 $\supset$ E |
| 12 | $Hkk \supset (\exists y)Gy$ | 9-11 $\supset$ I |
| 13 | $(\forall x)(Hxx \supset (\exists y)Gy)$ | 12 $\forall$I |
| 14 | $(\forall x)(Hxx \supset (\exists y)Gy) \equiv ((\exists x)Hxx \supset (\exists y)Gy)$ | 1-7, 8-13 $\equiv$ I |

During the derivation we made several assumptions, but by the end of the derivation the assumptions were all discharged. There are no primary assumptions in the derivation. Hence the sentence on the last line is a theorem in *PD*.

Equivalence in *PD* is defined as follows:

> Sentences $\mathscr{P}$ and $\mathscr{Q}$ of *PL* are *equivalent in PD* if and only if $\mathscr{Q}$ is derivable in *PD* from $\{\mathscr{P}\}$ and $\mathscr{P}$ is derivable in *PD* from $\{\mathscr{Q}\}$.

To show that the two sentences

$$(\forall x)(Ax \supset Bx)$$

and

$$(\forall x)(\sim Bx \supset \sim Ax)$$

are equivalent in *PD*, we construct two derivations. We derive the second sentence from the first

Derive: $(\forall x)(\sim Bx \supset \sim Ax)$

| | | |
|---|---|---|
| 1 | $(\forall x)(Ax \supset Bx)$ | Assumption |
| 2 | $\sim Ba$ | Assumption |
| 3 | $Aa$ | Assumption |
| 4 | $Aa \supset Ba$ | 1 $\forall$E |
| 5 | $Ba$ | 3, 4 $\supset$E |
| 6 | $\sim Ba$ | 2 R |
| 7 | $\sim Aa$ | 3-6 $\sim$I |
| 8 | $\sim Ba \supset \sim Aa$ | 2-7 $\supset$I |
| 9 | $(\forall x)(\sim Bx \supset \sim Ax)$ | 8 $\forall$I |

so that the only undischarged assumption is the first sentence. Then we derive the first sentence from the second

Derive: $(\forall x)(Ax \supset Bx)$

| | | |
|---|---|---|
| 1 | $(\forall x)(\sim Bx \supset \sim Ax)$ | Assumption |
| 2 | $Aa$ | Assumption |
| 3 | $\sim Ba$ | Assumption |
| 4 | $\sim Ba \supset \sim Aa$ | 1 $\forall$E |
| 5 | $\sim Aa$ | 3, 4 $\supset$E |
| 6 | $Aa$ | 2 R |
| 7 | $Ba$ | 3-6 $\sim$E |
| 8 | $Aa \supset Ba$ | 2-7 $\supset$I |
| 9 | $(\forall x)(Ax \supset Bx)$ | 8 $\forall$I |

so that the only discharged assumption is the second sentence. Hence the two sentences are equivalent in *PD*.

Inconsistency in *PD* is defined as follows:

> A set Γ of sentences of *PL* is *inconsistent in PD* if and only if both a sentence $\mathscr{P}$ of *PL* and its negation $\sim\mathscr{P}$ are derivable in *PD* from Γ. A set Γ of sentences of *PL* is *consistent in PD* if and only if it is not inconsistent in *PD*.

In Chapter One we claimed that the following set of sentences is inconsistent:

Anyone who takes astrology seriously is a lunatic.

Alice is my sister, and no sister of mine has a lunatic for a husband.

Higgins is Alice's husband, and he reads the horoscope column every morning.

Anyone who reads the horoscope column every morning takes astrology seriously.

This set of sentences can be symbolized in *PL* as:

(∀z)(Az ⊃ Lz)

Sa & (∀z)[Sz ⊃ ~(∃y)(Hyz & Ly)]

Hha & Rh

(∀z)(Rz ⊃ Az)

Now we have the techniques to show that this symbolized version of the set of sentences is inconsistent in *PD*. We take the members of the set as primary assumptions and construct a derivation like this one:

| | | |
|---|---|---|
| 1 | (∀z)(Az ⊃ Lz) | Assumption |
| 2 | Sa & (∀z)[Sz ⊃ ~(∃y)(Hyz & Ly)] | Assumption |
| 3 | Hha & Rh | Assumption |
| 4 | (∀z)(Rz ⊃ Az) | Assumption |
| 5 | (∀z)[Sz ⊃ ~(∃y)(Hyz & Ly)] | 2 &E |
| 6 | Sa ⊃ ~(∃y)(Hya & Ly) | 5 ∀E |
| 7 | Sa | 2 &E |
| 8 | ~(∃y)(Hya & Ly) | 6, 7 ⊃E |
| 9 | Rh ⊃ Ah | 4 ∀E |
| 10 | Rh | 3 &E |
| 11 | Ah | 9, 10 ⊃E |
| 12 | Ah ⊃ Lh | 1 ∀E |
| 13 | Lh | 11, 12 ⊃E |
| 14 | Hha | 3 &E |
| 15 | Hha & Lh | 14, 13 &I |
| 16 | (∃y)(Hya & Ly) | 15 ∃I |

Since we have derived a sentence '(∃y)(Hya & Ly)' on line 16 and its negation on line 8 and since both of these sentences occur in the scope of only the primary assumptions, we have shown that the set of sentences is inconsistent in *PD*.

Since *PD* is a syntactic system, it is not essential that we have any interpretation of the formulas in mind when testing for the properties just defined. Recall that the derivation rules allow us to manipulate symbols on the basis of the forms of the sentences alone, rather than on the basis of their truth-conditions. Although syntax and semantics are distinct, the results of one parallel the results of the other. The following claims are proved in Chapter Eleven:

> A sentence $\mathscr{P}$ is derivable in *PD* from a set Γ of sentences of *PL* if and only if $\mathscr{P}$ is quantificationally entailed by Γ.
>
> An argument of *PL* is valid in *PD* if and only if the argument is quantificationally valid.
>
> A sentence $\mathscr{P}$ of *PL* is a theorem of *PD* if and only if $\mathscr{P}$ is quantificationally true.
>
> Sentences $\mathscr{P}$ and $\mathscr{Q}$ of *PL* are equivalent in *PD* if and only if $\mathscr{P}$ and $\mathscr{Q}$ are quantificationally equivalent.
>
> A set Γ of sentences of *PL* is inconsistent in *PD* if and only if Γ is quantificationally inconsistent.

## 10.4 STRATEGIES FOR CONSTRUCTING DERIVATIONS IN *PD*

In Chapter Five we pointed out that we could (if we wanted) develop a decision procedure for constructing derivations in *SD*. However, the situation with *PD* is different. We could not (even if we wanted) develop a decision procedure for *PD*. As a result, the need for using strategies in constructing derivations in *PD* is all the more important.

Once again we use goal analysis in constructing derivations. The sentence that we hope ultimately to derive is taken as the goal sentence, and we look for subgoal sentences such that if we can derive them, we can in turn derive our goal sentence. These subgoal sentences become our new goal sentences, and the process is repeated until we are able to derive the goal sentences easily from the assumptions, if any. Consider an example of this approach. Suppose we wish to construct a derivation that shows that the following argument is valid in *PD*:

(∀z)(Szz ⊃ Tz)
(∀y)[(Ty ∨ Uyy) ⊃ Wy]
________________________________
(∀z)[(Szz & ~Kz) ⊃ (Wz & ~Kz)]

The derivation is begun by listing the premises as assumptions. Next the conclusion is entered farther down the page.

Derive: $(\forall z)[(Szz \;\&\; \sim Kz) \supset (Wz \;\&\; \sim Kz)]$

| | | |
|---|---|---|
| 1 | $(\forall z)(Szz \supset Tz)$ | Assumption |
| 2 | $(\forall y)[(Ty \vee Uyy) \supset Wy]$ | Assumption |
| | | |
| | $(\forall z)[(Szz \;\&\; \sim Kz) \supset (Wz \;\&\; \sim Kz)]$ | |

Using the goal-analysis approach, we next ask ourselves what sentences, if we could derive them, would allow us to derive the goal sentence, which in this case is the conclusion. A universally quantified sentence can be derived in many ways, but one possibility is to derive it by using Universal Introduction. Pursuing this strategy, we enter a substitution instance of the universally quantified sentence on the immediately preceding line as a subgoal. Of course, we must be careful not violate any of the restrictions on the use of Universal Introduction. When the derivation is completed, we must be sure that the instantiating constant does not occur in any undischarged assumption on a prior line, and we must be sure that it does not occur in the derived universally quantified sentence. We choose the constant 'j' as our instantiating constant. We can also enter '∀I' in the justification column for the last sentence, although the line reference for the justification is still unknown.

Derive: $(\forall z)[(Szz \;\&\; \sim Kz) \supset (Wz \;\&\; \sim Kz)]$

| | | |
|---|---|---|
| 1 | $(\forall z)(Szz \supset Tz)$ | Assumption |
| 2 | $(\forall y)[(Ty \vee Uyy) \supset Wy]$ | Assumption |
| | | |
| | $(Sjj \;\&\; \sim Kj) \supset (Wj \;\&\; \sim Kj)$ | |
| | $(\forall z)[(Szz \;\&\; \sim Kz) \supset (Wz \;\&\; \sim Kz)]$ | _ ∀I |

Our new goal sentence is '$(Sjj \;\&\; \sim Kj) \supset (Wj \;\&\; \sim Kj)$'. Since this sentence is a conditional, Conditional Introduction should be helpful. Thus we construct a subderivation that has the antecedent of the goal sentence as its assumption and the consequent of the goal sentence as its last sentence. The derivation under construction is

Derive: (∀z)[(Szz & ~Kz) ⊃ (Wz & ~Kz)]

| | | |
|---|---|---|
| 1 | (∀z)(Szz ⊃ Tz) | Assumption |
| 2 | (∀y)[(Ty ∨ Uyy) ⊃ Wy] | Assumption |
| 3 | Sjj & ~Kj | Assumption |
| | Wj & ~Kj | |
| | (Sjj & ~Kj) ⊃ (Wj & ~Kj) | 3-_ ⊃I |
| | (∀z)[(Szz & ~Kz) ⊃ (Wz & ~Kz)] | _ ∀I |

Notice that although ‘j’ is the individual constant used in the assumption on line 3, the assumption is discharged before Universal Introduction is applied to derive the last sentence. Hence there will be no violation of the restrictions put on the use of Universal Introduction. Our new goal is to derive ‘Wj & ~Kj’ on the basis of the two primary assumptions and the auxiliary assumption just made. This is not difficult, since we can instantiate the universally quantified assumptions using ‘j’. With the line references filled in, the completed derivation looks like this:

Derive: (∀z)[(Szz & ~Kz) ⊃ (Wz & ~Kz)]

| | | |
|---|---|---|
| 1 | (∀z)(Szz ⊃ Tz) | Assumption |
| 2 | (∀y)[(Ty ∨ Uyy) ⊃ Wy] | Assumption |
| 3 | Sjj & ~Kj | Assumption |
| 4 | Sjj ⊃ Tj | 1 ∀E |
| 5 | Sjj | 3 &E |
| 6 | Tj | 4, 5 ⊃E |
| 7 | (Tj ∨ Ujj) ⊃ Wj | 2 ∀E |
| 8 | Tj ∨ Ujj | 6 ∨I |
| 9 | Wj | 7, 8 ⊃E |
| 10 | ~Kj | 3 &E |
| 11 | Wj & ~Kj | 9, 10 &I |
| 12 | (Sjj & ~Kj) ⊃ (Wj & ~Kj) | 3-11 ⊃I |
| 13 | (∀z)[(Szz & ~Kz) ⊃ (Wz & ~Kz)] | 12 ∀I |

In this example goal analysis has led us to the proper auxiliary assumption: ‘Sjj & ~Kj’. But, if the ultimate goal were ignored, then it might be tempting to assume ‘(∀z)(Szz & ~Kz)’ and try to derive ‘(∀z)(Wz & ~Kz)’. This would be a mistake. The conditional derived by using Conditional Introduction would be

(∀z)(Szz & ~Kz) ⊃ (∀z)(Wz & ~Kz)

which is *not* the sentence we are seeking. With regard to making the proper assumptions, it is instructive to compare where goal analysis led us in the last example with where it leads us in the next.

Suppose we wish to construct a derivation to show

$\vdash ((\exists x)Fx \vee (\exists x)Gx) \supset (\exists x)(Fx \vee Gx)$

In constrast to our last example, in this one our ultimate goal is not to derive a quantified sentence, a sentence that begins with a quantifier whose scope extends over the entire sentence, but rather to derive a conditional. Hence we can enter the skeleton of a subderivation in the derivation under construction. The assumption of the subderivation is the antecedent of the desired conditional, and the last sentence of the subderivation is the consequent of the conditional. If the subderivation can be completed, our goal sentence can be obtained by Conditional Introduction.

Derive: $((\exists x)Fx \vee (\exists x)Gx) \supset (\exists x)(Fx \vee Gx)$

| | | |
|---|---|---|
| 1 | $(\exists x)Fx \vee (\exists x)Gx$ | Assumption |
| | | |
| | $(\exists x)(Fx \vee Gx)$ | |
| | $((\exists x)Fx \vee (\exists x)Gx) \supset (\exists x)(Fx \vee Gx)$ | 1-_ ⊃I |

The goal now is to derive '$(\exists x)(Fx \vee Gx)$' from the assumption. Since the assumption is a disjunction, a promising approach is to apply Disjunction Elimination.

Derive: $((\exists x)Fx \vee (\exists x)Gx) \supset (\exists x)(Fx \vee Gx)$

| | | |
|---|---|---|
| 1 | $(\exists x)Fx \vee (\exists x)Gx$ | Assumption |
| 2 | $(\exists x)Fx$ | Assumption |
| | | |
| | $(\exists x)(Fx \vee Gx)$ | |
| | $(\exists x)Gx$ | Assumption |
| | | |
| | $(\exists x)(Fx \vee Gx)$ | |
| | $(\exists x)(Fx \vee Gx)$ | 1, 2-_, _-_ ∨E |
| | $((\exists x)Fx \vee (\exists x)Gx) \supset (\exists x)(Fx \vee Gx)$ | 1-_ ⊃I |

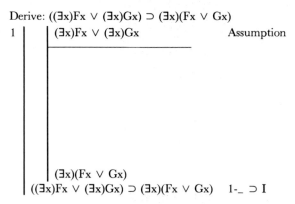

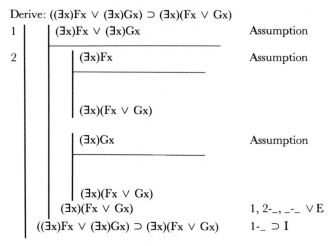

Now our goal is to derive '$(\exists x)(Fx \vee Gx)$' within each of the subderivations. This presents us with a very common situation in constructing derivations. Our goal sentence must be derived from an existentially quantified sentence. Whenever this situation occurs, a good procedure is to take a substitution instance of the existentially quantified sentence as an assumption, planning to derive the goal sentence by Existential Elimination.

Derive: ((∃x)Fx ∨ (∃x)Gx) ⊃ (∃x)(Fx ∨ Gx)

| | | |
|---|---|---|
| 1 | (∃x)Fx ∨ (∃x)Gx | Assumption |
| 2 | (∃x)Fx | Assumption |
| 3 | Fb | Assumption |
| | (∃x)(Fx ∨ Gx) | |
| | (∃x)(Fx ∨ Gx) | 2, 3-_ ∃E |
| | (∃x)Gx | Assumption |
| | Gb | Assumption |
| | (∃x)(Fx ∨ Gx) | |
| | (∃x)(Fx ∨ Gx) | _, _-_ ∃E |
| | (∃x)(Fx ∨ Gx) | 1, 2-_, _-_ ∨E |
| | ((∃x) Fx ∨ (∃x)Gx) ⊃ (∃x)(Fx ∨ Gx) | 1-_ ⊃ I |

Our new goal is to derive '(∃x)(Fx ∨ Gx)' from the most recent assumptions: 'Fb' in the upper subderivation and 'Gb' in the lower subderivation. The sentence '(∃x)(Fx ∨ Gx)' can be obtained from 'Fb ∨ Gb' by Existential Introduction, and 'Fb ∨ Gb' is easy to derive from the given assumptions.

Derive: ((∃x)Fx ∨ (∃x)Gx) ⊃ (∃x)(Fx ∨ Gx)

| | | |
|---|---|---|
| 1 | (∃x)Fx ∨ (∃x)Gx | Assumption |
| 2 | (∃x)Fx | Assumption |
| 3 | Fb | Assumption |
| 4 | Fb ∨ Gb | 3 ∨I |
| 5 | (∃x)(Fx ∨ Gx) | 4 ∃I |
| 6 | (∃x)(Fx ∨ Gx) | 2, 3-5 ∃E |
| 7 | (∃x)Gx | Assumption |
| 8 | Gb | Assumption |
| 9 | Fb ∨ Gb | 8 ∨I |
| 10 | (∃x)(Fx ∨ Gx) | 9 ∃I |
| 11 | (∃x)(Fx ∨ Gx) | 7, 8-10 ∃E |
| 12 | (∃x)(Fx ∨ Gx) | 1, 2-6, 7-11 ∨E |
| 13 | ((∃x) Fx ∨ (∃x)Gx) ⊃ (∃x)(Fx ∨ Gx) | 1-12 ⊃ I |

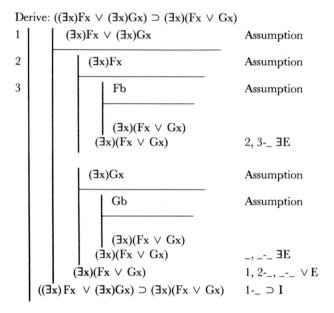

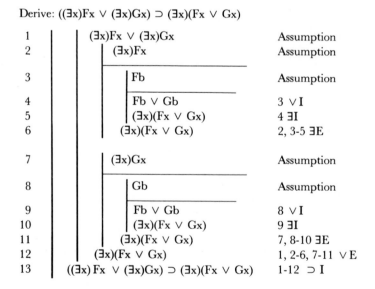

Notice that although the assumptions on lines 3 and 8 both contain the constant 'b', these assumptions are discharged when Existential Elimination is applied. Hence the restrictions on Existential Elimination are not violated.

Of the rules for introducing and eliminating quantifiers, Existential Elimination is probably the most difficult to apply, for this rule requires the construction of a subderivation. A good rule of thumb to follow is this: If it looks as if an existential quantifier must be eliminated in order to derive a goal sentence, set up the structure of a subderivation that has a substitution instance of the existentially quantified sentence as its assumption and the goal sentence as its last sentence. Of course, we must be careful to select a proper substitution instance of the existentially quantified sentence (i.e., an instance that will not violate any of the restrictions on Existential Elimination). Once the subderivation is filled in, the goal sentence can be derived by Existential Elimination. For instance, suppose we want to construct a derivation to show that the following argument is valid:

(∃x)(∀y)Nxxy
(∃y)(∃z)(Bzy & ~ Py)
(∀z)(∀w)[(Nzzw & ~ Pw) ⊃ Sz]
___
(∃z)Sz

Our goal sentence is '(∃z)Sz', and it is likely we shall have to eliminate some existential quantifiers in deriving this sentence. Thus, after listing the premises as primary assumptions, we can take a substitution instance of the assumption on line 1 as an auxiliary assumption.

Derive: (∃z)Sz

| | | |
|---|---|---|
| 1 | (∃x)(∀y)Nxxy | Assumption |
| 2 | (∃y)(∃z)(Bzy & ~ Py) | Assumption |
| 3 | (∀z)(∀w)[(Nzzw & ~ Pw) ⊃ Sz] | Assumption |
| 4 |     (∀y)Naay | Assumption |
| |     (∃z)Sz | |
| | (∃z)Sz | 1, 4-_ ∃E |

Ultimately we plan to derive the goal sentence by Existential Elimination but now our objective is to derive the goal sentence within the subderivation. However, the second assumption is an existentially quantified sentence, and thus we can repeat the process by setting up the structure of another subderivation whose assumption is a substitution instance of the assumption on line 2.

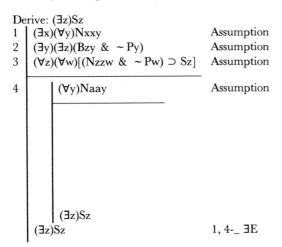

```
Derive: (∃z)Sz
1  | (∃x)(∀y)Nxxy                       Assumption
2  | (∃y)(∃z)(Bzy & ~Py)                Assumption
3  | (∀z)(∀w)[(Nzzw & ~Pw) ⊃ Sz]        Assumption
   |---------------------------------
4  |   | (∀y)Naay                       Assumption
   |   |-----------------------------
5  |   |   | (∃z)(Bzb & ~Pb)            Assumption
   |   |   |-------------------------
   |   |   |
   |   |   | (∃z)Sz
   |   | (∃z)Sz                         2, 5-_ ∃E
   | (∃z)Sz                             1, 4-_ ∃E
```

Notice that in making the assumption on line 5, we picked an instantiating constant other than 'a'. The use of Existential Elimination on the second to last line of the derivation would not be legitimate if 'a' were used, for at that point 'a' would occur in the undischarged assumption on line 4. The current goal is to derive '(∃z)Sz' within the innermost subderivation. But the assumption of the innermost subderivation is an existentially quantified sentence, and consequently we can set up another subderivation and plan to obtain the goal sentence by another application of Existential Elimination.

```
Derive: (∃z)Sz
1  | (∃x)(∀y)Nxxy                       Assumption
2  | (∃y)(∃z)(Bzy & ~Py)                Assumption
3  | (∀z)(∀w)[(Nzzw & ~Pw) ⊃ Sz]        Assumption
   |---------------------------------
4  |   | (∀y)Naay                       Assumption
   |   |-----------------------------
5  |   |   | (∃z)(Bzb & ~Pb)            Assumption
   |   |   |-------------------------
6  |   |   |   | Bcb & ~Pb              Assumption
   |   |   |   |---------------------
   |   |   |   |
   |   |   |   | (∃z)Sz
   |   |   | (∃z)Sz                     5, 6-_ ∃E
   |   | (∃z)Sz                         2, 5-_ ∃E
   | (∃z)Sz                             1, 4-_ ∃E
```

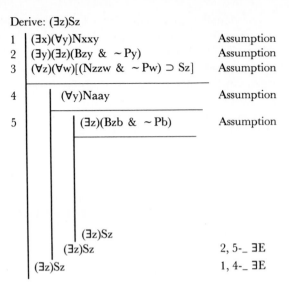

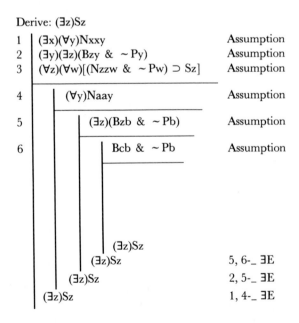

At line 6 an instantiating constant new to the derivation, 'c', is used. It is a good practice to pick an instantiating constant that is completely new to the derivation when making an assumption of a subderivation that will later be appealed to in using Existential Elimination. If the instantiating constant is completely new to the derivation, then there is no chance that it occurs in earlier undischarged assumptions or in the existentially quantified sentence that is appealed to in using Existential Elimination. The derivation at hand can easily be completed by deriving the goal sentence '(∃z)Sz' within the innermost subderivation.

Derive: (∃z)Sz

| | | |
|---|---|---|
| 1 | (∃x)(∀y)Nxxy | Assumption |
| 2 | (∃y)(∃z)(Bzy & ~ Py) | Assumption |
| 3 | (∀z)(∀w)[(Nzzw & ~ Pw) ⊃ Sz] | Assumption |
| 4 | (∀y)Naay | Assumption |
| 5 | (∃z)(Bzb & ~ Pb) | Assumption |
| 6 | Bcb & ~ Pb | Assumption |
| 7 | Naab | 4 ∀E |
| 8 | ~ Pb | 6 & E |
| 9 | Naab & ~ Pb | 7, 8 & I |
| 10 | (∀w)[(Naaw & ~ Pw) ⊃ Sa] | 3 ∀E |
| 11 | (Naab & ~ Pb) ⊃ Sa | 10 ∀E |
| 12 | Sa | 9, 11 ⊃ E |
| 13 | (∃z)Sz | 12 ∃I |
| 14 | (∃z)Sz | 5, 6-13 ∃E |
| 15 | (∃z)Sz | 2, 5-14 ∃E |
| 16 | (∃z)Sz | 1, 4-15 ∃E |

Using individual constants that already occur in a derivation to guide the application of Universal Elimination is an important technique in constructing derivations. Consider the following:

Derive: (∃x)Cx

| | | |
|---|---|---|
| 1 | (∀x)(∀y)[Gxy ≡ (Ky ⊃ Cx)] | Assumption |
| 2 | (∀w)Giw | Assumption |
| 3 | (∃z)Kz | Assumption |
| 4 | Kg | Assumption |
| | (∃x)Cx | |
| | (∃x)Cx | 3, 4-_ ∃E |

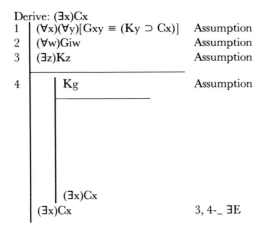

Our goal is to derive '(∃x)Cx'. Since it is likely that we shall need to eliminate an existential quantifier, we have followed the rule of thumb given in the last example and set up a subderivation for use with Existential Elimination. We can derive '(∃x)Cx' by Existential Introduction if we can obtain a substitution instance of that sentence. Since the predicate 'C' occurs in the first assumption, it is likely that the substitution instance we are seeking will be derived in some way from this sentence. Thus Universal Elimination must be applied to this universally quantified assumption, but which instantiating constant should we pick? The choice is important because we hope to derive sentences with similar sentential components so that the derivation rules for sentential connectives can be applied. Therefore we should allow the individual constants that already occur in the derivation to guide our choice. Since 'i' occurs in 'Giw' (line 2) where 'x' occurs in 'Gxy' (line 1), 'i' is a good choice as an instantiating constant.

Derive: (∃x)Cx

| | | |
|---|---|---|
| 1 | (∀x)(∀y)[Gxy ≡ (Ky ⊃ Cx)] | Assumption |
| 2 | (∀w)Giw | Assumption |
| 3 | (∃z)Kz | Assumption |
| 4 |     Kg | Assumption |
| 5 |     (∀y)[Giy ≡ (Ky ⊃ Ci)] | 1 ∀E |
| |     (∃x)Cx | |
| | (∃x)Cx | 3, 4-_ ∃E |

Now it is clear that 'Ci' is the substitution instance of '(∃x)Cx' that we are seeking. It is also clear that more universal quantifiers must be eliminated in order to derive it. Since 'g' occurs in 'Kg' (line 4) where 'y' occurs in 'Ky' (line 5), it is wise to use 'g' as the instantiating constant when applying Universal Elimination to the sentence on line 5.

Derive: (∃x)Cx

| | | |
|---|---|---|
| 1 | (∀x)(∀y)[Gxy ≡ (Ky ⊃ Cx)] | Assumption |
| 2 | (∀w)Giw | Assumption |
| 3 | (∃z)Kz | Assumption |
| 4 |     Kg | Assumption |
| 5 |     (∀y)[Giy ≡ (Ky ⊃ Ci)] | 1 ∀E |
| 6 |     Gig ≡ (Kg ⊃ Ci) | 5 ∀E |
| |     Ci | |
| |     (∃x)Cx | _ ∃I |
| | (∃x)Cx | 3, 4-_ ∃E |

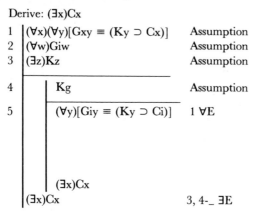

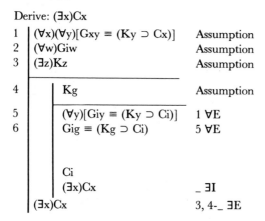

Similarly, since 'g' occurs in 'Gig' (line 6) where 'w' occurs in 'Giw' (line 2), Universal Elimination should be applied to the sentence on line 2, with 'g' as the instantiating constant.

Derive: (∃x)Cx

| | | |
|---|---|---|
| 1 | (∀x)(∀y)[Gxy ≡ (Ky ⊃ Cx)] | Assumption |
| 2 | (∀w)Giw | Assumption |
| 3 | (∃z)Kz | Assumption |
| 4 | Kg | Assumption |
| 5 | (∀y)[Giy ≡ (Ky ⊃ Ci)] | 1 ∀E |
| 6 | Gig ≡ (Kg ⊃ Ci) | 5 ∀E |
| 7 | Gig | 2 ∀E |
| | Ci | |
| | (∃x)Cx | _ ∃I |
| | (∃x)Cx | 3, 4-_ ∃E |

Since we have chosen the instantiating constants carefully, we can finish the derivation by application of the derivation rules for sentential connectives.

Derive: (∃x)Cx

| | | |
|---|---|---|
| 1 | (∀x)(∀y)[Gxy ≡ (Ky ⊃ Cx)] | Assumption |
| 2 | (∀w)Giw | Assumption |
| 3 | (∃z)Kz | Assumption |
| 4 | Kg | Assumption |
| 5 | (∀y)[Giy ≡ (Ky ⊃ Ci)] | 1 ∀E |
| 6 | Gig ≡ (Kg ⊃ Ci) | 5 ∀E |
| 7 | Gig | 2 ∀E |
| 8 | Kg ⊃ Ci | 6, 7 ≡ E |
| 9 | Ci | 4, 8 ⊃ E |
| 10 | (∃x)Cx | 9 ∃I |
| 11 | (∃x)Cx | 3, 4-10 ∃E |

As mentioned in Section 10.2, the introduction and elimination rules for quantifiers are rules of inference that must be applied to entire sentences on single lines. Therefore sentences that are negations of quantified sentences pose special difficulties. For example, Universal Elimination cannot be applied to '~(∀x)Fx'. In such situations the rules Negation Introduction and Negation Elimination are very useful. Consider their application in the following derivations:

Derive: (∃x) ~ Fx

| | | |
|---|---|---|
| 1 | ~ (∀x)Fx | Assumption |
| 2 |   ~ (∃x) ~ Fx | Assumption |
| 3 |     ~ Fc | Assumption |
| 4 |     (∃x) ~ Fx | 3 ∃I |
| 5 |     ~ (∃x) ~ Fx | 2 R |
| 6 |   Fc | 3-5 ~E |
| 7 |   (∀x)Fx | 6 ∀I |
| 8 |   ~ (∀x)Fx | 1 R |
| 9 | (∃x) ~ Fx | 2-8 ~E |

Derive: (∀x) ~ Fx

| | | |
|---|---|---|
| 1 | ~ (∃x)Fx | Assumption |
| 2 |   Fc | Assumption |
| 3 |   (∃x)Fx | 2 ∃I |
| 4 |   ~ (∃x)Fx | 1 R |
| 5 | ~ Fc | 2-4 ~I |
| 6 | (∀x) ~ Fx | 5 ∀I |

Using goal analysis and knowing the special techniques introduced in this section facilitate the construction of derivations in *PD*. But there is no substitute for practice in learning to construct derivations.

## 10.4E EXERCISES

**1.** Show that each of the following derivability claims holds in *PD*:

a. {(∀x)Kxx} ⊢ (∀z)Kzz
*b. {(∃x)Kxx} ⊢ (∃z)Kzz
c. {(∀z)(Gz ⊃ Hz), Gi} ⊢ (∃y)Hy
*d. {(∀x)Mx} ⊢ (∀x)(~ Mx ⊃ Mx)
e. {(∃y)Byyy} ⊢ (∃x)(∃y)(∃z)Bxyz
*f. {(∀x)[(Hx & ~ Kx) ⊃ Ix], (∃y)(Hy & Gy), (∀x)(Gx & ~ Kx)} ⊢ (∃y)(Iy & Gy)

**2.** Show that each of the following arguments is valid in *PD*:

a. (∀x)(∀y)Cxy
―――――――――
(Caa & Cab) & (Cba & Cbb)

*b. (∀x)(Tx ⊃ Lx)
~ Lb
―――――――――
~ Tb

c. (∀y)[(Hy & Fy) ⊃ Gy]
(∀z)Fz & ~ (∀x)Kxb
―――――――――
(∀x)(Hx ⊃ Gx)

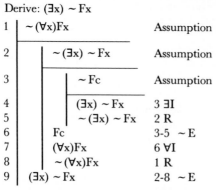

*d. $(\exists x)Cx \supset Ch$

---

$(\exists x)Cx \equiv Ch$

e. $(\forall x)(\sim Ax \supset Kx)$
$(\exists y) \sim Ky$

---

$(\exists w)(Aw \vee \sim Lwf)$

*f. $(\forall y)[Hy \;\&\; (Jyy \;\&\; My)]$

---

$(\exists x)Jxb \;\&\; (\forall x)Mx$

**3.** Show that each of the following is a theorem in *PD*:

a. $(\forall x)(\exists y)(Ay \supset Ax)$
*b. $(\forall x)(\forall x \supset \sim\sim Ax)$
c. $(\forall x)(Ax \supset Bx) \supset ((\forall x)Ax \supset (\forall x)Bx)$
*d. $(\exists x)(Ax \;\&\; Bx) \supset ((\exists x)Ax \;\&\; (\exists x)Bx)$
e. $(\forall x)(B \supset Ax) \equiv (B \supset (\forall x)Ax)$
*f. $(\forall x)(Ax \supset B) \equiv ((\exists x)Ax \supset B)$

**4.** Show that the members of each of the following pairs of sentences are equivalent in *PD*:

a. $(\forall x)Ax$
$(\forall x)(Ax \;\&\; Ax)$
*b. $(\forall x)(Ay)(Ax \;\&\; By)$
$(\forall x)Ax \;\&\; (\forall y)By$
c. $(\exists x)(Ax \vee Bx)$
$(\exists x)Ax \vee (\exists x)Bx$
*d. $(\forall x) \sim Ax$
$\sim (\exists x)Ax$
e. $\sim (\forall x)Ax$
$(\exists x) \sim Ax$
*f. $(\forall x)(\forall y)[(Axy \;\&\; Ayx) \supset Axx]$
$(\forall x)[(\exists y)(Axy \;\&\; Ayx) \supset Axx]$

**5.** Show that each of the following sets of sentences is inconsistent in *PD*;

a. $\{(\forall x)Hx, (\forall y) \sim (Hy \vee Byy)\}$
*b. $\{(\forall x)(Rx \equiv \sim Rx)\}$
c. $\{(\forall x)Rx, (\exists x) \sim Rx\}$
*d. $\{(\exists x)(\forall y)Fxy, \sim (\forall y)(\exists x)Fxy\}$
e. $\{(\forall w)(\forall z)(Jwz \equiv \sim Jwz)\}$
*f. $\{\sim (\exists y)Jy, \sim (\exists x) \sim Hx, (\forall z)(Jz \vee \sim Hz)\}$

**6.** Show that each of the following derivability claims holds in *PD*:

a. $\{(\forall x)(\sim Bx \supset \sim Wx), (\exists x)Wx\} \vdash (\exists x)Bx$
*b. $\{(\forall x)(\forall y)(\forall z)Gxyz\} \vdash (\forall x)(\forall y)(\forall z)(Gxyz \supset Gzyx)$
c. $\{(\forall x)(Hx \supset (\forall y)Rxyb), (\forall x)(\forall z)(Razx \supset Sxzz)\} \vdash Ha \supset (\exists x)Sxcc$
*d. $\{\sim (\forall x)(Fx \;\&\; Aix) \equiv \sim (\forall x)Kx, (\forall y)[(\exists x) \sim (Fx \;\&\; Aix) \;\&\; Ryy]\} \vdash \sim (\forall x)Kx$
e. $((\forall z)(\sim Lz \vee (\exists y)Ky)\} \vdash (\exists z)Lz \supset (\exists y)Ky$
*f. $\{(\exists x)(Jxa \;\&\; C), (\exists x)(Sx \;\&\; Hxx), (\forall x)[(C \;\&\; Sx) \supset \sim Ax]\} \vdash (\exists z)(\sim Az \;\&\; Hzz)$

**7.** Show that each of the following arguments is valid in *PD*:

a. $(\forall x)(Zx \supset (\exists y)Ky)$
$\overline{\phantom{xxxxxxxxxxxxxxxxxxxxxxxxx}}$
$(\forall x)(Zx \supset (\exists y)(Ky \vee Sy))$

*b. $(\forall y)(My \supset Ay)$
$(\exists x)(\exists y)[(Bx \ \& \ Mx) \ \& \ (Ry \ \& \ Syx)]$
$(\exists x)Ax \supset (\forall y)(\forall z)(Syz \supset Ay)$
$\overline{\phantom{xxxxxxxxxxxxxxxxxxxxxxxxx}}$
$(\exists x)(Rx \ \& \ Ax)$

c. $(\forall x)(\forall y)[(Hky \ \& \ Hxk) \supset Hxy]$
$(\forall z)(Bz \supset Hkz)$
$(\exists x)(Bx \ \& \ Hxk)$
$\overline{\phantom{xxxxxxxxxxxxxxxxxxxxxxxxx}}$
$(\exists z)[Bz \ \& \ (\forall y)(By \supset Hzy)]$

*d. $(\forall x)((Fx \ \& \ \sim Kx) \supset (\exists y)[(Fy \ \& \ Hyx) \ \& \ \sim Ky])$
$(\forall x)[(Fx \ \& \ (\forall y)[(Fy \ \& \ Hyx) \supset Ky]) \supset Kx] \supset M$
$\overline{\phantom{xxxxxxxxxxxxxxxxxxxxxxxxx}}$
$M$

e. $(\forall x)(\forall y)[(Gx \ \& \ Gy) \supset (Hxy \supset Hyx)]$
$(\forall x)(\forall y)(\forall z)([(Gx \ \& \ Gy) \ \& \ Gz] \supset [(Hxy \ \& \ Hyz) \supset Hxz])$
$\overline{\phantom{xxxxxxxxxxxxxxxxxxxxxxxxx}}$
$(\forall w)[[Gw \ \& \ (\exists z)(Gz \ \& \ Hwz)] \supset Hww]$

*f. $(\forall x)(\forall y)[(Ax \ \& \ By) \supset Cxy]$
$(\exists y)[Ey \ \& \ (\forall w)(Hw \supset Cyw)]$
$(\forall x)(\forall y)(\forall z)[(Cxy \ \& \ Cyz) \supset Cxz]$
$(\forall w)(Ew \supset Bw)$
$\overline{\phantom{xxxxxxxxxxxxxxxxxxxxxxxxx}}$
$(\forall z)(\forall w)[(Az \ \& \ Hw) \supset Czw]$

**8.** Show that each of the following is a theorem in *PD*:

a. $[(\forall x)(\forall y)Axy \ \& \ (\forall x)(Axx \supset B)] \supset B$
*b. $(\forall x)(\exists y)(Ax \supset By) \supset ((\forall x)Ax \supset (\exists y)By)$
c. $(\forall x)Ax \equiv \sim(\exists x) \sim Ax$
*d. $(\forall x)(Ax \vee B) \equiv ((\forall x)Ax \vee B)$
e. $(\exists x)(B \supset Ax) \equiv (B \supset (\exists x)Ax)$
*f. $(\exists x)(Ax \supset B) \equiv ((\forall x)Ax \supset B)$

**9.** Show that the members of the following pairs of sentences are equivalent in *PD*:

a. $(\forall x)(Ax \supset Ax)$
$(\forall x)(Bx \supset Bx)$
*b. $(\forall x)(Ax \vee Ax)$
$(\forall x)Ax$
c. $(\forall x)(\forall y)(Ax \supset By)$
$(\exists y) \sim By \supset (\forall x) \sim Ax$
*d. $(\exists x)Ax \supset ((\exists y)By \supset (\forall z)Cz)$
$(\forall x)(\forall y)(\forall z)[(Ax \ \& \ By) \supset Cz]$
e. $(\exists x)(\forall y)(Ax \supset By)$
$\sim(\forall x)Ax \vee (\forall y)By$
*f. $(\forall x)(\exists y) \sim(Axy \ \& \ Bxy)$
$(\forall x)(\sim(\forall y)Axy \vee \sim(\forall y)Bxy)$

**10.** Show that each of the following sets of sentences is inconsistent in *PD*:

a. {(∀y)(∃z)Byz, (∀w) ~ Baw}

*b. {(∃x)(Hx & Mxc), (∀x)(Lx ⊃ ~ Hx), (∃y)(Ly & Hy)}

c. {(∃x)( ~ Bx & Lxx), (∀z)(Cz & Bz), (∀y)[(By & ~ Cy) ≡ Lyy]}

*d. {(∀x)(∀y)[(Jx & Gy) ⊃ Hxy], (∃x)(∃y)[(Jx & ~ Jy) & ~ Hxy], (∀w)Gw}

e. {(∃x)(∃y)Fxy ∨ (∀x)(∀y)(∀z)Hxxyz, (∃x)(∃y)Fxy ⊃ ~ Haaab, (Hbbba ∨ ~ Haaab) ≡ (∀x) ~ (Ax ∨ ~ Ax)}

*f. {(∀x)(∃y)(Hx ⊃ By), ~ (∃y)(∀x)(Hx ⊃ By)}

**11.** Symbolize the following arguments in *PL* and show that the arguments are valid in *PD*:

a. Skiers are either very crazy or terrifically brave. George has a friend who is a skier but who is not terrifically brave. Thus George has a very crazy friend.

*b. Groucho Marx doesn't stay in any hotel that is willing to have him as a guest. Any hotel not willing to have Groucho Marx as a guest doesn't. Therefore Groucho Marx doesn't stay in any hotel.

c. Anybody who is loved by at least two persons is more fortunate than anyone who is loved by only one person. Hildegard and Gertrude are two people who love Norad. Since only Dora loves Manfred, Norad is more fortunate than Manfred.

*d. Everyone who know wine prefers every red wine to every equally or lower-priced white wine. Geribaldi Special is a red wine, but no one prefers it to anything. It follows that either no white wine is equally or lower-priced than Geribaldi Special or nobody knows wines.

e. Some hunters shoot deer. Other hunters don't shoot any deer. Anybody who shoots a deer or a hunter is a lawbreaker. Hunters are people who shoot only deer or hunters. Of course, every hunter shoots something. Hence, if no hunter shoots a hunter, then some lawbreakers shoot themselves.

*f. A baby is always cared for by his or her father, mother, or babysitter. A person is a parent of a baby if and only if the person is the baby's father or mother. Some babies are sometimes cared for by babysitters, for sometimes they are not cared for by their parents.

**12.** Symbolize the following passages in *PL* and show that the resulting sets of sentences of *PL* are inconsistent in *PD*;

a. Some psychiatrists understand those and only those who don't understand themselves.

*b. Nobody pleads guilty unless he or she is. Anybody who is guilty deserves punishment. However, there are some who plead guilty who do not deserve punishment.

c. Nobody who practices birth control acts morally. Any person who uses the rhythm method practices birth control. People who use the rhythm method act morally. There are, indeed, people who use the rhythm method.

*d. Everyone who likes some wine likes some red wine. Mike is a person who likes wine but only sauterne. No sauterne is a red wine.

## 10.5 THE DERIVATION SYSTEM *PD+*

We now enlarge the set of derivation rules and create the natural deduction system *PD+* . The additional derivation rules of *PD+* will not allow us to derive any more than can be derived in *PD*. However, the additional derivation rules will often allow us to construct derivations more easily. *PD+* contains all the derivation rules of *SD+* with the understanding that they are to be applied to the sentences of *PL*. The rules of replacement, unlike the rules of inference, can be applied to subformulas of sentences, as well as to sentences, of *PL*. Thus the rules of replacement are powerful rules for manipulating the internal structure of quantified sentences. The following is a correct derivation:

| | | |
|---|---|---|
| 1 | (∀x)[Mx ∨ (Kx ∨ (∃y)Nxy)] | Assumption |
| 2 | (∀x)[Mx ∨ ((∃y)Nxy ∨ Kx)] | 1 Com |
| 3 | (∀x)[(Mx ∨ (∃y)Nxy) ∨ Kx] | 2 Assoc |
| 4 | (∀x)[(~ ~ Mx ∨ (∃y)Nxy) ∨ Kx] | 3 DN |
| 5 | (∀x)[(~ Mx ⊃ (∃y)Nxy) ∨ Kx] | 4 Impl |

In this example each of the replacement rules has been applied to a subformula. For instance, Double Negation has been applied to the subformula 'Mx' of the sentence on line 3 to generate '~ ~ Mx', which is a subformula of the sentence on line 4.

*PD+* also contains the rules for introducing and eliminating quantifiers—Universal Introduction, Universal Elimination, Existential Introduction, and Existential Elimination. The only additional quantifier rule of *PD+* is *Quantifier Negation*. Quantifier Negation is a rule of replacement. Where $\mathscr{P}$ is an open sentence of *PL* in which $x$ occurs free, the rule is

*Quantifier Negation* (QN)

$$\sim(\forall x)\mathscr{P} :: (\exists x) \sim \mathscr{P}$$

$$\sim(\exists x)\mathscr{P} :: (\forall x) \sim \mathscr{P}$$

As with all rules of replacement, Quantifier Negation can be applied to subformulas within a sentence, as well as to an entire sentence on a line of a derivation. Quantifier Negation is a two-way rule in that a sentence (or subformula) that has the form of the expression on the left of the '::' can be replaced by a sentence (or subformula) that has the form of the expression on the right of the '::', and vice versa. All these are proper uses of Quantifier Negation:

| | | |
|---|---|---|
| 1 | (∀w) ~ (∃x)Hxw ∨ (∃y) ~ (∀z)Kyz | Assumption |
| 2 | ~ (∃w)(∃x)Hxw ∨ (∃y) ~ (∀z)Kyz | 1 QN |
| 3 | (∀w)(∀x) ~ Hxw ∨ (∃y) ~ (∀z)Kyz | 1 QN |
| 4 | (∀w) ~ (∃x)Hxw ∨ ~ (∀y)(∀z)Kyz | 1 QN |
| 5 | (∀w) ~ (∃x)Hxw ∨ (∃y)(∃z) ~ Kyz | 1 QN |

Care must be taken when applying the rules of replacement to the internal structure of quantified sentences to be sure that only sentences or subformulas are manipulated. The following is *not* correct:

| | | | |
|---|---|---|---|
| 1 | $(\forall x)[Lx \vee (\exists y)(Bxy \vee Jxy)]$ | Assumption | |
| 2 | $(\forall x)[(Lx \vee (\exists y)Bxy) \vee Jxy]$ | 1 Assoc | **MISTAKE!** |

For Association to be applicable to the sentence on line 1, the relevant subformulas must have the form $\mathscr{P} \vee (\mathscr{Q} \vee \mathscr{R})$. But the right disjunct of '$Lx \vee (\exists y)(Bxy \vee Jxy)$' is a quantified formula, not a disjunction. Consequently, Association cannot be applied to the sentence on line 1 to derive the sentence on line 2. In applying the rules of replacement it is important to identify correctly the main logical operators of the sentences and their subformulas.

The definitions of the basic concepts of *PD+* are exactly like the definitions for the basic concepts of *PD*, except that '*PD*' is replaced by '*PD+*'. Consequently, the tests for the various syntactic properties are carried out in the same way. The important difference between *PD* and *PD+* is that *PD*, with fewer rules, provides theoretical elegance and *PD+*, with more rules, provides practical ease.

### 10.5E EXERCISES

**1.** Show that each of the following derivability claims holds in *PD+* :

a. $\{\sim(\forall y)(Fy \,\&\, Gy)\} \vdash (\exists y)(\sim Fy \vee \sim Gy)$

*b. $\{(\forall w)(Lw \supset Mw), (\forall y)(My \supset Ny)\} \vdash (\forall w)(Lw \supset Nw)$

c. $\{(\exists z)(Gz \,\&\, Az), (\forall y)(Cy \supset \sim Gy)\} \vdash (\exists z)(Az \,\&\, \sim Cz)$

*d. $\{\sim(\exists x)(\sim Rx \,\&\, Sxx), Sjj\} \vdash Rj$

e. $\{(\forall x)[(\sim Cxb \vee Hx) \supset Lxx], (\exists y) \sim Lyy\} \vdash (\exists x)Cxb$

*f. $\{(\forall x)Fx, (\forall z)Hz\} \vdash \sim(\exists y)(\sim Fy \vee \sim Hy)$

**2.** Show that each of the following arguments is valid in *PD+* :

a. $(\forall x) \sim Jx$
$(\exists y)(Hby \vee Ryy) \supset (\exists x)Jx$
____________________
$(\forall y) \sim(Hby \vee Ryy)$

*b. $\sim(\exists x)(\forall y)(Pxy \,\&\, \sim Qxy)$
____________________
$(\forall x)(\exists y)(Pxy \supset Qxy)$

c. $(\forall x) \sim((\forall y)Hyx \vee Tx)$
$\sim(\exists y)(Ty \vee (\exists x) \sim Hxy)$
____________________
$(\forall x)(\forall y)Hxy \,\&\, (\forall x) \sim Tx$

*d. $(\forall z)(Lz \equiv Hz)$
$(\forall x) \sim(Hx \vee \sim Bx)$
____________________
$\sim Lb$

e. $(\forall z)[Kzz \supset (Mz \ \& \ Nz)]$
$(\exists z) \sim Nz$

---

$(\exists x) \sim Kxx$

*f. $(\exists x)[\sim Bxm \ \& \ (\forall y)(Cy \supset \sim Gxy)]$
$(\forall z)[\sim (\forall y)(Wy \supset Gzy) \supset Bzm]$

---

$(\forall x)(Cx \supset \sim Wx)$

g. $(\exists z)Qz \supset (\forall w)(Lww \supset \sim Hw)$
$(\exists x)Bx \supset (\forall y)(Ay \supset Hy)$

---

$(\exists w)(Qw \ \& \ Bw) \supset (\forall y)(Lyy \supset \sim Ay)$

*h. $(\forall y)(Kby \supset \sim Hy)$

---

$(\forall x)[(\exists y)(Kby \ \& \ Qxy) \supset (\exists z)(\sim Hz \ \& \ Qxz)]$

i. $\sim (\forall x)(\sim Px \vee \sim Hx) \supset (\forall x)[Cx \ \& \ (\forall y)(Ly \supset Axy)]$
$(\exists x)[Hx \ \& \ (\forall y)(Ly \supset Axy)] \supset (\forall x)(Rx \ \& \ (\forall y)Bxy)$

---

$\sim (\forall x)(\forall y)Bxy \supset (\forall x)(\sim Px \vee \sim Hx)$

**3.** Show that each of the following sentences is a theorem in *PD+* :

a. $(\forall x)(Ax \supset Bx) \supset (\forall x)(Bx \vee \sim Ax)$
*b. $(\forall x)(Ax \supset (Ax \supset Bx)) \supset (\forall x)(Ax \supset Bx)$
c. $\sim (\exists x)(Ax \vee Bx) \supset (\forall x) \sim Ax$
*d. $(\forall x)(Ax \supset Bx) \vee (\exists x)Ax$
e. $((\exists x)Ax \supset (\exists x)Bx) \supset (\exists x)(Ax \supset Bx)$
*f. $(\forall x)(\exists y)(Ax \vee By) \equiv (\exists y)(\forall x)(Ax \vee By)$

**4.** Show that the members of each of the following pairs of sentences are equivalent in *PD+* :

a. $\sim (\forall x)(Ax \supset Bx)$
$(\exists x)(Ax \ \& \sim Bx)$
*b. $(\exists x)(\exists y)Axy \supset Aab$
$(\exists x)(\exists y)Axy \equiv Aab$
c. $\sim (\forall x) \sim [(Ax \ \& \ Bx) \supset Cx]$
$(\exists x)[\sim Ax \vee (\sim Cx \supset \sim Bx)]$
*d. $\sim (\forall x)(\exists y)[(Ax \ \& \ Bx) \vee Cy]$
$(\exists x)(\forall y)[\sim (Cy \vee Ax) \vee \sim (Cy \vee Bx)]$
e. $(\forall x)(Ax \equiv Bx)$
$\sim (\exists x)[(\sim Ax \vee \sim Bx) \ \& \ (Ax \vee Bx)]$
*f. $(\forall x)(Ax \ \& \ (\exists y) \sim Bxy)$
$\sim (\exists x)[\sim Ax \vee (\forall y)(Bxy \ \& \ Bxy)]$

**5.** Show that each of the following sets of sentences is inconsistent in *PD+* :

a. $\{[(\forall x)(Mx \equiv Jx) \ \& \sim Mc] \ \& \ (\forall x)Jx\}$
*b. $\{\sim Fa, \ \sim (\exists x)(\sim Fx \vee \sim Fx)\}$
c. $\{(\forall x)(\forall y)Lxy \supset \sim (\exists x)Tz, \ (\forall x)(\forall y)Lxy \supset ((\exists w)Cww \vee (\exists z)Tz),$
$(\sim (\forall x)(\forall y)Lxy \vee (\forall z)Bzzk) \ \& \ (\sim (\forall z)Bzzk \vee \sim (\exists w)Cww), \ (\forall x)(\forall y)Lxy\}$

*d. $\{(\exists x)(\forall y)(Hxy \supset (\forall w)Jww), (\exists x) \sim Jxx \ \& \ \sim(\exists x) \sim Hxm\}$
e. $\{(\forall x)(\forall y)(Gxy \supset Hc), (\exists x)Gix \ \& \ (\forall x)(\forall y)(\forall z)Lxyz, Lcib \supset \sim Hc\}$
*f. $\{(\forall x)[(Sx \ \& \ Bxx) \supset Kax], (\forall x)(Hx \supset Bxx), (\exists x)(Sx \ \& \ Hx), (\forall x) \sim(Kax \ \& \ Hx)\}$

6a. Show that Universal Introduction and Universal Elimination are eliminable in *PD+* by developing routines that can be used in place of these rules to obtain the same results. Hint: Consider using Quantifier Negation, Existential Introduction, and Existential Elimination.
*b. Show that Existential Introduction and Existential Elimination are eliminable in *PD+* by developing routines that can be used in place of these rules to obtain the same results. Hint: Consider using Quantifier Negation, Universal Introduction, and Universal Elimination.

## 10.6 *PD* WITH IDENTITY

The derivation system *PD* can be enhanced by adding a pair of rules for introducing and eliminating the identity predicate, '$=$'. The symbolic language we use is *PLI*. Recall that the identity predicate is a two-place predicate, but unlike other predicates, the identity predicate is, by convention, written between the individual terms of the predicate.

The introduction rule for '$=$' is

*Identity Introduction* (= I)

$$(\forall \mathcal{x})\mathcal{x} = \mathcal{x}$$

Identity Introduction permits us to derive a sentence of the form $(\forall \mathcal{x})\mathcal{x} = \mathcal{x}$, where $\mathcal{x}$ is any individual variable. Hence sentences such as '$(\forall x)x = x$' and '$(\forall z)z = z$' can be entered on any new line of a derivation. These sentences claim that everything is identical with itself. Because that claim is always true, Identity Introduction is a truth-preserving derivation rule. Here is a very simple derivation of a theorem using the rule Identity Introduction:

Derive: $(\forall w)w = w$

| | | |
|---|---|---|
| 1 | $(\forall w)w = w$ | = I |

Identity Introduction is an axiom schema that allows us to enter any sentence of the form $(\forall \mathcal{x})\mathcal{x} = \mathcal{x}$ on any line of a derivation.

The elimination rule for '$=$' is

*Identity Elimination* (= E)

| | | |
|---|---|---|
| $\mathcal{a} = \mathcal{b}$ | | $\mathcal{a} = \mathcal{b}$ |
| $\mathcal{P}$ | or | $\mathcal{P}$ |
| $\mathcal{P}(\mathcal{a}//\mathcal{b})$ | | $\mathcal{P}(\mathcal{b}//\mathcal{a})$ |

The notation

$$\mathscr{P}(a//b)$$

means that at least one (but not necessarily all) occurrences of an individual constant $b$ in $\mathscr{P}$ has been replaced by an individual constant $a$. Similarly, $\mathscr{P}(b//a)$ means that at least one (but not necessarily all) occurrences of $a$ in $\mathscr{P}$ has been replaced by $b$. Identity Elimination is a truth-preserving rule. This rule permits the replacement of one name with another in a sentence only if both names occur in an identity sentence. Intuitively, whatever is true of something should be true of it regardless of its name. The application of this rule is illustrated by the following examples:

| | | |
|---|---|---|
| 1 | Rjjm | Assumption |
| 2 | j = m | Assumption |
| 3 | Rmjm | 1, 2 = E |

| | | |
|---|---|---|
| 1 | Rjjm | Assumption |
| 2 | j = m | Assumption |
| 3 | Rmmm | 1, 2 = E |

| | | |
|---|---|---|
| 1 | Rjjm | Assumption |
| 2 | j = m | Assumption |
| 3 | Rjjj | 1, 2 = E |

In constructing derivations using identity sentences it is often useful to obtain a sentence of the form $a = a$, where $a$ is some constant. This can be done by using the derivation rule Identity Introduction and then deriving the desired identity claim by the rule Universal Elimination as in the following derivation:

Derive: k = k

| | | |
|---|---|---|
| 1 | (∀z)z = z | = I |
| 2 | k = k | 1 ∀E |

An identity claim of the form $a = a$ also can be obtained by applying the rule Identity Elimination to an identity sentence of the form $a = b$, where $a$ and $b$ are different constants. The rule Identity Elimination is simply applied to the sentence itself! Consider the derivation

Derive: k = k

| | | |
|---|---|---|
| 1 | i = k | Assumption |
| 2 | k = k | 1, 1 = E |

Because i is identical to k by line 1 the rule Identity Elimination allows us to replace 'i' with 'k' wherever 'i' occurs in a sentence. In this derivation 'i' has been replaced with 'k' in the identity sentence 'i = k' itself to derive 'k = k' on line 2.

The derivation rules Identity Introduction and Identity Elimination together with the rules of *PD* form a new predicate derivation system, *PDI*. Notice that there is an important difference between *PD+* and *PDI*. The derivation system *PD+* , though it has more derivation rules than *PD*, is not stronger than *PD* in that everything derivable in *PD+* is derivable in *PD*. However, *PDI* with its two identity rules is stronger than *PD* in the sense that not everything derivable in *PDI* is derivable in *PD* alone. All of the derivations in this section furnish examples of this. Though we will not go through the details, it should be clear that all of the basic concepts of *PD*, such as being derivable in *PD*, being valid in *PD*, and being a theorem in *PD*, have straightforward analogues in *PDI* and that the two identity rules can be added to *PD+* to form still another derivation system *PDI+* .

Derivations systems, such as *PDI* and *PDI+* , are important for showing derivability claims that depend upon identity. Consider the following argument:

The Roman general who defeated Pompey conquered Gaul.
Julius Caesar was a Roman general, and he defeated Pompey.

---

Julius Caesar conquered Gaul.

We know this argument must be valid, for if Julius Caesar were a Roman general who defeated Pompey, then he must be the same person who conquered Gaul. We can show this argument is valid by symbolizing it in *PLI* and deriving the conclusion from the premises in *PDI*.

(∃x)[((Rx & Dxp) & (∀y)[(Ry & Dyp) ⊃ y = x]) & Cxg]
Rj & Djp

---

Cjg

Notice that the definite description 'the Roman general who defeated Pomey' has been captured in *PLI* by using the identity predicate. Here is a derivation which shows this argument is valid in *PDI*.

Derive: Cjg

| | | |
|---|---|---|
| 1 | (∃x)[((Rx & Dxp) & (∀y)[(Ry & Dyp) ⊃ y = x]) & Cxg] | Assumption |
| 2 | Rj & Djp | Assumption |
| 3 |     ((Ra & Dap) & (∀y)[(Ry & Dyp) ⊃ y = a] & Cag | Assumption |
| 4 |     (Ra & Dap) & (∀y)[(Ry & Dyp) ⊃ y = a] | 3 & E |
| 5 |     (∀y)[(Ry & Dyp) ⊃ y = a] | 4 & E |
| 6 |     (Rj & Djp) ⊃ j = a | 5 ∀E |
| 7 |     j = a | 2, 6 ⊃ E |
| 8 |     Cag | 3 & E |
| 9 |     Cjg | 7, 8 = E |
| 10 | Cjg | 1, 3-9 ∃E |

## 10.6E EXERCISES

**1.** Show that each of the following is a theorem in *PLI*:

a. $a = b \supset b = a$

*b. $(a = b \;\&\; b = c) \supset a = c$

c. $(\sim a = b \;\&\; b = c) \supset \sim a = c$

*d. $\sim a = b \equiv \sim b = a$

e. $\sim a = c \supset (\sim a = b \vee \sim b = c)$

**2.** Show that each of the following is valid in *PDI*:

a. $a = b \;\&\; \sim Bab$

---

$\sim (\forall x)Bxx$

*b. $Ge \supset d = e$

$Ge \supset He$

---

$Ge \supset Hd$

c. $(\forall z)[Gz \supset (\forall y)(Ky \supset Hzy)]$

$(Ki \;\&\; Gj) \;\&\; i = j$

---

$Hii$

*d. $(\exists x)(Hx \;\&\; Mx)$

$Ms \;\&\; \sim Hs$

---

$(\exists x)[(Hx \;\&\; Mx) \;\&\; \sim x = s]$

e. $a = b$

---

$Ka \vee \sim Kb$

**3.** Show that each of the following is a theorem in *PDI*:

a. $(\forall x)(x = x \vee \sim x = x)$

*b. $(\forall x)(\forall y)(x = x \;\&\; y = y)$

c. $(\forall x)(\forall y)(x = y \equiv y = x)$

*d. $(\forall x)(\forall y)(\forall z)[(x = y \;\&\; y = z) \supset x = z]$

e. $\sim (\exists x) \sim x = x$

**4.** Symbolize each of the following arguments in *PLI*, and show each argument is valid in *PDI*:

a. The number 2 is not identical to 4. The numbers 2 and 4 are both even numbers. Therefore there are at least two different even numbers.

*b. Hyde killed some innocent person. But, Jekyll is Hyde. Jekyll is a doctor. Hence some doctor killed some innocent person.

c. Shakespeare didn't admire himself, but the queen admired Bacon. Thus Shakespeare isn't Bacon since Bacon admired everybody who was admired by somebody.

*d. Rebecca loves those and only those who love her. The brother of Charlie loves Rebecca. Sam is Charlie's brother. So, Sam and Rebecca love each other.

e. Somebody robbed Peter and paid Paul. Peter didn't rob himself. Surely, Paul didn't pay himself. Therefore somebody else robbed Peter and paid Paul.

## GLOSSARY[1]

DERIVABILITY IN *PD*: A sentence $\mathscr{P}$ of *PL* is *derivable in PD* from a set Γ of sentences of *PL* if and only if there is a derivation in *PD* in which all the primary assumptions are members of Γ and $\mathscr{P}$ occurs in the scope of only those assumptions.

VALIDITY IN *PD*: An argument of *PL* is *valid in PD* if and only if the conclusion of the argument is derivable in *PD* from the set consisting of the premises. An argument of *PL* is *invalid in PD* if and only if it is not valid in *PD*.

THEOREM IN *PD*: A sentence $\mathscr{P}$ of *PL* is a *theorem in PD* if and only if $\mathscr{P}$ is derivable in *PD* from the empty set.

EQUIVALENCE IN *PD*: Sentences $\mathscr{P}$ and $\mathscr{Q}$ of *PL* are *equivalent in PD* if and only if $\mathscr{Q}$ is derivable in *PD* from $\{\mathscr{P}\}$ and $\mathscr{P}$ is derivable in *PD* from $\{\mathscr{Q}\}$.

INCONSISTENCY IN *PD*: A set Γ of sentences of *PL* is *inconsistent in PD* if and only if both a sentence $\mathscr{P}$ of *PL* and its negation $\sim\mathscr{P}$ are derivable in *PD* from Γ. A set Γ of sentences of *PL* is *consistent in PD* if and only if it is not inconsistent in *PD*.

[1] Similar definitions hold for the derivation systems *PD+*, *PDI*, and *PDI+*.

Chapter 11

# PREDICATE LOGIC: METATHEORY

## 11.1 SEMANTIC PRELIMINARIES

We have been tacitly assuming that our semantic and syntactic concepts of predicate logic coincide. For example, we have assumed that a sentence $\mathscr{P}$ of *PL* is quantificationally true if and only if $\mathscr{P}$ is a theorem in *PD*, and also that $\mathscr{P}$ is quantificationally true if and only if $\{\sim \mathscr{P}\}$ has a closed truth-tree. In this chapter we shall show that our semantic and syntactic concepts do coincide. We shall establish four major results: The soundness and completeness of the natural deduction systems *PD*, *PD+* , and *PDI*, and the soundness and completeness of the truth-tree method developed in Chapter Nine. The results we establish are part of the *metatheory* of predicate logic.

In our proofs of the adequacy of the natural deduction systems and the tree method, we shall use some fundamental semantic results that may seem obvious but that nevertheless must be proved. The purpose of this section is to establish these results. The reader may skim over this section on the first reading without working through all of the proofs, but should keep in mind that later metatheoretic proofs depend on the results presented here.

We first establish an important result that will enable us to prove several others. The result says, in effect, that if $\mathscr{P}$ is a formula of *PL*, and we replace each free occurrence of $\boldsymbol{x}$ in $\mathscr{P}$ with $\boldsymbol{a}$ to obtain $\mathscr{P}(\boldsymbol{a}/\boldsymbol{x})$, then any variable assignment **d** will treat $\mathscr{P}(\boldsymbol{a}/\boldsymbol{x})$ exactly as $\mathbf{d}[\mathbf{I}(\boldsymbol{a})/\boldsymbol{x}]$ treats $\mathscr{P}$. If **d** satisfies $\mathscr{P}(\boldsymbol{a}/\boldsymbol{x})$, then the variable assignment that is just like **d** except that it assigns the denotation of $\boldsymbol{a}$ to $\boldsymbol{x}$, will satisfy $\mathscr{P}$, and vice versa. This should not be surprising, for if $\boldsymbol{x}$ is used to refer to exactly the same thing as $a$, we would expect $\mathscr{P}$ and $\mathscr{P}(a/x)$ to behave the same way.

> 11.1.1. Let $\mathscr{P}$ be a formula of *PL*, let $\mathscr{P}(a/x)$ be the formula that results from replacing every free occurrence of $x$ in $\mathscr{P}$ with an individual constant $a$, let **I** be an interpretation, and let **d** be a variable assignment for **I**. Then **d** satisfies $\mathscr{P}(a/x)$ on **I** if and only if $\mathbf{d}[\mathbf{I}(a)/x]$ satisfies $\mathscr{P}$ on **I**.

To prove the result, we shall use mathematical induction on the number of occurrences of logical operators—truth-functional connectives and quantifiers—that occur in $\mathscr{P}$.

*Basis clause:* If $\mathscr{P}$ is a formula that contains zero occurrences of logical operators, then **d** satisfies $\mathscr{P}(a/x)$ if and only if $\mathbf{d}[\mathbf{I}(a)/x]$ satisfies $\mathscr{P}$.

Proof: If $\mathscr{P}$ contains zero occurrences of logical operators, then $\mathscr{P}$ is either a sentence letter or a formula of the form $\mathscr{A}t_1 \ldots t_n$, where $\mathscr{A}$ is a predicate and $t_1, \ldots, t_n$ are individual constants or variables. If $\mathscr{P}$ is a sentence letter, then $\mathscr{P}(a/x)$ is simply $\mathscr{P}$—a sentence letter alone does not contain any variables to be replaced. **d** satisfies $\mathscr{P}(a/x)$, then, if and only if $\mathbf{I}(\mathscr{P}) = \mathbf{T}$. And $\mathbf{d}[\mathbf{I}(a)/x]$ satisfies $\mathscr{P}$ if and only if $\mathbf{I}(\mathscr{P}) = \mathbf{T}$. So **d** satisfies $\mathscr{P}(a/x)$ if and only if $\mathbf{d}[\mathbf{I}(a)/x]$ satisfies $\mathscr{P}$.

If $\mathscr{P}$ has the form $\mathscr{A}t_1 \ldots t_n$, then $\mathscr{P}(a/x)$ is $\mathscr{A}t'_1 \ldots t'_n$, where $t'_i$ is $a$ if $t$ is $x$ and $t'_i$ is just $t_i$ otherwise. By the definition of satisfaction,

a. **d** satisfies $\mathscr{A}t'_1 \ldots t'_n$ if and only if $\langle \mathbf{u}'_1, \mathbf{u}'_2, \ldots, \mathbf{u}'_n \rangle$ is a member of $\mathbf{I}(\mathscr{A})$, where $\mathbf{u}'_i$ is $\mathbf{I}(t'_n)$ if $t'_i$ is a constant and is $\mathbf{d}(t'_i)$ if $t'_i$ is a variable,

and

b. $\mathbf{d}[\mathbf{I}(a)/x]$ satisfies $\mathscr{A}t_1 \ldots t_n$ if and only if $\langle \mathbf{u}_1, \mathbf{u}_2, \ldots, \mathbf{u}_n \rangle$ is a member of $\mathbf{I}(\mathscr{A})$, where $\mathbf{u}_i$ is $\mathbf{I}(t_i)$ if $t_i$ is a constant and is $\mathbf{d}[\mathbf{I}(a)/x](t_i)$ if $t_i$ is a variable.

But now we note that

c. $\langle \mathbf{u}'_1, \mathbf{u}'_2, \ldots, \mathbf{u}'_n \rangle = \langle \mathbf{u}_1, \mathbf{u}_2, \ldots, \mathbf{u}_n \rangle$.

Consider: If $t_i$ is a constant, then $t'_i$ is $t_i$ and so $\mathbf{u}'_i = \mathbf{I}(t_i) = \mathbf{u}_i$. If $t_i$ is any variable other than $x$, then $t'_i$ is $t_i$ and so $\mathbf{u}'_i = \mathbf{d}(t_i) = \mathbf{d}[\mathbf{I}(a)/x](t_i) = \mathbf{u}_i$—the variant does not affect the value assigned to $t_i$ in this case. If $t_i$ is the variable $x$, then $t'_i$ is $a$ and $\mathbf{u}'_i = \mathbf{I}(a) = \mathbf{d}[\mathbf{I}(a)/x](x) = \mathbf{u}_i$. (The variant $\mathbf{d}[\mathbf{I}(a)/x]$ ensures that the denotations of $x$ and of $a$ coincide.) Because the $n$-tuples are the same $n$-tuple, we conclude from (a) and (b) that **d** satisfies $\mathscr{A}t'_1 \ldots t'_n$ if and only if $\mathbf{d}[\mathbf{I}(a)/x]$ satisfies $\mathscr{A}t_1 \ldots t_n$.

The basis clause, in particular, the case where an atomic formula has the form $\mathscr{A}t_1 \ldots t_n$, is the crux of our proof. Having shown that at the atomic level the thesis we are proving holds, it is straightforward to show that the addition of connectives and quantifiers to build larger formulas does not change matters. The inductive step in the proof of 11.1.1 is:

*Inductive step:* If every formula $\mathscr{P}$ that contains $k$ or fewer occurrences of logical operators is such that **d** satisfies $\mathscr{P}(a/x)$ if and only if $\mathbf{d}[\mathbf{I}(a)/x]$ satisfies $\mathscr{P}$, then every formula $\mathscr{P}$ that contains $k+1$ occurrences of logical operators is such that **d** satisfies $\mathscr{P}(a/x)$ if and only if $\mathbf{d}[\mathbf{I}(a)/x]$ satisfies $\mathscr{P}$.

Proof: Letting $k$ be an arbitrary positive integer, we assume that the inductive hypothesis holds—that our claim is true of every formula with $k$ or fewer occurrences of logical operators. We must show that it follows that the claim is also true of every formula $\mathscr{P}$ with $k+1$ occurrences of logical operators. We consider each form that $\mathscr{P}$ may have.

Case 1: $\mathscr{P}$ has the form $\sim \mathscr{Q}$. Then $\mathscr{P}(a/x)$ is $\sim \mathscr{Q}(a/x)$, the negation of $\mathscr{Q}(a/x)$ (i.e., any replacements of $x$ that were made had to be made within $\mathscr{Q}$). By the definition of satisfaction,

a. **d** satisfies $\sim \mathscr{Q}(a/x)$ if and only if it does not satisfy $\mathscr{Q}(a/x)$.

Because $\mathscr{Q}(a/x)$ contains fewer than $k+1$ occurrences of logical operators, it follows from the inductive hypothesis that

b. **d** does not satisfy $\mathscr{Q}(a/x)$ if and only if $\mathbf{d}[\mathbf{I}(a)/x]$ does not satisfy $\mathscr{Q}$.

And, by the definition of satisfaction,

c. $\mathbf{d}[\mathbf{I}(a)/x]$ does not satisfy $\mathscr{Q}$ if and only if $\mathbf{d}[\mathbf{I}(a)/x]$ does satisfy $\sim \mathscr{Q}$.

So, by (a)–(c), **d** satisfies $\sim \mathscr{Q}(a/x)$ if and only if $\mathbf{d}[\mathbf{I}(a)/x]$ satisfies $\sim \mathscr{Q}$.

Case 2: $\mathscr{P}$ has the form $\mathscr{Q} \,\&\, \mathscr{R}$. Then $\mathscr{P}(a/x)$ is

$$\mathscr{Q}(a/x) \,\&\, \mathscr{R}(a/x)$$

—all replacements of $x$ occurred within $\mathscr{Q}$ and $\mathscr{R}$. By the definition of satisfaction,

a. **d** satisfies $\mathscr{Q}(a/x) \,\&\, \mathscr{R}(a/x)$ if and only if **d** satisfies $\mathscr{Q}(a/x)$ and **d** satisfies $\mathscr{R}(a/x)$.

Both conjuncts contain fewer than $k+1$ occurrences of logical operators so, by the inductive hypothesis,

b. **d** satisfies $\mathscr{Q}(a/x)$ if and only if $\mathbf{d}[\mathbf{I}(a)/x]$ satisfies $\mathscr{Q}$

and

c. **d** satisfies $\mathscr{R}(a/x)$ if and only if $\mathbf{d}[\mathbf{I}(a)/x]$ satisfies $\mathscr{R}$.

By the definition of satisfaction,

d. $\mathbf{d}[\mathbf{I}(a)/x]$ satisfies both $\mathscr{Q}$ and $\mathscr{R}$ if and only if $\mathbf{d}[\mathbf{I}(a)/x]$ satisfies $\mathscr{Q}$ & $\mathscr{R}$.

By (a)–(d), then, $\mathbf{d}$ satisfies $\mathscr{Q}(a/x)$ & $\mathscr{R}(a/x)$ if and only if $\mathbf{d}[\mathbf{I}(a)/x]$ satisfies $\mathscr{Q}$ & $\mathscr{R}$.

Cases 3–5: The proofs for the case in which $\mathscr{P}$ has one of the forms $\mathscr{Q} \vee \mathscr{R}$, $\mathscr{Q} \supset \mathscr{R}$, and $\mathscr{Q} \equiv \mathscr{R}$ are similar to that of case 2 and are left as exercises.

Case 6: $\mathscr{P}$ has the form $(\forall y)\mathscr{Q}$. We must consider two possibilities. If $y$ is not the variable $x$ that $a$ is replacing in $(\forall y)\mathscr{Q}$, then $\mathscr{P}(a/x)$ is $(\forall y)\mathscr{Q}(a/x)$—all replacements of $x$ are made within $\mathscr{Q}$. By the definition of satisfaction,

a. $\mathbf{d}$ satisfies $(\forall y)\mathscr{Q}(a/x)$ if and only if for every member $\mathbf{u}$ of the U.D., $\mathbf{d}[\mathbf{u}/y]$ satisfies $\mathscr{Q}(a/x)$.

Because $\mathscr{Q}$ contains fewer than $k + 1$ occurrences of logical operators, it follows from the inductive hypothesis that for every member $\mathbf{u}$ of the U.D.,

b. $\mathbf{d}[\mathbf{u}/y]$ satisfies $\mathscr{Q}(a/x)$ if and only if $\mathbf{d}[\mathbf{u}/y, \mathbf{I}(a)/x]$ satisfies $\mathscr{Q}$.

Each variant $\mathbf{d}[\mathbf{u}/y, \mathbf{I}(a)/x]$ is identical to $\mathbf{d}[\mathbf{I}(a)/x, \mathbf{u}/y]$, because $x$ and $y$ are not the same variable and hence neither of the assignments within the brackets can override the other. So every member $\mathbf{u}$ of the U.D. is such that

c. $\mathbf{d}[\mathbf{u}/y, \mathbf{I}(a)/x]$ satisfies $\mathscr{Q}$ if and only if $\mathbf{d}[\mathbf{I}(a)/x, \mathbf{u}/y]$ satisfies $\mathscr{Q}$.

And, by the definition of satisfaction again,

d. Every member $\mathbf{u}$ of the U.D. is such that $\mathbf{d}[\mathbf{I}(a)/x, \mathbf{u}/y]$ satisfies $\mathscr{Q}$, if and only if $\mathbf{d}[\mathbf{I}(a)/x]$ satisfies $(\forall y)\mathscr{Q}$.

So by (a)–(d), in the case where $y$ is not the variable $x$ that $a$ is replacing, $\mathbf{d}$ satisfies $(\forall y)\mathscr{Q}(a/x)$ if and only if $\mathbf{d}[\mathbf{I}(a)/x]$ satisfies $(\forall y)\mathscr{Q}$.

If $\mathscr{P}$ is $(\forall x)\mathscr{Q}$, where $x$ is the variable that $a$ is replacing, then $\mathscr{P}(a/x)$ is also $(\forall x)\mathscr{Q}$. Because $a$ replaces only *free* occurrences of $x$ in $\mathscr{P}$, and $x$ does not occur free in $\mathscr{P}$, no replacements are made within $\mathscr{Q}$. By the definition of satisfaction,

a. $\mathbf{d}$ satisfies $(\forall x)\mathscr{Q}$ (which is our $\mathscr{P}(a/x)$) if and only if for every member $\mathbf{u}$ of the U.D., $\mathbf{d}[\mathbf{u}/x]$ satisfies $\mathscr{Q}$

and

b. $\mathbf{d}[\mathbf{I}(a)/x]$ satisfies $(\forall x)\mathscr{Q}$ (which is our $\mathscr{P}$) if and only if for every member $\mathbf{u}$ of the U.D., $\mathbf{d}[\mathbf{I}(a)/x, \mathbf{u}/x]$ satisfies $\mathscr{Q}$.

What is $\mathbf{d}[\mathbf{I}(a)/x, \mathbf{u}/x]$? This variable assignment is just $\mathbf{d}[\mathbf{u}/x]$—the first assignment made to $x$ within the brackets gets overridden by the second. So

c. every member $\mathbf{u}$ of the U.D. is such that $\mathbf{d}[\mathbf{I}(a)/x, \mathbf{u}/x]$ satisfies $\mathcal{Q}$ if and only if every member $\mathbf{u}$ of the U.D. is such that $\mathbf{d}[\mathbf{u}/x]$ satisfies $\mathcal{Q}$.

Therefore, by (a)–(c), $\mathbf{d}[\mathbf{I}(a)/x]$ satisfies $(\forall x)\mathcal{Q}$ if and only if $\mathbf{d}$ satisfies $(\forall x)\mathcal{Q}$.

Case 7: $\mathcal{P}$ has the form $(\exists y)\mathcal{Q}$. Again, we consider two possibilities. If $y$ is not the variable $x$ that $a$ is replacing, then $\mathcal{P}(a/x)$ is $(\exists y)\mathcal{Q}(a/x)$. By the definition of satisfaction,

a. $\mathbf{d}$ satisfies $(\exists y)\mathcal{Q}(a/x)$ if and only if for some member $\mathbf{u}$ of the U.D., $\mathbf{d}[\mathbf{u}/y]$ satisfies $\mathcal{Q}(a/x)$.

By the inductive hypothesis, because $\mathcal{Q}(a/x)$ contains fewer than $k + 1$ occurrences of logical operators,

b. $\mathbf{d}[\mathbf{u}/y]$ satisfies $\mathcal{Q}(a/x)$ if and only if $\mathbf{d}[\mathbf{u}/y, \mathbf{I}(a)/x]$ satisfies $\mathcal{Q}$.

Because $y$ and $x$ are different variables, $\mathbf{d}[\mathbf{u}/y, \mathbf{I}(a)/x]$ is the same variable assignment as $\mathbf{d}[\mathbf{I}(a)/x, \mathbf{u}/y]$. So

c. $\mathbf{d}[\mathbf{u}/y, \mathbf{I}(a)/x]$ satisfies $\mathcal{Q}(a/x)$ if and only if $\mathbf{d}[\mathbf{I}(a)/x, \mathbf{u}/y]$ satisfies $\mathcal{Q}$,

and by the definition of satisfaction,

d. $\mathbf{d}[\mathbf{I}(a)/x, \mathbf{u}/y]$ satisfies $\mathcal{Q}$ if and only if $\mathbf{d}[\mathbf{I}(a)/x]$ satisfies $(\exists y)\mathcal{Q}$.

It follows from (a)–(d) that in the case where $y$ and $x$ are different variables, $\mathbf{d}$ satisfies $(\exists y)\mathcal{Q}(a/x)$ if and only if $\mathbf{d}[\mathbf{I}(a)/x]$ satisfies $(\exists y)\mathcal{Q}$.

If $\mathcal{P}$ is $(\exists x)\mathcal{Q}$, where $x$ is the variable that $a$ is replacing, then $\mathcal{P}(a/x)$ is $(\exists x)\mathcal{Q}$—no replacements are made within $\mathcal{Q}$, because $x$ is not free in $(\exists x)\mathcal{Q}$. So we must show that $\mathbf{d}[\mathbf{I}(a)/x]$ satisfies $(\exists x)\mathcal{Q}$ if and only if $\mathbf{d}$ satisfies $(\exists x)\mathcal{Q}$. By the definition of satisfaction,

a. $\mathbf{d}[\mathbf{I}(a)/x]$ satisfies $(\exists x)\mathcal{Q}$ if and only if for some member $\mathbf{u}$ of the U.D., $\mathbf{d}[\mathbf{I}(a)/x, \mathbf{u}/x]$ satisfies $\mathcal{Q}$.

$\mathbf{d}[\mathbf{I}(a)/x, \mathbf{u}/x]$ is just $\mathbf{d}[\mathbf{u}/x]$—the second assignment to $x$ overrides the first—and so

b. $\mathbf{d}[\mathbf{I}(a)/x, \mathbf{u}/x]$ satisfies $\mathcal{Q}$ if and only if $\mathbf{d}[\mathbf{u}/x]$ satisfies $\mathcal{Q}$.

By the definition of satisfaction,

c. $\mathbf{d}[\mathbf{u}/x]$ satisfies $\mathcal{Q}$ if and only if $\mathbf{d}$ satisfies $(\exists x)\mathcal{Q}$.

Therefore, by (a)–(c), $\mathbf{d}[\mathbf{I}(a)/x]$ satisfies $(\exists x)\mathcal{Q}$ if and only if $\mathbf{d}$ satisfies $(\exists x)\mathcal{Q}$.

With the basis clause and the inductive step established, the conclusion of the argument is also established—every formula $\mathcal{P}$ is such that $\mathbf{d}$ satisfies $\mathcal{P}(a/x)$ on $\mathbf{I}$ if and only if $\mathbf{d}[\mathbf{I}(x)/a]$ satisfies $\mathcal{P}$ on $\mathbf{I}$. And that completes the proof of result 11.1.1.

The second result will enable us to prove a claim that was made in Chapter Eight, that for any interpretation and any sentence of *PL*, either all variable assignments satisfy the sentence or none do. We used this claim in defining truth and falsehood for sentences: A sentence is true on an interpretation if it is satisfied by all variable assignments and false if it is satisfied by none. The reason that this claim turns out to be true is that there are no free variables in sentences. Result 11.1.2 assures us that only the values that a variable assignment assigns to the variables that are free in a formula play a role in determining whether the formula is satisfied:

11.1.2. Let $\mathbf{I}$ be an interpretation, $\mathbf{d}$ a variable assignment for $\mathbf{I}$, and $\mathcal{P}$ a formula of *PL*. Then $\mathbf{d}$ satisfies $\mathcal{P}$ on $\mathbf{I}$ if and only if $\mathcal{P}$ is satisfied on $\mathbf{I}$ by every variable assignment that assigns the same values to the free variables in $\mathcal{P}$ as does $\mathbf{d}$.

Proof: Let $\mathbf{I}$ be an interpretation, $\mathbf{d}$ a variable assignment for $\mathbf{I}$, and $\mathcal{P}$ a formula of *PL*. We shall prove 11.1.2 by mathematical induction on the number of occurrences of logical operators in $\mathcal{P}$.

*Basis clause:* If $\mathcal{P}$ is a formula that contains zero occurrences of logical operators, then $\mathbf{d}$ satisfies $\mathcal{P}$ if and only if $\mathcal{P}$ is satisfied by every variable assignment that assigns the same values to the free variables in $\mathcal{P}$ as does $\mathbf{d}$.

Proof of basis clause: If $\mathcal{P}$ contains zero occurrences of logical operators, then $\mathcal{P}$ is either a sentence letter or a formula of the form $\mathcal{A}t_1 \ldots t_n$. If $\mathcal{P}$ is a sentence letter, then any variable assignment satisfies $\mathcal{P}$ on $\mathbf{I}$ if and only if $\mathbf{I}(\mathcal{P}) = \mathbf{T}$. Therefore $\mathbf{d}$ satisfies $\mathcal{P}$ if and only if every variable assignment that assigns the same values to the free variables in $\mathcal{P}$ as $\mathbf{d}$ satisfies $\mathcal{P}$.

If $\mathcal{P}$ has the form $\mathcal{A}t_1 \ldots t_n$, then by the definition of satisfaction,

a. $\mathbf{d}$ satisfies $\mathcal{P}$ if and only if $\langle \mathbf{u}_1, \ldots, \mathbf{u}_n \rangle$ is a member of $\mathbf{I}(\mathcal{A})$, where $\mathbf{u}_i$ is $\mathbf{I}(t_i)$ if $t_i$ is a constant and $\mathbf{d}(t_i)$ if $t_i$ is a variable;

and, where $\mathbf{d}'$ is a variable assignment that assigns the same values to the free variables in $\mathcal{P}$ as does $\mathbf{d}$,

b. $\mathbf{d}'$ satisfies $\mathcal{P}$ if and only if $\langle \mathbf{u}'_1, \ldots, \mathbf{u}'_n \rangle$ is a member of $\mathbf{I}(\mathcal{A})$, where $\mathbf{u}'_i$ is $\mathbf{I}(t_i)$ if $t_i$ is a constant and $\mathbf{d}'(t_i)$ if $t_i$ is a variable.

But now we note that

c. $\langle \mathbf{u}_1, \ldots, \mathbf{u}'_n \rangle$ and $\langle \mathbf{u}_1, \ldots, \mathbf{u}'_n \rangle$ are the same $n$-tuple.

For if $t_i$ is a constant, then $\mathbf{u}_i = \mathbf{I}(t_i) = \mathbf{u}'_i$. If $t_i$ is a variable, then it is free in $\mathcal{A}t_1 \ldots t_n$ and is therefore assigned the same value by $\mathbf{d}'$ as it is assigned by $\mathbf{d}$. That is, $\mathbf{u}_i = \mathbf{d}(t_i) = \mathbf{d}'(t_i) = \mathbf{u}'_i$. So by (a)–(c), we conclude that $\mathbf{d}$ satisfies $\mathcal{A}t_1 \ldots t_n$ if and only if every variable assignment $\mathbf{d}'$ that assigns the same values to the free variables in $\mathcal{A}t_1 \ldots t_n$ as $\mathbf{d}$ satisfies $\mathcal{A}t_1 \ldots t_n$.

*Inductive step:* If every sentence $\mathcal{P}$ that contains $k$ or fewer occurrences of logical operators is such that $\mathbf{d}$ satisfies $\mathcal{P}$ on $\mathbf{I}$ if and only if $\mathcal{P}$ is satisfied by every variable assignment that assigns the same values to the free variables in $\mathcal{P}$ as $\mathbf{d}$, then every sentence $\mathcal{P}$ that contains $k + 1$ occurrences of logical operators is such that $\mathbf{d}$ satisfies $\mathcal{P}$ on $\mathbf{I}$ if and only if $\mathcal{P}$ is satisfied by every variable assignment that assigns the same values to the free variables in $\mathcal{P}$ as $\mathbf{d}$.

Proof of inductive step: Assume that, for an arbitrary positive integer $k$, the inductive hypothesis is true. We shall show that on this assumption, our claim must also be true of every sentence $\mathcal{P}$ that contains $k + 1$ occurrences of logical operators. Let $\mathbf{I}$ be an interpretation and $\mathbf{d}$ a variable assignment for $\mathbf{I}$. We consider each form that $\mathcal{P}$ may have.

Case 1: $\mathcal{P}$ has the form $\sim \mathcal{Q}$. By the definition of satisfaction,

a. $\mathbf{d}$ satisfies $\sim \mathcal{Q}$ if and only if $\mathbf{d}$ does not satisfy $\mathcal{Q}$.

Because $\mathcal{Q}$ contains fewer than $k + 1$ occurrences of logical operators, it follows from the inductive hypothesis that

b. $\mathbf{d}$ does not satisfy $\mathcal{Q}$ if and only if every variable assignment that assigns to the free variables in $\mathcal{Q}$ the same values as $\mathbf{d}$ assigns to those variables does not satisfy $\mathcal{Q}$

and, by the definition of satisfaction,

c. every variable assignment that assigns to the free variables in $\mathcal{Q}$ the same values as $\mathbf{d}$ assigns to those variables fails to satisfy $\mathcal{Q}$ if and only if every such assignment does satisfy $\sim \mathcal{Q}$.

The variable assignments that assign the same values to the free variables of $\mathcal{Q}$ as does $\mathbf{d}$ are the variable assignments that assign the same values to the free variables of $\sim \mathcal{Q}$ as does $\mathbf{d}$, because $\mathcal{Q}$ and $\sim \mathcal{Q}$ contain the same free variables. So by (a)–(c), $\mathbf{d}$ satisfies $\sim \mathcal{Q}$ if and only if every variable assignment that assigns the same values to the free variables in $\sim \mathcal{Q}$ as does $\mathbf{d}$ satisfies $\sim \mathcal{Q}$.

Case 2: $\mathcal{P}$ has the form $\mathcal{Q} \vee \mathcal{R}$. By the definition of satisfaction,

a. $\mathbf{d}$ satisfies $\mathcal{Q} \vee \mathcal{R}$ if and only if either $\mathbf{d}$ satisfies $\mathcal{Q}$ or $\mathbf{d}$ satisfies $\mathcal{R}$.

Because $\mathscr{Q}$ and $\mathscr{R}$ each contain fewer than $k + 1$ occurrences of logical operators, it follows by the inductive hypothesis that

b. **d** satisfies $\mathscr{Q}$ if and only if every variable assignment that assigns to the free variables in $\mathscr{Q}$ the same values as **d** satisfies $\mathscr{Q}$,

and

c. **d** satisfies $\mathscr{R}$ if and only if every variable assignment that assigns to the free variables in $\mathscr{R}$ the same values as **d** satisfies $\mathscr{R}$.

By (a)–(c),

d. **d** satisfies $\mathscr{Q} \vee \mathscr{R}$ if and only if either every variable assignment that assigns to the free variables in $\mathscr{Q}$ the same values as **d** satisfies $\mathscr{Q}$ or every variable assignment that assigns to the free variables in $\mathscr{R}$ the same values as **d** satisfies $\mathscr{R}$.

Because every variable that is free in $\mathscr{Q}$ is also free in $\mathscr{Q} \vee \mathscr{R}$,

e. every variable assignment that assigns the same values as **d** to the free variables in $\mathscr{Q} \vee \mathscr{R}$ is a variable assignment that assigns the same values as **d** to the free variables in $\mathscr{Q}$

(the converse does not hold), and for a similar reason,

f. every variable assignment that assigns the same values as **d** to the free variables in $\mathscr{Q} \vee \mathscr{R}$ is a variable assignment that assigns the same values as **d** to the free variables in $\mathscr{R}$.

Assume now that **d** satisfies $\mathscr{Q} \vee \mathscr{R}$. By (d), either (i) every variable assignment that assigns to the free variables in $\mathscr{Q}$ the same values as **d** satisfies $\mathscr{Q}$ or (ii) every variable assignment that assigns to the free variables in $\mathscr{R}$ the same values as **d** satisfies $\mathscr{R}$. If (i) is the case, then, by (e), we may conclude that every variable assignment that assigns the same values as **d** to the free variables in $\mathscr{Q} \vee \mathscr{R}$ satisfies $\mathscr{Q}$ and hence $\mathscr{Q} \vee \mathscr{R}$. If (ii) is the case, then by (f), we may conclude that every variable assignment that assigns the same values as **d** to the free variables in $\mathscr{Q} \vee \mathscr{R}$ satisfies $\mathscr{R}$ and hence $\mathscr{Q} \vee \mathscr{R}$. Either way, then, we conclude that if **d** satisfies $\mathscr{Q} \vee \mathscr{R}$, then every variable assignment that assigns the same values to the free variables in $\mathscr{Q} \vee \mathscr{R}$ as **d** satisfies $\mathscr{Q} \vee \mathscr{R}$.

Conversely, if every variable assignment that assigns the same values to the free variables in $\mathscr{Q} \vee \mathscr{R}$ as does **d** satisfies $\mathscr{Q} \vee \mathscr{R}$, then, trivially, **d** satisfies $\mathscr{Q} \vee \mathscr{R}$.

Cases 3–5: $\mathscr{P}$ has one of the forms $\mathscr{Q} \,\&\, \mathscr{R}$, $\mathscr{Q} \supset \mathscr{R}$, or $\mathscr{Q} \equiv \mathscr{R}$. These cases are left as an exercise.

Case 6: $\mathscr{P}$ has the form $(\forall x)\mathscr{Q}$. By the definition of satisfaction,

a. **d** satisfies $(\forall x)\mathscr{Q}$ if and only if every member **u** of the U.D. is such that $\mathbf{d}[\mathbf{u}/x]$ satisfies $\mathscr{Q}$.

Because $\mathscr{Q}$ contains fewer than $k + 1$ occurrences of connectives, it follows from the inductive hypothesis that

b. each member **u** of the U.D. is such that **d**[**u**/$x$] satisfies $\mathscr{Q}$ if and only if every variable assignment that assigns the same values to the free variables in $\mathscr{Q}$ as **d**[**u**/$x$] satisfies $\mathscr{Q}$.

It follows from (a) and (b) that

c. **d** satisfies $(\forall x)\mathscr{Q}$ if and only if for each member **u** of the U.D., every variable assignment that assigns the same values to the free variables in $\mathscr{Q}$ as **d**[**u**/$x$] satisfies $\mathscr{Q}$.

Because the variables other than $x$ that are free in $\mathscr{Q}$ are also free in $(\forall x)\mathscr{Q}$, every variable assignment that assigns the same values to the free variables in $\mathscr{Q}$ as **d**[**u**/$x$] is a variant **d**′[**u**/$x$] of a variable assignment **d**′ that assigns the same values to the free variables in $(\forall x)\mathscr{Q}$ as **d**, and vice versa. So (c) is equivalent to

d. **d** satisfies $(\forall x)\mathscr{Q}$ if and only if for each member **u** of the U.D., every variable assignment **d**′ that assigns the same values to the free variables in $(\forall x)\mathscr{Q}$ as **d** is such that **d**′[**u**/$x$] satisfies $\mathscr{Q}$.

It follows by the definition of satisfaction that

e. **d** satisfies $(\forall x)\mathscr{Q}$ if and only if every variable assignment that assigns the same values to the free variables in $(\forall x)\mathscr{Q}$ as **d** satisfies $(\forall x)\mathscr{Q}$.

Case 7: $\mathscr{P}$ has the form $(\exists x)\mathscr{Q}$. This case is left as an exercise.

It follows immediately from 11.1.2 that

11.1.3. For any interpretation **I** and sentence $\mathscr{P}$ of *PL*, either every variable assignment for **I** satisfies $\mathscr{P}$ or no variable assignment for **I** satisfies $\mathscr{P}$.

Proof: Let **d** be any variable assignment. Because $\mathscr{P}$ is a sentence and hence contains no free variables, every variable assignment for **I** assigns the same values to the free variables in $\mathscr{P}$ as does **d**. By result 11.1.2, then, **d** satisfies $\mathscr{P}$ if and only if every variable assignment satisfies $\mathscr{P}$. Therefore either every variable assignment satisfies $\mathscr{P}$ or none does.

Each of the following results, which can be established using results 11.1.1–11.1.3, states something that we would hope to be true of quantified sentences of *PL*.

11.1.4. For any universally quantified sentence $(\forall x)\mathscr{P}$ of *PL*, $\{(\forall x)\mathscr{P}\}$ quantificationally entails every substitution instance of $(\forall x)\mathscr{P}$.

Proof: Let $(\forall x)\mathscr{P}$ be any universally quantified sentence, let $\mathscr{P}(a/x)$ be a substitution instance of $(\forall x)\mathscr{P}$, and let **I** be an interpretation on which

$(\forall x)\mathscr{P}$ is true. Then, by 11.1.3, every variable assignment satisfies $(\forall x)\mathscr{P}$ and so for every variable assignment **d** and every member **u** of the U.D., $\mathbf{d}[\mathbf{u}/x]$ satisfies $\mathscr{P}$. In particular, for every variable assignment **d** the variant $\mathbf{d}[\mathbf{I}(a)/x]$ must satisfy $\mathscr{P}$. By 11.1.1, then, every variable assignment **d** satisfies $\mathscr{P}(a/x)$, so $\mathscr{P}(a/x)$ is also true on **I**.

11.1.5. Every substitution instance $\mathscr{P}(a/x)$ of an existentially quantified sentence $(\exists x)\mathscr{P}$ is such that $\{\mathscr{P}(a/x)\} \vDash (\exists x)\mathscr{P}$.

Proof: See Exercise 3.

11.1.4 and 11.1.5 are results that were used to motivate informally two of the quantifier rules in Chapter Ten, Universal Elimination and Existential Introduction, and they will play a role in our proof of the soundness of *PD*. We shall also want to ensure that the motivations for Universal Introduction and Existential Elimination were correct. Prior to showing this, we establish two further results that we shall need:

11.1.6. Let **I** and **I′** be interpretations that have the same U.D. and that agree on the assignments made to each individual constant, predicate, and sentence letter in a formula $\mathscr{P}$ (i.e., **I** and **I′** assign the same values to those symbols). Then each variable assignment satisfies $\mathscr{P}$ on interpretation **I** if and only if it satisfies $\mathscr{P}$ on interpretation **I′**.

In stating result 11.1.6, we have made use of the fact that if two interpretations have the same U.D., then every variable assignment for one interpretation is a variable assignment for the other—because the collection of objects that can be assigned to the variables of *PL* is the same. The result should sound obvious; if two interpretations with identical universes of discourse treat the nonlogical symbols of $\mathscr{P}$ in the same way, and if the free variables are interpreted the same way on the two interpretations, then $\mathscr{P}$ says the same thing on both interpretations. The values that **I** and **I′** assign to other symbols of *PL* have no bearing on what $\mathscr{P}$ says; $\mathscr{P}$ must either be satisfied by the variable assignment on both interpretations or be satisfied on neither.

Proof of 11.1.6: Let $\mathscr{P}$ be a formula of *PL* and let **I** and **I′** be interpretations that have the same U.D. and that agree on the values assigned to each nonlogical symbol in $\mathscr{P}$. We shall now prove, by mathematical induction on the number of occurrences of logical operators in $\mathscr{P}$, that a variable assignment satisfies $\mathscr{P}$ on interpretation **I** if and only if it satisfies $\mathscr{P}$ on interpretation **I′**.

*Basis clause:* If $\mathscr{P}$ contains zero occurrences of logical operators, then a variable assignment satisfies $\mathscr{P}$ on **I** if and only if it satisfies $\mathscr{P}$ on **I′**.

Proof of basis clause: Let **d** be a variable assignment. If $\mathscr{P}$ is a sentence letter, then **d** satisfies $\mathscr{P}$ on **I** if and only if $\mathbf{I}(\mathscr{P}) = \mathbf{T}$, and **d** satisfies $\mathscr{P}$ on **I′** if and only if $\mathbf{I}'(\mathscr{P}) = \mathbf{T}$. $\mathbf{I}(\mathscr{P}) = \mathbf{I}'(\mathscr{P})$, because we have stipulated that **I** and **I′** assign the same values to the nonlogical symbols in $\mathscr{P}$. So **d** satisfies $\mathscr{P}$ on **I** if and only if **d** satisfies $\mathscr{P}$ on **I′**.

If $\mathscr{P}$ is an atomic formula $\mathscr{A}t_1 \ldots t_n$, then by the definition of satisfaction,

a. **d** satisfies $\mathscr{P}$ on **I** if and only if $\langle \mathbf{u}_1, \ldots, \mathbf{u}_n \rangle$ is a member of $\mathbf{I}(\mathscr{A})$, where $\mathbf{u}_i$ is $\mathbf{I}(t_i)$ if $t_i$ is a constant and $\mathbf{d}(t_i)$ if $t_i$ is a variable,

and

b. **d** satisfies $\mathscr{P}$ on **I′** if and only if $\langle \mathbf{u}'_1, \ldots, \mathbf{u}'_n \rangle$ is a member of $\mathbf{I}'(\mathscr{A})$, where $\mathbf{u}'_i$ is $\mathbf{I}'(t_i)$ if $t_i$ is a constant and $\mathbf{d}(t_i)$ if $t_i$ is a variable.

We note that

c. $\langle \mathbf{u}_1, \ldots, \mathbf{u}_n \rangle = \langle \mathbf{u}'_1, \ldots, \mathbf{u}'_n \rangle$

because if $t_i$ is a constant then $\mathbf{u}_i$ is $\mathbf{I}(t_i)$ and $\mathbf{u}'_i$ is $\mathbf{I}'(t_i)$—which are the same value if **I** and **I′** assign the same values to the nonlogical symbols in $\mathscr{P}$, and if $t_i$ is a variable then $\mathbf{u}_i$ is $\mathbf{d}(t_i)$ and so is $\mathbf{u}'_i$. Moreover,

d. $\mathbf{I}(\mathscr{A}) = \mathbf{I}'(\mathscr{A})$, by our assumption about **I** and **I′**. So by (c) and (d),

e. $\langle \mathbf{u}_1, \ldots, \mathbf{u}_n \rangle$ is a member of $\mathbf{I}(\mathscr{A})$ if and only if $\langle \mathbf{u}'_1, \ldots, \mathbf{u}'_n \rangle$ is a member of $\mathbf{I}'(\mathscr{A})$ and by (a), (b), and (e) it follows that **d** satisfies $\mathscr{A}t_1 \ldots t_n$ on **I** if and only if it does so on **I′**.

*Inductive step:* If every formula $\mathscr{P}$ that contains $k$ or fewer occurrences of logical operators is such that a variable assignment satisfies $\mathscr{P}$ on **I** if and only if it satisfies $\mathscr{P}$ on **I′**, then every formula $\mathscr{P}$ that contains $k + 1$ occurrences of logical operators is such that a variable assignment satisfies $\mathscr{P}$ on **I** if and only if it satisfies $\mathscr{P}$ on **I′**.

Proof of inductive step: We shall consider the forms that $\mathscr{P}$ may have.

Case 1: $\mathscr{P}$ has the form $\sim \mathscr{Q}$. By the definition of satisfaction,

a. a variable assignment **d** satisfies $\sim \mathscr{Q}$ on **I** if and only if it does not satisfy $\mathscr{Q}$ on **I**.

Because $\mathscr{Q}$ contains fewer than $k + 1$ occurrences of logical operators, it follows from the inductive hypothesis that

b. a variable assignment fails to satisfy $\mathscr{Q}$ on **I** if and only if it fails to satisfy $\mathscr{Q}$ on **I′**.

By the definition of satisfaction again,

c. a variable assignment fails to satisfy $\mathscr{Q}$ on **I′** if and only if it does satisfy $\sim \mathscr{Q}$ on **I′**.

So, by (a)–(c), a variable assignment satisfies $\sim \mathscr{Q}$ on **I** if and only if it satisfies $\sim \mathscr{Q}$ on **I′**.

Case 2: $\mathscr{P}$ has the form $\mathscr{Q} \& \mathscr{R}$. By the definition of satisfaction,

a. a variable assignment satisfies $\mathscr{Q} \& \mathscr{R}$ on **I** if and only if it satisfies both $\mathscr{Q}$ and $\mathscr{R}$ on **I**.

$\mathscr{Q}$ and $\mathscr{R}$ each contain $k$ or fewer occurrences of logical operators and so, by the inductive hypothesis,

b. a variable assignment satisfies both $\mathscr{Q}$ and $\mathscr{R}$ on **I** if and only if it satisfies both $\mathscr{Q}$ and $\mathscr{R}$ on **I′**.

By the definition of satisfaction again,

c. a variable assignment satisfies both $\mathscr{Q}$ and $\mathscr{R}$ on **I′** if and only if it satisfies $\mathscr{Q} \& \mathscr{R}$ on **I′**.

By (a)–(c), a variable assignment satisfies $\mathscr{Q} \& \mathscr{R}$ on **I** if and only if it satisfies $\mathscr{Q} \& \mathscr{R}$ on **I′**.

Cases 3–5: $\mathscr{P}$ has the form $\mathscr{Q} \vee \mathscr{R}$, $\mathscr{Q} \supset \mathscr{R}$, or $\mathscr{Q} \equiv \mathscr{R}$. We omit proofs for these cases as they are strictly analogous to case 2.

Case 6: $\mathscr{P}$ has the form $(\forall x)\mathscr{Q}$. By the definition of satisfaction,

a. a variable assignment **d** satisfies $(\forall x)\mathscr{Q}$ on **I** if and only if for every member **u** of **I**'s U.D., **d**[**u**/$x$] satisfies $\mathscr{Q}$ on **I**

and

b. **d** satisfies $(\forall x)\mathscr{Q}$ on **I′** if and only if for every member **u** of **I′**'s U.D. (which is the same as **I**'s U.D.), **d**[**u**/$x$] satisfies $\mathscr{Q}$ on **I′**.

Because $\mathscr{Q}$ contains fewer than $k + 1$ occurrences of logical operators, it follows from the inductive hypothesis that

c. for each member **u** of the common U.D., **d**[**u**/$x$] satisfies $\mathscr{Q}$ on **I** if and only if **d**[**u**/$x$] satisfies $\mathscr{Q}$ on **I′**.

By (a)–(c), it follows that a variable assignment satisfies $(\forall x)\mathscr{Q}$ on **I** if and only if it satisfies $(\forall x)\mathscr{Q}$ on **I′**.

Case 7: $\mathscr{P}$ has the form $(\exists x)\mathscr{Q}$. This case is similar to case 6.

That completes the proof of the inductive step, and we may now conclude that 11.1.6 is true of every formula $\mathscr{P}$ and pair of interpretations that agree on their assignments to nonlogical symbols in $\mathscr{P}$.

Result 11.1.7 follows as an immediate consequence of 11.1.6:

11.1.7. Let **I** and **I′** be interpretations that have the same U.D. and that agree on the assignments made to each individual constant, predicate, and sentence letter in a sentence $\mathscr{P}$. Then $\mathscr{P}$ is true on **I** if and only if $\mathscr{P}$ is true on **I′**.

Proof: Let **I** and **I′** be as specified for a sentence $\mathscr{P}$. If $\mathscr{P}$ is true on **I**, then, by 11.1.2, $\mathscr{P}$ is satisfied by every variable assignment on **I**. By 11.1.6, this is the case if and only if $\mathscr{P}$ is satisfied by every variable assignment on $\mathbf{I}'$, that is, if and only if $\mathscr{P}$ is true on $\mathbf{I}'$.

With results 11.1.6 and 11.1.7 at hand, we may now show that our motivations for the rules Universal Introduction and Existential Elimination are correct:

11.1.8. Let $a$ be a constant that does not occur in $(\forall x)\mathscr{P}$ or in any member of the set $\Gamma$. Then if $\Gamma \vDash \mathscr{P}(a/x)$, $\Gamma \vDash (\forall x)\mathscr{P}$.

11.1.9. Let $a$ be a constant that does not occur in the sentences $(\exists x)\mathscr{P}$ and $\mathscr{Q}$ and that does not occur in any member of the set $\Gamma$. Then if $\Gamma \vDash (\exists x)\mathscr{P}$ and $\Gamma \cup \{\mathscr{P}(a/x)\} \vDash \mathscr{Q}$, $\Gamma \vDash \mathscr{Q}$ as well.

Result 11.1.8 says, in effect, that if a sentence containing a constant is quantificationally entailed by a set of sentences, and if no sentence in the set contains that constant (no specific assumptions were made about the individual designated by that constant), then what $\mathscr{P}$ says with that constant may be said about everything. And result 11.1.9 says that if a set of sentences quantificationally entails an existentially quantified sentence, and if we can take a substitution instance of that sentence involving a new constant, add it to the set, and find that a sentence making no mention of the individual designated by the constant is quantificationally entailed, then $\mathscr{Q}$ must have been entailed by the set without the substitution instance thrown in. Intuitively, this is so because $\mathscr{Q}$ does not draw any conclusion about the individual designated by the constant in the substitution instance and so all that was really needed to entail $\mathscr{Q}$ was the existential claim that the set entails rather than a specific claim about the individual in question. We shall prove 11.1.8 here; 11.1.9 is left as an exercise.

Proof of 11.1.8: Assume that $\Gamma \vDash \mathscr{P}(a/x)$, where $a$ does not occur in $(\forall x)\mathscr{P}$ or in any member of $\Gamma$. We shall assume, contrary to what we want to show, that $\Gamma$ does not quantificationally entail $(\forall x)\mathscr{P}$—that there is at least one interpretation, call it $\mathbf{I}$, on which every member of $\Gamma$ is true and $(\forall x)\mathscr{P}$ is false. We shall use $\mathbf{I}$ as the basis for constructing an interpretation $\mathbf{I}'$ on which every member of $\Gamma$ is true and the substitution instance $\mathscr{P}(a/x)$ is false, contradicting our original assumption. Having done so, we may conclude that if $\Gamma$ does quantificationally entail $\mathscr{P}(a/x)$, it must also quantificationally entail $(\forall x)\mathscr{P}$.

So assume that $\mathbf{I}$ is an interpretation on which every member of $\Gamma$ is true and on which $(\forall x)\mathscr{P}$ is false. Because $(\forall x)\mathscr{P}$ is false, there is no variable assignment for $\mathbf{I}$ that satisfies $(\forall x)\mathscr{P}$. That is, for every variable assignment $\mathbf{d}$, there is at least one member $\mathbf{u}$ of the U.D. such that $\mathbf{d}[\mathbf{u}/x]$ does not satisfy $\mathscr{P}$. Choose one of these members, calling it $\mathbf{u}$, and let $\mathbf{I}'$ be the interpretation that is just like $\mathbf{I}$ except that it assigns $\mathbf{u}$ to $a$ (all other assignments made by $\mathbf{I}$ remain the same). It is now straightforward to show that every member of $\Gamma$ is true on $\mathbf{I}'$ and $\mathscr{P}(a/x)$ is false. That every member of $\Gamma$ is true on $\mathbf{I}'$ follows from 11.1.7, because $\mathbf{I}$ and $\mathbf{I}'$

assign the same values to all of the nonlogical symbols of *PL* other than $a$, and, by stipulation, $a$ does not occur in any member of $\Gamma$. **I** and **I**$'$ therefore agree on the values assigned to the nonlogical symbols of each sentence in $\Gamma$, and each of these sentences must be true on **I**$'$ because it is true on **I**.

On our assumption that $\mathbf{d}[\mathbf{u}/x]$ does not satisfy $\mathcal{P}$ on **I**, it follows from 11.1.6 that $\mathbf{d}[\mathbf{u}/x]$ does not satisfy $\mathcal{P}$ on **I**$'$ (again, **I** and **I**$'$ assign the same values to all the nonlogical constants in $\mathcal{P}$; $a$ does not occur in $\mathcal{P}$). By the way we have constructed **I**$'$, **u** is $\mathbf{I}'(a)$ and so $\mathbf{d}[\mathbf{u}/x]$ is $\mathbf{d}[\mathbf{I}'(a)/x]$. Result 11.1.1 tells us that $\mathbf{d}[\mathbf{I}'(a)/x]$ satisfies $\mathcal{P}$ on **I**$'$ if and only if **d** satisfies $\mathcal{P}(a/x)$ on **I**$'$. So because $\mathbf{d}[\mathbf{I}'(a)/x]$ does not satisfy $\mathcal{P}$ on **I**$'$, **d** does not satisfy $\mathcal{P}(a/x)$ on **I**$'$. By 11.1.3, then, no variable assignment satisfies $\mathcal{P}(a/x)$ on **I**$'$, and it is therefore false on this interpretation. But this contradicts our first assumption, that $\Gamma \vDash \mathcal{P}(a/x)$, and so we conclude that if $\Gamma \vDash \mathcal{P}(a/x)$ then $\Gamma \vDash (\forall x)\mathcal{P}$ as well.

As a consequence of 11.1.8, we know that the rule Universal Introduction is indeed truth-preserving.

We shall state four more semantic results that are important in the sections that follow, and that the reader should now be able to prove. The proofs are left as exercises. The first result relies on 11.1.6 and 11.1.7 much as the proofs of 11.1.8 and 11.1.9 do:

11.1.10. If $a$ does not occur in any member of the set $\Gamma \cup \{(\exists x)\mathcal{P}\}$, and if the set is quantificationally consistent, then the set $\Gamma \cup \{(\exists x)\mathcal{P}, \mathcal{P}(a/x)\}$ is also quantificationally consistent.

Results 11.1.11 and 11.1.12 concern interpretations of a special sort: interpretations on which every member of the U.D. has a name.

11.1.11. Let **I** be an interpretation on which each member of the U.D. is assigned to at least one individual constant. Then if every substitution instance of $(\forall x)\mathcal{P}$ is true on **I**, so is $(\forall x)\mathcal{P}$.

11.1.12. Let **I** be an interpretation on which each member of the U.D. is assigned to at least one individual constant. Then if every substitution instance of $(\exists x)\mathcal{P}$ is false on **I**, so is $(\exists x)\mathcal{P}$.

Result 11.1.13 says that if we rename the individual designated by some individual constant in a sentence $\mathcal{P}$ with a constant that does not already occur in $\mathcal{P}$, then, for any interpretation on which $\mathcal{P}$ is true there is a closely related interpretation (one that reflects the renaming) on which the new sentence is true:

11.1.13. Let $\mathcal{P}$ be a sentence of *PL*, let $b$ be an individual constant that does not occur in $\mathcal{P}$, and let $\mathcal{P}(b/a)$ be the sentence that results from replacing every occurrence of the individual constant $a$ in $\mathcal{P}$ with $b$. Then if $\mathcal{P}$ is true on an interpretation **I**, $\mathcal{P}(b/a)$ is true on the interpretation **I**$'$ that is just like **I** except that it assigns $\mathbf{I}(a)$ to $b$ ($\mathbf{I}'(b) = \mathbf{I}(a)$).

### 11.1E EXERCISES

***1.** Prove cases 3–5 in the proof of result 11.1.1.

***2.** Prove cases 3–5 and 7 in the proof of result 11.1.2.

***3.** Prove result 11.1.5.

***4.** Prove result 11.1.9.

**5.** Prove result 11.1.10.

**6.** Prove result 11.1.11.

***7.** Prove result 11.1.12.

***8.** Prove result 11.1.13.

---

## 11.2 THE SOUNDNESS OF *PD*, *PD+*, AND *PDI*

We shall now establish the soundness of our natural deduction systems. A natural deduction system is said to be *sound* for predicate logic if every rule in that system is truth-preserving—that is, if no derivation that uses the rules of that system can lead from true assumptions to a false conclusion. The *Soundness Metatheorem* for *PD* is

| Metatheorem 11.1: if $\Gamma \vdash \mathscr{P}$ in *PD*, then $\Gamma \vDash \mathscr{P}$. |
|---|

(If $\mathscr{P}$ is derivable from $\Gamma$ in *PD*, then $\mathscr{P}$ is quantificationally entailed by $\Gamma$.) To establish Metatheorem 11.1, we shall prove that each sentence in a derivation is quantificationally entailed by the set of undischarged assumptions within whose scope the sentence lies. It will then follow that the last sentence of any derivation is quantificationally entailed by the set of undischarged assumptions of that derivation—hence that $\Gamma \vDash \mathscr{P}$ if $\Gamma \vdash \mathscr{P}$. (As in Chapter Six, we drop 'in *PD*' when we use the single turnstile here, and we use the double turnstile to signify *quantificational* entailment.) The proof is by mathematical induction and is, in outline, like the proof that we presented in Chapter Six establishing the soundness of *SD* for sentential logic. In fact, we shall see that much of the proof in Chapter Six can be used here—for in Chapter Six, we showed that the rules for the truth-functional connectives are all sound for sentential logic, and with a change from talk of truth-value assignments to talk of interpretations, those rules are established to be sound for predicate logic in the same way. The bulk of the proof will therefore concentrate on the rules for quantifier introduction and elimination.

In our proof we shall use several semantic results that were presented in Section 11.1 along with the following result:

11.2.1. If $\Gamma \vDash \mathscr{P}$ and $\Gamma^*$ is a superset of $\Gamma$, then $\Gamma^* \vDash \mathscr{P}$.

Proof: If every member of $\Gamma^*$ is true on an interpretation **I**, then every member of its subset $\Gamma$ is true on **I**. And if $\Gamma \vDash \mathscr{P}$, then $\mathscr{P}$ is also true on **I**. Hence $\Gamma^* \vDash \mathscr{P}$.

Letting $\mathscr{P}_i$ be the sentence at position $i$ in a derivation and letting $\Gamma_i$ be the set of assumptions that are undischarged at position $i$ (and hence within whose scope $\mathscr{P}_i$ lies), the argument by mathematical induction is:

*Basis clause:* $\Gamma_1 \vDash \mathscr{P}_1$.

*Inductive step:* If $\Gamma_i \vDash \mathscr{P}_i$ for every position $i$ in a derivation such that $i \leq k$, then $\Gamma_{k+1} \vDash \mathscr{P}_{k+1}$.

---

*Conclusion:* Every sentence in a derivation is quantificationally entailed by the set of undischarged assumptions in whose scope it lies (for every position $k$ in a derivation, $\Gamma_k \vDash \mathscr{P}_k$).

The basis clause is straightforward to prove: The first sentence in any derivation in *PD* is an assumption, and it lies in its own scope. $\Gamma_1$ is just $\{\mathscr{P}_1\}$, and it is trivial that $\{\mathscr{P}_1\} \vDash \mathscr{P}_1$.

To prove the inductive step, we choose an arbitrary position $k$ and assume the inductive hypothesis: For every position $i$ such that $i \leq k$, $\Gamma_i \vDash \mathscr{P}_i$. We must now show that the same holds for position $k + 1$. We shall show this by considering the justifications that might be used for the sentence at position $k + 1$, establishing that the entailment claim holds no matter which justification is used.

Cases 1–12: $\mathscr{P}_{k+1}$ is justified by one of the rules of *SD*. For each of these cases, use the corresponding case from the proof of the soundness of *SD* in Section 6.3, changing talk of truth-value assignments to talk of interpretations, and talk of truth-functional concepts (inconsistency and so on) to talk of quantificational concepts.

Case 13: $\mathscr{P}_{k+1}$ is justified by Universal Elimination. Then $\mathscr{P}_{k+1}$ is a sentence $\mathscr{Q}(a/x)$ derived as follows:

| | | |
|---|---|---|
| $h$ | $(\forall x)\mathscr{Q}$ | |
| $k + 1$ | $\mathscr{Q}(a/x)$ | $h$ ∀E |

where every assumption that is undischarged at position $h$ is also undischarged at position $k + 1$ (because $(\forall x)\mathscr{Q}$ at position $h$ is accessible at position $k + 1$)—so $\Gamma_h$ is a subset of $\Gamma_{k+1}$. By the inductive hypothesis, $\Gamma_h \vDash (\forall x)\mathscr{Q}$. It follows, by 11.2.1, that the superset $\Gamma_{k+1} \vDash (\forall x)\mathscr{Q}$. By 11.1.4, which says that a universally quantified sentence quantificationally entails every one of its substitution instances, $\mathscr{Q}(a/x)$ is true on every interpretation on which $(\forall x)\mathscr{Q}$ is true. So $\Gamma_{k+1} \vDash \mathscr{Q}(a/x)$ as well.

Case 14: $\mathcal{P}_{k+1}$ is justified by Existential Introduction. Then $\mathcal{P}_{k+1}$ is a sentence $(\exists x)\mathcal{Q}$ derived as follows:

| | | |
|---|---|---|
| $h$ | $\mathcal{Q}(a/x)$ | |
| $k+1$ | $(\exists x)\mathcal{Q}$ | $h$ $\exists$I |

where every assumption that is undischarged at position $h$ is also undischarged at position $k+1$. So $\Gamma_h$ is a subset of $\Gamma_{k+1}$. By the inductive hypothesis, $\Gamma_h \vDash \mathcal{Q}(a/x)$ and so, by 11.2.1, $\Gamma_{k+1} \vDash \mathcal{Q}(a/x)$. By 11.1.5, we know that $(\exists x)\mathcal{Q}$ is true on every interpretation on which $\mathcal{Q}(a/x)$ is true, so $\Gamma_{k+1} \vDash (\exists x)\mathcal{Q}$ as well.

Case 15: $\mathcal{P}_{k+1}$ is justified by Universal Introduction. Then $\mathcal{P}_{k+1}$ is a sentence $(\forall x)\mathcal{Q}$ derived as follows:

| | | |
|---|---|---|
| $h$ | $\mathcal{Q}(a/x)$ | |
| $k+1$ | $(\forall x)\mathcal{Q}$ | $h$ $\forall$I |

where every assumption that is undischarged at position $h$ is also undischarged at position $k+1$—so $\Gamma_h$ is a subset of $\Gamma_{k+1}$—and in addition $a$ does not occur in $(\forall x)\mathcal{Q}$ or in any member of $\Gamma_{k+1}$, because $\forall$I can be applied only if $a$ does not occur in $(\forall x)\mathcal{Q}$ or in any assumption that is undischarged at position $k+1$. By the inductive hypothesis, $\Gamma_h \vDash \mathcal{Q}(a/x)$. Because $\Gamma_h$ is a subset of $\Gamma_{k+1}$, it follows from 11.2.1 that $\Gamma_{k+1} \vDash \mathcal{Q}(a/x)$. And because $a$ does not occur in $(\forall x)\mathcal{Q}$ or in any member of $\Gamma_{k+1}$, it follows from 11.1.8, which we repeat here, that $\Gamma_{k+1} \vDash (\forall x)\mathcal{Q}$ as well:

> 11.1.8. Let $a$ be a constant that does not occur in $(\forall x)\mathcal{P}$ or in any member of the set $\Gamma$. Then if $\Gamma \vDash \mathcal{P}(a/x)$, $\Gamma \vDash (\forall x)\mathcal{P}$.

Case 16: $\mathcal{P}_{k+1}$ is justified by Existential Elimination. Then $\mathcal{P}_{k+1}$ is derived as follows:

| | | |
|---|---|---|
| $h$ | $(\exists x)\mathcal{Q}$ | |
| $j$ |     $\mathcal{Q}(a/x)$ | |
| $m$ |     $\mathcal{P}_{k+1}$ | |
| $k+1$ | $\mathcal{P}_{k+1}$ | $h$, $j$–$m$ $\exists$E |

where every member of $\Gamma_h$ is a member of $\Gamma_{k+1}$ and every member of $\Gamma_m$ except $\mathcal{P}(a/x)$ is a member of $\Gamma_{k+1}$ (if any other assumptions in $\Gamma_m$ were discharged prior to position $k+1$, then the subderivation $j$-$m$ would not be accessible at position $k+1$). Because every member of $\Gamma_m$ except $\mathcal{P}(a/x)$ is a member of $\Gamma_{k+1}$, $\Gamma_m$ is a subset of $\Gamma_{k+1} \cup \{\mathcal{P}(a/x)\}$. Moreover, $a$ does not occur in $(\exists x)\mathcal{Q}$, $\mathcal{P}_{k+1}$, or any member of $\Gamma_{k+1}$—otherwise, $\exists$E would not have been permissible. By the inductive hypothesis, $\Gamma_h \vDash (\exists x)\mathcal{Q}$ and so, because $\Gamma_h$ is a subset of $\Gamma_{k+1}$, it follows from

11.2.1 that $\Gamma_{k+1} \vDash (\exists x)\mathcal{Q}$. Also by the inductive hypothesis, $\Gamma_m \vDash \mathcal{P}_{k+1}$ and so, because $\Gamma_m$ is a subset of $\Gamma_{k+1} \cup \{\mathcal{P}(a/x)\}$, it follows from 11.2.1 that $\Gamma_{k+1} \cup \{\mathcal{P}(a/x)\} \vDash \mathcal{P}_{k+1}$. Because $a$ does not occur in $(\exists x)\mathcal{Q}$, $\mathcal{P}_{k+1}$, or any member of $\Gamma_{k+1}$, it follows from the last two entailments noted that $\Gamma_{k+1} \vDash \mathcal{P}_{k+1}$, by 11.1.9, which we repeat here:

> 11.1.9. Let $a$ be a constant that does not occur in the sentences $(\exists x)\mathcal{P}$ and $\mathcal{Q}$ and that does not occur in any member of the set $\Gamma$. Then if $\Gamma \vDash (\exists x)\mathcal{P}$ and $\Gamma \cup \{\mathcal{P}(a/x)\} \vDash \mathcal{Q}$, $\Gamma \vDash \mathcal{Q}$ as well.

That completes the proof of the inductive step; all of the derivation rules of *PD* are truth-preserving. Note that in establishing that the two quantifier rules $\forall$I and $\exists$E are truth-preserving, we made essential use of the restrictions that those rules place on the instantiating constant $a$—the restrictions were included in those rules to ensure that they would be truth-preserving. Having established that the inductive step is true, we may conclude that every sentence in a derivation of *PD* is quantificationally entailed by the set of undischarged assumptions in whose scope it lies. Therefore, if $\Gamma \vdash \mathcal{P}$ in *PD*, then $\Gamma \vDash \mathcal{P}$. This establishes Metatheorem 11.1, the Soundness Metatheorem for *PD*.

The proof that *PD+* is sound for predicate logic involves the additional steps of showing that the rules of replacement of *SD+*, the three derived rules of *SD+*, and the rule Quantifier Negation are all truth-preserving. The steps in the soundness proof for *SD+*, which show that its rules are truth-preserving for sentential logic can, with appropriate adjustments to quantificational talk, be converted into steps that show that the rules are truth-preserving for quantificational logic. We leave the proof that the additional rule of replacement in *PD+*, Quantifier Negation, is truth-preserving as an exercise.

Finally, we can prove that *PDI* is sound for predicate logic with identity by extending the inductive step of the proof for *PD* to cover the two identity rules, Identity Introduction and Identity Elimination. We note that all of the semantic results in Section 11.1.1 are true of predicate logic with identity as well as predicate logic without identity. (Each proof by induction over the number of occurrences of logical operators in a formula must now cover, in the basis clause, formulas of the form $\mathbf{a} = \mathbf{b}$—we leave these changes as an exercise.) So we may freely use those results in establishing the soundness of *PDI* for predicate logic with identity.

There is one change that we must make in the basis clause of the soundness proof, that we shall look at first. In the basis clause for *PD*, we said that the first sentence in a derivation is an assumption. This is not always the case in *PDI*; the first sentence *can* be an assumption but it can also be a sentence of the form $(\forall x)x = x$, introduced by Identity Introduction. So the proof of the basis clause will look like:

> The first sentence in a derivation in *PDI* is either an assumption or a sentence introduced by Identity Introduction. If the first sentence is an assumption, then it lies in its own scope. In this case $\Gamma_1$ is just $\{\mathcal{P}_1\}$, and it is trivial that $\{\mathcal{P}_1\} \vDash \mathcal{P}_1$.

If the first sentence is introduced by Identity Introduction, then $\Gamma_1$ is empty—there are no assumptions, and hence no undischarged assumptions, at that point. So it remains to be shown that $\varnothing$ truth-functionally entails every sentence of the form $(\forall x)x = x$, that is, every such sentence is quantificationally true. This was proved in Exercise 10.a of Section 8.7E.

We add the following two cases to the proof of the inductive step for *PD*:

Case 17: $\mathcal{P}_{k+1}$ is introduced by Identity Introduction. Then $\mathcal{P}_{k+1}$ is a sentence of the form $(\forall x)x = x$ derived as follows:

| | | |
|---|---|---|
| $k+1$ | $(\forall x)x = x$ | II |

We have already noted that the empty set quantificationally entails every sentence of the form $(\forall x)x = x$. And the empty set is a subset of $\Gamma_{k+1}$, so, by 11.2.1, $\Gamma_{k+1} \vDash (\forall x)x = x$.

Case 18: $\mathcal{P}_{k+1}$ is introduced by Identity Elimination. Then $\mathcal{P}_{k+1}$ is derived as follows:

| | | | | | | |
|---|---|---|---|---|---|---|
| $h$ | $a = b$ | | | $h$ | $a = b$ | |
| $j$ | $\mathcal{P}$ | | or | $j$ | $\mathcal{P}$ | |
| $k+1$ | $\mathcal{P}(a//b)$ | $h, j$ IE | | $k+1$ | $\mathcal{P}(b//a)$ | $h, j$ IE |

where both $\Gamma_h$ and $\Gamma_j$ are subsets of $\Gamma_{k+1}$ (because the sentences at positions $h$ and $j$ are accessible at position $k+1$). By the inductive hypothesis, $\Gamma_h \vDash a = b$ and $\Gamma_j \vDash \mathcal{P}$. Because these are both subsets of $\Gamma_{k+1}$, it follows, by 11.2.1, that $\Gamma_{k+1} \vDash a = b$ and $\Gamma_{k+1} \vDash \mathcal{P}$. To conclude that $\Gamma_{k+1}$ also quantificationally entails $\mathcal{P}_{k+1}$, we will use the result

> 11.2.2. For any constants $a$ and $b$, if $\mathcal{P}$ is a sentence that contains $a$, then $\{a = b, \mathcal{P}\} \vDash \mathcal{P}(b//a)$, and if $\mathcal{P}$ is a sentence that contains $b$, then $\{a = b, \mathcal{P}\} \vDash \mathcal{P}(a//b)$.
>
> Proof: See Exercise 4.

For let $\mathcal{I}$ be any interpretation on which all the members of $\Gamma_{k+1}$ are true. Then $a = b$ and $\mathcal{P}$ are both true, because they are quantificationally entailed by $\Gamma_{k+1}$. It follows from 11.2.2 that the sentence at position $k+1$ is true as well. So $\Gamma_{k+1} \vDash \mathcal{P}_{k+1}$.

These changes establish that *PDI* is sound for predicate logic with identity; like *PD* and *PD+* , *PDI* will never lead from true premises to a false conclusion.

## 11.2E EXERCISES

**1.** Using Metatheorem 11.1, prove the following:
a. Every argument of *PL* that is valid in *PD* is quantificationally valid.
b. Every sentence of *PL* that is a theorem in *PD* is quantificationally true.
*c. Every pair of sentences $\mathcal{P}$ and $\mathcal{Q}$ of *PL* that are equivalent in *PD* are quantificationally equivalent.

**2.** Prove the following (to be used in exercise 3) by mathematical induction:

11.2.3. Let $\mathcal{P}$ be a formula of *PL*, and let $\mathcal{Q}$ be a subformula of $\mathcal{P}$. Let $[\mathcal{P}](\mathcal{Q}_1//\mathcal{Q})$ be a sentence that is the result of replacing one or more occurrences of $\mathcal{Q}$ in $\mathcal{P}$ with a formula $\mathcal{Q}_1$. If $\mathcal{Q}$ and $\mathcal{Q}_1$ contain the same nonlogical symbols and variables and if on any interpretation $\mathcal{Q}$ and $\mathcal{Q}_1$ are satisfied by exactly the same variable assignments, then on any interpretation $\mathcal{P}$ and $[\mathcal{P}](\mathcal{Q}_1//\mathcal{Q})$ are satisfied by exactly the same variable assignments.

**3.** Using 11.2.3, show how we can establish, as a step in an inductive proof of the soundness of *PD*+ , that Quantifier Negation is truth-preserving for predicate logic.

***4.** Prove result 11.2.2.

***5.**a. Suppose that the rule ∀I did not have the restriction that the instantiating constant $\boldsymbol{a}$ in the sentence $\mathcal{P}(\boldsymbol{a}/\boldsymbol{x})$ to which ∀I applies must not occur in any undischarged assumption. Explain why *PD* would *not* be sound for predicate logic in this case.
b. Suppose that the rule ∃E did not have the restriction that the instantiating constant $\boldsymbol{a}$ in the assumption $\mathcal{P}(\boldsymbol{a}/\boldsymbol{x})$ must not occur in the sentence $\mathcal{Q}$ that is derived. Explain why *PD* would *not* be sound for predicate logic in this case.

***6.** Show the changes that must be made in the basis clauses of the proofs of the following results so that they will hold for predicate logic with identity:
a. Result 11.1.1.
b. Result 11.1.2.
c. Result 11.1.6.

## 11.3 THE COMPLETENESS OF *PD*, *PD*+ , AND *PDI*

In this section we prove that our natural deduction systems are *complete* for predicate logic. A natural deduction system is complete for predicate logic if whenever a sentence is quantificationally entailed by a set of sentences, there is at least one derivation of the sentence from members of that set in the natural deduction system. Metatheorem 11.2 is the *Completeness Metatheorem* for *PD*:

| |
|---|
| Metatheorem 11.2: If $\Gamma \vDash \mathcal{P}$, then $\Gamma \vdash \mathcal{P}$ in *PD*. |

We shall prove the Completeness Metatheorem for *PD* in a manner analogous to that in which the completeness of *SD* for sentential logic was shown in Chapter Six.

We note that that the Completeness Metatheorem follows almost immediately from the Inconsistency Lemma for predicate logic:

| Lemma 11.1: If a set $\Gamma$ of sentences of *PL* is quantificationally inconsistent, then $\Gamma$ is also inconsistent in *PD*. |
|---|

To see how Metatheorem 11.2 follows, assume that for some set $\Gamma$ and sentence $\mathscr{P}$, $\Gamma \vDash \mathscr{P}$ (this is the antecedent of the metatheorem). Then the set $\Gamma \cup \{\sim \mathscr{P}\}$ is quantificationally inconsistent (see Exercise 1). It follows, from Lemma 11.1, that $\Gamma \cup \{\sim \mathscr{P}\}$ is also inconsistent in *PD*. And from this it follows that $\Gamma \vdash \mathscr{P}$ in *PD* (see Exercise 2).

So the bulk of this section is devoted to proving Lemma 11.1. We shall do so by proving its contrapositive:

> If a set $\Gamma$ of sentences of *PL* is consistent in *PD*, then $\Gamma$ is quantificationally consistent.

If the contrapositive is true, then we may conclude of any set that is quantificationally *in*consistent that it is also inconsistent in *PD*. The proof of the contrapositive is in four steps. First, we shall show that for any set $\Gamma$ that is consistent in *PD*, if we double the subscript of every individual constant in $\Gamma$ (so every resulting subscript will be even), then the resulting set $\Gamma_e$ is also consistent in *PD*. We shall call such a set an *evenly subscripted* set. For our purposes, the interest of these sets lies in the fact that there are infinitely many individual constants—namely, all the oddly subscripted constants—that do not occur in the sentences of any evenly subscripted set. We shall use this fact in the second step of our proof, which is that every evenly subscripted set $\Gamma$ that is consistent in *PD* is a subset of a set that is *maximally consistent in PD* and that is *∃-complete*. Maximal consistency is defined as it was for *SD*, except that we are now talking about *PL* and *PD*:

> A set $\Gamma$ of sentences of *PL* is *maximally consistent in PD* if and only if $\Gamma$ is consistent in *PD* and for every sentence $\mathscr{P}$ of *PL* that is not a member of $\Gamma$, $\Gamma \cup \{\mathscr{P}\}$ is inconsistent in *PD*.

If a set is maximally consistent in *PD*, then adding even one new sentence to the set will make it inconsistent in *PD*. ∃-completeness (read aloud as *existential-completeness*) is a new concept, but a simple one:

> A set $\Gamma$ of sentences of *PL* is *∃-complete* if and only if for each sentence in $\Gamma$ that has the form $(\exists \mathscr{x})\mathscr{P}$, at least one substitution instance of $(\exists \mathscr{x})\mathscr{P}$ is also a member of $\Gamma$.

If, for example, '(∃x)Gx' is a member of a set that is ∃-complete, then at least one of 'Ga', 'Gb', 'Gc', . . . is also a member of the set. We want to prove that every evenly subscripted set that is consistent in *PD* is a subset of a set that is both maximally consistent in *PD* and ∃-complete because there is a straightforward way to construct an interpretation on which every member of such as set is true—showing this will be the third step of our proof of Lemma 11.1. With an interpretation at hand we may then conclude that the maximally consistent, ∃-complete set is quantificationally consistent, and hence that every one of its subsets is quantificationally consistent. Having thus shown that every evenly subscripted subset is quantificationally consistent, our final step will be to show that the set whose individual constant subscripts were doubled (to obtain an evenly subscripted set) must be quantificationally consistent as well.

First, then, we need

11.3.1. Let $\Gamma$ be a set of sentences of *PL*, and let $\Gamma_e$ be the set that results from doubling the subscript of every individual constant that occurs in any member of $\Gamma$. Then if $\Gamma$ is consistent in *PD*, $\Gamma_e$ is also consistent in *PD*.

Proof: Assume that $\Gamma$ is consistent in *PD* and that, contrary to what we wish to prove, $\Gamma_e$ is *in*consistent in *PD*. Then there is a derivation of the sort

$$
\begin{array}{r|l}
1 & \mathscr{P}_1 \\
2 & \mathscr{P}_2 \\
\cdot & \cdot \\
n & \mathscr{P}_n \\
\hline
\cdot & \cdot \\
k & \mathscr{Q} \\
\cdot & \cdot \\
p & \sim \mathscr{Q}
\end{array}
$$

where $\mathscr{P}_1, \mathscr{P}_2, \ldots, \mathscr{P}_n$ are members of $\Gamma_e$. We shall convert this derivation into a derivation that shows that $\Gamma$ is inconsistent in *PD*, contradicting our first assumption. Our strategy, not surprisingly, will be to halve the subscript of every evenly subscripted individual constant occurring in the derivation, thus converting each of $\mathscr{P}_1, \mathscr{P}_2, \ldots, \mathscr{P}_n$ back into a member of the original $\Gamma$. There is a complication, though—in so doing we may end up with a sequence in which either an ∃E restriction or an ∀I restriction is violated. If, for example, $\mathscr{P}_1$ in the derivation above is '$\text{Ba}_2$' and later in the derivation the sentence '(∀x)Lx' is legally derived from the sentence '$\text{La}_1$' by ∀I (note that an odd subscript *may* occur in the above derivation *after* the primary assumption), then in changing $\mathscr{P}_1$ to '$\text{Ba}_1$' we shall have introduced an individual constant into a primary assumption that *prevents* the later use of ∀I. Our first step is thus to ensure that this will not happen.

When the rule ∃E is used to justify a sentence, let the constant $\boldsymbol{a}$ that is the instantiating constant in the substitution instance $\mathscr{P}(\boldsymbol{a}/\boldsymbol{x})$ that begins the subderivation cited be called the *instantiating constant for that use of ∃E*. Similarly, the *instantiating constant for a use of ∀I* is the instantiating constant $\boldsymbol{a}$ in the sentence $\mathscr{P}(\boldsymbol{a}/\boldsymbol{x})$ cited. Let $\boldsymbol{a}_1, \ldots, \boldsymbol{a}_m$ be the distinct constants that are instantiating constants for uses of ∃E and ∀I in the above derivation. Let $a_{m+1}, \ldots, a_{m+m}$ be distinct constants that have odd subscripts that are larger than the subscript of any constant occurring in the derivation. (Because every derivation is a finite sequence, we know that of the constants occurring in our derivation there is one that has the largest subscript—and, whatever this largest subscript may be, there are infinitely many odd numbers that are larger.) We replace each sentence $\mathscr{R}$ in the original derivation with a sentence $\mathscr{R}^*$ that is the result of first replacing each occurrence of $a_i$ in $\mathscr{R}$, $1 \leq i \leq m$, with $a_{m+i}$, and then halving every even subscript in a constant in the resulting sentence.

We claim that the resulting sequence is a derivation in *PD* of $\mathscr{Q}^*$ and $\sim \mathscr{Q}^*$ from members of the set $\Gamma$. First note that for every new primary assumption $\mathscr{P}_i^*$, $\mathscr{P}_i^*$ is a member of $\Gamma$. This is because none of $a_1, \ldots, a_m$ can occur in a primary assumption of the original derivation (lest an instantiating constant restriction be violated—for these are the instantiating constants for uses of ∃E and ∀I in that derivation) and so $\mathscr{P}_i^*$ is just $\mathscr{P}_i$ with all of its individual constant subscripts halved—that is, a member of the set $\Gamma$ from which $\Gamma_e$ was constructed by doubling subscripts. It remains to be shown that the resulting sequence counts as a derivation in *PD*—that every sentence in that sequence can be justified. This is left as an exercise.

We now turn to proving the Maximal Consistency Lemma for predicate logic:

> Lemma 11.2: If $\Gamma$ is an evenly subscripted set of sentences that is consistent in *PD*, then $\Gamma$ is a subset of at least one set of sentences that is both maximally consistent in *PD* and ∃-complete.

We shall establish this lemma by showing how, beginning with $\Gamma$, to construct a superset that has the two properties. We assume that the sentences of *PL* have been enumerated, that is, they have been placed in a one-to-one correspondence with the positive integers so that there is a first sentence, a second sentence, a third sentence, and so on. The enumeration can be done analogously to the enumeration of the sentences of *SL* in Section 6.4; we leave proof of this as an exercise (Exercise 4). We shall now build a sequence of sets $\Gamma_1, \Gamma_2, \Gamma_3, \ldots$, starting with an evenly subscripted set $\Gamma$ that is consistent in *PD* and considering each sentence in the enumeration, adding the sentence if it can consistently be added and, if the added sentence is existentially quantified, adding one of its substitution instances as well. The sequence is constructed as follows:

1. $\Gamma_1$ is $\Gamma$.
2. $\Gamma_{i+1}$ is

(i) $\Gamma_i \cup \{\mathscr{P}_i\}$, if $\Gamma_i \cup \{\mathscr{P}_i\}$ is consistent in *PD* and $\mathscr{P}_i$ does not have the form $(\exists x)\mathscr{P}$, or

(ii) $\Gamma_i \cup \{\mathcal{P}_i, \mathcal{P}_i^*\}$, if $\Gamma \cup \{\mathcal{P}_i\}$ is consistent in *PD* and $\mathcal{P}_i$ has the form $(\exists x)\mathcal{Q}$, where $\mathcal{P}_i^*$ is a substitution instance $\mathcal{Q}(a/x)$ of $(\exists x)\mathcal{Q}$ and $a$ is the alphabetically earliest constant that does not occur in $\mathcal{P}_i$ or in any sentence in $\Gamma_i$, or

(iii) $\Gamma_i$, if $\Gamma_i \cup \{\mathcal{P}_i\}$ is inconsistent in *PD*.

As an example of (ii), if $\Gamma_i$ is the set {(∀x)(Fxa ⊃ Gx), ~ Hc ∨ (∃y)Jyy} and $\mathcal{P}_i$ is '(∃z)(Kz & (∀y)Fzy)', then $\Gamma_i \cup \{\mathcal{P}_i\}$ is quantificationally consistent and so $\mathcal{P}_i$ will be added to the set—but we must add a substitution instance of $\mathcal{P}_i$ as well. The alphabetically earliest constant that does not occur in $\mathcal{P}_i$ or in any member of $\Gamma_i$ is 'b', and so this will be the instantiating constant. $\Gamma_{i+1}$ is therefore

{(∀x)(Fxa ⊃ Gx), ~ Hc ∨ (∃y)Jyy, (∃z)(Kz & (∀y)Fzy), Kb & (∀y)Fby}

The reason for using an instantiating constant that does not already occur in $\Gamma_i$ will become clear shortly, when we prove that each set in the sequence is consistent in *PD*. Here it is important to note that, for any set in the sequence, there will always be at least one individual constant that does not already occur in that set. This is because the set that we started with is evenly subscripted, so we know that infinitely many oddly subscripted individual constants do not occur in Γ; and each subsequent set adds at most one new individual constant, still leaving infinitely many individual constants yet to be used. Thus the requirement in condition (ii), that $a$ be a *new* constant, is a requirement that can always be satisfied.

Because the sequence $\Gamma_1, \Gamma_2, \Gamma_3, \ldots$ is infinitely long, there is no last member in the set. We want a set that contains all of the sentences in these sets, so we let Γ* be the set that contains every sentence that occurs in some set in the infinite sequence $\Gamma_1, \Gamma_2, \Gamma_3, \ldots$ . We shall show that Γ* is both maximally consistent in *PD* and ∃-complete. To show that Γ* is maximally consistent in *PD*, we first prove that each set $\Gamma_i$ in the sequence is consistent in *PD*, using mathematical induction.

*Basis clause:* $\Gamma_1$ is consistent in *PD*.

Proof: By definition, $\Gamma_1$ is Γ, a set that is consistent in *PD*.

*Inductive step:* If for every $i \leq k$, $\Gamma_i$ is consistent in *PD*, then $\Gamma_{k+1}$ is consistent in *PD*.

Proof: If $\Gamma_{k+1}$ is formed in accordance with condition (i), then $\Gamma_{k+1}$ is obviously consistent in *PD*. If $\Gamma_{k+1}$ is formed in accordance with condition (ii), then $\Gamma_i \cup \{\mathcal{P}_i\}$ is consistent—as stipulated by condition (ii). We need to show that it follows that $\Gamma_i \cup \{\mathcal{P}_i, \mathcal{P}_i^*\}$, which is what $\Gamma_{k+1}$ was defined to be in this case, is also consistent in *PD*. Because the instantiating constant in $\mathcal{P}_i^*$ does not occur in any member of $\Gamma_i \cup \{\mathcal{P}_i\}$, the consistency of $\Gamma_{k+1}$ follows immediately from result 11.3.2, the proof of which is left as an exercise:

11.3.2. If $a$ does not occur in any member of the set $\Gamma \cup \{(\exists x)\mathcal{P}\}$, and if the set is consistent in *PD*, then the set $\Gamma \cup \{(\exists x)\mathcal{P}, \mathcal{P}(a/x)\}$ is also consistent in *PD*.

(This is why condition (ii) stipulated that $\boldsymbol{a}$ be a new constant—the fact that $\boldsymbol{a}$ does not occur in the set $\Gamma \cup \{(\exists \boldsymbol{x})\mathcal{P}\}$ is crucial to the proof of the inductive step.) Finally, if $\Gamma_{k+1}$ is formed in accordance with condition (iii), then $\Gamma_{k+1}$ is $\Gamma_k$ and $\Gamma_k$ is, by the inductive hypothesis, consistent in *PD*. So no matter which condition was applied in its construction, $\Gamma_{k+1}$ is consistent in *PD*.

Having established both premises, we conclude that every set in the sequence $\Gamma_1, \Gamma_2, \Gamma_3, \ldots$ is consistent in *PD*.

Now assume that $\Gamma^*$ is not consistent in *PD*. Then there is a finite nonempty subset $\Gamma'$ of $\Gamma^*$ that is inconsistent in *PD* (the proof is analogous to that in the proof of 6.4.3). Because $\Gamma'$ is finite, some sentence in $\Gamma'$, say $\mathcal{P}_j$, occurs later in our enumeration of the sentences of *PL* than any other sentence in $\Gamma'$. Every member of $\Gamma'$ is thus a member of $\Gamma_{j+1}$, by the way we constructed the sets in the sequence. (If the $i$th sentence gets added to one of the sets, it gets added by the time that $\Gamma_{i+1}$ is constructed.) It follows that $\Gamma_{j+1}$ is also inconsistent in *PD* (the proof is analogous to that in Exercise 3 of Section 6.4E). But we have just proved that every set in the sequence is consistent in *PD*, so we conclude that, contrary to our assumption, $\Gamma^*$ is also consistent in *PD*. That $\Gamma^*$ is *maximally* consistent in *PD* is proved in exactly the manner that the parallel result in Section 6.4 was proved—for any sentence $\mathcal{P}_k$, if $\Gamma^* \cup \{\mathcal{P}_k\}$ is consistent in *PD*, then the subset $\Gamma_k$ of $\Gamma^*$ is such that $\Gamma_k \cup \{\mathcal{P}_k\}$ is consistent in *PD* and so, by the construction of the sequence of sets, $\mathcal{P}_k$ is a member of $\Gamma_{k+1}$ and hence of $\Gamma^*$. Finally, the proof that $\Gamma^*$ is $\exists$-complete is left as an exercise. This completes the proof of Lemma 11.2—because every member of the original set $\Gamma$ is also a member of $\Gamma^*$, it follows that every evenly subscripted set $\Gamma$ of sentences of *PL* that is consistent in *PD* is a subset of at least one set of sentences that is both maximally consistent in *PD* and $\exists$-complete.

We shall now prove the Consistency Lemma for predicate logic:

| |
|---|
| Lemma 11.3: Every set of sentences of *PL* that is both maximally consistent in *PD* and $\exists$-complete is quantificationally consistent. |

Once Lemma 11.3 is established, Lemma 11.1 will be established as well—every evenly subscripted set $\Gamma$ that is consistent in *PD* can be extended to a set that is maximally consistent in *PD* and $\exists$-complete, and every set of the latter sort is quantificationally consistent; so every set $\Gamma$ that is consistent in *PD* is quantificationally consistent.

We shall prove Lemma 11.3 by showing how to construct, for any set of sentences that is both maximally consistent in *PD* and $\exists$-complete, an interpretation on which every member of the set is true. Before doing so, however, we present two results that we shall need later:

11.3.3. If $\Gamma \vdash \mathcal{P}$ and $\Gamma$ is a subset of a set $\Gamma^*$ that is maximally consistent in *PD*, then $\mathcal{P} \in \Gamma^*$.

Proof: See Exercise 9.

11.3.4. Every set $\Gamma^*$ of sentences that is both maximally consistent in *PD* and $\exists$-complete has the following properties:

a. $\mathcal{P} \in \Gamma^*$ if and only if $\sim \mathcal{P} \notin \Gamma^*$.

b. $\mathcal{P} \,\&\, \mathcal{Q} \in \Gamma^*$ if and only if $\mathcal{P} \in \Gamma^*$ and $\mathcal{Q} \in \Gamma^*$.

c. $\mathcal{P} \vee \mathcal{Q} \in \Gamma^*$ if and only if either $\mathcal{P} \in \Gamma^*$ or $\mathcal{Q} \in \Gamma^*$.

d. $\mathcal{P} \supset \mathcal{Q} \in \Gamma^*$ if and only if either $\mathcal{P} \notin \Gamma^*$ or $\mathcal{Q} \in \Gamma^*$.

e. $\mathcal{P} \equiv \mathcal{Q} \in \Gamma^*$ if and only if either $\mathcal{P} \in \Gamma^*$ and $\mathcal{Q} \in \Gamma^*$ or $\mathcal{P} \notin \Gamma^*$ and $\mathcal{Q} \notin \Gamma^*$.

f. $(\forall x)\mathcal{P} \in \Gamma^*$ if and only if for every individual constant $\boldsymbol{a}$, $\mathcal{P}(\boldsymbol{a}/x) \in \Gamma^*$.

g. $(\exists x)\mathcal{P} \in \Gamma^*$ if and only if for at least one individual constant $\boldsymbol{a}$, $\mathcal{P}(\boldsymbol{a}/x) \in \Gamma^*$.

Proof: The proofs that (a)–(e) hold for sets of sentences that are maximally consistent in *PD* and $\exists$-complete parallel exactly the corresponding proofs in Section 6.4, using result 11.3.3 instead of 6.4.5. (In those proofs we did not appeal to a property like $\exists$-completeness, and we do not need to appeal to it here in establishing (a)–(e).)

Proof of f: Assume that $(\forall x)\mathcal{P} \in \Gamma^*$. For any substitution instance $\mathcal{P}(\boldsymbol{a}/x)$ of $(\forall x)\mathcal{P}$, $\{(\forall x\}\mathcal{P}\} \vdash \mathcal{P}(\boldsymbol{a}/x)$ (by $\forall$E); so, by 11.3.3, every substitution instance is a member of $\Gamma^*$ as well. Now assume that $(\forall x)\mathcal{P} \notin \Gamma^*$. Then $\sim (\forall x)\mathcal{P} \in \Gamma^*$, by (a). The following derivation shows that $\{\sim (\forall x)\mathcal{P}\} \vdash (\exists x) \sim \mathcal{P}$:

| | | |
|---|---|---|
| 1 | $\sim (\forall x)\mathcal{P}$ | Assumption |
| 2 | $\quad \sim (\exists x) \sim \mathcal{P}$ | Assumption |
| 3 | $\quad\quad \sim \mathcal{P}(\boldsymbol{a}/x)$ | Assumption |
| 4 | $\quad\quad (\exists x) \sim \mathcal{P}$ | 3 $\exists$I |
| 5 | $\quad\quad \sim (\exists x) \sim \mathcal{P}$ | 2 R |
| 6 | $\quad \mathcal{P}(\boldsymbol{a}/x)$ | 3-5 $\sim$E |
| 7 | $\quad (\forall x)\mathcal{P}$ | 6 $\forall$I |
| 8 | $\quad \sim (\forall x)\mathcal{P}$ | 1 R |
| 9 | $(\exists x) \sim \mathcal{P}$ | 2-8 $\sim$E |

(We assume that the constant $\boldsymbol{a}$ does not occur in $\mathcal{P}$.) Therefore, by 11.3.3, $(\exists x) \sim \mathcal{P}$ is also a member of $\Gamma^*$. Because $\Gamma^*$ is $\exists$-complete, some substitution instance $\sim \mathcal{P}(\boldsymbol{a}/x)$ of $(\exists x) \sim \mathcal{P}$ is a member of $\Gamma^*$ as well, and it therefore follows from (a) that $\mathcal{P}(\boldsymbol{a}/x) \notin \Gamma^*$. So if $(\forall x)\mathcal{P} \notin \Gamma^*$, then there is at least one substitution instance of $(\forall x)\mathcal{P}$ that is not a member of $\Gamma^*$.

Proof of g: Assume that $(\exists x)\mathscr{P} \in \Gamma^*$. Then, because $\Gamma^*$ is $\exists$-complete, at least one substitution instance of $(\exists x)\mathscr{P}$ is also a member of $\Gamma^*$. Now assume that $(\exists x)\mathscr{P} \notin \Gamma^*$. If some substitution instance $\mathscr{P}(a/x)$ of $(\exists x)\mathscr{P}$ were a member of $\Gamma^*$, then, because $\{\mathscr{P}(a/x)\} \vdash (\exists x)\mathscr{P}$ (by $\exists$I), it would follow from 11.3.3 that, contrary to our assumption, $(\exists x)\mathscr{P}$ was also a member of $\Gamma^*$. So if $(\exists x)\mathscr{P}x \notin \Gamma^*$, then none of its substitution instances is a member of $\Gamma^*$.

We now construct, for a set $\Gamma^*$ that is both maximally consistent in *PD* and $\exists$-complete, an interpretation $\mathbf{I}^*$ on which every member of $\Gamma^*$ is true. We begin by associating with each individual constant a distinct positive integer—the positive integer $i$ will be associated with the alphabetically $i$th constant subscript. The number 1 will be associated with 'a', 2 with 'b', . . . , 22 with 'v', 23 with 'a1', and so on. $\mathbf{I}^*$ is then defined as follows:

1. The U.D. is the set of positive integers.
2. For each sentence letter $\mathscr{P}$, $\mathbf{I}^*(\mathscr{P}) = \mathbf{T}$ if and only if $\mathscr{P} \in \Gamma^*$.
3. For each individual constant $a$, $\mathbf{I}^*(a)$ is the positive integer associated with $a$.
4. For each $n$-place predicate $\mathscr{A}$, $\mathbf{I}^*(\mathscr{A})$ includes all and only those $n$-tuples $\langle \mathbf{I}^*(a_1), \ldots, \mathbf{I}^*(a_n)\rangle$ such that $\mathscr{A}a_1, \ldots, a_n \in \Gamma^*$.

The major feature of this interpretation is that for each atomic sentence $\mathscr{P}$ of *PL*, $\mathscr{P}$ will be true on $\mathbf{I}^*$ if and only if $\mathscr{P} \in \Gamma^*$. That is why we defined condition 4 (as well as condition 2) as we did. And to be sure that condition 4 can be met, we must have condition 3, which ensures that each individual constant designates a different member of the U.D. This is necessary because, for example, if 'Fa' is a member of $\Gamma^*$ and 'Fb' is not a member, then if 'a' and 'b' were to designate the same integer, say 1, condition 4 would require that the 1-tuple $\langle 1 \rangle$ both be and not be in the extension of 'F'. (In addition, condition 3 ensures that every member of the U.D. is named by a constant, which we shall shortly see is also important when we look at the truth-values that quantified sentences receive on $\mathbf{I}^*$.) With all the atomic sentences in $\Gamma^*$ true, and all other atomic sentences false, it will follow that truth-functionally compound and quantified sentences are true on $\mathbf{I}^*$ if and only if they are members of $\Gamma^*$. We shall now prove, by mathematical induction on the number of occurrences of logical operators in sentences of *PL*, that each sentence $\mathscr{P}$ of *PL* is true on $\mathbf{I}^*$ if and only if $\mathscr{P} \in \Gamma^*$.

*Basis clause:* Each sentence $\mathscr{P}$ that contains zero occurrences of logical operators is true on $\mathbf{I}^*$ if and only if $\mathscr{P} \in \Gamma^*$.

Proof: Either $\mathscr{P}$ is a sentence letter on $\mathscr{P}$ has the form $\mathscr{A}a_1, \ldots, a_n$. If $\mathscr{P}$ is a sentence letter, then, by part 2 of the definition of $\mathbf{I}^*$, it follows that $\mathscr{P}$ is true on $\mathbf{I}^*$ if and only if $\mathscr{P} \in \Gamma^*$.

If $\mathscr{P}$ has the form $\mathscr{A}a_1, \ldots, a_n$, then $\mathscr{P}$ is true on $\mathbf{I}^*$ if and only if $\langle \mathbf{I}^*(a_1), \ldots, \mathbf{I}^*(a_n)\rangle \in \mathbf{I}^*(\mathscr{A})$. Part 4 of the definition of $\mathbf{I}^*$ stipulates that $\langle \mathbf{I}^*(a_1), \ldots, \mathbf{I}^*(a_n)\rangle \in \mathbf{I}^*(\mathscr{A})$ if and only if $\mathscr{A}a_1, \ldots, a_n \in \Gamma^*$. So in this case as well, $\mathscr{P}$ is true on $\mathbf{I}^*$ if and only if $\mathscr{P} \in \Gamma^*$.

*Inductive step:* If each sentence $\mathscr{P}$ that contains $k$ or fewer occurrences of logical operators is such that $\mathscr{P}$ is true on $\mathbf{I}^*$ if and only if $\mathscr{P} \in \Gamma^*$, then each sentence $\mathscr{P}$ that contains $k + 1$ occurrences of logical operators is such that $\mathscr{P}$ is true on $\mathbf{I}^*$ if and only if $\mathscr{P} \in \Gamma^*$.

Proof: We assume that, for an arbitrary positive integer $k$, the inductive hypothesis is true. We must show that on this assumption, it follows that any sentence $\mathscr{P}$ that contains $k + 1$ occurrences of logical operators is such that $\mathscr{P}$ is true on $\mathbf{I}^*$ if and only if $\mathscr{P} \in \Gamma^*$. We consider the forms that the sentence $\mathscr{P}$ may have.

Cases 1–5: $\mathscr{P}$ has one of the forms $\sim \mathscr{Q}$, $\mathscr{Q} \,\&\, \mathscr{R}$, $\mathscr{Q} \vee \mathscr{R}$, $\mathscr{Q} \supset \mathscr{R}$, or $\mathscr{Q} \equiv \mathscr{R}$. The proofs for these five cases are analogous to the proofs for the parallel cases for *SL* in Section 6.4; so we omit them here.

Case 6: $\mathscr{P}$ has the form $(\forall x)\mathscr{Q}$. Assume that $(\forall x)\mathscr{Q}$ is true on $\mathbf{I}^*$. Then every substitution instance $\mathscr{Q}(a/x)$ of $(\forall x)\mathscr{Q}$ is true on $\mathbf{I}^*$, because, by 11.1.4, $\{(\forall x)\mathscr{Q}\}$ quantificationally entails every one of its substitution instances. Each substitution instance contains fewer than $k + 1$ occurrences of connectives and so, by the inductive hypothesis, each substitution instance is a member of $\Gamma^*$ since it is true on $\mathbf{I}^*$. It follows from part (f) of 11.3.4 that $(\forall x)\mathscr{Q}$ is also a member of $\Gamma^*$.

Now assume that $(\forall x)\mathscr{Q}$ is false on $\mathbf{I}^*$. In this case we shall make use of result 11.1.11, which we repeat here:

11.1.11. Let $\mathbf{I}$ be an interpretation on which each member of the U.D. is assigned to at least one individual constant. Then if every substitution instance of $(\forall x)\mathscr{P}$ is true on $\mathbf{I}$, so is $(\forall x)\mathscr{P}$.

$\mathbf{I}^*$ is an interpretation of the type specified in 11.1.11: Every positive integer in the U.D. is designated by the individual constant with which we have associated that integer. It follows, then, that if every substitution instance of $(\forall x)\mathscr{Q}$ is true on $\mathbf{I}^*$, then so is $(\forall x)\mathscr{Q}$. Therefore, if $(\forall x)\mathscr{Q}$ is false on $\mathbf{I}^*$, at least one of its substitution instances $\mathscr{Q}(a/x)$ must also be false on $\mathbf{I}^*$. Because $\mathscr{Q}(a/x)$ contains fewer than $k + 1$ occurrences of logical operators, it follows from the inductive hypothesis that $\mathscr{Q}(a/x) \notin \Gamma^*$. And so, by part (f) of 11.3.4, $(\forall x)\mathscr{Q} \notin \Gamma^*$.

Case 7: $\mathscr{P}$ has the form $(\exists x)\mathscr{Q}$. Assume that $(\exists x)\mathscr{Q}$ is true on $\mathbf{I}^*$. Then it follows from 11.1.12, which we repeat here, that at least one substitution instance $\mathscr{Q}(a/x)$ of $(\exists x)\mathscr{Q}$ is true on $\mathbf{I}^*$, for every member of the U.D. is designated by an individual constant:

11.1.12. Let $\mathbf{I}$ be an interpretation on which each member of the U.D. is assigned to at least one individual constant. Then if every substitution instance of $(\exists x)\mathscr{P}$ is false on $\mathbf{I}$, so is $(\exists x)\mathscr{P}$.

Because the substitution instance $\mathscr{Q}(a/x)$ contains fewer than $k + 1$ occurrences of logical operators, it follows from the inductive hypothesis that $\mathscr{Q}(a/x) \in \Gamma^*$. So, by part (g) of 11.3.4, $(\exists x)\mathscr{Q}$ is also a member of $\Gamma^*$.

Now assume that $(\exists x)\mathscr{Q}$ is false on $\mathbf{I}^*$. Because each substitution instance $\mathscr{Q}(a/x)$ is such that $\{\mathscr{Q}(a/x)\} \vDash (\exists x)\mathscr{Q}$ (this is result 11.1.5), it follows that every substitution instance $\mathscr{Q}(a/x)$ is also false on $\mathbf{I}^*$. Each of these substitution instances contains fewer than $k + 1$ occurrences of logical operators, and so it follows from the inductive hypothesis that no substitution instance of $(\exists x)\mathscr{Q}$ is a member of $\Gamma^*$. Finally, by part (g) of 11.3.4, it follows that $(\exists x)\mathscr{Q}$ is not a member of $\Gamma^*$ either.

That completes the proof of the inductive step, and we may now conclude that every sentence $\mathscr{P}$ of *PL* is such that it is true on $\mathbf{I}^*$ if and only if it is a member of $\Gamma^*$. So all of the members of $\Gamma^*$ are true on $\mathbf{I}^*$, and we conclude that $\Gamma^*$ is quantificationally consistent. Lemma 11.3 is therefore true; every set that is both maximally consistent in *PD* and ∃-complete is quantificationally consistent. Lemmas 11.2 and 11.3 together establish that every evenly subscripted set of sentences of *PL* that is quantificationally consistent is also consistent in *PD*. Lemma 11.1—that *every* quantificationally consistent set is consistent in *PD*—follows from 11.3.1, Lemmas 11.2 and 11.3, and the following result:

11.3.5. Let $\Gamma$ be a set of sentences of *PL* and let $\Gamma_e$ be the set that results from doubling the subscript of every individual constant that occurs in any member of $\Gamma$. Then if $\Gamma_e$ is quantificationally consistent, $\Gamma$ is quantificationally consistent as well.

Proof: See Exercise 8.

And Lemma 11.1 establishes the completeness of *PD* for predicate logic. If $\Gamma \vDash \mathscr{P}$, then $\Gamma \cup \{\sim\mathscr{P}\}$ is quantificationally inconsistent. By Lemma 11.1, $\Gamma \cup \{\sim\mathscr{P}\}$ is also inconsistent in *PD*, and hence $\Gamma \vdash \mathscr{P}$ in *PD*.

Because *PD* is complete for predicate logic, so is *PD*+ . Every rule of *PD* is a rule of *PD*+ , and so every derivation in *PD* is a derivation in *PD*+ . So if $\Gamma \vDash \mathscr{P}$, then $\Gamma \vdash \mathscr{P}$ in *PD*+ because we known, by Metatheorem 11.2, that $\Gamma \vdash \mathscr{P}$ in *PD*.

We also want to be sure that *PDI* is complete for predicate logic with identity. The completeness proof for *PDI* is similar to the completeness proof for *PD*, but there are some important changes. Results 11.3.1 and 11.3.5 must take into account statements containing the identity predicate; the necessary changes are left as an exercise. Maximal consistency and ∃-completeness are defined for *PDI* as they were for *PD*, and the proof of Lemma 11.2 for *PDI*—that every evenly subscripted set of sentences that is consistent in *PDI* is a subset of a set of sentences that is both maximally consistent in *PDI* and ∃-complete—is just like the proof for *PD* except that *PLI* and *PDI*, rather than *PL* and *PD*, are spoken of. However, the proof of Lemma 11.3 for *PDI* is different because the interpretation $\mathbf{I}^*$ that is constructed for a maximally consistent and ∃-complete set of sentences must be defined differently.

The interpretation $\mathbf{I}^*$ of the maximally consistent and ∃-complete set $\Gamma^*$ that we constructed in the proof of Lemma 11.3 stipulated that a distinct positive integer be associated with each individual constant, and that

3. For each individual constant $\boldsymbol{a}$, $\mathbf{I}^*(\boldsymbol{a})$ is the positive integer associated with $\boldsymbol{a}$.

This will not do in the case of *PDI*, for suppose that $\Gamma$, and consequently its superset $\Gamma^*$, contains a sentence $\boldsymbol{a} = \boldsymbol{b}$, where $\boldsymbol{a}$ and $\boldsymbol{b}$ are different constants. If we interpret the constants of *PLI* in accordance with condition 3, $\boldsymbol{a}$ and $\boldsymbol{b}$ will denote *different* members of the U.D. and hence $\boldsymbol{a} = \boldsymbol{b}$ will be false. But the interpretation is supposed to make all members of $\Gamma^*$, including $\boldsymbol{a} = \boldsymbol{b}$, true. So we shall have to change condition 3 to take care of the case where a sentence like $\boldsymbol{a} = \boldsymbol{b}$ is a member of the set $\Gamma^*$.

Before turning to the construction of an interpretation for $\Gamma^*$, however, we establish the following useful results about sets of sentences that are maximally consistent in *PDI*:

11.3.6. For every individual constant $\boldsymbol{a}$, $\boldsymbol{a} = \boldsymbol{a} \in \Gamma^*$.

Proof: Let $\boldsymbol{a}$ be any constant. $\varnothing \vdash \boldsymbol{a} = \boldsymbol{a}$, by II and $\forall$E. Because the empty set is a subset of $\Gamma^*$, it follows from 11.3.3 that $\boldsymbol{a} = \boldsymbol{a} \in \Gamma^*$.

11.3.7. If a sentence $\boldsymbol{a} = \boldsymbol{b}$ is a member of $\Gamma^*$, then

a. if $\mathcal{Q}$ is a sentence in which $\boldsymbol{a}$ occurs, $\mathcal{Q} \in \Gamma^*$ if and only if every sentence $\mathcal{Q}(\boldsymbol{b}//\boldsymbol{a})$ (every sentence obtained by replacing one or more occurrences of $\boldsymbol{a}$ in $\mathcal{Q}$ with $\boldsymbol{b}$) is a member of $\Gamma^*$, and

b. if $\mathcal{Q}$ is a sentence in which $\boldsymbol{b}$ occurs, $\mathcal{Q} \in \Gamma^*$ if and only if every sentence $\mathcal{Q}(\boldsymbol{a}//\boldsymbol{b})$ is a member of $\Gamma^*$.

Proof: Let $\boldsymbol{a} = \boldsymbol{b}$ be a sentence that is a member of $\Gamma^*$, and let $\mathcal{Q}$ be a sentence in which $\boldsymbol{a}$ occurs. Assume that $\mathcal{Q} \in \Gamma^*$. Every sentence $\mathcal{Q}(\boldsymbol{b}//\boldsymbol{a})$ is derivable from the set $\{\boldsymbol{a} = \boldsymbol{b},\ \mathcal{Q}\}$ by IE. Therefore, by 11.3.3, every sentence $\mathcal{Q}(\boldsymbol{b}//\boldsymbol{a})$ is a member of $\Gamma^*$. Now assume that $\mathcal{Q} \notin \Gamma^*$. Every sentence $\mathcal{Q}(\boldsymbol{b}//\boldsymbol{a})$ is such that $\{\boldsymbol{a} = \boldsymbol{b},\ \mathcal{Q}(\boldsymbol{b}//\boldsymbol{a})\} \vdash \mathcal{Q}$, by IE—use $\boldsymbol{a}$ to replace every occurrence of $\boldsymbol{b}$ that replaced $\boldsymbol{a}$ in $\mathcal{Q}(\boldsymbol{b}//\boldsymbol{a})$, and the result is $\mathcal{Q}$ once again. So if any sentence $\mathcal{Q}(\boldsymbol{b}//\boldsymbol{a})$ is in $\Gamma^*$, then, by 11.3.3, $\mathcal{Q}$ must be as well. Therefore, if $\mathcal{Q} \notin \Gamma^*$, then no sentence $\mathcal{Q}(\boldsymbol{b}//\boldsymbol{a})$ is a member of $\Gamma^*$.

Similar reasoning shows that if $\boldsymbol{a} = \boldsymbol{b} \in \Gamma^*$ and $\mathcal{Q}$ is a sentence in which $\boldsymbol{b}$ occurs, then $\mathcal{Q} \in \Gamma^*$ if and only if every sentence $\mathcal{Q}(\boldsymbol{a}//\boldsymbol{b})$ is a member of $\Gamma^*$.

We now turn to the proof of Lemma 11.3 for *PDI*—that every set of sentences of *PLI* that is both maximally consistent in *PDI* and $\exists$-complete is also quantificationally consistent. Let $\Gamma^*$ be a set of sentences that is both maximally consistent in *PDI* and $\exists$-complete. We associate positive integers with the individual constants of *PLI* as follows:

> First associate the positive integer $\boldsymbol{i}$ with the alphabetically $\boldsymbol{i}$th individual constant of *PLI*. Let '**p**' designate this association, and let $\mathbf{p}(\boldsymbol{a})$ stand for the integer that has been associated with the constant $\boldsymbol{a}$. Thus $\mathbf{p}$('a') is 1, $\mathbf{p}$('b') is 2, and so on.
>
> Now we define a second association, which we shall designate with '**q**'. For each constant $\boldsymbol{a}$, $\mathbf{q}(\boldsymbol{a}) = \mathbf{p}(\boldsymbol{a}')$, where $\boldsymbol{a}'$ is the alphabetically earliest constant such that $\boldsymbol{a} = \boldsymbol{a}'$ is a member of $\Gamma^*$.

Note that for each constant $\boldsymbol{a}$, 11.3.6 assures us that $\boldsymbol{a} = \boldsymbol{a} \in \Gamma^*$, and so we can be certain that **q** assigns a value to $\boldsymbol{a}$ because there will always be at least one $\boldsymbol{a}'$ such that $\boldsymbol{a} = \boldsymbol{a}' \in \Gamma^*$. According to the definition, $\mathbf{q}$('a') will always be 1, since result 11.3.6 assures us that 'a = a' is a member of $\Gamma^*$, and, because 'a' is the alphabetically earliest constant of *PLI*, there can be no earlier constant that stands to the right of the identity predicate in a sentence containing 'a' to the left. But for any other constant, the value that it receives from **q** depends on the identity sentences that the particular set $\Gamma^*$ contains. Suppose that 'b = a', 'b = b', 'b = e', and 'b = $m_{22}$' are the only identity sentences in $\Gamma^*$ that contain 'b' to the left of the identity predicate—in this case, there is an alphabetically earlier constant to the right, namely, 'a', and this is the alphabetically earliest constant so occurring. So $\mathbf{q}$('b') = $\mathbf{p}$('a') = 1. If 'c = c', 'c = f', and 'c = $g_3$' are the only identity sentences in $\Gamma^*$ that contain 'c' to the left of the identity predicate then 'c' is the alphabetically earliest constant occurring to the right and so $\mathbf{q}$('c') = $\mathbf{p}$('c') = 3. The definition of **q** will play a role in ensuring that identity sentences come out true on the interpretation that we shall construct if and only if they are members of $\Gamma^*$, as a consequence of

> 11.3.8. For any constants $\boldsymbol{a}$ and $\boldsymbol{b}$, $\mathbf{q}(\boldsymbol{a}) = \mathbf{q}(\boldsymbol{b})$ if and only if $\boldsymbol{a} = \boldsymbol{b} \in \Gamma^*$.
>
> Proof: Let $\boldsymbol{a}'$ be the alphabetically earliest constant such that $\boldsymbol{a} = \boldsymbol{a}' \in \Gamma^*$. (Remember that 11.3.6 guarantees that there is at least one such constant.) Then
>
> a. $\mathbf{q}(\boldsymbol{a}) = \mathbf{p}(\boldsymbol{a}')$.
>
> Let $\boldsymbol{b}'$ be the alphabetically earliest constant such that $\boldsymbol{b} = \boldsymbol{b}' \in \Gamma^*$. Then
>
> b. $\mathbf{q}(\boldsymbol{b}) = \mathbf{p}(\boldsymbol{b}')$.
>
> It follows from (a) and (b) that
>
> c. $\mathbf{q}(\boldsymbol{a}) = \mathbf{q}(\boldsymbol{b})$ if and only if $\mathbf{p}(\boldsymbol{a}') = \mathbf{p}(\boldsymbol{b}')$.
>
> And, because **p** associates different values with different constants,
>
> d. $\mathbf{p}(\boldsymbol{a}') = \mathbf{p}(\boldsymbol{b}')$ if and only if $\boldsymbol{a}'$ and $\boldsymbol{b}'$ are the same constant.
>
> From (c) and (d) we conclude that
>
> e. $\mathbf{q}(\boldsymbol{a}) = \mathbf{q}(\boldsymbol{b})$ if and only if $\boldsymbol{a}'$ and $\boldsymbol{b}'$ are the same constant.

Assume that $\mathbf{q}(a) = \mathbf{q}(b)$. It follows from (e) that $a'$ and $b'$ are the same constant. Therefore, because $b = b' \in \Gamma^*$, it follows trivially that $b = a'$, which is the same sentence, is a member of $\Gamma^*$. And because $a = a' \in \Gamma^*$, it follows from 11.3.7 that $a = b \in \Gamma^*$ ($a = b$ is a sentence $a = a'(b//a')$).

Now assume that $a = b \in \Gamma^*$. Then, because $a = a' \in \Gamma^*$, it follows from 11.3.7 that $b = a' \in \Gamma^*$; and because $b = b' \in \Gamma^*$ as well, it also follows from 11.3.7 that $a = b' \in \Gamma^*$. $a'$ was defined to be the alphabetically earliest constant that appears to the right of the identity predicate in an identity statement containing $a$ and so from the fact that $a = b' \in \Gamma^*$ we conclude that $b'$ is not alphabetically earlier than $a'$. $b'$ was defined to be the alphabetically earliest constant that appears to the right of the identity predicate in an identity statement containing $b$ and so from the fact that $b = a' \in \Gamma^*$ we conclude that $a'$ is not alphabetically earlier than $b'$. These two observations establish that $a'$ and $b'$ must be the same constant. So, from (e), we may conclude that $\mathbf{q}(a) = \mathbf{q}(b)$.

Result 11.3.8 guarantees that if there is an identity statement in $\Gamma^*$ that contains $a$ and $b$, then $\mathbf{q}(a) = \mathbf{q}(b)$, and if there is no identity statement in $\Gamma^*$ that contains $a$ and $b$, then $\mathbf{q}(a) \neq \mathbf{q}(b)$. And this fact will be crucial in our construction of an interpretation on which every member of a set that is both maximally consistent in *PDI* and ∃-complete is true. We turn now to the construction.

Let $\Gamma^*$ be a set that is both maximally consistent in *PDI* and ∃-complete, and define the interpretation $\mathbf{I}^*$ as follows:

1. The U.D. is the set of positive integers that $\mathbf{q}$ associates with at least one individual constant of *PLI*.
2. For each sentence letter $\mathscr{P}$, $\mathbf{I}^*(\mathscr{P}) = \mathbf{T}$ if and only if $\mathscr{P} \in \Gamma^*$.
3. For each individual constant $a$, $\mathbf{I}^*(a) = \mathbf{q}(a)$.
4. For each $n$-place predicate $\mathscr{A}$ other than the identity predicate, $\mathbf{I}^*$ is the set that includes all and only those $n$-tuples $\langle \mathbf{I}^*(a_1), \ldots, \mathbf{I}^*(a_n) \rangle$ such that $\mathscr{A}a_1, \ldots, a_n \in \Gamma^*$.

We must ensure that condition 4 can be met, that is, there are not two atomic sentences $\mathscr{A}a_1, \ldots, a_n$ and $\mathscr{A}a'_1, \ldots, a'_n$ such that one is in $\Gamma^*$ and the other is not in $\Gamma^*$, yet $\langle \mathbf{I}^*(a_1), \ldots, \mathbf{I}^*(a_n) \rangle = \langle \mathbf{I}^*(a'_1), \ldots, \mathbf{I}^*(a'_n) \rangle$. In the case of *PD*, it was simple to show this, for distinct constants were interpreted to designate distinct individuals. However, $\mathbf{q}$ may assign the same positive integer to more than one constant and as a consequence, condition 3 may interpret several constants to designate the same value. Here our previous results will be useful. Suppose that the constants $a_1, \ldots, a_n$ and $a'_1, \ldots, a'_n$ are such that $\langle \mathbf{I}^*(a_1), \ldots, \mathbf{I}^*(a_n) \rangle = \langle \mathbf{I}^*(a'_1), \ldots, \mathbf{I}^*(a'_n) \rangle$. Then, by clause 3 of the definition of $\mathbf{I}^*$, we know that for each $i$, $\mathbf{q}(a_i) = \mathbf{q}(a'_i)$. It follows from 11.3.8 that for each $i$, $a_i = a'_i \in \Gamma^*$. Because $a_1 = a'_1$ is a member of $\Gamma^*$, 11.3.7 assures us that $\mathscr{A}a_1, \ldots, a_n$ is a member of $\Gamma^*$ if and only if $\mathscr{A}a'_1a_2, \ldots, a_n$ is a member of $\Gamma^*$. And because $a_2 = a'_2$ is also a member of $\Gamma^*$, 11.3.7 assures us that $\mathscr{A}a'_1a_2, \ldots, a_n$ is a member of $\Gamma^*$ if and only if $\mathcal{A}a'_1a'_2, \ldots, a_n$ is a member of $\Gamma^*$, and so on until we note that because $a_n = a'_n$ is in $\Gamma^*$, $\mathcal{A}a'_1a'_2, \ldots, a_n$ is a member of $\Gamma^*$ if and only if $\mathcal{A}a'_1a'_2, \ldots, a'_n$ is a member of $\Gamma^*$. We conclude that if $\langle \mathbf{I}^*(a_1), \ldots, \mathbf{I}^*(a_n) \rangle = \langle \mathbf{I}^*(a'_1), \ldots, \mathbf{I}^*(a'_n) \rangle$, then $\mathcal{A}a_1, \ldots, a_n \in \Gamma^*$ if and only if $\mathcal{A}a'_1, \ldots, a'_n \in \Gamma^*$. So condition 4 can indeed be met.

To establish Lemma 11.3 for *PDI*—that every set $\Gamma^*$ that is both maximally consistent in *PDI* and $\exists$-complete is also quantificationally consistent—we can prove by mathematical induction that a sentence $\mathcal{P}$ of *PDI* is true on $\mathbf{I}^*$ if and only if $\mathcal{P} \in \Gamma^*$. The proof is similar to that for *PD*, with only the following change. The basis clause must consider sentences of the form $a = b$, in addition to the forms that were considered in the proof for *PD*. So we add the following to the basis clause:

> If $\mathcal{P}$ has the form $a = b$, then $\mathcal{P}$ is true on $\mathbf{I}^*$ if and only if $\mathbf{I}^*(a) = \mathbf{I}^*(b)$. By the way in which $\mathbf{I}^*$ was constructed, $\mathbf{I}^*(a) = \mathbf{I}^*(b)$ if and only if $\mathbf{q}(a) = \mathbf{q}(b)$. By result 11.3.8, $\mathbf{q}(a) = \mathbf{q}(b)$ if and only if $a = b \in \Gamma^*$. So $a = b$ is true on $\mathbf{I}^*$ if and only if $a = b \in \Gamma^*$.

Because every member of $\Gamma^*$ is true on $\mathbf{I}^*$, $\Gamma^*$ is quantificationally consistent. And, with Lemmas 11.2 and 11.3 established for *PDI*, we know that Lemma 1.1 is also true for *PDI* and hence that *PDI* is complete for predicate logic with identity.

## 11.3E EXERCISES

***1.** Prove that if $\Gamma \vDash \mathcal{P}$, then $\Gamma \cup \{\sim \mathcal{P}\}$ is quantificationally inconsistent.

**2.** Prove that if $\Gamma \cup \{\sim \mathcal{P}\}$ is inconsistent in *PD*, then $\Gamma \vdash \mathcal{P}$.

**3.** Using Metatheorem 11.2, prove the following:
a. Every argument of *PL* that is quantificationally valid is valid in *PD*.
b. Every sentence of *PL* that is quantificationally true is a theorem in *PD*.
*c. Every pair of sentences $\mathcal{P}$ and $\mathcal{Q}$ of *PL* that are quantificationally equivalent are equivalent in *PD*.

**4.** Prove that the sentences of *PL* can be enumerated. (Hint: See Section 6.4.)

**5.** Prove the following:

If $\Gamma \vdash \mathcal{P}$ and $\Gamma$ is a subset of $\Gamma'$, then $\Gamma' \vdash \mathcal{P}$.

**6.**a. Prove 11.3.2.
b. Prove that any set $\Gamma^*$ constructed as in our proof of Lemma 11.2 is $\exists$-complete.

**7.** Prove that the sequence of sentences constructed in the proof of 11.3.1 is a derivation in *PD* by showing (by mathematical induction) that each sentence in the new sequence can be justified with the same rule as the corresponding sentence in the original derivation.

***8.** Prove 11.3.5, using result 11.1.13.

***9.** Prove 11.3.3.

**10.** Explain why, in Lemmas 11.2 and 11.3, we constructed a set that is both ∃-complete and maximally consistent in *PD*, rather than a set that is just maximally consistent in *PD*.

**11.** Let system *PD** be just like *PD* except that the rule ∀E is replaced by the following rule:

*Universal Elimination** (∀E*)

$(\forall x)\mathscr{P}$

$\sim(\exists x) \sim \mathscr{P}$

Prove that the system *PD** is complete for predicate logic.

***12.** Let system *PD** be just like *PD* except that the rules ∃E and ∃I are replaced by the following two rules:

*Existential Elimination** (∃E*)

$(\exists x)\mathscr{P}$

$\sim(\forall x) \sim \mathscr{P}$

*Existential Introduction** (∃I*)

$\sim(\forall x) \sim \mathscr{P}$

$(\exists x)\mathscr{P}$

Prove that system *PD** is complete for predicate logic.

**13.** Using the results in the proof of Metatheorem 11.2, prove the following theorem (known as the *Löwenheim Theorem*):

If a sentence $\mathscr{P}$ of *PL* is not quantificationally false, then there is an interpretation with the set of positive integers as the U.D. on which $\mathscr{P}$ is true.

***14.** Prove the following metatheorem (known as the *Löwenheim-Skolem Theorem*):

If a set Γ of sentences of *PL* is quantificationally consistent, then there is an interpretation with the set of positive integers as the U.D. on which every member of Γ is true.

***15.** Show the changes that must be made in the proofs of 11.3.1 and 11.3.5 so that these results will hold for *PLI* and *PDI*. (Hint: Exercise 8 suggested that you use result 11.1.13 in proving 11.3.5; so you must check whether 11.1.13 needs to be changed.)

**16.** Show that the Löwenheim Theorem (and consequently the more general Löwenheim-Skolem Theorem) does *not* hold for *PLI*.

We have presented the tree method as a means of testing for semantic properties of sentences and sets of sentences in both sentential logic and predicate logic. In this section and the next we shall prove that the tree method of Chapter Nine fulfills a claim we have made: A finite set of sentences of *PL* is quantificationally inconsistent if and only if every systematic tree for that set closes. In this section we shall prove that the tree method is *sound* for predicate logic—that if a systematic tree for a set of sentences of *PL* closes, then the set is quantificationally inconsistent. We shall prove the same for predicate logic with identity. In both cases, we can then be assured that if we pronounce a set of sentences inconsistent because a tree for that set closes, our pronouncement is correct. In the next section we shall prove that the tree method is *complete* for predicate logic—that if a set of sentences is quantificationally inconsistent, then every systematic tree for that set is bound to close. Knowing that the method is complete, we shall also know that open systematic trees do establish quantificational consistency. (With a simple adaptation of parts of our proofs, the soundness and completeness of the tree method for sentential logic can also be established. This will be addressed in the exercises.)

Our *Soundness Metatheorem* for the tree method is:

| Metatheorem 11.3: If a systematic tree for a set Γ of sentences of *PL* closes, then Γ is quantificationally inconsistent. |
|---|

(As we shall see in the exercises for this section, soundness also holds for nonsystematic trees.) Our proof of Metatheorem 11.3 will rely heavily on the following observation about the decomposition rules used in constructing trees: Each rule is consistency-preserving in the sense that if we have a consistent set of sentences, and apply a decomposition rule to one of the sentences in that set, at least one of the sentences that results (there will be only one in the case of a nonbranching rule) can consistently be added to the set. As we build a tree for a set of sentences we are, in effect, building supersets of the one we started with—the set of sentences occurring on a branch is a superset of the original set. Given the sense in which the decomposition rules are consistency-preserving, at least one of the supersets formed on a branch by repeated application of decomposition rules will be quantificationally consistent. This will be important in establishing Metatheorem 11.3, for the supersets that comprise the branches of a closed tree are all quantificationally inconsistent, each such branch containing some literal and its negation. Because the decomposition rules are consistency-preserving in the sense described, it follows that the only way we can end up with every superset being quantificationally inconsistent (with a closed tree) is by starting with a set that is quantificationally inconsistent. And that is what Metatheorem 11.3 says.

Our observation that the decomposition rules are consistency-preserving must, of course, be proved. To facilitate our proof, we introduce the concept of a *level* of a tree. The first (occurrence of a) sentence on any tree is at level 1. For any other sentence $\mathscr{P}$, $\mathscr{P}$ is at level $i + 1$, where $i$ is the level of the sentence occurring immediately before $\mathscr{P}$ on the same branch of the tree. The line numbers used to annotate trees in Chapters Four and Nine do not always correspond to levels, because we adopted the convention in those chapters that only one decomposition rule can be cited on each line. Consider, for example, the tree on page 000. Lines 1–3 do correspond directly to levels 1–3 of that tree. Line 4, however, displays only one of the sentences occurring at level 4. The sentence in line 10 on the right-hand branch is *also* at level 4, for the sentence that occurs immediately before it on the same branch is at level 3. Similar observations hold for sentences further down the branches of the tree.

We shall establish that our decomposition rules are consistency-preserving by showing that each level $i$ of a systematic tree for a quantificationally consistent set of sentences is such that either there is at least one branch that was completed prior to that level on which the sentences form a quantificationally consistent set (a quantificationally consistent superset has resulted from applying as many rules as could be applied), or there is at least one branch that extends at least as far as level $i$ such that the sentences on that branch up to and including level $i$ form a quantificationally consistent set (the rules thus far have preserved consistency).

As an example of what we want to prove, here is a completed open tree for the set {(∀x)Fx ∨ Ga, (∃y) ~ Fy}:

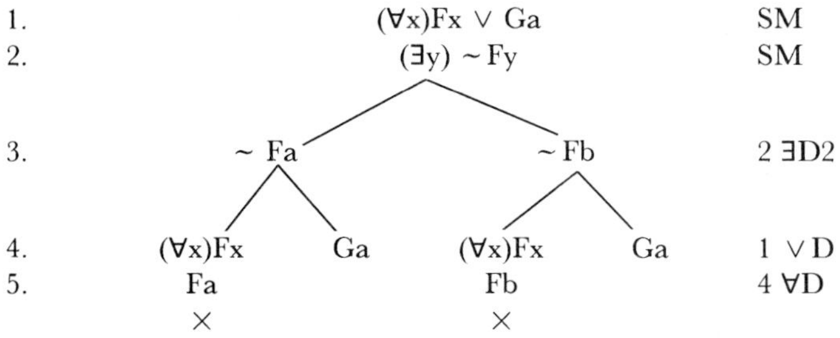


Each of the levels 1–5 is such that our claim holds. At level 1 there is at least one branch such that the set of sentences occurring on that branch through and including level 1 form a quantificationally consistent set: {(∀x)Fx ∨ Ga}. At level 2 there is at least one branch such that the set of sentences occurring on that branch form a quantificationally consistent set: {(∀x)Fx ∨ Ga, (∃y) ~ Fy}. At level 3 there are two (and so at least one) such branches: {(∀x)Fx ∨ Ga, (∃y) ~ Fy, ~ Fa} and {(∀x)Fx ∨ Ga, (∃y) ~ Fy, ~ Fb}. At level 4 there are also two such branches: {(∀x)Fx ∨ Ga, (∃y) ~ Fy, ~ Fa, Ga} and {(∀x)Fx ∨ Ga, (∃y) ~ Fy, ~ Fb, Ga}. The branches that include '(∀x)Fx' are not candidates, but we have not claimed that quantificationally consistent sets will be found on *all* branches. At level 5 there is no branch that extends to that level that contains a quantificationally consistent set of sentences, but there is at least one branch that was completed at an earlier level, level 4, on which the sentences form a quantificationally consistent set. So the claim is true of all levels of this tree.

The fact that the claim holds for every level of a systematic tree for a quantificationally consistent set will allow us to conclude that if a tree for a set of sentences closes, then the set must be quantificationally inconsistent. Consider: If a tree closes, then the tree has only a finite number of levels, and the longest branch ends at a finite level. In the following closed tree, the longest branch ends at level 4:

| | | | |
|---|---|---|---|
| 1. | (∀x)Fx ∨ Fa | | SM |
| 2. | ~ Fa | | SM |
| 3. | (∀x)Fx | Fa | 1 ∨D |
| 4. | Fa | × | 3 ∀D |
| | × | | |

No branch that closes before the last level contains a quantificationally consistent set of sentences (each such branch containing a literal and its negation), and the branch that closes at the last level does not contain a quantificationally consistent set. So at the last level of a closed tree our claim about the levels of a tree for a quantificationally consistent set is not true; and we may conclude that the set for which the tree was constructed is therefore quantificationally *in*consistent.

To prove our claim about the levels of any systematic tree for a quantificationally consistent set of sentences, we also introduce the concept of a path to a level of a tree. For any branch that extends to level $i$ or further, we call that part of the branch that extends to level $i$ a *path* to level $i$, and we say that the path *contains* the set of sentences that occur on it. In the last tree displayed, there is exactly one path to level 1, and it contains the set of sentences {(∀x)Fx ∨ Fa}. There is exactly one path to level 2, and it contains the set of sentences {(∀x)Fx ∨ Fa, ~ Fa}. There are two paths to level 3; one contains the set of sentences {(∀x)Fx ∨ Fa, ~ Fa, (∀x)Fx} and the other contains the set {(∀x)Fx ∨ Fa, ~ Fa, Fa}. There is one path to level 4, and it contains the set {(∀x)Fx ∨ Fa, ~ Fa, (∀x)Fx, Fa}. Finally, a *completed* path to level $i$ of a tree is a completed branch of that tree that ends at level $i$. We state our claim about the levels of a systematic tree for a quantificationally consistent set in terms of paths, in the Consistent Branch Lemma:

Lemma 11.4: Each level $i$ of a tree for a quantificationally consistent set of sentences of *PL* is such that either

a. there is at least one completed path to a level earlier than $i$ that contains a quantificationally consistent set of sentences.

or

b. there is at least one path to level $i$ that contains a quantificationally consistent set of sentences.

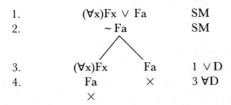

We shall prove Lemma 11.4 by establishing a more specific claim (which will later be useful in proving that systematic trees for sets of sentences with finite models always have a completed open branch). Let Γ be a finite set of sentences of *PL* that is quantificationally consistent, and let **I** be an interpretation. We call interpretation **I**′ a *path-variant* of **I** for path **p** of a tree for the set of sentences of Γ if **I**′ is just like **I** except that for each constant $\boldsymbol{a}$ that occurs in some sentence on the path but not in any member of Γ, there is a member **u** of the U.D. such that $\mathbf{I}'(\boldsymbol{a}) = \mathbf{u}$ and such that for every other constant $\boldsymbol{b}$ occurring on the path but not in Γ, $\mathbf{I}'(\boldsymbol{b}) \neq \mathbf{u}$. We shall show that

> 11.4.1. If a finite set of sentences of *PL* is true on an interpretation **I**, then each level $\boldsymbol{i}$ of a systematic tree from Γ is such that either
>
> a. there is at least one completed path **p** to a level earlier than $\boldsymbol{i}$ that contains a set of sentences all of which are true on a path-variant of **I** for **p**, or
>
> b. there is at least path **p** to level $\boldsymbol{i}$ that contains a set of sentences all of which are true on a path-variant of **I** for **p**.

We establish result 11.4.1 by mathematical induction on the levels of a systematic tree for a quantificationally consistent set of sentences of *PL*. Letting Γ be a finite set of sentences of *PL* and **I** an interpretation on which every member of Γ is true,

*Basis clause:* Level 1 of a systematic tree for Γ is such that either (a) or (b) holds.

*Inductive step:* If every level less than or equal to level $\boldsymbol{k}$ of a systematic tree for Γ is such that either (a) or (b) holds, then level $\boldsymbol{k}+1$ of a systematic tree for Γ is also such that either (a) or (b) holds.

---

*Conclusion:* Every level of a systematic tree for Γ is such that either (a) or (b) holds.

Proof of basis clause: There is exactly one path to level 1 of any tree, and that path contains the unit set $\{\mathcal{P}\}$, where $\mathcal{P}$ is a member of the set Γ for which the tree is being constructed. $\mathcal{P}$ is true on **I** since every member of Γ is, and **I** is in this case a path-variant of itself (since the path contains no constants that do not occur in Γ). So there is a path to level 1 that contains a set of sentences all of which are true on a path-variant of **I**, and (b) holds for level 1.

Proof of inductive step: We assume the inductive hypothesis for an arbitrary positive integer $\boldsymbol{k}$: For each level $\boldsymbol{i}$ less than $\boldsymbol{k}+1$ of a tree for Γ, either (a) or (b) holds. We must show that on this assumption, either (a) or (b) holds for level $\boldsymbol{k}+1$ of a tree for Γ as well. We first note that if (a) holds for an earlier level $\boldsymbol{i}$, then (a) holds for level $\boldsymbol{k}+1$ as well. That is, if there is at least one completed path to a level earlier than $\boldsymbol{i}$ that contains a set of sentences all of which are true on a path-variant of **I** for that path, then that path is also a completed path to a level earlier than $k + 1$.

Now we must consider the case where (a) does not hold for any level prior to $k + 1$. In this case, it follows from the inductive hypothesis that (b) holds for every level prior to $k + 1$, and, in particular, that (b) is true of level $k$. If, in addition, there is a *completed* path to level $k$ that contains a set of sentences all of which are true on a path-variant of **I** for that path, then (a) is true of level $k + 1$. If there is not such a path to level $k$, we still know, because (b) is true of level $k$, that at least one (noncompleted) path to level $k$ contains a set of sentences all of which are true on a path-variant of **I** for that path. Call this path $\Gamma_k$ and the variant $\mathbf{I}_{\Gamma_k}$. Because the path is not complete at level $k$, it is extended to level $k + 1$ by application of some tree rule. We shall now consider the rules that might be used to extend the path to level $k + 1$ and show that in each case application of the rule results in at least one path to level $k + 1$ that contains a set of sentences all of which are true on a path-variant of **I** for that path—thereby establishing that (b) holds for level $k + 1$ as well.

We divide the rules into six cases.

Case 1: The path $\Gamma_k$ is extended to level $k + 1$ by adding a set member at that level. Because decomposition rules apply *after* all set members have been entered, the only sentences on the path $\Gamma_k$ are members of $\Gamma$, and the sentence entered at level $k + 1$ is also a member of $\Gamma$. So there is a path to level $k + 1$ that contains a subset of $\Gamma$, all members of which are true in **I**, which in this case is a path-variant of itself.

Case 2: The path $\Gamma_k$ is extended to level $k + 1$ as a result of applying one of the nonbranching rules $\sim\sim$D, &D, $\sim\vee$D, $\sim\supset$D, $\sim\forall$D, or $\sim\exists$D to a sentence $\mathcal{P}$ on $\Gamma_k$. In each case, $\{\mathcal{P}\}$ quantificationally entails the sentence $\mathcal{Q}$ entered on level $k + 1$ (see Exercise 3). Therefore all of the sentences on $\Gamma_k$ and the sentence $\mathcal{Q}$ are true on $\mathbf{I}_{\Gamma_k}$, which is a path-variant of **I** for the extended path that we are considering (because none of the rules in this case add a new individual constant to the tree, and $\mathbf{I}_{\Gamma_k}$ itself was a path-variant of **I** for $\Gamma_k$). Thus there is a path to level $k + 1$—the path that extends $\Gamma_k$ to include $\mathcal{Q}$—that contains a set of sentences all of which are true on a path-variant of **I** for this path.

Case 3: The path is extended to form two paths to level $k + 1$ as a result of applying one of the branching rules $\sim$&D, $\vee$D, or $\supset$D to a sentence $\mathcal{P}$ on $\Gamma_k$. Letting $\mathcal{Q}$ be one of the sentences that was entered on level $k + 1$ and $\mathcal{R}$ the other, it can be shown that on any interpretation on which $\mathcal{P}$ is true, either $\mathcal{Q}$ is true or $\mathcal{R}$ is true (see Exercise 4). Therefore either all the sentences on $\Gamma_k$ plus $\mathcal{Q}$ are true on $\mathbf{I}_{\Gamma_k}$, which is a path-variant of **I** for the new path containing $\mathcal{Q}$, or all the sentences on $\Gamma_k$ plus $\mathcal{R}$ are true on $\mathbf{I}_{\Gamma_k}$, which is a path-variant of **I** for the new path containing $\mathcal{R}$. Thus there is a path to level $k + 1$—either the path that extends $\Gamma_k$ to include $\mathcal{Q}$ or the path that extends $\Gamma_k$ to include $\mathcal{R}$—that contains a set of sentences all of which are true on a path-variant of **I** for that path.

Case 4: The path is extended to level $k + 1$ as a result of applying either $\equiv$D or $\sim\equiv$D. See Exercise 5.

Case 5: The path is extended to level $k + 1$ as a result of applying $\forall$D. Then $\Gamma_k$ contains a sentence $(\forall x)\mathcal{P}$ such that $\mathcal{P}(a/x)$ is entered at level $k + 1$, where $a$ is either 'a' if no constants occur on $\Gamma_k$, or the alphabetically earliest constant that does occur. Because $(\forall x)\mathcal{P}x \vDash \mathcal{P}(a/x)$ (result 11.1.4), $\mathcal{P}(a/x)$ is true on $\mathbf{I}_{\Gamma_k}$. If no constant occurred on $\Gamma_k$ then $\mathbf{I}_{\Gamma_k}$ is also a path-variant of **I** for the new path to level $k + 1$, because $\mathbf{I}_{\Gamma_k}(a) \neq \mathbf{I}_{\Gamma_k}(b)$ for any other constant $b$ occurring on $\Gamma_k$ but not in $\Gamma$—there are no other constants $b$ occurring on $\Gamma_k$. If, on the other hand, $a$ is a constant that already occurs on $\Gamma_k$, then we have added no new constant to the path and so $\mathbf{I}_{\Gamma_k}$ is in this case also a path variant of **I** for the new path to level $k + 1$. Either way, there is a path to level $k + 1$ that contains a set of sentences all of which are true on a path-variant of **I** for that path.

Case 6: The path is extended to level $k + 1$ as a result of applying $\exists$D2. Then $\Gamma_k$ contains a sentence $(\exists x)\mathcal{P}$ such that $\mathcal{P}(a/x), \ldots, \mathcal{P}(m/x)$, $\mathcal{P}(n/x)$ are entered on distinct paths to level $k + 1$, where $a, \ldots, m$ are all the individual constants that occur in sentences on $\Gamma_k$ and $n$ is the alphabetically earliest constant that does not occur on $\Gamma_k$. We consider two possibilities:

a. If any one (or more) of $\mathcal{P}(a/x), \ldots, \mathcal{P}(m/x)$ is true on $\mathbf{I}_{\Gamma_k}$, then the path to level $k + 1$ on which that substitution instance was entered is a path that contains a set of sentences all of which are true on a path-variant of **I** for that path ($\mathbf{I}_{\Gamma_k}$ is a path-variant of the newly formed path because the substitution instance does not introduce a new constant).

b. Now consider the case where none of $\mathcal{P}(a/x), \ldots, \mathcal{P}(m/x)$ are true on $\mathbf{I}_{\Gamma_k}$. Because $(\exists x)\mathcal{P}$ is true on $\mathbf{I}_{\Gamma_k}$, and because $a$ does not occur in any sentence on $\Gamma_k$, our proof of result 11.1.10 (Exercise 5 of Section 11.1E) shows that $\mathcal{P}(n/x)$ is true on an interpretation $\mathbf{I}'_{\Gamma_k}$ that is just like $\mathbf{I}_{\Gamma_k}$ except that $\mathbf{I}'_{\Gamma_k}(n) = \mathbf{u}$, where **u** is a member of the U.D. such that $\mathbf{d}[\mathbf{u}/x]$ satisfies $\mathcal{P}$ on $\mathbf{I}_{\Gamma_k}$. This member **u** is not assigned to any other individual constant $a_i$ occurring on $\Gamma_k$ but not in $\Gamma$ (for, if it were, it would follow from result 11.1.13 that $\mathcal{P}(a_i/b)$ is true on $\mathbf{I}_{\Gamma_k}$, which contradicts our assumption here). Thus $\mathbf{I}'_{\Gamma_k}$ is a path-variant of **I** for the path extended to level $k + 1$ by the addition of $\mathcal{P}(n/x)$, and one on which every sentence in the new path is true.

Either way, then, there is a path to level $k + 1$ that contains a set of sentences all of which are true on a path-variant of **I** for that path.

We have considered each rule that might be used to extend the path $\Gamma_k$ to level $k + 1$, and have shown that in each case there is at least one path to level $k + 1$ that contains a set of sentences all of which are true on a path-variant of **I** for that path. That completes the proof of the inductive step.

Therefore, result 11.4.1 holds for every level of a tree for a set of sentences all of which are true on interpretation **I**.

Lemma 11.4 follows immediately from result 11.4.1, for in establishing the existence of paths containing sentences all of which are true on some path-variant of **I**, we have established that the sentences on each such path form a quantificationally consistent set.

Metatheorem 11.3 follows from Lemma 11.4 and from the fact that the null tree, which is the single tree for the empty set of sentences of *PL*, is not closed (the null branch does not contain any sentences and therefore does not contain some atomic sentence and its negation). If a tree for a set Γ of sentences is closed, then every branch on that tree is closed, and hence contains a literal and its negation. Any path to the last level of the tree is a closed branch and hence the set of sentences on that branch is quantificationally inconsistent (because it contains some literal and its negation). So (b) does not hold for the last level of such a tree. Nor does (a); all completed paths to earlier levels are closed branches and therefore the sets of sentences on those branches are also quantificationally inconsistent. Because the last level of any closed tree is such that neither (a) nor (b) holds, it follows, by Lemma 11.4, that the set for which the tree was constructed is quantificationally inconsistent. We conclude that the tree method is sound for predicate logic.

To establish that the tree method for predicate logic with identity is also sound, we need to add, to the proof of the inductive step for result 11.4.1, a case for paths that are extended by an application of = D:

Case 7: The path $\Gamma_k$ is extended to level $k + 1$ as a result of applying = D. Then $\Gamma_k$ contains sentences $a = b$ and $\mathcal{P}$ such that a sentence $\mathcal{P}(a//b)$ was entered at level $k + 1$. It follows from 11.2.2, which we repeat here, that $\mathcal{P}(a//b)$ is true on $\mathbf{I}_{\Gamma_k}$:

11.2.2. For any constants $a$ and $b$, if $\mathcal{P}$ is a sentence that contains $a$, then $\{a = b, \mathcal{P}\} \vDash \mathcal{P}(b//a)$, and if $\mathcal{P}$ is a sentence that contains $b$, then $\{a = b, \mathcal{P}\} \vDash \mathcal{P}(a//b)$.

In addition, $\mathbf{I}_{\Gamma_k}$ is a path-variant for the new path to level $k + 1$, because = D does not introduce new constants. Therefore there is a path to level $k + 1$ that contains a set of sentences all of which are true on some path-variant of **I** for that path.

Finally, we must note that a branch of a tree for predicate logic with identity will close in one of *two* cases: Either the branch contains some literal and its negation, or the branch contains a sentence of the form $\sim a = a$. In showing that Metatheorem 11.3 for predicate logic followed from Lemma 11.4, we made use of the fact that each closed branch contained a literal and its negation—arguing that the set of the sentences on that branch was therefore quantificationally inconsistent. In the present case we must also be sure that the set of sentences on a branch that closes because it contains a sentence $\sim \mathbf{a} = \mathbf{a}$ is quantificationally inconsistent. This is not hard to show: $\mathbf{a} = \mathbf{a}$ is quantificationally true, so $\sim \mathbf{a} = \mathbf{a}$ is quantificationally false, and therefore any set that contains $\sim \mathbf{a} = \mathbf{a}$ is quantificationally inconsistent. This and the addition of case 7 in the proof of result 11.4.1 suffice to show that the tree method is sound for predicate logic with identity.

Result 11.1.4 will also allow us to prove another claim made in Chapter Nine:

> Metatheorem 11.4: If a finite set Γ of sentences of *PL* has a finite model, that is, an interpretation with a finite U.D. on which every member of Γ is true, then every systematic tree for Γ will contain a *completed* open branch.[1]

In such a case, we will be able to conclude in a *finite* number of steps that the set is quantificationally consistent.

Proof of Metatheorem 11.4: Let Γ be a finite set of sentences such that there is an interpretation **I** with a finite U.D. on which every member of Γ is true. By result 11.1.4, every level $\mathbf{i}$ of a systematic tree for Γ is such that either (a) there is at least one completed path to a level earlier than $\mathbf{i}$ that contains a set of sentences all of which are true on a path-variant of **I** for that path, or (b) there is at least one path to level $\mathbf{i}$ that contains a set of sentences all of which are true on a path-variant of **I** for that path.

Consider, for any level $\mathbf{i}$, a path that satisfies either (a) or (b). There is a limit to the number of distinct individual constants not already occurring in Γ that can occur on this path (constants that were introduced by an application of ∀D or ∃D), namely, the size $\mathbf{n}$ of the finite U.D. for **I**. For if a path contains more than $\mathbf{n}$ new individual constants, it cannot meet the condition in the definition of path-variants that each of these constants be assigned a member of the U.D. that is *different* from the members assigned to other new constants; there would not be enough members of the U.D. to go around. In addition, because Γ only contains a finite number of constants, a path that satisfies either (a) or (b) can contain only a finite number of constants.

We now show that a path of a systematic tree that contains only a finite number of individual constants must be finitely long. Each of the decomposition rules & D, ~ & D, ∨ D, ~ ∨ D, ~ ⊃ D, ~ ≡ D, ~ ~ D, ∀D, and ∃D produces sentences with fewer occurrences of logical operators than the sentence being decomposed. The rules ⊃ D, ≡ D, ~ ∃D, and

[1] This metatheorem, along with result 11.1.4, is due to George Boolos, "Trees and Finite Satisfiability: Proof of a Conjecture of Burgess," *Notre Dame Journal of Formal Logic* 25(3), July 1984, 193–197.

$\sim\forall$D produce one or two sentences with the same number of occurrences of logical operators as the sentence being decomposed, but the sentences so produced have one of the forms $\sim \mathscr{P}$ (in the case of $\supset$D and $\equiv$D), $(\exists x) \sim \mathscr{P}$ (in the case of $\sim\forall$D), or $(\forall x) \sim \mathscr{P}$ (in the case of $\sim\exists$D). Each of the latter sentences, if not a literal, will be decomposed by a rule that produces only sentences with fewer occurrences of logical operators. Because subsequent applications of decomposition rules produce sentences with fewer and fewer occurrences of logical operators, literals are eventually reached. The only way in which a branch of a systematic tree can continue indefinitely is through repeated instantiation of one or more universally quantified sentences by $\forall$D, each instantiation containing a different instantiating constant. But this cannot be the case with a branch that contains a finite number of individual constants. Therefore the paths that we are guaranteed by result 11.1.4 can only be finitely long.

In addition, The System was designed to guarantee that if a path *can* be completed (or closed) after a finite number of applications of rules, it *will* be completed. Stages 1 and 2 (and stage 3, in the case of *PLI*) each require that we decompose *all* sentences on the tree of the specified sort before going to the next stage, and at each stage there are only finitely many sentences. The System does not allow one branch to be developed indefinitely while others are ignored, and so a branch that can be completed after a finite number of steps will be completed.

We conclude that at some finite level $i$ of a systematic tree for $\Gamma$, there will be a path that meets condition (a) of result 11.1.4. In addition, because this path meets (a), it is a completed *open* path. This establishes Metatheorem 11.4.

Metatheorem 11.4 is also true of *PLI*; this can be shown with trivial modifications.

## 11.4E EXERCISES

***1.** Show that Metatheorem 11.3 holds for nonsystematic trees as well as for systematic ones. (Result 11.4.1 is not generally true of nonsystematic trees, so you should prove Lemma 11.4 directly by mathematical induction.)

**2.** Using Metatheorem 11.3, prove the following:

a. If a sentence $\mathscr{P}$ of *SL* is such that $\{\mathscr{P}\}$ has a closed truth-tree, then $\mathscr{P}$ is quantificationally false.

b. If a sentence $\mathscr{P}$ of *SL* is such that $\{\sim \mathscr{P}\}$ has a closed truth-tree, then $\mathscr{P}$ is quantificationally true.

*c. If a set $\{\sim(\mathscr{P} \equiv \mathscr{Q})\}$ has a closed truth-tree, then $\mathscr{P}$ and $\mathscr{Q}$ are quantificationally equivalent.

d. If a set $\Gamma \cup \{\sim \mathscr{P}\}$ has a closed truth-tree, then $\Gamma \vDash \mathscr{P}$.

*e. If the set consisting of the premises and the negation of the conclusion of an argument has a closed truth-tree, then that argument is quantificationally valid.

3. Prove that if a sentence $\mathcal{Q}$ is obtained from a sentence $\mathcal{P}$ by application of one of the following tree rules, then $\{\mathcal{P}\} \vDash \mathcal{Q}$.
a. ~ ~ D
*b. & D
*c. ~ ∨ D
d. ~ ⊃ D
e. ∀D
*f. ~ ∀D
*g. ~ ∃D

4. Prove that if sentences $\mathcal{Q}$ and $\mathcal{R}$ are obtained from a sentence $\mathcal{P}$ by application of one of the following tree rules, then on any interpretation on which $\mathcal{P}$ is true, either $\mathcal{Q}$ is true or $\mathcal{R}$ is true.
a. ~ & D
*b. ∨ D
*c. ⊃ D

5. Prove case 4 in the inductive step of the proof of Lemma 11.4.

6. If we were to drop the rule ∀D from the tree method, would the method still be sound for predicate logic? Explain.

7. Explain how we can adapt the proof of Metatheorem 11.3 to establish that the tree method for *SL* is sound for sentential logic.

## 11.5 THE COMPLETENESS OF THE TREE METHOD

In the last section we established that the tree method is sound for predicate logic —if a tree for a set of sentences of *PL* closes, then that set is quantificationally inconsistent. In this section we shall prove that the tree method is also *complete* for sentential logic. The *Completeness Metatheorem* for the tree method is

> Metatheorem 11.5: If a finite set $\Gamma$ of sentences of *PL* is quantificationally inconsistent, then every systematic tree for $\Gamma$ closes.

Whereas soundness ensures that we are correct in pronouncing a set inconsistent if we can construct a closed tree for that set, completeness ensures that we are correct in pronouncing a set consistent if a systematic tree for that set does not close. The requirement that the tree be systematic is important, as we shall see; and the reader should remember that a tree that is constructed in accordance with The System but is abandoned before every branch closes and before at least one branch becomes a completed open branch does not count as a systematic tree.

We shall prove that the tree method is complete by establishing that the contrapositive of Metatheorem 11.5 is true—that if a systematic tree for a set of sentences of *PL* does not close, then the set is quantificationally consistent. There are three parts to the proof. First, we shall prove that if a systematic tree fails to close, and it does not contain a completed open branch after a finite number of steps in its construction, then it has at least one branch with infinitely many sentences. Second, we shall prove that for any completed open branch or infinite branch of a systematic truth-tree, the set of sentences occurring on that branch is a special sort of set known as a *Hintikka set*.[2] Finally, we shall present a method of constructing, for any Hintikka set, an interpretation on which every member of that set is true. This will establish that every Hintikka set is quantificationally consistent, and consequently that the set of sentences occurring on either a completed open branch or an infinite branch of a systematic truth-tree is quantificationally consistent. Because each sentence in the set Γ for which a tree is constructed occurs on every branch of that tree, it follows that if a systematic tree for Γ fails to close, Γ is a subset of a Hintikka set and is therefore also quantificationally consistent. Therefore, if a finite set Γ is quantificationally *in*consistent, then every systematic tree for Γ will close—and that is what Metatheorem 11.5 says.

Consider a systematic tree such that at no level $i$ does the tree contain a completed open branch and at no level $i$ is the tree closed. Our first task is to show that such a tree must contain an infinite branch. Because the tree fails to close or to contain a completed open branch at any level $i$, the tree must contain infinitely many sentences (strictly speaking, infinitely many *occurrences* of sentences—the sentences need not be distinct). The tree contains infinitely many sentences because it takes infinitely many steps to construct a systematic tree that neither is closed nor contains a completed open branch at any level, and each step in the construction involves adding at least one new sentence. It remains to be shown that a systematic truth-tree containing infinitely many sentences has at least one branch that is infinitely long—at least one branch that contains an infinite number of sentences. The reason that this needs to be *proved* is that a tree *could* contain infinitely many sentences and yet be such that each of its branches was only finitely long, *if* it contained infinitely many branches. So we need to establish the following lemma, the Infinite Branch Lemma:

> Lemma 11.5: Every systematic tree that contains an infinite number of occurrences of sentences has at least one branch that is infinitely long.[3]

Proof of Lemma 11.5: Some definitions will be useful for the proof. We will say that a sentence $\mathcal{P}$ (throughout, read *occurrence of a sentence* whenever we speak of a sentence) in a tree is *above* sentence $\mathcal{Q}$ just in case $\mathcal{P}$ and $\mathcal{Q}$ lie on the same branch of the tree and $\mathcal{P}$ is at an earlier level of the tree. $\mathcal{Q}$ is an *immediate successor* of $\mathcal{P}$ if $\mathcal{P}$ and $\mathcal{Q}$ lie on the same

[2] These sets were first studied by J. Hintikka, in "Form and Content in Quantification Theory," *Acta Philosophica Fennica*, 8 (Helsinki: 1955), 7–55; and "Notes on Quantification Theory," *Societas Scientiarum Fennica, Commentationes Physico-Mathematicae*, 17(12) (Helsinki: 1955).

[3] This follows as a special case of a famous lemma known as *König's Lemma* (D. König, *Theorie der endlichen und unendlichen Graphen*, Leipzig, 1936).

branch and $\mathscr{P}$ is one level earlier than $\mathscr{Q}$. Every sentence in a tree, except those that occur at the ends of branches, has a finite number of immediate successors—one if a nonbranching rule is applied, two if a branching rule other than ∃D2 is applied, and $m + 1$, where $m$ is the number of individual constants already occurring on the sentence's branch, if ∃D2 is applied.

We shall now show that if a systematic tree contains infinitely many sentences, then there is at least one infinite branch in the tree, by starting at level 1 and working down through the levels of the tree. The sentence at level 1 of such a tree—call it $\mathscr{P}_1$—is above every other sentence in the tree. Therefore this sentence is above infinitely many sentences (subtracting 1 from an infinite number leaves an infinite number). $\mathscr{P}_1$ has a finite number of successors at level 2. At least one of these immediate successors is above infinitely many sentences. Consider the possibility that each of the immediate successors—call then $\mathscr{Q}_1, \ldots, \mathscr{Q}_n$—is above only a finite number of sentences. Then $\mathscr{P}$ itself would be above only finitely many sentences: $\mathscr{Q}_1, \ldots, \mathscr{Q}_n$, $\mathscr{Q}_1$'s successors, . . . , and $\mathscr{Q}_n$'s successors together would constitute only a finite number of sentences. $\mathscr{P}_1$ must therefore have at least one immediate successor $\mathscr{P}_2$ that is above an infinite number of sentences. The reasoning that we have just used can be generalized: If a sentence at any level is above infinitely many sentences, then at least one immediate successor of that sentence is above infinitely many sentences. So $\mathscr{P}_2$, being above infinitely many sentences, has an immediate successor $\mathscr{P}_3$ that is above infinitely many sentences, and $\mathscr{P}_3$ has an immediate successor $\mathscr{P}_4$ that is above infinitely many sentences, and so on, for each positive integer. The sentences $\mathscr{P}_1, \mathscr{P}_2, \mathscr{P}_3, \mathscr{P}_4, \ldots$ constitute a branch with an infinite number of sentences. Therefore, if a systematic tree contains infinitely many sentences, then it has at least one branch that is infinitely long.

We may now conclude that a systematic tree that fails to close either has a completed open branch after a finite number of steps or has at least one infinite branch. This will be important in what follows.

Turning to the second step of the proof of Metatheorem 11.5, we define a *Hintikka set* to be a set Γ of sentences of *PL* that has the following properties:

a. There is no atomic sentence $\mathscr{P}$ such that both $\mathscr{P}$ and $\sim \mathscr{P}$ are members of Γ.

b. If $\sim \sim \mathscr{P} \in \Gamma$, then $\mathscr{P} \in \Gamma$.

c. If $\mathscr{P} \,\&\, \mathscr{Q} \in \Gamma$, then $\mathscr{P} \in \Gamma$ and $\mathscr{Q} \in \Gamma$.

d. If $\sim(\mathscr{P} \,\&\, \mathscr{Q}) \in \Gamma$, then either $\sim \mathscr{P} \in \Gamma$ or $\sim \mathscr{Q} \in \Gamma$.

e. If $\mathscr{P} \vee \mathscr{Q} \in \Gamma$, then either $\mathscr{P} \in \Gamma$ or $\mathscr{Q} \in \Gamma$.

f. If $\sim(\mathscr{P} \vee \mathscr{Q}) \in \Gamma$, then $\sim \mathscr{P} \in \Gamma$ and $\sim \mathscr{Q} \in \Gamma$.

g. If $\mathscr{P} \supset \mathscr{Q} \in \Gamma$, then either $\sim \mathscr{P} \in \Gamma$ or $\mathscr{Q} \in \Gamma$.

h. If $\sim (\mathscr{P} \supset \mathscr{Q}) \in \Gamma$, then $\mathscr{P} \in \Gamma$ and $\sim \mathscr{Q} \in \Gamma$.

i. If $\mathscr{P} \equiv \mathscr{Q} \in \Gamma$, then either $\mathscr{P} \in \Gamma$ and $\mathscr{Q} \in \Gamma$ or $\sim \mathscr{P} \in \Gamma$ and $\sim \mathscr{Q} \in \Gamma$.

j. If $\sim(\mathscr{P} \equiv \mathscr{Q}) \in \Gamma$, then either $\mathscr{P} \in \Gamma$ and $\sim \mathscr{Q} \in \Gamma$ or $\sim \mathscr{P} \in \Gamma$ and $\mathscr{Q} \in \Gamma$.

k. If $(\forall x)\mathscr{P} \in \Gamma$, then at least one substitution instance of $(\forall x)\mathscr{P}$ is a member of $\Gamma$ and for every constant $a$ that occurs in some sentence of $\Gamma$, $\mathscr{P}(a/x) \in \Gamma$.

l. If $\sim(\forall x)\mathscr{P} \in \Gamma$, then $(\exists x) \sim \mathscr{P} \in \Gamma$.

m. If $(\exists x)\mathscr{P} \in \Gamma$, then for at least one constant $a$, $\mathscr{P}(a/x) \in \Gamma$.

n. If $\sim (\exists x)\mathscr{P} \in \Gamma$, then $(\forall x) \sim \mathscr{P} \in \Gamma$.

We call a branch of a tree a *Hintikka branch* if the sentences on that branch constitute a Hintikka set. We now prove that every completed open branch and every infinite branch of a systematic tree is a Hintikka branch, which will establish the Hintikka Branch Lemma:

| |
|---|
| Lemma 11.6: Every systematic tree that is not closed has at least one Hintikka branch. |

Afterwards, we shall show that every Hintikka set is quantificationally consistent.

Proof of Lemma 11.6: If a systematic tree fails to close, then either the tree has a completed open branch or, by Lemma 11.5, the tree has an infinite branch. We will show that each of these two types of branches is a Hintikka branch, that is, the set of sentences occurring on such a branch has properties (a)–(n).

First consider completed open branches. By definition, a completed open branch is a finite branch that is open—there is no pair of literals $\mathscr{P}$ and $\sim \mathscr{P}$ such that both $\mathscr{P}$ and $\sim \mathscr{P}$ occur on the branch—and each sentence on that branch is one of the following:

1. a literal (an atomic sentence or the negation of an atomic sentence)

2. a sentence that is not universally quantified and that has been decomposed

3. a universally quantified sentence $(\forall x)\mathscr{P}$ such that at least one substitution instance of $(\forall x)\mathscr{P}$ occurs on the branch and for each constant $a$ occurring on the branch, $\mathscr{P}(a/x)$ occurs on the branch.

The set of sentences on a completed open branch has property (a) because there is no pair of literals $\mathscr{P}$ and $\sim \mathscr{P}$ occurring on the branch. Every sentence that has one of the forms described in properties (b)–(j) and (l)–(n) has been decomposed (part 2 of the definition of a completed open branch), and so it is easily verified that the set of sentences on a completed open branch has those properties. (For example, if a sentence $\sim\sim \mathscr{P}$ occurs on a completed open branch and has been decomposed by an application of $\sim\sim$D, then $\mathscr{P}$ also occurs on that branch—which establishes property (b)). Finally, the set of sentences on a completed open branch also has property (k), for part 3 of the definition of completed open branches stipulates that property (k) is satisfied. We conclude that the set of sentences occurring on a completed open branch has properties (a)–(n) and that the branch is therefore a Hintikka branch.

Now we turn to infinite branches. The System for tree construction was designed to guarantee that every infinite (nonterminating) branch is a Hintikka branch; we shall explain how it does so. First, a nonterminating branch is not closed (a branch that closes contains only finitely many sentences); so the set of sentences on such a branch must have property (a) of Hintikka sets. Second, the alternation of stages 1 and 2 of The System ensures that each nonliteral sentence that does not have the form $(\forall x)\mathscr{P}$ is decomposed a finite number of levels after the level on which it occurs, that for each universally quantified sentence $(\forall x)\mathscr{P}$ and constant $a$ on a branch of the tree, $\mathscr{P}(a/x)$ is entered within a finite number of levels, and that at least one substitution instance $\mathscr{P}(a/x)$ is entered. Each such addition yields only a finite number of levels, so every sentence on a branch must be decomposed if the branch is infinite. Therefore the set of sentences on a nonterminating branch satisfies properties (b)–(n) of Hintikka sets as well as property (a). Every infinite branch of a systematic tree is therefore a Hintikka branch.

Finally, we shall prove the Hintikka Set Lemma:

| Lemma 11.7: Every Hintikka set is quantificationally consistent. |
|---|

From this it will follow that if a systematic tree for a set $\Gamma$ of sentences does not close, then $\Gamma$ is quantificationally consistent—for one of the branches that contains the sentences in $\Gamma$ is a Hintikka branch.

Proof of Lemma 11.7: Let $\Gamma$ be a Hintikka set of sentences of *PL*. We first associate with each individual constant of *PL* a distinct positive integer—$i$ is associated with the alphabetically $i$th constant. We shall prove that every sentence of $\Gamma$ is true on the interpretation **I** defined as follows:

1. The U.D. is the set consisting of the positive integers that are associated with the individual constants occurring in members of $\Gamma$. If no member of $\Gamma$ contains an individual constant, let the U.D. be the set $\{1\}$.
2. For each sentence letter $\mathscr{P}$, $\mathbf{I}(\mathscr{P}) = \mathrm{T}$ if and only if $\mathscr{P} \in \Gamma$.
3. For each individual constant $a$ that occurs in some sentence in $\Gamma$, $\mathbf{I}(a)$ is the positive integer associated with $a$. For each constant $a$ that does not occur in any sentence of $\Gamma$, $\mathbf{I}(a)$ is the smallest positive integer in the U.D. (which, by specification 1, is nonempty).

4. For each $n$-place predicate $\mathscr{A}$, $\mathbf{I}(\mathscr{A})$ includes all and only those $n$-tuples $\langle \mathbf{u}_1, \ldots, \mathbf{u}_n \rangle$ such that for some constants $a_1, \ldots, a_n$, $\mathscr{A}a_1, \ldots, a_n \in \Gamma$ and $\langle \mathbf{I}(a_1), \ldots, \mathbf{I}(a_n) \rangle = \langle \mathbf{u}_1, \ldots, \mathbf{u}_n \rangle$.

We shall use mathematical induction to prove that every member of $\Gamma$ is true on **I**. Our induction will not be on the number of occurrences of logical operators in a sentence, since some of the clauses of the proof would not work in that case (see Exercise 5). Instead, we shall appeal to the *length* of a sentence. Where $\mathscr{P}$ is a formula of *PL*, let the *length* of $\mathscr{P}$ be the number of occurrences of sentence letters, predicates, and logical operators in $\mathscr{P}$. No sentence of *PL* has length 0, since every sentence contains at least one sentence letter or predicate. So the basis clause begins with length 1:

*Basis clause:* Every sentence $\mathscr{P}$ of length 1 is such that if $\mathscr{P} \in \Gamma$, then $\mathbf{I}(\mathscr{P}) = \mathbf{T}$.

*Inductive step:* If every sentence $\mathscr{P}$ of length less than or equal to $k$ is such that if $\mathscr{P} \in \Gamma$ then $\mathbf{I}(\mathscr{P}) = \mathbf{T}$, then every sentence $\mathscr{P}$ of length $k + 1$ is such that if $\mathscr{P} \in \Gamma$ then $\mathbf{I}(\mathscr{P}) = \mathbf{T}$.

---

*Conclusion:* Every sentence $\mathscr{P}$ is such that if $\mathscr{P} \in \Gamma$, then $\mathbf{I}(\mathscr{P}) = \mathbf{T}$.

The basis clause is simple to prove. A sentence of length 1 is an atomic sentence. (If a sentence contains any logical operators, then, because it also must contain at least one sentence letter or predicate, it has a length that is greater than 1.) If $\mathscr{P}$ is a sentence letter, then by part 2 of the definition of **I**, $\mathbf{I}(\mathscr{P}) = \mathbf{T}$ if $\mathscr{P} \in \Gamma$. If $\mathscr{P}$ is an atomic sentence of the form $\mathscr{A}a_1, \ldots, a_n$, then, by part 4 of the definition of **I**, if $\mathscr{A}a_1, \ldots, a_n \in \Gamma$ then $\langle \mathbf{I}(a_1), \ldots, \mathbf{I}(a_n) \rangle \in \mathbf{I}(\mathscr{A})$, and so $\mathbf{I}(\mathscr{P}) = \mathbf{T}$.

To prove the inductive step, we assume that the inductive hypothesis holds for some arbitrary positive integer $k$—that every sentence of length $k$ or smaller that is a member of $\Gamma$ is true on **I**. We must show that any sentence $\mathscr{P}$ of length $k + 1$ is also such that if it is a member of $\Gamma$ then it is true on **I**. It is easy to verify that $\mathscr{P}$, being nonatomic, must have one of the forms specified in properties (a)–(n) of Hintikka sets; and we shall consider each of these forms that $\mathscr{P}$ may have.

Case 1: $\mathscr{P}$ has the form $\sim \mathscr{Q}$, where $\mathscr{Q}$ is an atomic sentence. If $\sim \mathscr{Q} \in \Gamma$ then, by property (a) of Hintikka sets, $\mathscr{Q} \notin \Gamma$. If $\mathscr{Q}$ is a sentence letter then, by part 2 of the definition of **I**, $\mathbf{I}(\mathscr{Q}) = \mathbf{F}$ and so $\mathbf{I}(\sim \mathscr{Q}) = \mathbf{T}$.[4] If $\mathscr{Q}$ has the form $\mathscr{A}a_1, \ldots, a_n$ then, by part 4 of the definition of **I**, $\langle \mathbf{I}(a_1), \ldots, \mathbf{I}(a_n) \rangle \notin \mathbf{I}(\mathscr{A})$. This is because each constant that occurs in some member of $\Gamma$ designates a positive integer different from that

[4] Note that we have here bypassed the intermediate step of observing that a sentence is true on an interpretation if and only if it is satisfied by every variable assignment for that interpretation. We shall continue this practice until we reach cases 11–14; the reader who so desires may fill in the intermediate steps for cases 1–10 without much trouble.

designated by any other constant occurring in $\Gamma$ (by part 3), and so there is no other set of constants occurring in $\Gamma$ that also designate the members of the $n$-tuple $\langle \mathbf{I}(a_1), \ldots, \mathbf{I}(a_n)\rangle$ and consequently there can be no sentence $\mathcal{A}a'_1, \ldots, a'_n$ in $\Gamma$ such that $\langle \mathbf{I}(a_1), \ldots, \mathbf{I}(a_n)\rangle = \langle \mathbf{I}(a'_1), \ldots, \mathbf{I}(a'_n)\rangle$. We may therefore conclude, from the fact that $\mathcal{A}a_1, \ldots, a_n \notin \Gamma$, that the $n$-tuple $\langle \mathbf{I}(a_1), \ldots, \mathbf{I}(a_n)\rangle$ is not in the extension of $\mathcal{A}$. So $\mathbf{I}(\mathcal{A}a_1, \ldots, a_n) = \mathbf{F}$ and $\mathbf{I}(\sim \mathcal{A}a_1, \ldots, a_n) = \mathbf{T}$.

Case 2: $\mathcal{P}$ has the form $\sim\sim\mathcal{Q}$. If $\sim\sim\mathcal{Q} \in \Gamma$ then, by property (b) of Hintikka sets, $\mathcal{Q} \in \Gamma$. The length of $\mathcal{Q}$ is less than $k + 1$, so by the inductive hypothesis, $\mathbf{I}(\mathcal{Q}) = \mathbf{T}$. Therefore $\mathbf{I}(\sim\sim\mathcal{Q}) = \mathbf{T}$ as well.

Case 3: $\mathcal{P}$ has the form $\mathcal{Q} \,\&\, \mathcal{R}$. If $\mathcal{Q} \,\&\, \mathcal{R} \in \Gamma$ then, by property (c) of Hintikka sets, $\mathcal{Q} \in \Gamma$ and $\mathcal{R} \in \Gamma$. By the inductive hypothesis ($\mathcal{Q}$ and $\mathcal{R}$ both having lengths less than $k + 1$), $\mathbf{I}(\mathcal{Q}) = \mathbf{T}$ and $\mathbf{I}(\mathcal{R}) = \mathbf{T}$. So $\mathbf{I}(\mathcal{Q} \,\&\, \mathcal{R}) = \mathbf{T}$.

Case 4: $\mathcal{P}$ has the form $\sim(\mathcal{Q} \,\&\, \mathcal{R})$. If $\sim(\mathcal{Q} \,\&\, \mathcal{R}) \in \Gamma$ then, by property (d) of Hintikka sets, either $\sim\mathcal{Q} \in \Gamma$ or $\sim\mathcal{R} \in \Gamma$. The lengths of $\sim\mathcal{Q}$ and of $\sim\mathcal{R}$ are less than the length of $\sim(\mathcal{Q} \,\&\, \mathcal{R})$, so by the inductive hypothesis either $\mathbf{I}(\sim\mathcal{Q}) = \mathbf{T}$ or $\mathbf{I}(\sim\mathcal{R}) = \mathbf{T}$. If $\mathbf{I}(\sim\mathcal{Q}) = \mathbf{T}$ then $\mathbf{I}(\mathcal{Q}) = \mathbf{F}$, $\mathbf{I}(\mathcal{Q} \,\&\, \mathcal{R}) = \mathbf{F}$, and $\mathbf{I}(\sim(\mathcal{Q} \,\&\, \mathcal{R})) = \mathbf{T}$. If $\mathbf{I}(\sim\mathcal{R}) = \mathbf{T}$, then $\mathbf{I}(\sim(\mathcal{Q} \,\&\, \mathcal{R})) = \mathbf{T}$ as well. Either way, then, $\mathbf{I}(\sim(\mathcal{Q} \,\&\, \mathcal{R})) = \mathbf{T}$.

Cases 5–10: $\mathcal{P}$ has one of the forms $\mathcal{Q} \vee \mathcal{R}$, $\sim(\mathcal{Q} \vee \mathcal{R})$, $\mathcal{Q} \supset \mathcal{R}$, $\sim(\mathcal{Q} \supset \mathcal{R})$, $\mathcal{Q} \equiv \mathcal{R}$, or $\sim(\mathcal{Q} \equiv \mathcal{R})$. See Exercise 3.

Case 11: $\mathcal{P}$ has the form $(\forall x)\mathcal{Q}$. If $\mathcal{P} \in \Gamma$ then, by property (k) of Hintikka sets, for every constant $a$ that occurs in $\Gamma$, $\mathcal{Q}(a/x) \in \Gamma$ (and there is at least one such constant). Each substitution instance has a length smaller than $k + 1$ so it follows from the inductive hypothesis that for each of these sentences, $\mathbf{I}(\mathcal{Q}(a/x)) = \mathbf{T}$. Moreover, each member of the U.D. is designated by some constant occurring in $\Gamma$ (by part 1 on the definition of the interpretation $\mathbf{I}$—because at least one constant occurs in $\Gamma$), so for each member of the U.D. there is a constant $a$ such that $\mathcal{Q}(a/x) \in \Gamma$ and hence is true on $\mathbf{I}$. It therefore follows from 11.5.1 that $\mathbf{I}((\forall x)\mathcal{Q}) = \mathbf{T}$.

11.5.1. Let $\mathbf{I}$ be an interpretation on which for each member $\mathbf{u}$ of the U.D. there is at least one constant $a$ such that $\mathbf{I}(a) = \mathbf{u}$ and $\mathbf{I}(\mathcal{P}(a/x)) = \mathbf{T}$. Then $\mathbf{I}((\forall x)\mathcal{P}) = \mathbf{T}$.

Proof of 11.5.1: See Exercise 4.

Case 12: $\mathcal{P}$ has the form $\sim(\forall x)\mathcal{Q}$. If $\sim(\forall x)\mathcal{Q} \in \Gamma$ then, by property (l) of Hintikka sets, $(\exists x) \sim\mathcal{Q} \in \Gamma$ and, by property (m), $\sim\mathcal{Q}(a/x) \in \Gamma$ for some constant $a$. $\sim\mathcal{Q}(a/x)$ has a length less than $k + 1$, so by the inductive hypothesis, $\mathbf{I}(\sim\mathcal{Q}(a/x)) = \mathbf{T}$ and therefore $\mathbf{I}(\mathcal{Q}(a/x)) = \mathbf{F}$. Because $\{(\forall x)\mathcal{Q}\} \vDash \mathcal{Q}(a/x)$ (result 11.1.4), it follows that $\mathbf{I}((\forall x)\mathcal{Q}) = \mathbf{F}$ and so $\mathbf{I}(\sim(\forall x)\mathcal{Q}) = \mathbf{T}$.

Cases 13 and 14: $\mathcal{P}$ has one of the forms $(\exists x)\mathcal{Q}$ or $\sim(\exists x)\mathcal{Q}$. See Exercise 3.

That completes the proof of the inductive step. Therefore every sentence that is a member of the Hintikka set $\Gamma$ is true on $\mathcal{I}$, and this shows that $\Gamma$ is quantificationally consistent.

Lemmas 11.6 and 11.7 can now be used to establish Metatheorem 11.5. If a systematic tree for a set $\Gamma$ of sentences does not close, then the tree has at least one Hintikka branch (Lemma 11.6). The set of sentences on that Hintikka branch is quantificationally consistent (Lemma 11.7). Therefore, because every member of $\Gamma$ lies on that branch (as well as on every other branch), $\Gamma$ is quantificationally consistent. So if $\Gamma$ is quantificationally *inconsistent*, then every systematic tree for $\Gamma$ will close.

We note that the proof that we have just given is a *constructive* completeness proof. We have shown how, given a Hintikka branch of a systematic tree for a set of sentences $\Gamma$, to construct an interpretation on which every member of $\Gamma$ is true. This establishes a claim made in Chapter Nine: An interpretation showing the quantificational consistency of $\Gamma$ can always be constructed from a completed open branch of a tree for $\Gamma$.

Finally, the tree method for predicate logic with identity is also complete, and this can be shown by making a few changes in the proofs of Lemmas 11.6 and 11.7. We define a Hintikka set for *PLI* to be a set $\Gamma$ that has the properties (a)–(n) of our earlier definition and that also has the property

o. No sentence of the form $\sim \mathbf{a} = \mathbf{a}$ is a member of $\Gamma$.
p. If $\mathbf{a} = \mathbf{b} \in \Gamma$ and the sentence $\mathcal{P} \in \Gamma$ contains $\mathbf{b}$, then $\mathcal{P}(\mathbf{a}//\mathbf{b}) \in \Gamma$.

The proof of Lemma 11.6—that every systematic tree that does not close has a Hintikka branch—runs as before, except that we note in addition that by definition a branch that does not close does not contain a sentence of the form $\sim \mathbf{a} = \mathbf{a}$. The proof of Lemma 11.7 for predicate logic with identity is left as an exercise.

## 11.5E EXERCISES

**1.** Using Metatheorem 11.5, prove the following:

a. If $\mathcal{P}$ is quantificationally false, then every systematic tree for $\{\mathcal{P}\}$ closes.
b. If $\mathcal{P}$ is quantificationally true, then every systematic tree for $(\sim \mathcal{P}\}$ closes.
*c. If $\mathcal{P}$ and $\mathcal{Q}$ are quantificationally equivalent, then every systematic tree for $\{\sim(\mathcal{P} \equiv \mathcal{Q})\}$ closes.
d. If $\Gamma \vDash \mathcal{P}$, where $\Gamma$ is finite, then every systematic tree for $\Gamma \cup \{\sim \mathcal{P}\}$ closes.
*e. If an argument of *PL* is quantificationally valid, then every systematic tree for the set consisting of the premises and the negation of the conclusion of that argument closes.

**2.a.** What is the length of each of the following sentences?

$(\forall y)Wy \supset \sim (\forall y)Bya$
$(\exists x)Sxbc$
$(\forall x)(Mx \equiv \sim (\exists y)My)$

b. Show that the length of a sentence $\sim(\mathcal{Q} \;\&\; \mathcal{R})$ is greater than the length of $\sim\mathcal{Q}$ and greater than the length of $\sim\mathcal{R}$.

*c. Show that the length of a sentence $\mathcal{Q} \equiv \mathcal{R}$ is greater than the length of $\sim\mathcal{Q}$ and greater than the length of $\sim\mathcal{R}$.

d. Show that the length of a sentence $\sim(\forall x)\mathcal{Q}$ is greater than the length of $\sim\mathcal{Q}(a/x)$.

**3.** Complete the following clauses in the inductive proof of the completeness of the tree method:

a. 5

*b. 6

c. 7

*d. 8

*e. 9

f. 10

g. 13

*h. 14

***4.** Prove result 11.5.1.

**5.** Which clauses in the inductive proof of the completeness of the tree method would have broken down if our induction had been on the number of occurrences of logical operators in the sentences of *PL*?

**6.** If the rule ∃D were not included in our tree rules, where would the proof of Metatheorem 11.5 break down?

**7.** Suppose that our rule ~∀D were replaced by the following rule:

*Negated Universal Decomposition* (~∀D*)

$\sim(\forall x)\mathcal{P}$

$\sim\mathcal{P}(a/x)$

where $a$ is a constant foreign to all preceding lines of the tree.

Would the resulting system be complete for predicate logic? Explain.

**8.** Explain how we can adapt the proof of Metatheorem 11.5 to establish that the tree method for *SL* is complete for sentential logic.

**9.** Prove that every set of *PL* that is both maximally consistent and ∃-complete (as defined in Section 11.3) is a Hintikka set. Prove that every Hintikka set is ∃-complete. Prove that some Hintikka sets are not maximally consistent in *PD*.

***10.** Prove Lemma 11.7 for predicate logic with identity.

# *SELECTED BIBLIOGRAPHY*

The following books are suggested for further reading.


## INFORMAL LOGIC

Fogelin, Robert J., and Walter Sinnott-Armstrong. *Understanding Arguments*. 4th ed. New York: Harcourt Brace Jovanovich, 1990.

## ELEMENTARY LOGIC

Fraassen, Bas C. van, and Karel Lambert. *Derivation and Counterexample*. Encino, Calif.: Dickenson, 1972.

Jeffrey, Richard C. *Formal Logic: Its Scope and Limits*. 2nd ed. New York: McGraw-Hill, 1981.

Leblanc, Hugues, and William Wisdom. *Deductive Logic*. 2nd rev. ed. Boston: Allyn & Bacon, 1976.

Myro, George, Mark Bedau, and Tim Monroe. *Rudiments of Logic*. Englewood Cliffs, N.J.: Prentice-Hall, Inc., 1987.

Quine, W. V. O. *Methods of Logic*. 4th ed. New York: Holt, Rinehart and Winston, 1982.

Tennant, Neil. *Natural Deduction*. Edinburgh: Edinburgh University Press, 1978.

## INDUCTIVE LOGIC

Skyrms, Brian. *Choice and Chance*. 3rd ed. Belmont, Calif.: Wadsworth, 1986.

ADVANCED LOGIC

Grandy, Richard E. *Advanced Logic for Applications*. Holland: Kluwer Academic Publishers, 1979.
Hunter, Geoffrey. *Metalogic: An Introduction to the Metatheory of First-Order Logic*. Berkeley: University of California Press, 1971.
Kleene, Stephen Cole. *Introduction to Metamathematics*. New York: American Elsevier Publishing Company, 1974.
Quine, W. V. O. *Mathematical Logic*. Rev. ed. Cambridge, Mass.: Harvard University Press, 1951.
Smullyan, Raymond M. *First-Order Logic*. New York: Springer, 1968.

ALTERNATIVE LOGICS

Chellas, B. *Modal Logic*. New York: Cambridge University Press, 1975.
Hughes, G. E., and M. J. Cresswell. *An Introduction to Modal Logic*. London: Routledge, Chapman, & Hall, 1972.
Konyndyk, Kenneth. *Introductory Modal Logic*. Notre Dame: University of Notre Dame Press, 1986.
Rescher, N. *Many-Valued Logic*. New York: McGraw-Hill, 1969.

HISTORY OF LOGIC

Bochenski, I. M. *A History of Formal Logic*. Trans. and ed. by Ivo Thomas. New York: Chelsea, 1970.
Kneale, William, and Martha Kneale. *The Development of Logic*. Oxford: Clarendon, 1962.

PHILOSOPHY OF LOGIC

Gabbay, D., and Guenthner F., ed. *Handbook of Philosophical Logic*. 4 volumes. Holland: Kluwer Academic Publishers, 1983–1989.
Haack, Susan. *Deviant Logic*. New York: Cambridge University Press, 1975.
Haack, Susan. *Philosophy of Logics*. New York: Cambridge University Press, 1979.
Leblanc, Hugues. *Existence, Truth, and Provability*. SUNY Press, 1982.
Quine, W. V. O. *Philosophy of Logic*. Englewood Cliffs, N.J.: Prentice-Hall, Inc., 1970.

# *INDEX*

# *INDEX OF SYMBOLS*